THE INSTITUTE F(

The Institute for Polish–Jewish Studies in Oxford and its sister organization, the American Association for Polish–Jewish Studies, which publish *Polin*, are learned societies which were established in 1984, following the First International Conference on Polish–Jewish Studies, held in Oxford. The Institute is an associate institute of the Oxford Centre for Hebrew and Jewish Studies, and the American Association is linked with the Department of Near Eastern and Judaic Studies at Brandeis University.

Both the Institute and the American Association aim to promote understanding of the Polish Jewish past. They have no building or library of their own and no paid staff; they achieve their aims by encouraging scholarly research and facilitating its publication, and by creating forums for people with a scholarly interest in Polish Jewish topics, both past and present.

To this end, the Institute and the American Association help organize lectures and international conferences. Venues for these activities have included Brandeis University in Waltham, Massachusetts, the Hebrew University in Jerusalem, the Institute for the Study of Human Sciences in Vienna, King's College London, the Jagiellonian University in Kraków, the Oxford Centre for Hebrew and Jewish Studies, the University of Łódź, University College London, the Polish Cultural Centre and the Polish Embassy in London. They have encouraged academic exchanges between Israel, Poland, the United States, and western Europe. In particular they seek to help train a new generation of scholars, in Poland and elsewhere, to study the culture and history of the Jews in Poland.

Each year since 1987, the Institute has published a volume of scholarly papers in the series Polin: Studies in Polish Jewry under the general editorship of Professor Antony Polonsky of Brandeis University. Since 1994 the series has been published on its behalf by the Littman Library of Jewish Civilization, and since 1998 the publication has been linked with the American Association as well. In March 2000 the entire series was honoured with a National Jewish Book Award from the Jewish Book Council in the United States. More than twenty other works on Polish Jewish topics have also been published with the Institute's assistance.

For further information on the Institute for Polish–Jewish Studies or the American Association for Polish–Jewish Studies, contact <polin@littman.co.uk>.

THE LITTMAN LIBRARY OF
JEWISH CIVILIZATION

MANAGING EDITOR
Connie Webber

Dedicated to the memory of
LOUIS THOMAS SIDNEY LITTMAN
who founded the Littman Library for the love of God
and as an act of charity in memory of his father
JOSEPH AARON LITTMAN
יהא זכרם ברוך

'*Get wisdom, get understanding:*
Forsake her not and she shall preserve thee'
PROV. 4: 5

The Littman Library of Jewish Civilization is a registered UK charity
Registered charity no. 1000784

POLIN

STUDIES IN POLISH JEWRY

VOLUME EIGHTEEN

Jewish Women in Eastern Europe

Edited by
CHAERAN FREEZE, PAULA HYMAN
and
ANTONY POLONSKY

Published for
The Institute for Polish–Jewish Studies
and
The American Association for Polish–Jewish Studies

Oxford · Portland, Oregon
The Littman Library of Jewish Civilization
2005

wB

The Littman Library of Jewish Civilization
Chief Executive Officer: Ludo Craddock

PO Box 645, Oxford OX2 0UJ, UK

Published in the United States and Canada by
The Littman Library of Jewish Civilization
c/o ISBS, 920 N.E. 58th Avenue, Suite 300
Portland, Oregon 97213-3786

A catalogue record for this book is available from the British Library

Library of Congress Cataloging-in-Publication data applied for
ISSN 0268 1056
ISBN 1-874774-92-7
ISBN 1-874774-93-5 (pbk)

Publishing co-ordinator: Janet Moth
Production: John Saunders
Copy-editing: Laurien Berkeley
Proof-reading: Tamar Wang
Index: Bonnie Blackburn
Design: Pete Russell, Faringdon, Oxon.
Typeset by Footnote Graphics Limited, Warminster, Wilts.
Printed in Great Britain on acid-free paper by
Biddles Ltd., Kings Lynn. www.biddles.co.uk

Articles appearing in this publication are abstracted and indexed in
Historical Abstracts and *America: History and Life*

1/3/07

This volume of POLIN *is dedicated*
in affection and appreciation to

IRENE PIPES

long-standing President of the American Foundation for Polish-Jewish Studies, on her eightieth birthday

---

The volume benefited from grants from

THE AMERICAN SOCIETY FOR YAD VASHEM

ROBERT AND ROCHELLE CHERRY

TONY COREN

THE HANADIV CHARITABLE FOUNDATION

THE INTERNATIONAL SOCIETY FOR YAD VASHEM

THE LUCIUS N. LITTAUER FOUNDATION

and

THE TAUBE FOUNDATION FOR
JEWISH LIFE & CULTURE OF THE JEWISH COMMUNITY
ENDOWMENT FUND

Editors and Advisers

Preface

THIS volume of *Polin* is centred around a core of articles devoted to the position of Jewish women in eastern Europe, a developing field that we are conscious we have ourselves somewhat neglected. We are particularly grateful to the editors of this section, ChaeRan Freeze and Paula Hyman, who have worked so hard to produce a set of studies that lays the foundations for the further development of the field. As in previous volumes of *Polin*, the New Views section gives substantial space to new research into a variety of topics in Polish Jewish studies. These include an analysis, by Zenon Guldon and Waldemar Kowalski, of the distribution of the Jews in Poland–Lithuania in the second half of the eighteenth century; an examination by Jakub Goldberg of the views of the writer Julian Ursyn Niemcewicz on Jewish issues; an investigation by Susanne Marten-Finnis into how the Bund's propaganda was affected by its use of different languages; and an exploration by Martin Dean of the problem of the service of Poles in the German local police in former eastern Poland after 1941.

This will be the last volume in which we will have a section devoted to reviews and review essays. We have long been dissatisfied by the length of time it has taken for reviews to appear, and from now on they will be posted on our website, which will enable them to be published more quickly. We also intend to post other materials on this website, which can be found at <www.brandeis.edu/aapjs/>.

Polin is sponsored by the Institute of Polish–Jewish Studies, Oxford, an associated institute of the Oxford Centre for Hebrew and Jewish Studies, and by the American Association for Polish–Jewish Studies, which is linked with the Department of Near Eastern and Judaic studies, Brandeis University. As with earlier issues, this volume could not have appeared without the untiring assistance of many individuals. In particular, we should like to express our gratitude to Professor Jonathan Webber, treasurer of the Institute for Polish–Jewish Studies, to Professor Jehuda Reinharz, president of Brandeis University, and to Mrs Irene Pipes, president of the American Association for Polish–Jewish Studies. Their three institutions all made substantial contributions to the cost of producing the volume.The volume also benefited from grants from the Memorial Foundation for Jewish Culture and the Lucius N. Littauer Foundation. As ever, this issue of *Polin* could not have been published without the constant assistance and supervision of Connie Webber, managing editor of the Littman Library, Janet Moth, publishing co-ordinator, and the tireless copy-editing of Laurien Berkeley, Sarah Swartz, and Claire Rosenson.

Plans for future volumes of *Polin* are well advanced. Volume 19 will deal with Polish–Jewish relations in the United States, volume 20 will be devoted to recording and memorializing the Holocaust, and volume 21 will focus on the crisis of 1968 in Poland. Further volumes are planned—on Jews in pre-modern Poland–Lithuania, on the history of the Jews in Kraków, and on Jewish–Ukrainian relations. We should welcome articles for these issues, as well as for the New Views section. We should also welcome any suggestions or criticisms. In particular, we should be very grateful for assistance in extending the geographical range of our journal to Ukraine, Belarus, and Lithuania, both in the period in which these countries were part of the Polish–Lithuanian Commonwealth and subsequently.

We note with sadness the death of Father Stanisław Musiał, a tireless fighter for Christian–Jewish understanding, the Nobel laureate Czesław Miłosz, chairman of our Advisory Board, and of Dora Kacnelson of Drohobych, a fine scholar and contributor. We also mourn the tragic loss in a car accident of Katarzyna Więcławska, one of the most promising of our younger contributors.

POLIN

We did not know, but our fathers told us how the exiles of Israel came to the land of Polin (Poland).

When Israel saw how its sufferings were constantly renewed, oppressions increased, persecutions multiplied, and how the evil authorities piled decree on decree and followed expulsion with expulsion, so that there was no way to escape the enemies of Israel, they went out on the road and sought an answer from the paths of the wide world: which is the correct road to traverse to find rest for the soul? Then a piece of paper fell from heaven, and on it the words:

Go to Polaniya (Poland).

So they came to the land of Polin and they gave a mountain of gold to the king, and he received them with great honour. And God had mercy on them, so that they found favour from the king and the nobles. And the king gave them permission to reside in all the lands of his kingdom, to trade over its length and breadth, and to serve God according to the precepts of their religion. And the king protected them against every foe and enemy.

And Israel lived in Polin in tranquillity for a long time. They devoted themselves to trade and handicrafts. And God sent a blessing on them so that they were blessed in the land, and their name was exalted among the peoples. And they traded with the surrounding countries and they also struck coins with inscriptions in the holy language and the language of the country. These are the coins which have on them a lion rampant towards the right. And on the coins are the words 'Mieszko, King of Poland' or 'Mieszko, Król of Poland'. The Poles call their king 'Król'.

And those who seek for names say: 'This is why it is called Polin. For thus spoke Israel when they came to the land, "Here rest for the night [*Po lin*]." And this means that we shall rest here until we are all gathered into the Land of Israel.'

Since this is the tradition, we accept it as such.

S. Y. AGNON, 1916

POLIN
Studies in Polish Jewry

VOLUME 1 *Poles and Jews: Renewing the Dialogue* (1986)

VOLUME 2 *Jews and the Emerging Polish State* (1987)

VOLUME 3 *The Jews of Warsaw* (1988)

VOLUME 4 *Poles and Jews: Perceptions and Misperceptions* (1989)

VOLUME 5 *New Research, New Views* (1990)

VOLUME 6 *Jews in Łódź 1820–1939* (1991)

VOLUME 7 *Jewish Life in Nazi-Occupied Warsaw* (1992)

From Shtetl to Socialism (1993): selected articles from volumes 1–7

VOLUME 8 *Jews in Independent Poland, 1918–1939* (1994)

VOLUME 9 *Jews, Poles, Socialists: The Failure of an Ideal* (1996)

VOLUME 10 *Jews in Early Modern Poland* (1997)

VOLUME 11 *Aspects and Experiences of Religion* (1998)

VOLUME 12 *Galicia: Jews, Poles, and Ukrainians, 1772–1918* (1999)

Index to Volumes 1–12 (2000)

VOLUME 13 *The Holocaust and its Aftermath* (2000)

VOLUME 14 *Jews in the Polish Borderlands* (2001)

VOLUME 15 *Jewish Religious Life, 1500–1900* (2002)

VOLUME 16 *Jewish Popular Culture and its Afterlife* (2003)

VOLUME 17 *The Shtetl: Myth and Reality* (2004)

VOLUME 18 *Jewish Women in Eastern Europe* (2005)

VOLUME 19 *Polish–Jewish Relations in North America* (2006)

VOLUME 20 *Memorializing the Holocaust* (2007)

Contents

REVIEWS

OBITUARIES

Note on Place Names

POLITICAL connotations accrue to words, names, and spellings with an alacrity unfortunate for those who would like to maintain neutrality. It seems reasonable to honour the choices of a population on the name of its city or town, but what is one to do when the people have no consensus on their name, or when the town changes its name, and the name its spelling, again and again over time? The politician may always opt for the latest version, but the hapless historian must reckon with them all. This note, then, will be our brief reckoning.

The least problematic are those places that have a widely accepted English name, which we shall use by preference. Examples are Warsaw, Kiev, Moscow, St Petersburg, and Munich. As an exception, we maintain the Polish spelling of Kraków, which in English has more often appeared as Cracow.

Most other place names in east-central Europe can raise serious problems. The linguistic and contextual diversity encountered cannot adequately be standardized by editorial formula, and in practice the least awkward solution is often to let subject matter and perspective determine the most suitable spellings in a given chapter. The difficulty is well illustrated by Galicia's most diversely named city, and one of its most important, which boasts five variants: the Polish Lwów, the German Lemberg, the Russian Lvov, the Ukrainian Lviv, and the Yiddish Lemberik.

A particular difficulty is posed by Wilno/Vilnius/Vilna, to all of which there are clear objections: until 1944 the majority of the population was Polish; the city is today in Lithuania; 'Vilna', though least problematic, is an artificial construct. Our preference will be to use the common English form 'Vilna' until its first incorporation into Lithuania in October 1939, and 'Vilnius' thereafter.

Many place names have distinctive Yiddish forms, and sometimes context dictates that these should be given precedence. In such cases the corresponding Polish (Ukrainian, Belarusian, Lithuanian, Russian) name is given in parentheses at the first mention.

In all cases where context does not strongly suggest a preference, the following guidelines will apply by default for the period up to the Second World War:

1. Towns that were clearly part of a particular state and shared the majority nationality of that state will be given in a form which reflects that situation (e.g. Breslau, Danzig, Rzeszów, Przemyśl).

2. Towns that were in 'mixed' areas will take the form in which they are known today and which reflects their present situation (e.g. Poznań, Toruń, Kaunas).

Note on Transliteration

HEBREW

An attempt has been made to achieve consistency in the transliteration of Hebrew words. The following are the key distinguishing features of the system that has been adopted:

1. No distinction is made between the *aleph* and *ayin*; both are represented by an apostrophe, and only when they appear in an intervocalic position.
2. *Veit* is written *v*; *ḥet* is written *ḥ*; *yod* is written *y* when it functions as a consonant and *i* when it occurs as a vowel; *khaf* is written *kh*; *tsadi* is written *ts*; *kof* is written *k*.
3. The *dagesh ḥazak*, represented in some transliteration systems by doubling the letter, is not represented, except in words that have more or less acquired normative English spellings that include doublings, such as Hallel, kabbalah, Kaddish, rabbi, Sukkot, and Yom Kippur.
4. The *sheva na* is represented by an *e*.
5. Hebrew prefixes, prepositions, and conjunctions are not followed by a hyphen when they are transliterated; thus *betoledot ha'am hayehudi*.
6. Capital letters are not used in the transliteration of Hebrew except for the first word in the titles of books and the names of people, places, institutions, and generally as in the conventions of the English language.
7. The names of individuals are transliterated following the above rules unless the individual concerned followed a different usage.

YIDDISH

Transliteration follows the YIVO system except for the names of people, where the spellings they themselves used have been retained.

RUSSIAN AND UKRAINIAN

The system used is that of British Standard 2979:1958, without diacritics. Except in bibliographical and other strictly rendered matter, soft and hard signs are omitted and word-final -й, -ий, -ый, -ій in names are simplified to *-y*.

PART I

Jewish Women in Eastern Europe

Introduction
A Historiographical Survey

CHAERAN FREEZE and PAULA HYMAN

'ONE of the most corrosive assumptions of mainstream history is that it is only public events and lives which are important and meaningful,' the historian Megan Doolittle has observed.[1] Indeed, Jewish women's exclusion from the public domains of religious and civil life has been reflected in their near absence in the master narratives of the east European Jewish past. In his monumental *History of the Jews in Russia and Poland*, Simon Dubnow was content to note that not a 'single woman [attained] literary fame among the Jews of Poland and Lithuania'.[2] Moreover, attempts to highlight women's achievements (as students, workers, and revolutionaries) have not challenged or restructured the historical narrative; rather, the separate treatment of women has only served to 'fill in the gaps' (in a move known as compensatory history) and 'to confirm their marginal and particularized relationship to those (male) subjects already established as dominant and universal'.[3] Nor have Jewish women found their place in general studies of Polish and Russian women, which have often excluded women of other nationalities owing to the differences in their cultural, religious, and social development.[4] To be sure, there are a few exceptions, such as Barbara Engel's works on radical Russian women of the 1870s, which include a few well-known Jewish revolutionaries such as Gesia Gelfman (who was convicted in the assassination plot of Alexander II), and Laurie Bernstein's study of prostitution in tsarist Russia, which notes Jewish participation

[1] M. Doolittle, 'Close Relations? Bringing Together Gender and Family in English History', in L. Davidoff, K. McClelland, and E. Varikas (eds.), *Gender and History: Retrospect and Prospect* (Oxford, 2000), 124.

[2] S. Dubnow, *History of the Jews in Russia and Poland* (Philadelphia, 1975), i. 121.

[3] J. W. Scott, *Gender and the Politics of History* (New York, 1988), 10. Some early attempts to include stories of east European Jewish women can be found in S. Henry and E. Taitz, *Written Out of History: Our Jewish Foremothers* (New York, 1978), which highlighted the lives of a few educated women such as Rivka Tiktiner, author of *Meneket rivkah* (1602), notable hasidic women, and *firzogerins*, who read the synagogue prayers for women.

[4] See e.g. B. E. Clements, B. A. Engel, and C. D. Worobec (eds.), *Russia's Women: Accommodation, Resistance, and Transformation* (Berkeley, 1991), 3. Jewish women are only mentioned in passing as a statistic in R. Jaworski and B. Petrow-Ennker (eds.), *Women in Polish Society* (New York, 1992).

in the sex industry.[5] Even in these studies, however, Jewish women are marginal—perhaps more a reflection of their secondary roles in the broader story than a deliberate attempt to minimize their significance.

As a result, in contrast to the rich body of new knowledge about women in Europe and the United States, the study of Jewish women in eastern Europe is still in its infancy. The fundamental task of feminist historians to construct women as historical subjects, 'as a focus of inquiry, a subject of the story, an agent of the narrative',[6] has only recently begun. This neglect of women's experiences may be explained in part by the traditional preoccupation with political and intellectual history in east European Jewish studies. The near absence of social history (or the writing of history from the 'bottom up'), which has generated a mass of information and rich debate about women's experiences in other disciplines,[7] has meant that basic questions about everyday Jewish life have gone unanswered. Only small inroads have been made in the study of Jewish women's social experiences in reproduction (birth, contraception, and abortion), sexuality, the family (the household, marriage, divorce, motherhood, and widowhood), social deviance, charity, body and mind, popular culture, everyday life (material culture, clothing and fashion, food and diet), work, religion, and education—all of which have been staples of social history for decades.[8]

Methodologically, the field has recently begun to explore issues of gender and the new cultural history after the 'linguistic turn'. In 1986 Joan Scott proposed a

[5] B. A. Engel and C. N. Rosenthal (eds. and trans.), *Five Sisters: Women Against the Tsar: The Memoirs of Five Young Anarchist Women of the 1870s*, 2nd edn. (London, 1992); L. Bernstein, *Sonya's Daughters: Prostitutes and their Regulation in Imperial Russia* (Berkeley: University of California Press, 1995).

[6] Scott, *Gender and the Politics of History*, 17.

[7] In the field of Russian history, for example, see A. Bobroff-Hajal, *Working Women and the Hunger Tsars: Political Activism and Daily Life* (New York, 1994); Clements, Engel, and Worobec (eds.), *Russia's Women: Accommodation, Resistance, Transformation*; B. A. Engel, *Between the Fields and the City: Women, Work and Family in Russia, 1861–1914* (Cambridge, 1994); B. Farnsworth and L. Viola (eds.), *Russian Peasant Women* (New York, 1992); R. L. Blackman, *Russian Factory Women: Workplace and Society, 1889–1914* (Berkeley, 1984); M. Lamarche Marrese, *A Woman's Kingdom: Noblewomen and the Control of Property in Russia, 1700–1861* (Ithaca, NY, 2002); B. Meehan, *Holy Women of Russia: The Lives of Five Orthodox Women Offer Spiritual Guidance for Today* (New York, 1997); B. T. Norton and J. Heath (eds.), *An Improper Profession: Women, Gender, and Journalism in Late Imperial Russia* (Durham, NC, 2001); N. Pushkareva, *Women in Russian History: From the Tenth to the Twentieth Century*, trans. E. Levin (Armonk, NY, 1997); D. Ransel, *Mothers of Misery: Child Abandonment in Russia* (Princeton, 1988); R. Stites, *The Women's Liberation Movement in Russia: Feminism, Nihilism, and Bolshevism, 1860–1930* (Princeton, 1991); W. Wagner, *Marriage, Property, and Law in Late Imperial Russia* (Oxford, 1994); C. D. Worobec, *Peasant Russia: Family and Community in the Post-Emancipation Period* (Princeton, 1991); ead., *Possessed: Women, Witches, and Demons in Imperial Russia* (DeKalb, Ill., 2001).

[8] Some influential works in German women's history, for example, include U. Frevert, *Women in German History: Bourgeois Emancipation to Sexual Liberation* (Oxford, 1989); M. Kaplan, *The Making of the Jewish Middle Class: Women, Family, and Identity in Imperial Germany* (Oxford, 1991); I. V. Hull, *Sexuality, State and Civil Society in Germany, 1700–1815* (Ithaca, NY, 1996); A. Grossman, *Reforming*

new way of analysing the dynamics of gender in shaping history in her classic article 'Gender: A Useful Category of Historical Analysis'.[9] Influenced by the theories of Jacques Derrida, Michel Foucault, and others, she challenged historians to reconceptualize the binary opposition of 'male' and 'female' as historical constructions rather than as enduring categories. Instead of accepting gendered identities and norms as fixed and immutable, she argued that history could reveal *how* they had been constructed through symbolic representations, social institutions and organizations, and specific historical settings and culture. Gender, according to Scott, is the social organization of relationships based on sexual differences and a 'primary way of signifying relationships of power'.[10] It also goes beyond the categories of 'men and women' to assign meanings to all forms of concrete and symbolic human interaction including religion, politics, cultural production, sexuality, and the body. Judith Butler has also suggested that gender is not simply a social construction but a performance—the playing out of 'fantasy identifications' with one sex (male or female), with dress, language, and social codes appropriate for that role. In her own words: 'There is no gender identity behind the expressions of gender . . . identity is performatively constituted by the very "expressions" that are said to be its results.'[11] In other words, gender is not a fixed attribute or essence, but a variable that changes with different contexts.[12]

Scott and Butler's critique of 'universal womanhood' then raises a fundamental question about the very category of 'east European Jewish women' who resided across a vast geographic expanse in different cultural, political, and social settings. As European women historians have emphasized, categories such as social class, marital status, and geographic location created significant differences in women's experiences.[13] Jewish women were divided by all these factors and their identities, in terms of both their Jewishness and their understanding of appropriate female roles. To speak of an undifferentiated category labelled 'east European Jewish women' is to distort the self-definitions and the experiences of the millions of Jewish women who lived in Poland, Russia, and Galicia. Equally important is the question, posed by feminist historians who fear that gender theory relegates women to the 'relational

Sex (New York, 1995); R. Bridenthal, A. Grossman, and M. Kaplan (eds.), *When Biology Became Destiny: Women in Weimar and Nazi Germany* (New York, 1984); C. Koontz, *Mothers in the Fatherland: Women, Family, and Nazi Politics* (New York, 1987).

9 J. Scott, 'Gender: A Useful Category of Historical Analysis', in her *Gender and the Politics of History*, 28–50.

10 Ibid. 42.

11 J. Butler, *Gender Trouble: Feminism and the Subversion of Identity* (New York, 1990), 25.

12 For a critique of essentialism, see the classic study by D. Riley, *'Am I That Name?' Feminism and the Category of 'Women' in History* (Minneapolis, 1988).

13 See e.g. B. S. Anderson and J. P. Zinsser, *A History of their Own: Women in Europe from Prehistory to the Present*, 2 vols., 2nd edn. (Oxford, 1999); M. J. Boxer and J. H. Quataert (eds.), *Connecting Spheres: Women in the Western World, 1500 to the Present*, 2nd edn. (New York, 1999); K. Offen, R. R. Pierson, and J. Rendell (eds.), *Writing Women's History: International Perspectives* (Bloomington, Ind., 1990).

status that historians in general accorded them',[14] how does Jewish women's agency fit into these new paradigms of relational subjectivity? Despite these challenges, the chapters in this volume of *Polin* demonstrate that gender theory, with its attention to language, power, and formation of gendered identities, has already had a significant impact on the study of Jewish women in eastern Europe. It has provided a new understanding of how hierarchies of difference were constructed and legitimized[15] in east European Jewish society, as well as of the politics of gender in education, cultural production, religion, marriage, and other spheres of everyday life.

The following chapters investigate different aspects of Jewish women's experiences in Poland and Russia from the early modern period and through the inter-war years. They contribute new perspectives to a nascent historiography that has begun to tap new sources such as rabbinical responsa and other halakhic literature, Yiddish *tkhines* (prayers for women), newspapers, belletristic literature and memoirs by and about women, and newly declassified archival materials from the former Soviet Union. Although the historiography has developed unevenly owing to the nature of the source base, as we shall see below, there is now a solid foundation on which to build new scholarship and to consider how to incorporate the new findings into the master narratives of the east European Jewish past.

THE EARLY MODERN PERIOD

In her comprehensive study *Women and Gender in Early Modern Europe*, Merry Wiesner noted the paucity of literature on women in eastern Europe and on Jewish women in particular.[16] Indeed, very little is known about Jewish women's lives during the period of the Polish–Lithuanian Commonwealth, which represented a paradoxical era of security (at least until the late 1640s) and vulnerability for the Jews. On the one hand, some viewed it as a golden age characterized by unprecedented religious tolerance, economic prosperity based on extensive rights and privileges, and communal autonomy based on local, regional, and central administrative institutions. As Rabbi Moshe ben Yitshak Mintz (Maharam) saw it, the lands of Poland were 'a refuge for the exiled sons (of Israel)'.[17] On the other hand, Moshe Rosman has also noted a 'profound sense of apprehension' in the sources that recognized the precariousness of the Jewish position in Poland, which was contingent on the ability to justify the goodwill of the rulers and nobility and the mood of the general Christian population.[18]

The majority of Jews, who numbered around 750,000 by 1765, lived in towns

[14] B. G. Smith, 'Gender Theory', in *Encyclopedia of European Social History from 1350–2000* (New York, 2001), i. 99.

[15] Scott, *Gender and the Politics of History*, 4.

[16] M. Wiesner, *Women and Gender in Early Modern Europe*, 2nd edn. (Cambridge, 2000), 6.

[17] Cited by G. D. Hundert, 'Some Basic Characteristics of the Jewish Experience in Poland', *Polin*, 1 (1986), 19.

[18] M. J. Rosman, 'Jewish Perceptions of Insecurity and Powerlessness in 16th–18th-Century Poland', *Polin*, 1 (1986), 19–27.

owned by the Crown or powerful magnates. Despite their distinct religious and cultural lifestyle, Jews were hardly isolated from their Polish environment; indeed, as new studies have shown, Jewish architecture, music, language, dress, and culture occasionally reflected Polish influences.[19] By the close of the 'Nobleman's Republic', Polish Jewry was a society rife with conflict and dissension. Mounting social tensions between the oligarchic Jewish authorities and the lower social orders, combined with external political and economic calamities in Poland, all generated a profound sense of crisis on every level of Jewish life.

What were Jewish women's experiences during this period? The relatively few studies on Jewish women at the time have focused on several aspects of women's lives: their culture, economic activities, female piety, family, and sexuality. Moshe Rosman's chapter in this volume, which surveys the historiography, analyses distinct gendered spheres of culture that emerged in east European Jewish society, such as education, reading habits, methods of study, prayer, ritual observance, and economics. The underlying question of his study is 'Did women have power?' Rosman argues that while women were 'weak with respect to culture' in a patriarchal society dominated by the scholarly elites, there were 'women with social power'.[20] These were usually wealthy widows or householders with significant financial resources and economic privileges. Indeed, Gershon Hundert's study of Opatów, for example, demonstrates that women did act independently in their economic activities; more often than not, however, they worked in co-operation with their husbands. Edward Fram also suggests that rabbis like Solomon Luria sought to reconcile restrictive laws that limited women's power in the marketplace with the public realities where they made active decisions, if not controlled the business single-handedly.[21] Rosman concedes that it remains a matter of debate whether economic independence and power translated into social prestige, and more research needs to be conducted.

Another area of study has focused on Jewish women's piety and spirituality. The paucity of studies on women's religious experiences in eastern Europe is striking, given the sheer weight of the scholarship on Jewish religious movements, especially on hasidism.[22] This may not be surprising, however, since women were excluded from the major arenas of public religious life (such as the synagogue, where they

[19] See G. D. Hundert, Introduction, *Polin*, 10 (1997), pp. xxxi–xxxiv; E. Fram, *Ideals Face Reality: Jewish Law and Life in Poland, 1550–1655* (Cincinnati, 1997), 29–33.

[20] In general Polish historiography, similar questions have been raised about the status of noblewomen. In her study of the noble family structure, Bogna Lorence-Kot argues that Polish women occupied a contradictory position: on the one hand, they were 'equal' to men as members of the *szlachta*; on the other hand, they were subordinate to their husbands in the family. At the same time, the degree of control that a husband could exercise over his wife was limited owing to her financial independence (e.g. her entitlement to a fixed legacy in the form of monetary payments from her father's estate and dowry). See B. Lorence-Kot, *Childrearing and Reform: A Study of the Nobility in Eighteenth-Century Poland* (Westport, Conn., 1985), 47–9.

[21] *Fram, Ideals Face Reality*, 80.

[22] There is a rich collection of studies on Jewish religious movements and spirituality in Poland–Lithuania. The preponderance of works has focused on hasidism, a popular spiritual revival move-

sat separately in a balcony or behind a partition) and left only a 'scant literary legacy of their own'. But as Ellen Umansky has pointed out, to recognize 'study and communal worship as the heart and soul of traditional Judaism . . . minimizes or ignores the reality of women's religious lives'.[23]

Gender assumptions about the innate emotional nature of women versus the intellectual nature of men permeate the early studies on Jewish women's spirituality in hasidism.[24] According to S. A. Horodecky, women were not only receptive to hasidism because of its emotional character but they gained 'complete equality' in religious life in contrast to their sisters who remained oppressed by 'rabbinic' Judaism (e.g. mitnagdism). As he put it:

> Emotional religion (hasidism) which transcends all rules and regulations . . . accommodated the Jewish woman and allowed her much scope for direct involvement. . . . The Lurianic Kabbalah (Jewish mystical teachings) in particular had a great impact on the Jews of Poland in the sixteenth and seventeenth centuries, and the Polish-Jewish woman was emotionally receptive to it in full.

Horodecky concludes that hasidism ultimately strengthened the Jewish family by ameliorating the status of women, who were generally ignorant of Hebrew; it removed the obstacles to female knowledge of Judaism by producing religious literature in the vernacular Yiddish and allowed women to occupy key leadership roles in some instances.[25]

Ada Rapoport-Albert challenges these claims in her case study of Hannah Rachel Verbermakher (b. *c.*1815), 'the holy Maid of Ludmir'.[26] She argues that the

ment that originated in Podolia in the mid-18th century. See e.g. D. Assaf, *The Regal Way: The Life and Times of Rabbi Israel of Ruzhin* (Stanford, Calif., 2002); I. Etkes, *Tenuat haḥasidut bereshitah* (Tel Aviv, 1998); G. D. Hundert (ed.), *Essential Papers on Hasidism: Origins to Present* (New York, 1991); M. Idel, *Hasidism: Between Ecstasy and Magic* (Albany, NY, 1995); A. Rapoport-Albert (ed.), *Hasidism Reappraised* (London, 1996). Fewer studies have been devoted to the opponents of hasidism—the mitnagedim of Lithuania—who reinvigorated Torah studies by creating a culture founded on the supremacy of religious learning (for males), or to the *musar* (ethics) movement of the mid-19th century, which sought to 'grant higher priority to ethical education within Jewish life', especially in the arena of social relations. See I. Etkes, *The Gaon of Vilna: The Man and his Image* (Berkeley, 2002); id., *Rabbi Israel Salanter and the Mussar Movement: Seeking the Torah of Truth* (Philadelphia, 1993); M. Wilensky, *Ḥasidim umitnagedim: Letoledot hapulmus shebeneihem bashanim 1772–1815* (Jerusalem, 1990).

[23] E. Umansky, 'Spiritual Expressions: Jewish Women's Religious Lives in the United States in the Nineteenth and Twentieth Centuries', in J. Baskin (ed.), *Jewish Women in Historical Perspective*, 2nd edn. (Detroit, 1998), 337.

[24] See e.g. J. S. Minkin, *The Romance of Hassidism*, 3rd edn. (Los Angeles, 1971), 345–7; D. L. Mekler, *Fun rebins hoyf fun chernobyl biz talne* (New York, 1931), 209–45; H. Rabinowicz, *A Guide to Hassidism* (London, 1970), 102–13; ead., *The World of Hasidism* (Hartford, Conn., 1970), esp. ch. 21: 'Lady Rabbis and Rabbinic Daughters'; M. Feinkind, *Froyen rabonim un barimte perzenlekhkeytin in poylen* (Warsaw, 1937), 21–69.

[25] S. A. Horodecky, *Haḥasidut vehaḥasidim* (Tel Aviv, 1943), iv. 67–9.

[26] A. Rapoport-Albert, 'On Women in Hasidism, S. A. Horodecky and the Maid of Ludmir Tradition', in A. Rapoport-Albert and S. J. Zipperstein (eds.), *Jewish History: Essays in Honor of Chimen*

distinctive customs of hasidism detracted from a strong family life, as males abandoned their wives and children, especially during the sabbath and Jewish holidays, to spend months in the courts of their *rebbe*s (hasidic leaders). Women were generally excluded from these intimate moments with the *rebbe* and were left to 'fend for themselves'. Moreover, she demonstrates that the proliferation of Yiddish books—mainly hagiographies and popular literature—neither was intended explicitly for women nor enhanced their knowledge about more esoteric matters. In fact, the highly esteemed mystical and ethical literature was published exclusively in Hebrew, barring women from access to this important body of knowledge that shaped the theology and practices of hasidism. More importantly, she demonstrates that hasidism retained traditional gender boundaries, making it impossible for women to assume positions of leadership or to practise 'male' forms of piety. The story of the Maid of Ludmir, a popular miracle-working figure who was born in Volhynia province, provides an excellent case in point. Ironically, she was well known for her strong intellectual proclivities as a student of the Bible, Talmud, and other rabbinic literature in Hebrew. After a traumatic betrothal, the death of her mother, and a mysterious illness, the Maid of Ludmir went into seclusion, began to observe all the male rituals, and gained a widespread reputation as a teacher and miracle worker. Her desire to embrace the ascetic lifestyle promoted by the mystical teachings so popular in her time met with strong opposition and social pressure from the hasidic establishment for her to marry. As Rapoport-Albert suggests, asceticism in Judaism had always been treated with ambivalence, but society had legitimized and even sanctified periods of sexual abstinence for men.[27] For Jewish women, however, this was not an option as it was for their Christian counterparts. After two failed unconsummated marriages, the Maid's reputation declined and she died in obscurity in the Holy Land. 'Had this tradition bestowed any legitimacy on the ascetic piety of women,' Rapoport-Albert concludes, 'the Maid might have found an outlet for it even within marriage as did men who managed to achieve it without altogether renouncing their . . . obligation toward worldly existence.'[28]

If Jewish society rejected expressions of ascetic piety by women, it promoted more traditional forms of female piety—the subject of Chava Weissler's *Voices of the Matriarchs*. Her study explores the *tkhines*, or supplicatory prayers, written by both sexes for 'women and men who are like women' (e.g. ignorant in Hebrew) in the seventeenth and eighteenth centuries. Weissler's exploration of the 'lived religion' of Jewish women leads her to consider the relationship between popular religion and the 'high tradition' of the educated male leadership of traditional Jewish communities. She makes it clear that despite the gender hierarchy of traditional Jewish life, the Judaism of uneducated, often barely literate, Jewish men

Abramsky (London, 1988), 498–525; see also N. Deutsch, *The Maid of Ludmir: A Holy Jewish Woman and her World* (Berkeley, 2003).

[27] See A. Rapoport-Albert, *Female Bodies, Male Souls: Asceticism and Gender in the Jewish Tradition* (forthcoming).

[28] Rapoport-Albert, 'On Women in Hasidism', 502–3, 508.

shared many features with that of women. Indeed, men and women read many of the same *musar* (ethics) books in Yiddish. As Weissler notes, women's spirituality was 'very much enmeshed in the very fiber of Ashkenazic Judaism' and represented 'female variants of male Jewish culture'.[29]

Weissler's examination of those 'female variants' provides a portrait of the spiritual world of women. For example, in contrast to the obligatory Hebrew liturgy that men recited at set times in a public congregation, the *tkhines* were voluntary, personal, and recited at home in Yiddish, the vernacular language of east European Jewry. Moreover, the prayers addressed issues of specific concern to women (such as pregnancy, childbirth, child-rearing, visiting the cemetery or ritual bathhouse, petitioning the dead, baking bread, and other domestic rituals) and invoked the biblical matriarchs as models of piety and advocates in times of trouble.[30]

The author also demonstrates that the *tkhines* (especially by female authors) provided a means for women to transcend traditional gender roles if only momentarily, while at the same time valorizing female rituals and domestic culture. In *Tkhine imrei shifre* ('The *Tkhine* of Shifrah's Words'), the author endowed the lighting of the sabbath candles (one of the three women's commandments[31]) with mystical meaning, countering the rabbinic view that this action served to compensate for Eve's sin when she 'extinguished the light of the world'. Employing kabbalistic (mystical) images and ideas, Shifrah explains that 'the earthly act of lighting candles corresponds to the kindling of lights in the realm of the divine, which is a symbol of the union and harmony of the *sefirot* [emanations of revealed divinity] that occurs on the Sabbath'.[32] As Weissler points out, Shifrah took a bolder step when she cast the woman in the symbolic role of the High Priest who facilitated the union of the male and female aspects of God (the lower seven *sefirot*) when he lit the candelabrum in the Temple. While women still performed the ritual in their domestic sphere, they symbolically assumed a role that would have been unimaginable in traditional Judaism.[33]

[29] Weissler, *Voices of the Matriarchs: Listening to the Prayers of Early Modern Jewish Women* (Boston, 1998), 175.

[30] Ibid. 121–5.

[31] The three *mitsvot* (religious commandments) that women were obliged to observe include: *ḥalah*, or burning a small portion of the dough during the baking of bread in memory of the priestly tithes; *nidah*, or the sexual separation from a husband during menstruation; and the kindling of candles on sabbath. Women were obliged to keep the majority of other commandments like men, but were exempt from certain positive time-bound commandments and other laws, such as the duty to study Torah. For more detail, see R. Biale, *Women and Jewish Law: The Essential Texts, their History, and their Relevance for Today* (New York, 1984), 10–43.

[32] According to kabbalah, which sought to understand the inner life of the Godhead, there were two aspects of God: the Ein Sof (Infinity), or the 'unknowable' aspect of God, and the ten *sefirot* (emanations from the Ein Sof), or revealed divinity. For more on gender and kabbalah, see E. R. Wolfson, *Circle in the Square: Studies in the Use of Gender in Kabbalistic Symbolism* (New York, 1995).

[33] Weissler illustrates how Shifrah appropriated the idea of the High Priest from two passages of *Nakhalas tsevi* that included a translation of the Zohar (*c.*1300), the classical work of Jewish mysticism.

The study of female spirituality and ritual is complemented by recent research on the 'this-worldly' concerns of women in the area of family, inheritance, economics, and other facets of daily life. Edward Fram's groundbreaking use of early modern responsa literature (legal questions to prominent rabbis and their responses) reveals how women may have been impacted by rabbinic decision-making. Scholars have been extremely cautious and even reluctant to use this body of rabbinic decisions as a source, because they pose numerous methodological problems, especially for those unfamiliar with Jewish law. Since these terse legal decisions were not meant to be historical documents, they leave out basic information with which one might reconstruct the past (names, dates, personal details); in fact, some responsa may have dealt with hypothetical rather than real social or religious concerns. Moreover, Fram points out that one needs to be careful in accessing what is novel since the entire genre of responsa dealt with exceptions. In some instances, it was merely the legal argument that was new, not the circumstances described in the text.[34]

Despite these challenges, Fram illustrates how rabbinic authorities navigated between the demands of religious law and social realities in their decision-making, often bending to protect women whose legal status was inferior in Jewish law. For example, in a case of an orphaned bride in Poland whose prospective groom attempted to cancel the wedding by refusing to marry until an hour after sunset on Friday (the beginning of sabbath), Rabbi Moses Isserles nevertheless performed the ceremony on the sabbath in apparent violation of religious laws in order to preserve the bride's dignity and to secure her marriage.[35] Fram attempts to uncover the extra-legal concerns that may have shaped judicial decisions like the one above by comparing two similar cases that resulted in diametrically opposed decisions by the same rabbi.[36] His case study examines the responsa of Rabbi Joel Sirkes of Kraków (d. 1640) on the status of two married women who were suspected of adultery. The central question was: should the adulteress be permitted to return to her husband? Based on an exhaustive examination of legal precedents, Rabbi Sirkes ruled that the husband would have to divorce his wife in the first case: not only were there two witnesses to the 'ugly act' and endless rumours about the wife's infidelity, but there was also an admission on the part of the wife. In contrast to the first case, the second suspected adulteress maintained her innocence, which 'Sirkes exploited to support her continued status as a faithful wife'. More importantly, Fram points out that concern for the welfare of the children was critical in the decision to be more lenient in the second case, in which the couple had children, unlike the first case. While Rabbi Sirkes conceded that the husband retained the right to divorce

As noted in the text, Shifrah did not view the commandment of candle-lighting as a punishment for Eve's sin, as explained in *Nakhalas tsevi*. See Weissler, *Voices of the Matriarchs*, 98–100.

34 Fram, *Ideals Face Reality*, 7–12.

35 Ibid. 70.

36 E. Fram, 'Two Cases of Adultery and the Halakhic Decision-Making Process', *AJS Review*, 26/2 (Nov. 2002), 277–300.

his wife with her consent, he was responsible for their financial maintenance. Fram observes that the rabbi may have been concerned not only for the children's financial welfare but for their personal status, for rumours about a woman's fidelity could taint her children's identity and their ability to marry in the future. In any case, while Fram's case studies focus primarily on the process of rabbinic decision-making, they nonetheless shed light on how women may have been impacted by their rulings.[37]

Insight into Jewish women's marital experiences and sexuality may also be found in Jakub Goldberg's study of Jewish marriage in eighteenth-century Poland. He argues that a growing perception of sexual permissiveness and moral laxity among Jews (e.g. premarital loss of virginity and adultery with Christians), although hardly widespread, prompted maskilim such as Jakub Kalmanson to advocate marital reform in order to preserve traditional family values and to raise the level of marital satisfaction.[38] It may be worthwhile to note that general studies of marital annulments by the Polish Catholic Church in the same period have also found a certain 'decline of morals' among the nobility. For example, Bogna Lorence-Kot's examination of annulment petitions shows a growing demand for personal happiness among noblewomen who rebelled against the prevailing aristocratic values (such as obedience of wives to husbands) of the eighteenth century to pursue their desires.[39]

Discussion of sexuality and the body is not limited to communal records that registered 'unkosher' brides who had accidentally lost their virginity or indictments against those who engaged in premarital sexuality. Rabbinic and ethical literature can also shed light on gendered views of sexuality in Jewish society. Chava Weissler has found that 'male' ethical literature (such as Isaiah Horowitz's *Shenei luḥot haberit* , 'Two Tables of the Covenant') was often dominated by discussions about sexual desire (the sins of masturbation and nocturnal emission), in contrast to the 'female' prayers (*tkhines*) which focused mainly on reproduction, not erotic sexuality. Weissler suggests that the 'popularization of Kabbalah during this period needs to be understood in the context of male guilt and fear, on the one hand, and of female lack of interest in, or suppression of, sexuality, on the other'.[40] In another comparison of two genres of literature on menstruation and childbirth, Weissler also discovered that the *musar* literature was more concerned with 'why women are the way they are, whence the archetypal nature of the irreducibly Other springs',

[37] Tamar Salmon utilizes a similar approach using rabbinic literature to explore the divorce of insane women in early modern Poland. See T. Salmon, 'Gerushei nashim lo shafuyot bepolin beme'ah ha-17 veha-18', *Gal-Ed*, 17 (2000), 37–61, and T. Salmon-Mack, 'Ḥayei nisuin beyahadut polin, 1650–1800', Ph.D. thesis (Hebrew University, 2002).

[38] He also discovered a high rate of mortality among Jewish women (which doctors of the time attributed to the dangers and frequency of childbirth) and examined its impact on the duration of Jewish marriages. See J. Goldberg, 'Jewish Marriage in Eighteenth-Century Poland', *Polin*, 10 (1997), 3–39.

[39] Lorence-Kot, *Child Rearing and Reform*, 55 ff.

[40] Weissler, *Voices of the Matriarchs*, 47.

while the *tkhines* 'wanted to understand how God's justice can require women's suffering'.[41]

JEWISH WOMEN IN THE RUSSIAN EMPIRE AND GALICIA (1772–1917)

The partitions of Poland (1772–95) by the Great Powers—Russia, Prussia, and Austria—brought Jewish women under very different sociopolitical and cultural milieus. The historiography has described broad gender patterns that distinguished Jewish women in eastern Europe from their counterparts in western and central Europe.[42] In the latter countries the experience of civic emancipation, economic integration, and high degree of acculturation 'enabled Jews to situate themselves securely in the bourgeoisie'.[43] The ideals of bourgeois domesticity prescribed specific gender roles: a woman was 'priestess of the home' who cultivated respectability (*Bildung*), preserved religious rituals, and managed the household and upbringing of children, while men fulfilled their roles in the public sphere of business, politics, and education.[44] Jewish women also increasingly participated in philanthropic activities and organizations, which not only gave them a voice in the public sphere without challenging conventional gender norms, but also helped them develop close friendships and ties with non-Jewish women who supported similar causes.[45]

In contrast, the vast majority of Jewish women who resided in 'eastern Europe', which has generally referred to the Russian empire and Galicia (often described as the backwaters of the Austro-Hungarian empire), followed a different historical trajectory during the long nineteenth century. As Ezra Mendelsohn has noted, although Galician Jewry received civil emancipation in 1868, they 'resembled in all other respects' their co-religionists who lived in the Pale of Settlement.[46] These areas underwent a belated, protracted process of modernization not only in the economic, but also in the social and cultural, spheres. Throughout the nineteenth

[41] C. Weissler, 'Mitzvot Built into the Body: *Tkhines* for *Niddah*, Pregnancy, and Childbirth', in H. Eilberg-Schwartz (ed.), *People of the Body: Jews and Judaism from an Embodied Perspective* (Albany, NY, 1992).

[42] See P. Hyman, 'Two Models of Modernization: Jewish Women in the German and the Russian Empire', in *Studies in Contemporary Jewry*, xvi: *Jews and Gender: The Challenge to Hierarchy*, ed. J. Frankel (Oxford, 2000), 39–53.

[43] P. Hyman, 'Gender and the Jewish Family in Modern Europe', in D. Ofer and L. J. Weitzman (eds.), *Women in the Holocaust* (New Haven, 1998), 25.

[44] M. Kaplan, *The Making of the Jewish Middle Class: Women, Family, and Identity in Imperial Germany* (Oxford, 1991).

[45] Ibid. 192–227; id., *The Jewish Feminist Movement in Germany: The Campaigns of the Jüdischer Frauenbund, 1904–1938* (Westport, Conn., 1979).

[46] E. Mendelsohn, 'Jewish Assimilation in Lvov: The Case of Wilhelm Feldman', *Slavic Review*, 28/4 (1969), 577.

century east European Jews retained a few distinguishing characteristics that accentuated their 'otherness': a common religion, language (Yiddish), dress, communal institutions, and economic pursuits (mainly in petty trade, commerce, and artisanry). Notwithstanding this collective identity, which was reinforced by ethnic and religious boundaries, as well as discriminatory state policies, Jewish society was composed of diverse subcultures—hasidim, mitnagdim, maskilim, the new *Bildungsbürgertum* or *obshchestvennost'* (educated society)—each with its own constellation of values, customs, and life ways.

Although it is impossible to generalize about Jewish women's lives in eastern Europe during this period, the historiography has emphasized several key themes, especially their paradoxical status, roles, and images. They were at once subordinate and domineering in the family, conservative and revolutionary in their politics, pious preservers of Judaism and 'engines of acculturation'. Unlike their sisters in the west, they participated actively in economic and public life, but were similarly excluded from formal leadership positions in the synagogue and community. To understand these paradoxes, the recent historiography has focused on how women sought to accommodate, resist, or negotiate their position in Jewish society, as well the broader forces that helped to perpetuate or challenge traditional gender hierarchies and relations.

Family Life

Until recently, portraits of Jewish women's status and roles in the family have relied primarily on childhood memories of east European immigrants to the United States. Studies such as Sidney Stahl Weinberg's *World of Our Mothers* (1988) and Susan Glenn's *Daughters of the Shtetl* (1990), for example, seek to understand how women's experiences in the Old World shaped their self-perception and identities in America as mothers, wives, workers, and political activists. In particular, both works emphasize the unique gender division of labour in eastern Europe that assigned the wife the task of earning a livelihood so that her learned husband could fulfil the cultural ideal of Torah study.[47] To be sure, this allocation of roles was more ideal than real; most men were not learned, and the majority of spouses could ill afford to subsist on women's earnings alone and shared the breadwinning responsibilities. Nonetheless, Paula Hyman notes that these cultural ideals served to legitimize women's work outside the household—a model and ethos that were easily transferred to other settings.[48] Moreover, Glenn points out that 'this flexibility in gender roles . . . helped modify patriarchal dominance and blurred the lines between gender roles'.[49]

[47] See also C. Baum, 'What Made Yetta Work? The Economic Role of East European Jewish Women in the Family', *Response: A Contemporary Jewish Review*, 18 (1973), 32–8.

[48] P. Hyman, *Gender and Assimilation*, 67.

[49] S. Glenn, *Daughters of the Shtetl: Life and Labour in the Immigrant Generation* (Ithaca, NY, 1990), 14.

The cultural ideal of Torah studies not only shaped the gender division of labour but created marital tensions, as Immanuel Etkes has shown in his study of the scholarly elites in nineteenth-century Lithuania. Basing his research primarily on letters and memoirs by distinguished rabbis, he argues that Torah scholars were often torn between their devotion to study and family responsibilities. During the early years of marriage they sometimes experienced tensions with in-laws who supported the young couple (a period known as *kest*), while their wives faced the impossible choice of siding with their husbands or parents. In addition, the common practice of travelling to remote yeshivas to study Torah imposed great strains on the wife, who was left not only to fend for the family, but also to bear the emotional pain of separation. Etkes notes the surprising absence of any discussion about the husband's duty to satisfy his wife's sexual needs (a marital obligation encoded in Jewish law) in the letters of fathers to sons. He also points out that leaders of the *musar* movement were silent about a wife's well-being, which should have been a concern for a movement so engrossed with the issue of personal morality. In fact, Rabbi Israel Salanter, the founder of the movement, wandered for over twenty years, leaving his wife alone to raise their children. Etkes suggests that elite society's ability to co-opt women's tacit acceptance of these cultural ideals and gender roles as a 'privilege' allowed this system to perpetuate itself for generations.[50]

The Haskalah movement's criticism of the traditional family and its vision for 'reordering power in Jewish society' has been the subject of several studies.[51] David Biale argues that the maskilim aimed to 'decommercialize' marriage by abolishing traditional early and arranged unions, which they portrayed as financial transactions, devoid of love and consent. Moreover, they castigated traditional gender roles that created 'unproductive', parasitic men who lived off their in-laws or wives and coarse, masculine women in the marketplace. In lieu of these roles, they propagated the cult of domesticity that would shelter Jewish women from the corrupting influences of commerce and refeminize them as mothers, wives, and homemakers in the private sphere. Biale suggests that behind 'this revolt against a perceived matriarchal family' lay a desire on the part of the maskilim to usurp power from the very women who had dominated them in their adolescent marriages.[52]

New archival sources, which have become accessible since the collapse of the Soviet Union in 1993, have also shed new light on Jewish women and family life. In *Jewish Marriage and Divorce in Imperial Russia*,[53] ChaeRan Freeze examines the precipitous decline in the number of divorces from extremely high rates in the early

50 I. Etkes, 'Marriage and Torah Study Among the *Lomdim* in Lithuania in the Nineteenth Century', in D. Kraemer (ed.), *Jewish Family: Metaphor and Memory* (Oxford, 1989), 153–78; id., *Lita biyerushalayim: Hailit halamdanit belita uvekehilat haperushim biyerushalayim le'or igerot ukhetavim shel r. shemuel mikelm* (Jerusalem, 1991).

51 D. Biale, *Eros and the Jews: From Biblical Israel to Contemporary America* (Berkeley, 1997), 150; id., 'Eros and Enlightenment: Love Against Marriage in the East European Jewish Enlightenment', *Polin*, 1 (1986), 63.

52 Ibid. 161.

53 Hanover, NH, 2002.

1830s to a comparatively lower one by 1910. She argues that this distinct pattern did not necessarily mean a decrease in marital breakdown, but rather reflected the legal, economic, and social difficulties in obtaining a formal divorce.

Her study shows that Jewish women became increasingly vulnerable and powerless in matters of divorce, not simply because halakhah (Jewish law) recognized the husband's unilateral prerogative to dissolve the marriage. More important was the breakdown of rabbinical control over these broad rights, which had previously served to protect women. While tsarist law recognized Jewish jurisdiction over marriage and divorce until 1917, it deprived halakhah of the basic mechanism that allowed it to function—namely, the rabbinic power of enforcement. State attempts to create an alternative authority (namely, the state rabbinate created in 1835) only generated more judicial and social chaos. As a result, women found it increasingly difficult to secure a divorce from husbands for reasons such as wife-beating and could be divorced against their will (despite a ban attributed to Rabbi Gershom of Mayence in the eleventh century). To ameliorate their position, Jewish women began to resort to new strategies by going outside the boundaries of the community to the secular courts, as well as to local and central government institutions, to enforce a rabbinic decision or to obtain their rightful monetary settlement (e.g. alimony and child support). Freeze shows that, despite these new venues, Jewish women still suffered from specific disabilities in Jewish law, especially as *agunot* ('anchored women' who were unable to remarry).[54]

Nancy Sinkoff has examined the divorce issue in the Galician context. She analyses an unpublished memorandum written by Joseph Perl to the Galician *Kreisamt* (district office) in the 1830s on the modification of Jewish law, particularly with regard to divorce regulations that required a convert to 'release' his former Jewish wife so she could remarry. In his argument for modifying Jewish divorce legislation, Perl appeals to its historical development. The memorandum not only sheds light on the dilemma felt by Polish maskilim who desired to modernize Polish Jewry while remaining faithful to the principles of rabbinic law, but also illustrates Perl's sensitivity to the vexing issue of *agunot* in the context of the possibility of Jews accepting a civil code that included marriage and divorce, and which could potentially liberate bound women.[55]

Preservers of Tradition or Agents of Acculturation

As the Haskalah, which advocated the reformation of Russian and Polish Jewry, gained strength during the nineteenth century, and as economic and political changes transformed Jewish life, the 'woman question' became an important issue

[54] The problem of the *agunah* is the subject of M. Baker's study 'The Voices of the Deserted Jewish Woman, 1867–1870', *Jewish Social Studies*, 2/1 (1995), 98–123.

[55] N. Sinkoff, 'The *Maskil*, the Convert, and the *Agunah*: Joseph Perl as a Historian of Jewish Divorce Law', *AJS Review*, 27/2 (Nov. 2003), 281–99. See also id., *Out of the 'Shtetl': Making Jews Modern in the Polish Borderlands* (forthcoming).

on the agenda of Jewish leadership, initially with the maskilim and other modernizers, and subsequently with the traditionalists. It did not attract the attention of Jewish specialists, however, until feminist scholarship in the academy had become too pervasive to ignore.

Shmuel Feiner's comprehensive re-examination of the Haskalah as a social as well as an intellectual movement has incorporated the 'woman question' as a component of Haskalah ideology and praxis. Indeed, his important article on the subject of women bears the subtitle 'A Test Case in the Relations of the Haskalah and Modernity'.[56] Feiner uses the complex attitudes of maskilim to women to point out their fundamental ambivalence towards modernity. Although they advocated secular education and a restructuring of Jewish economic pursuits, and although they saw Orthodox Judaism, particularly hasidism, as a major obstacle to the realization of their goals, they retained a measure of fondness for tradition, embracing Hebrew and sexual modesty. They were most uncomfortable with notions of women's equality. While they decried the oppression of women and their ignorance, which was due to limited access to education, women were not welcomed into their ranks. Indeed, as Feiner has shown in another article, women often appeared in their writings as prime examples of the 'pseudo-Haskalah', false maskilim who were characterized by superficiality, vulgarity, and materialism and gave the ideals of Haskalah a bad name.[57]

Literary scholars of the Haskalah have addressed both the representation of women in Haskalah writings and also women's roles in the Haskalah itself. Tova Cohen's book *One Beloved and the Other Hated: Between Fiction and Reality in Haskalah Depictions of Women*[58] is a major study of the various images of women in Haskalah literature both in Hebrew and, to a lesser extent, in Yiddish. In a feminist reading of Haskalah fiction and poetry, Cohen succeeds in linking the positive and negative female tropes to the broader social attitudes of the Haskalah. In her chapter in this volume, 'Hebrew Maskilot: Between Feminine and Feminist Writing', she addresses the ways that the few female authors who wrote in Hebrew encoded their gender concerns in their writing, even when they followed the generic patterns of Haskalah literature.

Iris Parush has pioneered in exploring the social role of women writers in the Haskalah and the succeeding generation and their impact on Jewish culture more generally.[59] A scholar of literature and literacy, she focuses on the consequences of

[56] S. Feiner, 'Ha'ishah hayehudit hamodernit: Mikreh-mivḥan beyaḥasei hahaskalah vehamodernah', *Zion*, 58 (1993), 453–99.

[57] S. Feiner, 'The Pseudo-Enlightenment and the Question of Jewish Modernization', *Jewish Social Studies*, 3/1 (Fall 1996), 62–88.

[58] T. Cohen, *Ha'aḥat ahuvah veha'aḥat senuah: Bein metsiut lebidyon bete'urei ha'ishah besifrut hahaskalah* (Jerusalem, 2002).

[59] I. Parush, *Nashim korot: Yitronah shel hashuliyut baḥevrah hayehudit bemizraḥ eiropah bame'ah hatesha-esreh* (Tel Aviv, 2001); trans. as *Reading Jewish Women: Marginality and Modernization in Nineteenth-Century Eastern European Jewish Society* (Hanover, NH, 2004).

the gendered division of the two Jewish languages, Hebrew and Yiddish. Like Naomi Seidman, whose *A Marriage Made in Heaven* analyses the cultural conflict of the two languages in terms of gender,[60] Parush interrogates the meaning of the subordinate status of women and 'their' language, Yiddish, in contrast to men and 'their' language, Hebrew. Fully at home in Haskalah literature, including the numerous essays that appeared in Haskalah journals, she expands the discussion of the attitudes of maskilim towards women and provides new information on the women who participated in maskilic culture.

Most importantly, Parush argues that the gendered nature of traditional Jewish society led to women acquiring secular culture to a greater degree than men. In middle-class Jewish homes, even among the Orthodox, women were taught foreign languages and their literatures. A small elite of girls also acquired mastery of Hebrew through private tutoring. Moreover, their literacy went substantially beyond the basic decoding of what they read. As they immersed themselves in modern secular culture and adopted modern values, they served as agents of acculturation in Jewish society. The benefit of marginality to which Parush alludes is that women could acquire secular culture because their Jewish education was irrelevant to traditional Jewish society in the nineteenth century, as was their education in general. It is not surprising that, as Michael Stanislawski points out, maskilim established girls' schools, not only because they wanted to counter the ignorance of women, but because they knew that the schools' modern curricula would arouse less hostility if they were designed for students who really did not matter—that is, for girls.[61]

Although the educated women that Parush studies constituted only a small percentage of the total population of Jewish women in eastern Europe, the subject of women's education loomed large in the public conversation about acculturation that preoccupied the Jewish community from the mid-nineteenth century until after the First World War. As Paula Hyman has argued, looking at the gender dimensions of the issue of acculturation uncovers the ambivalence and tensions inherent in the adaptation of Jews to modern secular societies.[62] The education of women, in which many women themselves were involved as teachers and principals, was a stage on which to enact different versions of the formation of a modern Jewry. Both Parush and Hyman relied in part on the path-breaking articles of Shaul Stampfer that addressed the gendered division of the education of Jews. Perhaps the most influential was the article that first documented the phenomenon of girls from traditional Jewish communities attending public schools while their brothers studied in *ḥeder*s and yeshivas.[63] But other articles on the nature of traditional

[60] N. Seidman, *A Marriage Made in Heaven: The Sexual Politics of Yiddish and Hebrew* (Los Angeles and Berkeley, 1997).

[61] M. Stanislawski, *For Whom Do I Toil? Judah Leib Gordon and the Crisis of Russian Jewry* (New York, 1988).

[62] Hyman, *Gender and Assimilation.*

[63] S. Stampfer, 'Gender Differentiation and the Education of the Jewish Woman in Nineteenth-Century Eastern Europe', *Polin*, 7 (1992), 63–85.

education and its social stratification are essential for an understanding of the status of women and their education in traditional Jewish society and the changes that occurred in the second half of the nineteenth century.[64]

The explosion of interest in Jewish women has led to the recovery of women writers who had never attracted attention or who had faded into obscurity, because women were of marginal interest. Cohen, Parush, and Hyman all provide information on women who were deemed marginal to history, and situate their lives within a historical or literary narrative. Hyman has brought to publication the memoirs translated into English of one such woman, Puah Rakovsky, under the title *My Life as a Radical Jewish Woman: Memoirs of a Zionist Feminist in Poland*.[65] Carole Balin, too, has illuminated the stories of five women writers who represent the possibilities open to upper-class Jewish women who acquired extraordinary education.[66]

Much of the information historians and literary scholars mine to explore the lives of women comes not only from a careful reading of the Jewish press, but also from attention to the memoirs through which life stories are transmitted. The 'literary turn' in historical interpretation and the recent interest in memory, both private and public, as a component of our understanding of the past have stimulated scholarly interest in memoirs. Like all documents, memoirs have to be analysed and interpreted. They cannot be taken at face value. But they offer an entrée into the consciousness of the writer and thus into social attitudes, especially when large numbers of memoirs of the same period and geographic area are consulted. Moreover, although memoirs cannot serve as the sole source of knowledge of a phenomenon, they often provide details about daily life that are delivered in passing or that serve no ideological purpose. Women not only penned their own memoirs, but of course they figure in men's memoirs as well. Comparison of men's and women's memoirs can yield fascinating glimpses of gender attitudes.

In addition to work that relies on memoirs as a source, this volume contains a chapter that offers a detailed analysis of perhaps the best-known memoir written by an east European Jewish woman, Pauline Wengeroff's *Memoirs of a Jewish Grandmother*.[67] In her chapter, entitled 'Sins of Youth, Guilt of a Grandmother:

[64] S. Stampfer, 'Heder Study, the Knowledge of Torah, and the Maintenance of Social Stratification in Traditional East European Society', *Studies in Jewish Education*, 3 (1988), 271–89, and 'What Did "Knowing Hebrew" Mean in Eastern Europe?', in L. Glinert (ed.), *Hebrew in Ashkenaz* (Oxford, 1998).

[65] Ed. P. E. Hyman, trans. B. Harshav with P. E. Hyman (Bloomington, Ind., 2002). See review in this volume.

[66] C. B. Balin, *To Reveal our Hearts: Jewish Women Writers in Tsarist Russia* (Cincinnati, 2000). Her study examines the works of Miriam Markel-Mosessohn (1839–1920), Chava Shapiro (1879–1943), Rashel Mironovna Khin (1861–1928), Feiga Israilevna Kogan (1891–1974), and Sofiya Dubnowa-Erlikh (1885–1986).

[67] P. Wengeroff, *Memoiren einer Grossmutter. Bilder aus der Kulturgeschichte der Juden Russlands im 19. Jahrhundert* (Berlin, 1913).

M. L. Lilienblum, Pauline Wengeroff, and the Telling of Jewish Modernity in Eastern Europe', Shulamit Magnus offers an insightful reading of Wengeroff's complex attitude towards the traditional society in which she grew up, as well as towards the path of assimilation her family embraced. Through her comparison of Wengeroff's and Lilienblum's narratives of the decline of Jewish tradition, Magnus highlights the different perspectives of educated Jewish men and women towards the modernization they experienced in their own lifetimes.

Two chapters in this volume expand our knowledge of the education of Jewish women in eastern Europe, which was so central to their acculturation. Eliyana Adler's 'Women's Education in the Pages of the Russian Jewish Press' demonstrates that, while maskilim decried the negative consequences of failing to educate Jewish girls, they were grudging in their praise of modern schools for girls that had been established in response. Her chapter reinforces Feiner's conclusions on the ambivalence of the Haskalah towards modernity. In 'The Call to Serve: Jewish Women Medical Students in Russia, 1872–1887', Carole Balin turns to the elite of women who received higher education. Discussing the factors that led to the disproportionate representation of Jews in Russian institutions of medical training for women, she raises questions about the gendered nature of integration among the educated elite of Russian Jews.

Even as they modernized and integrated somewhat into east European societies, the vast majority of Jews remained connected to the Jewish community and retained some form of Jewish identity. Some Jews, however, converted to Christianity as part of their assimilation into Russian and Polish society. Analysing conversion experiences permits historians to explore Jewish–Christian contacts and the strength or weakness of social supports for Jewish identity. Not surprisingly, there were gender differences in the motivation for, the process of, and the results of, conversion.

Two of the chapters in this volume address the phenomenon of conversion. In her chapter 'When Chava Left Home: Gender, Conversion, and the Jewish Family in Tsarist Russia', ChaeRan Freeze has used consistory records to illuminate and analyse the complexity of the process that resulted in conversion, as well as the complications when the convert was married or had children. She analyses the various 'narratives', particularly those that Jewish women constructed to present their conversion as liberation from Judaism or from a Jewish family, presented as oppressive. Parents, on the other hand, often told a narrative of abduction, which accounted for their daughter's alleged desire for baptism. Freeze also demonstrates how and why Jewish families maintained contact with children or other relatives seeking conversion. In many cases, familial bonds did not necessarily disappear after baptism, despite efforts on the part of converts to distance themselves from their kin (at least in their petitions) or the latter to disown their children or relatives. Her chapter illustrates how converts and their Jewish families employed ideas about gender in their struggle to redefine identity and family relationships.

In her consideration of the phenomenon of female Jewish conversion in Kraków at the turn of the twentieth century, 'The Lost Generation: Education and Female Conversion in *Fin-de-Siècle* Kraków', Rachel Manekin demonstrates how the analysis of one case can illuminate a more general issue. Her story of 18-year-old Deborah Lewkowicz enables us to see the interplay of forces that motivated the conversion, the institution that facilitated its initial steps, and the family ties that ultimately prevented its consummation. Based on a close reading of documents and also of literary sources, Manekin's chapter depicts the extreme tensions between a traditional family and society, and a young woman with aspirations for change.

As more Jewish women continued to acquire secular education and departed from traditional observance, they became increasingly active in the public political arena. They participated in the Russian revolutionary movement in both the late nineteenth and the early twentieth centuries. The scholar Robert H. McNeal has commented that a quarter of all women active in the Russian revolutionary movements at the end of the nineteenth century were Jewish,[68] and they continued to be prominent in the twentieth century as well. Women also participated in specifically Jewish venues, such as Zionist parties, though to a lesser degree. The role of women in Zionist parties in eastern Europe, however, has been largely ignored. Feminist scholarship on Zionism has focused on the Yishuv (settlement) in Palestine, not on the role of gender in the east European Zionist movement.[69]

Scholars have noted the increased political participation of Jewish women, but have yet to provide a narrative framework for the broad phenomenon of women's political activism. Instead, we must be content with the stories found in individual women's memoirs and in biography-based studies. Naomi Shepherd's *A Price Below Rubies* introduces the English reader to a diverse collection of Jewish women activists in eastern Europe, though the book is marred by frequent errors of fact.[70] Some studies of the Bund, the Jewish socialist party founded in Vilna in 1897 and enormously influential in both late tsarist Russia and inter-war Poland, mention that women were active in the party. In the biographies of Bundist leaders around the world that J. S. Hertz presents in his three-volume study of the Bund, women account for about 20 per cent of the total, but Bundist leaders in Poland lamented the small proportion of women members, which they estimated at no more than 10 per cent.[71]

Although the history of women in the Bund has yet to be written, the Israeli scholar Daniel Blatman has begun to address the issue, particularly in two articles

[68] R. H. McNeal, 'Women in the Russian Radical Movement', *Journal of Social History*, 5/2 (1971–2), 153.

[69] See, in particular, D. S. Bernstein (ed.), *Pioneers and Homemakers: Jewish Women in Pre-State Israel* (Albany, NY, 1992).

[70] N. Shepherd, *A Price Below Rubies: Jewish Women as Rebels and Radicals* (London, 1993).

[71] See information in H. Tobias, *The Jewish Bund in Russia until 1905* (Stanford, Calif., 1972); J. S. Hertz (ed.), *Doyres bundistn*, 3 vols. (New York, 1956–68).

in English, as well as in his recent book.[72] Focusing on the Bundist organization, YAF (Yidishe arbeter froy), established in the early 1920s, he points to the ways it tried to provide social assistance and information to women, but argues that the Bundist leadership, overwhelmingly male, never accepted the idea of women as a group with special needs and saw the YAF primarily as a means to recruit women into the party.[73]

The First World War wreaked devastation on the Jews of eastern Europe. Their homes in Poland were on the front line, and the civil war that accompanied the Russian Revolution and the establishment of the USSR led to tremendous Jewish losses. By 1931, 3.1 million Jews, of whom 1.6 million were women, lived in independent Poland, the state that was created in the wake of the war.

INTER-WAR POLAND AND LITHUANIA (1918–1939)

Although there is much still to learn about Jewish women under the tsarist regime, the situation of Jewish women during the First World War and in independent Poland has scarcely been studied at all. There are some exceptions. As a sociologist, Celia Heller devotes some attention to gender (and class) differences in her study of inter-war Polish Jewry *On the Edge of Destruction*.[74] She is particularly attuned to the transformation of women's roles as they acculturated to Polish society and experienced diverse economic constraints. The pictorial record of inter-war Polish Jewry *Image Before My Eyes* depicts women of all classes engaged in daily life.[75] The recent publication of teenage autobiographies (selected from those submitted to YIVO-sponsored writing contests in the 1930s), entitled *Awakening Lives: Autobiographies of Jewish Youth in Poland before the Holocaust*,[76] includes six entries by young women. These provide insight into the self-understanding and experience of adolescent girls coping with poverty and intergenerational tension in the inter-war years. They also depict the politicization of young Jewish women, a subject studied by Dahlia Sabina Elazar.[77] She explores the formation of a political generation of

[72] D. Blatman, 'Women in the Jewish Labour Bund in Interwar Poland', in Ofer and Weitzman (eds.), *Women in the Holocaust*, 68–84, and id., 'National-Minority Policy, Bundist Social Organizations, and Jewish Women in Interwar Poland', in Z. Gitelman (ed.), *The Emergence of Modern Jewish Politics: Bundism and Zionism in Eastern Europe* (Pittsburgh, 2003), 54–70; id., *For our Freedom and Yours: The Jewish Labour Bund in Poland, 1939–1949* (London, 2003).

[73] For a first take on the subject, see H. Davis-Kram, 'The Story of the Sisters of the Bund', *Contemporary Jewry*, 5/2 (1980), 27–43.

[74] C. S. Heller, *On the Edge of Destruction: Jews of Poland Between the Two World Wars* (New York, 1977).

[75] L. Dobroszycki and B. Kirshenblatt-Gimblett (eds.), *Image Before My Eyes* (New York, 1977). Women are not equally represented in this volume.

[76] J. Shandler (ed.), *Awakening Lives: Autobiographies of Jewish Youth in Poland Before the Holocaust* (New Haven, 2002).

[77] D. S. Elazar, 'Engines of Acculturation: The Last Political Generation of Jewish Women in Interwar East Europe', *Journal of Historical Sociology*, 15/3 (Sept. 2002), 366–94.

Jewish women in inter-war eastern Europe, using data obtained from the survivors of the Ravensbrück concentration camp for women. She argues that Jewish women who came of age in inter-war eastern Europe 'perhaps for the first time formed a distinct political generation, as evidenced by high rates of political participation and assimilation into the thriving secular nationalistic culture of their time'. In addition, Shaul Stampfer provides us with important demographic information on the structure of Polish Jewish families between the wars as revealed in the 1931 census.[78]

Ewa Plach's chapter in this volume, 'Feminism and Nationalism in the Pages of *Ewa: Tygodnik*, 1928–1933', offers an unparalleled opportunity to explore the interests of those women whom Celia Heller first brought to the attention of scholars of Jewish history, that is Polonized Jewish women. In her examination of a Polish-language, feminist, and Zionist women's weekly newspaper, Plach demonstrates the concerns of cosmopolitan bourgeois and intellectual Jewish women, who were socially, culturally, and religiously distant from the milieu of the majority of the Jewish community, but were still participants in the communal discourse. It reminds us of the heterogeneity of Polish Jewry, its women included, and of the hybrid nature of Jewish identity. Although *Ewa* existed for only five years, it voiced the aspirations of the most modernized sector of Polish Jewish women.

Finally, Ellen Kellman's chapter, 'Feminism and Fiction: Khane Blankshteyn's Role in Inter-War Vilna', explores the life of a prominent feminist activist who has remained obscure until now. Kellman shows how the devastating impact of the First World War shaped Khane Blankshteyn's political and social activism, especially her involvement in two important feminist organizations in Vilna: the Yidisher froyen-fareyn (Jewish Women's Union) and Froyen-shuts (Society for the Protection of Women). Her weekly magazine *Di froy* ('The Woman') also provided an important forum in which Jewish working women could articulate their concerns about family life, economic and personal independence, and a host of other issues. Kellman aptly illustrates how Blankshteyn's unique ability to combine her ideology of feminism and Jewish autonomism in her social activism, literary endeavours, and politics made her a 'unique figure in her generation'.

NEW DIRECTIONS

As this historiographical survey has shown, scholars have only begun to explore the multifaceted lives of Jewish women in eastern Europe; indeed, this volume represents the first collection of essays devoted exclusively to the study of Jewish women's experiences. It seeks to 'recover' lost achievements and voices, and place

[78] S. Stampfer, 'Marital Patterns in Interwar Poland', in Y. Gutman, E. Mendelsohn, J. Reinharz, and C. Shmeruk (eds.), *The Jews of Poland Between the Two World Wars* (Hanover, NH, 1989), 173–97. See also L. Dobroszycki, 'The Fertility of Modern Polish Jewry', in P. Ritterband (ed.), *Modern Jewish Fertility* (Leiden, 1981).

these empirical findings into a broader analytical framework. In response to the cutting-edge gender theories proposed by Joan Scott, Judith Butler, and others, the contributors to this volume have gone beyond a description of 'what' women experienced to explore 'how' gender constructed distinct experiences, identities, and meanings. The challenging task ahead is how to integrate these new findings in the master narratives of the past, to deconstruct old paradigms and models, and to rethink east European Jewish history with the aid of new insights gleaned from the research on gender.

The History of Jewish Women in Early Modern Poland: An Assessment

MOSHE ROSMAN

IN the huge volume of research and publications on the history of women in the early modern period, little has been written on the historical experience of Jewish women in the Polish–Lithuanian Commonwealth in the sixteenth, seventeenth, and eighteenth centuries. There are virtually no Polish Jewish analogues to the detailed analyses of women's family, economic, social, and religious life that can be read for Christian women in Europe and elsewhere.[1] This lack is the more regrettable in view of the fact that the case of early modern Polish Jewish women neatly encapsulates many of the key issues that have been debated over the course of the last thirty years in the process of shaping the approaches, methodologies, and substance of women's history. Questions of the existence and nature of historical material relevant to women's experience, how to recover it, how to evaluate its significance, and how the incorporation of women into historiography transforms

This chapter is dedicated to the doctors, nurses, and staff of the Departments of Bone Marrow Transplantation and Hematology at the Hadassah University Medical Center in Jerusalem. They have been, for me, the fourth partner (*Midrash Job*).

Most of the work on this essay was done in Spring semester 2003 while I was fortunate to enjoy a term as the Herbert and Ellie Katz Distinguished Fellow and member of the research group on Jewish History and Culture in Eastern Europe at the Center for Advanced Judaic Studies (CAJS) of the University of Pennsylvania. I cannot express enough gratitude to the staff of CAJS for doing their utmost to enable me to work in ideal conditions. I am deeply indebted to my colleagues at CAJS who offered the opportunity for learning new things and testing my ideas on a daily basis. Particularly helpful was a seminar session held on 22 January 2003 where I presented some of the material that appears here and benefited from the other fellows' responses. Colleagues whose counsel contributed directly to the final form of this chapter are Gershon Bacon, David Engel, Jack Kugelmass, Olga Litvak, Rachel Manekin, Benjamin Nathans, Adam Teller, Magdalena Teter, and Beth Wenger. I am also grateful to Shira Wolosky for her critique and stylistic suggestions based on an earlier draft, and to Elisheva Baumgarten, who has been a perceptive critic of my work and a guide to some of the medieval and gender-related sources I drew upon.

[1] For example, a guided keyword computer search of the University of Pennsylvania Library catalogue, using 'early', 'modern', and 'women', located 383 book titles; 279 of these were published from 1990 on. A search of article titles would doubtless turn up several times as many items. Some significant studies are B. S. Anderson and J. P. Zinsser, *Women in Early Modern and Modern Europe* (Washington, 2001); N. Z. Davis (ed.), *Renaissance and Enlightenment Paradoxes*, vol. iii of G. Duby

the master narrative are all exemplified by the study of the subject of Polish Jewish women.

In order to clarify these issues I will begin with analysis of three pioneering studies, each of which is of overriding importance for the specific topic which it treats, but which—in view of the dearth of scholarship on our subject—also attain status as vehicles to help us arrive at a conception of what life was like for Polish Jewish women before 1800. This is the case despite the fact that none of these studies purports to survey specifically the place and period under discussion here. Two of them focus on the nineteenth century, not the earlier period; and the third treats Ashkenaz as a whole, rather than Poland in particular. Nonetheless, at least by implication, these three studies have established an agenda, both methodological and substantive, for the historical study of Polish Jewish women, and have postulated some basic theses that seem to apply to early modern Poland as well as to either the later period or larger Ashkenaz. Review and analysis of these precedential studies can lead to the identification of some basic questions that have been or still need to be pursued and to consideration of alternative approaches to finding answers. While, in the nature of things, I will assume a critical stance towards parts of what my predecessors have asserted, it is only their path-breaking work that has

and M. Perrot (eds.), *A History of Women in the West* (Cambridge, Mass., 1992); id., *Women on the Margins: Three Seventeenth-Century Lives* (Cambridge, Mass., 1995); S. Cavallo and L. Warner (eds.), *Widowhood in Medieval and Early Modern Europe* (New York, 1999); B. J. Whitehead (ed.), *Women's Education in Early Modern Europe: A History 1500–1800* (New York, 1999); S. Marshall, *Women in Reformation and Counter-Reformation Europe* (Bloomington, Ind., 1989); M. E. Wiesner, *Women and Gender in Early Modern Europe* (Cambridge, 1993). On women in the Polish–Lithuanian Commonwealth, see M. Bogucka, *Białogłowa w dawnej Polsce: Kobieta w społeczenstwie polskim XVI–XVIII wieku na tle porównawczym* (Warsaw, 199); C. Kuklo, *Kobieta samotna w społeczeństwie miejskim u schyłku Rzeczypospolitej szlacheckiej* (Białystok, 1998); L. Charewiczowa, *Kobieta w dawnej Polsce do okresu rozbiorów* (Lwów, 1938); B. Jedynak (ed.), *Kobieta w kulturze i społeczeństwie* (Lublin, 1990); A. Karpiński, *Kobieta w mieście polskim w drugiej połowie XVI i w XVII wieku* (Warsaw, 1995). (The reader will note that a much-needed comparison of Jewish and non-Jewish women in Poland is beyond the scope of this study. That is a task I hope to undertake in the future.) On Jewish women in the Commonwealth, see E. Fram, 'Glimpses into the Religious World of Jewish Women in Poland, *circa* 1600', ch. 1 in his forthcoming monograph introduction to and translation of Benjamin Slonik's *Seder mitsvot nashim*; J. Goldberg, 'Jewish Marriage in Eighteenth-Century Poland', *Polin*, 10 (1997), 3–39; T. Salmon-Mack, 'Ḥayei nisu'im beyahadut polin, 1650–1800', Ph.D. thesis (Hebrew University, Jerusalem, 2002); M. Rosman, 'Lehiyot ishah yehudiyah bepolin-lita bereishit ha'et haḥadashah', in I. Bartal and I. Gutman (eds.), *Kiyum vashever: Yehudei polin ledoroteihem*, ii (Jerusalem, 2001). Chava Weissler's book *Voices of the Matriarchs: Listening to the Prayers of Early Modern Jewish Women* (Boston, 1998), which will be discussed below, relates to the religious lives of all Ashkenazi Jewish women in this period, including those who lived in Poland. For treatments of Jewish women's history in various contexts, see J. Baskin (ed.), *Jewish Women in Historical Perspective*, 2nd edn. (Detroit, 1998); Y. Atzmon (ed.), *Eshnav leḥayeihen shel nashim beḥavarot yehudiyot* (Jerusalem, 1995); E. Baumgarten, *Mothers and Children: Jewish Family Life in Medieval Europe* (Princeton, 2004); H. Edelman, *Jewish Women in Early Modern Italy* (forthcoming). For a survey of feminist-inspired scholarship on the history of modern Jewish women to the early 1990s, see P. Hyman, 'Feminist Studies and Modern Jewish History', in L. Davidman and S. Tenenbaum (eds.), *Feminist Perspectives on Jewish Studies* (New Haven, 1994).

enabled me to arrive at my own positions. My criticism certainly does nothing to change their fundamental importance to the study of this subject.[2]

The three studies are: Shaul Stampfer, 'Gender Differentiation and Education of the Jewish Woman in Nineteenth-Century Eastern Europe'; Chava Weissler, *Voices of the Matriarchs*; and Iris Parush, *Nashim korot: Yitronah shel shuliyut* ('Reading Women: The Benefit of Marginality in Nineteenth-Century East European Jewish Society').[3]

METHODOLOGY

The first question all of these studies imply is one that was settled long ago in general feminist historiography, but is still sometimes raised in Jewish scholarship:[4] Is it methodologically possible to add women to the narrative of Polish Jewish history? The classic works of Polish Jewish historiography from Dubnow, Bałaban, Schiper, Schorr, and Mahler to Baron and Weinryb lent scant attention to the lives of women.[5] While a few exceptionally wealthy and powerful women were highlighted,[6] the rhythm of women's lives was not incorporated into the narrative. Among the various reasons (excuses?) offered for this shortcoming was a methodological one: women are simply invisible in the sources. After our three studies, such a claim can no longer be credibly maintained.

Most dramatically, Weissler discovered (in plain sight) a Yiddish literature written by and/or for women and used by them, centring on the *tkhines*, topical supplicatory prayers that women said either at home, or in the synagogue, *mikveh*, or cemetery. The existence of these prayers (and other female-oriented Yiddish literature) was certainly no secret before Weissler; but with barely an exception,[7] scholars dismissed the *tkhines* out of hand as having nothing to contribute to knowledge about 'significant' Jewish culture. With great interpretative sensitivity Weiss-

[2] The reader should bear in mind that I am using these studies to relate to a topic—Jewish women in early modern Poland—that is other than what they were originally intended to illuminate. I also do not pretend to present an overall assessment of these works. To appreciate fully their scope, subtlety, and import, they must be read in the contexts in which they were first proffered.

[3] S. Stampfer, 'Gender Differentiation and Education of the Jewish Woman in Nineteenth-Century Eastern Europe', *Polin*, 7 (1992), 63–87; C. Weissler, *Voices of the Matriarchs* (Boston, 1998); and I. Parush, *Nashim korot: Yitronah shel hashuliyut baḥevrah hayehudit bemizraḥ eiropah bame'ah hatesha-esreh* (Tel Aviv, 2001).

[4] Hyman, 'Feminist Studies and Modern Jewish History', 120–1, 132–3.

[5] For bibliographical details on the works of these authors, see the introductory essays and alphabetically arranged bibliographies in G. D. Hundert and G. Bacon, *The Jews in Poland and Russia: Bibliographical Essays* (Bloomington, Ind., 1984).

[6] See M. Bałaban, *Historja Żydów w Krakowie i na Kazimierzu, 1304–1868*, i (Kraków, 1931; repr. 1991), 71, 101, 108–10, 280, 547–52; pub. in Hebrew as *Toledot hayehudim bekrakuv uvekazhimiezh, 1304–1868*, i (Jerusalem, 2002), 57, 62, 90, 92, 214, 417–22, on Raszka (Rachel) Fiszel and Gitl Kożuchowska (and see below, in the text near nn. 90–1).

[7] S. Freehof, 'Devotional Literature in the Vernacular', *CCAR Yearbook*, 33 (1923), 375–424.

ler showed how the *tkhines* could be construed as reflecting women's interests and concerns, women's *mentalité*, women's social and religious roles, and how women responded to male-defined cultural stereotypes.[8]

Stampfer, in his article, as well as in much of his other work, showed that women often show up in statistics.[9] True, statistics in pre-partition Poland were much less abundant and much less sophisticated than in the succeeding regimes in the nineteenth century. Yet the earlier period did produce lists—of town residents, of property owners, of petitioners, of taxpayers, of people fined in court, of borrowers or lenders, of those counted in the 1764–5 census of Polish Jewry—and perusal of these often yields names and other information about women. This leads to the larger point that several types of both Polish and Jewish archival sources—communal *pinkasim* (minute books), court protocols, nobility correspondence, subject petitions, loan records, tax records, property inventories—are likely to contain material relating to women.[10]

Iris Parush has taught us a different methodological lesson: that to discover information about women we must concentrate on the background, rather than the foreground, of literary sources. As she put it,

> Discovering the riveting and compelling images of the women who read was the result of reading the memoir literature of the period 'around the edges'. This reading did not focus on the obvious themes of this literature, on its central narratives or the ideas reflected in it; but precisely on the asides and on the biographical details that insinuated themselves into the descriptive fabric . . . this book thus aims the spotlight precisely at the 'background' and

[8] The book *Voices of the Matriarchs* is largely a collection of articles and lectures that Weissler had written beginning in the mid-1980s. While she did add the introduction, ch. 7 on Leah Horowitz, and the epilogue, and revised some of the older articles, it is evident from ch. 10, 'The Feminist Scholar and the *Tkhines*', that by the mid-1990s Weissler had re-evaluated the basic significance of the *tkhine* prayers but did not change the earlier articles to conform to her new approach. (See below, text near nn. 33–6); cf. J. W. Joselit, B. Gibbs, E. Wolfson, and A. Bernstein-Nahar, 'The Uses of History in Contemporary Jewish Historical Writing: A Roundtable', *Jewish Book Annual*, 55–6 (1997–9), 4–37, esp. 10–12; and Weissler's response to this discussion of her book, 'For Whom Do I Toil?', in the same volume.) Weissler alluded to her decision to adopt the strategy of leaving the viewpoint of the earlier articles unchanged in the preface, pp. xii–xiii, and perhaps as well in her thanks to the editor, Susan Worst, on p. 262. While this approach can be defended (Carole Balin, in a review (*AJS Review*, 26 (2002), 370–1), termed the book an 'anthology' on the subject of the *tkhines*), it does make for inconsistency in the book and creates the need to distinguish between the earlier and later Weissler when discussing her work in the present context.

[9] 'Gender Differentiation and Education of the Jewish Woman', 66–8, 77–80; see also his 'Remarriage Among Jews and Christians in Nineteenth-Century Eastern Europe', *Jewish History*, 3 (1988), 85–114; and various chapters in his book *Families, Rabbis and Education: Essays on Traditional Jewish Society in Eastern Europe* (London, forthcoming).

[10] For examples of archival material related to women, see G. D. Hundert, *The Jews in a Polish Private Town: The Case of Opatów in the Eighteenth Century* (Baltimore, 1992), 71–5; Rosman, 'Lehiyot ishah yehudiyah bepolin-lita bereishit ha'et haḥadashah'; Salmon-Mack, 'Ḥayei nisu'im beyahadut polin'; A. Teller, *Kesef, ko'aḥ vehashpa'ah: Hayehudim be'aḥuzot beit radzivil belita bame'ah hashemoneh-esreh* (Jerusalem, forthcoming), ch. 6.

traces the 'minor details' that were shunted into the description of the ambiance, ancillary to the main subject.[11]

Parush applied this method to nineteenth-century memoirs; but it is also valid for the earlier period when dealing with such classic sources as the memoirs of Dov Ber of Bolechów and the Life of Solomon Maimon or with various genres of rabbinic literature.[12]

RESTRUCTURING THE HISTORICAL NARRATIVE

All three of our studies also imply an additional question that has been a venerable one in feminist historical scholarship: How should the addition of women to the historical narrative be structured?

All three authors—Weissler explicitly and the others implicitly—rejected both what might be termed 'additive' or 'compensatory' history on the one hand and 'herstory' on the other.[13] The first approach takes the conventional historiographical categories that have been used to describe men's experience and attempts to fit women into them. For example, we know what the rabbis said about men's marital obligations; what did they say about women's? X number of men loaned money; how many women loaned money? There were men who were courtiers of

[11] Parush, *Nashim korot*, 9.

[12] Dov Ber of Bolechów, *The Memoirs of Ber of Bolechów*, ed. and trans. M. Vishnitzer (London, 1922; repr. 1973); *Solomon Maimon: An Autobiography*, ed. and trans. J. Clark Murray (Boston, 1888); new edn. with introd. M. Shapiro (Urbana, Ill., 2001); the very popular Schocken Books edition of the Murray translation, ed. M. Hadas (New York, 1947), is abridged. Rabbinic responsa and halakhic codes are a particularly rich source of information about women and about how men related to women, topics that are often in the foreground of these types of texts. E. Fram, *Ideas Face Reality: Jewish Law and Life in Poland, 1550–1655* (Cincinnati, 1997), id., 'Two Cases of Adultery and the Halakhic Decision-Making Process', *AJS Review*, 26 (2002), 277–300, and Salmon-Mack, 'Ḥayei nisu'im be-yahadut polin', provide good examples of the methodology of working with these types of sources for topics related to women. The 'background reading' technique could be applied with utility to other genres of rabbinic literature in early modern Poland, such as homiletics and commentaries. A model can be found in the feminist scholarship on classic rabbinic sources, e.g. J. Hauptman, *Rereading the Rabbis: A Woman's Voice* (Boulder, Colo., 1998); D. Boyarin, *Carnal Israel: Reading Sex in Rabbinic Culture* (Berkeley, 1993); S. Valler, *Women and Womanhood in the Talmud* (Atlanta, 1999); T. Ilan, *Jewish Women in Greco-Roman Palestine* (Tübingen, 1995); G. Hasan-Rokem, *Web of Life: Folklore and Midrash in Rabbinic Literature* (Berkeley, 2000).

[13] *Voices of the Matriarchs*, 36–44; cf. J. W. Scott, *Gender and the Politics of History* (1st pub. New York, 1988; rev. 1999), 15–50 (for her discussion of 'herstory', see esp. pp. 18–21); J. Kelly-Gadol, 'Did Women Have a Renaissance?', in R. Bridenthal and C. Koonz (eds.), *Becoming Visible: Women in European History* (Boston, 1977); G. Bock, 'Challenging Dichotomies: Perspectives on Women's History', in K. Offen, R. R. Pierson, and J. Rendall (eds.), *Writing Women's History: International Perspectives* (Bloomington, Ind., 1991). For Jewish historiography, see S. Magnus, 'Out of the Ghetto: Integrating the Study of Jewish Women into the Study of "The Jews"', *Judaism*, 39 (1990), 28–36; M. Shoub, 'Jewish Women's History: Development of a Critical Methodology', *Conservative Judaism*, 35 (1982), 33–46.

the Polish kings; were there also women who were close to the monarchy? Weissler called this approach 'filling in the blanks' and it can result in the discovery of many new facts about women.[14] The main problem with this approach is that it is a variety of me-tooism: women also wrote poetry, women also led political movements, women also ran businesses. By leaving men as the normative case, women's experience is significant only to the extent that it mirrors men's. This means that we will probably overlook topics that might be significant for a description of women in history, but that men were absent from or only peripherally involved in. Where, for example, do things like mothering and home-making fit in? Did they remain basically unchanging and thus ahistorical? While such questions are beyond the scope of the present chapter, they are fundamental to the writing of social history.[15]

Herstory is based on the proposition that there is a women's story that does not necessarily correspond to the rubrics that the men's story has made conventional. For example, one of the main topics in west European Jewish history is emancipation. Women, however, were unemancipated—both within Jewish society and within the state—long after Jewish men received their rights. In relating to the historical experience of Jewish women it would be more meaningful to speak of the process of *embourgoisement*.[16] Another example is hasidism. This religious movement profoundly changed men's religious practice in Jewish eastern Europe. At least in its first generations, however, it apparently had little effect on women's spiritual lives and may have made women's day-to-day life more difficult.[17] For women a more relevant religious factor was practical kabbalah. A herstory approach might investigate how women became conversant with practical kabbalah and how they put it into practice.[18]

[14] Some important examples of this approach are the scholarly A. Grossman, *Ḥasidot umoredot: Nashim be'eiropah bimei habeinayim* (Jerusalem, 2001), and the popular S. Henry and E. Taitz, *Written Out of History: Our Jewish Foremothers*, 2nd edn. (Fresh Meadows, NY, 1983); E. Taitz, S. Henry, and C. Tallan, *The JPS Guide to Jewish Women, 600 BCE–1900 CE* (Philadelphia, 2003).

[15] Various studies have taken up the challenge of incorporating these types of questions into the master narrative; e.g. S. Shahar, *The Fourth Estate: A History of Women in the Middle Ages* (London, 1983), 140–5, 183–9, 230–6; U. A. Robertson, *The Illustrated History of the Housewife, 1650–1950* (New York, 1997); Baumgarten, *Mothers and Children*.

[16] M. Kaplan, *The Making of the Jewish Middle Class: Women, Family and Identity in Imperial Germany* (New York, 1991), pp. viii–ix, 3–21; id., 'Tradition and Transition: The Acculturation, Assimilation and Integration of Jews in Imperial Germany—A Gender Analysis', *Leo Baeck Institute Yearbook*, 28 (1983), 263–300; id., 'Gender and Jewish History in Imperial Germany', in J. Frankel and S. Zipperstein (eds.), *Assimilation and Community: The Jews in Nineteenth-Century Europe* (Cambridge, 1992).

[17] A. Rapoport-Albert, 'On Women in Hasidism: S. A. Horodecky and the Maid of Ludmir Tradition', in A. Rapoport-Albert and S. J. Zipperstein (eds.), *Jewish History: Essays in Honor of Chimen Abramsky* (London, 1988).

[18] On women and kabbalah, see A. Rapoport-Albert, *Female Bodies, Male Souls: Asceticism and Gender in the Jewish Tradition* (London, forthcoming); *Voices of the Matriarchs*, 89–93, 180–2; cf. S. S. Sered, *Women as Ritual Experts: The Religious Lives of Elderly Jewish Women in Jerusalem* (Oxford, 1992), 50–8.

Herstory has the virtue of making women the normative case, but by separating from men's history it runs the risk of marginalization. It can be analogous to the histories of various ethnic groups, which often seem to be of value only to those with special interests.[19]

In adding women to the narrative of the story of the Jews in eastern Europe, these three authors opted for what Weissler called the 'transformative' approach. That is, by adding women to the story one does not merely add more facts to known rubrics, or establish that women had a history of their own. Learning about women affects how we interpret what we know about men as well. Women transform the entire story, not just the parts where they appear.[20] When we look at the totality of human historical experience (male and female), we realize the significance of the observation made by the cultural anthropologist M. Z. Rosaldo: 'Every known society recognizes and elaborates some differences between the sexes . . . it is everywhere the case that there are characteristic tasks, manners, and responsibilities primarily associated with women or with men.'[21] These culturally determined differences between the sexes are commonly referred to as 'gender' and represent one of the fundamental organizing principles of every society.

Each of our authors believed that conceptualizing east European Jewish society in terms of gender could lead to a better understanding of how it was structured and how it functioned. Each described east European Jewish culture as constituted by separate male and female activities in various categories of experience. Jewish culture did not consist only of what men did while women helped or observed; rather in Jewish culture there were different sectors and in each of them there were distinct male and female styles.

In Table 1 I have extruded and summarized the main features of the differential cultural realms that the three studies characterized. The table implies a neat division and a high degree of complementarity in the differential cultural realms of east European Jewish men and women. In traditional society, each gender had its own characteristic way of acquiring education, studying, praying, and observing rituals; and its own ideal with respect to economic activities.

Weissler and Stampfer asserted that this complementarity ultimately resulted in both men and women being initiated sufficiently into the culture to be loyal practitioners of it. With their different forms of education and different libraries, both men and women knew rudimentary Jewish theology, biblical cosmogony and cosmology, the doctrine of reward and punishment, rabbinic morality and values, and halakhic obligations.[22]

[19] Scott, *Gender and the Politics of History*, 20–1; Bock, 'Challenging Dichotomies', 16.

[20] Scott, *Gender and the Politics of History*, 22, 26, 29–31; N. Z. Davis, '"Women's History" in Transition: The European Case', in J. W. Scott (ed.), *Feminism and History* (Oxford, 1996), 88–9.

[21] M. Z. Rosaldo, 'Women, Culture and Society: A Theoretical Overview', in M. Z. Rosaldo and L. Lamphere (eds.), *Women, Culture and Society* (Stanford, Calif., 1974), 18.

[22] 'Gender Differentiation and Education of the Jewish Woman', 70–1; *Voices of the Matriarchs*, 41–2.

Table 1. Male and female cultural spheres in Jewish eastern Europe (based on Stampfer, Weissler, and Parush)

Cultural sphere	Male	Female traditional (Stampfer—Weissler)	Female modernizing (Parush)
Education	Hebrew–Aramaic language; formal school institutions	Yiddish language; informal schooling and/or minimal formal schooling	Yiddish, European languages; secularized schools
	Objectives: to be a faithful Jew, and participate in public ritual and in public study; for some: to study independently	Objectives: to be a faithful Jew and observe 'women's rituals'	Objectives: practical knowledge, modernization
Library	Mostly Hebrew–Aramaic, some Yiddish: Siddur, Pentateuch, Rashi, Mishnah, Talmud, *Ein ya'akov*, kabbalah manuals, *musar* books	Yiddish: Bible translations, epic poems, midrashic retellings, halakhic compendiums on women's mitsvot, *musar* books, stories, prayer collections (*tkhines*)	Classics of Russian, French, German, and Polish literature; new Hebrew literature; Yiddish and other romantic novels; lyric poetry
Main functional texts	Rashi (rabbinic Bible interpretation); *Pirkei avot* (moral instruction); *Ein ya'akov* (aggadah); halakhic literature	*Tsenerene* (rabbinic Bible interpretation); *Brantspiegel* (moral instruction); *Mayse-bukh* (aggadah); women's mitsvot compendiums (halakhah)	(Traditional Jewish literature often scorned)
Study method	Public, traditional institutionalized setting; study requires strenuous effort	Home setting; private, pious reading at leisure	Public, secular Jewish or non-Jewish institutions
Prayer	Determined by calendar and clock; fixed liturgy; universal content; public	Determined by contingency and biology; flexible liturgy; topical content; private	
Ritual observance	Mainly in public or semi-public (synagogue, home in presence of entire family)	Mainly in private or semi-private (home, *mikveh*, cemetery, some synagogue attendance)	
Economics	Ideal man unburdened by economic obligations	Ideal woman assumed responsibility for making a living	Bourgeois woman was to be educated home-maker and social activist

As we shall see, Parush, while recognizing that women were inducted into traditional culture to some degree, rejected the idea that women had a meaningful share in it. Mostly deprived of formal traditional education and the cultural capital it supplied, women were more easily initiated into an anti-traditional, secularist, modernist cultural posture by way of reading non-traditional literature; a practice which the traditional elite largely ignored (see the third column in the table). It was these 'reading women', not men, who broke free enough to make the first popular assaults on traditional culture.[23]

THE IMPLICATIONS OF SEPARATE SPHERES

The three pioneering authors disagreed, however, on how the existence of these separate spheres, or worlds, actually transformed the historical story.

Weissler said, in her earlier work, 'Ashkenazic Judaism in fact offered multiple possibilities for the cultural construction of gender, possibilities that may still be explored and reclaimed.'[24] In other words, the existence of a separate women's cultural sphere rendered possibilities for women to be empowered in traditional Ashkenazi culture (and today). For the earlier Weissler, the significant historical story is not only about how men controlled women, but how women expressed themselves and made claims on men. Cultural creativity, cultural institutions, and ritual life—i.e. cultural capital—were to be found not solely among men, but among women too. In her early work Weissler used the terms 'women's religion' and 'women's culture'.[25] Neither women's nor men's culture, however, could be fully comprehended without reference to its relationship to its complement.

Stampfer understood the significance of women's historical experience in eastern Europe differently:

> In most cases, this system of limited formal education for most women was appropriate for the realities of traditional Jewish society. . . . Lack of 'school education' was part of a system that functioned to condition women to accept their role in the family and society with a minimum of conflict . . . most women apparently accepted this role and found fulfillment in the parallel culture that was theirs—and was meaningful to them.[26]

[23] Parush, *Nashim korot*, 14–17, 62–74.

[24] *Voices of the Matriarchs*, 50. On the distinction between Weissler's earlier and later work, see n. 8.

[25] e.g. pp. 36, 37, 38, 44; cf. pp. 4, 9. Later (pp. 175–80, 185–6; cf. pp. ix–xii) Weissler strongly qualified her use of these terms. Also, as she made clear by using the word 'reclaimed' in the above citation and in her remarks in 'For Whom Do I Toil?', Weissler aimed for her work to have practical consequences, especially feminist ones, for the contemporary Jewish community: 'I certainly regard my own work . . . as providing historical information to Jews today, in order to enrich their understanding of the Jewish past, and thus to broaden the possibilities for the Jewish future' (p. 55). 'I do hope that knowledge of the prayers of Jewish women in the past will lead to a more just vision of the possibilities for Jews and women in the present' (p. 61).

[26] Stampfer, 'Gender Differentiation and Education of the Jewish Woman', 74.

For Stampfer, recognition of a separate female cultural sphere enables us to understand how Jewish society and culture actually functioned. Only by introducing women into the story is it possible to understand how the components of society fit together to make it work ('a system that functioned'). Both men and women were supplied with the basic education needed to function in the culture. Society depended, however, on women to fulfil certain gender roles in the family and in the economy if society were to work. It was important, therefore, that women not be distracted from their proper social work by creating other expectations. As compensation for their being denied access to elite culture, they were given cultural tools to express themselves, but not ones so sophisticated as to lead to frustration and possible rebellion. The cultural configuration served to convince both men and women that only those who excelled in learning deserved to be among the elite. So unlearned men accepted communal authority; women accepted the authority of men; and society functioned as a harmonious whole. Stampfer emphasized that their 'parallel culture' was something women accepted and found fulfilment in.

As if in anticipation of this functionalist analysis, Joan W. Scott, in her landmark essay 'Gender: A Useful Category of Historical Analysis', criticized those who write 'to endorse a certain functionalist view, ultimately rooted in biology and to perpetuate the idea of separate spheres. . . . Subsequent history is written as if these normative positions were the product of social consensus rather than conflict.'[27] Scott might say to Stampfer that the modus vivendi he described was not a felicitous accommodation, or a social Darwinian adaptation to improve Jewish traditional society's chances of survival, but the result of a power struggle.[28]

While Scott could not have been reacting specifically to Stampfer's work, Parush did respond directly to him by negating the benign nature of the gender division of cultural labour he described:

> The emergence of these patterns of living reflected the value priorities of traditional society and the gender hierarchy within it. It expressed the preference for the spiritual over the material, the superiority of the male over the female and the critical importance of the religious destiny that the man was to fulfil . . . [The educational system] was careful to preserve clear distinctions between the genders with respect to the language of literacy and the tools of literacy in order to prevent equal access to the canonical texts and equal distribution of 'cultural capital'.[29]

[27] The essay appears in Scott, *Gender and the Politics of History*; the citations are from pp. 32, 43.

[28] To which Stampfer has replied, in informal communication: When and where did this struggle take place? Who were the protagonists?

[29] Parush, *Nashim korot*, 44, 66. In her analysis Parush adapted some of the categories explicated by Pierre Bourdieu (e.g. 'The Forms of Capital', in J. J. Richardson (ed.), *Handbook of Theory and Research for the Sociology of Education* (New York, 1986)). It should be stressed that her critique of functionalist analysis is not necessarily feminist. She also objected to Stampfer's functionalist explanation of the male educational curriculum. Parush's critique was closer to that of social scientists in general against functionalism (for discussion and criticism of functionalism in the social sciences, see e.g. G. W. Stocking, Jr., *Functionalism Historicized: Essays on British Social Anthropology* (Madison, 1984); J. C.

For Parush, the separate female sphere was not a means to release tensions and maintain social equilibrium and stability. It was not even, as Scott had implied, the result of conflict. It was, rather, a tool of patriarchy to keep men powerful and prestigious and women as social facilitators and cultural inferiors. The introduction of women's experience into the historical story underscores just how zealously men guarded their power and utilized the oppression of women as one of the main ways to do so.

Parush insisted that the apparent functional equivalence of the male–female spheres that Stampfer (and Weissler) had pointed out was overshadowed by the hierarchical relationship of those spheres. The fact that as late as the end of the nineteenth century more than half of Jewish women could not read, even in Yiddish, and that—according to Parush—women bore the economic brunt, without the right to shape public discourse and policy, was not a result of a harmonious functionalism. There was a clear hierarchy, and the male sphere was higher and more prestigious. Women were prevented from entering the men's arena by being deprived of formal traditional Jewish education; men had no temptation to go into the women's sphere because it was culturally degraded. The appropriation of Hebrew literacy by men was not just a functional convention, but part and parcel of male identity. Knowing Hebrew was essential to maleness; allowing females to know it would let them have access to maleness and threaten male identity and the gender hierarchy.[30]

Parush spurned Stampfer's justification of women's deprivation of cultural capital in the name of functionalism. Contrary to such a view, she asserted that the (inferior) female role was not constructed in order to compensate women or to supply them with cultural means of expression, but to ensure that, despite their importance in the family and the economy, they would forever remain in an inferior position in the social hierarchy. The gender configuration was actually a way of compensating

Alexander, *Neofunctionalism and After* (Malden, Mass., 1998). In reflecting on the Stampfer–Parush controversy, I realized that in the context of depicting Jewish culture in Poland, I, too, had proffered a functionalist explanation of gender relations (is this perhaps a function of the gender I share with Stampfer?): 'We can also understand how these roles interlocked to undergird the structure of meaning and practice that supported Jewish culture. The elaborate Sabbath and holiday rituals were well-served by the combination of women's "freedom" to serve as facilitators and men's "obligation" to serve as performers, which in turn reinforced the facilitator/performer dichotomy in the family, social, and political realms. Children's initiation into the culture was premised on the mother having a flexible ritual schedule and the father, a more regularized one' (M. Rosman, 'A Prolegomenon to Jewish Cultural History', *Jewish Studies: An Internet Journal*, 1 (2002), 125). This is a functionalist position that posits that society, however genderized it was, functioned as a whole with each gender playing its part. Whatever judgement was merited by Stampfer's explanation applies to mine as well. In response to that critique I would say that, following Scott and Parush, we should not take the functionalist approach as a causal explanation, nor as a justification of the status quo, but only as a description. After offering a functional description, we must ask: How was the differentiated gender structure created? Was it the product of conflicts? What were its objectives? How was it maintained? What were its consequences? How did it change and why did it change?

[30] Parush, *Nashim korot*, 44–7, 62–7.

the males for giving up power to women in the economic arena. The potential of female economic power was vitiated by its lack of reinforcement by cultural capital.[31]

To summarize, all three authors employed gender analysis to put traditional east European Jewish society in a new light. The earlier Weissler demonstrated that there was a women's religious universe that paralleled men's, empowered women, and affected men. Stampfer showed how men's and women's parallel cultures in education and religion allowed society to function in other areas. Parush insisted that the cultural construction of separate spheres was insidious and guaranteed that women would remain in an inferior position to men.

THE PROBLEMATICS OF SEPARATE SPHERES DISCOURSE

The conceptual scheme of differential male and female cultural spheres has been one of the main focuses of modern feminist historical scholarship, the thrust of which has been to refute the discourse of separate spheres and to dissolve the dichotomies—such as state–family, work–family, public–private, work–sexuality, nature–culture—that sustain it. Most feminist scholars today would maintain that men and women's cultural and social activities cannot be neatly divided into mutually exclusive categories, which inevitably imply a hierarchical relationship, with women in the inferior position. Rather, both genders can be found to participate on each side of these binary oppositions, although not always in obvious ways.[32]

The problematic nature of a separate spheres construct is exemplified by our three studies. In her later work Weissler wrote:

> After futile attempts to separate women's culture from men's culture, folk culture from elite culture, that is, to isolate single voices in this multivocal mess, I realized it was more important to attend to the way different layers of the culture related to each other. But once I began to do that, I found I could no longer avoid seeing the power relations embedded and reproduced within my texts. My efforts to define and valorize an Ashkenazic women's culture—and thus at some level to get 'Judaism' off the hook—began to seem naïve, as I recognized that the gender representations that controlled women's lives were enmeshed in the very fiber of Ashkenazic Judaism . . . traces of an independent female culture have been quite scarce.[33]

This sounds close to Parush. Women were not empowered in traditional culture; they were 'controlled' (manipulated?) by the patriarchal cultural constructs. Men determined the parameters of women's religious experience. This was so because

[31] Parush, *Nashim korot*, 63.

[32] Scott, *Gender and the Politics of History*, 26, 32, 40, 43, 49; Davis, '"Women's History" in Transition', 90–1. For a cogent attack on the public–private dichotomy in the 19th-century American context, see S. Wolosky, 'Public Women, Private Men: American Women Poets and the Common Good', *Signs*, 28 (2003), 665–94.

[33] *Voices of the Matriarchs*, 175, 178. On the distinction between Weissler's earlier and later work, see n. 8.

Women's Judaism did not exist in a vacuum; its terms are set by 'Judaism,' to which women must respond. The religious world we can infer from the *tkhine* literature is, essentially, a set of female variants of male Jewish culture. It does not comprise a Judaism that takes women as its starting point.[34]

By 1995 Weissler was no longer speaking of separate cultures, but of distinct roles in a *common* culture that men controlled. True, there were differential study styles and differential prayer styles; however, overall cultural goals were the same, and these, as well as the methods by which women would go about realizing them, were set by men. We may be able to speak of separate cultural roles or multiple cultural voices ('multivocality' in Weissler's lexicon) or 'layers of the culture', but not separate cultures.[35]

Moreover, boundaries between the domains of the roles seem permeable. For example, Weissler had originally singled out the *tkhines* as a peculiarly female mode of expression; but there were *tkhines* for men and, as she herself pointed out,[36] there were many *tkhines* composed for female recital in the synagogue (especially in eighteenth-century Poland)—the supposed preserve of men. Moreover, despite Weissler's heroic efforts at identifying female *tkhine* authors, a critical reading of the evidence she adduced leads to the conclusion that most *tkhines*, in both western and eastern Europe, were probably written by men.[37] These men did seem to try to express and appeal to female sensibilities,[38] but they also crafted their works according to male-determined religious norms. In the marketplace men and women could share and even exchange roles; and the Yiddish literature that earlier Weiss-

[34] *Voices of the Matriarchs*, 185. [35] Ibid. 175. [36] Ibid. 19–23, 25, 27.

[37] By my count, Weissler identified eight possible female authors: Anonymous and Beila bat R. Ber ben Hezekiah Horowitz (p. 24), Rachel bat R. Mordecai Sofer of Pinczów (p. 25), Leah Dreyzl bat Moses (pp. 10, 26–7), Serl bat Jacob Kranz (pp. 10, 145–6, 177–8), Shifrah bat Joseph (ch. 6 and *passim*), Sarah Rebecca Rachel Leah Horowitz (ch. 7 and *passim*), Sarah bat Tovim (ch. 8 and *passim*); cf. S. Niger (H. Leyvik), 'Tsu der geshikhte fun der yudishe literatur, A: Di yudishe literatur un di lezerin', in S. Niger (ed.), *Der pinkas* (Vilna, 1912; repr. 1913); repr. in S. Niger, *Bleter geshikhte fun der yidisher literatur* (New York, 1959); abridged trans. S. Zucker in J. Baskin (ed.), *Women of the Word: Jewish Women and Jewish Writing* (Detroit, 1994), 88–94. Of these, there is some doubt as to whether the first three were authors, in the conventional sense, of the works associated with them while the historicity of Sarah bat Tovim and Shifrah bat Joseph is subject to question (pp. 92, 94). Over time Weissler became more and more certain of Sarah's existence, although the evidence base did not change; cf. *Voices of the Matriarchs*, 236–7; id., 'The Traditional Piety of Ashkenazic Women', in A. Green (ed.), *Jewish Spirituality from the Sixteenth-Century Revival to the Present* (New York, 1987), 271; id., 'Prayers in Yiddish and the Religious World of Ashkenazic Women', in J. Baskin (ed.), *Jewish Women in Historical Perspective* (Detroit, 1991), 174, 181; '"For the Human Soul Is the Lamp of the Lord": The *Tkhine* for "Laying Wicks" by Sarah bat Tovim', *Polin*, 10 (1997), 40–2. In the preface to *Voices of the Matriarchs*, on p. xxii, Weissler stated that 'most Eastern European *tkhines* were written by women'; however, on pp. 7, 10, 23, 25, 37, 66, 67, and 94 her assertions in this regard were more cautious, usually claiming, in each context, only that 'some' *tkhines* were written by women. In any case she offered no list of *tkhines* definitely or probably written by women and no guidelines for determining or even speculating on the gender of *tkhine* authors.

[38] *Voices of the Matriarchs*, 37, 53.

ler had claimed was primarily directed at women[39] was actually shared to a large extent by members of both sexes. (See below.)

Similarly, upon closer examination, Parush's conclusions warrant modification. She was convincing in describing the cultural elite's objectives of maintaining power largely at the expense of women, of depriving women of cultural capital, and of preserving a gender hierarchy. Her claims of cultural segregation and absolute hierarchy successfully attained by the efforts of the elite, however, bear qualification. Parush's argument runs aground on its analysis of: (1) the institution of *eshet ḥayil*, i.e. women who were the breadwinners for their families while their husbands spent their days in full-time scholarship; and (2) women's particular deprivation of cultural capital due to their lack of formal education.

Parush was careful not to claim that in general reality women were the breadwinners and most men engaged in scholarship in Jewish eastern Europe. In fact, from the early modern period through the nineteenth century and beyond, the overwhelming majority of Jewish men in eastern Europe did work—as did their wives.[40] Most women, even working ones, were economically dependent on their husbands, a condition apparent in the decline of living standards endured by most widows and divorcees.[41]

There seems to have been a surge in popularity of the *eshet ḥayil* arrangement in the nineteenth century, although there are no statistics or systematic study of this phenomenon.[42]

If, however, the impression is accurate, then the reasons why *eshet ḥayil* grew may be connected to two economic and social developments. First, as the rabbinate declined, rabbis came to be paid more and more with certain commercial monopoly rights rather than salaries, and it was usually their wives who exercised these monopolies in practice.[43] Secondly, haskalah, modernization, and industrialization probably made it more difficult for young Talmud scholars to attract wealthy

[39] *Voices of the Matriarchs*, 5, 36.

[40] Parush, *Nashim korot*, 44 and *passim*; cf. J. Katz, *Tradition and Crisis: Jewish Society at the End of the Middle Ages*, trans. and afterword B. D. Cooperman (New York, 1993), 113, 313 n. 2.

[41] Elsewhere (Rosman, 'Lehiyot ishah yehudiyah bepolin-lita bereishit ha'et haḥadashah', 426–8) I have demonstrated this for the earlier period; see also Salmon-Mack, 'Ḥayei nisu'im beyahadut polin', 54–60. That this situation also obtained in the 19th century is clear from ChaeRan Freeze, *Jewish Marriage and Divorce in Imperial Russia* (Hanover, NH, 2002), 207–9; see also *tkhines* on the subjects of earning a living and widowhood, e.g. T. Guren Klirs *et al.* (eds. and trans.), *The Merit of our Mothers* (Cincinnati, 1992), 118–23; Weissler, *Voices of the Matriarchs*, 22.

[42] I. Etkes, *Lita biyerushalayim* (Jerusalem, 1991), is the study that most fully presents this phenomenon, but it is based on the analysis of only one case.

[43] On the decline of the rabbinate in this period, see S. Stampfer, 'Inheritance of the Rabbinate in Eastern Europe in Modern Times: Causes, Factors, and Development Over Time', *Jewish History*, 13 (1999), 45–6. On monopoly rights in lieu of salary, see I. Levitats, *The Jewish Community in Russia, 1772–1844* (New York, 1943; repr. 1970), 154; id., *The Jewish Community in Russia, 1844–1917* (Jerusalem, 1981), 90. My thanks to Shaul Stampfer for these references and for suggesting that this was a mechanism whereby women became the breadwinners.

fathers-in-law. Traditionally, these were willing to support sons-in-law who were Torah scholars for a number of years after marriage (an arrangement called *kest*), and supply them with a large enough dowry to enable them to take up a livelihood after the period of support. Ideally this occupation would be capital-intensive (e.g. money-lending, real estate) rather than requiring huge investments of time and effort. Alternatively, such post-*kest* men might become paid communal rabbis. By the mid-nineteenth century many rich men preferred sons-in-law who were university students rather than yeshiva students. In addition, during the course of the nineteenth century the number of rabbinic posts significantly decreased, meaning that those with insufficient capital would likely have a hard time finding a paying rabbinic post. Consequently, the age of marriage of yeshiva students rose; once they finally did get married, it was often, apparently, their wives who filled the economic breach.[44]

However, those who lived this way could never be more—and probably were less—than the total number of full-time scholars, and therefore a thin layer of the overall Jewish population. Parush held, however, that, regardless of their actual number, women who fulfilled the *eshet ḥayil* role represented a normative ideal that had practical consequences. 'It was sufficient that Jewish society strived to realize the ideal vision—according to which the men were to dedicate all of their time to fulfilling their religious destiny—in order to concretize norms of behaviour that placed the concerns of making a living on the shoulders of the women.' She judged that such norms, delineated by the talmudist and literary critic Daniel Boyarin, were indeed the accepted ones in nineteenth-century Jewish eastern Europe. This judgement relied on both Boyarin's unhistorical argument and the prominence of supposed east European Jewish gender reversal (which at least *preached* that women be the breadwinners and men scholars at leisure) as a target of haskalah literature's criticism. Parush also dwelt on (and criticized) the negative literary portrayal of the 'Cossack'—the aggressive, gruff, tough Jewish woman of the marketplace—as corroborating the general devaluation of women in this society.[45]

44 On the problems of attracting wealthy fathers-in-law and the diminution of rabbinic positions, see Stampfer, 'Inheritance of the Rabbinate in Eastern Europe in Modern Times', 46–7. On the marriage age of yeshiva students, see S. Stampfer, 'Shalosh yeshivot lita'iyot bame'ah hatesha-esreh', Ph.D. thesis (Hebrew University, Jerusalem, 1981), 220–30*c*.

45 Parush, *Nashim korot*, 44–52, 138–9, 241–2, 260, 288 (the quotation is on p. 45). In her introduction, p. 20, Parush recognized the need to confirm literary images with extra-literary sources before declaring them historical; in practice she did little in the way of such confirmation. For the 18th century, which I have researched, there are sources that show that married women who worked as tavern-keepers still observed gender conventions, deferring to their husbands or other men to handle various business situations that would have required 'unladylike' behaviour (Rosman, 'Lehiyot ishah yehudiyah bepolin-lita bereishit ha'et haḥadashah', 429). Intensive searching would likely turn up 19th-century examples of the same phenomenon. Parush did find dubious affirmation for her claims about the putative normativity of *eshet hayil* in the work of Daniel Boyarin: 'Internal Opposition in Talmudic Literature: The Case of the Married Monk', *Representations*, 36 (1991), 87–113, which treats a literary trope of manhood from the talmudic period; and his *Unheroic Conduct: The Rise of*

To my mind, the maskilic portrayal of both gender reversal and 'Cossacks' are literary tropes—no proof of what Parush wanted to demonstrate in reality. Her assertion that in Jewish eastern Europe *eshet ḥayil* became the social ideal 'as expressed by customs and lifestyles that placed women in the store or in the marketplace and exposed them to daily contact with the non-Jewish environment'[46] is belied by non-maskilic assessment of women's economic activity and its relationship to men's. For example, in his memoirs Yekhezkel Kotik, after detailing women's roles as storekeepers and tavern-keepers in his town, Kamenets *c.*1850, turned to the men: 'So what did the men occupy themselves with? Surely they did not hang around idly.' He then described men's activities as agents of the hundreds of local middle-ranking noblemen and as artisans. Kotik's depiction makes it clear that the economic activities of men and women were complementary. Women were not sitting in their stores in service of some normative ideal of *eshet ḥayil* while their husbands attended or dreamed of attending the local *beit midrash* (study house). Women's economic contribution was parallel to—and usually subordinate to—men's, and both were required in order to make a living for the family; not because women were deemed primarily responsible for the physical side of life and men for the spiritual.[47]

Heterosexuality and the Invention of the Jewish Man (Berkeley, 1998), 151–85, which analyses talmudic tropes of manhood and womanhood and then breathtakingly assumes that they were upheld as ideal types from the Babylonian talmudic period through all of the periods of its 'cultural descendants' (p. 156). Barely pausing to adduce the supposed example of the famed Glikl of Hameln (1646–1723), whose husband was a businessman and not a scholar, Boyarin certainly did not deign to examine either the attitudes or the actual behaviour of Jews in the 19th century to test his assumptions. Parush, *Nashim korot*, 261, also cited S. Saltsman's description of *eshet hayil*-type women in his town, Seltz, in the late 19th century (*Ayarati* (Tel Aviv, 1947), 52–6). Close reading of this source indicates that Saltsman did not consider *neshei ḥayil* and 'Cossacks' to be typical, ideal, or negative. He portrayed them as exceptional women who often filled leadership and public roles in economic, social, and religious life, influenced the public sphere, and possessed more cultural capital than most women. He also implied that their husbands were not necessarily scholars, but working men.

46 Parush, *Nashim korot*, 44.

47 Y. Kotik, *Journey to a Nineteenth-Century Shtetl: The Memoirs of Yehezkel Kotik*, ed. D. Assaf (Detroit, 2002), 110–12. Parush cited this source in her notes (*Nashim korot*, 261 n. 6) without fully exploring its implications. The classic, although problematic, anthropologically oriented study of east European Jewish culture, M. Zborowski and E. Herzog, *Life Is With People: The Culture of the Shtetl* (New York, 1962), also presents a more balanced and realistic picture of male–female economic responsibilities: 'The earning of a livelihood is sexless, and the large majority of women, even among the sheynah [upper class], participate in some gainful occupation if they do not carry the chief burden of support. The wife of a "perennial student" is very apt to be the sole support of the family. . . . There are many instances in which the man carries the chief or the sole support of the household. *If he is not a scholar it is taken for granted that the primary economic responsibility is his*' (pp. 131–2; my emphasis). It is interesting to note that, to a small degree, Zborowski and Herzog anticipated Parush's insights with regard to the freedom of culturally marginal women to pursue secular education (p. 128) and the identification of cultural patterns making for gender hierarchy (pp. 129, 130, 133, 137, 140, and *passim*); although they, perhaps apologetically, theorized that this was largely negated by the coexistence

As to their being deprived of education, Parush knew that most men in Jewish eastern Europe were almost as poorly educated as the women were.[48] Most were not qualified for admission to the ranks of the learned elite and suffered from deprivation of cultural capital. If the elite discriminated educationally, it was against men as well as women. Parush also implied that her generalization that men were not tempted to cross over to female culture was not to be taken simplistically. Men, too, read Yiddish literature, even that explicitly intended for women.[49]

Overall, Parush's argument can be characterized as a form of synecdoche. Because in a small part of society—among the learned elite—women were largely responsible for economic matters while men were in charge of culture does not mean that this division of labour determined the whole of gender relationships throughout society. Also, Parush's description of culturally marginalized women as the avatars of modernization and secularization, while convincing as far as it goes, applies to a very small group that was itself an educated elite, even if not a traditional one.[50]

In real life, as opposed to haskalah literature, women did not dominate—and the social norm did not project their domination of—the economic sphere. If the elite was culturally manipulative, its victims included the vast majority of men. Moreover, it is my contention that over the *longue durée* ordinary east European Jewish women were taking an ever more active role in culture (see below). While there was undoubtedly a gender hierarchy, its machinations and oscillations among the vast majority of men and women has yet to be elucidated. It needs to be studied less impressionistically and on the basis of sources that reflect life in the period as it was lived and not as a small group of maskilic critics construed it for polemical purposes.

As Parush so vividly depicted, there were some women who succeeded in obtaining an education that gave them the tools to venture into secularized modernity. They did impress and influence the maskilic intelligentsia and other social opinion-makers; but they were a tiny minority.[51] For most women—and most men—modernization was a much less self-conscious and much more externally generated process, deriving from such trends as urbanization, industrialization, and emigration.

As for Stampfer, he himself undermined his claim that women had a separate culture that interlocked with the men's:

of formal (hierarchical) and informal (roughly egalitarian) status (cf. Davis, '"Women's History" in Transition', 82–3, 89). They summed up the situation by saying, 'The pattern prescribed by the culture, however, allows full scope for the "never-silent bell" to be a submissive partner or a vibrant force in her home and in the community' (p. 141). See also J. Katz, *Out of the Ghetto* (New York, 1973), 84, 86.

[48] Parush, *Nashim korot*, 14, 67–9, 71.

[49] Ibid. 148–9.

[50] Ibid., chs. 6–7 and *passim*. Parush's remarks, pp. 52–61, 171–2, about the matchmaking system and its contribution to both the subordination of women and the rise of women's subversive power also apply to a relatively small group within the population who could afford to assume the financial burden that marrying off young children imposed.

[51] Ibid. 180–206 and *passim*.

Jewish men and women could be seen as occupying adjacent but different cultural worlds in Eastern Europe. . . . To be sure there were many exceptions to this gender division and they did not extend to every sphere of life. Both men and women generally worked and contributed to the family income . . . many men read Yiddish material, while there were also women who could read literature published in Hebrew.[52]

If boundaries were so easily crossed, perhaps the separate cultures were not so discretely defined. Rather than parallel each other, they seem to have coincided at various points. We may conclude, then, that (as feminist scholarship has led us to expect) the separateness of the gender domains was less than each of the three scholars had initially enunciated.

EARLY YIDDISH LITERATURE: WOMEN'S OR MEN'S?

Early Yiddish literature, singled out by our three authors and many of their predecessors as an embodiment of the boundary between the genders, is a good example of the conflation of male and female domains. In this case the dichotomy that breaks down is male = Hebrew/female = Yiddish.

The common Yiddish terms *veibertaytsh* (women's translation) and *veibershrift* (women's typeface), referring respectively to Yiddish translations of Hebrew books, especially *Tsenerene*, and the special typeface used to print early Yiddish books, epitomized the idea that Yiddish literature was a women's literature. This thesis was elaborated in a Yiddish essay written some ninety years ago by Shmuel Niger, who made a case for the *essential femininity* of Yiddish literature. Even when written by men or for men, according to Niger, Yiddish maintained a feminine sensibility, feminine lyricism, feminine tendency to concreteness, etc.[53]

This position, maintaining that Yiddish literature was primarily a women's literature, was initially adopted, minus the now embarrassing essentialism, by Jewish feminist scholars like Naomi Seidman and Chava Weissler.[54] It was attractive, offering an articulated women's domain that was parallel to and in at least some ways equivalent, and even equal, to the male domain. With Yiddish literature east European Jewish women had found a room of their own. This view of Yiddish literature was, however, controvertible.

Even the earlier Weissler, for example, remarked on 'the splendid ambiguity' of some of the early Yiddish books as to their intended audience.[55] Much earlier, Max Weinreich had posited that the myth of Yiddish femininity was actually a deliberate fiction manufactured to provide cover for the male audience that was also reading

[52] Stampfer, 'Gender Differentiation and Education of the Jewish Woman', 71–2.

[53] Niger, 'Tsu der geshikhte fun der yudishe literatur'; cf. N. Seidman, *A Marriage Made in Heaven* (Berkeley, 1997), 3–5, 15.

[54] Seidman, *A Marriage Made in Heaven*, 5–7, 15, 18; Weissler, *Voices of the Matriarchs*, 5, 36.

[55] Weissler, *Voices of the Matriarchs*, 41.

this work and for whom it was indeed also intended. By pretending that Yiddish was written and published exclusively for women, one need not admit that there were in fact both men who needed a non-Hebrew literature and men who, although they may not have needed it, desired it and the pleasures it afforded.[56] Investigation of early Yiddish literature, however, makes one wonder if even this was true: that women were positioned as a front to camouflage the male readers. The problem is that the men don't seem very camouflaged.

One way that the audience for Yiddish literature has been assessed is by interpretation of the title pages of Yiddish books. Some of them, characterizing their potential readers, contain phrases like 'for women and girls', seeming indeed to be addressed to a female readership. However, Israel Zinberg reported that out of more than seventy such title pages he checked, only nine were addressed exclusively to women. Most contain phrases like: 'men and women and the pious girls', 'for women and maidens to read with joy, boys and householders—all together' , 'dear men and women' , 'women or men' , 'men, youths, girls, and women'.[57]

Even books that seem obviously addressed to women can be problematic. For example, *Seder mitsvot nashim* (1577) is a book ostensibly directed at women to explain to them how they should attain righteousness, largely—but not exclusively—by means of observance of the commandments which are especially incumbent upon them. Yet the author, Benjamin Slonik, expected that some husbands would read this book and explain it to their wives:

A man may also take delight [in this booklet] for there are some wives who cannot read. Such a wife must often err. Therefore, her husband may instruct her so that she will take care of her matters well and not sin away both worlds [i.e. this world and the world to come] and not follow the evil inclination altogether.[58]

In addition, there are several passages in the book addressed explicitly to men.[59]

The oft-cited, quintessential women's book *Tsenerene* was written by Ya'akov ben Yitzhak of Yanov. In the introduction to his second book, *Melits yosher*, he noted that he was moved to write this book because of the popularity of his first one.

[56] M. Weinreich, *History of the Yiddish Language*, trans. S. Noble (Chicago, 1980), 277; cf. Seidman, *A Marriage Made in Heaven*, 17.

[57] I. Zinberg, *Di geshikhte fun der literatur bei yidn* (Vilna, 1935; New York, 1943), vi. 411–13. (This section is not included in the English translation of this work.)

[58] For analysis of this book and its antecedents, see A. Romer Segal, 'Sifrei mitsvot hanashim beyidish bame'ah hashesh-esreh', MA thesis (Hebrew University, Jerusalem, 1979) (Romer Segal summarized her thesis in English in A. Romer Segal, 'Yiddish Works on Women's Commandments in the Sixteenth Century', *Studies in Yiddish Literature and Folklore* (1986), 37–59); and Edward Fram's forthcoming translation and analytical introduction of this work (see n. 1). I am grateful to Professor Fram for allowing me to read parts of his work in manuscript and to utilize his translation of the passage from the introduction (p. 2a) presented here; see also *Seder mitsvot nashim*, para. 105.

[59] Romer Segal, 'Sifrei mitsvot hanashim beyidish bame'ah hashesh-esreh', 25, 29. She noted that earlier redactions of the material in the book contained additional male-directed passages; ibid. 8, 13.

He wrote: 'and I want to benefit the people, for God helped me with the *Tsenerene* and I benefited *men and women*; thus should I be privileged to continue to do'.[60]

Also in this book there are occasional passages that seem addressed to men.

Are such references here and on title pages just devices intended to expand the potential audience and, with it, book sales? Are they but meaningless repetition of conventional phrases? Are they included to help with the rhyme scheme? Or do they express the author's sincere conviction as to whom his book was written for and who actually read it? As with the issue of *eshet ḥayil*, systematic analysis is still awaited.[61] It behoves us, therefore, to take to heart the criticism voiced by Michael Stanislawski: 'The vast majority of premodern Yiddish texts have never been subjected to any serious scholarly examination. To cite only one, though crucial, example . . . the *Tsena U-Rena* . . . We still lack a comprehensive study of the contents of this work . . .'.[62] At present we must say that the connection between early Yiddish literature and women has yet to be fully explicated.[63]

Another approach to Yiddish literature has been to say that it was not intended just for women, but for women and other uneducated people. In the most famous phrase cited in Weissler's book: 'This book is written in Yiddish for women and for men who are like women in not being able to learn much.'[64] Weissler noted that the locution 'for women and for men who are like women' is a variation on the more traditional phrase *nashim ve'amei ha'arets* ('women and ignorant men').[65] To gain perspective, it is worth briefly examining the history of this expression.

First of all, this phrase is more traditional than contemporary scholarship on Yiddish literature might lead readers to think. It goes back to the Talmud, where in BT, *Meg.*, it says:

Mishnah: 'A foreigner who heard the Megilah in Hebrew has fulfilled his obligation.' Gemara: 'But he does not know what they are saying. It is like the case of women and ignorant

[60] Ya'akov ben Yitzhak of Yanov, *Melits yosher* (Lublin, 1622), introd.; quoted by C. Shmeruk, *Sifrut yidish bepolin* (Jerusalem, 1981), 39 (my emphasis). Like *Seder mitsvot nashim*, *Tsenerene* contains occasional passages that seem to be addressed to men.

[61] A start has been made by C. Turniansky (ed.), *Sefer ma'asah umerivah: 387 (1627), lerabi aleksander ben rabi yitsḥak fafin hofin* (Jerusalem, 1985), 133.

[62] 'The Yiddish *Shevet yehudah*: A Study in the "Ashkenization" of a Spanish-Jewish Classic', in E. Carlebach, J. M. Efron, and D. N. Myers (eds.), *Jewish History and Jewish Memory: Essays in Honor of Yosef Hayim Yerushalmi* (Hanover, NH, 1998), 136.

[63] Some important steps in this direction have been taken by Romer Segal, 'Sifrei mitsvot hanashim beyidish bame'ah hashesh-esreh'; id., 'Sifrut yidish vekahal koreiha bame'ah hashesh-esreh', *Kiryat sefer*, 53 (1978), 779–90; Fram, introd. to *Seder mitsvot nashim*; D. Roskies, 'Yiddish Popular Literature and the Female Reader', *Journal of Popular Studies*, 13 (1979), 852–8; Shmeruk, *Sifrut yidish bepolin*, 11–74, 147–64; C. Turniansky, 'On Old Yiddish Biblical Epics', *International Folklore Review*, 8 (1991), 26–33.

[64] Moshe Henokh Altshuler, *Brantspiegel* (Kraków, 1596), ch. 3; trans. C. Weissler in *Voices of the Matriarchs*, 53; cf. p. 38.

[65] *Voices of the Matriarchs*, 38. There are other variants of this phrase, such as *noshim un proste folk* (lit. 'women and simple people').

men. Ravina objected to it: Do we understand the words האחשתרנים בני הרמכים?[66] Rather the *mitsvah* is reading and publicizing the miracle. Here too the *mitsvah* is reading and publicizing the miracle.'[67]

The connotations of this phrase changed significantly from talmudic to medieval times. As utilized in the cited talmudic passage, it implied: the uneducated don't know and don't have to know. Later, in some contexts, it still meant this; but in other contexts it was deemed important for this sector of the community to be informed. Rashi, commenting on a talmudic discussion of the proper method of reading out to the congregation the Targum (the Aramaic translation of the Scriptures) during the public reading of the Torah and Haftarah, said: 'The purpose of the Targum is to communicate to women and ignorant men who do not understand the holy tongue . . . and we must repeat the Torah in translation so they will understand the *mitsvot*.'[68]

From this it appears that by the Middle Ages there were certain types of knowledge that the elite decided unlearned women and men were required to know and, consequently, had a right to know.[69] If so, the publication of Yiddish books for the uneducated does not seem very revolutionary, but rather can be seen as a link in a long-evolving process of bringing knowledge to the common people. Also, classifying uneducated women and men together in one category was a traditional expedient reaching back into antiquity and maintaining its relevance through the early modern period.[70]

[66] Ravina's example of an ill-understood biblical text is apt: *Tanakh*, the 1985 Jewish Publication Society of America translation of the Bible, translates this phrase from Esther 8: 10 'steeds used in the King's service, bred of the royal stud', but immediately adds that the meaning of the Hebrew here is uncertain.

[67] BT, *Meg.* 18*a*; trans. based on Schottenstein edn. (Brooklyn, 1991).

[68] Rashi on BT, *Meg.* 21*b*. Rashi (1040–1105) adds that it is not so important for the women and men in question to understand the Haftarah texts, which are taken from the books of the Prophets, presumably because no practical *mitsvot* are to be found in them. Similarly, a statement included in Zedekiah ben Abraham Rofe Anav (13th century), *Shibolei haleket*, ed. S. Buber (Vilna, 1887), sect. 78, pp. 28*b*–29*a*, affirms that translation of the Torah text is necessary because the unlearned need to know its contents. A different part of this passage specifies some circumstances where translation for the unlearned women and men is not appropriate because they might misunderstand the real meaning of the text or the text might seem prima facie derogatory. In such a case the 'honour of God' requires not revealing the particular text. (My thanks to Sol Cohen of CAJS for this reference.) Also *Sefer ḥasidim* (13th century), ed. Y. Wistinetzki and Y. Freimann (Jerusalem, 1969), p. 211, para. 435 notes: 'A man is required to teach his daughters the *mitsvot*, such as halakhic decisions. . . . If she will not know the rules of the sabbath, how will she observe the sabbath?'

[69] It is interesting to note what may be a Christian parallel to this phenomenon. According to A. Vauchez, *The Laity in the Middle Ages: Religious Beliefs and Devotional Practices*, ed. D. E. Bornstein, trans. M. J. Schneider (Notre Dame, Ind., 1993), 99–106, in the 13th century European Catholic clergy recognized the need to actively teach correct belief and correct behaviour to the lay masses. As Vauchez put it, clerics in this period were beginning to identify ignorance with error.

[70] Terming these people 'the intellectual middle class', as Weissler does (*Voices of the Matriarchs*, 10–12), is in my opinion not appropriate. This appellation would be better applied to so-called *ba'alei batim* (lit. 'householders'), those laymen who, having studied somewhat intensively in their youth,

Moreover, in the process of the democratization of knowledge and cultural upheaval that began in the sixteenth century—which Elhanan Reiner and Zeev Gries have pointed to as a function of several vectors such as humanism, printing, and Reformation ideology[71]—Yiddish lagged behind Hebrew. To illustrate quantitatively: according to Chone Shmeruk, between 1535 and 1648 approximately 200 Yiddish books were printed. In her recently completed doctorate on all of the Hebrew books published in 1540–1639, Anat Gueta has shown that out of a total of some 5,600 published Hebrew imprints, almost 500, approximately 9 per cent, were printed by Christians for Christian purposes; that is about 2½ times the number of books published in Yiddish at approximately the same time.[72] So, quantitatively speaking, the Yiddish literary revolution took place after the mid-seventeenth century.

FACILITATORS, BYSTANDERS, AND PERFORMERS

To return to the question of the cultural relationship between men and women, perhaps the beginnings of a formulation can be arrived at from further analysis of the *nashim ve'amei ha'arets* stereotype. Weissler's highlighting of the 'men who are like women' phrase implied that this cliché should be subsumed as part of the larger stereotype of what women are like, i.e. uneducated and all that is concomitant with that. This presumption, however, runs into the problem that the men are attached. Claims about women's literature, women's *mentalité*, women's concerns, or about the treatment women received always clash with the fact that the phrase in question mentions men and that in fact many, if not most, men were in the same situation as women.

I would like to try to cut this knot by asserting that culturally speaking there were two different governing stereotypes about women that Polish Jewry inherited from

could study elementary books, like Rashi's Bible commentary, independently; and could understand an erudite lesson in Talmud or other rabbinic literature. S. Assaf, 'Teshuvah neged ḥibur sifrei dinim beyidish', *Kiryat sefer*, 20 (1943), 41–2, quoted a 15th-century responsum, probably written by R. Jacob Levi (the Maharil) in Ashkenaz, that explicitly distinguishes between *ba'alei batim* who can understand Rashi and other texts and *think* they understand halakhic codes such as *Arba'ah turim*, *Sha'arei dura*, and *Sefer mitsvot katan* (and therefore they also think they can determine halakhah by themselves), and *amei ha'arets* and *nashim* who can only understand texts written in Yiddish; cf. Romer Segal, 'Sifrei mitsvot hanashim beyidish bame'ah hashesh-esreh', 2. According to this schema it was the *ba'alei batim* who really were, intellectually speaking, the middle class, in between the scholarly elite and the poorly educated women and men who read only Yiddish.

71 E. Reiner, 'The Ashkenazi Élite at the Beginning of the Modern Era: Manuscript Versus Printed Book', *Polin*, 10 (1997), 85–98; id., 'The Attitude of Ashkenazi Society to the New Science in the Sixteenth Century', *Science in Context*, 10 (1997), 589–603; Z. Gries, *Sifrut hahanhagot* (Jerusalem, 1989), introd.

72 Shmeruk, *Sifrut yidish bepolin*, 11–74; A. Gueta, 'Hasefarim hamudpasim shel shenot hashin kemakor leḥeker ḥayei haru'aḥ shel haḥevrah hayehudit', Ph.D. thesis (Bar-Ilan University, Ramat Gan, 2003), 94–7, 213–16.

its Ashkenazi forebears. These were created and promoted by men, were patronizing and even demeaning, but were shared to a large extent by women as well.

One was *nashim*: women *qua* women were supposed to participate in the culture as *facilitators* (while men were to be *performers*). The classic talmudic formulation 'How do women gain merit? By bringing their sons to the synagogue [to learn Torah] and by sending their husbands to the study hall and waiting for them until they come from the study hall' (BT, *Ber.* 17*a*; my translation), was expressed in Poland by Isserles: 'If she helps her son or her husband occupy themselves with Torah she shares the reward with them.'[73]

The second stereotype is *nashim ve'amei ha'arets*. These, culturally speaking, are bystanders.[74] They did not possess the cultural capital that would empower them culturally and enable them to play significant roles in elite culture. With respect to elite culture they were supposed to remain on the sidelines.

Women, therefore, were thought of as both facilitators and bystanders relative to the male-dominated, patriarchal culture. As bystanders, women were supposed to be non-participants; as facilitators they were participants, albeit low-status, unempowered ones; but inextricably involved in the dominant culture.

The relationship of each gender to early Yiddish literature illustrates the difficulty of delimiting separate cultural domains for men and women. There seems to have been a very long cultural process at work that was continually effacing cultural boundaries that supposedly separated women from men. As cultural bystanders, women were in the same category as many men and, like them, while initially deprived of cultural capital, were continually gaining more of it. With respect to the job of women as facilitators, the male performers could not afford to let the cultural gap between them and their female helpmates grow so wide that the meaning behind the role of women would disappear. Facilitators who could not understand the significance of what they were supposed to foster would not be very dedicated to the task. This also required endowing them with more cultural capital.

How, then, did the conception of women's cultural role change in Poland through the early modern period? My contention is that the expectation that women would be cultural facilitators did not change significantly. Women remained theoretically responsible for the physical and spiritual welfare of their families, 'managing the

[73] *SA*, *Mapah*, 'Yoreh de'ah', 246: 6.

[74] However, analogously to the case presented by Sered in *Women as Ritual Experts*, Jewish women in Poland may have had their own, autonomous religious culture where they were active performers, and which was expressed orally and with gestures, rather than in written texts. Being unfamiliar to men, this culture remained unexpressed in the sources available to us that were written by men. As Sered points out in her book (pp. 47–9), when cultural segregation between men and women breaks down, the existing autonomous female culture tends to disappear as women adopt and adapt many of the elements of the male culture. So the *tkhines* that Weissler described, which are related to normative rabbinic culture shaped by men, may actually have come in place of a previous, more autonomous women's culture. But, lacking the means to study today what was in the past only oral and ephemeral, we cannot know.

household in cleanliness'[75] and creating a situation conducive to their husbands' religious and material success. The *tkhines* illustrate this nicely. They are laden with women's petitions that they be allowed to promote the health, welfare, and both material and religious success of husbands and children.[76]

However, the *bystander* construct was ameliorated. The patriarchal elite allowed and even advanced (through the books they wrote) the formal incorporation of more of women's (and uneducated men's) behaviour into the dominant culture. Women came to be seen less as bystanders and more as performers in various ways. Books in Yiddish, alluded to above, aimed to involve bystanders, women and men, in the elite culture. Some of these books were new codifications of women's specific halakhic duties, especially the three *mitsvot* of separating a part of the dough when baking bread (*ḥalah*), observing the restrictions and obligations incumbent upon menstruants (*nidah*), and lighting candles at the onset of the sabbath and major holidays (*hadlakat nerot*). Such codes denoted a new concern for how women were to perform their cultural duties. Sometimes these books emphasized other religious obligations on women as well, such as refraining from oaths and gossip, observing the sabbath, raising children, honouring parents, praying, giving charity, and being punctilious in *kashrut* observance.[77] Likewise, the appearance of *books* of *tkhine* prayers, beginning in the late sixteenth century, betokened a new institutionalization of women's prayer and a new significance assigned to it. Yiddish fiction, which was popular among women (and men too)—much of which was translated from non-Jewish sources—was adapted and 'Judaized'. A sprinkling of pious Jewish sentiments, the deletion of Christological references and themes, and the addition of Jewish ones, ensured that readers were reading material that was 'religiously correct'.[78]

There are several indicators that in the synagogue in the same period women went from being occasional guests to being regular participants. Polish synagogue architecture beginning in the sixteenth century began to include women's annexes (*weibershule*) and, later, women's sections (*ezrat nashim*) as integral parts of the physical synagogue structure.[79] In halakhah some authorities were prepared to allow

[75] J. Emden, *Megilat sefer*, ed. J. Bik (Shauli) (Jerusalem, 1979), 93.

[76] Klirs *et al.* (eds.), *The Merit of our Mothers*, 116–23, 130–7, and *passim*.

[77] Romer Segal, 'Sifrei mitsvot hanashim beyidish bame'ah hashesh-esreh', 9, 11, 13, 16, 19, 21.

[78] I. Zinberg, *A History of Jewish Literature*, ed. and trans. B. Martin, vii (Cincinnati, 1975), 50–1, 55, 68, 74, 79–81.

[79] On the building of *weibershule* in Poland, see Fram, introd. to *Seder mitsvot nashim*, ch. 1; on *ezrat nashim*, C. Krinsky, *Synagogues of Europe: Architecture, History, Meaning* (Mineola, NY, 1985), 28–31; R. Wischnitzer, *The Architecture of the European Synagogue* (Philadelphia, 1964), 76–124. There is evidence both for the existence of *weibershule* and for women's regular synagogue attendance and involvement in synagogue life in Ashkenaz in the Middle Ages; see *Das Martyrologium des Nürnberger Memorbuches*, ed. S. Salfeld (Berlin, 1898), 87; *Sefer ḥasidim*, p. 70, para. 172, pp. 132–3, paras. 464, 465, 468; A. M. Haberman (ed.), *Sefer gezerot ashkenaz vetsarefat* (Jerusalem, 1971), 165; E. Baumgarten, 'Imahot veyeladim baḥevrah hayehudit bimei habeinayim', Ph.D. thesis (Hebrew University, Jerusalem, 2000), 313. It appears, however, that in the 13th century there was a move, led by Rabbi

more women to attend synagogue.[80] With regard to liturgy, as noted previously, in eighteenth-century Poland there was a trend towards the composition of *tkhines* to be said by women in the synagogue.[81]

There also was apparently an increasing ritualization of certain women's activities as exemplified by the practice of measuring graves with candlewick (*kneytlach leygn*). This converted what began in the distant past as popular customs into sacral acts.[82]

Just as there are *tkhines* that reflect the continuity of the facilitator stereotype, others manifest changes in the bystander construct. As Weissler has observed, some *tkhines*, apparently written by women, valorized women's behaviour, presenting women in more empowered roles than they enjoyed in real life, imbuing women's activities with greater sacral significance, and implying protest against misogynist trends in traditional rabbinic exegesis.[83] These vectors in the *tkhines* might be seen as approaching the logical conclusions of the ameliorative trend set in motion by the male elite described above.[84]

Meir of Rothenburg, to discourage women's participation in the synagogue and public ritual in eastern Ashkenazi communities in general; see Baumgarten, 'Imahot veyeladim baḥevrah hayehudit bimei habeinayim', 125–36; D. Sperber, *Minhagei yisra'el*, i (Jerusalem, 1990), 64–6. What lasting effects this action had needs to be investigated. My claim is that, whatever earlier precedents exist, from the 16th century in Poland (and in areas to the west), it is apparent that the intensification and spread of public participation by women in ritual life was something that was being debated and revitalized; cf. Yuspa Shamash (17th-century Ashkenaz), *Minhagim de-k'k vermeisa*, ed. B. S. Hamburger and Y. Zimmer, pt. 1 (Jerusalem, 1988), 221.

[80] *SA*, *Mapah*, 'Oraḥ ḥayim', 88: 1; *Seder mitsvot nashim*, trans. Fram, para. 77; M. Rosman, 'Prolegomenon', *Jewish Studies: An Internet Journal*, 1(2002), 111–12.

[81] *Voices of the Matriarchs*, 25, 27; cf. text above, near n. 36 above.

[82] Ibid. 133–46; cf. Sered, *Women as Ritual Experts*, 84–96, 139–141. The key word is perhaps 'increasing'. Here, too (see n. 79), there are certainly precedents for various female rituals in the Middle Ages; however, I think that in the early modern period these became more numerous, more institutionalized, and more widespread.

[83] *Voices of the Matriarchs*, e.g. pp. 62–5, 70–4, 77–85, 96–103. The alternative biblical exegesis in the *tkhines* which Weissler explicates has an interesting American analogue. This is biblical interpretation incorporated in women's poetry in 19th-century America, where 'the interpretive project in women's poetry reaffirms a shared biblical discourse as fundamental to both personal identity and American cultural continuity. It demonstrates the way biblical interpretation both reasserted tradition and acted as an arena of disagreement and protest'; S. Wolosky, 'Women's Bibles: Biblical Interpretation in Nineteenth-Century American Women's Poetry', *Feminist Studies*, 28 (2002), 191–211 (the quotation is on p. 194).

[84] Another sign of this ameliorative trend may be the apparent change in the role of women in hasidism in the period immediately following the time-frame of this chapter. Earlier I alluded to the case made by Ada Rapoport-Albert concerning the virtual exclusion of women from the early hasidic groups in the late 18th century (see above, n. 17). However, in his recent dissertation Glenn Dynner ('"Men of Silk": The Hasidic Conquest of Polish Jewry, 1754–1830', Ph.D. thesis (Brandeis University, 2002)), has emphasized how at the end of the 18th century and in the early 19th century mitnagedim, maskilim, and Polish critics of hasidism all attacked various tsadikim for keeping too much company with, pandering to, or exploiting female devotees (pp. 130, 132, 269, 271, 272, 283, 290). There are also hasidic sources which indicate that with time some hasidic leaders paid much

With regard to Haskalah, Shmuel Feiner has pointed out that maskilim's advocacy of certain liberal reforms with respect to women did not mean that these men were interested in women becoming fully educated and truly enlightened. They were willing to entertain women's modernization only to the extent that it enhanced the role of female facilitator within the new modernizing context.[85] In the early modern period, too, giving women more opportunities to be cultural performers rather than bystanders bound them more tightly to the culture, worked against their straying after the new alien temptations of the post-Renaissance and post-Reformation world, and ultimately guaranteed their continuation in their traditional facilitator role. This, not very coincidentally, strengthened the position of the elite. Recognition and institutionalization of women's cultural activities were means to control them better.[86]

WOMEN OF POWER?

Having just asserted that the amelioration of the bystander stereotype was not intended to empower women but to control them more efficiently and reinforce existing gender hierarchical structures, the question remains: Whatever the male establishment's intentions were, did women have power?

Here feminist scholars have answered, 'No!' Parush, more secularist than feminist, refined this accusation to read that in traditional society women were not *intended* to have meaningful power, but that they successfully transformed their structural powerlessness into freedom and a subversive kind of power as agents of social, secularly oriented, change. While at first Weissler gave a qualified yes to the question of female empowerment,[87] later she decided to say no; but more in resignation than in anger as she saw women as complicit in their own powerlessness: 'Yet women do acquiesce to such ideologies and we must try to understand why. . . . a recognition that women are often relatively powerless, that they often acquiesce to this condition, and that otherwise valuable institutions, cultures, religions are implicated in women's powerlessness and acquiescence.'[88]

attention to prescribing proper behaviour (mainly restrictive) for female followers and made themselves accessible to female petitioners, particularly prominent and affluent ones (pp. 316–21). Dynner also documented how Temerel Sonnenberg, daughter-in-law of the Jewish magnate Samuel Zbytkower (she was married to his son Berek) used her wealth and influence to promote Polish hasidism, endowing various institutions, giving commercial opportunities to hasidic leaders, and intervening with the government to obtain favourable administrative decisions on behalf of hasidic groups and their leaders (pp. 126, 150–64).

[85] S. Feiner, 'Ha'ishah hayehudit hamodernit: Mikreh-mivḥan beyaḥasei hahaskalah vehamodernah', *Zion*, 58 (1993), 453–99.

[86] And perhaps contributed to the disappearance of a previous autonomous women's culture; see above, n. 74.

[87] See above, near and in nn. 24–5, 83.

[88] *Voices of the Matriarchs*, 173, 175. This issue of women's complicity in their own deprivation of power is an inveterate problem in modern feminist scholarship going back at least to Simone de

So women willingly supported—facilitated—gender hierarchy. In this Weissler seemed to give a nod to the functionalist position of Stampfer. He also claimed that women acquiesced in what he identified as their semi-deprivation of cultural capital. He thought that this was in exchange for the compensation of (inferior) cultural tools and in the name of the efficient functioning of society as a whole. Weissler had a different and somewhat more salutary explanation:

> Like all great religious traditions, Judaism contains rich and profound texts, traditions, rituals, and customs. This helps us understand why women—and nonlearned men—would acquiesce to a system of meaning that, in part, disempowers them. It offers them something in return. . . . in order to get the good things inherent in an institution or social practice, one agrees, though not always freely or consciously, to accept some of the bad things . . . [89]

For Weissler, the compensation that women got in exchange for acquiescence in their own subordination was the meaningfulness that Jewish tradition offered.

I think that in order to clarify the question of female empowerment in Polish Jewish society some further analysis is called for. The sixteenth- to eighteenth-century Jewish community in Poland was a patriarchy where the cultural elite was exclusively male. However, some other features of this society should be added to the analysis.

As observed above, culturally speaking, most men were as powerless as women. The norms and ideals that determined meaning and values were not open to popular debate. The arbiters of meaning in the culture tried to maintain the powerlessness of most men as well as women.

While women were usually weak with respect to *culture*, there were women with *social* power. Review of the list of Jewish taxpayers in any town in the Polish–Lithuanian Commonwealth in these centuries reveals a significant proportion of households (approximately 5–15 per cent) headed by women, virtually always widows. Often these women housed young married children and while they did not have political rights in the community, their status as householders and taxpayers meant that they bore responsibility for the people in their household and towards the public economy and polity. The financial importance of some affluent

Beauvoir's *The Second Sex*, ed. and trans. H. M. Parshley (1st pub. 1953; New York, 1993), where, in my opinion, it is the engine driving the argument of the book; see e.g. pp. xliv–lx, 628–60, 751–67. This question may be anachronistic, seeing that there is little evidence that the issue of women's complicity was raised in the period being studied. However, the discovery of patterns and questions in the past that were relevant to what happened, but that contemporaries were not aware of—and that might be inspired by the investigator's own sensibilities—is certainly part of the historian's stock-in-trade, and is a major source for innovations in research and conceptualization.

[89] *Voices of the Matriarchs*, 176. Compare Weissler's contention with the problem of women's complicity in their own devaluation with de Beauvoir (see previous note) and S. Ortner, 'Is Female to Male as Nature Is to Culture?', in M. Z. Rosaldo and L. Lamphere (eds.), *Woman, Culture and Society* (Stanford, Calif., 1974), 76, 84–5.

widows in society may be reflected by the fact that frequently Polish Jews bore not patronymics but matronymics, such as Rivkes, Sirkes, Rachlin, Rivlin, Feiglin, Etkes. This, however, is another female-related historical issue that awaits elucidation.

A few women were legendarily wealthy and powerful. Raszka (Rachel) Fishel, in the late fifteenth and early sixteenth centuries, was a major moneylender to the courts of three Polish kings, her business enterprises beginning while her husband, Moses, was still alive. She was the only Jew that King Jan Olbracht allowed to remain in Kraków when the Jews were expelled in 1495. She was also involved in power struggles within the Jewish community, particularly in connection with her son-in-law Rabbi Jacob Pollack's battle to retain his position as rabbi of Kraków in the wake of various controversies.[90]

Upon the death of her husband, David Todros, in 1648, Gitl Kożuchowska became one of the richest Jews in Kraków. By the terms of her husband's will she controlled all of his business enterprises and real estate. As his will put it: 'She is to deal in all business that there is according to her desire and will, as she has always done, for her benefit and for the benefit of the heirs in general . . . because she is the lady of the house, dominant and ruling over the entire estate and the business for all of her days.' She was to decide, as well, whom her children would marry, which of them would receive houses and places in the synagogue, and which would be taken into the business.[91]

Judyta Jakubowiczowa, who flourished in the late eighteenth and early nineteenth centuries, was the third wife of the notorious Samuel Zbytkower, army purveyor and royal factor extraordinaire. She was her husband's main negotiator in his dealings with the Polish king, Stanisław August Poniatowski, and his partner in other business enterprises, such as supplying the Russian troops in Poland, serving as Prussian court agents, and various import–export schemes. After Samuel's death Judyta eventually became the largest purveyor to the Polish and French armies during the period of the Duchy of Warsaw. Upon her death she left a prodigious estate.[92]

There were also women, often arrendators of estates or monopoly rights on them, who were not as stupendously wealthy as the women mentioned above, but who nevertheless enjoyed power and high status on a less grandiose scale. In the Pinsk area the most important arrendators in the 1640s were the Szimszic family. When her husband, Eliezer, died in 1645, Devora Szimszic became the lessee and

[90] Bałaban, *Historja Zydów w Krakowie i na Kazimierzu*, i. 71, 101, 108–10; *Toledot hayehudim bekrakuv uvekazhimiezh*, i. 57, 62, 90–2.

[91] *Historja Zydów w Krakowie i na Kazimierzu*, i. 280, 547–52; *Toledot hayehudim bekrakuv uvekazhimiezh*, i. 214, 417–22. The comment in the will 'as she has always done' implies that, like Glikl of Hameln, Gitl was an active business partner to her husband while he was alive.

[92] A. Eisenbach and J. Kosim, 'Akt masy spadkowej Judyty Jakubowiczowej', *Biuletyn Żydowskiego Instytutu Historycznego*, 39 (1961), 88–143; Dynner, 'Men of Silk', 134–47.

manager of three large nobility latifundia that included forests with their produce and hunting game; waterways with their fish and tax possibilities; agricultural lands; and various monopoly rights. She held authority over more than a thousand townspeople and peasants, collecting taxes in money, kind, and labour. She also controlled a sizeable staff and asserted her rights, occasionally by force, when faced with recalcitrant peasants or threatening nobles.[93]

In the early eighteenth century one of the largest and wealthiest landowners in Poland was the politically well-connected aristocratic magnate Elżbieta Sieniawska. In the second and third decades of the century one of her three most important arrendators was the Jewish woman Feyga Lejbowiczowa, who was active mainly in the Końskowola section of Sieniawska's latifundium. Whether officially in partnership with her husband or in her own name, she held the leases at various times to different important properties and monopoly rights, lent large sums of money, and was involved in commercial enterprises. Her business activities brought her into conflict with administrators, peasants, townspeople, and Jewish rivals. However, she was able to maintain Sieniawska's favour and, in the main, successfully fend off those who threatened her, at least until Sieniawska's death in 1729 (Lejbowiczowa died in 1730).[94]

The list of female arrendators, merchants, factors, and moneylenders could easily be extended.[95] In addition, women were active in the public domain in fields other than the economy. Archival documents indicate women testifying in court, and signing as guarantors for bail and loans or on public petitions.[96]

There were even women in institutionalized public roles in the Jewish community. Gershon Hundert found women supervisors (Hebrew: *gabaot*; Yiddish: *gabates*) in charge of collecting women's charity funds in Poznań; and women appointed by the Lithuanian Jewish Council helped poor women properly observe menstrual restrictions.[97] Tamar Salmon-Mack identified women supervisors in

[93] M. Nadav, 'Toledot kehilat pinsk 1506–1880', in Z. Rabinowitsch (ed.), *Pinsk*, i (Tel Aviv, 1973), 63–5.

[94] J. Nowak, 'Feyga Lejbowiczowa, arendarka w Końskowoli Sieniawskich: Z dziejów gospodarczej aktywności kobiet żydowskich w początkach XVIII wieku', *Rocznik Biblioteki Naukowej PAU i PAN w Krakowie*, 48 (2003), 211–36; cf. M. J. Rosman, *The Lords' Jews* (Cambridge, 1990), 138–9.

[95] Nowak mentions several other female arrendators active in Poland in the first half of the 18th century. Teller, *Kesef, ko'aḥ vehashpa'ah*, ch. 6, gives information on women merchants and suppliers to the Radziwiłł family. On women lending money, see Rosman, 'Lehiyot ishah yehudiyah bepolin-lita bereishit ha'et haḥadashah', 428–9. For a survey of some economic activities among women, see Salmon-Mack, 'Ḥayei nisu'im beyahadut polin', 92–6.

[96] Rosman, 'Lehiyot ishah yehudiyah bepolin-lita bereishit ha'et haḥadashah', 434.

[97] G. D. Hundert, 'Approaches to the History of the Jewish Family in Early Modern Poland–Lithuania', in S. M. Cohen and P. E. Hyman (eds.), *The Jewish Family* (New York, 1986), 23 and sources in nn. 23–4 there. With regard to women in charge of women's (but not men's) charity, there are medieval precedents; see Yonah Gerondi (13th-century Spain–Provence), *Sha'arei teshuvah* (Jerusalem, 1967), *Igeret hateshuvah*, para. 95, p. 211; cf. Yuspa Shamash, *Minhagim de-k'k vermeisa*, 221.

Kórnik who were in charge of charity collection from the men as well as the women and were also responsible for distributing the money.[98]

The social significance of all of this economic and public activity of women—whether large-scale and dramatic or merely common and mundane, whether it involved married women subject to their husbands' authority or autonomous widows—is a matter of some debate. The anthropologist Sherry B. Ortner insisted that any power or influence that women have or contributions they make in society and culture are rendered trivial by the overarching gender ideology and deep assumptions of culture that devalue women and determine their true (inferior) status.[99]

The historian Mary Beth Norton, studying colonial American society, disagreed, at least with reference to women of high social and economic status who regularly wielded power over men. Such women were located at the intersection of class and gender. Norton maintained that they represented a contradiction between the class and gender conventions that early modern patriarchal societies were based on. This might make them flashpoints for social conflict, which could lead to profound social change.[100]

In this light, it is interesting that the careers of the powerful arrendators Devora Szimszic and Feyga Lejbowiczowa were so marked by conflicts with men who challenged their power.[101] However, as yet there is no evidence that these struggles, or ones like them, led to anything new of significance for Jewish society as a whole.

Furthermore, there are traces of resistance to the amelioration of the cultural role of bystander that, I have argued, existed in this period. As already observed, women in the early modern period were attending synagogue more frequently than formerly, but the restrictions on menstruating women that some authorities relaxed still had their advocates,[102] and in the community of Iwaniec in 1759, for example, women were required to leave the synagogue before the men did, evidently to avoid informal, unsupervised mingling of the sexes. Likewise one can find enactments

[98] Salmon-Mack, 'Ḥayei nisu'im beyahadut polin', 97–9. See also Fram, introd. to *Seder mitsvot nashim*, ch. 1. The best-documented institutionalized communal role for Jewish women, at least in the Middle Ages, is that of midwife; see E. Baumgarten, '"Kakh omerot hameyaldot haḥakhamot": Meyaldot umeyaldut be'ashkenaz bame'ah hashelosh-esreh', *Zion*, 65 (2000), 45–74; cf. H. Marland (ed.), *The Art of Midwifery: Early Modern Midwives in Europe* (London, 1993). It is reasonable to assume that the midwife was a central figure in early modern Poland as well. Discovering sources about midwives' activity would make an important contribution to our understanding of gender roles and relationships in the period.

[99] Ortner, 'Is Female to Male as Nature Is to Culture?', 69. In her later critique of the article, S. Ortner, 'So *Is* Female to Male as Nature Is to Culture?', in her *Making Gender* (Boston, 1996), Ortner did not change her position on this point. Parush's emphasis on the ideology and ideals of east European Jewish society being determinative of women's status is consonant with this position.

[100] M. B. Norton, *Founding Mothers and Fathers: Gendered Power and the Forming of American Society* (New York, 1996), 10; cf. Davis, '"Women's History" in Transition', 82–3, 89, 90.

[101] Prominent male arrendators and administrators were also involved in numerous conflicts. Only close study of a representative sample of cases can establish the significance of gender in this sphere; cf. *Lords' Jews*, 165–70.

[102] See sources in n. 80.

mandating that women not participate in the *tashlikh* ritual on Rosh Hashanah (in which people symbolically cast away their sins at a body of water), that men and women visit cemeteries on different days, and even that they not buy in butchers' shops on the same day of the week. There were also attempts to limit women's economic activities, restricting the movements of female pedlars.[103] While such expedients might be rationalized as guarding morality and ensuring sexual modesty, they surely served to undermine trends leading to significant change in women's cultural status as well as to structure the economy and control competition. With this dialectic at work, it is not surprising that it took approximately 400 years for Polish Jewish women, in the form of their descendants in America, western Europe, and modern Israel, to move from outside the synagogue to taking a central place in the public life and ritual that transpired there.

CONCLUSION

In this preliminary study I have tried to understand better the relationship between women's and men's lives in this period. I have found that attempts, like Table 1, to define separate female and male spheres are not very productive. Gender boundaries were continually criss-crossed, women are found in unexpected roles and spaces, most men were not scholars or even would-be scholars and needed Yiddish almost as much as women did, and men and women seem to have been much more similar than historiography has usually proposed.

In economic life there was little of the gender reversal that has often been touted as characterizing Jewish society in eastern Europe. Both men and women worked to earn money, typically in economic partnership, with women usually more economically dependent on their husbands than vice versa. With regard to culture, there was gender hierarchy, but with the onset of the age of print, the male cultural elite changed its approach to the uneducated. Both women and men in this category were allowed opportunities to participate more actively in elite-governed cultural life and they used similar cultural tools to do so.

But while male and female spheres were not dichotomous, women did face conflicting expectations. Their evolving role as cultural performers had to be assumed while they still maintained their role as facilitators for family and community, and while the gender hierarchy was still firmly in place. As women became more active in public cultural life, the tension between their two roles presumably grew.

[103] Rosman, 'Lehiyot ishah yehudiyah bepolin-lita bereishit ha'et haḥadashah', 425–6, 429–30; cf. Fram, introd. to *Seder mitsvot nashim*, ch. 1. These regulations might be seen as part of a general European trend among both Christians and Jews in the early modern period to reform popular culture, distance the sacred from the profane, and intensify piety (although they are probably not only that); see E. Horowitz, 'The Eve of the Circumcision: A Chapter in the History of Jewish Nightlife', *Journal of Social History*, 23 (1989), 51–5, repr. in D. B. Ruderman (ed.), *Essential Papers on Jewish Culture in Renaissance and Baroque Italy* (New York, 1992), 563–7.

Documenting expressions of this tension might be a promising direction for new research.

In addition to what I have considered here, the work of Stampfer, Weissler, and Parush suggests other research subjects. With regard to power, we must ascertain what different types of power were available in this society (perhaps, for example: autonomy, coercive power, influence). What was their relative importance? To what extent did women share in each type? Did women exercise meaningful power in 'informal' ways? Was women's power, as Ortner contended, trivial? How did women's relationship to power shape the community?

Following Norton, we should ask: What happens when basic social organizing principles, like gender and class, intersect? What was the relationship between women of high status and men of low status? How were gender roles and gender relations different for people in different classes?

In addition, we might investigate the relationships between women and leadership. What was the relationship between women and various male elite groups; between women and the rabbinic leadership; between women and the political leaders of the *kahal*; between women and *ba'alei shem*; and between women and the earliest hasidic leaders?

This chapter has ignored one of the most obvious and important directions for research: the comparison of Jewish women with other women. What was the relationship between Jewish women's circumstances in Poland and those of women belonging to other estates, ethnic groups, and religions? To what extent were gender roles and gender boundaries shaped by particular cultures and to what extent by a common culture?

We have seen that questioning the conventional separate spheres construct and exploring women's economic and cultural roles leads to reconsideration of both men's and women's roles. What other additional information, new categories, re-evaluations of old conceptions, and revisions of the master narrative of Polish Jewish history will result from the engagement with women's historical experience?

The Maskilot: Feminine or Feminist Writing?

TOVA COHEN

LESS than a decade ago, the conventional wisdom was that nineteenth-century Haskalah literature was exclusively masculine: historians and literary critics, not to mention the maskilim themselves, assumed that all the canonical authors, as well as their readers and the enlightened public, were male. Given this male-oriented framework, the maskilim did not direct their works at women. Thus, for example, when Miriam Markel-Mosessohn reprimanded Moshe Leib Lilienblum for using obscene language in his writing, he explained: 'You should bear in mind that *you are the only woman who reads my book*. Do I have to guard my mouth and the tongue that speaks our holy language (which is not alien to such expressions, forged in the spirit of the ancient land) *in a book read by no gentle woman but you*?'[1] Women were certainly not seen as belonging among Haskalah writers. Even a century after Lilienblum's declaration, Dan Miron echoed similar sentiments when he denied that the maskilot (enlightened women) existed as a significant phenomenon: 'Throughout the nineteenth century, Hebrew *maskilot* were a random phenomenon, which occurred only once or twice. . . . These were the poor aftergrowths in the corners of the fields of rational Haskalah poetry and the sentimental poetry of Hibbat Zion.'[2]

To be sure, we cannot deny the fact that the great majority of the Haskalah community—both writers and readers—were male, first and foremost because of the inherent connection between the Haskalah and Hebrew, a language that belonged more or less exclusively to men. This linguistic division in traditional Jewish society resulted from a gendered educational system that reserved the privilege of studying Hebrew (the 'holy tongue') and Torah for men. Conversely, women were excluded from Torah study, the ultimate ideal of Jewish religious society, by a ruling based on the statement of R. Eliezer, 'Whoever teaches his daughter Torah,

[1] Moshe Leib Lilienblum's letter to Anshel Markel-Mosessohn and his wife, Miriam Markel-Mosessohn (Odessa, 1870), *Ketuvim* (26 Heshvan 1926), 3–4; the emphasis here and throughout is my own unless otherwise noted.

[2] D. Miron, *Imahot meyasdot, aḥayot ḥoregot: Al shetei hatḥalot beshirah ha'erets-yisra'elit hamodernit* (Tel Aviv, 1991), 11.

it is as though he teaches her *tiflut* [immorality].'[3] The 'masculine' character of the Hebrew language continued into the Enlightenment period, for its Hebraism was based on the knowledge of Hebrew and the canonical texts that men acquired within the framework of traditional learning, so that women were automatically excluded.[4] The Haskalah movement was masculine from a social perspective as well: the maskilim, who were a minority in their own society, created a male fraternity that provided its members with a network of social relations and mutual support by means of extensive correspondence as well as through the Haskalah periodicals.[5]

Nevertheless, this basic assumption about the exclusive male gendering of the Haskalah community has recently been somewhat undermined. Miriam Markel-Mosessohn (1841–1920), the Hebrew translator who corresponded with the great maskilim of her time, has always been well known: the historian Joseph Klausner, for instance, refers to her on several occasions.[6] Klausner also devotes a short chapter to the Italian Jewish poet Rachel Morpurgo (1790–1871)[7] and mentions Devorah Ephrati,[8] who corresponded with Abraham Mapu. However, the maskilim, like the historians of the period, regarded each of these women as an exceptional phenomenon who deserved to be singled out because of her uniqueness. Expressions of amazement about women who wrote in Hebrew were common in Haskalah journals: 'Behold, *this is new,* which our eyes have seen, a letter in the Hebrew language written by a Hebrew woman . . . which we intend to present to our distinguished readers so that they too can see this *wondrous thing*'—thus the publisher of Devorah Ephrati's letter to Abraham Mapu in the Hebrew periodical *Hamagid*.[9] Or, to take another example, 'It is *a rare sight* in these days, to see a young woman writing in

[3] Mishnah, *Sot.* 3: 4. For an explanation and details of this passage, see E. G. Ellinson, *Bein ha'ishah leyotserah* (Jerusalem, 1974), 143–65. On the restrictions on Torah study by women, see also Y. Azmon, 'Mavo: Hayahadut vehahadarah shel nashim min haseferah hatsiburit', in Azmon (ed.), *Eshnav leḥayeihen shel nashim beḥevrot yehudiyot* (Jerusalem, 1995); I. Parush, *Nashim korot: Yitronah shel shuliyut baḥevrah hayehudit bemizraḥ eiropah bame'ah hatesha-esreh* (Tel Aviv, 2001), 62–3.

[4] In addition to women, a large proportion of men who had received only a basic education in the *ḥeder* were also excluded from Haskalah literature. Only male scholars who had studied in yeshiva had sufficient knowledge of Hebrew and the canonical texts (the Bible, Talmud, and Midrash) to become potential maskilim. See T. Cohen, 'The Maskil as Lamdan: The Influence of Jewish Education on Haskalah Writing Techniques', in G. Abramson and T. Parfitt (eds.), *Jewish Education and Learning* (London, 1994); N. Seidman, *A Marriage Made in Heaven: The Sexual Politics of Yiddish and Hebrew* (Los Angeles and Berkeley, 1997).

[5] According to David Biale, the strength of the male fraternity of the Haskalah resulted in part from the maskilim's frustration over their relationships with women (D. Biale, *Eros and the Jews* (New York, 1992), 157–8).

[6] See e.g. J. Klausner, *Hahistoriyah shel hasifrut ha'ivrit haḥadashah*, 4 vols. (Jerusalem, 1949–54), iv. 344–6. Some of her letters were published in A. Ya'ari, *Tseror igerot yalag el miriam markel-moseson* (Jerusalem, 1937). These have been republished in *Yedidato shel hameshorer: Igerot miryam markel-moseson el yehudah leib gordon*, ed. S. Werses (Jerusalem, 2004).

[7] Klausner, *Hahistoriyah shel hasifrut*, iv. 38–49. [8] Ibid. iii. 296. [9] *Hamagid*, 2/12 (1858), 46.

Hebrew; we must therefore grant a place for her words, although we do not agree with her ideas.' This is what the editor of the periodical *Ha'ivri* wrote about an essay by Toybe Segal called 'She'elat hanashim' ('The Question of Women').[10] None of the maskilim or the historians ever considered collecting these 'wondrous things' together and examining them as part of a growing and meaningful phenomenon.

Shmuel Feiner first posed a challenge to the assumption about the purely masculine character of the Haskalah in his pioneering article 'Modern Jewish Women: A Test Case in the Relationship between Haskalah and Modernity'.[11] In this study, Feiner compiled the first list of maskilot, including many names in addition to those I have already mentioned, who wrote letters and articles and published them in Hebrew periodicals. This compilation constituted a significant step towards a new understanding of the phenomenon, which no longer appears to have been as limited as the maskilim assumed. My joint research with Feiner has uncovered the writings of some thirty Hebrew women writers from the period of the Haskalah.[12] Meanwhile, Iris Parush, Carole Balin, and Shmuel Werses, although they have not added any new names, have now contributed further information about some of these women: Parush has provided more literary and non-literary evidence of their existence, while Balin and Werses have described the life and works of Miriam Markel-Mosessohn in great detail.[13] All these studies focus on the historical aspects of the phenomenon, the identity of the authors, their Hebrew education, and how they were seen by the maskilim. In addition, they ask how our new knowledge of these maskilot changes our understanding of the Haskalah movement.

In this chapter I propose to examine the writings of the maskilot from a literary perspective and to ask to what extent their writing was 'feminine'—not only as a biographical fact but also as a literary characteristic of their works. Did they write as women? Did their experience as women and their struggles and doubts as female creative writers influence how they wrote? And, as a result of all this, to what extent should the discovery of female texts change our understanding of Haskalah literature, and of modern Hebrew literature in general?

Only a small proportion of the writings of the maskilot can be described as literary in the conventional sense of the term. We know of three poets in the Haskalah period: Rachel Morpurgo, Hannah Bluma Sultz, and Sarah Shapira.[14] Only one woman, Sarah-Feiga Foner Meinkin, wrote a novel, *Ahavat yesharim* ('The Love of the Righteous'), of which only the first half was ever published, as well as a short

[10] The article was published in instalments in *Ha'ivri*, 16 (1879), 69, 78–9, 85, 94, 101–2.

[11] S. Feiner, 'Ha'ishah hayehudiyah hamodernit: Mikreh mivḥan beyaḥasei hahaskalah vehamodernah', *Zion*, 58 (1993), 453–9; repr. in Y. Bartal and Y. Gafni (eds.), *Eros eirusin ve'isurim: Miniyut umishpaḥah bahistoriyah* (Jerusalem, 1998).

[12] See T. Cohen and S. Feiner, *Kol almah ivriyah: Nashim bitenuat hahaskalah beme'ah hatesha-esreh* (Tel Aviv, forthcoming).

[13] See Parush, *Nashim korot*; C. Balin, *To Reveal our Hearts: Jewish Women Writers in Tsarist Russia* (Cincinnati, 2000); *Yedidato shel hameshorer*, ed. Werses.

[14] The latter two poets wrote only a few poems.

novella, *Beged bogedim* ('The Treachery of Traitors').[15] The other texts written by women in Hebrew were letters and articles. Some of the letters have been preserved in archives,[16] while others were printed in Haskalah periodicals by editors who were excited about the very existence of women who were able to write in Hebrew.[17] Several essays written by women were printed in Hebrew periodicals: some of these essays address conventional Haskalah themes such as the importance of the Enlightenment to the individual and to society as a whole,[18] or the struggle between the European and Jewish Enlightenments,[19] while others concentrate on the subject of Jewish girls' education.[20]

In examining this body of literature from a literary standpoint, I hope to show that the central characteristics of feminine literary writing, typical of the first stages of literary writing by women, can be found in the established works as well as in the non-canonical writings of the maskilot. I will focus on the works of Rachel Morpurgo, Miriam Markel-Mosessohn, and Sarah-Feiga Foner Meinkin, who I would argue made the most important literary contribution. In addition, I will illustrate certain characteristics of women's writing from other texts, including poetry and fiction, as well as letters and articles.

A SHARED FEMALE EXPERIENCE AMONG WOMEN WRITERS?

The attempt to define the unique characteristics of texts written by women was the central subject of debate in feminist literary-critical circles in the 1970s and 1980s. The goal of this criticism (which the literary critic Elaine Showalter has called 'gynocritics') is 'to develop new models based on the study of female experience, rather than to adapt male models and theories . . . and to focus instead on the newly visible

[15] *Ahavat yesharim* (Vilna, 1881); only the first part of the novel was published. *Beged bogedim* (Warsaw, 1891).

[16] Only one archive of a maskilah is known to us: that of Miriam Markel-Mosessohn. All the letters of the other women writers are preserved in the collections of men. Letters from female admirers can be found in the collection of Y. L. Gordon. There are also letters by women in the archival collections of Shneur Sacks and Yehuda Landau. The letters of lesser-known women were not preserved in archives, which does not mean that they did not exist. For example, one of the letters of Miriam Markel-Mosessohn (Nov. 1878), which opens with the words 'My best and most honoured female friend', is clearly a reply to a letter from one of her female friends, which was almost certainly in Hebrew but which was not preserved.

[17] For example, letters of Yenta Vollerner were printed in *Kokhavei yitsḥak*, 18 (1853), and 28 (1862); a letter by Leah Bermzon appeared in *Hashaḥar*, 5 (1874); Berta Kreidman's letter appeared in *Hamagid*, 14 (1870), and Merka Altshuler's letter appeared in *Haboker or*, 4 (1880).

[18] See e.g. M. Altshuler, 'Hegyonai leyom tu be'av', *Haboker or*, 4 (1880), 1456–60.

[19] See e.g. the speech by Rivka Lifshits in memory of Peretz Smolenskin, published in *Hamelits*, 33 (1890), 1–2.

[20] See e.g. an untitled letter written by O. Belkind in *Hashaḥar*, 4 (1880), in which she explains the importance of professional training for Jewish women. See also T. Segal, 'She'elat nashim', *Ha'ivri*, 16 (1880), 69, 77–8, 85, 94, 101–2.

world of female culture . . . and to stop trying to fit women between the lines of male tradition'.[21] A fundamental assumption of gynocritics is that there is a common denominator in texts written by women based on their shared 'female experience'. It is through such a common denominator that we can define the criteria on which we should base our examination of women's texts. Since the early 1990s, however, this approach has come under criticism, as feminist scholars have challenged the concept of a 'shared female experience' and called for a greater recognition of the class and ethnic differences that divide women.[22] Despite these criticisms, I would argue that the assumption of the reality of a 'shared female experience' is still valid for women writing in Hebrew in the period under discussion, and also, to a large extent, for women writers in Europe as a whole.

'Shared female experience' was certainly characteristic of women writing in Hebrew in this period: they not only experienced the world through a female body and consciousness, but shared a common social and cultural milieu. All these writers were middle-class European Jews who lived at a time when the age of marriage had risen. As a result, they had a certain amount of free time, as well as the economic wherewithal to study, read, and write. In addition to their social background, these writers shared a common upbringing. They were all daughters of enlightened fathers who fostered the Hebrew education of all their children, male and female.[23] Furthermore, they all experienced the problem of penetrating a masculine culture where women's voices had never been given expression, as well as the parallel problem of the attempt to penetrate the androcentric field of Haskalah Hebrew literature.

The 'female experience' of the maskilot also shared some characteristics with the experience of their non-Jewish counterparts in European society of the time, despite the great distance between the two cultures. This was not simply because they were women: other important factors included their common experience of social class—more specifically, the middle class—and a level of education unusual for women of the period. Both groups of writers similarly attempted to become part of a male culture and both experienced the difficulties involved in trying to be accepted by an androcentric culture that perceived literary writing as an act appropriate only to men. These similarities allow us to examine the writing of maskilot in the nineteenth century using the criteria established for research into the writing of European women of the same period. Here I will rely on the classic research by Elaine Showalter ('Toward a Feminist Poetics' and *A Literature of their Own*), and

[21] E. Showalter, 'Toward a Feminist Poetics', in M. Jacobus (ed.), *Women, Writing, and Writing about Women* (London, 1979), 28.

[22] See e.g. C. West and S. Fenstermaker, 'Doing Difference', *Gender and Society*, 9 (1995), 8–37.

[23] For details and examples of this shared social background, see T. Cohen, 'Min hateḥum haprati el hateḥum hatsibori: Kitvei maskilot ivriyot bame'ah hatesha-esreh', in D. Assaf *et al.* (eds.), *Mivilna liyerushalayim: Meḥkarim betoledoteihem uvetarbutam shel yehudei mizraḥ eiropah mugashim leprofesor shmuel verses* (Jerusalem, 2002).

on Sandra Gilbert and Susan Gubar's *The Madwoman in the Attic*, on women's literature in England in the eighteenth and nineteenth centuries.[24] I will propose that the processes and characteristics discussed by these authors can be used to describe the development of Hebrew writing by women in this period, even though each society had its own specific character.

Showalter defines three periods in the development of English women's writing from the nineteenth century to the present: *feminine*, *feminist*, and *female*. She differentiates them as follows:

> During the *Feminine* phase (1849–80), women wrote in an effort to equal the intellectual achievements of the male culture, and internalised its assumptions about female nature. . . . In the *Feminist* phase (1880–1920), women are historically enabled to reject the accommodating postures of femininity and to use literature to dramatise the ordeals of wronged womanhood. . . . In the *Female* phase, ongoing since 1920, women reject both imitation and protest—two forms of dependency—and turn instead to female experience as the source of autonomous art.[25]

The activities of the maskilot in the nineteenth century and the nature of their writings parallel the feminine phase described by Showalter; I will therefore use the conventions that characterize the literature of this stage to analyse their writings. Only at the end of the nineteenth century did some Hebrew women writers set themselves free from their fears of overt feminist/female expression and begin to pen a feminist protest equivalent to the second stage of Showalter's periodization.

THE PSYCHOLOGICAL BASE OF FEMININE HASKALAH WRITING: THE 'ANXIETY OF AUTHORSHIP'

In *The Madwoman in the Attic*, Gilbert and Gubar define what they see as the main psychological and creative problem for women who wrote in this period: the 'anxiety of authorship', which is a 'radical fear that she cannot create'.[26] They explain as follows: 'She confronts precursors who are exclusively male and therefore significantly different from her. . . . They attempt to enclose her in a definition of her person and her potential which, by reducing her to extreme stereotypes . . . drastically conflict with her own sense of self—that is, of her subjectivity, her autonomy, her creativity.'[27]

This 'anxiety of authorship' was especially reinforced in the consciousness of the Hebrew women writers of the nineteenth century. Not only was the female writer 'invading' the male sphere of culture by the very fact that she was writing in Hebrew and as a result endangering her feminine being, but she was also violating a religious ban—at least in society's eyes. The silencing of women in traditional

[24] E. Showalter, *A Literature of their Own: British Women Novelists from Brontë to Lessing*, 2nd edn. (Princeton, 1999); S. Gilbert and S. Gubar, *The Madwoman in the Attic: The Woman Writer and the Nineteenth Century Literary Imagination* (New Haven, 1979).

[25] 'Toward a Feminist Poetics', 35–6. [26] *The Madwoman in the Attic*, 49. [27] Ibid. 48.

Jewish society had religious force: women were not only banned from studying Torah, but also from expressing themselves aloud in the public religious arena. A woman could not be called up to the Torah in the synagogue or serve as a reader, as this would violate the principle of *kevod hatsibur* (the honour of the community).[28] Her singing in public was also banned, since *kol be'ishah ervah* (the voice of a woman is indecent).[29] The words of a woman in a printed text which appeared in public could be considered in the same vein. Her 'voice' in the public arena violated both religious and social conventions, even if it was not expressly forbidden by Jewish law.

Indeed, Hebrew women writers of the time expressed a deep fear about publishing their works. Miriam Markel-Mosessohn, for example, made a connection between her fear of publishing and her abstention from writing literature:

> I am still of two minds: should I present this to the public or will it never see the light of day? . . . moreover, should a woman dare to insert her head between these two mountains? Surely I will soon be stoned . . . and also my soul knows full well that never will I achieve great things in literature and *belles lettres*.[30]

Unlike Markel-Mosessohn, who nonetheless seems to have found ways to express herself, Berta Kreidman was silenced by her 'anxiety of authorship'. In a letter addressed to the 'lover of the Hebrew language', Kreidman demonstrates a rich knowledge of Hebrew and a superb facility of expression; nonetheless, she refuses to answer the request of the addressee to publish her works in the periodical. She explains her refusal with the characteristic argument of female 'anxiety of authorship':

> Who am I to dare approach the holy and to mingle with the writers of our time? . . . Will the fly dare to make his buzzing heard among the lions and tigers, whose roars would weaken the very cedars of Lebanon? I am merely a young girl who in sadness and suffering has assembled a little knowledge. It is therefore only right for me to curb my pen and seal my thoughts that they may not be seen outwardly. I will choose to sit in the tranquillity of the quiet of my house and to indulge in my studies rather than make my voice heard without profit.[31]

As a result of this fear, and in the context of a patriarchal society that viewed their writing with great suspicion, women writing in Hebrew, like their English sisters, were forced to adopt strategies that would permit them to participate in the masculine Haskalah culture, despite their female identity.

The strategy of English writers of the time was to work within the conventions

[28] For discussion and sources, see Ellinson, *Bein ha'ishah leyotserah*, 70–1.

[29] For discussion and sources, see E. G. Ellinson, *Hatsne'a lekhet: Ha'ishah vehamitsvot*, ii (Jerusalem, 1984), 78–80.

[30] Letter from Miriam Markel-Mosessohn to Yehuda Leib Gordon (1868), Jewish National and University Archive, Hebrew University of Jerusalem, no. 77455.

[31] *Hamagid*, 14 (1870), an addition to issue no. 7. There is no page numbering.

of the period that took it for granted that women's literary capacity was limited, resorting to one of two options. One was to write literature deemed 'suitable for women' according to the norms of patriarchal society: 'silly novells by Lady Novellists', as George Eliot put it.[32] In other words, they would write on subjects of secondary importance in a form which was in accordance with the accepted image of women in a patriarchal society. The second option—also a form of submission to societal norms—was to hide behind a male pseudonym in an attempt to erase the writer's female self. These two strategies of self-denial, according to Gilbert and Gubar, led many writers to write 'literature of bad faith and inauthenticity'. In the words of Virginia Woolf, because the writer 'had altered her values to the opinions of others', her writings became 'Like small pock-marked apples in an orchard . . . it was the flaw in the centre that had rotted them.'[33]

These two strategies, it should be noted, were seldom adopted by women writing in Hebrew. They hardly wrote 'literature suitable for women', according to the conventions of their times and rarely imitated in blind fashion the writings of men. Perhaps a few of Rachel Morpurgo's poems in *Shirei hizdamnut* ('Poems on Special Occasions') demonstrate this kind of modest and incidental women's writing, though she certainly did not confine herself to this genre,[34] while an example of the imitation of male writing is the poetry of Hannah Bluma Sultz.[35] These few examples of feminine writing, which women produced 'in an effort to equal the intellectual achievements of male culture and [internalize] its assumptions about female nature', are the exception in the writings of the maskilot. In my view, this was because Jewish women's struggle to enter into Hebrew culture and Jewish public life was especially hard. This meant that only resolute women participated in the process—individuals who were not willing to surrender their identity so easily, either as women or as intellectuals.

'PALIMPSESTIC' WRITING: THE STRATEGY OF THE MASKILOT

The maskilot who dared to break through into the public sphere of the Hebrew Haskalah employed a strategy that was characteristic of the best of the English women writers: writing in multiple layers, which Gilbert and Gubar have called a

[32] Quoted in Gilbert and Gubar, *The Madwoman in the Attic*, 72.

[33] *A Room of One's Own* (1929; repr. New York, 1989), 74.

[34] All the poets of the period wrote verses in honour of various events. However, out of all Morpurgo's poems, Miron, *Imahot meyasdot, aḥayot ḥoregot*, discusses only these, unimportant, ones, and on that basis mocks her writing: 'between a wedding and a funeral, she wrote, as could be expected, rhymes for weddings births, deaths and sycophantic praise of those in power' (p. 11). Thus he sees her as a negligible poet.

[35] Sultz published two long poems: 'Hamaḥazeh' (*Hashaḥar*, 5 (1882), 1–10), and 'Gei ḥizayon' (*Hashaḥar*, 11 (1883), 69–72).

palimpsest—a parchment on which the writing is erased so that it can be written on again, but where it is still possible to reconstruct the first layer of writing. In other words, palimpsests are writings in which the internal and hidden layer, the female authentic one, is completely different from the external layer, the conventions of patriarchal society. 'Works whose surface designs conceal or obscure deeper, less accessible (and less socially acceptable) levels of meaning . . . achieve true female authority by simultaneously conforming to and subverting patriarchal literary standards.'[36]

During the Haskalah, 'palimpsestic' writing was characteristic not only of women but also of men, especially at the beginning of the period. The first maskilim (like the maskilot in the following generations) were a minority group, expressing opinions that were not acceptable in traditional society. Thus they often chose to formulate their opinions in a hidden, less accessible, and less socially acceptable layer in their writings. Naphtali Hertz Wessely, for example, subverts the biblical description of the image of Moses in the epic poem *Shirei tiferet* ('Songs of Splendour'), but this is carefully concealed and can only be discovered through a detailed comparison with the biblical descriptions. Similarly, Adam Hakohen (Abraham Dov Lebensohn) hides secular meanings in works that appear on the surface to be religious poems.[37] The satirical works of the Haskalah were also frequently hidden behind near-perfect imitations of the texts they were criticizing. It is probable that the maskilot also chose palimpsestic writing because they were familiar with this Haskalah style.

LETTER-WRITING: CONCEALING AUTHENTIC EXPRESSION IN A 'FEMININE' GENRE

It was mainly in the hidden layers of their texts that the maskilot were able to raise new subjects which had never before been discussed in Haskalah literature to express a new understanding of ideal womanhood and to criticize the concept of the woman in Jewish society. They hid their authentic voice under an external layer of 'literature appropriate for women', and under the guise of imitating male expression—but only externally—through the revision, or 're-vision', of androcentric canonical culture.

Literary expression within the canonical framework was especially difficult for women writers in the nineteenth century. To write within these boundaries made women writers all the more strongly aware of their encroachment into the (public and forbidden) male sphere, and of the danger that this posed for their 'female' nature (as they had been socialized to think of it). Moreover, this canonical framework already had a tradition of stereotypes that governed the portrayal of women

[36] Gilbert and Gubar, *The Madwoman in the Attic*, 73.

[37] On the poems of Wessely and Adam Hakohen, see T. Cohen, 'Hatekhnikah halamdanit: Tsofan shel sifrut hahaskalah', *Meḥkarei yerushalayim besifrut ivrit*, 13 (1992), 138–69.

from a male perspective, making it more difficult for women writers to create within it.[38] It is thus hardly surprising that, in both European and Hebrew literature, many women writers shied away from tackling the well-established canonical genres, and turned to less respected, non-canonical ones such as children's books, letters, and diaries.[39]

We do not have any surviving examples of diaries written by maskilot of this period.[40] However, letters in Hebrew (some published in nineteenth-century periodicals, others found in various archives) attest to the fact that the maskilot, like their European sisters, found in letter-writing a legitimate form of expression that facilitated personal feminine expression. In European culture the letter was considered a 'female' form of expression that did not harm the writer's image as a woman and which was even considered 'appropriate'.[41] The private letter addressed to a single reader did not violate the convention of public silence that was considered proper for a woman and thus did not evoke in her any anxiety of authorship. The letter draws its vitality from personal, daily events, as well as personal and emotional experience, not necessarily from the masculine subjects that were seen as proper to canonical literature.[42] The language that was appropriate for use in a personal letter was precisely the natural language of daily life, rather than the language characteristic of high canonical culture.

The prevalence of Hebrew letters between maskilot was certainly part of this general European cultural phenomenon. As I have noted, Jewish women did not generally write letters in Hebrew, but there were a number of maskilot who turned the Hebrew letter into their central form of expression. Some confined themselves to private letters, but others agreed to publish them in Hebrew periodicals. There were even those who wrote letters expressly for publication in a journal.

[38] For examples of how different conventions in canonical literature were shaped in a masculine fashion that did not permit 'a subsistence area' to the female writer, see Gilbert and Gubar, *The Madwoman in the Attic*, 67–71.

[39] For the factors that prevented women from writing in the canonical genres and led to their being sidelined into less canonical ones, see J. Donovan, 'The Silence is Broken', in S. McConnell-Ginet, R. Borker, and N. Furman (eds.), *Women and Language in Literature and Society* (New York, 1980).

[40] It is worth noting that in *Limdu heitev* (the first version of the novel *Ha'avot vehabanim*) S. J. Abramowitz quotes from the heroine's diary. Although this is described in the novel as being written in Yiddish, this still suggests that educated Jewish women wrote diaries, and that some of them could have been in Hebrew.

[41] On the letter as a socially accepted style of writing between women in England beginning in the 17th century, see Donovan, 'The Silence is Broken', 210–11. On the popularity of letter-writing between women in Europe in general during the same period, see E. C. Goldsmith, *Writing the Female Voice* (Boston, 1989), p. vii. This entire collection of articles is dedicated to the art of female letter-writing and its influence on European literature.

[42] See the analysis of Virginia Woolf, who argues that, in the canonical literature, 'it is the masculine values that prevail . . . Football and sport are "important"; the worship of fashion, the buying of clothes "trivial" . . . This is an important book, the critic assumes, because it deals with war. This is an insignificant book because it deals with the feelings of women in a drawing room' (*A Room of One's Own*, 73–4).

Letter-writing could be seen as the surrender of the maskilot to the conventions of androcentric society, which viewed this genre as an appropriate way of restricting women to the private sphere and limiting their capacity for self-expression. However, I would like to propose that it was by composing letters in Hebrew that women writers gained a noteworthy entrance into the world of the Haskalah.

Jewish women who wrote such letters differed from their female contemporaries who wrote in English, French, German, or Russian: these women wrote in their everyday language (Yiddish being the equivalent for Jewish women), whereas the maskilot wrote in a language of canonical culture from which they had been excluded. By their use of the 'masculine' Hebrew, they had already penetrated the sphere of the male Hebrew Enlightenment. Moreover, as a result of the geographical dispersal of maskilim in remote places (often in areas where there was no Haskalah society), letter-writing had become a well-established means of communication in the male Haskalah world. Women were making an attempt to be included in this world of letters. Thus it is no surprise that maskilot corresponded primarily with men, often members of their family, and frequently with famous Haskalah authors. They were aware that the letter enabled them to enter an arena that was traditionally not feminine; hence, in their letters they emphasized this by choosing to discuss subjects deemed to be masculine, such as Hebrew culture and language, and public matters.

Thus, for example, in 1871 Bertha Rabinowits begins a letter to her father with a personal, 'feminine' description of the fact that she did not need to prepare the house for Passover that year:

> And the days of freedom and liberty are also such for me, since all the household preparations, cleaning the walls of the rooms and their furnishings, sewing the clothes and koshering the spoons and forks, in which I took part in previous years have been lifted from my shoulders this year.[43]

However, in the rest of the letter Rabinowits moves on to a detailed intellectual discussion (certainly unfeminine by the standards of the time) on the meaning of the hidden liberation of the Passover holiday:

> These days, revered father, the very days of our festival of freedom [Passover] should serve as an example for every thinking man and for every man who perceives and understands the history of his people, that he is not alone, and that he should not despair of hope in time of trouble, even if his troubles seem insurmountable and his sorrows overtake him between the straits. For what man from the old or the new generation would have believed that those few who went down to Egypt, with no laws or regulations and no communal order, oppressed harshly and devoid of any sense of freedom or lofty heroism—that they should escape their suffering through strength of hand, that they would have true laws and statutes and be governed by such lofty communal order and that they would inherit a wide and fertile land from mighty kings and princes.

[43] *Hashaḥar*, 2 (1871), 364–6.

Bertha Rabinowits uses the personal, feminine letter, a 'legitimate' genre for women, but it becomes a typical male Haskalah letter: a nationalist discussion that demonstrates her desire to deal with masculine Haskalah subjects and to be included in the male fraternity. Thus, consciously or not, the Hebrew letter became the gateway to the literature of the Haskalah for the maskilot.

The Hebrew letter of the maskilah was often structured as a palimpsest. Under the outer layer of legitimate women's writing in the appropriate style as defined by androcentric culture, the writer often hid an additional layer where she revealed the authentic identity that she did not dare to express openly. A fascinating example is a letter from Miriam Markel-Mosessohn to her brothers Yosef and Shimon.[44] In its external layer, it is a personal, family letter where she describes for her brothers an event in the town of Suvalk where she lived, the sort of daily community gossip that is typical of personal letters: 'Listen, my brothers, and I will tell of the scandal that took place in our town.' Under the guise of personal, gossipy, women's writing, Markel-Mosessohn conceals the first 'feminist' Haskalah story, to which she even gives a title: 'Ḥokhmat ha'ishah hasuvalkit keḥokhmat ha'ishah hateko'it' ('The Wisdom of the Woman of Suvalk—Like the Wisdom of the Woman of Teko'a'). This story is well constructed both linguistically and in terms of its plot, and describes a gendered social confrontation between the religious establishment, in the shape of a man—the rabbi—and the simple people, personified as a woman. It is an encounter that ends with the woman's victory.

The story takes place in the private sphere, as was characteristic of women's writing in the nineteenth century.[45] It begins with a description, the first in the literature of the Haskalah, of house-cleaning before the Passover festival, with 'everything upside down; all the belongings from the houses of the poor lying outside—tables, chairs, and beds'. The story indeed continues in the public sphere (the matzah bakery), but the bakery is described as an extension of the private sphere of the home and the baking that takes place there, 'And one wise woman has had an oven and a stove for twenty years and she bakes the most beautiful matzahs.'

Markel-Mosessohn's strategy of limiting the story to the private and semi-private spheres, however, like the concealment of a hidden message under the layers of the familial, feminine letter, does not cancel its clear feminist message. Although she limits herself to a sphere with which she is familiar (the private sphere), she pre-

[44] Letters of Miriam Markel-Mosessohn to her brothers Yosef and Shimon (n.d.), Jewish National and University Archive, Hebrew University of Jerusalem, Schwadron Collection, Autobiography, no. 77455.

[45] On this subject, see Virginia Woolf, 'Women and Fiction', in her *Collected Essays*, ii (London, 1966), in which she describes the way in which the first English Romantic women writers concentrated on the description of the home. On the importance of the home and its rituals in the literature of the 19th century, see also A. Romines, *The Home Plot: Women, Writing, and Domestic Ritual* (Amherst, Mass., 1992). Romines demonstrates that, through the description of 'trivial' events such as those of home life, American women storytellers also considered all the central social problems of their time.

sents the story as an important means through which we can understand society (the public sphere). She does not present the details of daily life (such as the preparations for the Passover festival or baking the matzahs) as a diminution of the Jewish world, but rather as its focus from within which one can understand the Jew.

In terms of its content and didactic message, this is a typical feminist story. The heroine is a wise woman, a baker of matzot, who opposes the excessive prohibitions of the communal rabbi which are intended to enhance his reputation without any consideration for the increased suffering of the poor: in the cynical language of the writer, 'good and useful decrees which the majority of the community cannot bear'. This woman confronts the rabbi in a long dialogue from which she emerges as the victor, while 'the face of the rabbi was covered [with fury] and his lips fell silent because a woman had silenced him; he hastened home, sullen and displeased'. The feminist message is combined with a social class protest against the abuse of the simple people by the religious establishment. As in other works of Haskalah literature, the oppression of women and the poor go hand in hand.[46] However, in contrast to the male Haskalah tendency to identify female suffering with economic and social woes, and to turn women into central figures of passive and resigned suffering, Markel-Mosessohn creates a woman who responds stormily and goes out to defend her workers and herself.

The description of the heroine in this story is completely different from that of any other female figure in the male Haskalah literature. She is economically independent and is not described within a family framework (which, in fact, is not mentioned at all). She is active, assertive, and successful in her struggle with the rabbi and his prohibitions. Her image and behaviour are a combination of both 'feminine' and 'masculine' traits. On the one hand, through her role as a baker, she extends her work as a housewife. She is also described as using a feminine style of management, being personally involved with the workers, rather than supervising them from above. She 'commands, orders, rebukes, and entreats'. In her arguments with the rabbi, she also uses feminine tactics ('pleasant answers') when she tries to persuade him to withdraw his demands.[47] On the other hand, the heroine does not hesitate to use the kinds of behaviour that would be considered aggressive and masculine. She responds to the rabbi's rebukes with halakhic knowledge and a political understanding of the power arrangements in society ('surely there are two parties and sides in the town'). Her words are 'soft', but also 'bite like a sword'.

[46] See e.g. Y. L. Gordon's poem 'Ashka derispak', his story 'Aḥarit simḥah tugah', and Ben Avigdor's story 'Le'ah mokheret hadagim'. On the image of the 'suffering woman' in the literature of the Haskalah, see T. Cohen, *Ha'aḥat ahuvah veha'aḥat senuah: Bein metsiyut lebidyon bete'urei ha'ishah besifrut hahaskalah* (Jerusalem, 2002).

[47] On the idea of women as builders of a network of relationships and as preferring tactics of persuasion, as opposed to men, who immediately storm to the head of the pyramid, see C. Gilligan, *In a Different Voice: Psychological Theory and Women's Development* (Cambridge, 1982).

The combination of masculine and feminine qualities in the heroine is especially poignant when the author uses biblical images: 'Only the woman who baked alone did not move or stir (*lo na'ah velo za'ah*); her courage did not leave her. She stationed herself (*vateitatsav*) standing up with great courage (*beruaḥ kabir*) to hear and discover what would be done to her.' Markel-Mosessohn incorporates references to the courage of Mordecai,[48] the power of expression of Job,[49] and the patience of Miriam[50] to describe the ideal woman, who displays the positive traits of both genders.

In contrast, she describes the rabbi through references to Haman and Ahab: 'The face of the rabbi was covered [with fury] . . . he hastened home, sullen and displeased.'[51] The author's enmity towards the rabbi, demonstrated in the satirical use of sources (a tactic characteristic of Haskalah satire), is ubiquitous in the story. In the opening, she mocks his ignorance by quoting his halakhic judgment, which is based on his mistaken identification of the verb *yaḥam* (to be hot with sexual passion) with *ḥamam* (to heat, to warm) due to his lack of knowledge of Hebrew: 'Lest the pan be in heat like the sheep of Jacob our patriarch, may he rest in peace.' The knowledgeable and ironic author derides the ignorance of the male religious authority and is thus identified with the heroine, who points out the rabbi's ignorance.[52]

The letter ends with a sentence that may be understood in various ways by different readers: 'All of this transpired and I saw it here in the town of Suvalk and the chroniclers will remain silent [about it] so that the coming generations will know nothing of it in the future.' Perhaps the original addressees of the letter would have seen in this an innocent and feminine explanation for including the story in a family letter. However, if we read the letter as a palimpsestic text of a feminist writer, we can see in this sentence a subversive statement against traditional historiography that does not include 'herstory' in the historical description. The final sentence of Miriam Markel-Mosessohn's letter embodies, in miniature, the palimpsestic techniques of the letter as a whole, in which a subversive, authentic feminist layer is hidden within a feminine letter.

On the other side of Europe, in the generation prior to Markel-Mosessohn, the Italian Jewish poet Rachel Morpurgo also used the 'feminine' genre of personal letters for the purpose of authentic personal expression. Included in the extensive

[48] 'But when Haman saw Mordecai in the palace gate, and Mordecai did not rise or even stir on his account . . .' (Esther 5: 9).

[49] 'How long will you speak such things? Your utterances are a mighty wind [*ruaḥ kabir*]' (Job 8: 2).

[50] 'And his sister stationed herself at a distance, to learn what would befall him' (Exod. 2: 4).

[51] 'And Haman's face was covered' (Esther 7: 9); 'Haman hurried home, his head covered in mourning' (Esther 6: 12); 'And Ahab came to his house, heavy and displeased' (1 Kgs. 21: 4).

[52] The lack of knowledge of Hebrew among the Orthodox is the subject of ironic criticism by Markel-Mosessohn in another letter to a woman friend in which she mocks the cantor's lack of knowledge of Hebrew (unnumbered letter, Jewish National and University Archive, Hebrew University of Jerusalem, Schwadron Collection, Arc 4° 761).

correspondence between Morpurgo and her famous maskil cousin, Shmuel David Luzzatto, are a number of verse letters.[53] Morpurgo adopted a genre that was conventional in medieval Judaeo-Spanish poetry, finding in it a mixture of an appropriate feminine genre and canonical poetic expression.

Thus, for example, in an early poetic dialogue between the cousins ('Torah, daughter of the maker of all things, daughter of the Creator of wind' and 'Torah brings light from every direction', 1816),[54] Morpurgo responds to Luzzatto's question about her refusal to marry. In the poem, she displays a degree of assertiveness and determination in her desire to marry a man whom she herself will choose. Her verse letter illustrates her complex technical ability: it is written purposefully, precisely in the form of the verse letter that Luzzatto had sent to her, and repeats the exact words with which he finished his lines. However, the identical line-endings undermine the original meaning through their expression of feminine protest. Thus, for example, Luzzatto uses the word *shevet* (tribe) in his humorous description of his cousin's wide-ranging search for a husband: 'And she went to seek a lover among the tribes.' However, in Morpurgo's context—'What shall I do, then | If I do not bend myself under the rod (*shevet*)'—the word takes on a different meaning and becomes an expression of protest against the oppression of a girl by the accepted norms of society and her family. Moreover, Morpurgo does not hesitate to describe in detail her rebellion against her parents in the choice of her own spouse: 'This time, I found a goodly youth . . . | But my parents refused him . . . | My answer is . . . | I shall never get married, not even to the messiah.'

For the maskilah, the genre of the letter thus functioned as an excellent tool for self-expression. On the one hand, letter-writing in Hebrew served as a widespread means of communication between the maskilim, and provided an opportunity to discuss intellectual subjects; this made it possible to overcome the linguistic gender barrier that stood between the maskilah and the Hebrew Haskalah. On the other hand, the letter was also considered a legitimate feminine genre, so that the maskilah was free to use it and indeed exploit it as a double-layered palimpsest in which she concealed authentic personal feminine expressions.

CONCEALING AUTHENTIC FEMININE EXPRESSION IN CANONICAL GENRES

There are a number of Hebrew prose texts by women writers which at first sight could be classified within the accepted canonical genres, apparently because of their authors' attempt to participate in the androcentric culture through the complete

[53] See Y. Berlowitz, 'Rachel Morpurgo: Hateshukah el hamavet, hateshukah el hashir: Letivah shel hameshoreret ha'ivrit harishonah ba'eit haḥadashah', in Z. Shamir (ed.), *Sadan: Meḥkarim besifrut ivrit*, ii (Tel Aviv, 1996), 11–39.

[54] R. Morpurgo, *Ugav raḥel: Sefer kolel shirim ve'igerot umikhtavim shonim* (Kraków, 1890), 50–1.

negation of their authentic female self. However, as I will try to show, palimpsestic texts can also be found in this group of works, texts which include a hidden authentic feminine layer that often undermines the accepted norms of the genre under whose name-tag they appear. I will use two texts as examples of this phenomenon: an essay and a novel.

Merka Altshuler, 'Hegyonai leyom tu be'av'

The first example is the essay by Merka Altshuler, 'Hegyonai leyom tu be'av' ('Meditations on the Fifteenth of Av'), which was published in the journal *Haboker or* in 1880. It is written as a *derashah* (homily) about 15 Av (which was also the author's birthday), and appears at first glance to be a typical Haskalah essay. As is usual in the *derashah*, the essay opens with a link to a specific textual passage, in this instance the description of Joseph's release from prison through his interpretation of the cupbearer's and baker's dreams (Genesis 41). Taking this story, the author infers from it the importance of knowledge and Haskalah for the whole Jewish people, who suffer from 'disgrace and contempt', and for each individual among them 'who has achieved none of the world's pleasures and delights but has diligence, intelligence, a cultured soul, and a heart full of knowledge'. To the importance of knowledge, she adds the significance of a belief in God and the hope for redemption that gives the people of Israel the strength to continue to exist: 'Why do they not stumble and fall . . . surely it is their belief in God; surely their hope and deliverance in God is their strength.' This is a theme which is characteristic of conservative male Haskalah writing, without any authentic personal expression by the author. Perhaps it is her effort to express these general conventional values that makes Altshuler's style verbose, florid, and itself conventional.

I would like to suggest, however, that Altshuler is using the imitation of masculine writing as the external layer of her essay, to make it acceptable to the journal and its readers. Within a hidden layer, in a language that is more lively and natural, she gives expression to her authentic female identity in two places: in the second paragraph she describes her studies, and in the last paragraph she inserts her personal commentary on making 15 Av into a holiday 'in the time of the Mishnah'. Even in these two paragraphs she does not dare to express herself openly, but rather conceals her thought under wrappings

Altshuler begins the description of her studies with a relatively short sentence: 'For I was my father's daughter, soft and delicate when I came forth from the womb, and he raised me in the lap of science and reason and taught me knowledge.' She describes her unconventional education in simple, clear, and personal words. Immediately thereafter, however, as if she were frightened by the direct and revolutionary description of a girl's education 'in the lap of science and reason', she quotes her father about the difficulty of attaining Haskalah. Thus she does not endanger herself with the expression of feminist opinions about equality of education for women and men. It is for the reader to link her father's words with the fact that they are addressed to his daughter and to conclude that herein lies a feminist statement about the importance of education for women.

The second expression of her personal feminine opinion is also hidden. In the concluding paragraph of the essay she deals with the question of why the people of Israel sanctified 'the fifteenth day of this month and made it a day of feasting and celebration'. This is indeed a conventional, masculine kind of discussion of a canonical (talmudic) text. However, the very fact that it was written by a woman makes a feminist statement about the ability of a woman to learn Torah as a result of her attainment of knowledge. Moreover, the writer interprets the canonical text in a new way by emphasizing the woman's point of view—an act of female appropriation of a canonical text, a female tactic characteristic of the time, as I shall demonstrate below.

Sarah-Feiga Meinkin, Ahavat yesharim

Another example of a palimpsestic text is Sarah-Feiga Meinkin's *Ahavat yesharim* ('The Love of the Righteous'), the first Hebrew novel to be written by a woman.[55] The genre of the social novel was developed by the prose writers of the Hebrew Haskalah from the mid-nineteenth century onward. It began with the influential prose romance by Abraham Mapu, *Ayit tsavuah* ('The Hypocrite', 1857–64), and continued with the social novels of S. Y. Abramowitz, Peretz Smolenskin, and Reuven Braudes. In spite of the differences between the works, we can identify a standard pattern in the Haskalah social novel during these years: these are didactic works overtly preaching Haskalah values through descriptions of the conflict between the maskilim and conservative society.

The Haskalah social novel is strongly influenced by the conventions of prose romance in its Mapu incarnation. Like the romance, its plot is complex and includes numerous sub-plots, which describe the many different faces (usually negative) of Jewish society. The protagonist, the ideal male maskil who stands in opposition to conservative society, embarks on a quest to attain enlightenment as well as personal happiness through union with his beloved. The heroine is also shaped on the model of the romance: she is accomplished and passive, the object of the hero's dreams. On the few occasions that the literature depicts her as an enlightened woman, her education serves only as an embellishment and does not determine her fate.[56]

In its external layer, Sarah-Feiga Meinkin's novel is shaped by the conventions of the genre of the social novel. *Ahavat yesharim* sets positive Haskalah heroes against negative conservative antagonists. The fundamental elements of the romance are also present: the complicated plot, the various sub-plots and complex intrigues, the love-story of the Haskalah hero and heroine who are separated from each other, and the extreme black and white construction of negative traditional characters and

55 *Ahavat yesharim*, or *Hamishpaḥot hamordafot: Sipur min ha'et haḥadashah* (Vilna, 1881). Only the first part of the novel is available; the novel was published before her marriage to Meir Foner.

56 See Cohen, *Ha'aḥat ahuvah veha'aḥat senuah*, chs. 4 and 6.

positive enlightened heroes. The subjects criticized in the novels, such as forced betrothals, hasidism, and Galician Jewry, are also conventional themes that dominated the genre during this period. It is evident that the author, in her desire for acceptance, attempts to imitate the conventional genre through her use of common literary elements.

The strength of the novel, however, is not in its conventional, male foundations, in which one immediately recognizes the weakness of the inauthentic imitation, but rather in the author's successful ability to conceal another layer; in this it differs from earlier examples of the genre. In this hidden layer is the story of the woman in both societies described in the novel: the enlightened and the conservative. Meinkin conveys this story both through the characteristics of the heroine, Finalia, and through the depiction of the world of women, which she, the author, knows intimately.

The image of Finalia is not different on the surface from that of the typical Haskalah heroine. She is a member of the aristocracy, perfect in her beauty and enlightened character. She also rebels against the betrothal proposed to her and instead chooses the ideal maskil hero. However, beyond these characteristics, a new image of an ideal woman emerges for the first time in a Haskalah social novel—a woman who is also the protagonist of the story.[57] She is not constructed as the 'Other' who complements the primary male hero; rather, she stands at the centre of the plot as its prime mover. The story begins with a description of Finalia:

> At this moment as the sun is going down and the stars are yet hiding their power, there walks a figure wrapped in black garments . . . Who is she? We cannot know, as she has covered her face, but her bearing and refined step inform us that she is of the loftiest daughters of the land.[58]

Thereafter the author presents the characters as they appear to Finalia. Thus Victor begins a conversation with her in the street immediately after her first appearance.[59] In the next scene her parents are described as anxiously anticipating her return that same evening.[60] Moreover, the central intrigue of the plot is the story of Finalia's kidnapping and escape.

Meinkin portrays Finalia as active and resourceful, characteristics expressed in her frequent departures from her home. Visits to friends and invitations to parties (where she develops a network of relationships) and the meeting with Victor, her beloved, all take place outside the home. Her resourcefulness becomes most apparent when, having been kidnapped from her home in Italy and brought to Galicia, she manages to escape with the help of a manservant, Azariah. She is the initiator of

[57] It is worth noting that the woman is the protagonist of several short stories of the time (for example, in the stories of M. Brendershteter and Ben Avigdor); however, she was never the 'ideal heroine'. Heroines of these stories are the 'suffering woman' or the 'satirized woman'.

[58] Meinkin, *Ahavat yesharim*, 9–10. For the English translation, see 'The Way of the Righteous', in M. Rosenthal (ed.), *A Woman's Voice: Sarah Foner, Hebrew Author of the Haskalah* (Wilbraham, Mass., 2001), 151.

[59] *Ahavat yesharim*, 9.

[60] Ibid. 15–18.

the escape, persuading Azariah to free her and escape with her to Vienna. The first part of the novel (which is all we have) ends with a powerful declaration by Finalia, as she embarks on the train to Vienna: 'Now I can breathe the air of freedom and liberty and I can go wherever I want.'[61]

The centrality of Finalia to the story and, no less important, the ability of the woman writer to depict a female character so persuasively, influence her formation. As a rule, the female heroine in the male Haskalah novel is a stereotypical character, one-sided and simple. If a Haskalah writer succeeded in developing complexity in a character, it was always in the male hero. In Meinkin's novel, however, while the male characters, and even the enlightened hero Victor, are cast in a hackneyed and simple mould, the heroine Finalia is a complex and rounded character. She is a developing character too, thrust into complicated circumstances that force her to change, manoeuvring between different relationships.

Two examples of the different construction of the male and female heroes can be found in chapter 14, 'The Ball', and chapter 15, 'The Next Day'. In the first instance, Finalia receives an invitation to a magnificent ball from the Minister of Justice, Emmanuel, a friend of her father's. To preserve her father's honour, she is obliged to respond to Emmanuel's courtship to some degree; at the same time, she maintains her loyalty to Victor, and her behaviour at the ball reflects her emotional complexity. Victor, who observes these events, comprehends only the external actions, believes that she has betrayed him, and responds with a childish quarrel. The juxtaposition of Finalia's maturity and Victor's naivety, as well as the complex formation of her character and the flat depiction of his, become all the more poignant when she explains the different obligations that have dictated her behaviour.[62] Her words reflect a deep understanding of the complexity of her situation, her strength to claim what is rightfully hers, her powers of persuasion, and the intricacies of her literary formation. In contrast to the traditional Haskalah author, who identifies with the male hero and regards the heroine from afar, Meinkin clearly identifies with her heroine and is able to describe her world from within.

A parallel gender construction can be seen in the formation of the secondary characters. For example, in addition to the kidnapper, Yahede'el, who serves as the negative antagonist of Victor ('his heart full of fraud and deceit and his eyes sparkling as he sought out any lies or deception'[63]), Meinkin also describes his mother, who is appointed to watch over the kidnapped Finalia. Surprisingly, the author casts the mother in contrast to her son, as a woman of honour who relates to Finalia with empathy and gentleness. Her love for her son does not preclude empathy for Finalia and the recognition that it will be impossible to force the girl to marry, 'because she will only cry, and she is so delicate that in a few days she'll become ill, and then you'll be forced to set her free'.[64] Even a negative female character such as Bonah, Rafiah's wife, who is 'thoroughly corrupt' with 'seven abominations in her heart', is hardly a prosaic, stereotypical character. The author

[61] Ibid. 149. [62] Ibid. 99. [63] Ibid. 35. [64] Ibid. 126.

takes pains to explain that Bonah's immorality in her adulthood resulted from her spoiled upbringing: 'Their love was like the love of all the Galician hasidim for their children. They never punished her or withheld from her anything that her heart desired.'[65]

This female author's empathy with women finds expression in great detail. Like a number of Haskalah writers, Meinkin is not afraid to express her opinions through the direct voice of the narrator: 'You men always behave the same. Whenever you see a young woman that you fancy, you turn yourselves into her slaves, prostrating yourselves before her, but if she falls into the trap that you have laid for her, even if you are miles away, she will languish under your yoke.'[66] The gender distinction here is biting and bitter and the author expresses caustic generalizations about men.[67]

The female experience of the author influences not only the formation of her women characters, but also the realistic depiction of their daily lives, with which she is familiar. Meinkin, like the English women authors described by Virginia Woolf, portrays 'what happens when she goes into a room'[68]—both when Finalia enters a room in her own home and when she enters the ballroom. She also depicts the details of a woman's life at home: housework, kitchen chores, her dress, and so forth. Finalia is described cleaning the house,[69] repairing her dress after the ball,[70] and enthusiastically reading *The Ruins of Troy* by Schiller. Meinkin also unabashedly includes apparently trivial details such as a description of Finalia's delicate and unadorned dress when she arrives at the ball, which provides the opportunity to insert a didactic conclusion: 'pure conduct, nobility of soul, grace and comely beauty: these are the precious jewels of every maiden'.[71] To paraphrase Virginia Woolf, it can be said that Meinkin 'lighted a torch in that vast chamber where nobody has yet been' of the lives of women which had not been depicted in the Haskalah novel before.

These descriptions of 'household rituals' not only serve as background to the plot, but also constitute a code for understanding the moods of the heroine and the changes that the family undergoes. As Ann Romines notes: 'Rituals performed in a house . . . possess most of the qualities that . . . are common to all rituals: regular recurrence, symbolic value, emotional meaning . . . It can be an ordinary household task such as serving a meal or sewing a seam. All such rituals help to preserve the shelter.'[72]

The Edelberg house is described at the beginning of the novel through the household rituals that characterize daily life: standard chores, such as baking and

[65] *Ahavat yesharim*, 133.

[66] Ibid. 42.

[67] Her attitude to men was afterwards justified in view of her truly bitter life experience: in a letter to Gordon (Hebrew University Y. L. Gordon Archive, n.d.), she complains about the maskil who married her in a private ceremony and afterwards denied the fact of their marriage.

[68] Woolf, *A Room of One's Own*, 87.

[69] *Ahavat yesharim*, 68.

[70] Ibid. 97.

[71] Ibid. 89.

[72] Romines, *The Home Plot*, 12.

cleaning, are carried out by Finalia and her mother, Dinah. The performance of orderly work reflects the permanence and security of the family's life and the relationships of mutual love and respect that exist between the family members. One scene, for example, shows Finalia and Dinah in the kitchen, baking *hamentaschen*; Finalia's father, the baron, comes in to speak to them. It is here in the kitchen that they have a friendly and humorous discussion about the importance of women's work.[73] The whole scene expresses the feeling of security of a warm loving home with fixed rituals. This warmth and order is similarly expressed in the ritual of cleaning the silver, as performed by Finalia: 'There stood Finalia cleaning all the household utensils, the candelabras, the spoons, knives, forks. She arranged the flowers and everything else in the proper order . . . Then the humble dwelling was like a palace of joy in its purity and beauty.'[74]

These household rituals, which represent the normal passage of life, are disrupted by the kidnapping of Finalia and her mother's illness, induced by sorrow. The narrator, who 'enters' the room with the baron, describes what happens there with the eyes of a woman who understands the meaning of the room's appearance and the disruption of the permanent household rituals:

> The flowers were withered, the window curtains were blackened, the whole house was in disarray. Here and there a couple of chairs were grouped together while another area was entirely empty. The table was not in its place, and neither were any of the household furnishings. The baron's bookcase was covered with dust on every side, but who paid attention to this? . . . Every glimmer of happiness had left the house with them and who noticed the wilted flowers or furniture?[75]

Rather than describing the great agitation of the baron and his wife, the narrator chooses to describe the room. With the help of these seemingly trivial details, she conveys her heroes' emotional state and their feelings about the tragedy are expressed by the disruption of the rituals.

No less important is Meinkin's exploration of the relationships between women: between Finalia and her mother, and between Finalia and her friend Henrietta. These relationships are carried through the entire novel, especially in the two chapters that are devoted to specific conversations between the heroines (chapters 17, 'Henrietta and Finalia', and 18, 'Mother and Daughter'). To be sure, Meinkin is not the first writer in Haskalah literature to depict the relationship between mother and daughter or between girlfriends; such relationships appear in several Haskalah novels written by men.[76] However, in Meinkin's novel they are central relationships, and accompany the heroine throughout the story. Moreover, in the novels

[73] *Ahavat yesharim*, 68. [74] Ibid. 69. [75] Ibid. 116.

[76] See e.g. the description of the relationship between Tamar and her mother, Tirzah, in A. Mapu, *Ahavat tsiyon* (Vilna, 1853); the relationship between Yehosheva and Miriam in A. Mapu, *Ashmat shomeron* (Vilna, 1866); the relationship between Rachel and her mother, Sarah, in S. J. Abramowitz, *Ha'avot vehabanim* (Odessa, 1868); the relationship between Shifra and Chava in P. Smolenskin, *Simḥat ḥanef* (Vilna, 1882).

by male writers these female relationships are portrayed in stereotypical terms, primarily through the opposition between mother and daughter, or between the heroine and her girlfriend, each representing a particular social and ideological position. In contrast, in *Ahavat yesharim* these relationships are shown in a vital and realistic manner, without the burden of class or ideological representation. For Finalia, the relationship with her mother is a source of love and support, as is her friendship with Henrietta. Their conversations are much more natural and realistic than those of their male counterparts, which often consist of long speeches that serve to fill in information that the reader is lacking.[77]

By making these empathetic relationships the focus of the novel, Meinkin directs the reader to her central innovation. In terms of the connection between personal relationships and ideological representation this novel represents the complete opposite of the conventional Haskalah pattern: Haskalah novels by men usually present personal relationships as representations of societal relationships, as a result of the romance pattern on which they are based.[78] In contrast, while *Ahavat yesharim* still uses the same stock figures, the framework of relationships is much less representational and stereotypical. The focus of the novel is not on ideology, but rather on the human and emotional side of life. The social developments serve as a background, often as a stimulus, for the plot, but not as the primary focus.

Meinkin's novel, therefore, constitutes a unique maskilic attempt to write a woman's novel that captures the struggles of the Haskalah from a female perspective. It departs from the conventional genre with its unusual focus on the framework of relationships in general, and on the world of women in particular. It may have been the fact that this was such a new and different perspective which prompted the author to conceal it under the external layer of the conventional Haskalah novel that deals with the tensions between maskilim and conservatives. But it is worth our while to scratch the upper layer of this palimpsest to reveal the female story underneath.

THE FEMININE SUBVERSIVE USE OF CANONICAL RELIGIOUS TEXTS

'Re-vision', or the reading anew of the androcentric culture from a feminine viewpoint, is the means by which, Adrienne Rich suggests, women writers find their place and means of expression within canonical patriarchal culture.[79] Based on this

[77] See e.g. ch. 8, 'Victor's History' (pp. 47–57); ch. 13, 'The History of Baron Edelberg' (pp. 78–83).

[78] On the shaping of heroes in the novels of Mapu, see D. Miron, *Bein ḥazon le'emet: Nitsanei haroman ha'ivri vehayidi beme'ah hatesha-esreh* (Jerusalem, 1979), 112–24. See also T. Cohen, *Tsevu'im veyisharim, elilot veliliyot: Iyunim beyetsirato shel avraham mapu* (Tel Aviv, 1990), 29–41.

[79] 'Re-vision—the act of looking back . . . of entering an old text from a new critical direction—is for women . . . an act of survival' (A. Rich, 'When We the Dead are Awakened', in Rich (ed.), *On Lies, Secrets, and Silence, Selected Prose, 1966–1978* (New York, 1979), 35).

theory, Alicia Ostriker has described how female writers have appropriated 'Fathers' speech' to access authentic feminine expression. This is accomplished through the process of 'revisionist mythmaking'—namely, the deconstruction of existing myths by challenging or correcting the 'gender stereotypes embodied [in them]' and their reconstruction for 'altered ends'.[80] This alteration of the canonical texts provides a woman with the means to express the 'I' by fusing the two circles of culture in which she lives—the national, canonical culture and the female experience.[81]

Appropriation of canonical texts for personal expression—often in opposition to their original meaning—has long been an accepted literary technique for both men and women.[82] It was an especially popular practice among Haskalah writers, who used this approach to rejuvenate, but also often to undermine, biblical texts.[83] It is no wonder, therefore, that women writers of the Haskalah also resorted to the appropriation of biblical texts. Their central innovation was to infuse the androcentric texts with new feminine and feminist content and thus read anew or 'revise' these male canonical texts. There are numerous examples of this approach, which was also to become part of the tradition of twentieth-century Hebrew writing by women.[84]

Examples of the appropriation of biblical texts can be found frequently in the writings of the women authors discussed in this chapter: for example in the letters of Markel-Mosessohn, discussed above. Merka Altshuler's 'Hegyonai leyom tu be'av' also offers examples of the way in which women appropriate canonical texts. As I have already shown, Altshuler hides an authentic personal feminine layer beneath the external male genre of the *derashah*; this dual layering is also evident, I would argue, in her commentary on BT *Ta'anit* 31*a*. While she does not expressly cite this text, the last paragraph of her letter constitutes a personal woman's appropriation of it. At first sight it looks as if her words are simply a paraphrase of the talmudic passage—'There were no better days for Israel than those of the Fifteenth of Av and Yom Kippur . . . the Fifteenth of Av, what is it?'—but the changes she inserts constitute a personal interpretation.

80 Ostriker's definition of myth is broad and actually identical to 'cultural tradition'. In her words, 'Whenever a poet employs a figure or a story previously accepted and defined by a culture, the poet is using a myth' (A. Ostriker, 'The Thieves of Language', in E. Showalter (ed.), *The New Feminist Criticism* (New York, 1985), 317).

81 For a definition of the woman as an actor from within two cultures that partially overlap, see E. Showalter, 'Feminist Criticism in the Wilderness', in Showalter (ed.), *The New Feminist Criticism*, 262–7.

82 Alicia Ostriker devotes most of 'The Thieves of Language' to the different ways in which men and women appropriate canonical texts.

83 T. Cohen, 'Appropriating the Bible: Women and Haskalah in the 19th Century', in R. Elior (ed.), *Men and Women: Gender, Judaism and Democracy* (Jerusalem, 2004).

84 On this topic, see T. Cohen, 'Betokh hatarbut umiḥutsah lah: Al nikhus "sefat ha'av" kederekh le'itsuv intelektuali shel he'ani hanashi', in Z. Shamir (ed.), *Sadan*, ii (Tel Aviv, 1997), 69–110.

Altshuler's commentary first makes a connection between the first and second parts of the passage. The Talmud describes the different characteristics of 15 Av but does not make a connection between them: 'The sun grew weaker and wood for burning was not being chopped . . . The daughters of Israel would go out to dance in the vineyards.' Altshuler, however, links the beginning and end of this description: in her opinion, the source of the day's festivities lies in the people's fear about the decreasing hours of sunlight now that summer's peak is past: '[The summer] is helpless and our strength has gone too.' Opposed to this helplessness, 'those who worried about their people' are wise to establish a day of hope to counteract this despair: 'How pleasant it is to breathe hope into the understanding heart so that it knows not to despair.' Her woman's perspective clearly influences Altshuler's description: the focus of the day—i.e. hope—is translated into the female hope of marriage. 'All of them together, each and every woman, the pretty and the despised poor, have found through their hope which is focused on this one day, that exalted One who chose them and lifted them out of the dung-heaps and turned them into a blessing to all.'

The female perspective also influences Altshuler's characterization of the different women, all of whom are searching for their match on this day. Like the Talmud, she depicts the beautiful women as emphasizing the importance of female beauty. However, her analysis of the rest of the women, the 'noble' and the 'ugly', is different. In the Talmud the noble women emphasize the importance of family pedigree as a virtue that a woman will pass on to her sons: 'Look at the family because women are for nothing if not to bear sons.' Altshuler, in contrast, turns the value of lineage into a virtue of *the woman herself* and connects lineage to education, 'an educated woman and daughter of a noble family, she is a gift of God'.

Even more innovative is the way in which she revises the category of 'the ugly'. In the words of the Talmud: 'And what do the ugly women say? You may marry us for nothing, only cover us with gold coins.' In other words, ugly women abandon any dream of marrying a man of their personal liking and will be satisfied with achieving solid financial status through marriage. Altshuler refrains from using the word 'ugly' in such an abrupt and humiliating way, out of female empathy for the poor girls who are neither pretty nor noble. She tones down the description by drawing it out: 'The girl to whom God did not distribute this and that [i.e. beauty and nobility], she who is of displeasing appearance, and the daughter of the margins of the people'. Moreover, she goes even further in refusing to countenance the idea that these women must reject all hope of love, esteem, and intimacy in marriage. Thus she puts words in the mouths of these girls to emphasize the importance of the woman as a mother, and her role in the creation of the family and home: 'Pedigree and beauty mean nothing and women's wisdom is folly; for a woman's worth is measured in her ability to bear sons and bring forth offspring! She is all glorious within, she sits at home to nurse her young and give food to the mouth that eats.' While this may be an essentialist description of the woman, and even reductive from a feminist perspective, Altshuler is trying to give expression to the femininity of thousands of years ago. She thus reads the traditional male text with a woman's eyes and tries to revise it by joining its main characteristics to a new feminine perspective.

A third example of female appropriation of canonical texts can be found in the poetry of Rachel Morpurgo, who often appropriated expressions from the canonical literature of her time—the Bible, Talmud, kabbalah, and liturgical hymns. Morpurgo's wide knowledge of these Jewish sources was unusual, especially for a woman of her time. Apart from the Bible, Talmud, and kabbalah, it appears that she was also familiar with many liturgical hymns through the connection with her cousin, Shmuel David Luzzatto, one of the greatest collectors of liturgical poetry. Thus, unlike other women of her time, she was able to draw upon a very wide range of Jewish sources.

I will consider Morpurgo's appropriation of two texts—one biblical, the other liturgical—in one stanza of her sonnet entitled 'Ve'eleh divrei raḥel bevo le'ozneiha ki shemah nizkar letehilah bemikhtevei ha'itim' ('These are the words of Rachel when she heard her name was praised in the papers', 1847).[85] The poem begins with the speaker's surprised response to the words of praise that have reached her ears: 'Woe to me, says my soul, it is bitter to me, bitter.' What follows is the author's attempt to explain her response, which draws on the inherent contradiction between the words of praise for her poems and Judaism's perception of women as frivolous and unintellectual. In the third and fourth stanzas she cites the Talmud: 'Women's ideas are frivolous', and 'Women have no wisdom except in spinning'.[86] She concludes with bitterness that all the praise of her poems will be quickly forgotten and, therefore, she does not rejoice over it: 'After a few years why should my name be remembered in every city and country any more than that of a dead dog?'

In the second stanza she describes her feelings of bitterness on hearing herself praised; she feels that this is but fleeting fame and her name will be quickly forgotten. The full meaning of the feminine protest at the core of this stanza can be seen by comparing it with the two canonical sources that Morpurgo appropriates: a biblical verse and a liturgical poem. The biblical verse is Jeremiah 48: 11: 'Moab hath been at ease from his youth, and he hath settled on his lees, and hath not been emptied from vessel to vessel, *neither hath he gone into exile: therefore his taste remained in him and his scent is not changed.*' Morpurgo uses some of the same key words as this verse:

> Woe to me says my soul.
> My spirit then replies
> *My scent has changed*
> *Exile after exile*, my skin has stood on edge
> *My taste has not remained in me*, my vineyard has been cut down
> Afraid of being shamed, I sing no more.

[85] Morpurgo, *Ugav raḥel*, 54. For a full analysis of the poem, see Cohen, 'Betokh hatarbut umiḥutsah lah', 77–85

[86] BT, *Shab.* 33*b*; BT, *Yoma* 66*b*.

The 'I' in the poem is formed in complete opposition to the biblical image, the latter preserving his vigour for a long period, while the 'I' immediately loses vitality and flavour. Moab's 'scent is not changed', while her 'scent has changed'; he has never 'gone into exile', while she wanders from 'exile to exile'; he is described as one whose 'taste remained in him', while hers 'has not remained'. A comparison of the biblical image with Morpurgo's adaptation here also clarifies the reason for this contrast. The one described in the Bible is 'at ease' and does not suffer the vicissitudes of fate. Thus, he displays strength, vigour, and the preservation of his identity. In contrast, the subject of the poem loses her vivacity and identity—'my scent has changed'—because she goes through 'exile after exile'. The verse speaks explicitly about Moab, but its description is all in masculine language as opposed to the female 'I', the speaker. The gender contrast is striking—the quiet, serene male achieves success while the woman never attains tranquillity or accomplishment. Her fundamental position is one of fear and insecurity, hence her inability to sing or write poetry. The poet thus revises the biblical verse to depict her female identity in complete opposition to the original text.

Another canonical text that Morpurgo appropriates in this stanza is the medieval *piyut* (liturgical poem) of Solomon ibn Gabirol, which opens: 'For the third time I am praying the third prayer'.[87] Morpurgo's whole poem is written as a feminine echo of this *piyut*. There are clear linguistic connections between them; for example, she deliberately quotes a number of its unusual words and expressions: 'stood on edge', 'it is bitter to me, bitter', 'my scent has changed', and others. However, while the liturgist uses the conventional image of a suffering woman as a metaphor for the people of Israel awaiting their redemption ('Will I languish in Exile for ever? | Has God forgotten me?'), Morpurgo, describing herself, returns the description to the level of the original image—the suffering woman. In this way she manages to find a canonical source for her description of the female 'I' through a hidden protest that the image of the suffering woman is not depicted in canonical culture for herself, but only as a literary image for the whole people, as demonstrated above. Moreover, the reader is called upon to continue the analogy and to project into Morpurgo's poem the detailed description of the suffering of the Jewish people in ibn Gabirol's *piyut*: 'She cries out of the mire, out of the muddy well | Her years have passed in agony and woe.' In the *piyut*, this is a description of the Jewish people, but is it not also a description of the suffering of the woman writer who speaks in the poem?

Morpurgo thus brings to a peak the palimpsestic technique of concealing feminine protest by using canonical sources in an apparently traditional and innocent way, but one which expresses the female 'I' rather differently from the original. Only the reader who delves deeper into the text, beyond the shallow layer of what is proper to female poetry, will realize the depth of protest and pain expressed in this poem.

[87] See D. Yarden, *Shirei haḥol lerabi shelomoh ibn gabirol*, i (Jerusalem, 1984), 303–4.

THE OVERT APPEARANCE OF FEMINISM IN THE WRITINGS OF THE MASKILOT

As we have seen so far, when the maskilot expressed feminist protest they did so in covert and half-hidden ways, and the reader is required to decipher the different layers of the palimpsest in order to reveal the feminine criticism hidden within. Only at the end of the period, perhaps due to the increasing influence of Russian feminism of the 1860s and 1870s,[88] do we find more overtly feminist expression. Toybe Segal's essay 'She'elat hanashim' ('The Question of Women') is one example of this new trend.[89] In this long and articulate essay, which was published in 1879 in five parts, the author does not spare Jewish men in any segment of society—the maskilim, the Orthodox, and the 'in-betweens'. Her claims are based on the radical Russian feminist theories of the time that emphasized the need to provide woman with an education equal to that of men, so that they could support themselves and become independent. It is important to note that a small minority of radical male maskilim of the time, including Moshe Leib Lilienblum and Yehuda Leib Levin, shared similar views, albeit not with the same intensity and focus.[90] They saw the question of women as part of the general demand for equality, to be achieved through social revolution.

Segal's article was innovative on many levels. Written at a time when women's voices were still rare in the public arena, the whole essay is focused on the question of women. Moreover, Segal was not afraid to pen sharp criticism of the maskilim's attitude to women, arguing that, despite the rhetoric of gender equality which allegedly stood at the centre of the Haskalah revolution, in reality it excluded women: 'The ideas of the Haskalah, on what were they forged? Was it not the call for freedom for all who are oppressed and suffering?'[91] This revolution does not include women, and the maskilim, like all men, oppress women by luring them with their erudition (Haskalah) and then take financial advantage of them:

> Why therefore do you oppress women and triumph over them? . . . Why do you raise yourselves above them and put them under your feet to trample them? . . . What good is the Haskalah of our maskilim who make Haskalah into a lifeless idol to lure a multitude of the daughters of Jacob, who hasten to bow down before them . . .

Another innovation in the article is Segal's criticism of the excitement that the maskilim expressed over the phenomenon of a woman who was educated and able to write in Hebrew. Here it seems to me that she gets to the heart of the cultural discrimination of the maskilim against women: the exaggerated enthusiasm of the men

[88] On Russian feminism beginning in the 1860s, see R. Stites, *The Women's Liberation Movement in Russia* (Princeton, 1978). See also Feiner, 'Ha'ishah hayehudiyah hamodernit', 294–303.

[89] Feiner, 'Ha'ishah hayehudiyah hamodernit', 299–300.

[90] See M. L. Lilienblum, 'Mishnat elisha ben avuyah', in Y. Friedlander (ed.), *Bemistarei hasatirah*, iii (Ramat Gan, 1994), 196–215; Y. L. Levin, 'She'elot hazeman', in his *Ketavim nivḥarim* (Warsaw, 1914), 98.

[91] 'She'elat hanashim', 77.

over every woman who wrote in Hebrew clearly demonstrates that they did not see maskilot as their equals in intellectual ability:

> People like this, if they read this essay of mine, would say: How wonderful it is to see a young woman writing in Hebrew! How fortunate she is! How rare it is in these days to see a woman writing in the Holy Tongue! But how upsetting it is to realize that they express this admiration about anything a woman does or says as if it were the wisdom of a small child . . . Why are you so surprised? Are we apes and not thinking human beings that men should be so surprised to find something good in us? Who can vouch for me that if given the chance, women would not have done as well as men in all matters useful to them and to others?[92]

The ironic tone of the writer is not new. As we have seen above, similar irony could be found in the letters and story by Markel-Mosessohn, as well as the poetry of Morpurgo. However, in this case, it stands out because of its forcefulness. For Segal, the treatment by Jewish men of women in general, and their education in particular, is a source not only of criticism but also of mockery. However, as in every satire the irony is based on pain, the pain of a feminist who understands only too well the subjugated position of women, and especially the misery and loneliness of the maskilah.

Thus, while in the external layer of the article Segal seems secure in her views, articulate in her writing, and capable of ridiculing all the men around her, in the hidden layer the attentive reader will discover the feelings of loneliness experienced by a woman who is cut off from all the worlds around her. She is certainly aware of the distance between herself and the male maskilim who do not accept her as an equal among equals, but even when she turns to other women she reveals the distance between them and herself: 'To you, respectable girls, safe in your parents' homes, to you, too, I address my words.'[93] Segal writes to women with greater empathy than to men, and includes herself among them ('*for us* it was twenty years that *we* had to wait impatiently until the time when the messiah would come to save *us*'). Nonetheless, it is clear that she also sees herself as an outsider, feeling the difference between herself, who understands, and the innocence of other young women.

It is no wonder that, despite Segal's efforts to conclude on an optimistic note by suggesting remedies (for example, the woman must learn 'wisdom or a craft'; the educated man must appreciate a woman according to her 'worthiness, beauty of soul, and wisdom'), the last sentence conveys her pessimism in the style of Ecclesiastes: 'Therefore at every time and in every place you will find them acting to deceive us and to lead us astray, the wisest of the wise, the richest of the rich, will not save us and there is no advantage in the trained charmer.'[94]

[92] 'She'elat hanashim', 94.

[93] Ibid. 101.

[94] The sentence refers to Ecclesiastes in several ways. First, Segal uses the word 'wisdom', which is mentioned twenty times in the book. Secondly, she describes the disappointing nature of wisdom and riches. Thirdly, she utilizes specific expressions: 'let your clothes always be freshly washed' (9: 8), and (the sentence that ends the passage) 'no advantage in the trained charmer' (10: 11).

Segal articulates her accusations against patriarchal society more sharply and clearly than any of the other women writers; however, she is not so very far removed from the rest of the Hebrew maskilot. Indeed, not every woman who wrote in Hebrew at the time had a revolutionary feminist consciousness, but it is also clear that the women who wrote in Hebrew were not content with being confined to an intellectual Ladies' Gallery. The women who wrote in Hebrew at the end of the Haskalah period made a conscious effort to appropriate the 'fathers' speech' and to participate in the circles of the maskilim and in the literature and public life of the Haskalah.

I have defined the works of the maskilot as 'women's writing' not simply because of the sex of the authors but also because of the characteristics of their texts, since these texts reveal both their conscious need for a means of authentic female expression and their ability to create one. On the basis of this new understanding it is now possible to change the historical description of modern Hebrew literature in two areas:

Haskalah literature and the Haskalah movement. Women should be seen as members of the Haskalah movement and their writing in Hebrew as an integral part of Haskalah literature. This changes our picture of the entire subject. The Haskalah movement, like most social and cultural movements of its time, was truly a 'masculine' phenomenon in terms of its goals and characteristics. However, as we have seen in this chapter, not only did educated women attempt to participate in the production of Hebrew Haskalah literature, but their writing has specific characteristics typical of the women writers of their time. Hence, a proper understanding of Haskalah literature will include the writings of these women, with their particular characteristics. Women's writing presents a different way of depicting women, culture, and society. It suggests its own ways of presenting the feminine and feminist protest in literature. By comparing the writings of men and women of this period we may discover the unique gender differences: the masculine elements of the canonical Haskalah literature and the feminine aspects that were novel and innovative.

The development of modern Hebrew literature. It is clear that writing by women who were fully conscious of their femininity and wanted to express it in a literary form began some decades earlier than is commonly believed. It is in the works of Rachel Morpurgo, rather than the four women poets of the early twentieth century who wrote in Hebrew—Rahel Bluvstein, Esther Raab, Elisheva, and Yokheved bat Miriam[95]—that we should see the first stage of women's Hebrew poetry, with many of its distinguishing characteristics. While women's prose fiction has its first real embodiment in the writings of Deborah Baron, there were already visible precedents in the conscious literary writings of the maskilot of the previous generation.

[95] On these poets, see Miron, *Imahot meyasdot, aḥayot ḥoregot.*

Literary feminism, too, began with the writings of these maskilot, rather than the better-known Baron or Nehama Pukhachevsky.

In this chapter I have attempted to restore the writings of the maskilot to their rightful place in the history of the both the Haskalah movement and modern Hebrew literature. It is my belief that reading their works, and the writings of the Haskalah in general, as gendered will give us a more complete understanding of this period and its literature.

Sins of Youth, Guilt of a Grandmother: M. L. Lilienblum, Pauline Wengeroff, and the Telling of Jewish Modernity in Eastern Europe

SHULAMIT S. MAGNUS

Pity my small world, destroyed before my eyes, which I am incapable of repairing.

(M. L. Lilienblum, *Ḥatot ne'urim*)

The conversion of my children was the most grievous blow that I suffered in my life. But the loving heart of a mother can endure so much. I forgive, and lay the blame on us parents.

(P. Wengeroff, *Memoirs of a Grandmother*)

THE nineteenth century was many things for the Jews of eastern Europe, but it was surely a time of writing. There was an explosion in types of genres and in the sheer volume of what was produced. This was true within both major groups of the religious world, the hasidim and the mitnagedim, as well as in the latter's offshoot, the Musar movement, all of which had distinct literatures and readers as well as institutions in which particular texts formed a curriculum and a canon. The Haskalah, or Jewish Enlightenment, the first secular movement of eastern Europe, produced its own vast corpus of writing. There were searing essays critical of the practices, beliefs, and the very authority of the traditional Jewish community, and calls for intellectual and economic reform. There were biting satires and fiction:

This is for Liba, daughter of Leah Juda and Salomon Grossman, whose memory is a blessing, with love and gratitude.

My work on Wengeroff has benefited over the years from discussions, suggestions, and critical readings by Ruth Sporer, Edie Gelles, Steven Zipperstein, Paula Hyman, Michael Stanislawski, Marion Kaplan, Shmuel Feiner, and David Assaf, who have my thanks. I, of course, bear sole responsibility for what I say here. This article is based on my unabridged, critical edition of the memoirs of Pauline Wengeroff, to be published by the University of California Press, and a work in progress entitled 'A Woman's Enlightenment: Pauline Wengeroff and the Voice of Jewish Modernity'.

short stories, novels, and poetry. There was history and, not least, memoir and autobiography.

Published as books or as entries in maskilic journals, themselves an innovation in their nature and breadth, Haskalah literature, produced mostly in Hebrew but also in Yiddish and, eventually, in Russian as well, blazed new terrain in the consciousness of Jewry. Despite traditionalist opposition and tsarist censorship, there was unprecedented communication, linking Jewish writers in the Pale of Settlement with one another, with those of Germany, in particular, and with intellectual currents in Russia and Europe, all of which accelerated the pace and radicalized the content of social change in Russian Jewish society. By the end of the century there was a plethora of Jewish nationalist and socialist alternatives as well as a strident Orthodoxy girded for battle against a veritable sea of infidels. All these streams competed through writing in an extraordinarily vigorous marketplace of ideas. The very languages of Jewish eastern Europe—Hebrew, Yiddish—were transformed in the course of their new uses in the torrent of literary output that marked Jewish modernity in eastern Europe and, indeed, can be considered one of the defining characteristics of the age.[1]

Of Haskalah literature, autobiography has garnered particular interest, in its own time and since.[2] The personal nature of the probing and the revelations, from communal and family feuds to sexual impotence, guaranteed as much, as was of course the intent. Probing the self, charting evolving consciousness, was to serve the goal of ruthlessly honest self-knowledge and personal growth, one of the central tenets of the movement. Publication of such probing, of course, had other implications. Maskilic autobiography, however, was not merely an exercise in self-absorbed exhibitionism, though the narcissism of its authors is at times breathtaking. This genre was also intended to serve programmatic purposes by illustrating through the drama of frustrated and failed lives the bankruptcy and depravity of the social order

[1] On the literature of the Haskalah, see the classic works of Y. Klausner, *Historiyah shel hasifrut ha'ivrit haḥadashah* (Jerusalem, 1955) and *Kitsur toledot hasifrut and ivrit ha hadashah* (Tel Aviv, 1934); M. Waxman, *A History of Jewish Literature*, vols. iii and iv (New York, 1945, 1947); and I. Zinberg, *A History of Jewish Literature* (Cincinnati, 1978), vols. xi–xii. On the uses of Yiddish and Hebrew in this period, see N. Seidman, *A Marriage Made in Heaven* (Berkeley, 1997), and I. Parush, *Nashim korot: Yitronah shel shuliyut baḥevrah hayehudit bemizraḥ eiropah bame'ah hatesha-esreh* (Tel Aviv, 2001), which also treats Jewish (women's) uses of other languages during the Haskalah. See, too, Y. Slutsky, *Tenuat hahaskalah beyahadut rusyah* (Jerusalem, 1977), 64–7, on attitudes to the Russian language.

[2] See Zinberg, *A History of Jewish Literature*; S. Vilnai, 'Darkhei ha'otobiyografyah bitekufat hahaskalah', *Gilyonot*, 17 (1945), 175–83; S. Werses, 'Autobiography During the Haskalah Period', in his *Trends and Forms in Haskalah Literature* (Jerusalem, 1990); A. Mintz, 'Guenzburg, Lilienblum, and the Shape of Haskalah Autobiography', *Association for Jewish Studies Review*, 4 (1979), 71–110; id., *'Banished from their Father's Table': Loss of Faith and Hebrew Autobiography* (Bloomington, Ind., 1989); M. Moseley, 'Jewish Autobiography in Eastern Europe: The Pre-History of a Literary Genre', Ph.D. thesis (Oxford University, 1990); D. Biale, *Eros and the Jews* (New York,1992), 149–75; M. Graetz, 'Autobiography: On the Self-Understanding of the Maskilim', in M. Meyer (ed.), *German Jewish History in Modern Times* (New York, 1996), vol. i.

run by 'benighted, sanctimonious obscurantists' (to cite Peretz Smolenskin), that the Haskalah came to reform or later, in more radical versions, to uproot.[3] The men who wrote autobiography also composed essays and reviews; some wrote fiction and poetry as well. But self-reflection and self-revelation were suited, as were no other types of expression, to reach the masses of the yet unconverted through recognition. No longer would Jewish youths suffer as atomized individuals the outrages of arranged early marriage, primitive religious teachers, superstition masquerading as faith, and frustrated desires for larger horizons, broader education, European learning. Through the shock of seeing their own lives, the most personal intimacies, writ large in those of others (whatever the differences in particulars), they would recognize that their misery was systemic—cultural. It was not this or that marriage match that was at fault, not the felicity (or lack thereof) of the families into which they were wed, or born; not fortune, in other words, but social forces, humanly forged and capable of being forged differently. Such a radical perception, going to the guts of (intended male) readers through tales of woe they would find startlingly familiar, would surely ignite a current of opposition to the social structures producing the misery and swell the ranks of the Haskalah. At the very least, it would stimulate interest in the other kinds of explicitly programmatic writing by the maskilim, where solutions to the misery were offered.

Of all the nineteenth-century autobiographies of east European maskilim, those of Mordecai Aaron Guenzberg, Abraham Ber Gottlober, and Moshe Leib Lilienblum are the most prominent, with Lilienblum's the 'central one of the generation'.[4] Lilienblum's *Hatot neurim* ('The Sins of Youth') is an epic tale of one maskil's life from his teens into his thirties, as he fought the battles of Jewish modernity. It is a dizzying story chronicling several abrupt and drastic reversals of position on central issues: religious beliefs; educational and economic programmes to revitalize Russian Jewry; the efficacy of Haskalah itself; the right Zionist project.[5] Lilienblum assumes each dogmatically and self-righteously, only to reject it just as rigidly in

[3] Smolenskin, cited in S. Feiner, *Haskalah and History*, trans. C. Naor and S. Silverston (Oxford, 2002), 318, and in id., *Haskalah vehistoriyah* (Jerusalem, 1995), 431.

[4] Vilnai, 'Darkhei', 180. Mintz (*'Banished from their Father's Table'*, 25) calls Lilienblum's 'the monumental autobiography of the Haskalah period', to which, of all the maskilic autobiographies, 'and perhaps [to] it alone', modernists returned as a 'living and inspiring text' (Mintz, 'Guenzberg', 74). Solomon Maimon's *Lebensgeschichte* (Berlin, 1793) was the first in the genre of maskilic autobiographies, but Maimon, who died in 1800, having left Poland for Germany as a youth, pre-dated the east European Haskalah and the modernization of Jewry in eastern Europe. His work was a pivotal model, even a paradigm, for later maskilim, but is clearly in a different category from those of the 19th century mentioned here: Mordechai Aron Guenzberg's *Avi'ezer* (Vilna, 1863), Avraham Ber Gottlober's *Zikhronot miyemei ne'urai* (Warsaw, 1881, 1886), and Lilienblum's. There were many other autobiographical works by maskilim, some quite brief, e.g. by Mr. Letteris, Eliezer Zweifel, Rashi Fuenn, and Y. L. Gordon, but those of Guenzburg, Gottlober, and Lilienblum are the closest to a maskilic canon in their prominence and influence.

[5] Lilienblum's shifts of position on Zionism are to be found in his autobiographical sequel *Derekh teshuvah* (Warsaw, 1899), on which see further below.

favour of the new position, with no articulated perspective on the meaning of the changes in his thinking.

This pattern of reversal is so striking a feature of Lilienblum's writing that his mental stability, or at very least his emotional maturity, seem very much in question. Yet in fairness, this very inconstancy, this erratic quality, well evokes the confusion of an age when those Jews who did not simply accept tradition and wish its unquestioning perpetuation considered a bewildering set of unprecedented possibilities to better the Jewish situation—culturally, economically, politically—but lacked a way to assess the efficacy of any of them. Lilienblum was not the only maskil to change his position radically on basic tenets of the Haskalah; several prominent maskilim reversed themselves on the 'women's question' in Jewish society, renouncing in the 1860s and 1870s the critical positions they had articulated decades earlier, arguing for parental authority and even arranged marriage.[6] Beginning in the 1860s, the movement was riven into camps of 'moderates' and 'radicals' on such questions as the place of Hebrew, the role of scholarship in Haskalah, and religious reform. As Shmuel Feiner notes, the radicals lost faith in the century they were living in well before the pogroms of the 1880s, a sharp departure from the optimism that was a hallmark of Haskalah since its inception in Prussia in the late eighteenth century.[7] Lilienblum belonged to both camps over the course of his life, but obviously, if there were 'camps', he had company. This very instability and divergence of opinion was one of the chief weaknesses of the Haskalah against the claims of hoary, allegedly unchanging, 'tradition', which had been with (and traditionalists argued, responsible for the survival of) the Jews in the long years of their improbable survival in exile.

The Haskalah in eastern Europe lasted from the early nineteenth century into the 1890s, a far longer duration than the movement in German lands.[8] The very longevity of the Russian movement virtually guaranteed that it would change rather than be a fixed set of ideas and ideals. It also meant that more than one generation of Jews grew up with Haskalah and that generational conflict, even literary parricide by younger maskilim over the direction and the meaning of 'enlightenment' itself,

[6] See S. Feiner, *Eros, erusin, ve'isurim* (Jerusalem, 1998), 275–87.

[7] Feiner, *Haskalah and History*, 288. On the crisis of maskilic ideology in the second half of the 19th century, see M. Stanislawski's biography of Judah Leib Gordon, *For Whom Do I Toil?* (New York, 1988).

[8] On the nature and duration of the German Haskalah, see M. Meyer, *German-Jewish History in Modern Times* (New York, 1996), i. 261–380. On the beginnings and development of Haskalah in Russia, see M. Stanislawski, *Tsar Nicholas I and the Jews* (Philadelphia, 1983), 49–122; for a study of an important centre where Lilienblum spent a formative period, see S. Zipperstein, *The Jews of Odessa* (Stanford, Calif., 1985), and id., 'Remapping Odessa', in his *Imagining Russian Jewry* (Seattle, 1999). While, as Stanislawski notes (*For Whom Do I Toil?*, 6), 'the essential issues articulated by the Haskalah, its basic quest for educational, social and religious reform of the Jews', continued to preoccupy east European Jews 'until the end', in Russia the sense was widespread at the century's end that 'the days of the Haskalah are behind us', in the words of a radical maskil in 1897, a view shared by Ahad Ha'am and Micha Joseph Berdichewski; cited by Feiner, *Haskalah and History*, 346, 348.

would emerge, besetting the later Haskalah, just as revolt of the first generation of maskilim against their fathers, biological and cultural, had beset traditionalist society in the early decades of the century.[9] To be sure, Jews did not just generate change but were buffeted by change coming at them from the outside, as one of the memoirs discussed here, that of Pauline Wengeroff, makes dramatically clear: government policy to the Jews underwent many abrupt shifts over the course of the Haskalah, periodically leaving Jews—traditionalist and modern, in turn—reeling.[10] Lilienblum's autobiography definitely reads like that of a mercurial and unstable man, but it was a mercurial and unstable age.

The complexity of the problems and the unknowns with which maskilim and their adherents were faced in this era was enormous. Acculturate to the non-Jewish world, yes, but how much and where to draw limits? What aspects of traditional culture were to be retained and how could a new Jewish culture be created? How could a Jewish identity be 'sold' to a younger generation accustomed (in the 1860s and 1870s) to educational opportunity in Russian institutions and contemptuous of an increasingly ineffectual Jewish community?[11] How to assess the intentions of the government and respond to its policies as well as to the schemes of Russian social theorists? Given this complexity and the inevitability of mistakes about what the writers considered the most important issues of their age, regret and nostalgia, guilt and blame are to be expected in autobiographical retrospectives by maskilim.

Lilienblum's work is one of the major statements of Jewish modernity, conveying the pathos of one who struggled with his age and himself. The memoirs of Pauline Wengeroff are another. Wengeroff, born Pessele Epstein in 1833 in Bobruisk (in Belarus, an area Jews called Lithuania), produced an extraordinary retrospective on the age of Haskalah in her *Memoiren einer Grossmutter* ('Memoirs of a Grandmother'). Composed in 1898, when that age had come to a close, the memoirs richly depict traditional Jewish society and family life in Russia, including the ritual world of women, the unravelling of this society during the nineteenth century, and the devastating impact of this dissolution on families and, especially, on women.

[9] See Feiner, *Haskalah and History*, 306–40. Feiner cites 'ferment and rethinking' among the maskilim particularly during the reign of Alexander (p. 339). On the Oedipal aspect of the first generation of maskilic assertion, see Biale, *Eros and the Jews*, 149–75, and id., *Power and Powerlessness in Jewish History* (New York, 1987), 87–117. See also Feiner, *Mehaskalah loḥemet lehaskalah meshameret* (Jerusalem, 1993).

[10] On 19th-century tsarist policy towards the Jews, see Stanislawski, *Tsar Nicholas I and the Jews*; id., 'Russian Jewry, the Russian State, and the Dynamics of Jewish Emancipation', in P. Birnbaum and I. Katznelson (eds.), *Paths of Emancipation* (Princeton, 1995); H. Regger, *Jewish Policies and Right-Wing Politics in Imperial Russia* (Berkeley, 1986); J. D. Klier, *Russia Gathers her Jews* (DeKalb, Ill., 1986); id., *Imperial Russia's Jewish Question, 1855–1881* (Cambridge, 1995); and B. Nathans, *Beyond the Pale: The Jewish Encounter with Late Imperial Russia* (Berkeley, 2002).

[11] On the weakening of Jewish communal authority in this era in which government policy had a direct hand, see Stanislawski, *Tsar Nicholas I and the Jews*, 123–54, and A. Schohat, 'Hahanhagah bekehilot rusiyah im bitul ha-"kahal"', *Zion* (1979), 143–223.

Wengeroff's writing is extraordinary in many ways. It is not a mere chronicle of her life, though this would have been important in itself given the dearth of such statements from women of this (or any previous) era of Jewish history. Rather, Wengeroff presumes to tell her life through the biography of an era, and the story of an era through the biography of her life. This assertion of microcosm–macrocosm is conveyed in the full title of the memoirs, whose subtitle is *Bilder aus der Kulturgeschichte der Juden Russlands im 19. Jahrhundert* ('Scenes from the Cultural History of the Jews of Russia in the Nineteenth Century'). Wengeroff omits some very basic personal and family data and, unlike the memoirs of the maskilim, does little probing of Self. A highly astute social observer and a gifted writer who carefully crafts her narrative, Wengeroff instead weaves personal narrative, cultural and anthropological description, and selective historical contextualization to create a powerful statement on the period and perhaps the most dramatic treatment of personal experience of a major historical event before the memoirs of the Holocaust.

In Wengeroff's case, the personal is also female and this makes her work the more extraordinary. Wengeroff does not claim to write a 'cultural history of Jewish women in the nineteenth century' (an unimaginable focus, certainly for anyone who wished to be published), but a cultural history of the Jews—yet she does this through the lens of female experience, hers and (she says) that of other Jewish women. In refracting an entire age in Jewish history through female perceptions and experience, Wengeroff's memoirs are unprecedented in the annals of Jewish literature. The now famous memoirs of her literary forebear Glikl Hamel (1646– 1724) were originally intended purely for private, family consumption. They are certainly a rich source of information about Jewish society as a whole and about women's religion, economic activities, and familial roles in her time, but this is not because Glikl presents them in this way or for this purpose. Readers must seek other sources with which to identify the court Jews (including women) mentioned in Glikl's writing, much less appreciate their actions or those of other women, including Glikl herself. Glikl does not write with a historical perspective on either her times or herself as an author. The former view is precluded by the reigning religious outlook, which saw Jewish existence in the Diaspora as theological rather than historical, as a state of 'exile because of sin, awaiting divine redemption'. The latter view is precluded by a profound, gendered piety, which could not admit the notion of a woman pronouncing publicly about anything. Glikl does not write from the perspective of women; of *a woman*, yes, but purely an individual, again, with the expectation that no one outside her family would read her.[12] Wengeroff writes with a radically different perspective.

Portrayals of traditional Jewish family life and women are central features of the autobiographies of the maskilim, with their depictions of tyrannical, conniving,

[12] On Glikl and her writing, see N. Z. Davis, *Women on the Margins* (Cambridge, 1995), 5–62, 215–16. Glikl's work was first published by D. Kaufmann under the title *Die Memoiren der Glickel von Hameln, 1645–1719* (Frankfurt am Main, 1896); its best English translation is B.-Z. Abrahams, *The Life of Glickel of Hameln, 1646–1724; Written by Herself* (London, 1962).

sadistic mothers-in-law and clutching, suffocating wives. Lilienblum himself provides much material here. The maskilim made reform of the Jewish family, of Jewish marriage patterns, and, to a lesser extent, of Jewish women's education, main planks in their reform programme. There certainly are in maskilic memoirs (and in fiction) portraits of women, including in Lilienblum's writings, even an adored 'modern' type of woman, the incomparable 'N' of his unconsummated obsession. (Of course, there are also rich portraits of men—of male behaviour and male culture, traditional and maskilic—but the maskilim do not look upon men as gendered. Women are Other, men are simply Jews.) But making portrayals of women prominent in a narrative does not mean telling a story through a female lens, and this is precisely what Wengeroff does.[13]

Despite several requisite and unconvincing demurrals in both volumes about her unworthiness and surprise that anyone would find her work interesting—this, after she had peddled the first volume with determination and notable success—Wengeroff's writing, in marked contrast to Glikl's, is suffused with a sense (albeit, deterministic) of history, and with ego, testimony to its modern spirit.[14] Women are not unconscious backdrop but prime subjects (if not agents) in the drama of Jewish modernity. Wengeroff's memoirs are a rich source of information about women in traditional and modernizing Jewish societies, a treasure trove of detail about their childhood, informal and formal education, socialization, dress, religious rituals and outlook, and acculturation. They provide extremely important insight into arranged marriage, that staple of maskilic grievance, from the perspective of the brides (Wengeroff and an older sister). But they do more than record women's experience (or rather, to be sure, Wengeroff's representation of it). They make women's experience central to the tale of emerging Jewish modernity and to grasping what Wengeroff asserts is the fundamental tragedy of modern Jewish history: the loss of traditional Jewish culture. This catastrophe, she insists, illustrating with tragedies of her own life, is a consequence of women's loss of power in the modern Jewish family, and thereby in modern Jewish culture, and a consequence of the arrogance and short-sightedness of modernizing Jewish men.

[13] On depictions of women in maskilic writing, see T. Cohen, 'Reality and its Refraction in Descriptions of Women in Haskalah Fiction', in S. Feiner and D. Sorkin (eds.), *New Perspectives on the Haskalah* (London, 2001),144–65; id., *Ha'aḥat ahuvah veha'aḥat senuah* (Jerusalem, 2002), and S. Feiner, 'Ha'ishah hayehudit hamodernit, mikreh mivḥan beyaḥasei hahaskalah vehamodernah', *Zion*, 58 (1993), 453–99. On the very different subject of women as consumers and producers of literature in this era, see Parush, *Nashim korot*. In his poem 'Kotso shel yud', one of the Haskalah's most searing and important statements on the position of women in traditional Jewish society, Yehuda Leib Gordon, as Biale notes (*Eros and the Jews*, 160), writes from the perspective of the woman. On this classic poem, see Stanislawski, *For Whom Do I Toil?*, 5, 95, 104, 125–9, 140, 202, 210, 213–14. On the history of the Jewish family, see S. Cohen and P. Hyman (eds.), *The Jewish Family* (New York, 1986), and D. Kraemer (ed.), *The Jewish Family* (New York, 1989).

[14] On Wengeroff's determined efforts to get her work published, see my 'Kol Isha: Women and Pauline Wengeroff's Writing of an Age', *Nashim korot* (2004), 30–1, and my forthcoming work (see n. 17 below).

Wengeroff's narrative, then, does three things with regard to women, gender, and Russian Jewish modernity. It gives precious information about women; it accords their experience unprecedented historical importance; and it provides a gendered account of Jewish modernity, making the story of relations between men and women, and of modern, radically altered rules of gendered behaviour, central to understanding Jewish modernity. For all her omissions, at times so significant they amount to distortion, Wengeroff's memoirs are not fragmentary recollections. Rather, they are a systematic, chronological, and thematic treatment of Jewish modernity from the time of her birth to the 1890s—*the* years of the heyday of Haskalah up to its decline—with a clear, if not abstract, theory about what went wrong: women's loss of cultural power and the Jews' progressive deracination. In terms of culture, the fate of women in modernity and that of 'the Jews' was synonymous: loss, with the two in a causal relationship.

The audacity of this coupling is breathtaking, but so is the very existence of nineteenth-century 'memoirs of a grandmother'. As men, the maskilim were heirs to a tradition of elite male writing. They themselves came from the circles of this elite, having all had traditional yeshiva education; some, like Lilienblum, having been groomed for the rabbinate. They were rebels against this world and suffered persecution for their rebellion, but the issue was which men would control official Jewish culture; that men did so was a given. Maskilic writing drew from and stimulated that of other maskilim, cross-fertilization they assiduously encouraged in media they created and controlled. With a very few, if highly significant, female exceptions, the entire burst of publication mentioned above—the enormous expression that defined the age—was male.

As a woman writer in the nineteenth century, Wengeroff had absolutely no such context. On the contrary, she had to counter embedded, explicit cultural norms that discounted women's intellectual capacities even as consumers, let alone producers, of the fruits of intellect. The act of forthright, public pronouncement by a female out of such a context is therefore quite remarkable. While it is clear that Wengeroff did not emerge full-blown from her own head, an impression casual reading of her memoirs, with their lack of any cited precedent for her work (such as Glikl, whose memoirs were published for the first time two years before Wengeroff says she began to write hers), might convey, neither did she have anything approaching an institutional context, much less support, for her writing, whose audacity, therefore, is the more noteworthy.

In this chapter I wish to lay these two epic narratives of Russian Jewish modernity, Lilienblum's and Wengeroff's, side by side and see what the juxtaposition can tell us about that era and the act of writing about it. The possible objections to such a juxtaposition are manifold: the two authors and their narratives are so different as to preclude comparison. Lilienblum wrote self-consciously as one of the more important members of a movement, citing the precedent of the memoirs of earlier maskilim, especially Guenzberg's *Aviezer*, as inspiration and foundation for his own. By the time Lilienblum published *The Sins of Youth*, in 1876, he was a public figure known for essays, letters, and reviews, published especially in *Hamelits*, one of the foremost organs of Haskalah expression, but in *Hakarmel*, another maskilic journal, as well. Wengeroff, too, published before the appearance of her memoirs: a Russian-language version of what would become volume I of the *Memoirs* appeared in *Voskhod*, the most important Russian-language Jewish periodical of its time, in 1902.[15] But clearly, there is no comparison in terms of their output or audience. We know of Wengeroff because of her memoirs; she was no public figure. Lilienblum's memoirs would also be significant in their own right, as testimony to this convulsive era, but the connection in his case between personal experience and public role is surely part of their interest and importance.

Lilienblum was severely critical of traditional Jewish society. Wengeroff evokes that society with love and nostalgia, and scathingly criticizes certain practitioners of Haskalah—those who ran maskilic schools—for badly mishandling their mandate.[16] We know who Lilienblum's intended and actual audience was: maskilim and would-be (or perhaps we should say should-be) maskilim. Wengeroff's intended audience is harder, though not impossible, to identify. One thing about which we can be absolutely certain is that it was not her grandchildren, of whom she mentions not one, nor her children—the four she records, that is, not the three she omits—with whom (especially the girls) she is clearly furious. While I am convinced that Wengeroff's intended audience was broad (as opposed to familial) from the beginning, she, unlike he, did not have a ready, ideologically identified readership.[17] Wengeroff appears to write entirely retrospectively (in fact, she kept a diary which she cites in the memoirs and, like Lilienblum though to a far lesser degree, cites letters from the time of events she depicts), while Lilienblum's account has the ring

[15] Published in two parts in October and November 1902. I learned of the existence of this material from C. B. Balin, *To Reveal our Hearts: Jewish Women Writers in Tsarist Russia* (Cincinnati, 2000), 2–3.

[16] See P. Wengeroff, *Memoiren einer Grossmutter. Bilder aus der Kulturgeschichte der Juden Russlands im 19. Jahrhundert*, 2 vols., vol. i (Berlin, 1908), vol. ii (Berlin, 1910), ii. 181, 183, for important observations about the poor quality of instruction by teachers of Judaica in both state and Jewish-run schools. All translations of this work are mine.

[17] The question of Wengeroff's intended and actual audience is beyond the scope of this chapter; I treat it in my forthcoming work, an unabridged translation of and commentary on Wengeroff's memoirs, in which context I discuss her complex relationship to her children and her husband. I explored the complicated and crucial question of Wengeroff's omissions in my 'Of Myth and Memory: Pauline Wengeroff's Cultural History of Russian Jewry in the Nineteenth Century', paper presented at the Conference on Memory and the Invention of Jewish History, Meyerhoff Center, University of Maryland, College Park, 14 Apr. 2002, and do so more fully in my 'Kol Isha', and in my forthcoming edition of Wengeroff's memoirs. Scattered but crucial information about Wengeroff's other children is in the memoirs of one of her grandchildren, Nicholas Slonimsky, *Perfect Pitch: A Life Story* (Oxford, 1988), esp. pp. 1–50; see also n. 27 below. For family information, see my 'Pauline Wengeroff', in P. Hyman and D. Ofer (eds.), *Jewish Women: A Comprehensive Historical Encyclopedia* (Jerusalem, forthcoming). Cf. *Rememberings*, trans. H. Wenkart (Bethesda, 2000), an abridged translation of Wengeroff's memoirs with other changes to the original, esp. the afterword by B. Cooperman, on which see my 'Kol Isha'.

of close contemporaneity to the events he describes, which lends them a particular air of authenticity.

Not least, Lilienblum wrote in Hebrew, one of the hallmarks of Russian maskilic autobiography and a clear sign that the maskilim (all of whose mother tongue was Yiddish, universally denigrated in maskilic circles) saw themselves as continuing an elite (male) intellectual tradition.[18] Their use of Hebrew for autobiographical and other writing was Hebrew's first sustained foray into the secular domain and itself constitutes one of the more significant cultural developments of Jewish modernity.[19]

Wengeroff, like the vast majority of Jewish women, knew how to read and understand at least some of the Hebrew of the prayers (she inserts translations and commentaries to some of them in moving sections about the meaning of the high holy days), but was not educated to a level that enabled her to compose in that language. She wrote largely in German, with some phrases in Yiddish and Hebrew, and a few in Polish. A strict construction of 'Haskalah' would omit Wengeroff from a discussion of its memoir literature, as indeed, has been the case. While scholars of this period know of her memoirs and cite them as a source for a variety of things, the memoirs themselves have never been admitted into the canon of nineteenth-century Russian Jewish writing about self and era, tradition and enlightenment.[20]

There are solid reasons for considering maskilic autobiography a genre of its

[18] All works on the Haskalah discuss the language question; see esp. Seidman, *A Marriage Made in Heaven*, and M. Weinreich, *The History of the Yiddish Language*, trans. S. Noble and J. Fishman (Chicago, 1973, 1980); Slutsky, *Tenuat hahaskalah beyahadut rusyah*; and Stanislawski, *For Whom Do I Toil?*

[19] The Berlin Haskalah began using Hebrew but switched to German before petering out; see Meyer, *German-Jewish History in Modern Times*.

[20] See S. Ginsburg, *Historische Verke* (New York, 1937), ii. 82–90, who interviewed Wengeroff at the end of her life; M. Beregovksi, 'Yidishe klezmer, zeiner shafn un shteiger', *Sovetish*, 12 (1941), 412–17; E. Steinman (ed.), *Brisk delita* (Tel Aviv, 1954), 294; S. Leichter, 'Toledot hakehilah hayehudit beminsk', 'Zikhronoteiha shel savta miska'it, polina vengrov', and 'Tenuat ḥibat tsiyon beminsk uvasevivah', in S. I. Shoshan (ed.), *Minsk, ir va'em* (Tel Aviv, 1975), 31, 172, 200–1; see also p. 651; L. Greenberg, *The Jews in Russia: The Struggle for Emancipation* (New York, 1976), i. 57, 62. More recent scholars have often cited Wengeroff. See the many references in M. Levin, *Arkhei ḥevrah vekalkalah be'ide'ologiyah shel tekufat hahaskalah* (Jerusalem, 1975), which uses Wengeroff extensively to illustrate various points about Jewish culture and society in this era; Biale, *Eros and the Jews*, 156, which asserts, erroneously, that all her children converted and that her memoirs are a 'lament' directed at her grandchildren (see n. 27 below, and my forthcoming work for a full treatment of her intended audience); Balin, *To Reveal our Hearts*, 2–3; Feiner, 'Ha'ishah hayehudit', 289 n. 133; Parush, *Nashim korot*, 20, 136, 167, 177–8, 252, 287, 293, 294, 299; Nathans, *Beyond the Pale*, 89, 128 n. 13, 147–8, 234. The earlier works use Wengeroff as a source of cultural history or folklore; more recently, the fact of her writing is also noted. Lucy Dawidowicz, *The Golden Tradition* (New York, 1967), 160–8, was the first to translate Wengeroff into English and introduce Wengeroff to a wide audience since her own times. Dawidowicz's focus in the excerpts she chooses to translate is on Wengeroff's sons' 'quest for education' (i.e. on Wengeroff's sons). None of these scholars situates Wengeroff's writing in the context of 19th-century Jewish writing about self and era in a time of radical social transformation, or explores Wengeroff's complex attitudes to modernity, as well as tradition.

own. Without disregarding these, I wish to broaden consideration of that literature, and Wengeroff's writing, by considering Lilienblum's and Wengeroff's works together. Maskilic autobiography has stamped our impression of traditionalism and Haskalah, of youth and coming of age in this era, to such an extent that we fail to see how atypical or even how male these accounts are.[21] Wengeroff's, to be sure, is no more typical, if for no other reason than that she came from a very wealthy family, her father, a building contractor to the government, having also attained an advanced level of talmudic learning beyond the means and intellectual abilities of most Jewish men.[22] Obviously, writing, much less publishing, memoirs was no typical female pursuit—and I have repeatedly characterized Wengeroff's as extraordinary. But most Jewish men did not write memoirs either. Typicality, then, is not the criterion for judging either of these narratives (or the genre of maskilic memoirs) significant. Yet in the case of maskilic memoirs, the very fact of articulation against the silence of the vast majority of Jews and, equally crucially, the attribution of significance to them by contemporaries and by scholars, has created an impression of normativeness. We have before us dramatic, explicit tales of the odyssey from traditionalism to modernity: this is 'the story'.

Seeing the clear differences in the account of tradition and its demise between Wengeroff's narrative and those of the maskilim, in this instance, Lilienblum, adds a critical nuance to our understanding of this period, which can no longer be depicted simply as one of 'Oedipal rebellion'—that is, of maskilic (or male) experience writ large on Jewish society as a whole. That impression of course, is one the maskilim very much wished to convey: a teleological path leading the Jews from obscurity to Enlightenment, with them, persecuted heroes, leading the way. But it is not one historians can adopt uncritically and Wengeroff's account offers a serious counterpoint, not because she simply opposed Haskalah—she didn't—but precisely because she shared and lived out many of its core values. In this, her memoirs are in a different category from the Yiddish-language memoirs of Yekhezkel Kotik (1847–1921), which are extremely rich testimony to the culture of the shtetl and the transformations of this age, but which are not written with enlightenment per se as a lens.[23] Wengeroff and Lilienblum, her younger contemporary by ten years, wrote

[21] See my 'Pauline Wengeroff and the Voice of Jewish Modernity', in T. M. Rudavsky (ed.), *Gender and Judaism: The Transformation of Tradition* (New York, 1995); on male issues in maskilic autobiography, see Biale, *Eros and the Jews*, who notes the success of 'this admittedly small movement of writers . . . in defining tradition and in creating a set of images that dominates the discourse of Jewish sexuality to this day' (p. 151).

[22] On Wengeroff's father, see my 'Pauline Wengeroff and the Voice of Jewish Modernity' and 'Kol Isha'.

[23] See D. Assaf (ed.), *Journey to a Nineteenth-Century Shtetl: The Memoirs of Yekhezkel Kotik*, with notes and introd. (Detroit, 2002). In Kotik's memoirs the defining issue is his own conflict regarding hasidism and mitnagedism; there are particularly rich depictions of relations between Jews and non-Jews, especially with Polish lords. Kotik devotes substantial space to 'recollection' of events that occurred well before he was born and so, unlike Wengeroff, notes that memory was not his strong suit. As Assaf says, Kotik's 'real interest' as a memoirist lies in 'documenting his family history, in re-

of traditionalism and the passage to modernity with an explicit, central focus on Haskalah, as they each understood and experienced this, their perceptions moulded pivotally by gender. Both hone their tales so that their narrative is oriented to specific purposes. What they each have to say about their lives and era enriches our reading of the other.

Wengeroff's writing specifically throws open the question of gender in the experience and telling of Russian Jewish modernity and, in doing so, puts the writing of the maskilim in fresh relief. We cannot but notice that her memoirs are by a woman, not only because of her title (what other status could she possibly have claimed for herself as an author?), but because of the rarity of female voice. Juxtaposed to hers, we see more clearly that maskilic accounts do not depict the emergence of Jewish modernity, but the peculiar odysseys of certain extraordinary men. Juxtaposition removes the veil of gender invisibility that so marks maskilic writing, a veil that is the unconscious prerogative of the privileged gender. While Wengeroff's memoirs (despite her claims) cannot be said to speak for the experience of women in this era any more than Lilienblum's (or that of other maskilim) can be said to speak for men, both represent signally important accounts by the articulate minority of Jews in this period who were able to and for complicated reasons chose to write about the Jewish passage from traditionalism to modernity.

THE TALES OF TWO MEMOIRS

The structures of Lilienblum's and Wengeroff's narratives are fundamentally different and, in themselves, say much about their respective purposes. Wengeroff's has two volumes, the first of which evokes the years of her childhood, from earliest consciousness until her mid-teens (roughly, 1835–46). The bulk of it richly details a year's cycle of Jewish festivals in her parents' home. It is here that we get the rich depiction of female ritual and piety, her mother's especially, but also that of a class of women who are semi-official religious functionaries, serving other women. She describes girlhood in traditional society; her pranks, friendships, and not least, given the centrality in maskilic autobiography of depraved, incompetent *melamedim* (elementary school teachers), her induction into a girl's *ḥeder*, run by a kindly, impoverished *melamed*, accorded respect at her learned father's table. Report of a *ḥeder* for girls at this time (the 1830s), something Wengeroff records with no special note, is significant in itself. Girls in the Pale, we often assume and are sometimes told explicitly, did not have avenues for formal education at this time and were educated solely at home.[24]

creating the shtetl life that was . . . in portraying different personalities', in the course of which he uses his imagination and occasionally 'spout[s] absurdities', writing 'with artless naiveté' (p. 84); see further characterization of the limitations of Kotik's writing style, ibid. 85.

[24] On the education of girls and women in the Pale in the 19th century, see E. Adler, 'Educational Options for Jewish Girls in Nineteenth Century Europe', *Polin*, 15 (2002), 301–10, who notes: 'Traditional Jewish historiography evinced little interest in this subject partly because of the assumption

There is an extremely important, substantial section on the disruptive effects in her family and in the larger society of the first phase of organized Haskalah: Max Lilienthal's government-sponsored tour of the Pale in 1841–2 to promote educational reform. Not surprisingly, the importance of this part of her memoirs was recognized from the time Wengeroff first circulated volume I of her memoirs for publication.[25] Significantly, the disruption she portrays is not only intergenerational, with young people of both sexes violating various norms and seeking outside worlds, but also between her parents—with her father more culturally open (to be sure, up to distinct limits) and her mother steadfastly hostile to Haskalah and ominously suspicious of change. This is her first mention of a gender disparity about enlightenment.[26]

Finally, Wengeroff includes several sections on decrees under Nicholas I that traumatized the Jews: one, forcing the Jews of Brest-Litovsk (or Brisk, as Jews called it), a commercial and administrative centre to which her family had moved when she was an infant, to move to a new part of town in order to make way for the building of a fortress. Wengeroff portrays the harrowing disinterment of the Jewish cemetery, the Jews transporting the remains for reburial to prevent their desecration in the building project. Much personal hardship and financial loss, including to her father's business, resulted from the move, and her description of the misery, especially of poor Jews, is very gripping. Wengeroff also describes the impact of Nicholas's decree that forced Jews to give up traditional Jewish dress (described in detail) in favour of European fashion. In sum, volume I is a very rich evocation of the period as lived by people: a personal and family memoir that is also, indeed, cultural history.

Volume II is devoted to the story of Pessele's engagement in 1848 and marriage to Chonon Wengeroff of Konotop, Ukraine; Chonon's loss of faith while on pilgrimage to his *rebbe* and his progressive estrangement from tradition; the birth of

that girls received no education' (p. 103); D. Weissman, 'Bais Yaakov: A Historical Model for Jewish Feminists', in E. Koltun (ed.), *The Jewish Woman* (New York, 1976); P. Hyman, *Gender and Assimilation in Modern Jewish History: The Roles and Representation of Women* (Seattle, 1995); S. Stampfer, 'Gender Differentiation and Education of the Jewish Woman in Nineteenth-Century Europe', *Polin*, 7 (1992), 63–87; and A. Greenbaum, 'Ḥeder habanot uvanot beḥeder habanim bemizraḥ eiropah lifnei milḥemet ha'olam harishonah', in R. Feldhay and I. Etkes (eds.), *Ḥinukh vehistoriyah* (Jerusalem, 1999). On the *ḥeder* and the maskilim, see S. Zipperstein, 'Transforming the Heder: Maskilic Politics in Imperial Russia', in A. Rapoport-Albert and S. Zipperstein (eds.), *Jewish History* (London, 1988), and id., 'Reinventing Heders', in his *Imagining Russian Jewry*. On Jewish education in general in this period, see G. Abramson and T. Parfitt (eds.), *Jewish Education and Learning* (Chur, 1994).

[25] Gustav Karpeles, the editor of German-speaking Jewry's most important journal, *Allgemeine Zeitung des Judentums*, and one of Wengeroff's most important backers, underscored the importance of her depiction of Lilienthal's tour of the Pale in a letter to Wengeroff, dated 25 Jan. 1906, repr. in vol. 2 (1910), 3–4. On Karpeles, see my 'Kol Isha'.

[26] Wengeroff does not note this in recording the conflict, which is consistent with her (non-)treatment of gender as a dividing line in traditional society, quite unlike her treatment of modern Jewish society. On this, see my 'Kol Isha'.

children; and their wanderings in and outside the Pale (they lived for a time in a fort in Helsinki and in St Petersburg) while Chonon sought and largely failed to achieve business success. Wengeroff's portrayal of acculturating and assimilating, as well as traditional, Jews in the Jewish communities in which they lived is an invaluable portrait of Russian Jewish society in transition in the 1850s and 1860s. Wengeroff cites Chonon's aspirations and frustration in the context of the cultural changes of the time as the backdrop to his crude, cruel coercion of her to relinquish her observance—her marriage wig and, most traumatic, her kosher kitchen. She writes of her tormented inability to pass on Jewish traditions to her children and the children's (specifically two sons') choice of secular education and career opportunity over Judaism to the point of the latter's conversions.[27]

It is here that Wengeroff asserts that her personal tragedy—conversion, of course, considered worse than death and an unimaginable failure for a woman like her, raised in a deeply pious home—is to be put squarely in the context of the culture of the 1860s and 1870s (when, scholars now agree, assimilatory pressures were at a peak because of the then-liberal policies of Alexander II). And it is here that Wengeroff asserts that Jewish men as a class mindlessly abandoned tradition, while Jewish women as a class struggled to maintain it—not as unenlightened obscurantists (the maskilic portrait of their wives)—but while also affirming the best of European culture. This 'best' was not fickle values, such as fashion, whose superficiality Wengeroff contrasts with the dignity and significance of traditional Jewish dress, but weighty ones, such as literature and science. Women, she says, were capable of such a fusion; men, incapable of moderation, were not. Indeed, Wengeroff portrays the Jewish men of her time (only once qualifying this with a reference to specific class and region—the concessionaires of White Russia[28]) as hypocrites, who preached liberal ideas—'liberty, fraternity, equality' (*sic*)—outside the home, while behaving like despots within it, towards their wives.[29] Against the desperate wishes of these wives, they not only purged the home of any meaningful Judaism (pale reflections, which she describes with contempt, remained to mock her memories of the rituals of her youth), but forced them to desist from participation in the family livelihood, despite their experience and (in her case, she asserts, superior) ability.

By the 1880s, as cultural wreckage lay all around them, even Chonon regretted his rashness, shamed by the conversion of his eldest son (she does not record his reaction to that of the second) and by his own collusion in the assimilation of others. 'Ach!' she records him remarking after one of their dinner parties, 'sixty Jewish children sat here together and ate *tref*!'[30] By the end of his life Chonon was a

[27] Another child, an unrecorded daughter, also converted—two of Wengeroff's striking omissions; in all, three out of seven of her children converted. In the memoir, she speaks only of the conversions of her two sons (and mentions only four children). See above, n. 17.

[28] Wengeroff, *Memoiren einer Grossmutter*, ii. 114.

[29] Ibid. 136.

[30] Ibid. 215. Cf. the striking musing of Ahad Ha'am in the 1880s, which Steven Zipperstein characterizes as a semi-autobiographical 'elegy' to traditionalism lost and to urban ennui: 'During those long

respected banker in Minsk and member of its city council—extraordinary achievements. Appropriate to their station under the bourgeois ethic, both Chonon and Pauline became civic Jews, supporting Jewish artists, and especially founding and staying actively involved with two trade schools for impoverished Jewish boys and girls, respectively. The food in these schools was kosher (unlike that in their own home); the sabbath and other festivals were observed; there was religious instruction. Wengeroff makes a point of saying that the mishnaic tractate *Pirkei avot* was taught to the girls at her initiative.

Volume II evokes the trauma and horror of the era of pogroms, the growing antisemitism of the streets and of officialdom. Her sons convert, she explains at length, when their brilliant paths are blocked in the 1880s by anti-Jewish quotas in the universities. Chonon dies in 1892 after delivering an impassioned address, despite illness, to the Minsk City Council on behalf of the city's Jews who were wrongly over-assessed for municipal works. The memoirs end abruptly, with a distraught account of his death and with the final, seemingly surprising pronouncement that Chonon, despite having 'disregarded many Jewish practices in his life . . . loved his people, Israel'.[31] Six years later, she says, she gathered her yellowed pages of preserved materials—letters, diary entries—and, sitting 'under an oak tree on a small bench in the woods' outside Minsk, began sorting her memories, 'the wish stirring in me', she says in one of several places where she states different motives for writing, 'to record for my children all that I had lived through, as a remembrance of their mother'.[32]

The opening and closing of the memoirs of self-conscious, purposeful authors, as Wengeroff and Lilienblum both were, are very significant. They are signature statements that encapsulate the author's intent and summarize her or his fundamental message. Thus, it is highly significant that Wengeroff's opening section—the first we hear about the life of a 'grandmother'—is a loving, powerful evocation of her father's early morning religious devotions, before she proceeds to one of the chief themes of volume I: the order and 'calm' that, she repeatedly asserts, pervaded her parents' home. It is equally telling that she also closes the volume with a loving depiction of the sound of her father's study and prayer. The narrative of her childhood is bracketed with the reassuring tropes of tradition.

'I was a tranquil child, deeply moved by every happy and sad event,' Wengeroff begins her preamble to volume I, introducing herself as narrator of memoirs by

winter evenings, at times when I am sitting in the company of enlightened men and women, sitting at the table with *tref* food and cards . . . suddenly then . . . before me is a very old table with broken legs, full of tattered books, torn and dusty books of genuine value, and I'm sitting alone in their midst, reading them by the light of a dim candle . . . and the whole world is like the Garden of Eden' (cited in Zipperstein, *Imagining Russian Jewry*, 84).

[31] Wengeroff, *Memoiren einer Grossmutter*, ii. 220. Wengeroff quotes the Maggid of Minsk speaking these words at Chonon's funeral, but, of course, it is she who records them for us, obviously approvingly (I would say, desperately).

[32] Ibid. 29.

stating her credentials, and yet a different motive for writing than the one we just saw above:

Many incidents are imprinted in my memory like wax, so that I remember them even now with perfect clarity. Indeed, what happened is fresh and alive before me as if it were yesterday. With every passing year, my need to record my experiences and observations grows, and now this rich material that I have gathered provides me with the most beautiful and consoling hours of my life, which, in old age, have become so lonely. They are joyous hours for me, when I take my notes in hand and often, with a silent teardrop or a restrained smile, leaf through them. Then I am no longer alone, but in good and beloved company. Before my mind's eye, seven decades full of turmoil and stress march past as if in a kaleidoscope and the past becomes living present: a joyful, carefree childhood in my parents' home; in later years, more serious scenes of sorrow as well as joy from the lives of the Jews of that time, and so many scenes from my own home. These memories help me over lonely, difficult hours and over the bitter disappointments of life, from which no one is spared.

Wengeroff entitles the first section of volume 1 'A Year in My Parents' House', a house whose pleasant physical appearance she describes with the touch of an artist: yellow exterior and green shutters, Venetian window, flower garden, surrounding wooden fence. A fitting site for the family life within it, which was 'as in other Jewish homes' in the first half of the nineteenth century, 'very peaceful, pleasant, earnest and sensible . . . harmonious', she asserts.

Lilienblum, in stark contrast, opens his memoir with a section entitled 'The Days of Chaos', with the blunt sentence 'After my father divorced his first wife without giving her her *ketubah* [financial divorce settlement] because she had stayed overnight in the house of a Gentile without supervision, he married a second wife, and after five years with her, their first and only son was born to them, the author of this book.'[33]

If this were not enough to establish Lilienblum as anti-hero and to rip any mists of nostalgia off the past, he proceeds to contrast his father's extensive rabbinic lineage and hopes that Lilienblum himself would follow in this path with the reality that emerged, observing sardonically: 'To what degree the merit of his rabbinic and wealthy forebears successfully disposed his efforts to make me great in Torah and fear of sin, the reader [who, of course, was well aware of what Lilienblum had become] will see below.'

Lilienblum then turns to his main first task: depicting the cruelty and depravity of traditional Jewish society. He was taken at the tender age of 4 to his grandfather's *ḥeder*, where, after quickly learning the Hebrew alphabet, he was initiated to the study of Bible—with Leviticus (the *ḥeder*'s standard initiating curriculum). By the

[33] M. L. Lilienblum, *Ḥatot ne'urim* (Vienna, 1876), 9; translations are my own unless otherwise noted. I thank Jeffrey Green, Jerusalem, for graciously providing me with a copy of his unpublished translation of this work, written in often torrid Hebrew, full of biblical and rabbinic allusions, and borrowing heavily from traditional forms of *melitsah*, all of which makes the work a considerable challenge to English translation.

age of 10 he had begun lessons in Talmud and soon proceeded to its commentaries. His mother died that same year despite an amulet to ward off evil, but he barely noticed this since his father, a man then 40 years old, quickly married his deceased wife's 16-year-old sister. As for secular study, there was a school in Lilienblum's town (Kėdainiai, near Kovno), which some Jewish boys even attended, but his father thought it madness to send his only son, destined to become a great rabbi, to the gymnasium to learn things any Talmud scholar can pick up effortlessly in the bathroom. 'Secular' knowledge was imparted by his father and grandfather, who tutored him in astronomy, using traditional sources marbled with fables and fantasies.

Having impugned traditional society within four pages of opening his narrative, Lilienblum condemns the first crime it commits against young boys, including himself:

[The] education . . . [that] is the cause of the dreadful, dark folly that haunts my townsfolk to this day . . . Robbed of childhood [an oft-repeated plaint in this and other maskilic autobiographies], I was imprisoned in my study room all day . . . not allowed to enjoy the pleasant days of . . . youth . . . my strength . . . not nurtured in freedom and childish games . . . deprived of all knowledge of any subject not connected with Talmud study . . . my head clouded with awful nonsense . . . filled with corrosive poison . . . They did not even teach me the letters of the Gentiles' alphabets . . . I did not even know how to distinguish Russian from Polish print.[34]

But this crime is swiftly followed by the next: arranging a marriage match for him when he was 14 years old. Lilienblum learned of this when his father woke him one morning with news that his 'mother-in-law' was on her way, news that the boy thought a joke. He was roused from this illusion with the news that the bride was 11. His objections made no difference and shortly thereafter there was an engagement ceremony where he beheld a 'little girl who looked to me as if she were three years and a day old': his intended. The wedding was set for three years hence, during which time Lilienblum was to continue his rabbinical studies. The wedding actually took place when he was 15 and she, 13, after which, Lilienblum moved to Vilkomir (Ukmergė), where his in-laws lived, to be supported by them while he continued yeshiva study.[35]

Lilienblum proceeds to his wedding within a few pages of the opening of his memoirs. His pithiness here is in marked contrast to the overdrawn, overwrought repetition that marks (and mars) much of the rest of the book, which goes on for almost 300 more pages (not including the later memoir, *Derekh teshuvah* ('The Path of Repentance'), which he appended to *The Sins of Youth* in 1899). Lilienblum is succinct in the initial section of the book, summarizing his education and referring readers to Guenzberg's autobiography for details because, he says, the traditional education of Jewish boys is the same, but especially because his individual story

[34] Lilienblum, *Ḥatot ne'urim*, pt. 1, pp. 15–16.

[35] Ibid. 33. This was the traditional system called *kest*, in which one or both sets of parents supported a young couple for several years after the marriage to enable the groom to study Talmud.

does not matter. What is crucial is that the mistakes which 'wove' the fabric of his life, mistakes by his 'fathers' and by himself (which have so aged him that, at the age of 29, he writes as if his life were over) be made known so that others can profit. 'This is why I write the story of my life,' he says, in a book whose subtitle is *Vidui hagadol* ('The Great Confession') (a play on a central piece of Jewish liturgy for the Days of Awe).[36]

He describes the progressive disintegration of his faith in almost obsessive detail, like a pathologist delineating the stages of a disease.[37] Lilienblum is a rationalist by nature and fairly early on negates supernaturalism, at least in rabbinic sources, for which tendency he readily finds precedence in such traditional sources as Maimonides. Then, though, on the eve of Yom Kippur no less, he suddenly radically questions the very existence of God. In an unsystematic way, lacking a teacher, Lilienblum reads maskilic literature, which intensifies the process of questioning.[38] The autobiography is at its best in Lilienblum's depiction of his anguished struggle against his own heresy: a 'civil war within my heart'.[39] For all the vaunted optimism of the Haskalah, the loss of this innocence is no joyous moment, an important point that can get lost in discussions of maskilic writing, and Lilienblum's work is eloquent testimony to its pain. The death throes of traditional faith, in Lilienblum's case, go on for nine conflict-ridden years, as he attempts to stem his relentless slide into negation by ever more zealous immersion in traditional study. God laughs at him—uproariously, it would seem—when he has a nocturnal emission during the night of Yom Kippur after returning from some of the most solemn prayers of the year. (This is considered a particularly heinous event in general and, on that day, a most ominous portent for the new year to come.)

Persecution by traditionalists, including his mother-in-law, for his 'Berlinish' tendencies ensues, and description of it is another major element of the memoir: the cruelty, stupidity, and hypocrisy of his tormentors and his steadfast resistance to pressure and threats. But his struggles over faith continue and broaden—the Talmud, he concludes, is a human product of its time—even as he continues traditional study and fathers three children. He is soon considered a full-fledged heretic and entitles the second period of his life 'Days of Heresy'. He also begins to critique the alleged lack of Jewish economic productivity, another mainstay of the maskilic indictment of traditional Jewish society, influenced by the critiques of Russian positivism. Men, in this view, are wasted in pursuit of largely useless learning with which they are unable to support themselves and their families. (In his case, as in

36 Lilienblum, *Ḥatot ne'urim*, 22.

37 On areas of compression and detail in Lilienblum, see Mintz, 'Guenzberg, Lilienblum, and the Shape of Haskalah Autobiography', 79–80.

38 Aside from Guenzberg, he mentions Isaac Ber Levinsohn, *Hamagid*, Nachman Krochmal, Shumel David Luzzatto, and *Hamelits*.

39 Jeffrey Green's felicitous translation of Lilienblum's 'milḥemet penimit bekerev libi', his MS, fo. 220; Lilienblum, *Ḥatot ne'urim*, 132.

that of the learned elite in general, his mother-in-law and wife earned the family's livelihood.) Filled with self-contempt, he resolved to become a *melamed* or a shopkeeper (without secular education, there is nothing else he can do), but is hounded by his persecutors, who impeach his credentials as a religious teacher and promote boycotts of his mother-in-law's store. Yet, this very critique soon turns upon Haskalah, another body of learning that stresses the literary and has no practical application. What are poems to nature or odes to Hebrew but secularized *pilpul* (convoluted talmudic argumentation with no practical use)? Lilienblum's tendency to critique not only that which he opposed but also that which sustained him, clearly emerges: where could he turn if, having spurned hasidism, as did all maskilim, both the yeshiva world and Haskalah are also false?[40]

Significantly, despite heresy, Lilienblum remained observant in his behaviour. It was his articulated views and, even more, the fact that they were promoted by an organized movement, that made him an intolerable threat. These connections, whatever his criticisms of them, were also his lifeboat. After an article of his about the nature of Talmud and contemporary rabbinic authority caused a scandal, his maskilic friends from other towns rallied around him. (He reproduces letters and telegrams from them in his narrative.) They want to know how he is, all the details; they will fight for him if anyone dares to harm him. (He was threatened with economic and religious boycott, with expulsion; he was hounded when walking the streets—women, we should note, as well as children, taking the lead in this.) Most importantly, the maskilim, as well as their opponents, knew that the Russian government might enter into the fray on the side of the maskilim, which indeed, it did, through the government-appointed rabbi and an official. The rabbi was pressured by both sides but finally backed Lilienblum, who was neither expelled nor agreed to leave voluntarily; the official, too, backed Lilienblum. Nothing could more clearly convey the modern context of this heresy (as compared, for instance, with that of Uriel Da Costa in seventeenth-century Amsterdam, who cracked under similar tactics, unmitigated by any alleviating counter-force), or the crucial importance of the fact that Lilienblum had an active social context for his personal travails, comrades in arms, and a common ideology that sustained them all.

And a woman he loved. Not his wife, of course, but N, whom he meets in 1869 in Vilkomir, and with whom he carries on a correspondence for years, his letters, and extensive summaries of hers, reproduced in the autobiography. N, an enlightened young woman fluent in German, advocate of Haskalah, is a crucial character in his story.[41] She is the exemplar of what Jewish womanhood, freed from traditional

[40] Lilienblum was influenced in this phase of his ideological wanderings by N. Chernyshevsky's *What Is To Be Done?*; Feiner, *Haskalah and History*, 275. On radical maskilic critiques of Haskalah pedantry (and other shortcomings), see S. Feiner, '"Keyonek hanoshekh shedei imo": Posthaskalah bekets hame'ah hatesha-esreh', *Alpayim*, 21 (2000), 59–94, and id., *Haskalah and History*, 274–340.

[41] On the identity of N, see Mintz, *Banished from their Father's Table*, 34–5, and Feiner, 'Ha'ishah hayehudit', 293–4.

shackles, could be, and evidence that romantic, as opposed to arranged, coupling could have been possible for Lilienblum, if not for the benighted practices of his father and mother-in-law and the culture that spawned them. N, too, writes supportively to Lilienblum, an ally in spirit, if also the source of torment to him, a married man with children, mired in a traditionalism he cannot completely escape because he lacks secular education, and in a Haskalah which serves only to make him more aware of his misery. Still, Lilienblum has two critical sources of support: his male allies in the Haskalah, including its great poet Yehudah Leib Gordon, and his romantic alliance.[42] Indeed, Lilienblum records revelling not only in his triumph over his persecutors, but in the fact that he could share it with others.[43]

Lilienblum's friends soon suggest that he leave for Odessa, at Russia's southern frontier and city of seemingly unbounded horizons. There he would become 'a European man': finally receive a gymnasium education (qualifying for it through tutoring and self-study), and build a new life.[44] This means leaving his wife and children for years, about which Lilienblum expresses some sorrow and responsibility (he does consistently send his wife some of his meagre earnings), but which clearly gives him no serious pause. (Indeed, Lilienblum later records hearing about the deaths of two of his children, pointedly noting the moderation of his response, although one of these children, he also records, was sufficiently attached to him to have wept at his departure.) It also means leaving N. (He meticulously records and analyses the details of their final moments in a marvel of self-absorption.) Lilienblum enters another pivotal phase of his life in 1869. It is at this turning point that he resolves, at the age of 29, to write his memoirs, and he ends their first part with his departure for Odessa. He closes with an ode to hope. In Odessa, he, a prematurely married man, will recover the years of adolescence that his father had stolen from him.

Within a month, however, Odessa becomes the site of crushing disillusionment. Lilienblum's economic struggles continue; he does not find sponsors committed to subsidizing his maskilic remaking, as his in-laws had done to make him a rabbi. He is revolted by the materialism, crassness, and libertinism of the Jews of the city, who are freed of restraint in this place lacking even the remnants of a pre-modern *kehilah*, but who also lack enlightenment—knowledge of Hebrew, for instance. Lilienblum soon speaks of his former life as the good old days and comes to see faith in book-learning as a solution to his or other Jews' economic problems as absurd. Practical knowledge—studying medicine, surveying, bookkeeping, mechanics—makes sense, yet he has spent seven years 'dreaming dreams' in a state of 'drunkenness'.[45] Material change—betterment in Jewish political status, in standard of living—must precede and will be the basis for cultural change.

The Jews, he also realizes, are not the only people in need of internal reform. Other societies—including supposedly enlightened France (this, well before the

[42] On Gordon, see M. Stanislawski, *For Whom Do I Toil?*

[43] *Ḥatot ne'urim*, pt. 1, p. 116.

[44] See Zipperstein, *The Jews of Odessa*.

[45] *Ḥatot ne'urim*, pt. 2, p. 124.

Dreyfus affair)—are as corrupt and hypocritical. All is not rosy, in other words, in the Europe worshipped by maskilim. For the Jews, religious reform, in particular, is imperative because religion is the repository of their culture. There must be a loosening of gratuitous stringencies, a living connection 'between religion and life', so that the younger generation, who have the option and are increasingly electing it, will not abandon Judaism altogether. Religious leaders must take the initiative for the sake of Judaism itself, so that the culture is not lost. As early as 1870, not tradition but assimilation is Lilienblum's demon.

Odessa, however, seems to augur the Jewish future, and Lilienblum is haunted by the spectre that Jews and Judaism will disappear within a century. He is haunted, too, by the emptiness of his own loss of faith, which has now also manifested in behavioural infraction. Having skipped the Passover *seder*s in 1872, Lilienblum uses plays on the classic *seder* liturgy to write of poetry and prose and of the two once-sacred evenings, now robbed of their poetry: 'This night, which was once a Night of Watching and full of the highest poetry, was now an utterly prosaic night, like all other nights. But I am alive and I love poetry, yet where is my poetry? How terrible is this memory and how bitter the prosaic idea!'[46]

Moses-like, Lilienblum ceremoniously records completing his own 'biography', even while continuing to write, and sums up his life (at the age of 31) a failure and a mass of frustration.[47] Having been educated to be a great rabbi, he has become 'a slave in a commercial house' (where he eked out a living). Educated 'on illusion, to fear of sin and observance of commandment', he remains oppressed by that education even after illusion has been dispelled, able neither to live among the dead of his traditional studies nor to function among the living. Reared to family life, his spirit is far from this lifestyle. 'Pity my small world, destroyed before my eyes, which I am incapable of repairing!', he laments. In the end, Lilienblum writes in a concluding section, there 'shall be no reparation for the sins of my youth', which were several, some committed by him, others by his father. His father's were depriving him of a 'decent' education that would have made him fit to function in the world, and marrying him off as a child. His own sins derived from those of his father: He sought 'chaotic enlightenment' and allowed himself to become besotted with N (with whom he had broken off, having never intended to realize the relationship by divorcing his wife and marrying her). He did not correct what his father had wrought. His sojourn in Odessa only compounded his errors. Despairing, he finishes his 'eulogy of my life'. His only hope is that fathers and sons will read and learn from it.

Lilienblum's autobiographical sequel, *Derekh teshuvah* ('The Path of Repentance'), was published at the very end of the century, a year after Wengeroff says she began to write her memoirs. It brings his story through 1882, after the pogroms that shook Russian Jewry, of which he gives a harrowing account. Despite its distinctive features, Lilienblum clearly understood it as part of his autobiographical statement;

[46] Ibid. 111. [47] Ibid. 125.

he makes repeated reference to it as presenting the culmination of *The Sins of Youth*, something its title also announces.[48] The sequel shows that age does not confer emotional stability on Lilienblum, whose choppy course continues as he pursues European education (despite all he has said about this), making progress in Russian, German, science, and mathematics. He manages this despite ongoing financial difficulty and the fact that his wife joins him, against his will, with their children, several more of whom are born, burdening him further.

Although Lilienblum had already expressed deep concern about Jewish assimilation, in this segment of the autobiography Zionism per se is at centre stage. Neither tradition nor enlightenment is any longer his preoccupation. It is not Jewish activities, cultural or economic, that is the source of their problems, but Jewish alienness.[49] Jewish survival, which for Lilienblum is possible only in a new kind of Jewish society and in a revived Land of Israel, is now the core of his being.[50] He has found a new mission; significantly, his mood changes radically. 'The stony burden that had lain on my heart for so long has completely fallen away,' he writes. 'My eyes shine, my spirit soars, I am another man. The dew of rebirth has fallen on me again and it has melted the fearful ice that covered my heart for so many years.'[51] Most astonishing, he claims to have made peace with all the 'sins' that plagued him and has wiped the slate clean.[52] He is no longer angry about the education his father gave him, having corrected it with his studies. Had he not received that earlier education, 'I would not be what I am today.' Lilienblum does not make a similar statement about his personal life and those 'sins', but the note on which he chooses to end his narrative is almost absurdly upbeat, and certainly triumphant.

WHAT IS ENLIGHTENMENT?

Pauline Wengeroff uses the term 'enlightenment'—*Aufklärung*—to refer to a specific programme of cultural reform in Russian Jewry. Thus, in her first volume, under the chapter heading 'The Beginning of the Period of Enlightenment', she gives a detailed account of Max Lilienthal's tour of the Pale and the proposed educational changes that were at the very heart of Haskalah. In the second, she records telling (as she calls them, tragicomic) scenes of her brothers-in-law stealing time from Talmud study to read forbidden books hidden in the folios of the sacred texts and secretly conducting scientific experiments, to the grief of her mother, who spies

[48] The front page of *Derekh teshuvah* announces it as 'part three' (*Ḥatot ne'urim* is divided into two parts); at the end of *Derekh* (pp. 48–9) Lilienblum writes, 'After *Ḥatot ne'urim* ['Sins of Youth'], comes *Derekh teshuvah* ['The Path of Repentance'].' See Mintz, *Banished from their Father's Table*, 29–32, 45–50, on the relationship between the various parts of Lilienblum's autobiographical writings.

[49] *Derekh teshuvah*, 48. Lilienblum claims to have cracked the mystery of modern antisemitism using an analysis in fact originated by Leo Pinsker (Lilienblum's colleague in the Hovevei Zion (Lovers of Zion) movement), in the latter's famous essay *Autoemancipation* (1882). Indeed, the final section of *Derekh* shows the deep (and unacknowledged) influence of Pinsker's analysis.

[50] Ibid. 33–5.

[51] Ibid. 47; trans. J. Green, his MS, fo. 83.

[52] Ibid. 49, 51.

on them, sure that no good has or ever will come from Lilienthal's visit. In a section entitled 'Second Stage of the Enlightenment', she refers to Moses Mendelssohn, his Bible translation and philosophical works, and to the epithets—'Berliner', 'heretic' (*apikores*)—attached to the 'young spirits' (gender: masculine) who followed in his path in the Russian Pale during the 1840s.[53] She notes the proximity of 'Berlinism' to Lithuania and the ease of its transmission to the area of the Pale where she and her family lived, and cites 'L[eon] Mandelstamm', the first Jew to attend a Russian university, who, she says, followed Mendelssohn's example and translated the Bible into Russian. Thus, Wengeroff was well aware of the intellectual content and trajectory of Jewish 'enlightenment', in its German place of origin and in Russia.

However, Wengeroff also writes of changes in Jewish behavioural norms, such as dress and social customs, that are part of 'enlightenment', giving the term a social meaning as well: sisters who attempt to don European fashion, stroll with a husband on the sabbath, or meet a (selected) groom before the wedding, all of which are decisively quashed by both parents. In Wengeroff's experience, then, 'enlightenment' is not only an intellectual affair confined, we would note, all but exclusively to an elite of men. Its ripples and resonance are far broader than this, a judgement supported by contemporary scholarship.[54] Moreover, when Chonon had his radical loss of faith (whose causes, she says, he never shared with her), she records that he immediately manifested this in infraction of prescribed appearance as well as religious practice: a trimmed rather than the full beard of traditional male Jewish practice, a cultural signal of such unambiguous meaning that both she and his parents argued strenuously with him about it.

Although Wengeroff does make maddeningly brief mention of Chonon having entertained 'free ideas' some two years before his fateful trip to his *rebbe*,[55] from all she tells us (would that we had his memoirs), Chonon's odyssey was nothing like Lilienblum's. An intelligent man, Chonon was no intellectual driven by a relentless thirst for enlightenment. Rather, he was driven by desire for material success and recognition, and by a great chafing to be outside the confines of the traditional Russian Jewish world; I sense that he held himself up and competed against the example of Wengeroff's wealthy and successful father and paternal grandfather, as well as the small but conspicuous cohort of Jewish men of his generation who were achieving success, including Wengeroff's brother-in-law, the banker Avram Sack. In Wengeroff's depiction, Chonon and other Jewish men like him confused enlightenment with licence for unbridled self-absorption and self-indulgence. It is this—not enlightenment per se—that leads to disaster. Wengeroff, in short, does

[53] Wengeroff, *Memoiren einer Grossmutter*, ii. 14.

[54] See Zipperstein, *The Jews of Odessa*; Hyman, *Gender and Assimilation in Modern Jewish History*, esp. pp. 50–92; and M. Kaplan, *The Making of the Jewish Middle Class* (New York, 1991), which focuses on Germany and shows in exquisite detail how modernity for most Jews was expressed in behavioural and attitudinal, if not ideological, change.

[55] Wengeroff, *Memoiren einer Grossmutter*, ii. 98.

not write in uncritical defence of Jewish traditionalism nor in blanket condemnation of enlightenment. On the contrary, she, like some of the most prominent maskilim, writes in defence of enlightenment *properly understood*, and against what the latter termed 'false enlightenment'.[56] This and much else situates Wengeroff solidly in the maskilic camp, not as a practitioner of Haskalah, as Lilienblum and his colleagues were, but as a conscious consumer of Haskalah, a discriminating sympathizer.

It is quite clear from Wengeroff's depictions of her sisters' attempts to don European-style clothing, especially, to be able to stroll in public with a husband, and meet a groom before the wedding, and from her emphasis that she herself was able not only to meet her (selected) groom at the engagement formalities but spend time alone and correspond with him, that she disapproved of strictures against this and considered them unessential to Judaism. (She does cite these incidents as admirable examples of parental authority, the likes of which she is never able to wield with her own children about matters far more weighty.) Aside from the formal Jewish education she received, Wengeroff tells us that she was tutored in Russian and German (tutoring arranged, it should be stressed, by her mother). Her pious parents, then, held to a broad norm in the middle and wealthy classes of traditional Jewish society that allowed girls, but not boys, to learn European languages and to read literature and study such arts as music (since it would not detract from their Torah study, which was forbidden to girls). She reports that, as a young bride, she read a great deal, mostly in Russian but in German as well, and cites well-known authors, including the heroic staple of enlightened German-speaking Jews, Schiller.[57] Thus, some of the core expressions of enlightenment were not forbidden fruit to her as they were to her brother, brothers-in-law, and Lilienblum. This may well be the source of her and other women's alleged ability to be moderate with regard to tradition and enlightenment and a clue to male inability to situate similarly between these poles.

As we have seen, Wengeroff threw the liberal ideals of the French Revolution in the face of Jewish husbands who failed to practise them at home as they (allegedly) did in society. She did not reject these ideals; she wished them more, not less, broadly applied. Furthermore, this dichotomy—'home' and 'abroad'—that she cites, saying that she and other Jewish women were ready to 'allow' their husbands liberty outside the home in return for being allowed to maintain traditions within it, clearly shows familiarity with the famous poem of Y. L. Gordon 'Awake My People', with its line 'Be a man abroad and a Jew in your tent.' Gordon's poem was published in 1864, just as her family troubles were reaching their peak with her

[56] On maskilic critiques of 'false enlightenment', see S. Feiner, 'The Pseudo-Enlightenment and the Question of Jewish Modernization', *Jewish Social Studies*, 3/1 (Fall 1996), 62–88, and his 'Keyonek hanoshekh shedei imo'. On defining 'Haskalah', see Feiner, 'Towards a Historical Definition of the Haskalah', in S. Feiner and D. Sorkin (eds.), *New Perspectives on the Haskalah* (London, 2001).

[57] Wengeroff, *Memoiren einer Grossmutter*, ii. 97.

older children reaching adolescence, when Wengeroff, we surmise, would have been casting about for a modern rationale for her desperate desire to maintain tradition at home.[58] What better possible support than the poet laureate of Haskalah?

Wengeroff says that she and other women wished to impart 'the ethics of Judaism, the traditions of its faith, the solemnity of the sabbath and festivals, Hebrew, the study of the Bible'—a maskilic curriculum if ever there was one—'together with the lessons of European Enlightenment and the innovations of west European culture'. In introducing the 'Beginning of the Era of the Enlightenment', in volume I, she speaks of the 'great reforms under Tsar Nicholas I [that] brought about the spiritual, yes, even the physical regeneration of the Jews in Lithuania', and she goes on to editorialize:

> Whoever, like me, lived between the years 1838 and today, took part in all the religious battles in the family life of Lithuanian Jewry, and finally observed the great progress made, must express his admiration for the idea of that reform legislation and bless it. Indeed, you must speak of it enthusiastically if you compare the generally uncultivated, poor Jews of the forties with Lithuanian Jewry of the sixties and seventies, among whom today there are so many men of such perfect European refinement, who have outstanding accomplishments in the most diverse fields of literature, science and art, and who do not lack honours and titles from the outside world.[59]

To anyone familiar with Tsar Nicholas I's reputation among the masses of Russian Jews—he was feared and detested for his cantonist policy, which targeted young boys for a lifetime of army service, for conversion, and often, for death—this praise and the failure to qualify it by mention of Nicholas's responsibility for decades of grief is jarring, indeed.[60] But it is not the only such expression. When Wengeroff tells of her family's forced move from Old to New Brest, she opens the chapter with what can only be described as girlish flutters (this, from an elderly woman recalling the 1830s), as she details how handsome Nicholas and the tsarevich were when they came to survey the site for their new fortress. Her title for this chapter is 'It Was

[58] On the poem, see n. 13; see Wengeroff, *Memoiren einer Grossmutter*, ii. 136, where she herself characterizes the 'double life' she was proposing as an untenable solution.

[59] Wengeroff, *Memoiren einer Grossmutter*, i. 118.

[60] Wengeroff, of course, like every Russian Jew, knew of Nicholas's cantonist policy and of the grief and devastation it brought to Jewish society. As a married woman, she encountered a former cantonist living in Helsinki, and used the recollection of that encounter as the occasion to describe the cantonist episode and record Yiddish folklore about the trauma of that era; ibid. ii. 155–60. (For an excellent treatment of the cantonist era and its ravaging effects on Jewish society, see Stanislawski, *Tsar Nicholas I and the Jews*.) It is very telling, however, that she does this in vol. ii of her memoirs, not in vol. i, which covers the years in which the cantonist horrors actually occurred. Her father's wealth and relationship to the regime clearly put her own brother outside the reach of the cantonist conscription and allowed Wengeroff's emotional distancing in writing about it. She fails not only to criticize Nicholas I, but even to attribute the cantonist policy to him. The elderly cantonist she meets was in Helsinki—outside the Pale, that is—because this was a privilege awarded to them (and other exceptional Jews, like herself and Chonon), making Nicholas seem benevolent.

a Pretty Picture'.[61] Wengeroff does, as we have noted, depict the cruel effects of several of Nicholas's edicts, including the forced relocation from Old Brest. Never, however, does she criticize him for them. More significantly, she never impugns Haskalah—which Nicholas backed decisively and aggressively, his support proving pivotal in transforming a loose confederacy of persecuted mavericks into a movement—for its association with him. Rather, she refers to the 'great reforms' Nicholas propagated and the marvels of scientific and cultural attainment that these wrought in 'uncultivated' Lithuanian Jewish society. This—paeans to Nicholas—we do not get from Lilienblum even at the height of his Haskalah 'illusion' and 'drunkenness'.[62] Indeed, only the first generation of maskilim, a minuscule group of Jews indebted to Nicholas's policies and delusional about his supposedly progressive intentions, spoke of him in the way Wengeroff does.

Finally, we recall Wengeroff publishing in *Voskhod*, the most important Russian-language Jewish periodical, whose editorial slant was decisively pro-acculturation, though, equally decisively, against assimilation,[63] and the fact that she published her memoirs not in Yiddish, her native tongue and the language reviled by maskilim, but in German, the language of 'enlightenment'.[64]

Wengeroff, then, neither came from an obscurantist background, nor was she of this bent herself. The testimony she offers about wanting a combination of Judaism and European culture is made credible by many other details she provides, beginning with her childhood. Brest, where Wengeroff spent her formative years (unlike Konotop, where Chonon grew up), was an important city at the intersection of several major roads, where businesspeople, whom historians of the Haskalah have shown often carried cultural as well as material wares, came and went. Her brother and brothers-in-law were part of a circle of young maskilim in town.[65] Her father, she says, returned from synagogue with news of Max Lilienthal's imminent arrival—already understanding what this meant.[66] Indeed, Wengeroff tells us that her pious father himself was a sharp critic of traditional Jewish educational practices, sharing

[61] Wengeroff, *Memoiren einer Grossmutter*, i. 147.

[62] Wengeroff also lavishes praise on Alexander (ibid. ii. 129–30), though this attitude was much more common among Jews and understandable given his liberal policies, not least his abolition of his father's cantonist policy.

[63] See 'Voskhod', in *Encyclopaedia Judaica* (Jerusalem, 1971), xvi. 225–7; Waxman, *A History of Jewish Literature*, iv. 609; Greenberg, *The Jews in Russia*, ii. 63, 112–13, 125, 173; and Balin, *To Reveal our Hearts*, 2–3, 23, 84, 109, 157.

[64] I treat the question of Wengeroff's choice of language in my forthcoming work. It is, of course, a pivotally important one, tied not only to her intended and actual audience, but to her very sense of what her enterprise as memoir writer was about. Her other choices, aside from Yiddish, which was struggling for respectability as a literary medium at the end of the century and would have consigned her to insignificance, were Russian, which would have limited her audience to Russian readers, and German, which opened up the much larger audience of German-reading Jews, not only in Russia, but in Germany and Austria. Wengeroff's Hebrew, as noted, was not adequate for composition.

[65] Wengeroff, *Memoiren einer Grossmutter*, i. 126, 134–5.

[66] Ibid. 126. On Wengeroff's father and his perspective, see my 'Kol Isha'.

a central critique of the maskilim, and that he welcomed aspects (though not all) of Lilienthal's proposed reforms as a positive development. So secure was he in his understanding of what Haskalah meant and of his support for it (for him, this meant very limited pedagogical reforms), that he himself brought his sons-in-law, whom he housed and fed so that they could devote themselves to Talmud study, to see the German 'doctor', against his wife's objections.

'Enlightenment' was transmitted in writing largely, though not exclusively, in Hebrew (some works were in the far more popularly accessible Yiddish) to a coterie of almost exclusively male devotees. But this was hardly the extent of its diffusion, as Wengeroff, who we can safely assume did not read Hebrew Haskalah tracts directly, clearly shows in her use of the term 'Haskalah'. People, like the men in her father's synagogue, spread Haskalah by speaking of it. Men, like her brother and brothers-in-law, under the same roof as she, who read maskilic works, surely spoke of what they were reading, of what occupied them at the sabbath meetings they held. At the very least, she surely overheard them speaking among themselves, just as she overheard other things she reports in her memoir, like the discourse during her mother's spying expeditions on these same young men. As a married woman, Wengeroff had one of the literary lights of Haskalah under her roof. Abraham Mapu, creator of the modern Hebrew novel and activist for the reform of Jewish education, as she relates in some detail (she knew very well who he was, citing his most famous works), tutored her son Simon in Russian and German when the family lived in Kovno. Mapu, of whom she speaks warmly, often stayed for extensive conversations, which she says Chonon very much enjoyed.[67]

In marital matters, too, Wengeroff proves herself a modern. Unlike Lilienblum, who never had an emotional, companionate relationship with his wife (he writes a poem to imprisonment and deadening of the spirit on the occasion of their tenth wedding anniversary), Wengeroff expected her husband to be a 'friend' and a partner. It is because of these expectations that she experiences his insensitivity as betrayal, something Lilienblum, for all his unhappiness, can never feel about his spouse. Finally, Wengeroff, as well as Lilienblum (and other maskilim), effectively distinguishes between egotistical self-indulgence and Haskalah. Indeed, of the two of them, it is she who remains loyal to Haskalah, which Lilienblum rejects in favour of materialist economics and Zionism.

What we understand, then, by the term 'Haskalah' must be broadened to encompass its social dimension, a dimension far wider than the circle of maskilim, or their readers, alone. This is a dimension that includes women, not as mere victims of its social dislocations (as a simple reading of Wengeroff's memoirs would lead us to believe), nor as exceptional participants, but as lay participants and propagators, which is clearly what Wengeroff was.[68] Wengeroff's defence of an enlightened

[67] Wengeroff, *Memoiren einer Grossmutter*, ii. 143–4.

[68] On moderate Haskalah, see Feiner, *Mehaskalah loḥemet*; id., 'Hamifneh beha'arakhat haḥasidut, eli'ezer zweifel vehahaskalah hametunah berusyah', in I. Etkes, *Hadat vehaḥayim* (Jerusalem, 1993),

traditionalism hardly excludes her from the camp of Haskalah. On the contrary, it puts her solidly within it, since all but the most radical of maskilim, after the 1860s, advocated some version of precisely this.

Beyond this, however, careful reading of her memoirs shows that Wengeroff's claim of a straight gendered dichotomy about the place of Judaism in her and Chonon's home was simply not true. She herself provides evidence that subverts this assertion, which is central of course, to her myth of her own life and of Jewish modernity. This material, embedded in the narrative but not given headings that draw attention to its meaning, of which indeed, Wengeroff probably was not consciously aware, shows that Chonon did try to impart Judaism to his children, not only when they were grown and he, old and rueful, and that Wengeroff actively supported her children's immersion in settings that could only have put serious pressure on them to assimilate, if not actually convert. Thus, we read in volume II that Chonon tutored the eldest son, Simon, in Hebrew and read Bible and Mishnah with him during the short time that the family lived in Vilna, a Jewish heartland, a time when Chonon even returned to Talmud study and retreated somewhat from the path he had taken.[69] Simon also studied with a rabbi there.[70] While the family resided in Helsinki, Wengeroff says that she *and* Chonon sought a Jewish teacher for the older children ('wir suchten nach einem jüdischen Lehrer'),[71] and that, when they could not find one, Chonon himself taught Simon. He was a terrible teacher, given to striking and humiliating the boy, and the lessons soon stopped. But there is a difference between being a terrible pedagogue and utterly denying the need for religious instruction, leaving her to attempt to arrange this in beleaguered isolation—which is what Wengeroff asserts elsewhere.[72] Indeed, she says that she and Chonon continued to try to find a teacher (and that Simon 'received' tefillin and was bar mitzvah).

The family subsequently moved to St Petersburg, where it is clear that, among the city's small circle of highly assimilated Jews, Chonon's pressures on her to minimize her traditional observance and her anguish on this account reached a peak. Here, Simon was expelled from gymnasium for refusing, as a Jew, to kneel before an icon during chapel—hardly the behaviour of a child bereft of identification with Judaism.[73] Wengeroff was fiercely proud of this act but also frantic for the expulsion to be rescinded, dashing to the school to plead tearfully before its director,

336–79'; and I. Etkes, 'Parashat "hahaskalah mita'am" vehatemurah bema'amad tenuat hahaskalah berusyah', 167–216. We have already seen instances of female opposition to Haskalah, namely, that of Wengeroff's mother, in contrast with whose stance Wengeroff's is quite striking. Both of Chonon's parents opposed his modernizing behaviour. Prominent in Lilienblum's account of his travails over enlightenment (*Ḥatot ne'urim*, 108–9) are his mother-in-law's opposition to his education and the lead women (and children) took in persecuting him.

[69] Wengeroff, *Memoiren einer Grossmutter*, ii. 149–50. [70] Ibid. 151, 173. [71] Ibid. 161.

[72] Ibid. 135. Indeed, Wengeroff asserts that Jewish men in this era told their protesting wives, 'the children need no religion!' [73] Wengeroff, *Memoiren einer Grossmutter*, ii. 172–3.

'because I could see well enough the ruin of my son's happiness in life'. Simon had not meant to be disrespectful, she explained. He just wanted 'to be true to the education he had received in his parents' [*sic*] house and at school with the rabbi'.[74] She was not successful, though the school arranged for Simon to be admitted to another gymnasium. Wengeroff then attributes Simon's Jewish steadfastness to herself: 'He was flesh of my flesh.' But she knew very well that she could hardly 'hope that, amid alien influences, the children would always follow their mother's ways'. Despite this awareness, Wengeroff does not say that she reluctantly went along with Simon's gymnasium education. Rather, her own testimony is that she fervently supported it.

Finally, when the family lived in Minsk, a fire destroyed their house and possessions and Wengeroff reports leaving with the children for three years (while Chonon, presumably, continued his business and rebuilt).[75] They went—to Vienna, she says, about which time she says not a word further, resuming the narrative when she returns to Minsk.

Vienna? If not Minsk, why not . . . Pinsk?[76] Or better yet, the Jerusalem of Lithuania, Vilna? Perhaps, because several of her children were brilliant students of literature and music, and cosmopolitan Vienna offered far better opportunities for ambitious young people—and their mothers?[77]

I do not mean to suggest doubt about Wengeroff's main assertion—that the abandonment of traditional observance in her home was Chonon's doing and that he coerced her with relentless, crude pressure whose details lend utter credence to her story. I do mean to say that there is more to this story, as we learn mostly from careful reading of the memoirs themselves, as well as from material outside them. Wengeroff's own behaviour feeds her guilt, which I submit is one major motive (albeit, among several) for her writing her memoirs.

SINS, GUILT, BLAME

For all their manifold differences, Lilienblum's and Wengeroff's tales share one significant trait: an overwhelming sense of failure, regret, and guilt at the end of the century of Jewish enlightenment. Lilienblum, of course, makes all this central in his writing. But it is very clear in Wengeroff's as well. How could a woman raised in a home where *kashrut* was an obsession, who herself never lost attachment to the

[74] Ibid. 173.

[75] Although Wengeroff does not state a date, she may be referring to the catastrophic Minsk fire of 1881.

[76] I owe the marvellous formulation of this question to Ruth Sporer.

[77] On Wengeroff's children, several of whom became accomplished literary figures, see my 'Pauline Wengeroff and the Voice of Jewish Modernity'. One daughter, Isabelle, a brilliant pianist, studied in the Vienna Conservatory in the 1890s (she later taught at the Curtis Institute of Music in the United States, teaching Leonard Bernstein among others); a son, Vladimir (Volodya), was a gifted cellist (who died young, as Wengeroff reports, in *Memoiren einer Grossmutter*, ii. 193); Gdal Saleski, *Famous Musicians of Jewish Origin* (New York, 1949), 390.

dietary traditions, yet whose own kitchen was *tref*, not feel failure and guilt? (The one point on which Wengeroff insists, when she finally relinquishes her kosher kitchen, is observance of the dietary laws during Passover.) How could she not feel shame and guilt to have children who become Christians, even if, as she strains to point out, they did so opportunistically?[78]

Indeed, Wengeroff makes the mind-boggling disparity between her upbringing and world-view and that of her children an explicit theme in her memoirs, mentioning this in her preface to volume I and especially in a separate chapter in volume II, entitled 'My Wise Mother Said Two Things'. Her mother stated (Wengeroff doesn't tell us when) that she and her generation would surely live and die as Jews: that her grandchildren would not, the only question being the behaviour of her children.[79] Wengeroff's need to explain (or justify) how such radical change occurred in the space of two generations comes to expression in her writing of memoirs. Her work is a significant narrative for anyone trying to understand Jewish modernity, something Wengeroff and those who supported publication of her work grasped very well.[80] But clearly, Wengeroff also desperately needed to unburden herself of her sense of failure and guilt. She does so in some of the narrative strategies I have termed extraordinary: her adamant insistence that her personal tragedy had a wider, societal, grounding; that her story is not just the tale of one marriage but that of modern Jewish women and men as a whole. Whatever the truth of these assertions, they serve another vital purpose: to alleviate some of the personal burden of guilt for her failure to maintain a Jewish home.

Wengeroff's sense of guilt is evident in a number of comments. Describing her tenacity in fighting for the old traditions when she was forced to relinquish her kosher kitchen, Wengeroff writes of her emotional ties to her parents, bound up inextricably with their religious observance. She speaks of having betrayed them and of feared loss of their approval and love: 'It will surely strike a deep wound in my parents' hearts. I was, until now, a beloved daughter . . . Now, they have every right to curse me . . .'. Then, tellingly, she records her father's reaction (relayed by a 'good friend' who 'naturally' had told him of it) to the report of Wengeroff's *tref* kitchen: 'If my Pessele did this it is because she had to.'[81] Welcome absolution for a weighty sense of guilt, its significance to Wengeroff evident in the fact that she included it in her memoirs, from which so much else is omitted.

Wengeroff speaks of the failure of parents in her generation, singling out fathers.[82] Yet she reveals her own torment in recording the challenge of 'the greatest *tsadik*' (whom she does not identify) to Jewish youth who

[78] In fact, one of the children, Faina, omitted from the memoirs, apparently converted for more complicated reasons and at some point at least was a fervent Christian; see Slonimsky, *Perfect Pitch*, 14–18. On this and how it relates to Wengeroff's memoir writing, see my forthcoming work.

[79] Wengeroff, *Memoiren einer Grossmutter*, ii. 134.

[80] See Gustav Karpeles's letter to Wengeroff, repr. in *Memoiren einer Grossmutter*, ii. 3–4; about Wengeroff's backers, see my forthcoming work.

[81] Wengeroff, *Memoiren einer Grossmutter*, ii. 177.

[82] Ibid. 180.

had grown up without any tradition, far from Judaism, to renounce everything the future could offer him in success, honour, reputation, in the name of this, to him, unknown and hollow concept; to demand that he resist . . . temptations and retreat into the obscurity and narrowness of a little provincial town and spend there a wretched existence. He said—if he had the right and the boldness for it, *because I did not*![83]

Wengeroff, of course, had not made this demand of her children, as we saw from her reaction when Simon was expelled from gymnasium. It is significant, indeed, that she 'hears' the challenge of this *tsadik* as directed towards her, and feels the need to respond to it with the justification she offers in the memoirs. And she mourns. Her sons' conversions were 'the most grievous blow that I suffered in my life'. Wengeroff writes:

But the loving heart of a mother can endure so much—I forgive them, and lay the blame on us parents. Gradually, the grief lost significance as a personal experience for me and seemed ever more a national misfortune. I mourned not just as a mother, but as a Jew, for the whole Jewish people, which had lost so much of its precious energies.[84]

CONCLUSION

Wengeroff and Lilienblum both wrote tragic–heroic personal accounts of Haskalah and *fin-de-siècle* statements about the era of Jewish enlightenment in Russia. For all the differences between their narratives, there are some striking similarities, and both the differences and the similarities give us important insight into Jewish sensibility at this time. While it is common to depict post-1881 Russian Jewry as shaken by the pogroms of 1881 and the discriminatory May Laws, events stressed by both memoirs, more prominent in both works is a global sense of having been overwhelmed by social forces. For Lilienblum, it is his father and his father's culture. Then, it is enlightenment, which he himself chose to pursue, but which he came to see as a drunken illusion over which he had no control. We might observe that Haskalah was an irresistible force for a rationalist chafing the more unbearably in traditional culture for awareness of a dawning alternative outside it. He does not show that kind of insight, seeing himself instead as a victim of overwhelming forces. He says much the same about his obsession with N.[85]

Wengeroff fought against Chonon's deviations until demoralization broke her ability to resist. Their frequent moves as Chonon sought material success—something she, child of privilege, never claims to have resisted—surely made it more difficult for her to find a stable base in which to establish any kind of traditional life and must have added greatly to her isolation, loneliness, and sense of powerlessness.

[83] Ibid. 193.

[84] Ibid. 194.

[85] A stance that strikes this reader as a narcissistic indulgence without concern for either his wife (and children), about whose feelings in this regard he does not so much as speculate, or N, since Lilienblum never moves to actualize his relationship with her—the second time, as he knew, since he is our source of knowing it—that this young woman fares badly in love.

The children were far from the home of either set of grandparents, where they could have observed an 'organic', lived Judaism. There is no indication they even met any of them (though Wengeroff's omissions are not necessarily reliable indication of a non-event). But Chonon was seeking affirmation from assimilating, not traditional, Jews. His loss of faith coincided roughly with Alexander II's ascent to the throne in 1855 (Wengeroff was married in 1849) and the beginning of the brightest phase of Russian Jewry's hopes for increased rights and opportunities. While Chonon made some effort to give (at least) his sons some Jewish knowledge, he had clearly consigned an all-encompassing Jewishness to the past. To his children, Judaism was literally out of fashion. His appeal to 'the right of husbands' (*Herrenrechte*, literally seigneurial rights) to dictate practice in the home contrasts sharply with what we know about middle-class German Jewish society of this time, where men were content to leave Jewish practice to the domestic sphere as long as they were free to ignore it there, as well as outside the home—close to the compromise Wengeroff said she had offered.[86] This may or may not have been the widespread phenomenon in (middle-class) Russian Jewish society Wengeroff claims it was, but in her own case it was surely a traumatic invasion of turf that Wengeroff's upbringing gave her every reason to expect would be hers. She is also surely correct in saying that in the circles in which her family travelled, the children would follow their father's tastes—there was everything to support this and nothing to render her proclivities credible.[87] There is no way that gifted children seeking professional success in the world outside Jewish society could do so without serious compromise with Judaism and, after 1881, little chance of doing so without conversion. As Wengeroff notes of her children's generation, put under the antisemitic pressures of the 1880s: 'there were but two paths: either relinquish in the name of Judaism, all claim to everything that had become essential to [them]—or, choose freedom and all possible opportunities, like education, career—in other words, baptism. And hundreds of enlightened Jews chose the second route'.[88]

Lilienblum says he was robbed of his childhood and adolescence and the ability to make practical decisions about the rest of his life. Both tradition and its nemesis, enlightenment, share in this depiction, in depriving him of any practical sense or skills. Wengeroff, by contrast, was robbed of her majority. Having been groomed to be the matron of a Jewish home, like her mother and the other powerful female figures of her childhood, she is denied this inheritance.

Marriage and its failures is a central aspect of both narratives, responsible for frustration and misery that in the tellings of both authors are based in a larger social

[86] See Kaplan, *The Making of the Jewish Middle Class*, 64–84; P. Hyman, 'Two Models of Modernization, Jewish Women in the German and Russian Empires', in J. Frankel (ed.), *Jews and Gender* (Oxford, 2000).

[87] Wengeroff, *Memoiren einer Grossmutter*, ii. 175, 'And the children?', she writes (as if to Chonon), describing the trauma of relinquishing her kosher kitchen and of his cruelty to her. 'They were so young, yet they sided with you. They were children of their time!'

[88] Ibid. 192–3.

reality: for Lilienblum, traditionalism; for Wengeroff, modernity. One does wonder, in both cases, why there is no mention of considered divorce, which, as ChaeRan Freeze shows, was exceedingly common in Russian Jewish society at this time.[89] Divorce could have been an avenue to some greater and happier control of personal destiny and, for Wengeroff, a way to live in locations and social settings more conducive to Jewish life. Her circumstances were certainly letter-perfect grounds for divorce under rabbinic law. In Lilienblum's case, he even had an adoring 'modern' type of woman waiting anxiously in the wings. Lilienblum says he is unsuited for family life—with anyone, even a soulmate, an important admission after dozens of pages excoriating arranged marriage. Wengeroff never even hints about the possibility of divorce, not in the diary fragments she embeds in her memoir, recorded at a time of acute despair, when she relinquished *kashrut*, nor in the retrospective writing, the memoir itself. (After three years in Vienna she returns to Chonon.) It is very clear, not least from her description of his death, that for all his abusive behaviour and her rage at him, Wengeroff dearly loved and was dedicated to Chonon. Quite probably, she also wished to avoid the scandal that divorce would have meant in her circle of acculturated, bourgeois Jews. Here too, then, she seemed to be living out, rather than shaping, a destiny.

Lilienblum undergoes several drastic changes in orientation and self-definition over the course of his life. Significantly, Wengeroff retains a sense of herself as having remained fundamentally the same—religious—despite outward, behavioural change. After all, she had never undergone a loss of faith, as had Lilienblum, only of observance and this against her will. 'In the last years of his life', she says, speaking of Chonon, 'he became peaceful, gentle, and fell back into the mystical mood of his youth, becoming engrossed in the teachings of the kabbalah. I felt as if he envied me the fact that throughout all the turmoil of our life, I had maintained my religious soul.'[90]

She regards this constancy as one of several areas of superiority over Chonon. As she says after a section depicting the assimilating circles in which she and Chonon travelled:

> To live in this environment and remain impervious to its influence required a strength of character and a religious constancy that my husband, alas, did not possess. It would have left me untouched; my strong belief, my upbringing, and the religious fervour with which I remained attached to Jewish customs would have kept me from disloyalty. Indeed, I might have gone around proudly among the weaklings, proud and happy that I still possessed the spiritual riches that the others had long since lost. And I might have pitied them their poverty.[91]

Wengeroff's strange use of the subjunctive about herself in this passage, speaking as if she had not been in the same 'environment' as Chonon, may be indirect but power-

[89] C. Freeze, *Jewish Marriage and Divorce in Imperial Russia* (Hanover, NH, 2002).

[90] Wengeroff, *Memoiren einer Grossmutter*, ii. 24.

[91] Ibid. 169–70.

ful testimony to her claim that men's and women's realities were utterly different, with men much more exposed and susceptible to assimilatory pressures, to the point that she was not 'where' Chonon was, even if they were physically in the same place. Wengeroff never speculates about why women were so much more constant, more capable of moderation, and men so intemperate. Effectively, hers is an essentialist reading of gendered behaviour. Anything else—such as an economic or sociological reading—would have taken the sails out of her narrative, which is built on the assumption and even glorification of traditional gender roles.[92] The 'sin' of Jewish modernity is that it robbed women of their rightful turf and role, with cultural catastrophe the result.

For both writers, ultimately, it is Jewish nationalism that offers balm to the wounds of modernity and personal frustration. Having left Haskalah, Lilienblum becomes one of the leaders of Hovevei Zion (Lovers of Zion) in Russia, in which he finds salvation. But Wengeroff, too, takes great comfort in the resurgence of interest in Jewish culture among some young Jewish circles at the end of the century, and explicitly in Hovevei Zion—founded, she tells us, by Leo Pinsker and Moshe Leib Lilienblum.[93] She clearly wishes her own work to encourage this new, more hopeful trend at the end of a century marked by progressive assimilation; this is clearly another primary motive for her writing.

Reading Lilienblum's and Wengeroff's memoirs side by side, we see that for all the claims of Haskalah and its adherents that a new day was dawning for Russian Jewish society (*voskhod* literally means sunrise), Jews at the end of the century of enlightenment were consumed by a sense of terrible regret for what had been lost in their lifetime, and of failure and guilt for their part in that loss. For all the differences in their personalities and narratives, the sense of loss, regret, and a desperate desire to make some reparation is a striking common motif. For Lilienblum and Wengeroff, but also for Chonon, activism of some kind—for Wengeroff and Chonon, in the trade schools, for Wengeroff and Lilienblum, in the publication of didactic memoirs—helped serve the latter goal. For all the assertion of being overwhelmed by forces beyond their control, guilt is a function of perceived agency, which certainly in Wengeroff's case is closer to the complicated truth of her adult behaviour than an assertion of hapless victimization.

Wengeroff's and Lilienblum's paths to Jewish modernity are quite different, but together their narratives give us insight into the gendered nature of that odyssey and into important commonalities despite gender, complicating our understanding of Russian Jewish modernity and the fallibility and struggles of its pioneer generation.

[92] On this, see my 'Kol Isha'.

[93] Wengeroff, *Memoiren einer Grossmutter*, ii. 195.

Women's Education in the Pages of the Russian Jewish Press

ELIYANA R. ADLER

THIS chapter is an attempt to reconcile a contradiction I encountered while conducting research on private schools for Jewish girls in nineteenth-century Russia. On the one hand, published reports of the openings of such schools in locales throughout the Pale of Jewish Settlement were uniformly positive, zealously proud of the accomplishments of the Haskalah. On the other hand, full-length articles about Jewish women's education published in the very same periodicals displayed a far more ambivalent stance towards women's education and were dismissive of the new schools.

In this chapter I seek to characterize and to clarify the relationship between the Russian Jewish press and the new educational initiatives for Jewish women in the latter half of the nineteenth century. Building on previous scholarship, I have attempted to understand how the progressive Jewish periodical press simultaneously supported and dismissed concrete advances in Jewish women's education.[1]

WHY EDUCATE JEWISH GIRLS?

The Russian Jewish press, first in Hebrew and later in Russian and Yiddish, was both a product of and stimulus to the progress of enlightenment. The first Hebrew

I am grateful to the editors, Paula Hyman and ChaeRan Freeze, for their insightful and incisive comments on this chapter. My friend and colleague Sheila Jelen was kind enough to look at an earlier draft.

[1] I am indebted to other scholars who have used the Russian Jewish periodical press to access information about Jewish women and about attitudes towards Jewish women. Shmuel Feiner's groundbreaking essay on the maskilim and their relations with actual and imagined Jewish women, Iris Parush's careful attention to nuance and gender in contemporary writing, and Semion Kreiz's mining of Russian-language journals for references to schools have all served to enhance this work in terms of both methodology and content.

S. Feiner, 'Ha'ishah hayehudit hamodernit: Mikreh-mivḥan beyaḥasei hahaskalah vehamodernah', *Zion*, 58/4 (1993), 453–99; I. Parush, *Nashim korot: Yitronah shel shuliyut baḥevrah hayehudit bemizraḥ eiropah bame'ah hatesha-esreh* (Tel Aviv, 2001); and S. Kraiz, 'Batesefer yehudiim besafa harusit berusia hazarit', Ph.D. thesis (Hebrew University of Jerusalem, 1994).

journals were started by men committed to the goals of Haskalah and to their spread. The writers, often newly embarked on their paths as maskilim, struggled to make their formerly sacred tongue express new ideas in both fiction and belletristic writing. Although individual publications and individual contributors expressed different views, there were common themes. Chief among these was a desire for the 'normalization' or modernization of Russian Jewry. This was to be accomplished through innovations in such areas as education, dress, and occupational structure.

The press offered a forum for the promulgation and discussion of these grand ideas. Writers took part in a multilingual open-ended conversation, wherein proposals raised in one journal might be critiqued in another. There was thus broad consensus on the direction of progress, but debate on the particulars.

The need to reform traditional patterns of education figured prominently in the thought of the maskilim and their intellectual heirs.[2] In their autobiographies, published treatises, fiction, and journalistic writing, they decried the prevalent patterns and proposed changes. Given that the vast majority of writers, whether for the periodical press or other venues, were men, it is hardly surprising that their chief concern was the reform of the *ḥeder*.[3]

The venom spilled on the *ḥeder* is well known. But even as some were reviling this essential institution of the east European Jewish experience, others turned to imagining its replacement. Isaac Baer Levinsohn's *Te'udah beyisra'el*, published in 1828, explored what Jews should study and contained a critique of the current educational system. In *Beit yehudah*, published ten years later, Levinsohn outlined a five-point plan of improvement for the Jewish community in Russia. His first proposal was the creation of a modern educational system for boys and girls.[4]

Levinsohn was notable for placing the education of boys and girls on equal footing. Most of his contemporaries were consumed with the proper education of

The negative appraisal of women's education has been noted previously by Feiner, 'Ha'ishah hayehudit hamodernit', 22, as well as Tova Cohen, 'Reality and its Refraction in Descriptions of Women in Haskalah Fiction', in S. Feiner and D. Sorkin (eds.), *New Perspectives on the Haskalah* (London, 2001), 162, and Parush, *Nashim korot*, 75–6.

[2] The term 'maskilim' has often been used to encompass individuals supporting all modernizing ideologies within the Jewish community. However, this usage can erase very real differences between those advocating, for example, revitalizing Hebrew as the literary language of the Jews and those who sought to create a Russified Jewry. In this chapter I have tried to use the term 'maskilim' specifically to refer to those who supported the goals of the Russian Jewish Haskalah, and more general terms such as 'progressives' or 'modernizers' to refer to other ideologically motivated Jewish intellectuals. Nonetheless, I have assumed an overlap in these intellectual communities and read the Hebrew- and Russian-language Jewish newspapers as part of one conversation.

[3] The topic of maskilim and the *ḥeder* has been treated thoroughly elsewhere. See e.g. M. Avital, *Hayeshivah vehaḥinukh hamesorati basifrut hahaskalah ha'ivrit* (Tel Aviv, 1996), and M. Zalkin, *Ba'alot hashaḥar: Hahaskalah hayehudit ba'imperiyah harusit bame'ah hatesha-esreh* (Jerusalem, 2000). For more on the women who wrote for the Jewish press, see C. B. Balin, *To Reveal our Hearts: Jewish Women Writers in Tsarist Russia* (Cincinnati, 2000), esp. introd.

[4] Y. B. Levinsohn, *Beit yehudah* (1838; Vilna, 1858), pt. 2, ch. 146, 148–50.

boys. However, there was a tacit recognition that the transformation of the Jewish community would require modernizing the education of girls, as well. Indeed, raising a generation of enlightened boys would not be possible without the active co-operation of their mothers.

In this, the maskilim were clearly influenced by the west European notions of the bourgeois family. Both Marion Kaplan and Paula Hyman have written about the power of the surrounding society's discourse of gender over the rapidly acculturating Jews of western Europe.[5] These expectations had an influence on many Russian Jews as well.

To the writer Gornberg, writing for the Russian-language Jewish periodical *Rassvet* in 1860, the reason to educate Jewish women was simple and logical:

> In Jewish society the mother of the family has an even bigger influence on children than in Christian [families]. The head of the family, given all his concerns, spends almost all of his time outside of the house, leaving the children and their instruction to the mother; and therefore, so that this instruction will go correctly, it is necessary to think seriously about the education of Jewish women.[6]

Khaim Funt, in the transcript of a speech delivered on the tenth anniversary of the founding of his school for Jewish girls in Minsk, not only spoke at length about the need to train educated mothers but raised the stakes considerably: 'she must be reborn; she must prepare herself for this modest, but great mission; she must renounce superstition, improve her taste, ennoble her understanding, attach her soul to general human need'.[7] He claimed that women had the ultimate responsibility for the next generation.

In a long and persuasive piece on his school for Jewish girls in Kherson, Abram Yakov Bruk-Brezovsky, writing in the Russian-language periodical *Sion* in 1861, similarly extended the responsibility of women. He saw women as responsible not only for the education of the next generation, but also for the interaction between Jews and their neighbours:

> And thus, in the education of women is included the source of education for the whole people: in their hands rests the fate of the next generation. For our Jews the education of women holds yet another importance: only through them can we gradually supplant our jargon, and imperceptibly acquire for ourselves the national language—an exceedingly important step towards internal and external merging with the Russian people.[8]

Bruk-Brezovsky utilized the Bible and later rabbinic authorities to provide support for his position. His argument, although more complex than those above, still rests

[5] M. Kaplan, *The Making of the Jewish Middle Class* (New York, 1991); P. E. Hyman, *Gender and Assimilation in Modern Jewish History: The Roles and Representation of Women* (Seattle, 1995), esp. ch. 1.

[6] Gornberg, 'Zametka o evreiskikh uchilishchakh', *Rassvet*, 6 (1860), 87.

[7] K. Funt, 'Rech'', *Minskie gubernskie vedomosti*, 21 (27 May 1867), 116.

[8] A. Ya. Bruk-Brezovsky, 'Iz rechi skazannoi soderzhatelem evreiskogo devich'ego pansiona, v g. Khersone', *Sion*, 20 (17 Nov. 1861), 321.

on utilitarian presumptions. Women should be educated for what they can provide to the community.

Even female writers relied upon this instrumental justification for the education of Jewish girls. E. Yampolskaya, writing in 1880 for *Russkii evrei*, promised that two of Russian Jewish society's most intractable problems could be solved through educating Jewish women. Both the abandonment of the Jewish community by the Russified intellectuals and the obscurantism of the masses could be remedied in this manner. Yampolskaya ended her article with the following plea: 'Only the sublime development of Jewish women can serve as a true guarantee of the renewal and revival of our people.'[9]

Paula Hyman has pointed out the irony of this equation in the west European context.[10] Writers and communal leaders embraced the bourgeois ideal of the wife as 'priestess of the home', charged with raising and educating the next generation, as entirely natural. Yet they were undoubtedly aware that in Jewish law the responsibility for the education of sons falls squarely on the shoulders of the father.[11] In the east European setting the contrast was even more stark, as many women were far too busy supporting their families to have time to teach them.[12] Despite internal contradictions, the embrace of the Western bourgeois family was an integral part of the Haskalah ideology.

There were some writers for the Jewish press who advanced Jewish women's education as a cause for other reasons. The well-known educator and maskil Shmuel Yosef Fuenn, writing in 1867, began his brief article on women's education with a discussion of the unstoppable march of time. Progress, whether for good or ill, could not be reversed. Following a nostalgic reference to a past where men studied the Torah and women minded the home and business, Fuenn advanced the fact that such a system was no longer viable and that Russian Jews must now follow their German brethren, providing their daughters with both education and religious confirmation.[13]

Shalom Ya'akov Abramovitsh (Mendele Mokher Seforim), known best for his Yiddish and Hebrew fiction, also contributed to the debates of his day. He was among a small minority of writers publicly committed to advancing Jewish women's education as a goal in and of itself. In a lengthy article on the historical development of Judaism from the ancient Near East to the present, he ended his discussion of education with a truly egalitarian plea: 'The idea of education is not a choice, but a strict obligation, which the very survival of humanity depends upon, a positive

9 E. Yampolskaya, 'Nechto o zhenskom obrazovanii u evreev', *Russkii evrei*, 20 (1880), 781.

10 Hyman, *Gender and Assimilation in Modern Jewish History*, 47–8.

11 See e.g. *SA*, *Mapah*, 'Yoreh de'ah', 245: 1, 4.

12 For more on women as breadwinners in east European Jewish society, see I. Etkes, 'Marriage and Torah Study Among the *Lomdim* in Lithuania in the Nineteenth Century', in D. Kraemer (ed.), *The Jewish Family: Metaphor and Memory* (Oxford, 1989), and S. A. Glenn, *Daughters of the Shtetl: Life and Labor in the Immigrant Generation* (Ithaca, NY, 1990), ch. 1.

13 S. Y. Fuenn, 'Ḥinukh habanot', *Hakarmel*, 44 (1867), 346–7.

commandment, crucial to human welfare and all are obligated: men and women, sons and daughters, each according to his worth and strength!'[14]

But such views were not the norm. Most of the writers for the Russian Jewish periodical press wrote of women deserving education, not for their own sake, but for the sake of serving the community.

CRITIQUE OF THE STATUS QUO

Whatever the reasoning they applied, all agreed that the education of Jewish girls required attention. Many of the writers sought to highlight this point by describing the current educational status of women. According to D. Lazarev, writing for a non-Jewish periodical in 1864, Jewish women in the past had been taught only a few rites and prayers. Whereas Jewish boys always received a religious education, girls learned only the bare minimum: 'she knows that a spoon, once used in a meat dish, cannot be placed in a pot of milk; it is known to her, that when the window of the old synagogue shines forth softly with dregs of candles, she must throw off all wearisome work and take in the sabbath peace'.[15]

As enlightened ideas began to reach the male members of the Jewish community, this imbalance in educational levels led to marital problems:

> As stated, the wife, brought up in infernal terror, sees in every more or less free act of the husband—a great transgression, from which will follow horrible consequences. . . . This hostile relationship between the father and mother and the husband and wife has a pernicious influence on the raising of children. The father, with all his might trying to give to the children some amount of decent instruction, must often give in to the tears and entreaties of his fanatical wife and her tribe, and in catering to their old-fashioned understanding must sacrifice the happiness of his children.[16]

According to Lazarev, as new ideas reached the Jews of Russia, the literate and educated husband found himself at odds with his superstitious and traditional wife in matters ranging from religious practice to education of the next generation.

Most of the other contemporary writers who depicted the past educational status of Jewish women agreed with Lazarev's analysis. Jewish girls received only the most meagre education, this being limited to practical religious knowledge. Once they had mastered their household and ritual tasks, they were left without further education. The result, from the perspective of these authors, was generations of Jewish women mired in ignorance and superstition, opposed to general and personal betterment. At the same time that the authors were professing sympathy with Jewish women and their situation, the rhetoric of their articles suggests more complex sentiments.

M. G. Gershfeld, writing for *Russkii evrei* in 1880, pointed out that women,

[14] S. Y. Abramovitch, 'Ma anu?', *Hashaḥar*, 6 (1875), 534.

[15] D. Lazarev, 'O vospitanii i stepeni obrazovannosti evreiskikh zhenshchin', *Uchitel'*, 15/16 (1864), 558.

[16] Ibid. 559.

much more than men, have 'maintained a series of absurd prejudices and superstitions'.[17] He went so far as to blame the high divorce rate among Jews on this particular imbalance. A. Zeidler, writing for *Rassvet* in 1861, concurred with much of the analysis of Lazarev and Gershfeld, although his depiction of the results placed more blame on the society at large, stigmatizing the women less:

> Crude fears, fanaticism and idleness, this is what she is surrounded by; these are her elementary instructors and founding impressions! To reach in such circumstances healthy development? She knows nothing more than mangled morning prayers learned by heart, by rote, not having an understanding of the meaning or significance, not having any conception of to Whom these misplaced words are directed.[18]

These three writers for the Russian Jewish periodical press used dramatic and colourful language to depict Jewish women and their homes. In particular, all three relied heavily on direct and indirect accusations of fanaticism. For these self-professing progressive men, women served as symbols of the past they had overcome. Zeidler conflated women and the home to paint a picture of moral and intellectual darkness. They all relied upon prevalent notions of women as prone to superstition and exaggerated religiosity. At the same time as they explicitly expressed support for educating Jewish women, they demonstrated uncertainty over whether Jewish women were capable of reform.

Just as the theoretical justifications for educating Jewish women often relied upon an idealized image of what the Jewish family should be, the portrayal of women's current educational status built on a highly exaggerated trope of what Jewish women represented to the authors. In conflating the Jewish woman with the past, and a distant vision of bourgeois respectability with the future, these writers betrayed the degree to which they were cut off from the experiences of real Jewish women. How, then, did they respond to the transformations in Jewish women's education taking place around them?

REALITY MEETS THEORY: PRIVATE SCHOOLS FOR JEWISH GIRLS

At the same time as writers argued over the nature of the educational ills perpetrated on Jewish women and how best to heal the resultant societal wounds, enterprising educators across the Pale of Settlement opened modern private schools for Jewish girls for both ideological and economic reasons. Between 1844 and 1881 well over 100 Jewish girls' schools were opened in the highly populated Jewish areas of the Russian empire.[19] The growth and spread of these schools represented changing

[17] M. G. Gershfeld, 'K voprosu o zhenskom obrazovanii u evreev', *Russkii evrei*, 6 (1880), 206.

[18] A. Zeidler, 'O zhenskom obrazovanii', *Rassvet*, 40 (1861), 638.

[19] See my 'Private Schools for Jewish Girls in Tsarist Russia', Ph.D. thesis (Brandeis University, 2003), ch. 4 and pp. 279–83.

expectations and norms within the Jewish community, as well as trends in Russian society as a whole.

Throughout the second half of the nineteenth century the Russian state actively sought both to acculturate its minority populations through educational measures and to improve education for the Russian masses.[20] At the same time, growing grassroots attention to the plight of the peasants and the power of education meant that educated society became increasingly committed to spreading education to previously disfranchised groups, including women.

The period of great reforms, initiated by Tsar Alexander II in the 1860s, heightened these activities and witnessed the rise of the populist movement and the women's movement in Russia. Educated Russian women were soon advocating higher education and entering the teaching profession.[21]

The new private schools for Jewish girls must be understood as part of these broader processes, as well as a response to internal Jewish developments. A look at enrolment figures shows that these schools filled a need. Across the Pale of Settlement, as well as across the economic spectrum, Jewish families went to great efforts to get their daughters into private Jewish schools. The curriculum, composed mainly of Russian-language and religion courses, with some European languages and arithmetic, was attractive to Jewish families.

As the new schools spread, writers for the Jewish press could hardly fail to notice them. Surely, they would have been overjoyed at the progress evident around them. Indeed, in local reports, the press praised and fêted the new schools.

A common feature of many of the Hebrew and Russian-language Jewish periodicals of this era was a section providing news from around the Jewish world. In some cases, updates were provided regularly from correspondents living in St Petersburg, Berlin, Paris, and other major Jewish communities. Other papers simply printed letters from individuals reporting from far and near. Reports from abroad included international news, as well as news from within particular Jewish communities. Given the tenor of the papers, local reports often focused on the status of the Haskalah in a given community. It was in these letters that many new schools for Jewish girls were announced.

A thematically typical, yet idiosyncratically written, example came from Grodno to the Hebrew journal *Hakarmel* in 1866. The author opened with a somewhat messianic portrayal of the coming of the Haskalah:

[20] See e.g. H. D. Lowe, 'Poles, Jews, and Tartars: Religion, Ethnicity, and Social Structure in Tsarist Nationality Policies', *Jewish Social Studies*, 6/3 (2000), 52–96; M. Stanislawski, *Tsar Nicholas I and the Jews: The Transformation of Jewish Society in Russia, 1825–1855* (Philadelphia, 1983), ch. 4; B. Eklof, *Russian Peasant Schools: Officialdom, Village Culture, and Popular Pedagogy, 1861–1914* (Berkeley, 1986); and A. Sinel, *The Classroom and the Chancellery: State Educational Reform in Russia Under Count Dmitry Tolstoi* (Cambridge, 1973), ch. 9.

[21] R. Stites, *The Women's Liberation Movement in Russia: Feminism, Nihilism, and Bolshevism, 1860–1930* (Princeton, 1978), 29–88; B. A. Engel, *Mothers and Daughters: Women of the Intelligentsia in Nineteenth-Century Russia* (Cambridge, 1983), ch. 4; and C. Ruane, *Gender, Class and the Professionalization of Russian City Teachers, 1860–1914* (Pittsburgh, 1994).

Through all the generations that have come and gone, and the innumerable ages through which the eternal people have passed, from generation to generation knowledge grows, from day to day wisdom [*haskel*] is multiplied, and at the passing of the generation the wisdom [*haskalah*] goes on, there will arise a new generation which will also invigorate and add strength, because there is no end to understanding, and no limits to knowledge. . . . How pleasant for the soul and sweet to see the light of the Haskalah arriving. And how dear to pronounce that it dawns also in the windows of our city.[22]

After describing the general improvement, the author went on to catalogue specific changes to support his claim, including the school for Jewish girls, now in its eleventh year of existence. The author expressed joy and wonder at its success: 'Who would not rejoice to see his young daughter of seven or eight years standing for exams in the Russian language, and would not express wonder when young girls would show their knowledge in other languages?'[23]

Likewise, a more straightforward report was filed for the Russian paper *Rassvet* from the city of Kamenets-Podolsk in 1860. The author, who signed himself with the Russian letter 'Ya.', devoted his letter to advances in education (*prosveshchenie*) in his place of residence. Accordingly, not only was the government Jewish school growing, but a new private school for Jewish girls had just been opened. The school was off to such a good start that the curator of the Kiev educational circuit, N. I. Pirogov, had already visited and was very favourably impressed.[24]

These and other announcements for Jewish girls' schools in regional reports can be found throughout the Hebrew and Russian-language Jewish press, particularly during the 1860s and 1870s. The reports included a few details about the school—number of pupils, subjects of study, name of principal—and were almost always entirely positive. Even when local reports addressed faults with the schools, the blame was usually placed at the feet of larger societal concerns. A report filed from Ponevezh (Lithuanian: Panevėžys) in 1880 candidly stated that their school for Jewish girls was not on the highest level educationally. Nonetheless, the author praised the principal roundly for his efforts and decried the chronic poverty of the Jewish community, leading to is difficulties.[25] Likewise, a report from Berdichev rated local Jewish schools honestly, while blaming the slow progress on local hasidim.[26]

This generally optimistic view of Jewish women's education prevails in articles about specific schools as well. In the same vein as the local reports, writers would sometimes submit brief articles about specific institutions worthy of note for one reason or another. A few such pieces describe local private schools for Jewish girls. In 1860, nearly one year after Mr Dikker opened his private school for Jewish girls

[22] 'Grodno', *Hakarmel*, 30 (1866), 233.

[23] Ibid. 234.

[24] Ya., 'Kamenets-Podol'sk', *Rassvet*, 39 (1861), 619–20. The important Russian doctor and controversial educational theorist oversaw the Kiev educational circuit from 1858 until 1861.

[25] I. Tzedekh, 'Ponevezh', *Russkii evrei*, 31 (1880), 1214.

[26] 'Berdichev', *Sion*, 42 (1862), 661–2.

in Simferopol, I. Likub wrote in *Rassvet* about the successes of the school in that brief period. Likub expounded enthusiastically about the teachers and subjects, and described significant local support. The only problem, according to him, was financial.[27]

After attending the public examination at Aron Frud's school in Berdichev in 1860, an author who signed himself 'D.M.' was left with an overall favourable impression, but with certain concerns. Chief among these was the power wielded by wealthy families. According to D.M., the school's financial situation was unstable enough to require the principal to cater to the vanity of the donor families at the expense of academic integrity: 'Mr. Frid [*sic*] knows only too well the local so-called civilized society, not to perceive that the deprivation of mediocre pupils of their undeserved awards threatens his school with the loss of pupils and the mortal animosity of its parents.'[28] In the author's view, the result was that awards were given to almost every pupil and therefore lost their value. Even worse, the overall educational level had to be limited, so that even mediocre pupils could succeed. Nonetheless, D.M. praised the school's curriculum and the tireless efforts of Mr Frud.

In local reports, whether devoted to all aspects of progress or specifically to a particular school, the new private schools for girls were evidence of the success of the Haskalah in Russia. The schools were the antidote to the superstition and ignorance of the past. But at the same time that the new schools merited praise in these short and largely descriptive pieces, longer articles in the very same journals demonstrated an entirely different attitude towards private schools for Jewish girls. This is true even in pieces written by those involved in educating girls. In a speech delivered at the twelfth anniversary celebration of his own school for Jewish girls, and later printed in *Sion*, Abram Bruk-Brezovsky attacked the other educational institutions for Jewish girls:

> In recent times, *ḥeder*s and schools have begun to open also for girls, teaching elementary Hebrew reading and writing, and occasionally also Russian, and some arithmetic. The principals of these schools lack all knowledge, except good Hebrew handwriting. These *melamedim*, or teachers, do not pay any attention to the development of the intellectual talents of the pupils, nor to their morality, nor to the teaching of the country's language; there was no trace of teaching crafts. Calligraphy received all the effort.[29]

By referring to the other schools and teachers with the traditional Hebrew terms *ḥeder* and *melamed*, Bruk-Brezovsky meant to belittle their claim to reform and suggest that they were no better than the traditional schools. Yet, in mentioning their typical curricula, clearly far broader than a traditional *ḥeder*, he betrays the modern aspirations of the schools, though he dismisses them as only concerned with penmanship.

[27] I. Likub, 'Chastnoe evreiskoe devich'e uchilishche v Simferopole', *Rassvet*, 4 (1860), 54.

[28] D.M., 'Berdichev', *Rassvet*, 28 (1860), 447.

[29] Bruk-Brezovsky, 'Iz rechi', 321.

L. Dreizen, a seminary-educated man serving as a private tutor in the city of Minsk, wrote to the Russian-language supplement in the Hebrew periodical *Hakarmel* about an incident he experienced. One of his private students in Russian and German asked why they were not studying the German Romantic writer Johann Christoph Schiller. She had recently left the third class of a local Jewish girls' school and was surprised not to be continuing with her reading of the works of Schiller. The thrust of Dreizen's article was that educators should be paying more attention to teaching basics and appropriate works to Jewish girls. He was outraged that Schiller was being taught to girls who lacked both the linguistic skills and maturity to understand the work.[30]

Dreizen was not the only writer to express concern specifically about Jewish girls reading Schiller. Khaim Funt dismissed the popularity of Schiller's works as follows: 'Previously only the rich educated their daughters, limited almost to the reading of Schiller and Goethe and including elegant French phrases.'[31] Lazarev also complained about women's 'chatter about Schiller'.[32] The anxiety of these writers seems to have stemmed from a concern that the women were enjoying the romantic tales without grasping their deeper messages.

Another common complaint levelled at both schools and wealthy families who hired tutors for their daughters was the 'useless' content of the education, in particular the effort devoted to learning French, as opposed to Russian or Hebrew. A. Zeidler went so far as to question whether such study was in fact educational training:

> A girl, in order to gain for herself an advantageous match—her parents imagine—must speak French and play the pianoforte, just as she needs a luxurious wardrobe, diamonds, and so on. This conclusion is reinforced when the matchmaker comes to them with offers of marriage. Already in the [18]50s their daughters were educated. However, is it possible to call their . . . crude materialism an education?[33]

A St Petersburg correspondent for *Russkii evrei* ridiculed the results of the gendered expectations for education among wealthy religious Jews: 'And these two systems exist simultaneously within the same family, sister dressed in the latest fashion, speaking several languages and playing piano, and brother in a long garment, with longer *peyot*, not knowing how to write in even one language, even ancient Hebrew.'[34]

For these writers, women no longer stood for tradition. Yet, instead of finding promise in the new knowledge and skills available to Jewish women, they saw the knowledge as superficial and the skills as misplaced. To them, the arrogance and ignorance of the wealthy society girl had replaced the arrogance and ignorance of her traditional mother.

[30] L. Dreizen, 'O vospitanii devich', *Hakarmel*, suppl.: *Prilozhenie k evreiskomu zhurnalu Gakarmelyu*, 1 (1864), 3–4.

[31] Funt, 'Rech'', 116.

[32] Lazarev, 'O vospitanii', 561.

[33] Zeidler, 'O zhenskom obrazovanii', 638.

[34] 'Sankt-Petersburg', *Russkii evrei*, 31 (1880), 1204.

This new image of the superficially educated Jewish girl relied on an evaluation of her educational training as inappropriate. These writers were not contesting the existence of new educational initiatives for Jewish girls, but rather their worthiness. Despite the overwhelmingly positive reception of the new schools for girls in local reports, essayists saw them as fundamentally flawed.

CONCLUSION: THE SCHOOLS AND THEIR DETRACTORS

One might have expected that those writing for the Russian Jewish press, largely outside the traditional camp, would have offered overwhelming support for the new trends in education for Jewish girls. After all, the new schools, while imperfect, offered a great deal more access to languages and literacy than had previously been available. In fact, many anonymous writers lauded their local schools for Jewish girls as bastions of enlightenment in otherwise backward towns. However, those authors who explicitly treated the subject of Jewish women's education were surprisingly dismissive of the new options.

Authors derided the private schools for Jewish girls as either devoting attention to the wrong subjects or aiming at an inappropriate level. There was concern that European languages and culture, in particular French, were valued over learning either Hebrew or Russian. Other writers committed to Jewish women's education found that the new schools catered to the wealthy and taught impractical subjects.

In point of fact, these criticisms were often justified. The private schools for Jewish girls of the 1860s and 1870s occupied a precarious position. On the one hand, their principals were well educated and committed to modernization and Russification of the Jewish community. On the other hand, the schools operated within largely traditional communities and could not hope to survive if their constituents were antagonized.

Not only did the schools rely on the goodwill of the community at large, but they counted on direct support from a variety of diverse groups. Private schools for Jewish girls throughout the Pale of Jewish Settlement could not hope to fill their enrolment and tuition needs only from daughters of the wealthy and enlightened members of their communities. They had to appeal to a broader market of families who sought literacy in Russian and a Jewish education for their daughters without the trappings of modernity. Both the moderate nature of the Judaic studies curricula and the sliding-scale tuition options provide evidence of this need to attract students broadly. Serving the needs of the daughters of the poor as well as the wealthy, the progressive as well as the traditional, required careful compromise.

That such schools would not entirely satisfy the most progressive elements of the Russian Jewish community is hardly surprising. Between their chronic lack of funds and the unique role these schools served in their communities, radical educational experiments were out of the question. What is surprising is the emotional and exaggerated rhetoric of many of the schools' detractors in their scorn for the private schools. Even if the new schools were not overly ambitious ideologically, surely they were a great improvement over the past and worthy of some praise.

The majority of articles written about Jewish women's education expressed a fervent desire for change, but motivations differed. Most of the writers for the Russian Jewish press supported improved women's education as a means towards achieving a modernized Russian Jewish community. The next generation of Jewish boys depended on what they were taught in their homes by their mothers. Creating a cadre of rational, nurturing modern mothers was thus key. A smaller number of writers supported teaching Jewish women as a goal in itself.

What all the contributors shared was a commitment to advancing Jewish women's education. Concrete changes, in the form of new private schools for Jewish girls springing up all over the Pale of Settlement, found favour in the eyes of the local correspondents of the Jewish papers. In descriptions of one to two sentences in Hebrew and Russian-language papers, these new schools served as an expression of local pride. This suggests that members of the educated and enlightened elite could appreciate the degree to which the schools were both new and important. However, while these positive views continued to appear in the periodical press, they were overshadowed in tone and quantity by the overwhelmingly negative full-length articles about Jewish women's education.

The conservative nature of the schools, the teaching of French and German literature instead of advanced Jewish studies, is not sufficient in explaining the disproportionate critique they received. Examination of the rhetoric of some of the writings shows that progressive Jewish men had enormous difficulty in positing the existence and necessity of progressive Jewish women. For many enlightened men, Jewish women, on the whole, represented the past they were struggling to overcome. In their minds, Jewish women embodied the backward traditional home. Thus, even well-educated Jewish women were tainted in their eyes, unable to merit the transformation of modernity. The extreme anxiety of these authors shows clearly in their treatments of Jewish women's education.

In the ongoing debate about Jewish women's education, these voices of derision were joined by the voices of those advocating a variety of solutions to the problems of the status quo. This chapter has focused on the period from the 1860s to the early 1880s. By the end of the century the immediacy of Jewish politics would turn the discussion away from women's education and towards more ideological solutions to educational issues as a whole.

The Call to Serve: Jewish Women Medical Students in Russia, 1872–1887

CAROLE B. BALIN

'Do you sincerely think that every woman who enrols on the courses feels called to medicine?'[1] This question posed by a *kursistka*—as a student at women's courses was commonly known—reverberated throughout educated Russian society in the 1870s and 1880s, as record numbers of women, especially Jewish women, flocked to St Petersburg to gain entry to medical courses designed specifically for females. Medical training was one of several paths open to women seeking higher education in Russia and the most popular choice among Jewish women.[2]

Initially a four-year programme, the courses for advanced midwives (*uchenye akusherki*) admitted four Jews among its first class of eighty-nine students when the programme opened in 1872. The first class performed so admirably that the courses were upgraded in 1876 to a five-year programme, equivalent to that of a university medical school. To signify that it required students to master more information and acquire more clinical experience than mere midwifery, it received the official designation 'Women's Medical Courses' (*zhenskie vrachebnye kursy*). By that time Jews comprised nearly 24 per cent of all students in the programme; and Jewish enrolment continued apace so that by 1879 one in three students was a Jew.

The Women's Medical Courses (WMC) were short-lived. In 1882, a decade

I wish to thank the following individuals for their generous assistance: Eliyana Adler, Felice Batlan, Michelle DenBeste, Ruth Dudgeon, Barbara Engel, Irina Gordon, Diana Greene, Rebecca Kobrin, and Andrea Weiss. Unless otherwise indicated, all translations from the Russian are my own.

[1] R. F-va, 'Iz storony v storonu', *Drug zhenshchin*, 3 (1883), 1. The question appears in a serialized novella by Rashel Feldshtein, who was herself a medical student on the Women's Medical Courses (WMC) before abandoning them for literary training.

[2] Jews constituted 21 per cent of the total matriculants at the WMC offered in conjunction with St Petersburg's renowned Medical-Surgical Academy, while making up 18 per cent of those on the rarefied Bestuzhevskie Higher Courses for Women in St Petersburg and 16 per cent of those on both the Kiev Higher Courses and the Lubyanskie Mathematics and Science Courses in Moscow. See R. Dudgeon, 'The Forgotten Minority: Women Students in Imperial Russia, 1872–1917', *Russian History/Histoire Russe*, 9 (1982), 16.

after opening, the courses stopped accepting new students. In 1887 they ceased operation altogether. Along with other institutions of higher learning, they fell victim to reactionary policies that swept Russia following the tsar's assassination. Women's medical education would not be revived in the empire until 1897 with the founding of the Women's Medical Institute in St Petersburg, where Jewish enrolment was limited to 3 per cent.

Despite their short tenure, the WMC trained a contingent of women doctors far outnumbering that of any contemporary European state. By the beginning of the twentieth century the Russian Medical Register listed 740 female physicians, of whom at least 200 were Jews.[3] Although smaller in absolute numbers, Jewish women doctors were to become even more of a presence in late imperial Russia, proportionately, than Jewish male doctors. In 1889, for instance, while Jewish men represented 13.4 per cent of Russian male physicians, Jewish women represented 24 per cent of female physicians—this, at a time when Jews accounted for less than 4 per cent of the total population in the Russian empire.[4]

Notably, neither male nor female doctors garnered much pay or prestige in nineteenth-century Russia. In fact, according to one historian, a sure sign of the physician's lowly status was the prevalence of (male) Jews in the profession, giving the Russian doctor a stigma of racial, as well as social, inferiority.[5] But medicine meant something entirely different to Russia's Jews—and to Russia's women. Both populations regarded medicine as a worthy profession that would help them to attain their common goal of reconfiguring Russian society at the end of the nineteenth century.

Like the inquisitive *kursistka* mentioned above, this chapter will scrutinize the motives driving women to medical school. Did these women feel called to medicine? What forces prompted women, especially Jewish women, to dedicate themselves to such a lengthy and arduous course of study? What do the abundant statistical data on the Jews enrolled on the WMC, the handful of their extant

[3] 'Alfavitnyi spisok zhenshchin-vrachei', *Rossiiskii meditsinskii spisok* (St Petersburg, 1904), 416–31. In contrast, France in 1900 had only ninety-five female physicians, while England lagged behind Russia with 258 doctors. Comparative figures are in C. Johanson, *Women's Struggle for Higher Education in Russia, 1855–1900* (Kingston, 1987), 90. I am grateful to Barbara Engel for providing me with the register.

[4] N. M. Frieden, *Russian Physicians in an Era of Reform and Revolution, 1856–1905* (Princeton, 1981), 333, based on V. I. Grebenshchikov, 'Opyt razrabotki rezul'tatov registratsii vrachei v Rossii', *Spravochnaya kniga dlya vrachei* (St Petersburg, 1890), i. 111–13.

[5] Johanson, *Women's Struggle for Higher Education in Russia*, 77–8. Medicine's lowly status was largely due to its low placement in the Table of Ranks, the ordering of professions and positions instituted by Peter the Great. Until the late 19th century, most physicians were restricted to government service, where they had little freedom or mobility. Popular associations of healing with women indubitably led to a further denigration of medicine's status, even as it became increasingly controlled by men over the course of the 19th century.

memoirs, and the Russian Medical Registers of women doctors from subsequent years reveal about their desire to become physicians? An examination of the pages of the Russian Jewish press and the records of Russian Jewry's chief philanthropic organization of the day show that educated Jewish men, by and large, encouraged the medical training of Jewish women in word and deed. Why did they endorse these future doctors? Did their motives for supporting them coincide with the motives of those whom they supported? Generally speaking, what larger historical lessons begin to be illuminated by focusing on the modest phenomenon of Jewish women entering professional medicine in late imperial Russia?[6] What might the study of Jewish medical *kursistki* teach us about the integration into progressive Russian society of educated Jewish women, on the one hand, and Jewish men, on the other?

ADVANCES IN EDUCATION AMONG WOMEN AND JEWS

As if in a Venn diagram, educated Jewish women of late imperial Russia stood in the overlap between two intersecting communities: women and Jews. As such, they were the beneficiaries of strides made in higher education within each community over the course of the nineteenth century. Briefly surveying the relevant educational gains made by women, and then by Jews, will provide the necessary context for exploring the motives of Jewish women pursuing medical training at the WMC.

The extensive debate on enhancing women's education that ensued among Russia's progressive society in the 1860s was part of a larger discussion on the role and status of women in the Russian empire. Known as the 'woman's question' (*zhenskii vopros*), this controversy pitched those who applauded women's pursuit of university study as a first step towards their emancipation, leading ultimately to equality of the sexes, against those who warned that higher education would divert women from their conventional roles of wives and mothers, thereby imperilling both the family and the entire social order. While this debate raged in the abstract, the loosening of state control over educators permitted the actual admission of women to higher educational institutions. Enjoying their new freedom and caught up in the reformist spirit of the day, professors and administrators embarked upon a series of liberal experiments in higher education, including the admission of women to university lectures and medical laboratories as auditors (*slushatel'nitsy*) beginning in 1859. Such privileges were swiftly curtailed, however, with the University

[6] Paula Hyman's use of gender as a category of study to point out differing rates of assimilation among Jewish men and women is particularly instructive here, as is Benjamin Nathans's reinterpretation of the Russian Jewish encounter that focuses on Jewish men's entry into civil society via professionalization. See P. E. Hyman, *Gender and Assimilation in Modern Jewish History: The Roles and Representation of Women* (Seattle, 1995) and B. Nathans, *Beyond the Pale: The Jewish Encounter with Late Imperial Russia* (Berkeley, 2002).

Statute of 1863, which banned women from all Russian universities. In the wake of student disturbances in 1861–2, the government acted on its fears that women's presence at universities was becoming a threat to social morality and a factor contributing to the rebelliousness of the student community.[7]

A notable exception to the 1863 statute was Varvara Aleksandrovna (Nafanova) Kashevarova-Rudneva (1842–99), an orphan of Jewish descent who is mentioned in nearly every history of women in medicine as the 'mother' of all female doctors in Russia.[8] Born into a Jewish family in Vitebsk, she married a St Petersburg merchant who promised her the freedom and finances to study. When he opposed her plans to seek a medical career, the couple divorced and Kashevarova pursued midwifery studies in St Petersburg. In 1864, when the Medical-Surgery Academy banned women from its courses, she alone received permission to continue her studies on account of a previous agreement that after graduation she would treat Orenburg's Bashkir women, whose religion forbade the attendance of male physicians. Unlike her male counterparts, when she was awarded a medical degree, she was barred from state service, including in Orenburg's hospitals. Thus, she pursued and received a doctorate in 1878 and spent the rest of her life engaged in research with her second husband, M. M. Rudnev, the pathologist who came to teach (with his wife's assistance) at the WMC.

Unlike Kashevarova-Rudneva, considerable numbers of determined Russian women abandoned their homeland to seek higher education abroad, primarily in Switzerland and France.[9] A majority returned by the 1870s as 'Higher Women's Courses' (*vysshie zhenskie kursy*) were founded. Established in Moscow, St Petersburg, Kiev, and Kazan, they were meant to staunch the flow of Russian women leaving to study at European universities, where presumably they were at risk of being indoctrinated with revolutionary dogma. The Higher Women's Courses functioned like any other Russian state institution of learning. They had entrance requirements, a prescribed course of study, and traditional forms of administration. Featuring a curriculum and professors drawn largely from the local university, the courses admitted thousands of women to advanced study in the sciences and humanities.[10] However, in contrast to male university graduates, the women who completed the Higher Women's Courses did not receive employment commensurate with their academic preparation. Among those who found gainful employment, most occupied

[7] C. Johanson, 'Autocratic Politics, Public Opinion, and Women's Medical Education During the Reign of Alexander II, 1855–1881', *Slavic Review*, 38 (Sept. 1979), 426–43.

[8] She is also one of the few women to merit an entry in *Evreiskaya entsiklopediya* (St Petersburg, 1906), xiii. 715. Her biography is detailed in J. Tuve, *The First Russian Women Physicians* (Newtonville, Mass., 1984), 46–56, and S. M. Dionesov, *V. A. Kashevarova—pervaya russkaya zhenshchina-doktor meditsiny* (Moscow, 1965).

[9] They formed a virtual 'colony' in Zurich, where many studied medicine. See J. M. Meijer, *Knowledge and Revolution: The Russian Colony in Zurich, 1870–73* (Assen, 1955), 46–62.

[10] Johanson, *Women's Struggle for Higher Education in Russia*, 5.

positions that required only secondary education; the majority became teachers.[11] For Jewish women, who were barred from teaching in the Russian empire, medicine became a particularly alluring professional prospect.

In general, medicine was an attractive option for women. Some argued that 'feminine attributes', such as nurturing, compassion, and intuition, made women 'natural' healers and comforters of the sick. This was bolstered by women's enduring involvement in the healing arts, especially childbirth. But midwives had been left to their own devices in Russia until the mid-eighteenth century when two empresses undertook the development of formal midwifery courses as a means of improving skills and increasing numbers.[12] They accomplished neither until the following century when more midwifery programmes emerged and Russian law formally distinguished between the educational backgrounds of three different types of obstetric personnel.[13] In all of pre-revolutionary Russia there were only 6,000 trained midwives, all of whom were women.[14] A highly disproportionate number of midwives were Jews: they comprised 19 per cent of all midwives by the end of the nineteenth century.[15] But for some Jewish and Russian women, the limited nature of midwifery did not 'slake their thirst for knowledge' and so they opted for professional medical training.[16]

Medicine held special appeal for a generation that had come of age during a period of intellectual ferment and rising expectations in the Russian empire. The 1860s was a time of immense optimism when young women and men, eager to participate in the regeneration of their society, structured their lives according to a new ideology, labelled by conservative forces as 'nihilism'.[17] Nihilists believed in the power

[11] There is employment information on two-thirds of the more than 1,000 women who graduated from the Bestuzhevskie Courses from 1882 to 1889: 36 per cent became teachers; 20 per cent engaged in various types of literary, theatrical, laboratory, or clerical work; and 5 per cent entered the medical field, mainly as midwives, masseuses, and paramedics. Ibid. 73.

[12] V. A. Bazanov and A. V. Pavluchkova, 'Ot "babich'ikh shkol" k "zhenskim vrachebnym kursam"', *Akusherstvo i ginekologiya*, 48 (Nov. 1972), 74.

[13] The categories, in descending order, are *povival'nye babki*, *sel'skie* (rural) *povival'nye babki*, and *povitukhi*. The term *akusherka* (from the French *accoucheur*, meaning midwife), while frequently used in general discussions, did not exist in Russian legislation, except when appended to the term *fel'dsheritsa*, as in *fel'dsheritsa-akusherka* (paramedic–midwife). S. C. Ramer, 'Childbirth and Culture: Midwifery in the Nineteenth-Century Russian Countryside', in D. L. Ransel (ed.), *The Family in Imperial Russia: New Lines of Historical Research* (Urbana, Ill., 1978), 219.

[14] Ibid. 221.

[15] Yu. G., 'Meditsinskie professii v Rossii', *Evreiskaya entsiklopediya*, x. 779.

[16] [A.] Sh[abanova], 'Zhenskoe vrachebnoe obrazovanie v Rossii (K 35-letiyu pervykh zenshchin-vrachei v Rossii)', *Istoricheskii vestnik*, 131 (Mar. 1913), 953. Shabanova was among the first students admitted to the WMC, graduating in 1878. Her point was confirmed by the appearance of thirteen former midwifery students among those enrolled at the WMC. See E. Nekrasova, 'Zhenskie vrachebnye kursy v Peterburge: Iz vospominanii i perepiski pervykh studentok', *Vestnik Evropy*, 17 (Dec. 1882), 818.

[17] Turgenev coined the term in *Fathers and Sons* (1862). His hero was a medical student who disregarded the ways of his elders and adopted a belief that only the study of science was worthwhile. For a discussion of the maskilim's attitudes towards this new ideology and the women it produced, see

of science to help build the future and rejected all that relied on faith and custom, including men's subjugation of women. They proposed better educational and vocational opportunities for women and comradely relations between the sexes. Because their struggle for autonomy was in most cases linked with a desire to help others, they came to regard the practice of medicine as uniquely suited for acting on their principles.[18] In a country that suffered a chronic shortage of medical personnel, the social utility of medical education could not be underestimated.[19]

At the same time, medicine offered women the only route to a profession traditionally held by Russian men. Graduates of the WMC had served so admirably in the Russo-Turkish War of 1877–8 that the tsar granted them the title of 'woman doctor' (*zhenshchina-vrach*) and the right to independent medical practice. By 1882 female physicians were functioning as general practitioners in rural and urban hospitals, as well as interns and assistants at their alma mater.[20]

Medicine was one of the first areas of higher learning in which the Russian government began to loosen restrictions and extend privileges to Jewish men. The Medical-Surgical Academy in St Petersburg contained the greatest concentration of Jewish male students of any Russian institution of higher learning in the early part of the nineteenth century.[21] Still the numbers were meagre, and the government banned all Jews from state service, except those willing to convert. Over the course of the nineteenth century, however, governmental decrees made medical service more attractive to Jews, so that by the 1880s, one observer maintained, 'there was almost no occasion when a [male] Jewish gymnasium student applied to anything but a medical faculty'.[22]

Jewish men were drawn to medicine for a variety of practical and ideological reasons, not least of which was the influence of the Haskalah. As the Jewish Enlightenment movement expanded its reach to the Russian empire, it concerned itself with disseminating secular knowledge.[23] The maskilim were particularly

S. Feiner, 'Ha'ishah hayehudit hamodernit: Mikreh-mivḥan beyaḥasei hahaskalah vehamodernah', *Zion*, 58/4 (1993), 469–99.

[18] As illustrated by Vera Pavlova, the socially conscious heroine of Chernyshevsky's influential novel *What Is To Be Done?*, who studied medicine.

[19] By mid-century, Russia engaged in a campaign of *ozdorovlenie* ('health improvement') to rid itself of cholera and typhus and to reduce child mortality. See J. F. Hutchinson, *Politics and Public Health in Revolutionary Russia, 1880–1918* (Baltimore, 1990), p. xv.

[20] P. P. Sushchinsky, *Zhenshchina-vrach v Rossii: Ocherk desyatiletiya zhenskikh vrachebykh kursov, 1872–82* (St Petersburg, 1883), 17.

[21] Approximately forty Jewish men matriculated between 1835 and 1854; Nathans, *Beyond the Pale*, 60.

[22] H. Sliozberg, *Dela minuvshikh dnei* (Paris, 1933), i. 110–11, as quoted in L. R. Epstein, 'Caring for the Soul's House: The Jews of Russia and Health Care, 1860–1914', Ph.D. thesis (Yale University, 1995), 48.

[23] Maskilim promoted modern education for Jews of both sexes. For them, only the woman who had received a thorough grounding in secular subjects and who had fully developed her intellectual potential could properly fulfil her roles of wife and mother.

interested in science and its practical application in medicine. It offered a unique professional avenue for contributing, quite literally, to the general welfare of society, as well as a means of educating and moulding the so-called ignorant Jewish masses.[24]

Russian officials, too, were supremely confident in the power of education to draw Jews out of their traditional isolation and transform them into useful subjects. As early as 1804, legislation allowed Jews to enrol in 'all the public schools, secondary schools and universities in Russia, on equal terms with other children'.[25] This law did not, however, translate into any noticeable shift in Jewish enrolment in any Russian educational institution until later in the century when the Russian government and maskilim combined their efforts.[26] Over the course of the nineteenth century, increasing practical considerations led Jews to pursue education beyond traditional Jewish modes. In particular, a number of incentives were offered to Jewish male graduates of institutions of higher learning, such as reduction in military service from twenty-five to ten years and the right to apply for employment in the civil service. But these were little more than token changes that had little effect until 1861, when the Russian government granted all Jewish male university students and graduates unrestricted residential rights.[27] The privileges outlined in this legislation were later extended to Jewish women ascending to institutions of higher learning in the Russian empire.

For all their similarities, it is necessary to underscore a crucial difference in the history of higher education of women and Jews. In the Russian context, each was being educated for a different end. The writings of Nikolay Pirogov—the noted surgeon and pedagogue who advocated educating both women and Jews—are instructive in this regard. In his provocative article 'Questions of Life' (1856), Pirogov called for improvement in women's education so as to enhance their duties as teachers and guardians of children: 'Not the position of woman in society—but her education, which contains the education of all humanity—that is what needs to be changed.' Such reform, he implied, ought not to cause a transformation in women's status or family structure.[28] Not so the Jews. For them, according to Pirogov, education was the best method for elevating their status in Russian society and erasing barriers

[24] Of course, alterations proposed in health care challenged deeply rooted beliefs among Jews. After all, modern medicine demands that scientific authority be asserted over religious faith—a fundamental shift in orientation for a revelation-based tradition like that of the Jews. The hope was that modern medicine would help reform the Jews. See L. R. Epstein's excellent framing of the issue in 'Caring for the Soul's House', 1–2.

[25] P. Levanda, *Polnyi khronologicheskii sbornik zakonov i polozhenii kasayushchikhsya evreev* (St Petersburg, 1874), 53–9, as quoted in P. Mendes-Flohr and J. Reinharz (eds.), *The Jew in the Modern World* (New York, 1995), 375.

[26] M. Stanislawski, *Tsar Nicholas I and the Jews: The Transformation of Jewish Society in Russia, 1825–1855* (Philadelphia, 1983), 97–122.

[27] Nathans, *Beyond the Pale*, 214–15.

[28] As quoted in Johanson, *Women's Struggle for Higher Education in Russia*, 10–11. As noted above, this initial impetus for educating women was later expanded to include gainful employment, self-fulfilment, and even emancipation of women.

between them and their Russian peers. 'Enlightenment has such an ability to amalgamate, to humanize', maintained Pirogov in 1860, 'that Jews, Slavs and every other one-sided nationality yield to it.'[29] Such was the underlying aim of educating Russian Jewry: utility for the ultimate goal of social integration.

A PROFILE OF JEWISH WOMEN AT THE WOMEN'S MEDICAL COURSES

Despite the stringent entry requirements, Jews became a constituent element of women's professional medical training from the day the original four-year advanced midwifery courses started on 2 November 1872. Students needed to be at least 20 years of age (men could study medicine at 17, but women were considered not mature enough by that age), pass an examination on gymnasium subjects and show proof of (1) a gymnasium diploma or its equivalent; (2) parental or spousal permission to study; (3) a certificate of loyalty from police officials; (4) relationship to a family residing in St Petersburg that would presumably take responsibility for them; and (5) sufficient funds for tuition and other expenses during the entire four years of study.[30] All told, 109 women took the entrance exam and, of the ninety who passed, eighty-nine entered the programme.

Jewish enrolment started slowly but climbed steadily, so that by 1875 they comprised one-fifth of the student body (see Table 1). The jump in enrolment in 1876 (a 33.8 per cent rate of increase for non-Jews and a striking 63.2 per cent for Jews) may have been due to the age for admission being lowered. This change fulfilled the dreams of even larger numbers of parents eager to send their well-prepared teenage daughters to the capital to put their solid educational backgrounds to use. At a median age younger than their non-Jewish peers, 82 per cent of Jewish students entered the courses between the ages of 19 and 21. In their first eight years of operation, Jewish women accounted for over 20 per cent of students at the WMC and, by the time they closed in 1887, Jewish women comprised 24 per cent of all graduates.[31]

A composite portrait of the 169 Jewish students at the WMC during its first eight years of operation yields a very high percentage from the petit bourgeoisie.[32]

[29] As quoted in Nathans, *Beyond the Pale*, 257.

[30] R. Dudgeon, 'Women and Higher Education in Russia, 1855–1905', Ph.D. thesis (George Washington University, 1975), 106.

[31] G. M. Gertsenshtein, 'Zhenskie vrachebnye kursy i zhenshchiny-vrachi', *Real'naya entsiklopediya prakticheskikh meditsinskikh nauk: Mediko-khirurgicheskii slovar'*, 7 (St Petersburg, 1893), 224.

[32] Unless otherwise noted, all statistics are drawn from G. M. Gertsenshtein, 'Evreiki-studentki', *Rassvet*, 37 (1880), 1465–9. Gertsenshtein (1851–99) was an adjunct professor of medical geography and statistics at the Medical-Surgical Academy. His sister Anna was among the first Jews in Russia to study at an institution of higher learning abroad. See N. Rubinshtein, 'Pervaya evreika-studentka v Rossii', *Russkii evrei*, 27 (1880), 1071–2, and G. M. Gertsenshtein, 'Pis'mo v redaktsiyu', *Russkii evrei*, 29 (1880), 1140–1.

Table 1. Number of Jewish Women Students on the Women's Medical Courses, St Petersburg

Year	All students	Jewish students	%
1872	89	4	4.5
1873	89	13	14.6
1874	88	12	13.6
1875	93	19	20.4
1876	130	31[a]	23.8
1877	122	29[a]	23.8
1878	108	35	32.4
1879	77	26	33.8
Total	**796**	**169**	**21.2**

[a] The figure includes one Karaite.

Source: G. M. Gertsenshtein, 'Evreiki-studentki', *Rassvet*, 37 (1880), 1468.

That is, within Russia's social framework of legally defined estates, most Jewish students' fathers were classified as merchants (*kupechestvo*, 51 per cent) or artisans and petty traders (*meshchantsvo*, 40 per cent).[33] Six of the students were the daughters of doctors, who presumably encouraged their female offspring by example.[34] Like their middle-class counterparts elsewhere, the Jews of increasingly well-to-do families in Russia from the 1860s onwards were entering liberal professions and taking on both commercial and cultural roles. Subject to the 'twin process of Russification and embourgeoisement', they took their cues from the West and transformed their daughters from schoolgirls to properly educated ladies through attendance at Russian primary schools and gymnasiums.[35] While their brothers may have toiled under the religious obligation of Jewish study, they acquired an elite classical education with fluency in European languages and a thorough grounding in secular subjects, making them fully prepared for admission to the WMC.[36] In fact, nearly all Jewish matriculants at the WMC had received a gymnasium degree (79.3 per cent), and the remainder had earned diplomas through the assistance of

[33] Of the remaining fourteen students, six were daughters of doctors, three of foreign subjects, two of teachers and lower ranks, one of a civil servant, and two were wives of male students.

[34] For example, Evgeniya Nikolaevna Mandelshtam, the daughter of the chief obstetrician in Mogilev, who was also a key player in the development of midwifery courses, graduated from the WMC in 1881.

[35] The phrase is coined by M. Stanislawski in 'Russian Jewry, the Russian State, and the Dynamics of Russian Emancipation', in P. Birnbaum and I. Katznelson (eds.) *Paths of Emancipation* (Princeton, 1995), 276.

[36] Literacy among Jewish women was relatively widespread and those Jewish girls who were formally educated were far more likely to attend Russian primary schools than Jewish boys. See S. Stampfer, 'Gender Differentiation and Education of the Jewish Woman in Nineteenth-Century Eastern Europe', *Polin*, 7 (1992), 63–87.

home tutors (17.1 per cent) or training colleges (2.4 per cent) and institutes (1.2 per cent). In the words of Mariya Semenovna Kaufman, a Jew admitted to the courses in the 1880s, gymnasium studies had 'aroused in [them] a desire to satisfy the inquisitiveness of the mind'.[37]

Kaufman, who hailed from Odessa, travelled a considerable distance to satisfy her yearning for higher education, which was typical of Jewish students at the WMC, who largely originated from southern Russia. Although fewer than 14 per cent of Russia's Jews lived in New Russia in the 1870s, its four southern provinces furnished 45 per cent of the Jewish students at the WMC.[38] In contrast, the area of the Pale along the River Vistula, which counted 2½ million Jews among its population, provided only 29 per cent of Jews at the WMC. Twenty per cent of all non-Jewish students (and only nine Jews) were from St Petersburg.[39] Although the region north of the Black Sea known as New Russia (Novorossiya) was delineated in 1835 as part of the Pale of Settlement, secular education and modifications to traditional ways of Jewish life made greater inroads there than in other parts of the Pale. New Russia's Jews, who were largely engaged in commerce, were instrumental in the founding of such cities as Kherson and Odessa, which became the two largest training grounds for Jewish women entering the WMC. In fact, Odessa has become legendary in the historical literature for its huge Jewish enrolment of both boys and girls in gymnasia.[40]

The surge of Jews from the south to the WMC is only partially explained by the progressive nature of New Russia and its sizeable number of qualified candidates for admission. Some Jewish parents—even those of the petit bourgeoisie—were not eager to see their diploma-holding daughters enrol on the EMC. Teofiliya Polyak, for instance, waged such a bitter struggle with her Jewish middle-class parents that it left her, in the words of a friend, 'sarcastic, distrustful and pessimistic'.[41] Yet, even the Polyaks might have agreed that medical school provided Jewish women an escape from their restricted lives and a passport out of the Pale.

Enrolment on any of the Higher Women's Courses guaranteed a Jew temporary right of residence outside the Pale during the course of her study.[42] Only in 1911 was this right for women made permanent, as it had been for Jewish men since

[37] M. K[au]f[ma]n, 'Pis'mo v redaktsiyu', *Nedel'naya khronika Voskhoda*, 44 (30 Oct. 1882), 1186. She is registered as a female physician in 'Alfavitnyi spisok zhenshchin-vrachei', 421.

[38] While in 1847 only 2.5 per cent of Russia's Jews lived in the southern provinces, the proportion increased to 13.8 per cent in 1897; 'Russia', in *Encyclopedia Judaica*, CD-ROM version.

[39] G. M. Gertsenshtein, 'Zhenskie vrachebnye kursy (Statisticheskie materialy k istorii ikh)', *Vrach*, 34 (21 Aug. 1880), 556, and B. Engel, 'Women Medical Students in Russia, 1872–1882: Reformers or Rebels?', *Journal of Social History*, 12 (Spring 1979), 401.

[40] Jews accounted for over one-third of gymnasium students in Odessa's educational districts. See Nathans, *Beyond the Pale*, 218, as well as S. Zipperstein, *The Jews of Odessa: A Cultural History, 1794–1881* (Stanford, Calif., 1986).

[41] As quoted in Engel, 'Women Medical Students in Russia', 399.

[42] Nathans, *Beyond the Pale*, 222 n. 73.

1861.[43] Because Jewish women were barred from teaching, medicine promised them the longest protection of their residential rights. According to a law promulgated in 1879, any Jew of either sex studying or practising any medical profession enjoyed the right to live anywhere in the empire. This included those training to become doctors, doctors' assistants, midwives, pharmacists, and dentists.[44] Even a Jewish midwife married to a man without residential rights was permitted to live outside the Pale.[45] The 1879 legislation was likely responsible for the spike in Jewish enrolment in that same year, when Jews reached a robust 33.8 per cent of the entering class at the WMC.

While residential rights might have been one incentive for pursuing higher educational opportunities, some charged that Jewish women entered higher courses in order to 'catch a good husband'.[46] The statistics suggest otherwise: Jewish women arrived at the WMC single and remained so until after graduation. In fact, all but two of the Jewish students were single, and Jewish women were far less likely to marry during the course of their studies than their Christian counterparts. Of 167 unmarried Jewish students, only thirteen (8 per cent) married while engaged in their studies, while 103 (16 per cent) Christian students wed.[47] According to a professor who taught at the courses, 'The Jewish women [students] were practical' and eschewed marriage to remain exclusively focused on their studies, so as to finish their training in the shortest time possible.[48]

A DAY IN THE LIFE

Young or old, single or married, those who attended the courses were subject to restrictions meant to keep their behaviour in check. The government was especially uneasy about the potential for revolutionary activity among the student body and took precautions to ensure its utmost loyalty. Within the first week of classes, students received a set of regulations that covered even the most trivial aspects of daily life. They were instructed to behave properly at lectures, wear uniforms at all times, and observe strict decorum in their appearance. Both short hair and smoking were forbidden, as was contact with any of their male counterparts, who were reputed to be the most politically active of St Petersburg's student body. Should anything unusual occur, they were to report it at once to the inspector, M. C. Ermolova, a society woman of some standing whose presence helped to ensure the respectability

[43] R. Dudgeon, 'The Forgotten Minority', 19.

[44] G. Voltke, 'Meditsinskie professii po deistvuyushchemu russkomu zakonodatel'stvu', *Evreiskaya entsiklopediia*, x. 780.

[45] Ibid. 782.

[46] L. D. Lyakhovetsky, 'Zhenskoe obrazovanie (Pis'mo v redaktsiyu)', *Nedel'naya khronika Voskhoda*, 39 (25 Sept. 1882), 1071.

[47] Note that two female Jewish students married physicians. See Epstein, 'Caring for the Soul's House', 54 n. 13.

[48] Gertsenshtein, 'Evreiki-studentki', *Rassvet*, 37 (1880), 1468.

of the courses.[49] All in all, the government's suspicions were ungrounded. Only 10 per cent of the WMC graduates became involved with the police and only a fraction of these abandoned medical school for full-time political activity.[50]

Jewish students were especially prone to accusations of revolutionary involvement. Even those generally sympathetic to women medical students criticized the Jews for a predilection for revolutionary engagement. N. I. Kozlov, for instance, the chief military medical inspector of Russia who had played a key role in the founding of the WMC and whose own daughter became a graduate, asserted that serious study and the achievement of practical goals had a settling influence on even the 'radical Jewish women from the south-western regions'.[51] Indeed, records do reveal political engagement on their part, ranging from the casual commitments of WMC students Dora Tauber and Adelaida Klein, who lent their apartments to radicals, to the zealous actions of Sofiya Ginzburg, whose radicalism cost her life.[52] Ginzburg (1863–90) unsuccessfully sought to follow her elder sister Minona to the WMC from their home town of Ekaterinoslav, but wound up instead studying medicine in Bern when the WMC were shut down. Ultimately, she landed in prison for her involvement in revolutionary politics and took her own life after being sentenced to death.[53]

Radicalism was not the only charge levelled at the medical *kursistki*. Throughout their training and careers they had to contend with those who regarded them with, if not disdain, at least curiosity and distrust. Macabre rumours spread throughout St Petersburg that those studying at the WMC 'cut up corpses in the evenings and left their laboratories with bones in their hands and intestines in their pockets'.[54]

The *kursistki* themselves describe a far more mundane existence with days crammed with lectures and nights with preparation. One student chronicled her frenetic day that began before eight in the morning on one day and ended after one in the morning the following day.[55] Without a doubt, the course load was heavy. In the first year students attended twenty-two hours of lectures in physics, chemistry, botany, zoology, anatomy, and histology each week, and spent most evenings in the

[49] The strict regulations are mentioned in several memoirs, including A. Shabanova, 'Zhenskie vrachebnye kursy (Iz vospominanii vysshei slushatel'nitsy)', *Vestnik Evropy*, 1 (1886), 347–8; Sh[abanova], 'Zhenskoe vrachebnoe obrazovanie v Rossii', 955, and Nekrasova, 'Zhenskie vrachebnye kursy', 819.

[50] Engel, 'Women Medical Students in Russia', 408.

[51] As quoted in E. O. Likhacheva, *Materialy dlya istorii zhenskogo obrazovaniya v Rossii*, 2 vols. (St Petersburg, 1899–1901), ii. 632–4. See R. Dudgeon, 'Women and Higher Education in Russia', 171.

[52] Engel, 'Women Medical Students in Russia', 402, and M.Ch., 'K biografii S. M. Ginzburg', *Katorga i ssylka: Istoriko-revolyutsionnyi vestnik*, 8/24 (Moscow, 1926), 210–22.

[53] The Ginzburgs' younger sibling Liza received a midwifery diploma. The names of ten pairs of Jewish sisters are listed in 'Alfavitnyi spisok zhenshchin-vrachei'.

[54] Sh[abanova], 'Zhenskoe vrachebnoe obrazovanie v Rossii', 956. This rumour about women medical students, who were largely Jewish, evokes long-standing stereotypes, ranging from women's association with witchcraft to Jews' association with devil worship.

[55] Nekrasova, 'Zhenskie vrachebnye kursy', 837ff.

laboratory. With each successive year of study, the number of subjects and hours of practical training increased, so that by the final year students took classes in gynaecology, ophthalmology, dermatology, syphilis, and children's diseases, as well as clinical studies in obstetrics, surgical gynaecology, and internal medicine.

In light of the arduous course of study, some members of the Jewish community worried that 'their' women might not make the grade. They feared that the historic inattention to girls' education within Jewish society had resulted in a generation of girls now eligible for higher education 'on paper', but in reality insufficiently prepared for such. As one representative declared, despite their different dogmas, both 'orthodox and progressive Jews share an unforgivable neglect of women's education'.[56] That indifference was translating into failing grades for some Jews enrolled on the Higher Women's Courses.[57] Yet a *kursistka* retorted that the high Jewish enrolment on the WMC proved their competence. After all, she argued, 'the entry requirements are stiff, and no university official would make allowances for Jews'.[58] With or without adequate training, Jews were to comprise nearly one-quarter of all graduates of the courses.[59]

From matriculation to graduation, students were preoccupied by the quotidian task of making ends meet. In some cases, families, unwilling or unable to assist their daughters, left them in dire straits. Many students lived in abject poverty, sharing rented quarters that resembled hovels or subsisting for twenty-four hours without a piece of bread. Economic hardship and the general severity of daily life exacted the ultimate toll on dozens of women: of those enrolled in the first eight classes, twenty-seven non-Jews and three Jews died, of consumption, typhus, or suicide.[60] Others cobbled together a living from the largesse of recent graduates who had already secured gainful employment or aid provided by philanthropic societies founded to help students.

THE OPE AND THE GENDERED DIFFERENTIATION OF FINANCIAL SUPPORT

Generally, financial assistance was in short supply. No stipends were allotted to the first class, and only six to the second.[61] By 1879, 6 per cent of non-Jewish students received some form of aid, but the same could not be said of the Jews.[62] Articles

[56] Slushatel'nitsa vysshikh zhenskikh kursov, 'Golos iz sredi zabytykh', *Russkii evrei*, 41–2 (28 Nov. 1884), 3. The editor concurred with the writer in *Russkii evrei*, 45–6 (16 Dec. 1884), 2–5.

[57] G. M. Gertsenshtein, 'Evreiki-studentki', *Rassvet*, 38 (1880), 1511–13.

[58] K[au]f[ma]n, 'Pis'mo v redaktsiyu', 1186.

[59] In all, 959 women entered the courses. By 1887, 410 had finished and become doctors; of these, 24 per cent were Jews. Gertsenshtein, 'Zhenskie vrachebnye kursy i zhenshchiny-vrachi', 224.

[60] Gertsenshtein, 'Evreiki-studentki', *Rassvet*, 38 (1880), 1511.

[61] Engel, 'Women Medical Students in Russia', 401.

[62] Johanson, *Women's Struggle for Higher Education in Russia*, 83.

began to appear in the Jewish press describing the deleterious effects of financial hardship on the students in the hope that generous individuals and institutions would come forward to give full material support to their endeavours.[63] The most likely funding source of the day was the Society for the Spread of Enlightenment Among the Jews of Russia (Obshchestvo dlya rasprostraneniya prosveshcheniya mezhdu evreyami v Rossii, OPE), which was founded in 1863 by a cadre of affluent Jewish merchants and became essentially an organization devoted to financial aid for Jewish students. A steady stream of petitions made its way to the society's headquarters in St Petersburg from Jewish students throughout the empire. In response, it began doling out funds to needy students of all kinds, but privileged those at institutions of higher learning. Beginning in 1863, it provided university students (or the equivalent) with 3,000 roubles, which reached a high of 35,000 roubles by 1893.[64] Over the course of two decades (1864–84), more than 70 per cent of its financial aid was allocated to students enrolled specifically in St Petersburg's educational institutions (see Table 2).

That fact notwithstanding, the OPE gave meagre support to Jews studying at St Petersburg's WMC until an external goad prodded it into giving generously. Already during the early years of the WMC's operation, Jewish medical *kursistki* were petitioning the society for assistance. By 1875 it had responded favourably to merely five students, in amounts too minuscule to record.[65] A year later the actions of the newly founded Society for Assistance to Needy Women Enrolled on Medical Courses managed to wangle far more support out of the OPE.[66] On 9 May 1876 the OPE leadership reported that the non-sectarian society had provided stipends to more than half of the Jews enrolled on the WMC (twenty-six out of forty-five petitioning Jews received stipends totalling 1,420 roubles, equalling approximately 55 roubles per student).[67] Grateful for the society's open-mindedness, the OPE agreed to raise its allocation of stipends to Jewish *kursistki* and immediately sent 300 roubles to the society, along with a letter thanking its members for

[63] Gerstenshtein, 'Evreiki-studentki', *Rassvet*, 37 (1880), 1469.

[64] Nathans, *Beyond the Pale*, 227.

[65] I. M. Cherikover, *Istoriya Obshchestva dlya rasprostraneniya prosveshcheniya mezhdu evreyami v Rossii, 1863–1913* (St Petersburg, 1913), 152. The stipends are not represented in Table 2, which is based on data in Rosenthal's appendix (see the source note to the table).

[66] The society was founded in St Petersburg by Anna Pavlovna Filosofova and Mariya Vasilevna Trubnikova, important leaders in the women's movement in Russia. Filosofova's husband worked closely with the war minister D. A. Milyutin, the official largely responsible for founding the WMC; Dudgeon, 'Women and Higher Education', 158–9. The OPE's response to the society's generosity to Jewish women is recorded in Cherikover, *Istoriya Obshchestva dlya rasprostraneniya prosveshcheniya mezhdu evreyami v Rossii*, 152, and L. M. Rosenthal, *Toledot ḥevrat marbitsei haskalah beyisra'el be'erets rusyah*, 2 vols., vol. i (St Petersburg, 1885), vol. ii (St Petersburg, 1890), i. 129.

[67] Rosenthal, *Toledot ḥevrat marbitsei haskalah beyisra'el be'erets rusyah*, i. 129. A total of sixty-eight stipends were provided that year. See Engel, 'Women Medical Students in Russia', 401. Note as well the very significant number of Jews requesting assistance in that year: of seventy-nine Jewish students enrolled in the WMC by 1876, forty-five requested aid from the society.

Table 2. Value of stipends given to students at Russian institutions of higher learning by the OPE, 1864–84 (roubles)

Year	St Petersburg University	Moscow University	Kharkov University	Kiev University	Military–Surgical Academy, St Petersburg	Higher women's courses	Midwifery programmes
1864	978	600	255	190	637	—	50
1865	1,000	800	210	255	620	—	150
1866	1,000	800	200	—	720	—	205
1867	908	200	—	100	885	—	75
1868	900	100	300	100	900	—	69
1869	675	100	150	100	1,125	—	87
1870	375	—	150	—	775	—	56
1871	300	100	150	100	600	—	75
1872	300	—	150	100	600	—	31
1873	300	—	—	—	600	—	—
1874	300	—	—	—	600	—	—
1875	300	—	—	—	800	—	—
1876	300	100	—	—	800	—	—
1877	150	—	—	—	800	—	—
1878	150	—	—	—	800	300	—
1879	150	—	—	—	600	300	—
1880	807	—	—	—	1,045	1,320	—
1881	1,279	—	—	—	2,761	1,660	—
1882	405	—	50	—	317	965	—
1883	496	—	—	—	129	475	—
1884	525	—	—	—	100	—	—
Total	**11,598**[a]	**2,800**	**1,615**	**945**	**16,214**	**5,020**	**798**

[a] The original table records an incorrect total of 11,597.

Source: L. M. Rosenthal, *Toledot ḥevrat marbitsei haskalah beyisra'el be'erets rusiyah*, 2 vols. (St Petersburg, 1885, 1889), vol. i, appendix.

'not differentiating between girls of varying faiths'.[68] The OPE supported the society for six consecutive years, reaching a peak in 1881 and a total of 5,020 roubles overall.[69] Moreover, it began to open its coffers—and quite widely—to individual Jewish female students at institutions of higher learning in St Petersburg.[70] Beginning in 1878, it awarded stipends totalling 300 roubles, rising to 1,660 roubles in 1881 (see Table 2). In fact, allocations to female students at institutions of higher learning in St Petersburg totalled 5,020 roubles over six years (1878–83), which represents 35.8 per cent of the OPE's total giving in that period.[71] Remarkably, in other words, more than one-third of the OPE's contributions from 1878 to 1883 funded Jewish women's higher education.

At the same time, the OPE preserved its predilection for allocating stipends to professional students. As with male students, the OPE privileged female students engaged in higher education over those in vocational training. Thus, it provided more than six times as much assistance to those enrolled on the Higher Women's Courses (5,020 roubles) than to those involved in midwifery (798 roubles) (see Table 2). In fact, as recorded in its minutes on 17 November 1878, the OPE was partial to doctors in training.[72] After remarking on the rising numbers of female petitioners enrolled in either general science (Higher Women's Courses) or medical courses (WMC), the members questioned whether they should give preference to the latter, since, as the minutes spell out: 'Medical students have a hope [following graduation] of making a living in an honourable way and of having more opportunity than those studying other subjects.' Though the OPE deferred judgement on the matter in hand, their telling prioritization of women's higher education (doctors first, all others next) shows that they understood the purpose of education as not merely to enlighten but also to make Jews productive members of society. In other words, their generous support of students was motivated by a desire to elevate the Jews' stature by enabling them to contribute to the greater good. On their imagined ladder of priorities, professional training surpassed general studies and, of the professions, medicine was on the uppermost rungs. Thus, doctors—even female ones—were worthy of the OPE's support, for they were uniquely qualified to make a valuable contribution to society, which would in turn accrue merit to the larger Jewish community.

Thus, it is the similarity in the OPE's giving pattern between the two sexes—that is, its generous support of both male and female students, and its preference for

[68] Rosenthal, *Toledot ḥevrat marbitsei haskalah*, i. 129. Moreover, individual members pledged an additional 250 roubles for the society in the following year.

[69] See Table 2 and Cherikover, *Istoriya Obshchestva dlya rasprostraneniya prosveshcheniya mezhdu evreyami v Rossii*, 152.

[70] In the Rosenthal source, allocations to women's higher courses are not broken down by programme; rather, they are lumped together as one sum.

[71] Note that during this period (1878–83), the OPE only awarded stipends to students enrolled in St Petersburg's institutions, with the exception of a 50 rouble allocation to students in Kharkov in 1882.

[72] Rosenthal, *Toledot ḥevrat marbitsei haskalah*, ii. 169.

supporting those undertaking professional training, regardless of their sex—that raises the greatest potential for understanding how male Jews regarded the women they were supporting. The OPE invested in Jewish women medical students in the hope of a profitable return. They were banking on Jewish medical *kursistki* becoming doctors, alongside their male counterparts, as part of the larger enterprise of making Jews productive citizens. Similar sentiments were expressed in the press.

THE RUSSIAN JEWISH PRESS: DEBATING THE USES OF MEDICAL TRAINING

The pages of the Russian Jewish press are peppered with commentary on Jewish women medical students. In many ways, the opening paragraph of a single letter to the editor sets the parameters of the debate:

> It's hardly likely at the present time to find anyone among educated people who would strongly oppose women's higher education. It would be foolish to bar women—who possess the proper energy, ability, and passion—from [studying] science. They could become quite useful members of the educated segment of our society, and they have a full right to our sympathy and esteem, as well as to [our] material support and special attention. Those who value education must also value those involved in educating themselves, regardless of their sex. For us Jews, because [we are living at a time of heightened] antisemitism, it is important and necessary to fight for the survival of educated people. An educated woman at the very top of her game [literally: vocation] will make a good wife, a good mother, a good citizen. Who would dare not recognize in such a woman the jewel in our communal crown![73]

As the author suggests, nary a soul in late nineteenth-century progressive Jewish society questioned a woman's capacity for learning or her determination to improve her mind. Rather, the debate turned on the overarching purpose of women's education. Was education exclusively a means for transforming women into better wives and mothers? Or was there, as suggested above, something larger at stake? The answer, documented in a dozen or so pieces found in the press, is that a woman's education must lead her to work beyond her home. Those who expressed their opinions on the subject agreed that by doing so she would bring merit to herself and to the larger Jewish community.

Medical training of women was therefore viewed in practical terms. Expediency drove one writer, for instance, to counsel Jewish women 'to look deep inside and decide if you are really able' to undertake the training necessary to become a physician. He wondered if they might not be better off 'enrolling in midwifery courses that [like the WMC, at least] require a gymnasium diploma but [differ in that they require] less mental energy and time'.[74] But 'this is falsely optimistic', responded another writer. 'Everyone knows that even midwives, especially Jewish ones, cannot necessarily make ends meet.'[75] 'It's too late for this advice'; concurred a second

[73] Lyakhovetsky, 'Zhenskoe obrazovanie', 1071.

[74] Ibid. 1072.

[75] A. Kaufman, *Nedel'naya khronika Voskhoda*, 43 (23 Oct. 1882), 1154.

respondent, 'there are already enough midwives out there. It is not so easy for them to land a job.'[76] Evidently, the concern on readers' minds was not women's ability to complete medical training, but rather their prospects for productive employment upon completion.

The upsurge in professionally trained Jewish women was regarded as a sign of the Jewish community's becoming useful in society. In 1881 the editor of *Russkii evrei* called upon women to become active participants in public life and advocated the establishment of professional schools to train them. 'To sit at home is to waste her resources,' he claimed. Education could prepare a woman for the full range of her responsibilities, both inside and outside the home.[77] Involvement in public life, he insisted, must go hand in hand with being a wife and a mother; the two need not be at odds with each other. In closing, he laid out the dual value of training women professionally: 'First, it satisfies an extreme need in public life; and secondly, it spreads productive work among us Jews.'[78] Men, in other words, need not hold a monopoly on utility. Allow women, too, to contribute to the good of society and thereby bring honour to the Jewish community.

THE WOMEN SPEAK: THE PURPOSE OF MEDICAL TRAINING

Meanwhile, Jewish medical *kursiski* had different notions regarding the larger purpose of their education. Their words and actions speak volumes about the ways they imagined putting their medical training to use. Mariya Rashkovich, born the seventh of eight children in a Jewish family in Odessa in 1859, graduated with the first class of the WMC in 1876.[79] Her father, a textile wholesaler, died before she was 6 and she described her mother as a gymnasium graduate who was 'deeply religious' but observed no Jewish practice. Upon her father's death, her elder brothers—a jurist and a municipal official—assumed responsibility for her care. They sent her to gymnasium, where she became involved in a reading group that was, as she expressed it, 'the most illuminating spot of [her] gymnasium life'. Her exposure to the works of progressive thinkers like D. I. Pisarev, who unconditionally supported the emancipation of women, enabled her to feel 'completely independent'. Upon graduation from gymnasium, she worked for two years giving private lessons and teaching in a Hebrew school. Concurrently, she attended scientific

[76] K[au]f[ma]n, 'Pis'mo v redaktsiyu', 44 (30 Oct. 1882), 1188.

[77] In contrast, maskilim generally regarded the education of Jewish women exclusively as a means to make them better wives and mothers. See Feiner, 'Ha'ishah hayehudit hamodernit'.

[78] Editorial, *Russkii evrei*, 5 (28 Jan. 1881), 165. *Russkii evrei* was published in St Petersburg (1879–84) and edited by G. M. Rabinovich, Judah Kantor, and Lazar Behrmann. Behrmann (1830–93), an educator who founded St Petersburg's first Jewish school, was also an instructor in Jewish religion at a women's college in St Petersburg. See *The Jewish Encyclopedia* (New York, 1902), ii. 645–6.

[79] Mariya Rashkovich's memoirs are found in Ya. A. Kvyatkovskaya, *Vospominaniya vrachei Yulii Al. Kvyatkovskoi i Marii P. Rashkovich* (Paris, 1937), 151–234.

lectures offered by a local professor, read Marx and other Russian radicals, and moved in revolutionary circles.

Rashkovich's memoirs paint the portrait of a typical educated Russian woman of the day, influenced by the progressive spirit of her generation. Her motive for undertaking study on the WMC stemmed from her desire 'to be useful to the people through specialized knowledge'. 'People', to her, meant to the folk—rural populations, including mainly peasants, whom a generation of young people had idealized and sought to 'reform'. Like thousands of others, Rashkovich regarded medicine as the link between her own struggle for autonomy and a desire to help others achieve independence. So she headed to St Petersburg to attend the WMC. Despite intermittent breaks from the training to heal her 'destroyed nervous system', Rashkovich graduated, as mentioned above, with the first class in 1876 and subsequently accepted a post in a rural *zemstvo* hospital in the Moscow *guberniya* (province), providing free health care to an indigent population.[80]

Rashkovich was not alone. As of 1882 sixty-two women doctors were engaged by *zemstva*, including the first two Jewish graduates of the WMC. Clinics and hospitals employed fifty-four more, forty-six had set up private practice, and twelve had become interns or remained assistants in the hospital where they had recently trained.[81] *Zemstvo* work attracted the more idealistic women, such as Dora Aptekman, a Jewish graduate of 1879, who wrote that this humble practice would enable her 'to get to know the simple people, to observe them in their own homes, in the rural setting'.[82] Although their desire to serve was frustrated at every turn by the lack of proper medicine and equipment, Jews persevered in providing rural health care. By the turn of the century, one in every ten Jewish women doctors was involved in *zemstvo* work.[83] Their dedicated service did not go unnoticed, as in the case of Dr Teresa Zakgeim, a Jewish physician whose patients turned up by the thousands to mourn her death.[84]

From Rashkovich to Zakgeim, the evidence suggests that an idealistic, and in some cases self-sacrificing, Jewish woman entered the medical field to 'heal Russia's body and soul'.[85] For her, medical training was a calling—a response to progressive Russia's call to serve the people. She regarded this service as an end in itself, undertaken to be of immediate use to society.

Practicality was practically of no value to her. Such benefits as financial security, marital prospects, and residential rights could have been more expeditiously

[80] The tsar created *zemstva*, regions of rural self-government, in 1864. They did not include the western borderlands of the empire for fear of electoral domination by Poles and Jews.

[81] Engel, 'Women Medical Students in Russia', 407.

[82] D. Aptekman, 'Iz zapisok zemskogo vracha', *Russkaya mysl'*, 5 (Dec. 1884), 49.

[83] 'Alfavitnyi spisok'.

[84] 'Nekrolog—Teresa Zakgeim', *Nedel'naya khronika Voskhoda*, 20 (1887), 528.

[85] Rashkovich, in Kvyatkovskaya, *Vospominaniya vrachei*, 172.

obtained by pursuing other paths, including midwifery. However, she chose not to tread that downhill path. Instead, she pioneered an uphill course that required half a decade of arduous study, amid dire living conditions, but that suited her strong educational background and satiated a craving for both knowledge and service.

The Jewish medical *kursistka* was indifferent to the mission of making Jews useful to the society at large. While the Russian Jewish press lauded her and the OPE awarded her stipends in the hope that her actions would redound to the benefit of the Jewish community, she toiled away in the Russian landscape—in territory beyond the Pale, both physically and mentally. Her actions do not represent the humble offering of an anxious Jew seeking acceptance by a Russian society that kept her at arm's length, though she had done everything that was expected. Rather, in the Russian Jewish encounter of late imperial Russia, she had, as it were, already traversed to the 'other side'. Russian society embraced her and she returned that gesture in kind.

It is instructive to recall Varvara Kashevarova-Rudneva in this context. The 'mother' of all women doctors was a Jew by birth who 'passed' effortlessly into the Russian landscape. She was eventually stymied—but not by her Jewish roots. Russian society was ambivalent about women becoming doctors, not Jewish women per se.

So, in the end, the answer to the opening question is 'yes'. Generally, Jewish medical students enrolled at the WMC, like young idealists of late nineteenth-century Russia, did feel called to medicine and all that its practice implied.

This study of Jewish women's medical education in the 1870s and 1880s is a look at one specific moment in the Russian Jewish past through a gendered lens. It raises larger questions about the differing rates of integration into civil society among educated Jewish women and men in late imperial Russia. It challenges our understanding of both the process and results of professionalization among educated Jewry. The field is wide open and promises further exploration.

When Chava Left Home: Gender, Conversion, and the Jewish Family in Tsarist Russia

CHAERAN FREEZE

. . . because he apostatized, he has left the sanctity of Israel and the sanctity of his father.

Teshuvot hageonim

But how can he, a man like Dubnow, make peace with the thought that his daughter fattens calves for idol worship and that his descendants will be Gentiles and anti-semites? In this situation, there is only one way to escape the sorrow that consumes body and soul, and that is to tear out from the heart in one act all the ties which bind him to the sinful soul, and to consider her dead and non-existent. This is what our forefathers did, not out of cruelty, but because they could not otherwise bear the terrible pain, which for them was worse than death.

Ahad Ha'am to Alter Druianov about the conversion of Simon Dubnow's daughter, 24 October 1908

'Apostasy', a historian once observed, 'endangered the sanctity of the most hallowed relationships in the community—between parent and child, husband and wife, rabbi and disciple.'[1] Yet, this most fundamental aspect of conversion has been largely overlooked in the historiography, partly because of assumptions that the east European Jewish family and community simply severed all contacts with converts.[2] As Shmuel Leib Tsitron remarked, the apostate 'immediately became the enemy of the entire Jewish people'.[3] While this assertion may have described

The preparation and publication of this chapter have been made possible by generous grants from the Memorial Foundation for Jewish Culture, which has supported my numerous travels to archives of the former Soviet Union. I am grateful to David Biale, Todd Endelman, Sylvia Fuks Fried, and Eugene Shepperd for their suggestions.

[1] J. Cohen, 'The Mentality of the Medieval Jewish Apostate: Peter Alfonsi, Hermann of Cologne, and Pablo Christiani', in T. Endelman (ed.), *Jewish Apostasy in the Modern World* (New York, 1987), 22.

[2] For a social history of Jewish conversion in early modern Poland that addresses the family question, see J. Goldberg, *Hamumarim bemamlekhet polin-lita* (Jerusalem, 1985).

[3] S. L. Tsitron, *Meshumodim: Tipn un siluetn fun noentn over* (Warsaw, 1923), 3.

popular sentiments well, it nonetheless raises some vexing questions. Were family relations so easily torn asunder by the decision to convert? How did converts create new Christian families when their Jewish spouses and children refused to undergo baptism? Did they have to obtain a Jewish divorce? Finally, how did gender expectations shape family and societal attitudes towards Jews who chose to leave the fold?

Based on a close reading of archival texts from the nineteenth century, this study examines family relations suspended between Judaism and Christianity.[4] Like their predecessors in early modern Poland, Jewish converts in tsarist Russia initially sought to dissociate themselves from their kin and community; in fact, many emphasized family ruptures in their petitions to the Christian consistories to demonstrate their alienation from Judaism and Jewish life. Significantly, however, the ablution of baptism often failed to dissolve the old bonds that bound converts to the Jewish family and vice versa.[5] The very modes of employment, such as the 'abduction narrative' routinely employed by Jewish parents in their petitions to the Church and state, revealed both a profound disbelief in the possibility of conversion and an abiding hope for reconciliation with the 'kidnapped' convert. Little wonder that Christian authorities—and many spouses of Jewish converts—viewed any contact with former family members as inherently dangerous. Conversion also raised difficult halakhic and quotidian questions about marital status; that was especially true in the case of the *agunah* (perpetual grass widow) if the converted husband withheld her *get* (bill of divorcement) and the *yevamah* (childless widow), whose brother-in-law refused to perform his duty of *ḥalitsah* (levirate divorce). In all these cases, conversion challenged fundamental ideas about gender and family; it laid bare implicit social attitudes and drove the Russian state to address the problems of inter-faith marriage, divorce, and child custody between 'mixed couples'. By focusing on gender, this chapter seeks to place Jewish women's narratives in a broader context and to provide a comparative perspective.

Like many archival documents, conversion files pose special methodological problems because the 'facts of the case' are not only selective, but often elusive. Instead of attempting to 'peel away the fictive elements', this study will analyse how converts and their families crafted narratives to interpret, mediate, and give coherence to their experiences.[6]

After all, petitioners were not simply retelling actual events, but self-consciously refashioning them into a seamless story that ended at the baptismal font. As Paul

[4] This chapter uses archival files from four Russian Orthodox consistories (Vilna, Kherson, Zhitomir, and Odessa), the Roman Catholic consistory in Vilna, the chancellery of the governor-general of Vilna, the office of the chief procurator of the Holy Synod, and the Imperial Chancellery for the Receipt of Petitions in St Petersburg.

[5] For a comparative study of converts in German lands, see E. Carlebach, *Divided Souls: Converts from Judaism in Germany, 1500–1750* (New Haven, 2001).

[6] This study employs the narrative approach similar to Natalie Zemon Davis's analysis of royal letters of pardon and remission in 16th-century France in *Fiction in the Archives: Pardon Tales and their Tellers in Sixteenth-Century France* (Stanford, Calif., 1987).

Ricœur observes, this process 'draws a configuration out of a simple succession. [It] brings together factors as heterogeneous as agents, goals, means, interaction, circumstances, [and] unexpected results.'[7] The final product deliberately demarcated the boundaries between the 'Self' and the conflicting will of 'the family'—a term often used interchangeably with Judaism and community.

DISTANCING: CONVERSION NARRATIVES ABOUT THE JEWISH FAMILY

The first official step towards conversion was to file a written petition to the local Christian consistory (Russian Orthodox, Catholic, or Lutheran) for baptism.[8] These texts usually extolled the supremacy of Christianity over Judaism with phrases such as 'knowing that the promised Messiah of God has already come' or 'understanding the superiority of the Christian faith over other non-Christian [religions]'.[9] At the same time, each petition contained a personal narrative that mediated between these new declarations of faith, on the one hand, and the convert's Jewish past, on the other. Jews almost invariably began their journey into the Christian world with a statement about their motivations, which seldom dwelt on a spiritual awakening, but rather focused on family and economic concerns. A central theme in the petitions was the parallel estrangement from both their families and Judaism. In contrast to conversion narratives that 'fictionalize religious experience as self-engendered and separable from the authority of law and other institutions',[10] these petitions consciously indicted 'the family' (or its absence) as the force that alienated them from the Jewish faith and community.

Children's Narratives

Perhaps the most mediated type of conversion narratives was the deposition of Jewish children, who no doubt were highly susceptible to external prompting and influence. When a Jewish child under the age of 14 desired to convert without parental approval, it was not uncommon to undergo an oral interview with Church or state officials, especially if the family demanded a formal hearing.[11] The final text, preserved in the archive, was nominally dictated by the child, but doubtlessly

[7] P. Ricœur, *Time and Narrative*, trans. K. M. Blamey and D. Pellauer, 3 vols. (Chicago, 1984–8), i. 65.

[8] M. Stanislawski, 'Jewish Apostasy in Russia: A Tentative Typology', in Endelman (ed.), *Jewish Apostasy in the Modern World*, 193.

[9] See e.g. Lietuvos Valstybės Istorijos Archyvas (LVIA), *fond* 605, *opis'* 2, *delo* 1912, fos. 2–2^{v}. (Hereafter the standard Russian archival notation will be used: *f.* (*fond*), *op.* (*opis'*), *d.* (*delo*).

[10] G. Viswanathan, *Outside the Fold: Conversion, Modernity, and Belief* (Princeton, 1998), 84.

[11] On 4 Dec. 1862 the state ruled that 'Jews who are fourteen years old may convert to the Christian faith without permission from their parents or guardians' (*Sbornik uzakonenii kasayushchikhsya evreev* (St Petersburg, 1872)).

reflected the coaching and manipulation of the interrogators. However, texts often preserved the personal 'I' or at least placed direct statements in quotation marks. Moreover, multiple depositions of the child in the presence of different people (the parish priest, the parents, the local rabbi) produced different, sometimes 'undesirable' answers, at least from the perspective of the Church—a hint that the investigators 'let the story stand'. As Natalie Zemon Davis notes, although some would assume 'that the minute a learned agent of the state puts his hand on another's words, they are so remade and reshuffled that their original form is effaced', this was not always the case. The written version had to conform in some form to the personal nature of oral testimonies in order to be credible.[12]

Children's conversion narratives generally relied on two archetypal family plots. The first, utilized mainly by impoverished young girls, juxtaposed abusive and neglectful Jewish parents to generous Christian peasants. A typical case involved 10-year-old Tsipa Mendak, who ran away from home to convert to Catholicism in 1861. In the presence of Catholic clergy and Iona Gershtein (a learned Jew from Vilna),[13] Mendak offered this motive for baptism: 'From [my] very infancy [*mladenchestva*], I was cruelly persecuted by my mother, who not only mercilessly beat and despised me, neglecting my upbringing and placing me lower than my other sisters, but at times, out of malice, did not give me daily bread to satisfy [my] hunger.'[14]

Deprived of 'maternal love in my parent's home', Tsipa continued, 'I often visited the peasant village, which lies close to our village, where I found welcome shelter, gracious satisfaction of [my] hunger, sympathy for my pitiful position, and consolation for my sufferings from the cruelties [at home].' She claimed that this sequence of events led to 'a decline in my observance of Judaism and to adopt the Christian rites'. In the end, the girl announced to her interrogators: 'A year or half a year ago, I decided to reject the religion of my parents completely and to adopt the Christian faith.'[15] She then fled to a nearby monastery to seek asylum and prepare for conversion.

The recourse to infancy as the beginnings anchors Mendak's narrative in a 'mythic zero-point',[16] followed by a cycle of abuse at home and relief in the peasant village, leading directly to her decision to convert. Her ordering of events cites a prolonged period of time (namely, from birth), whereas the testimonies of the peasants and parents only refer to a two-year time-frame. The basic plot is reminiscent of the Cinderella tale (a theme prevalent in Yiddish children's stories[17]) in which the victim suffers from physical mistreatment, deprivation of food, and the mother's

[12] Davis, *Fiction in the Archives*, 20–2.

[13] 'Iona G. Gershtein', *Evreiskaya entsiklopediya*, vi (repr. St Petersburg, 1991), 428.

[14] LVIA, *f.* 378, *op.* 78, *d.* 353 (1860), fo. 4^v, report of the 'learned Jew' Iona Gershtein and Adjutant Captain Tolstoy to the Vilna governor-general, 22 Jan. 1861.

[15] Ibid., fo. 9^v, B 10.

[16] M. de Certeau, *The Writing of History* (New York, 1988), 88–92.

[17] See B. S. Weinreich (ed.), *Yiddish Folktales* (New York, 1988), 51–2.

favouritism of the other siblings. This is not to suggest that Mendak invented her story, but only that she may have drawn upon 'approaches to narrative learned in past listening to and telling of stories'.[18]

The process of separation from both her family and Judaism is the central theme in her narrative. She argues that the denial of food at home forced her to partake in peasant meals (a violation of the laws of *kashrut*), while her deprivation of motherly love led her to kiss the cross and embrace Christianity. Although her testimony is silent about her father's role, Mendak notes that the peasants were reluctant to take her to the Roman Catholic priest because they were 'afraid of the hardship on my father'—perhaps a revelation of her own fears. When deposed again in her father's presence, the girl changed her mind and declared that she wished 'to remain Jewish but to live in another Jewish home'.[19] Denied that option, Tsipa Mendak converted to Christianity in July 1862 and assumed a new Christian name, Ulina.

A second, related narrative also focused on the lack of parental supervision, as well as the influence of Christian children, who are described as playmates and friends. When 14-year-old Khana Prais applied to convert to Catholicism, she maintained that she had always lived in the village of Arel and had grown up among Christian children. Their daily interaction, she asserted, had instilled in her a 'love of Christian prayers' and 'the desire to become Catholic'.[20] The only mention of her family was a statement that she did not desire to return home. Not even a visit from her mother, 'who firmly [sought to] coerce her to return to Judaism', could persuade her to leave the monastery

In a similar case, Feiga Baikovskaya informed her parents that her desire for conversion stemmed from 'frequent interactions with Christian children'.[21] The civil governor of Grodno, who attended the meeting with her parents, confirmed this explanation but observed: 'Her poor parents, who are constantly working to earn a living, were deprived of the possibility to teach her the Ten Commandments.' As a result, the girl 'was often found among Christian children, even learning a few prayers from them'. He maintained that, despite Feiga's apparent sincerity about her devotion to Catholicism and rejection of Judaism, 'she does not have any understanding of the Jewish faith let alone the Christian faith'.[22]

Female narratives about close interaction with Christians, along with references to the lack of parental or communal supervision, may have reflected the gendered system of socialization in the small Lithuanian shtetl. Avraham Sachs, a Zionist activist who grew up in this very region, decried the fate of poor Jewish girls who rarely received the formal education available to their brothers:

[18] Davies, *Fiction in the Archives*, 4.

[19] LVIA, *f.* 378, *op.* 78, *d.* 353 (1860), fo. 10v, report of Adjutant Captain Tolstoy and 'learned Jew' Gershtein, 22 Jan. 1861.

[20] LVIA, *f.* 378, *d.* 185 (1862), fos. 7–8, report of the police of Kovno province, 20 Feb. 1863.

[21] LVIA, *f.* 378, *d.* 207 (1862), fo. 4v, report of the civil governor of Grodno to the governor-general of Vilna, 14 Sept. 1862.

[22] Ibid., fo. 1v.

There was still a lower class of girls who were on everybody's lips, and whom no one dared to have anything to do with, 'the dissolute ones' (*di tsulozene*). These were mostly the daughters of female water-carriers, washerwomen, and matzah-rollers, poor widows who lived in hovels on the outskirts of town and went without bread, fuel, or candles. The sons of these widows were usually under the supervision of the community. Up to the bar mitzvah they were sent to Talmud Torah and after that they were apprenticed to some artisan. But no one looked after the girls. They wandered on the streets, went about in tatters until, because of our many sins, they became wanton and dissolute.[23]

To be sure, the number of private schools and charitable organizations for indigent Jewish girls increased by the late nineteenth century, especially in urban centres like Vilna, Odessa, and Minsk. Such philanthropy, however, often did not extend to those living in distant villages, isolated taverns, and inns.[24] Moreover, unlike daughters of privileged or rabbinical families (such as Dvora Baron, Puah Rakovsky, and Miriam Markel-Mosessohn) who did receive private tutoring, these girls lacked even a modicum of knowledge of Judaism, as revealed by the governor's observations about Feiga Baikovskaya.[25]

The theme of parental neglect or rejection was also prominent in the testimonies of Jewish boys, but they offered a plot that was differently gendered. One common narrative foregrounded their premature initiation into the adult world—a theme also prominent in maskilic memoirs. If the latter often attributed the trauma of early marriage to their 'heretical' turn to Haskalah, converts depicted the untimely separation from their parents as the definitive push towards apostasy.[26] For example, following the death of his father, 15-year-old Khaim Ioinovich described the plight of his widowed mother and her three 'orphans' to the local priest of Antopol, in Vilna province. 'Living in complete poverty and without any means of support,' he explained, 'she entered service [as a domestic servant] in Congress Poland and took the small children with her, but left me here to support myself by my own labour.'[27] Not only had his mother left him without support ('due to my young age, I do not earn anything'), but the local Jewish prayer house had refused his request for alms and food. As a result, he turned to a Russian Orthodox priest, who took him into his

[23] A. Zaks, *Horuve velten* (New York, 1917), 45.

[24] V. E. Kelner and D. A. Elyashevich, *Literatura o evreiakh na russkom iazyke, 1890–1947* (St Petersburg, 1995), 346–67.

[25] See P. E. Hyman, *Gender and Assimilation in Modern Jewish History: The Roles and Representation of Women* (Seattle, 1995), 50–92; id., 'East European Jewish Women in an Age of Transition, 1880–1930', in J. Baskin (ed.), *Jewish Women in Historical Perspective*, 2nd edn. (Detroit, 1998), 270–86; S. Stampfer, 'Gender Differentiation and Education of the Jewish Woman in Nineteenth Century Eastern Europe', *Polin*, 7 (1992), 63–87. On Miriam Markel-Mosessohn, see C. Balin, 'Jewish Women Writers in Tsarist Russia, 1869–1917', Ph.D. thesis (Columbia University, 1998), 21–79; on Puah Rakovsky, see P. Rakovsky, *Zikhroynes fun a revolutionerin* (Buenos Aires, 1954); on Dvora Baron, see N. Govrin, *Hamaḥatsit harishonah, devorah baron ḥayeiha veyetsiratah* (Jerusalem, 1988).

[26] D. Biale, 'Eros and Enlightenment: Love Against Marriage in the East European Jewish Enlightenment', *Polin*, 1 (1986), 49–67.

[27] LVIA, *f.* 605, *op.* 4, *d.* 145, fo. 3, testimony of Khaim Ioinovich, 20 Feb. 1866.

home to prepare for conversion (i.e. instruction in Christian prayer and dogma). In another case, Iosel Finkelshtein of Brest-Litovsk declared that his father's decision to apprentice him to a 'cruel master' had forced him to turn to the Russian Orthodox Church for shelter.[28] Similarly, young boys sent to work in Jewish taverns also invoked their difficult experiences in their applications for baptism.[29]

To demonstrate alienation from their families, some male petitioners cited parental favouritism in dealing with Jewish conscription in the tsarist military. For example, 12-year-old Lipman Levinson, who had been sent to prison for vagrancy, informed the Russian Orthodox consistory that his father intended to send him as a recruit to protect his other six male siblings.[30] 'I do not have any desire to evade the draft,' he declared. 'On the contrary, I am prepared to enter into [the army] but not as a Jew but a Christian.'[31] After meeting with his relatives, Levinson (whom the police described as speaking Russian 'without a Jewish accent') recanted his desire to convert, but decided to sacrifice himself as the family recruit 'out of pity for his younger brother . . . and his mother who lamented over the latter sibling'.[32]

Paradoxically, orphaned Jewish boys whose lack of ties to family or community made them prime candidates for baptism in the eyes of the Church faced a more rigorous investigation by the state, which suspected them of seeking to evade prosecution for crimes. For instance, when Osher Abramovich Beber filed a petition for baptism, the Kovno provincial board warned Church officials that the orphaned boy sought to escape not only from conscription, but from imprisonment for fraud.[33] Whereas the state associated the absence of family ties with the breakdown of parental authority and lawful order, the Church emphasized the petitioner's social dislocation, poverty, and persecution by the Jewish community. In other words, estrangement from Jewish folk and kin gave some guarantee of loyalty to his new faith.

Adult Narratives

In contrast to children's depositions, adults wrote their own conversion petitions or requested a literate representative to draft it for them. In general, petitions to the Lithuanian Russian Orthodox consistory differed significantly by gender, both in content and in length. Male candidates focused almost exclusively on the 'theological' motives for baptism and offered little, if any, personal narrative. Typical was the laconic petition from Yakov Berenshtein (a fourth-year student at the Vilna rabbinical seminary), who confessed: 'From my soul and heart, I wish to see the

[28] LVIA, *f.* 605, *op.* 4, *d.* 825, fo. 4, testimony of Iosel Finkelshtein, 1867.

[29] LVIA, *f.* 605, *op.* 2, *d.* 244, fos. 2–3. See also the case of Mordukh Tsigelnitsky of Lida, who resided in a tavern (*f.* 601, *op.* 4, *d.* 783).

[30] LVIA, *f.* 605, *op.* 2, *d.* 2079, fo. 1.

[31] Ibid., fo. 1^{v}, petition of Lipman Levinson to Archbishop Iosif [Semashko], 1851.

[32] Ibid., fo. 22.

[33] LVIA, *f.* 605, *op.* 2, *d.* 1569, fo. 4, Kovno provincial board to the Lithuanian Orthodox consistory, 1848.

light of holy baptism according to the rites of the Russian Orthodox Church; thus I fall at the feet of Your Grace to request permission for baptism and lodging until this event.'[34]

If the male petitioner gave the Jewish family or community any attention, it was merely to castigate them as obstacles to his conversion. Movsha Nokhimovich of Eishishki, in Vilna province, for instance, informed the local bishop that his mother had tried to prevent his baptism by sending him after his father's death to live with an uncle in a neighbouring village. The report of his mother's recent death implied that no barriers remained.[35] In the same vein, the merchant Zelman Nurok explained that after living separately from his parents for at least ten years, he was fully independent, and hence ready for baptism.[36]

In some cases, the petitioner probably added personal details about the family to dispel doubts about his sincerity or real motives. Srol Zaks of Kovno province admitted his desire to leave the Pale of Settlement, but emphasized that his former spouse had obstructed his desire for baptism in the past. Like many husbands, he offered no account of their marriage—in contrast to female converts, as we shall see.[37] Some cases did raise official eyebrows about sincerity; for example, Moishe Koronevsky was an Odessa merchant incarcerated in a Vilna prison for falsifying banknotes when he suddenly 'grasped the truth of Christianity'.[38] Since baptism automatically reduced or rescinded the sentence for Jewish criminals until 1862, doubts about his genuine conviction were only natural.[39] Perhaps to assuage suspicions about his ulterior motives, Koronevsky insisted that 'my ardent wish to [convert] to the Christian faith of the Russian Orthodox confession took root within me from early childhood, which because of the hindrance of my parents, I could under no condition realise'.[40] Even after his parents died, he asserted that the Jewish community conspired to thwart his conversion at all costs:

> But when I lost them [the parents], I still did not succeed in preparing to fulfil this [desire] because my co-religionists began to persecute me for my deviation from their mistaken beliefs. When I set out for commercial business in the city of Vilna, where Jewish fanaticism is more prevalent, I was persecuted even more. They wanted to compel me, through coercion, into the business of forged banknotes.

The merchant claimed that his attempts to thwart this 'crime against our government' failed when he was arrested unfairly for his participation in fraudulent activities. 'From this, I clearly see that God dealt me this punishment,' Koronevsky

[34] LVIA, *f.* 605, *op.* 4, *d.* 124, fo. 1, Yakov Berenshtein to the bishop of Kovno, 22 Apr. 1866.

[35] LVIA, *f.* 605, *op.* 2, *d.* 244, fo. 3, petition of Movsha Nokhimovich, 18 Dec. 1841.

[36] LVIA, *f.* 605, *op.* 2, *d.* 64, fo. 2, petition of Zelman Nurok, 1840. Levin Mikhelson of Mitava made a similar declaration, stating that he had been divorced from his wife for over a decade; *f.* 605, *op.* 2, *d.* 500, petition of Levin Mikhelson in 1845.

[37] LVIA, *f.* 605, *op.* 4, *d.* 142, fo. 3, testimony of Srol Yankelevich Zaks, 20 Sept. 1866.

[38] LVIA, *f.* 605, *op.* 4, *d.* 94, fos. 1–2.

[39] Stanislawski, 'Jewish Apostasy in Russia', 197.

[40] LVIA, *f.* 605, *op.* 4, *d.* 94, fo. 2.

concluded, 'because of my prolonged vacillation towards the truth of the Russian Orthodox faith.'[41]

In some rare cases, petitioners candidly admitted that they had been driven to the baptismal font because of corrupt Jewish communal leaders, who had planned to sacrifice them as military recruits. As Litman Shvartsbord of Izabelin, in Grodno province, explained: 'I wish to be baptized based on [my] conviction of the truth of the Russian Orthodox faith to receive a discharge from military service into which the Vilna Jewish community unjustly subjected me, even though I was not in the queue.'[42] Shaul Gintsburg related a similar narrative about Yakov Brafman, who allegedly converted to evade conscription by the Kletzker *kahal* (communal authority).[43] Velvel Portnoy of Vilkiya, in Kovno province, attributed the 'banishment from his father's table' on Passover eve as the reason for his alienation from Judaism. His wealthy father, he complained, 'did not love him very much' and threw him out of the house with these words: 'I will not give you anything to eat, go wherever you want.'[44] When the 22-year-old threatened to convert, his father allegedly retorted: 'Go ahead and do whatever you desire.' That the family rupture occurred on Passover eve (mentioned in the first line of the document) heightened the poignancy of the break. Since the file breaks off without the usual confirmation of the final conversion, it may well be that Portnoy threatened to convert simply to gain paternal attention and reconciliation, if only to avert the scandal of apostasy in the family.

Apart from such unusual admissions, most male petitioners remained reticent about family relations. Perhaps they had less need to prove estrangement: most 'typical converts' (Jewish soldiers, imprisoned criminals, Russified students, merchants) had already established a certain distance from Jewish life.[45] Hence, they tended to focus on their knowledge of Christian prayers, command of the Russian language and culture, and ties with non-Jewish society. Conversely, they denied their Jewish roots. When Izrael Bernburg converted to Catholicism in 1848, he demonstrated his break with the Jewish community by describing his rootless wanderings and made no mention of co-religionists.[46] Srol Zaks vowed that he had not observed 'the Jewish faith of the mitnagedim' for three months to show that he too had sundered ties to Judaism.[47]

By contrast, Jewish women usually came to the monastery or local church directly from their homes with little spatial or temporal separation between their everyday

41 Ibid., fos. 2–3, petition of Moishe Koronevsky, 16 Feb. 1863.

42 LVIA, *f.* 605, *op.* 2, *d.* 1914, fo. 18, petition of Litman Shvartsbord, 15 Mar. 1851. See also *f.* 694, *op.* 1, *d.* 1859, case of N. Davidovich Leizerovich's conversion to Catholicism, 1848.

43 S. Gintsburg, *Meshumodim in tsarishn rusland* (New York, 1946), 67–8.

44 LVIA, *f.* 605, *op.* 4, *d.* 819, fo. 10.

45 For a typology of Jewish converts in Russia, see Stanislawski, 'Jewish Apostasy in Russia', 195–203.

46 LVIA, *f.* 694, *op.* 1, *d.* 1854, testimony of Izrael Zelik Bernburg, 12 Feb. 1848.

47 LVIA, *f.* 605, *op.* 4, *d.* 142, fo. 2, petition of Srol Yankelevich Zaks, 20 Sept. 1866.

Jewish existence and preparation for baptism. Women like Sora Dovginovna were still living in their parental home when they requested baptism.[48] To demonstrate their detachment from Judaism, they invoked narratives of family discord that sowed a psychological and spiritual separation from their Jewish past. These tales of failed marriages, unfulfilled dreams of higher education, and clandestine love affairs with Christian soldiers or peasants all ended with pleas for 'salvation'—namely through a de facto divorce, the opportunity to pursue intellectual aspirations, and the right to select a new spouse.

Paradoxically, these veiled demands for self-determination challenged not only traditional hierarchies of power in Jewish society but also the very foundations of imperial family law, which upheld 'patriarchal authority, unequal status, patrilineal kinship, and broad ecclesiastical jurisdiction'.[49] According to the imperial Digest of Laws, the passport system gave parents and husbands broad rights over the residence, employment, and education of children and wives; only with patriarchal consent could 'dependants' embark on an independent path.[50]

State law obliged a wife to live with her husband 'in all circumstances except his exile to Siberia'. In the same vein, children who entered into a marriage without parental consent could be prosecuted for 'disobedience and disrespectful behaviour'.[51] The law also empowered institutionalized religion; it gave the member of each religious confession the right to 'marry according to their laws and customs', without the participation of civil authorities.[52] In the case of Jews, halakhah (Jewish law) controlled every aspect of marital life—from its formation to its dissolution. Not surprisingly, bitter disputes over legal and religious authority arose when female converts sought to renegotiate their new marital status, obligations, and rights.

In the majority of cases, female petitioners constructed narratives that portrayed a powerless woman subjected to the abuse of capricious parents, the Jewish community, or a cruel husband. By depicting Jewish family practices as despotic, even destructive, they cast themselves as victims, not as rebellious daughters and wives. Although the Orthodox Church and Russian family were no less patriarchal (as some neophytes would discover not long after their baptism), this trope of the tyrannized woman provided grounds for Church intercession.

One plot common to female petitioners revolved around the sufferings of a young girl who was forced into an arranged marriage in order to subvert her desire to convert—an intention she had allegedly harboured since early childhood. The narrative discursively denounced coerced marriages and combined conversion

[48] LVIA, *f.* 605, *op.* 4, *d.* 800, testimony of Sora Dovginovna, 24 Mar. 1867.

[49] W. G. Wagner, *Marriage, Property and Law in Late Imperial Russia* (Oxford, 1994), 61.

[50] Ibid. 63. See *Svod zakonov* (St Petersburg, 1857), vol. x, bk. 1, pt. 1, arts. 100–18, 2202; vol. xi, pt. 2.

[51] Wagner, *Marriage, Property and Law in Late Imperial Russia*, 63. See *Svod zakonov*, vol. x, bk. 1, pt. 1, arts. 1, 6–7, 164–95, 226, 229–30, 294–5, 995, 2203.

[52] *Polnoe sobranie zakonov Rossiiskoi imperii*, 1st ser., 45 vols. (St Petersburg, 1830), x. 90. See also Rossiisskii gosudarstvennyi istoricheskii arkhiv (RGIA), *f.* 821, *op.* 9, *d.* 17.

motives with family oppression. Golda Perlshtein of Pruzhany, for example, reported to Metropolitan Iosif of Lithuania in 1867 that 'from the age of three, I had thought of receiving enlightenment through holy baptism'.[53] When her parents learned of this intention, she claimed, they sought to marry her off as quickly as possible with the assistance of a matchmaker. This particular ordering of events placed less emphasis on Perlshtein's aversion to the arranged union and assigned greater importance to the malicious attempt to prevent conversion. Perhaps the petitioner also hoped that the emphasis on her childhood yearning to convert would also overshadow her more 'worldly' motive to thwart an undesirable match.

Mirema Mermel of Kovno resorted to a similar narrative in 1867 (but casting the Jewish community as the chief antagonist) to justify not only her conversion to Russian Orthodoxy but her desertion of her husband.

> Since I was an orphaned minor, without a father and mother, I have possessed a constant inclination to convert to the Christian faith, but did not have the means to achieve this [goal]. But the Jews, seeing that I had these wishes, tried every means to marry me off and gave me to some Jew, Mordkhelia Girshovich, who constantly engaged in drunkenness, card-playing, leading a depraved live, and squandering the entire dowry; he constantly beat me without mercy. Although I wanted to obtain a divorce from him many times, he will not give me a divorce. I am subjected to constant abuse and cannot lead a tranquil life.[54]

By articulating the limits of intolerable treatment at the hands of her community and spouse, Mermel linked Judaism with the sufferings she desired to leave behind. Unable to free herself under Jewish law, she deserted her husband and entered a woman's monastery in Vilna to prepare for baptism.[55] It bears emphasizing that the Russian Orthodox Church rejected hundreds of petitions like hers from its own flock, for it did not recognize spousal abuse as a valid ground for divorce.[56] In fact, even legal separation from abusive spouses was virtually impossible until the 1880s, when the Imperial Chancellery in St Petersburg began to grant women separate passports for exceptional cases of wife-beating and abuse.

Mermel's petition thus used conversion to overturn conventional power relations. Not only did she reject the community's insistence on marriage as the only 'solution' to her single status and 'rebelliousness', but she also challenged her husband's sole prerogative to dissolve their marriage.[57] According to tsarist law, wives who ordinarily resided separately from their husbands risked forcible return to the

[53] LVIA, *f.* 605, *op.* 4, *d.* 828, fo. 4, petition of Golda Perlshtein, 22 Feb. 1867.

[54] LVIA, *f.* 605, *op.* 4, *d.* 722, fo. 1, petition of Mirema Mermel of the Bolotovskii Jewish community in Kovno province, 24 Oct. 1867.

[55] In another case Freida Polyakova left her husband in Minsk and converted with her daughter in the town of Kovno; LVIA, *f.* 605, *op.* 4, *d.* 485, fo. 1, petition of Polyakova, wife of a merchant's son, 29 July 1866.

[56] For a comparative perspective on the Russian Orthodox Church and divorce, see G. Freeze, 'Bringing Order to the Russian Family: Marriage and Divorce in Imperial Russia, 1760–1860', *Journal of Modern History*, 64/4 (1990), 709–46.

[57] See also LVIA, *f.* 605, *op.* 2, *d.* 1570, fo. 1, case of Toube Avgustskaya.

spouse or even exile to Siberia for vagrancy (living without a valid passport). In this instance, however, the petitioner secured her right to reside separately from her husband without his consent, even the option to remarry, since the Orthodox Church allowed the convert to remarry and finalize the break with the Jewish world.

A second narrative, employed regularly by prospective converts who planned to marry a non-Jew, depicted a defenceless woman taking refuge in a Christian home or monastery to escape the fanatical wrath of a family that vowed to kidnap, even murder, the offender planning to commit apostasy. 'Only God knows how much I endured different kinds of troubles and threats from my Jewish relatives, when they learned about my desire to convert,' lamented Fruma Mukhova, who had deserted her husband to marry a Russian soldier. She claimed that relatives had attempted to persuade her to change her mind with promises of monetary rewards, but then resorted to 'threats of eternal punishment'. If it were not for the armed guards around the priest's home where she awaited her baptism, she wrote, 'the 'throng of Jews who surrounded the house' would have abducted her.[58]

Similarly, Ita Kaminskaya reported to the Lida district police that, when her parents first discovered her intent to convert, 'they pleaded with her to abandon the idea'. One evening, when everyone had gone to bed, the daughter claimed to have overheard a conversation between her 'former parents' who had decided that, in the event she refused to change her mind, 'there remained only one [option]—to poison her'.[59] Kaminskaya allegedly fled that night to the home of an Orthodox deacon to prepare for a hasty baptism and marriage to a certain Karl Vysotsky.

Despite such tales of persecution, this second group of petitioners rarely made disparaging remarks about their family life prior to the conflict over marriage. Sara Goldshtein, who had run away from home to marry a clerk in the Klementev infantry, even remarked that 'things for her were good at home and that she was already spoken for by some young, wealthy Jew'.[60] To avoid painful confrontations and pressures to recant, brides-to-be sought to rebuff pleas by parents and husbands for one final, private meeting. Church officials were also averse to such confrontation, fearing a tendency of potential converts to vacillate after a face-to-face encounter with family members. One bishop, for instance, reported with alarm that Tsivya Zhmudskaya (who intended to marry a Cossack officer) 'unexpectedly' met her father on her way to retrieve some belongings at the sacristan's home. 'As she revealed to me completely,' he informed his superiors in Vilna, 'Shmuil Zhmudsky took her into the apartment and spoke with her for half an hour in Yiddish,

58 LVIA, *f.* 605, *op.* 4, *d.* 85, fo. 13, petition of Fruma Shliomovna Mukhova, 8 Dec. 1863. In 1867 Gena Rivka Taube also argued that she needed to be baptized immediately because 'her family had already found out where she was staying and would abduct her' (LVIA, *f.* 605, *op.* 4, *d.* 849, fo. 1).

59 LVIA, *f.* 447, *op.* 1, *d.* 3079, fo. 8, report of the court investigator of the Lida district court, including depositions, 4 June 1869.

60 LVIA, *f.* 378, *d.* 221 (1862), fo. 3, report of the civil governor of Grodno to the governor-general, 25 Sept. 1862.

persuading her to renounce her intention to convert to Christianity, promising her all possible blessings for this.'[61] Less than a month later the daughter surreptitiously left the local priest's house and allegedly returned to her parental home. Some priests used incidents like this as a pretext for hastily baptizing prospective converts before they were adequately prepared (that is, instructed in the basic prayers and essentials of the faith) or prior to receiving permission from their superiors.[62]

FAMILY RESPONSES TO CONVERSION

As these cases suggest, Jewish families rarely responded to conversion by simply severing ties with their children or kin, especially during the preparatory period for baptism, but even after the dreaded act. As the fiction writer Rashal Khin recalled, her father simply refused to accept the conversion of her sister, who worked as a governess for one of most prominent gentry families in Russia. 'Papa was forcing her to renounce her Christianity, which was as impossible for her as abandoning the Sheremetev family . . . [and thus] denied herself the pleasure of seeing him and her family until a later time.'[63] Even the historian Simon Dubnow, whose daughter Olga converted and married a Christian, eventually corresponded with her after an initial period of silence.[64]

When verbal persuasion and physical coercion failed, desperate parents appealed to the state courts or governor-general for assistance. Their carefully constructed petitions adopted variations of the 'abduction plot'—namely, the kidnapping and forced baptism of a Jewish child—to mediate between events and their meaning. Through these narratives, 'they made sense of the unexpected and built coherence into immediate experience'.[65] As Peter Brooks put it, plot serves as 'a structuring operation peculiar to those messages that are developed through temporal succession, the instrumental logic of a specific mode of human understanding'.[66]

Indeed, the choice of the abduction narrative was by no means accidental. After all, tales of children kidnapped by Christian zealots were deeply entrenched in Jewish historical memory and still haunted the imagination. R. Jacob Maze fondly recalled how his nurse Rosha filled his after-*ḥeder* hours with wondrous stories of demons and heroes, including one about the miraculous deliverance of a poor orphan boy who had been seized by a Catholic priest and imprisoned in a woman's monastery while he awaited baptism.[67]

[61] LVIA, *f.* 605, *op.* 3, *d.* 78, fo. 5, report of Bishop Viktor [Tomomitsky], 6 Sept. 1863.

[62] See e.g. LVIA, *f.* 605, *op.* 4, *d.* 343. The priest Berezskoy argued that he had baptized 19-year-old Kaplan before he was ready because he was in danger from the wrath of the Jews.

[63] Ivan Turgenev, *Pisma Turgenevu: Shchukinskii sbornik* (1909), 207–10, as cited in Balin, 'Jewish Women Writers in Tsarist Russia', 148.

[64] K. Goldberg and A. Greenbaum (eds.), *A Missionary for History: Essays in Honor of Simon Dubnow* (Minneapolis, 1998), 36.

[65] Davis, *Fiction in the Archives*, 4.

[66] P. Brooks, *Reading for the Plot: Design and Intention in Narrative* (New York, 1984), 10.

[67] J. Maze, *Zikhronot*, 3 vols. (Tel Aviv, 1936), i. 30–4.

In many respects, parental petitions were no different from Rosha's tales for their 'fictional' qualities. As Natalie Zemon Davis points out, this does not mean 'their feigned elements, but rather the broader sense of the root word *fingere*, their forming, shaping, and molding elements: the crafting of a narrative'.[68] To give credence to the story (what Roland Barthes has called the 'reality effect'), petitioners provided a precise timeline and minute details, even when the 'abduction' had occurred in the absence of eyewitnesses.[69]

In one poignant case, Yankel Kushlyansky of Oshmyany informed the governor of Vilna in 1865: '[The peasant] Vitsekhovsky [and others] succeeded in taking my daughter secretly away from the parental home and, in order to disguise their steps, they cut her hair and dressed her in men's clothing.' That very day, he added, 'when my wife was absent from the house', the peasant and his friend stole several items from his home. With a court order in hand, the father claimed that he pursued the captors with his wife, brother, and brother-in-law and succeeded in rescuing the daughter only to be driven off with 'violent force' by Vitsekhovsky and his co-workers. '[They] managed to drag off my daughter to the post office in the town of Oshmyany,' Kushlyansky concluded, 'where they hastily drew up a document addressed to the mother superior of the Vilna monastery of St Steropa the Nun about her alleged desire to convert to the Catholic faith.'[70]

Fearing that claims of abduction alone would not gain the intercession of state officials, petitioners routinely added charges of theft to emphasize the gravity of the case and its 'non-religious' character. Thus, Shloima Rogalsky accused a Catholic priest of 'smashing the window [to his house] to pieces and breaking the lock to the trunk and chest of drawers' to steal 3,000 roubles, as well as some personal items, in the process of kidnapping his daughter. According to the investigation by the Vilna criminal court, however, there was no evidence of forced entry through the window and the furniture from which the money was allegedly stolen appeared old and 'already broken'. Rogalsky's own daughter Pai testified that nothing had been stolen and that she had run away from home to prepare for baptism in order to marry a Catholic peasant. She attributed all her father's accusations to his 'malice towards her for conversion'. Since the father refused to itemize the stolen property, the court rejected his suit, but gave him the option to appeal the case if he provided further evidence.[71] In desperation, one parent even asked the police to arrest his daughter Eta Kagan when he found out that she 'been kidnapped by a converted Jewish soldier', whom he charged with stealing money and his son's property. To prevent her conversion, the family employed every means to keep her in prison

[68] Davis, *Fiction in the Archives*, 3.

[69] R. Barthes, 'Introduction to the Structural Analysis of Narratives', in S. Sontag (ed.), *A Barthes Reader* (New York, 1982), 266.

[70] LVIA, *f.* 378, *op.* 66, *d.* 579 (1865), fo. 25, petition of Yankel Kushlyansky to the governor-general of Vilna, 14 Feb. 1865.

[71] LVIA, *f.* 378, *d.* 409 (1862), fo. 23, case of Pai Rogalskaya, 1862–5.

until they could secure her release into their custody. Their efforts, however, came to naught; she was baptized with her full consent on October 1862.[72]

Implicit assumptions about age and gender also informed the choice of narrative. Of the twenty complaints about abduction for conversion filed in Vilna between 1820 and 1870, only four pertained to boys (all under the age of 13); the other cases involved teenage girls, as well as young women who planned to marry Christians. By portraying conversion as abduction or deception, parents rejected agency on the part of the 'kidnapped victims' on the grounds that they were minors or female. Thus, when Shifra Lebovich discovered that her 15-year-old daughter was waiting to be baptized at the monastery of St Stephen in Vilna, she protested: 'But how can she—a minor, illiterate, and completely uneducated because she has always resided in the village—possibly desire to convert to this faith [Russian Orthodoxy]? It could not be out of sincerity but only because someone convinced her about the luxurious and easy lifestyle that does not require one to work.'[73]

Similarly, Moishe Faivelevich insisted that because his daughter 'was born and raised among Jews, it is impossible that she, an eleven-year-old, could prefer an alien faith from her own religion without the influence of someone else'.[74]

Notions about 'natural' differences between the sexes also informed these narratives. Whereas parents blamed a son's 'rebelliousness' (a deliberate act of defiance) for his desire to convert,[75] they attributed that same desire to a daughter's 'feeble-mindedness', 'lack of mental capacity', or 'mental illness'. They treated female converts not only as dependants (even when they had reached their maturity), but also as the 'weaker sex' and in need of social control for their own benefit. In 1861, for example, the prominent maskil and learned Jew of Vilna Samuel Fin (Fuenn) filed a complaint about the abduction of his 17-year-old daughter Pera Rivka (Rivekka), who was 'locked up in the Vizitok monastery'. Despite a thorough investigation (facilitated by Fin's connection to influential bureaucrats in Vilna), as well as several family visits, the daughter remained resolute in her decision to embrace Catholicism. She also warned the local bishop (in a handwritten petition in Polish) that, because of her father's influential position, she would be subjected to great troubles (*nepriyatnosti*) at the hands of the police.[76] On several other occasions she complained about the harassment that she suffered at the hands of her father and relatives who 'caused her trouble to the point where it made her ill'.

Nevertheless, Fin adamantly rejected his daughter's verbal and written claims that she deliberately chose the Catholic faith out of conviction and understanding.

[72] LVIA, *f.* 378, *d.* 190 (1862), fos. 3–20, case of Eta Kagan, 1862.

[73] LVIA, *f.* 378, *d.* 2067 (1862), fo. 3, petition of Shifra Lebovich, 11 July 1852.

[74] LVIA, *f.* 378, *d.* 198 (1862), fo. 3, report of the Kovno provincial board to the governor-general, 21 Aug. 1862.

[75] See e.g. LVIA, *f.* 378, *d.* 314 (1863), fo. 1, petition of Vulf Potrukha, 5 Aug. 1863.

[76] LVIA, *f.* 378, *d.* 322 (1861), fo. 58, petition of Rivka Fin, 15 Oct. 1861. The authorities relied on the Russian translation of the Polish petition.

In a letter to the governor-general of Vilna he cited Rivka's minority and her inability to think for herself:

> If I proposed that she were in a condition to differentiate between confessions and be persuaded in the Roman Catholic faith, then she would be acting according to a pure conscience and healthy common sense. But being convinced, on the contrary, that she cannot even have the understanding to choose for herself something other than [what] her parents [want] due to her minority, weak aptitude, and the sickly condition of her faculties from which she has suffered for many years, I cannot but propose that she decided to take this step as a result of an ephemeral, unclear, and dark feeling, which was successfully instilled in her by fanatical people who have colluded with my personal enemies.[77]

Fin added that he had medical certification of his daughter's 'mental illness, which was often accompanied by fits with the loss of healthy rationale', although there is no evidence that he ever produced the document.

If most parents did not go so far as to attribute their daughter's 'wayward' behaviour to mental illness, they sought to convince the state that female converts were easily 'seduced through deception', in the words of one father.[78] In a similar petition to the governor of Vilna, Feiga Goldshtein complained that her daughter had been 'talked into conversion' by the infantry soldier Klematov, who had persuaded her to marry him, even though she was already betrothed to a respectable Jewish man.[79]

Finally, the abduction narrative served to shift responsibility for the 'shameful' act from the parents to the kidnapper or seducer. In all but two cases, the parents insisted that they had provided a decent upbringing for their children. As Yankel Kushlyansky put it, he had 'a fourteen-year-old daughter, who received an excellent education [and] was his sole delight'.[80]

Shifra Lebovich, on the other hand, was more introspective about her daughter's disappearance. 'Due to my extreme poverty, I moved with my family to Vilna to earn a living,' the distressed mother explained. That new environment opened the door to family disaster: 'On 14 July [1852], my daughter Khaika, who is fifteen years old, left the apartment that we rented in Vilna and I did not know until now where she had gone.'[81] While Lebovich blamed the family's dire economic straits for her inability to supervise the girl, the abduction narrative also allowed her to shift part of the blame to the Christians who had deceived her.

Petitioners had not only to construct a credible narrative that would capture the attention of state authorities, but also to devise a political strategy to win their case. In the Lithuanian provinces, where the dominant Catholic faith competed with the Russian Orthodox Church for believers, one tactic was to play the latter against the

77 LVIA, *f.* 378, *d.* 322 (1861), fo. 34, petition of Samuel Fin, 17 Oct. 1861.

78 LVIA, *f.* 378, *op.* 66, *d.* 579 (1865), fo. 25, petition of Yankel Kushlyansky to the governor-general of Vilna, 14 Feb. 1865.

79 LVIA, *f.* 378, *d.* 221 (1862), fos. 3ᵛ–4.

80 LVIA, *f.* 378, *op.* 66, *d.* 579 (1865), fo. 5ᵛ, report of the Vilna provincial board, 22 Mar. 1865.

81 LVIA, *f.* 378, *d.* 2067 (1852), fo. 3.

former. Thus, in a complaint to the Russian governor of Vilna in 1865, Yankel Kushlyansky castigated the official appointed to investigate his daughter's abduction: 'But as an individual professing the Roman Catholic faith, he conducted the investigation with a great deal of bias. Instead of taking measures to find out the truth, he chided me for allegedly trying to prevent my daughter from converting to the Catholic faith and sternly obliged me to sign [a document] that I would never leave [this place].'

In a dramatic gesture, Kushlyansky asserted that 'if my daughter's sincere desire was to turn to the prevailing Russian Orthodox faith, because of her minority, I am prepared to give her my blessing willingly.'[82] That disingenuous declaration was probably a ploy to delay the conversion by inducing the Vilna administration, already deeply enmeshed in a campaign to tame the Catholic Church and promote Russian Orthodoxy, to intercede.

Whereas the state rarely intervened in Russian Orthodox conversions, it did intercede on several occasions when Jewish parents accused the Catholic Church of kidnapping and forced baptisms, especially in the case of minors. When Samuel Fin filed a complaint about the abduction of his daughter, the state went so far as to appoint an official commission composed of relatively high-ranking bureaucrats to investigate the matter 'due to the importance of this case'.[83] Even those without Fin's political influence could expect assistance. The civil governor of Grodno, for example, personally attended the deposition of 14-year-old Feiga Baikovskaya to determine whether her baptism was indeed voluntary. When he discovered that she understood neither Judaism nor Catholicism, the governor ordered that the child be returned to her parents' custody. 'To prevent any abuses [against Feiga] by her co-religionists,' he reported, 'I ordered the chief of police and police official to keep guard [over her], and the parents and rabbi to sign [that they agreed to this].'[84] In another case, the same governor facilitated the meeting between a distraught mother and her daughter at a women's monastery, much to the chagrin of Catholic clergy, who had sought to prevent the reunion at all costs.[85]

The state also required birth certificates (metrical book records) or poll tax records to verify the age of prospective converts in order to counteract the tendency of minors like Khana Prais (a 13-year-old claiming to be 19) to exaggerate their age. To prevent forced child baptisms, the governor of Vilna even warned the Catholic consistory that the law dictated 'extreme caution and circumspection in these times in order that the holy cause of conversion not be denigrated in the eyes of the non-Orthodox and non-Christians'.[86]

In contrast to the state, the Russian Orthodox Church and society harboured little sympathy towards the Jewish family, which they viewed as a menace not only

[82] LVIA, *f.* 378, *op.* 66, *d.* 579 (1865), fo. 25^{v}.

[83] LVIA, *f.* 378, *d.* 322 (1861), fo. 2, governor-general of Vilna to the Roman Catholic spiritual consistory in Vilna, 21 Oct. 1861.

[84] LVIA, *f.* 378, *d.* 207 (1862), fos. 2^{v}–3.

[85] LVIA, *f.* 378, *op.* 221 (1862), fo. 3^{v}.

[86] Ibid., fos. 9–10^{v}.

to the successful conversion of new members, but to their spiritual welfare and physical safety *after* baptism. To a large degree, Jewish converts themselves exploited such suspicions with hair-raising tales of violent persecution at the hands of their former co-religionists. Casting themselves as Christian martyrs, they related counter-narratives of abduction, attempted murders, heroic escapes, and their resolute faith throughout these trials and tribulations.

In 1830, for example, Marianna Kvatkovskaya (formerly Mnukha Klebinskaya) accused her family and local Jews of kidnapping her twice after her conversion. In the first instance, she claimed that in 1821 her father's acquaintances confronted her at an inn in Lida and they pressured her to return to Judaism. When she resisted, they allegedly 'placed a drug in her beer so that she fell into a deep slumber and did not feel them place her in a *brichka* [light carriage]'. Moments before the drug took effect, she heard the conspirators 'reach an understanding with some other Jews that if she screamed on the way or refused to renounce her Christian faith, they would strangle her and dispose of [the body] in a river or forest'. Not long after she regained consciousness, Kvatkovskaya recalled that 'a group of Jews cut her hair and disguised her in Jewish clothing', before her father secretly moved her from town to town, all the while urging her to abandon her new faith. After great suffering, which she described in vivid detail (including concealment in a cemetery for several weeks), Kvatkovskaya reported that she succeeded in fleeing to the Bernardine monastery in Kovno.[87]

The second abduction, Kvatkovskaya complained, came two years later (1823) as she was passing out tickets for a gymnastic show organized by the Jew Pinkhas late at night at an inn in Kaidan, when her cousin Leizer Leibovich Klebansky came by 'on the pretext of some necessity'. He allegedly forced her to come to a local rabbi, who performed an ancient Jewish ritual to revert her back to Judaism, chanting 'amen, amen, *mazel tov*!' The cousin then forced her to travel from 'one unknown shtetl to another, until they reached Shtabin in tsarist Poland where she was given in marriage to a Jew named Eina from Sukhovolsk'.[88]

Whether accurate or invented (to divert attention away from her frequent interaction with Jews), accounts like Kvatkovskaya's provided ammunition for the Church and the secular Russian press to condemn the physical violence and coercion by 'fanatical Jews'. From the mid-nineteenth century the secular press (such as the Kiev newspaper *Kievlyanin*) as well as the ecclesiastical press (*Kievskie eparkhial'nye vedomosti, Moskovskie tserkovnye vedomosti*) regularly published sensational accounts about young Jewish women who were found murdered or beaten violently after their baptism.[89] So common were such stories that in 1879 the editors of the Jewish newspaper *Rassvet* urged local Jews to confirm whether these reports were indeed

[87] LVIA, *f.* 378, *d.* 65 (1821), fos. 184–93^{v}, complaint of Marianna Kvatkovskaya, 25 Sept. 1830.

[88] Ibid.

[89] 'The Case Against the Jew Prizent', *Kievlyanin*, no. 283 (1885), as cited in M. Agursky, 'Conversion of Jews to Christianity in Russia', *Soviet Jewish Affairs*, 20/2–3 (1990), 83–4.

factual or simply vicious rumours. It cited two recent articles in the *Vilenskii vestnik* and *Vek* about the 'ignorance and fanaticism of the Jewish masses'. According to these accounts, Jews had tortured one female convert from Bobruisk district by holding her a prisoner in a cellar for many days, and had murdered another from the village of Pozvilya, in Ponevezh district.[90] The focus on women may have reflected the disproportionate number of female converts, but also a gendered construction of the helpless female victim in need of protection.

These kinds of reports, whether genuine or bogus, provided grounds for the Church to discourage new converts from socializing with former co-religionists and even to require some to sign a sworn statement to that effect. In a private interview with a Russian Orthodox bishop, 17-year-old Sofia Avgustonovich (formerly Rokha Rudlinova of Rezhitsa) promised that she would 'never speak with her relatives and Jews or meet with them [in the future]'.[91]

In another case, when Girsh (Hirsh) Stolper expressed a desire to return to his home town after his baptism, the Lithuanian Orthodox consistory requested the local bishop in Novo-Aleksandrovsk to keep the new convert under surveillance to ensure that he meticulously observed Christian rites. Despite these precautions, immersion in the baptismal waters did not automatically terminate ties between Jewish converts and their families.

POST-CONVERSION NUPTIALS: CREATING A NEW CHRISTIAN FAMILY

Unlike much of western Europe, civil marriage did not exist in tsarist Russia; marriage and divorce remained under the control of each religious confession until the Bolshevik revolution of 1917. Although marriage between Russian Orthodox and other Christians had been legalized since the early eighteenth century, that rule did not extend to non-Christians. Such unions—of Russian Orthodox with Jews, Muslims, and Karaites—were expressly prohibited.[92] The only means to legitimize a mixed marriage was if the non-Christian converted to Orthodoxy. Although marriages between Jews and Protestants were not strictly banned, a protracted list of conditions reflected the ambivalence towards such unions. For example, Protestant parents could prevent grown children from marrying the spouse of their choice, if they could produce 'reasonable' grounds for their objection, which included 'marriage to a member of a non-Christian faith'.[93] Given the legal and social pressures against mixed marriages in tsarist Russia, conversion was as much a tool to legalize inter-faith marriages as a means to 'personal salvation'.

As archival sources suggest, however, few chose this path. As the state gradually

[90] 'Vnutrennyaya khronika', *Rassvet*, 1 (1879).

[91] LVIA, *f.* 605, *op.* 2, *d.* 499, fo. 3.

[92] V. O. Levanda, *Polnyi khronologicheskii sbornik zakonov i polozhenii kasayushchikhsya evreev* (St Petersburg, 1874), 726–7.

[93] Ibid. 322.

abandoned prosecution for 'illegal [extramarital] cohabitation' others simply chose a 'common-law marriage' over apostasy, especially in the late nineteenth century.[94]

Until 1905, for example, unions between Jews and Christians in St Petersburg remained at a low rate—only one or two mixed marriages per year. According to the *St Petersburg Yearbook*, out of 537 mixed marriages (9.87 per cent of all marriages in the city) in 1892, only two Jewish women married Christian (Protestant) men.[95] These numbers rose slightly following the Law of Religious Toleration (17 April 1905), which unintentionally encouraged converts to return to Judaism. Hence, in 1907 twenty Jews (ten males and ten females) married Protestants in St Petersburg out of 200 total marriages involving at least one Jewish spouse.[96]

A gender analysis reveals that prior to 1904 women comprised a disproportional number of those who married non-Jews in St Petersburg. After 1905 the male quotient increased, perhaps because of the possibility of reconversion, as well as greater secularization and social interaction with non-Jews. Elsewhere in the empire, especially in Ukraine and Lithuania, more women converted than men (mainly to Russian Orthodoxy and Catholicism) to enter a mixed marriage. While historians have argued that Jewish women were driven to convert by forces of demographic and economic circumstances beyond their control, archival sources indicate a more deliberate exercise of agency in the decision.[97] In other words, the majority of mixed marriages did not represent a final act of desperation by 'pariah women' with diminishing marital prospects.[98]

To be sure, factors such as poverty, place of residence, and acculturation were more conducive to rendezvous with non-Jewish suitors. For example, Khena Perlshtein became acquainted with Konstantin Berezovsky, an employee at her father's tavern in the remote village of Nemonyany in Vilna province.[99] Others developed liaisons with passing soldiers who were billeted in their towns.[100]

According to Mikhail Agursky, Jews and non-Jews developed close social

[94] See e.g. RGIA, *f.* 1412, *op.* 3, *d.* 325, fos. 1–7. In this case a Jewish lawyer, Rafail Lvov Veisman, sent a petition to the Imperial Chancellery requesting permission to adopt his two illegitimate sons from his six-year relationship with a Russian Orthodox widow. Although he remained with their mother, Veisman indicated no intention to convert in order to marry her. He did concede, however, to baptizing the two boys. See also *f.* 1412, *op.* 213, *d.* 101, case of Leia Broun, who had a long-term extramarital affair with a Russian doctor; *f.* 1412, *op.* 3, *d.* 391, case of Peisakh Moseivich Vulfovich, who had a daughter from a relationship with a Russian Orthodox woman.

[95] *Statisticheskii ezhegodnik Sankt-Peterburga za 1892* (St Petersburg, 1894), 143.

[96] *Statisticheskii ezhegodnik Sankt-Peterburga za 1907* (St Petersburg, 1913), 7.

[97] See Agursky, 'Conversion of Jews to Christianity in Russia'; id., 'Ukrainian–Jewish Intermarriages in Rural Areas of the Ukraine in the Nineteenth Century', *Harvard Ukrainian Studies*, 9 (1985), 139–44.

[98] Agursky, 'Ukrainian–Jewish Intermarriages in Rural Areas of the Ukraine', 140.

[99] LVIA, *f.* 398, *op.* 78, *d.* 291 (1870).

[100] A large proportion of Jewish women who converted for the sake of marriage would wed soldiers. For examples, see LVIA, *f.* 605, *op.* 4, *d.* 123 (Khaika Essim married a soldier in the third battalion of the Vladimir infantry); *d.* 78 (Tsivya Zhmudskaya wed a Cossack officer); *d.* 122 (Polina Moriovich married a military doctor).

relations in some Ukrainian villages. As the Brotherhood of St Vladimir reported, '[Jewish] girls who married [Orthodox] peasants, being already accustomed to the peasant way of life and to physical work, directly entered into peasant families'.[101] In urban centres such as St Petersburg, highly acculturated women like Matilda Lissanevich hosted a salon 'frequented by guard officers and young *chinovniki* [state bureaucrats]', and she herself married the powerful minister of finance (1892–1903), Sergey Witte, a highly publicized 'scandal' in high society. In the words of one German ambassador, Witte had settled for the daughter of an obscure postmaster from Lithuania, 'eine kluge, sehr intrigante Jüden [*sic*] [a smart, very intriguing Jewess]'.[102]

There is good reason to challenge the notion that conversion was a last recourse for undesirable *alte moydn* (spinsters). Contrary to previous assumptions, the median age of female converts was not greater, but sometimes even less, than that of Jewish brides at first marriage.[103] In Lithuania the pattern of youthful conversions was the norm; the median age for converts was 18 for women and 21 for men.[104] More specifically, of approximately a dozen women who applied for the sake of marriage between 1850 and 1870, the ages ranged between 15 and 22.[105] According to the Vilna metrical books of marriage, the average age of brides at first marriage was 19 in 1851 and 21 in 1870.[106]

Similarly, the Brotherhood of St Vladimir reported that of the thirty-one Jewish women in Kiev province who converted to Russian Orthodoxy in 1882, twenty-two were between the ages of 14 and 19; five between 20 and 24; only four were older but none was over 30. Based on these estimates, Agursky concluded that 'Jewish girls who did not marry by the age of sixteen or seventeen were considered unsuitable brides for Jewish boys or men, and so were probably more open to marriage with gentiles.'[107]

As recent demographic studies have shown, however, child marriages (brides under 16 years old) were the exception among Jews, even in small Ukrainian shtetls.[108] In fact, by the later decades of the nineteenth century, the proportion of

[101] Agursky, 'Ukrainian–Jewish Intermarriages in Rural Areas of the Ukraine', 140.

[102] T. H. von Laue, *Sergei Witte and the Industrialization of Russia* (New York, 1973), 143.

[103] For example, Agursky has argued that 'the majority of Jewish female converts listed [in the St Vladimir brotherhood reports] were *above* the average marital age for Jewish brides'; see 'Ukrainian–Jewish Intermarriages in Rural Areas of the Ukraine', 143.

[104] This estimate is based on Michael Stanislawski's study of 244 Jewish converts, combined with my own calculations of over 100 remaining Jewish conversion files in the Lithuanian State Archive in Vilnius; Stanislawski, 'Jewish Apostasy in Russia', 200.

[105] LVIA, *f.* 605, *op.* 2, *dd.* 826, 925; *op.* 4, *dd.* 784, 122, 849, 85, 78, 123, 878; *f.* 378, *d.* 409 (1862); *d.* 221 (1862); *f.* 447, *op.* 1, *d.* 3079; *f.* 398, *op.* 78, *d.* 281.

[106] LVIA, *f.* 728, *op.* 3, *d.* 6, metrical book of marriage for the residents of Vilna, 1851; *d.* 81, metrical book of marriage, 1870.

[107] Agursky, 'Ukrainian–Jewish Intermarriages in Rural Areas of the Ukraine', 124–43.

[108] S. Stampfer, 'Hamashma'ut haḥevratit shel nisu'ei boser bemizraḥ eiropah', in E. Mendelsohn and C. Shmeruk (eds.), *Kovets meḥarim al yehudei polin: Sefer lezikhro shel paul glikson/Studies in*

married females under the age of 21 declined sharply, falling from 42.2 per cent in 1887 to 25 per cent by 1897.[109] All this suggests that age played a minor role, if any, in the decision to enter a mixed marriage.

Significantly, petitioners like Sara Goldshtein stressed that they were already betrothed or had shunned arranged matches—assertions confirmed by their parents.[110] Thus, they consciously and voluntarily accepted marriage proposals from Christian men whom they had been courting in secret. If some women married outside the faith due to limited options, their decisions could have been shaped more by pragmatic considerations than by simple desperation. For example, some may have preferred a single Christian man to a widowed or divorced Jewish husband with several children. Others may have sought a partner whose social status offered certain legal advantages, such as residence and work outside the Pale of Settlement—an option that may have been attractive to orphaned women without strong ties to their home towns.

SOURCES OF TENSION IN MIXED MARRIAGES

Mixed marriages, even those based on 'love', were hardly free from religious and cultural tensions. Christians often suspected that their converted spouses were tempted to abandon their new faith and marriage, especially when conversion resulted in a traumatic break with parents and other family members. Such anxiety was particularly characteristic of male spouses, who attributed any 'wavering faith' to the emotional weaknesses of their wives.

According to Aleksandr Kunik, his wife, Maria's, intense desire to be reconciled with her family had nearly led her to revert to Judaism. The husband noted with satisfaction that her resolution broke down when he confronted her at the train station and dragged her before the local priest. In a complaint to the Russian Orthodox consistory in Kherson, Kunik explained that some Jews (including Maria's first husband) had conspired to turn his wife away from Christianity and had only succeeded by manipulating the painful relationship with her Jewish family: 'They took her to her father and started crying and screaming words in the dogmas of Judaism, until she swore to leave me and the children.'[111] In a signed confession, the wife admitted that the 'proselytizing Jews' had provided food and money for her to travel to Akkerman so that she could quietly reconvert to the Jewish faith. The local priest testified that the wife's father and other Jewish acquaintances had

Polish Jewry (Jerusalem, 1987); C. Y. Freeze, *Jewish Marriage and Divorce in Imperial Russia* (Hanover, NH, 2002).

[109] S. Rabinovich [Rabinowitsch], 'K voprosu o nachal'nom remeslennom obrazovanii evreiskikh zhenshchin', *Novyi Voskhod*, 5 (4 Feb. 1910), 9–10; id., 'Heiraten der Juden im europäischen Russland vom Jahr 1857 bis 1902', *Zeitschrift für Demographie und Statistik der Juden*, 5 (1909), fasc. 9–12.

[110] LVIA, *f.* 378, *d.* 221 (1862).

[111] Derzhavnyi arkhiv Odes'koyi oblasti, *f.* 37 (Kherson religious consistory), *opys* 1, *sprava* 3553.

persuaded Maria to return to Judaism, but boasted that, after his admonishments and exhortations, he had persuaded the woman to change her mind.

By no means was the Church always so successful. In a case from the village of Lukashevka, in Kiev province, in 1845, Eta, the tavern-keeper, not only deserted her peasant husband and son, but returned to Judaism and married a Jew. Much to the state's dismay, it was unable to ascertain her whereabouts and to prosecute the woman for apostasy and bigamy.[112] While such cases may have been exceptional, they still reinforced fears about the dangerous influence of family ties on neophytes.

Another problem involved the hostility of some Christian spouses towards the convert's Jewish family, which they regarded as a harmful and undesirable influence, particularly on the children. When Rosa Nakhmanova first converted to Protestantism to marry Emil Gustavovich Vilken, she believed that they would be socially and intellectually compatible. The bride came from a highly acculturated family, received an elite education at the Riga City Institute for Girls, and held a music degree from the St Petersburg Conservatory. But she soon discovered that neither her fluent German nor her cultivated manner impressed her husband; nor would he countenance her desire to maintain contact with her Jewish family. As Rosa Vilken complained to the Imperial Chancellery in 1887: 'Whenever he is dissatisfied with me, he prohibits me to see my closest relatives. So this past winter, he forbade me to correspond with my cousins, who were abroad, and now he does not permit them to visit me or (for that matter) me to call on them.'[113]

Emil Gustavovich denied mistreating his wife but openly admitted that he despised her relatives, whom he blamed for the breakdown of their marriage. Even before the marriage there had been 'such unpleasant exchanges and misunderstandings because of the dowry' that 'I did not want to become related to them.'[114] Throughout their nine-year marriage the husband complained that Rosa's sisters constantly borrowed money, imposed on their hospitality for several months at a time, and, worst of all, so poisoned his wife against him that she took the children and moved out. To add to his indignation, Emil added: 'After our falling out, her sisters even broke their own promise to their dying mother that they would not convert to Christianity and embraced Russian Orthodoxy, just to paralyse my anticipated protest that my children were in Jewish hands.'[115] Several of his letters made disparaging remarks about their insincere conversion to Orthodoxy for residence rights in St Petersburg. To be sure, the Vilkens' basic marital problems may have not been different from any ordinary couple; however, in this case, the husband translated his 'superior' position as the 'true' Christian spouse to justify his assertion of power. By forbidding his wife to maintain ties with Jewish relatives, he sought to re-establish his dominance in a marriage that both spouses acknowledged had already broken down.

[112] Tsentral'nyi derzhavnyi istorychnyi arkhiv Ukrayiny, Kiev, *f.* 442, *opys* 153, *sprava* 1044, fos. 1–13.

[113] RGIA, *f.* 1412, *op.* 215, *d.* 104, fo. 8.

[114] Ibid., fo. 60, petition of Emil Gustavovich Vilken, 24 Jan. 1888.

[115] Ibid., fo. 152.

Assertion of a spouse's residual 'Jewishness' informed the petition of a Russian Orthodox woman who accused her husband of wife-beating and adultery. The court investigator assigned to the case recycled her accusations: 'German [Herman] Trakhtenburg, the son of a Jew, is without education or upbringing, lacks every moral principle, and is capable of every form of despicable behaviour.'[116] He added that the wife had married against the wishes of her parents and advice of good friends. Despite his conversion to Christianity (Lutheranism), the investigator ascribed Trakhtenburg's deficient moral character to his inherent Jewish identity. When the Holy Synod granted his wife a divorce, it forbade the husband as the 'guilty party' to remarry.

Applications for divorce thus attributed the moral depravity of converted spouses to lingering Jewishness, a narrative strategy designed to elicit consistorial sympathy and a quick resolution of their suits. In 1917, for example, Ivan Patsevich reported that his wife, Olga Kaplan (a convert from Judaism), had not only deserted him five years ago, taking their only daughter with her, but recently informed him that 'she loved another and could not live with me'.[117] As one witness who testified on his behalf recalled: 'People said that Olga Patsevich did not love her husband very much and left him to go to America.' The husband requested a divorce on the grounds of desertion and permission for him 'as the innocent party' to remarry.

Some Russian Orthodox husbands included letters from their converted 'Jewish' spouses, who tearfully admitted their adulterous affairs with great regret. 'Vasya,' read one letter to Vasily Safonov from his wife, Elena, 'today, on 4 May (1909), I received a summons [for a divorce hearing], but I did not completely understand it.' She proceeded to describe her miserable existence with her new lover in St Petersburg:

> I began to remember how I used to live at home with you—that you never beat me, when suddenly he [the lover] jumped up and beat me with such force that blood flowed from my neck and nose. When he began to throw out my belongings, I began to search for a revolver and wanted to kill myself, but could not find one.[118]

Blaming herself entirely for the breakdown of the marriage, the wife assured Safonov that she would not attempt to sabotage the divorce proceedings. Based on the letter and other evidence of Elena's unfaithfulness, which allegedly began while the husband was away to attend his father's funeral, the Lithuanian Orthodox consistory granted the divorce.

Tension also permeated mixed marriages because of the social ostracism sometimes directed at converted spouses by Orthodox Russians. That hostility was salient in the case of Count Sergey Witte and Matilda Lissanevich: 'When I married

[116] RGIA, *f.* 1412, *op.* 215, *d.* 104, fo. 8.

[117] LVIA, *f.* 605, *op.* 9, *d.* 2196, fos. 149–52, journal of the Lithuanian Orthodox consistory, 14 Dec. 1917.

[118] LVIA, *f.* 605, *op.* 9, *d.* 1241, fo. 5, letter from Elena Safonova to Vasily Safonov, n.d.

a divorced woman, my wife was not accepted into court for more than ten years, and I considered this completely natural and correct', Witte rationalized, 'because at that time the court in general did not permit the introduction of divorced wives.'[119] According to state controller I. I. Filippov, however, the issue was not just her divorced status but Lissanevich's Jewish background. Their loathing only intensified, he observed, when Witte 'transferred her sisters' husbands—the engineer Bykhovets and the doctor Levi, who were living in Novgorod—to a new position with enormous salaries and travelling expenses, much to the surprise of all in Novgorod'.[120] Witte was already a highly controversial figure, profoundly detested by the noble landowning élite for his merciless industrialization—in their view, at the expense of the countryside. Witte's outsider status—Baltic German, economist, and railway executive—was only compounded by the marriage to a convert and a divorcée.

SPOUSES AND CHILDREN AFTER CONVERSION

Conversion served as a pragmatic solution not only for Jews who chose to marry Christians, but also for Jews seeking to dissolve a marriage without a formal Jewish divorce. This avenue held a special appeal for wives whose husbands refused to issue them a *get* (bill of divorcement), but it also offered advantages to men seeking to avoid a legal divorce hearing in rabbinical court and attendant financial risks. In the case of lower-ranking Jewish soldiers, the state offered to pay full child support (15 to 30 silver roubles regardless of sex) in the event of conversion and divorce from a Jewish spouse.[121] Some simply sought to evade the repayment of the wife's *ketubah* (marriage contract) and other monetary obligations. As a certain 'Dr F' told one Roman Catholic priest, he dreaded the 'troublesome negotiations' regarding the support of his first family.[122] When the latter informed him that conversion would 'automatically dissolve his previous Jewish marriage' and liberate him from all such obligations, he seized upon the opportunity and converted.

From the Russian Orthodox Church's standpoint, baptism did not automatically annul existing marriages between converts and their non-Christian spouses. However, it permitted the Christian spouse to divorce the 'unbelieving partner', regardless of the latter's wishes, under the three broad conditions (based on the resolutions of the Seventh Ecumenical Council in 680 and 690): (1) 'if the latter does not wish to live in agreement or refuses to fulfil marital obligations'; (2) if the Christian is convinced of the impossibility of winning over the unbelieving spouse

119 S. I. Witte, *Vospominaniya*, 13 vols. (Moscow, 1960), i. 422–3.

120 Ibid. 536 n. 63.

121 RGIA, *f.* 821, *op.* 8, *d.* 355, fo. 1. The law was taken from *Svod voennykh postanovlenii* (1859), bk. 1, pt. 11, ch. 2340, app. 129.

122 V. Maksimov, *Zakony o razvode pravoslavnogo i nepravoslavnogo ispovedanii i o razdel'nom zhitel'stve suprugov, s raz"yasneniami Pravitel'stvuyushchego Senata i tsirkulyarnymi i separatnymi ukazami Svyateishego Sinoda* (Moscow, 1909), 264.

to the faith'; and (3) 'if the unbelieving spouse hinders the religious duties [of the Christian]'.[123]

If these terms were met, the convert was absolved of former marital ties and free to marry an Orthodox spouse. The Roman Catholic Church followed a similar policy. Thus, when Sheine Litvak converted, the consistory in Mogilev permitted her to marry a Christian engineer and rejected the remonstrations of her Jewish husband, who appealed but lost his suit in 1887.[124]

If the various Christian confessions upheld the right of converts to remarry, state laws were more ambiguous. According to a statute of 1825, 'if the wife adamantly remains in her [Jewish] faith upon the conversion of her husband to the Christian faith and does not wish to cohabit with him, in such a case their marriage is completely dissolved and her husband is allowed to marry another Russian Orthodox woman'.[125] Not only did this ruling refer exclusively to Russian Orthodox conversions, it did not stipulate how to resolve cases in which one spouse desired to maintain the union. Bewildered by the exact terms of the law, Nadezhda Maksimovna (formerly Mnula Mendeliovna of Volkovysk, Grodno province) appealed personally to Tsar Nicholas I, in 1844, for permission to remarry against the wishes of her Jewish husband. The wife complained that an enormous age difference made her spouse, who was 'over sixty years old', completely unattractive to her: 'He is completely grey (*sovershenno sedoi*) in appearance. I [on the other hand] appear no older than thirty to all who know me, even though the Grodno district police has me registered as thirty-three years old.' If the state forced her 'to remain married to this old man (*starik*)', she threatened, 'I am afraid that this coercion will be an accomplice to the possible violation of my sexual probity.'[126]

Quite apart from her candid expression of sexual dissatisfaction, Maksimovna argued that profound religious differences between them made it impossible to cohabit with her Jewish spouse, despite 'Christ's commandment to love your enemies'. 'Can I live with him in love and harmony when he thanks God daily in his morning prayers according to the Jewish customs, and will most certainly always thank God that He did not make him a Christian or heathen (which is all the same to them) but a Jew?'[127] Not only would she be forced to tolerate his antipathy towards Christians, the wife argued, but she would invariably cause her husband to violate Jewish laws. During the Passover *seder*, for instance, she would be obliged 'to pour and pass a glass of wine to my husband. But as a Jew, he should not drink, let alone take in his hand a vessel touched by a Christian if he does not want to violate the laws of his faith.' Finally, his wife admitted that their sexual relations had never

[123] M.Sh., 'K voprosu o razvode mezhdu suprugami evreyami pri perekhode odnogo iz nikh v pravoslavie', *Voskhod*, 1 (1892), 6.

[124] *Khronika Voskhoda*, 24 (13 June 1899), 737.

[125] Levanda, *Polyni khronologicheskii sbornik*, 161. The same conditions applied when the wife converted to Christianity.

[126] LVIA, *f.* 605, *op.* 2, *d.* 456, fo. 10, petition of Nadezhda Nikolaevna Maksimovna to Tsar Nicholas I, 6 July 1844.

[127] Ibid., fo. 11.

been 'fully sanctified', because 'I did not succeed in preparing myself for the rite of immersion [the *mikveh*].' As a new Christian, she completely rejected the Jewish laws of purity, making it impossible for her husband to have sexual relations with her. In this case, the plaintiff clearly prevailed; the last document in the file, a bitter complaint from the Jewish husband, cited rumours that she had already remarried a Christian and demanded the unconditional return of Maksimovna as his lawful wife.

In response to such cases, the state sought to clarify its position. According to a revised version of the 1857 law, 'if either the husband or wife does not wish to remain in the former marital union, then the marriage is dissolved and the baptized individual is permitted to remarry a person of the Russian Orthodox faith'.[128] This ruling appeared to resolve the question of remarriage among converts, but remained susceptible to later rulings and interpretations. In an effort to make it more difficult for the convert to dissolve a marriage unilaterally against the will of the Jewish spouse, the senate issued an order requiring the written consent of the latter starting in 1891–2.[129]

Not surprisingly, this new resolution led to new inconsistencies at the local level. For example, in Zvenigorod, Kiev province, one fastidious priest insisted on strict adherence to the senate ruling. Brukha Shnaiderman claimed that, although the priest Ivan had reassured her—before her conversion in 1903—that there were no obstacles to her remarriage, he now demanded proof of a Jewish divorce. 'The Jew [her husband] knows that I am baptized', she protested, 'and will not give me a divorce out of spite.'[130] In this instance, the Volhynia Orthodox consistory sided with the priest and requested the local police to determine whether the husband consented to the dissolution of the marriage. Whether voluntarily or out of coercion, he finally agreed: 'I declare that I do not desire to live with Brukha, who converted to Russian Orthodoxy.' Not long after Shnaiderman submitted the document, Bishop Antony declared the 'marriage dissolved' and permitted the wife to remarry.[131] The Lithuanian consistory in Vilna, by contrast, declared an 1887 ruling of the Holy Synod, which gave the Russian Orthodox Church the sole prerogative to dissolve inter-faith marriages, as more binding than the senate resolution.[132] Hence, when Raisa Glikman (formerly Riva Leizerovna) petitioned to remarry in 1911, Church authorities noted that if the wife converted to the Russian Orthodox faith and her husband 'remained in his unbelief', their marriage was dissolved.[133]

As already noted, these conditions applied exclusively to converts of the Russian Orthodox faith, while other Christian confessions adopted their own policy and rules. The state's benign negligence, however, came to an end in 1905 when the

[128] *Sbornik uzakonenii kasayushchikhsya evreev*, citing *Svod zakonov*, vol. x, bk. 1, pt. 1, chs. 3 and 79.

[129] Derzhavnyi arkhiv Zhytomyrs'koyi oblasti, *f.* 1, *opys* 31, *sprava* 827, fos. 3^{v}–4. See also *Tserkovnye vedomosti*, no. 11 (1892).

[130] GAZhO, *f.* 1, *opys* 31, *sprava* 827, fos. 1–2, petition of Brukha Shnaiderman, 1903.

[131] Ibid., fos. 3–7.

[132] LVIA, *f.* 605, *op.* 9, *d.* 1376, fo. 18, decree of the Holy Synod, 16 June 1887.

[133] Ibid.

wife of 'Dr F' filed a suit with the Department of Spiritual Affairs of Foreign Faiths protesting the illegal dissolution of her marriage by the Catholic Church. She claimed that when her husband left for the Russian–Japanese front, he sent regular support for family. After his transfer to Manchuria, she had expected to join him but was aghast to discover that he had decided to create a new family. To avoid the 'long, tedious, and unpleasant explanations for the unexpected rupture and troublesome negotiations' regarding his family's support, the husband decided to convert to Catholicism.[134]

The process of discarding his first family was not as simple as the husband had anticipated. He first attempted—without success—to secure a formal statement from his wife that she no longer desired to remain married (as required by the senate ruling). To the Church's enquiries about her intention to convert, the wife offered an equivocal statement 'that she did not dismiss the possibility in the future', thus undermining any arguments about the impossibility of winning her over to the Christian faith. Failing to coerce her into capitulation or conversion, the Roman Catholic Church granted a special papal dispensation that unilaterally annulled the marriage and permitted the convert to remarry. Despite the wife's protests about the illegality of the whole affair, the Department of Spiritual Affairs admitted that it had no authority to overturn the papal dispensation since it did not threaten the political interests of the state (the one condition stipulated in the law allowing the government to intercede in such matters).[135]

To compound the confusion, state laws provided no explicit guidelines on how to dissolve the first marriage; in most cases, Church officials simply declared that the marriage 'was dissolved'. If the consequences were inconvenient for Jewish husbands, who could still resort to the *heter me'ah rabanim* (literally, permission of one hundred rabbis) in order to remarry, it was tragic for abandoned wives—who were condemned as *agunot* until they secured a proper Jewish divorce.[136] To be sure, some converted spouses consented to a formal Jewish divorce, as in one case that took place in Rabbi Chaim Tchernowitz's home town of Shebiz, in Vitebsk province. The husband, who had become the village policeman shortly after his conversion, treated the whole divorce proceedings with *ḥutspah* by responding to the rabbi's questions only in Russian. When the haughty official failed to clarify whether he was of priestly origins (a Cohen or a Levy), the rabbi lost his patience and retorted angrily: 'You, a convert, do you think that I am intimidated by your shining buttons?' Bewildered by the sudden reversal of roles, the husband began to reply more modestly in Yiddish and the divorce ended peacefully.[137]

For more unfortunate wives, however, the obstacles to obtaining a Jewish divorce were poignantly apparent, as in the case of Perl Goldbergova of Minsk,

[134] Maksimov, *Zakony o razvode*, 264–5.

[135] Ibid. 268.

[136] An *agunah* could never remarry because her first marriage was not legally terminated, either through divorce or through the death of her husband.

[137] C. Tchernowitz, *Pirkei ḥayim* (New York, 1954), 64.

whose husband entered a monastery in Vilna with the intent to convert. Although the wife assured the local bishop that she did not seek to prevent her husband's baptism, but only desired a Jewish divorce, he simply rejected the case without any investigation based on formalistic grounds: 'She wrote her petition on plain paper,' that is, without attaching the proper stamp tax.[138]

In another case, the St Petersburg consistory permitted Fedor Ivanov (formerly Khaim Salomonsky) to marry a Russian Orthodox woman in 1886, but issued no directives about the necessity of dissolving his first marriage with his Jewish wife. When Ester Salomonskaya received word of her husband's actions, she protested that, without a formal Jewish divorce, she would not be permitted to remarry.[139] The Ministry of the Interior noted that according to the law, 'a Jewish marriage dissolved by a Russian Orthodox consistory is no longer considered legitimate'.[140]

But by permitting the convert to remarry without the dissolution of the first marriage, it argued, the law in effect 'induces one spouse to commit bigamy and unjustly condemns the other to celibacy'. If the final decision had rested with the Department of Spiritual Affairs of Foreign Faiths (within the Ministry of the Interior), the outcome might have been different. Given its broader experiences with Jewish marriage and divorce matters, more than any other branch of the state bureaucracy, it may have compelled Jewish converts to divorce their spouse before they remarried, as the sympathetic tone of the above-mentioned report suggests.[141]

However, the jurisdiction over converts rested with the Church, which was concerned exclusively with the moral and spiritual welfare of the new believer, not the fate of the unconverted spouse. As the Church's top lay official replied: 'I cannot help but notice that, although the petitioner was prompted to [send] her request on the grounds that it was impossible for her to remarry, not only does she lack evidence for this [assertion], but she does not appear to have attempted to obtain permission to remarry.'[142] Clearly, this office was neither informed about the Jewish laws of divorce, nor cognizant of the plight of the *agunah*, who had begun to capture the attention of state bureaucrats in the Department of Spiritual Affairs of Foreign Faiths.

A similar problem afflicted a Jewish widow whose converted brother-in-law refused to perform the ceremony of *ḥalitsah* (levirate divorce), which some considered a 'primitive and degrading ritual'.[143] On 22 May 1886 the governor of

[138] LVIA, *f.* 605, *op.* 4, *d.* 1427, fo. 456–456^{v}.

[139] RGIA, *f.* 797, *op.* 90, *d.* 47, fo. 4, Department of the Imperial Chancellery for the Receipt of Petitions to the chief procurator of the Holy Synod, 22 Aug. 1886.

[140] Ibid., fo. 4^{v}.

[141] For more on the involvement of the Department of Spiritual Affairs of Foreign Faiths in Jewish family matters, in particular, with the activities of the Rabbinic Commission, see Freeze, *Jewish Marriage and Divorce in Imperial Russia*, ch. 2.

[142] RGIA, *f.* 797, *op.* 90, *d.* 47, fo. 17^{v}, letter from K. P. Pobedonostsev to the Imperial Chancellery, 15 Nov. 1886.

[143] A woman whose husband died before she had borne children was 'chained' to the husband's brother. According to an ancient Israelite custom, the brother-in-law was obliged to marry the child-

Odessa received a complaint from Sara Gener against three rabbis who rejected her petition to remarry until she produced evidence of her levirate divorce. An investigation revealed that the former state rabbi of Odessa, S. L. Schwabacher (who received his doctorate from Lwów) had erroneously instructed her to remarry on the grounds that a convert was not permitted to perform the ritual of *ḥalitsah*. Despite Gener's protests about the inequity of her circumstances, the Rabbinic Commission[144] in St Petersburg rejected her suit on the grounds that 'a *yevamah* [childless widow] is chained to her levir until he releases her through the rite of *ḥalitsah*'—an onerous requirement since neither the Church nor the state enforced it.[145]

Equally controversial was the case of converted Jews, who had accepted Christianity to obtain legal and professional advantages, but elected *not* to divorce their Jewish spouses. Here, state law was unequivocal: according to one statute of 1835 (reiterated in 1851), in such mixed marriages 'neither the husband nor wife are permitted to maintain permanent residency outside the Pale of Settlement'.[146] In other words, although baptized Jews normally had the right to reside in cities such as St Petersburg and Moscow, they forfeited that privilege if they chose to remain married to a Jewish spouse. This was a recurring and important problem for many Jewish converts. For example, when Iosef Rubenshtern (originally from Mitava) and Aleksandr Brozgal (from Vitebsk) converted to Orthodoxy, they obtained the right to register in the communities of St Petersburg and Orenburg respectively.[147] However, once they informed local authorities that they had no intention of divorcing their Jewish wives, both immediately lost their new residence permits.

This law revealed a deep ambivalence on the part of authorities. On the one hand, it did not directly mandate the dissolution of marriages when one spouse converted; unless one party insisted, the marriage remained in force. To be sure, the converted spouses were required to swear that they would proselytize to the 'unbelieving spouse' and ensure that their children would 'not be led away to the Jewish faith'.[148] This qualified tolerance of inter-faith marriages between Jews and

less widow and to name the firstborn after the deceased 'so that his name is not obliterated from Israel', or to release the widow through the ceremony of *ḥalitsah*. In Russia the option of marriage (*yibum*) was not available, so *ḥalitsah* was the only alternative. The ceremony of *ḥalitsah* required the widow to remove a shoe from her brother-in-law, spit on the ground, and declare, 'Thus shall be done to the man who will not build up his brother's house!' If the surviving brother-in-law refused to perform this ritual, as in this case, the widow automatically became an *agunah*, unable to remarry for the rest of her life.

[144] The Rabbinic Commission was a consultative body under the MVD, which regulated Jewish rituals, examined divorce cases, advised rabbis about ambiguous religious and state laws, and adjudicated charges brought against local rabbis.

[145] RGIA, *f.* 821, *op.* 8, *d.* 291, fos. 42–45ᵛ. For a more detailed discussion about the rite of *ḥalitsah* in the event that a levir converted to Christianity, see RGIA, *f.* 821, *op.* 9, *d.* 14, fos. 1–15.

[146] RGIA, *f.* 797, *op.* 92, *d.* 120, fo. 7, statute of 9 Apr. 1851, citing a law first enacted in 1835.

[147] Ibid., fos. 8 ob–9, decision of the Senate on the Rubenshtern and Brozgal cases, 27 Aug. 1852.

[148] *Sbornik uzakonenii kasayushchikhsya evreev*, arts. 79–91.

converts gave lip-service to the Pauline principle that 'if any brother has a wife who is an unbeliever, and she consents to live with him, let him not send her away' (1 Corinthians 7: 12). On the other hand, the law clearly penalized those who chose to remain married to a Jewish partner, perhaps from fear of pressure on the convert and their children to return to the Jewish faith. Here, too, the Church could find suitable scriptural justification, such as Paul's injunction not to be 'bound together with unbelievers; for what partnership have righteousness and lawlessness?' (2 Corinthians 6: 14).[149]

It was not until a flurry of similar cases reached the Holy Synod and Senate in the late 1890s that the state began to reconsider the contradictions in the laws on interfaith marriages. One such suit involved Dr Mikhail Nyurenberg, who had converted from Judaism in 1899 with the expectation of enjoying the full rights and privileges of Orthodox subjects. To his dismay, however, he discovered that the Moscow police would not give him a passport until he brought a certificate verifying that he had divorced his Jewish wife.[150] As Nyurenberg explained in his appeal, prior to baptism he had enjoyed the privilege of residency in Moscow as a physician—as did his wife, who had obtained residency in the capital before their marriage.[151] If the police decision was upheld, he complained, he had more rights as a Jew than as a Christian. A second case involved a first-guild merchant, Isaak Gurkov. Like the Nyurenbergs, he complained that the police had expelled him from St Petersburg when they discovered that he had converted to Lutheranism but had not divorced his Jewish wife.[152] Similar actions also transpired in provincial towns. Aleksandr Khokhlov, a mechanic and foreman in the city waterworks of Perm, filed an appeal against the local authorities; although the couple had lived in the city for thirty years (because of his occupational speciality), city officials had expelled them both once he converted to Orthodoxy but chose to remain with his Jewish wife.[153]

At first, authorities were reluctant to dismantle the 1835 rule. Thus, in 1901 the chief procurator of the Holy Synod (representing the Church) and the senate initially rejected the Nyurenbergs' appeal on the grounds that tolerance of 'mixed marriages' would have a 'morally harmful' impact on the rest of the population.[154]

Two years later, however, secular authorities took up the issue again. Some senators (such as P. M. Lazarev, N. M. Anichkov, and N. P. Smirnov) reaffirmed the earlier ruling and defended the 'religious-moral character' of the original law. They noted that the law applied only to converts who chose 'to maintain the marital union with an individual of the Jewish faith'. In other words, the converts forfeited their

149 M. Sh., 'K voprosu o razvode', 1–11.

150 RGIA, *f.* 797, *op.* 92, *d.* 120, fo. 4, report of the governor of Moscow, 31 Aug. 1899.

151 For more on the rights of certain groups of Jews to live outside the Pale of Settlement, see B. I. Nathans, *Beyond the Pale: The Jewish Encounter with Late Imperial Russia* (Berkeley, 2002).

152 RGIA, *f.* 797, *op.* 92, *d.* 120, fo. 11, case of Isaak Gurkov, who filed his first petition on 18 Mar. 1892.

153 Ibid., fo. 10–10^{v}.

154 Ibid., fos. 5^{v}–6^{v}, proposal of the chief procurator and Senate, 2 Jan. 1901.

rights by making a morally 'wrong' decision to remain with the non-Christian spouse.[155] But this time a strong alternative view emerged, with adherents from the senate (F. F. Trepov and I. V. Meshchaninov) and even from the Church (lay officials who included V. K. Sabler, A. I. Petrov, and A. A. Melnikov). They noted the 1835 ruling, which pre-dated later legislation liberalizing the right of certain categories of Jews (retired soldiers, first-guild merchants, university graduates, skilled artisans) to reside outside the Pale of Settlement. The original law, they argued, should be modified to take into account these new legal realities. Specifically, they rejected the decision to deprive the Nyurenberg couple of their residency rights in Moscow. In 1904 the Senate formally ruled in favour of the latter, recognizing their right to reside as an inter-faith couple in Moscow.[156] By the time their case had been resolved, however, the Nyurenbergs had already divorced, apparently in order to retain their residence permits. Upon the dissolution of their marriage, they could not remarry unless the wife converted to Christianity. Similarly, in the Rubenshtern and Brozgal cases cited above, the senate decided to allow the wives, Tsira and Gita, to register in their husbands' towns of residence, but enjoined the local police to verify that the wives actually resided with their husbands.[157]

CHILD CUSTODY AFTER CONVERSION

The thorny issue of child custody also confronted families in which only one parent converted to Christianity. In this event, the law mandated a gendered division of the children between the spouses: 'Upon the baptism of Jews, they can baptize their children as long as they are under seven years old. If only the father or mother converts, in the former case, the sons can be baptized; in the latter case, the daughters can be baptized.'[158] Hence, when Peter Lipkin's Jewish wife (from whom he was still not divorced) refused to surrender their children for baptism in 1864, the authorities in Mogilev gave the father sole custody of his 5-year-old son. Based on a strict interpretation of the law, they rejected his bid for their 3-year-old daughter Khana, who was permitted to remain with her mother.[159]

Whereas state law reflected a dichotomous view about the 'natural' gender division of parental responsibilities prevalent in Russian society, the Church dismissed such notions and proposed to grant child custody of both sexes to the converted parent. Moishe Polinshy, for example, succeeded in baptizing two sons and one daughter (between the ages of 5 and 14) in 1867, perhaps because the second wife had little power over the fate of her stepchildren.[160] In another case, the Church

155 RGIA, *f.* 797, *op.* 92, *d.* 120, fos. 21–22^{v}. 156 Ibid., fos. 22^{v}–23. 157 Ibid., fos. 33–36^{v}.

158 *Svod zakonov*, vol. ix, art. 1385. 159 LVIA, *f.* 378, *d.* 310 (1864), fos. 1–2.

160 LVIA, *f.* 605, *op.* 4, *d.* 813, fos. 4–9. See also LVIA, *f.* 605, *op.* 4, *d.* 758 (1867), case of Fai Lazarova, who was baptized with her 9-year-old son. Although Lazarova revealed that her wealthy and influential father (an honorary citizen) opposed her decision, neither he nor the husband could apparently prevent the baptism of the boy.

approved Iosel Stengrod's petition to baptize his son *and* daughter; the monastery reported that the father only arrived 'with his eight-year-old son and without his daughter, Khana, who remained with her mother due to an illness'.[161] Apparently, the wife prevailed in her struggle to retain custody over her two daughters—the elder adamantly refused to convert and the 1-year-old girl mysteriously fell ill just before the father entered the monastery.

Not all Jewish parents were as successful in preventing their children's baptism. Shaul Gintsburg described the fate of Avraham Perets's children, who were not only separated from their mother to reside with their father in St Petersburg, but also forced to convert with him. 'It was said in St Petersburg', Gintsburg noted, 'that the daughter [Tsirel] used to light the candles every Friday night after her baptism.'[162] The struggle to protect young children proved even more challenging for close relatives, who had no legal authority over their welfare. In 1872 the newspaper *Vestnik russkikh evreev* reported a case in which Leizer Rabinovich left his two children with their grandparents in Berdichev after the death of his wife. When the father later converted to Lutheranism, he 'suddenly remembered his sons [who were now aged 13 and 10] and demanded their return'.[163] Although the grandfather contended that the boys should be able to choose their own religion since they were over 7 years of age, the governor-general of Kiev and court procurator sided with the father. The author of the article decried this decision as a blatant violation of the law and urged that local officials be required to read the most recent *Collection of Laws Pertaining to Jews* to prevent such a miscarriage of justice from recurring.

The final question was guardianship for converted children whose Jewish parents demanded that they reside at home until they reached their majority. This issue first came to the attention of the central government in 1873 when the governor of Kiev protested the decision of the Cherkassy Justice of the Peace Court to return a baptized child (Taube Yanopolskaya) to her Jewish mother's charge. 'Given the deep-rooted religious fanaticism of the Jewish population of the south-western region [hasidic enclaves], which incites various persecutions against their own who convert to Russian Orthodoxy', the governor asserted that the state should 'not allow converted Jewish children to reside with their parents'.[164]

The Holy Synod concurred with this recommendation, noting that 'due to religious fanaticism, Jews could not but exert a pernicious influence on their converted children by living with them'.[165] Since the existing laws provided no guidance on this matter, it proposed that the state enact appropriate legislative measures to ensure the protection of converted Jewish minors.

[161] LVIA, *f.* 605, *op.* 2, *d.* 1919.

[162] Gintsburg, *Meshumodim in tsarishn rusland*, 47–8.

[163] *Vestnik russkikh evreev*, 2 (1872), 54.

[164] RGIA, *f.* 821, *op.* 9, *d.* 110, fo. 1, report of the Ministry of Justice to the Ministry of the Interior, 25 May 1873.

[165] Ibid., fo. 4, report of the chief procurator of the Holy Synod, 11 Mar. 1874. For the full discussion in the Holy Synod, see RGIA, *f.* 796, *op.* 154, *d.* 1471.

In principle, the Second Section of His Imperial Majesty's Chancellery (an active participant of the legal reforms of the 1860s and 1870s) was reluctant to revise the fundamental civil laws concerning parent–child relations.[166] It argued that separation of parents and children 'would be completely opposed to the general spirit of our existing laws about the mutual relationship between parents and children and, in light of the general regulations, could even turn out to be unjust in many instances'.[167] Even though no specific laws stipulated the custody of child converts, the Second Section maintained that Russian legislation provided protective measures against the abuses of parental power fostered by Jewish fanaticism. For instance, children under 14 years of age who desired to convert without the consent of their parents could be educated in Church dogma and teachings only after their decision was established as sincere and valid.[168] Moreover, civil law freed children from the obligation to obey their parents if the latter 'forced them to act against their conscience'.[169] However, it recommended that 'if these established measures are not sufficient for some districts, especially those densely populated by Jews', then it was possible to adopt other measures without giving them 'the character of a universal and binding law'. In other words, given the difficulties of revising the existing laws, they could simply reinterpret certain judicial statutes to accommodate new circumstances. As one prelate so aptly observed, 'In our fatherland, there is a tried and tested, most reliable method for annulling the effect of unsuccessful legislation: exceptions, limitations, explanations, permissions, etc.'[170] This was typical of the 'counter-reform' period of the 1880s and 1890s, when it was difficult to pass general statutes.

After considering all these reports, the minister of justice concurred with the reasoning of the Second Section, save in one matter: 'I cannot agree as consistent with justice the establishment of any special laws with respect to the Jewish population that would exempt them from the current general rules regulating all confessions that protect children in matters of faith and conscience from parental coercion.'[171] He argued that the 'categorical removal' of converted children from their living at home would completely undermine the legal concept of parental power. Moreover, in many instances separation 'would not correspond to their mutual wishes, as it proved to be in the case of the baptized Jewess Yanopolskaya',

[166] For more on the function of the Second Section of His Imperial Majesty's Chancellery, see N. P. Eroshkin, *Istoriya gosudarstvennykh uchrezhdenii dorevolyutsionnoi Rossii* (Moscow, 1968), 206–7.

[167] RGIA, *f.* 821, *op.* 9, *d.* 110, fo. 8, report of the Second Section of His Imperial Majesty's Chancellery to the chief procurator of the Holy Synod, 14 Aug. 1874.

[168] Ibid., fo. 10–10^{v}. The Second Section cited the regulation of 4 Dec. 1862 regarding the conversion of non-Russian subjects.

[169] Ibid., fo. 10^{v}. It cited the *Svod zakonov* (civil law section), vol. x, pt. 1, ch. 169.

[170] Otdel rukopisei, Gosudarstvennaya biblioteka im. V. I. Lenina, *f.* 230, *kollektsiya* 9804, *d.* 2, fos. 5–6^{v}.

[171] Ibid., fo. 13, report of the Ministry of Justice to the Ministry of the Interior, 7 July 1875.

who apparently wished to reside at home.[172] Hence, the Ministry of Justice concluded that only in cases involving the abuse of parental power from religious intolerance or neglect should these rules be applied on an ad hoc basis and through a court of law.

CONCLUSION

Conversion was not merely a matter of legal advantage (that is, residency outside the Pale of Settlement and professional advancement) or escape from destitution and social displacement, as generally depicted in the literature. It also involved—as cause or consequence—critical quotidian questions involving marriage and family. In many cases, familial bonds did not necessarily disappear after baptism, despite efforts on the part of converts to distance themselves from their kin (at least in their petitions) or the kin to disown their children or relatives. Perhaps Tevye the Milkman captured this sentiment best in a darker vignette of the shtetl when his daughter Chava converted to marry a Russian Orthodox peasant: 'I burned with anger against her and against him and against the whole world, but mostly against myself because I wasn't able to forget her even for a minute. Why couldn't I forget her? Why couldn't I tear her out of my heart completely?'[173]

Indeed, such ties represented the very force that Church and society feared would lure converts back to Judaism. To be sure, some Jewish families severed all relations with their converted kin, as in the case of Olga Kaplan, whose mother terminated all communication after her marriage to Ivan Patsevich.[174] But immediate disavowal was hardly the only response to conversion. Complaints about the 'abduction' of children (which often included those who had reached their majority), for example, alerted Catholic monasteries that zealous parents and relatives had no intention of acquiescing. Parents, relatives, and even entire Jewish communities resorted to extreme measures to prevent baptism or induce a convert to return to Judaism. As one priest in Simferopol reported to the Holy Synod, he was forced to lock the church during the baptism of a Jewish girl as a precautionary [measure] due to the frequent disorder on the part of the Jews'.[175] Afterwards, he was afraid to come out to face some 500 Jews who appeared on the verge of rioting.

Social constructions of gender also shaped responses to conversion. As this study has illustrated, Jewish parents and society often depicted the conversion of Jewish women as the consequence of their unstable constitution, easily seduced by deception. While petitioners countered these assumptions with bold declarations about their long-standing conscious decision to convert, they too invoked popular tropes—that of the 'victimized woman' seeking to abandon an abusive husband or

[172] Ibid., fo. 14^{v}.

[173] 'Tevye the Milkman', ed. I. Howe and R. Wisse, in *The Best of Sholem Aleichem* (Washington, 1979), 176.

[174] LVIA, *f.* 605, *op.* 9, *d.* 2196, fos. 149–52.

[175] RGIA, *f.* 796, *op.* 154, *d.* 1471, fos. 13–14, report of the Holy Synod, 12 Dec. 1873.

undesirable arranged marriage. In contrast, parental petitions treated converting sons as rebellious youths or seeking advantage to escape the confines of Jewish life. To demonstrate their sincerity, male petitioners often described a 'rational' path to conversion, such as their knowledge of Russian Orthodox tenets, prayers, and customs. For example, Moishe Polinshy informed the Lithuanian consistory that, because of his illiteracy, 'the light of truth' had been hidden from him, but his constant interactions with Christians had taught him the dogmas of the faith. He now believed that one could only be saved through Russian Orthodoxy.[176]

Finally, if some converts regarded baptism as an expeditious solution to their marital, occupational, or legal predicaments, state laws did not always accommodate their efforts. Thus, questions about the right to dissolve an existing Jewish marriage, residence rights for mixed couples, and child custody, for example, posed unforeseen dilemmas for both converts and Jewish family members. Not surprisingly, ambiguous regulations for multiple Christian confessions, compounded by ad hoc addenda (often viewed by their initiators as creative solutions to contemporary circumstances), created confusion and inconsistent practices throughout the empire. This resulted, in part, from the increasingly conflicting goals of Church and state—the former concerned more with the fate of its new flock and the latter with *raison d'état*, especially with the professionalization of judicial officials within the central government in the post-reform period.[177] As Jewish conversions to Russian Orthodoxy increased from 322 in 1835 to 938 in 1900, these issues became more urgent for Jews and converts alike, as they sought to negotiate the tangled legal web surrounding their marital and family circumstances.[178]

[176] LVIA, *f.* 605, *op.* 4, *d.* 813, fo. 2, petition of Moishe Polinshy to the bishop of Kovno, 11 Mar. 1867.

[177] For more on the role of professional jurists involved in reforming imperial law, see Wagner, *Marriage, Property and Law in Late Imperial Russia*.

[178] *Izvlechenie iz otcheta po vedomstvu dukhovnykh del pravoslavnogo ispovedaniya za 1836* (St Petersburg, 1837), 124–7; *Izvlechenie iz otcheta po vedomstvu dukhovnykh del pravoslavnogo ispovedaniya za 1900* (St Petersburg, 1901), 50–1.

The Lost Generation
Education and Female Conversion in *Fin-de-Siècle* Kraków

RACHEL MANEKIN

IN 1907 a Yiddish melodrama was published in Kraków called *Tate mames tsures* ('The Troubles of Father and Mother').[1] The popular play, by L. Gebel, was based on the true story of a young Jewish woman, the daughter of a tavern-keeper in a small Galician village, who fled from her parents' home on the first night of Passover, then converted to Christianity and married her Polish lover in 1889. In the theatrical version the Jewish woman elopes with her lover after her mother reveals to her the identity of her groom-to-be, a Jewish yeshiva student, and the date of her impending marriage. Unlike the story on which it was based, the play ends happily for the Jewish audience with the young woman returning to her family and her faith.[2]

A similar story was related by S. Y. Agnon in his novel *Hakhnasat kalah* (The Bridal Canopy'), although Agnon told his story from the standpoint of the rabbinical student rather than that of the Galician village woman. As in the case of *Tate mames tsures*, the marriage was quickly arranged after the girl's parents learned of their daughter's romantic attachment with a Pole. The parents invite the young student to their house for Passover *seder*, and the young couple spend time together after the meal. But later that night the young woman elopes with her Polish lover, leaving the yeshiva student dejected and desolate.[3]

1 L. Gebel, *Tate mames tsures: Lebens bild mit gezang in 4 akten* (Podgórze bei Krakau, 1907).

2 Gershom Bader relates in his memoirs that he was personally acquainted with the young woman on whom the play's heroine was based. In a private conversation she told him that from the time she had reached the age of intelligence she felt an aversion to all things Jewish, whereas she found anything Christian to be beautiful and noble. Bader adds that in Galicia during those times young women lived in fanatical homes with uneducated fathers and brothers who engaged in Torah study and in business. The girls felt more at home in the free and intelligent atmosphere outside their houses. Their stories ended in tragedy, with the girls escaping to convents or causing other problems. In either case 'they were lost to the Jewish people'. See G. Bader, *Mayne zikhroynos* (Buenos Aires, 1953), 331–5.

3 S. Y. Agnon, *The Bridal Canopy*, trans. I. M. Lask (New York, 1937), 68–79. The title of the tale is 'Jacob Solomon's Bed'.

Interestingly, neither the play nor the novel depicts the young women in a negative light. On the contrary, the authors reveal to their audience an unbridgeable gap between the reality in which the heroines live and the future lives that their parents have planned for them. The village woman in *Tate mames tsures* is a free spirit who reads philosophy and believes in a love that transcends religious and national differences, a love that symbolizes the 'spirit of the new times'. She knows that her mother belongs to a generation that is incapable of understanding this. Nevertheless, she loves her mother deeply and torments herself with the knowledge that her choice will break her mother's heart. After her mother reveals the identity of her intended bridegroom, she breaks down in tears, 'Mameniu! What are you talking about?! That yeshiva student, that idler! . . . No, no, mamele? What are you saying? How can you even imagine a thing like that, that I, so young . . . You did not ask me? With the son of Zalman Peseles? No, this cannot be. I am so unfortunate, so wretched.'[4] According to the author, there is no way that the young woman could find happiness within the framework of such a marriage.

In the Agnon story the daughter is a sensuous, determined woman with a strong physical presence, in sharp contrast to the wretched appearance and shy demeanour of the yeshiva student. She attempts to create some sort of bond with the yeshiva student after the Passover *seder* has concluded, but it is clear to the reader that the bond cannot hold. The responsibility for the failed engagement, implies Agnon, lies not with the young woman but with the yeshiva student. In commenting upon the unhappy ending one of the characters, an *epikoros* ('heretic') asks, 'Why was the bridegroom, who lived the life of a righteous man, punished in this manner? Because he only learned Torah. My son, a man has to learn language and writing, for whoever does not know language and writing is called contemptible.'[5] Not a word of criticism or censure of the woman is uttered by the author or the characters in the story.

Both authors portray the young village women as intelligent and modern, women who know what they want and who are not willing to lead the sort of life led by their mothers.[6] This point is important because there are historians who appear to assume

[4] Gebel, *Tate mames tsures*, 5.

[5] Especially since Agnon begins the story of the meeting between the two with the line 'But the Holy One, Blessed be He, does not withhold the reward of any youth' and then ends it with what appears to be a terrible divine injustice, something that demands an explanation.

[6] Cf. one of the heroines in Agnon's *A Simple Story*, a village girl whom the author describes in the following manner: 'It would be pointless to criticize Mina in order to praise Blume, for Mina too was a well-mannered and attractive young lady. Even though she had grown up in a village she had the graces of a city girl, having gone to a boarding school in Stanisław where she learned to speak French, embroider, and play piano, so that nothing about her so much as hinted that she was the daughter of a country Jew. When she accompanied her parents to Szybusz, her elegance contrasting with their simplicity and her leisurely gait with their hurried one, one might have thought her the daughter of a Polish nobleman besieged by two Jewish peddlers. The transformation undergone by her was so complete that her own father and mother scarcely seemed to belong to her anymore. Not that she was ashamed of them—it just could not be said that she was particularly proud of them either' (S. Y. Agnon, *A Simple Story*, trans. H. Halkin (New York, 1985), 41).

that women in Galician villages must have been ignorant country girls, who, if they converted, did so either to escape poverty or because they fell in love with an unlettered farmer or peasant.[7] As we shall see below, there is substantial historical evidence to refute this assumption. Here we merely note that in the play by L. Gebel the heroine elopes with a tax superintendent; in the story by Agnon, the heroine, whose father is a well-to-do tax collector, knows her Hebrew letters and, after the Passover meal, listens to the yeshiva student reading from the Song of Songs. It is reasonable to assume that such women did not dream of tending livestock or of working the soil alongside their Polish peasant husbands in order to escape from their parents' houses.

In fact, the two heroines appear to be typical of a large number of female converts from Judaism in western Galicia during the last decades of the nineteenth and the first decades of the twentieth centuries. In one fifteen-year period beginning in 1887 over 300 Jewish women converted in Kraków alone, almost all of them at the convent of the Felician sisters.[8] Fortunately, we are able to sketch a socio-economic profile of some of the converts, for according to the laws of the Habsburg empire, any citizen who wished to undergo a religious conversion had to appear before a municipal clerk in order to sign a 'protocol', i.e. a form with his or her personal data, which declared that the conversion was voluntary. Copies of this form were sent to the representatives of the two religions in the town in which the conversion was to take place; in the case of Kraków, this was the Catholic consistory and the Kraków rabbinate. In the state archives in Kraków there is a collection of such protocols that were sent to the municipal rabbis,[9] and these give us a fairly clear picture of the status of the families from which the converts came.

[7] See e.g. T. M. Endelman, 'Gender and Radical Assimilation in Modern Jewish History', in M. L. Raphael (ed.), *Gendering the Jewish Past* (Williamsburg, Va., 2002), 25–40, esp. pp. 34–7.

[8] See J. Thon, 'Austritte und Übertritte in Krakau', in his *Die Juden in Österreich* (Berlin, 1908), 77–8. According to Thon, 302 females and 142 males converted between the years 1887 and 1902. According to these numbers, women constituted 68 per cent of the converts; 92.8 per cent of the converts were not married; more than half of them were 20 years old or younger; 10.4 per cent were from Kraków and 66.2 per cent from other places in Galicia. In Lviv in eastern Galicia the number of the male and female converts was nearly equal; ibid. 76. Thon supplies data concerning the occupation not of the parents, but of the converts themselves. See also P. E. Hyman, *Gender and Assimilation in Modern Jewish History: The Roles and Representation of Women* (Seattle, 1995), 73–5.

[9] Archiwum Państwowe w Krakowie (APK), Pełnomocnik do spraw Metryk Izraelickich w Krakowie (PMI). The legal directives were not always observed with respect to converts, and not all of them were reported. *Ha'olam* (Vilna), 29 Sept. 1910, 20, states: 'This hunting for souls, under the protection of the police, has caused an increase of conversions at an alarming rate. The Kraków rabbis, for example, registered recently in their records forty conversions in one month. And how many conversions are not registered in the rabbinical records?!' Another newspaper writes that the abduction of women for the purpose of baptism has assumed 'catastrophic dimensions. Not a month passes, and occasionally not a week, without a young woman converting to Christianity.' See Dr Bloch's *Oesterreichische Wochenschrift*, 26 Nov. 1909, 824. Thon's statistics only go up to 1902. From the protocols discussed above I was able to locate about ninety-one young women who converted between the years 1903 and 1914, but, again, these data are incomplete.

An examination of the data from the protocols reveals that the vast majority of the Jewish converts to Catholicism in Kraków were young women between the ages of 15 and 20, most of whom came from the villages and towns of western Galicia surrounding Kraków. Virtually no women from the lower classes appear in the list of converts, i.e. daughters of cobblers or tinsmiths, or other low-income professions. Instead, their fathers worked as ritual slaughterers, wood merchants, landlords, livestock merchants, sausage purveyors, wheat merchants, dairy merchants, communal registrars, etc. A large number were tavern-keepers. The women's signatures on the protocols demonstrate a knowledge of Polish writing; most of the signatures are written in a steady and fine hand. All this suggests strongly that the village women who converted during this period came from lower middle-class and middle-class backgrounds.[10]

It should be noted that the conversion data from Kraków during the last decades of the nineteenth century and the first decades of the twentieth challenge several commonly held assumptions, e.g. that, as a universal rule, more Jewish males than females converted, or that Jewish women converts generally came from the lower classes, or that their conversion was designed to enable them to marry a member of their own class.[11] Study of the conversions in Kraków makes the obvious point, worth repeating, that social phenomena must be analysed within a particular temporal and regional context.[12]

We see, then, that a significant number of young Jewish women from villages around Kraków converted to Christianity at the turn of the nineteenth and beginning of the twentieth centuries. The phenomenon of their conversion raises the following questions:

1. Why was there an increase in conversion to Christianity among young Jewish females during this time?
2. How does one explain the large number of Jewish women from villages among the converts?
3. Why was the phenomenon more widespread in western Galicia than in other parts of Galicia, and why did Kraków serve as a magnet for the converts?

[10] This differs from the conclusion of Anna Lea Staudacher, '"Wenn Sie sich taufen lassen . . .". Über Kindesentführung, Verführung Minderjähriger und Zwangstaufen in Galizien um die Jahrhunderterwende', *Das jüdische Echo*, 40 (1991), 133–8, esp. p. 136. The author claims that most of the 'kidnapped' women came from a modest background and from poor families that were barely able to allow themselves recourse to legal assistance. Apparently she assumed that girls from villages and hamlets were poor.

[11] See Endelman, 'Gender and Radical Assimilation in Modern Jewish History', 36.

[12] Certainly in lieu of evidence one should not draw conclusions from one region to another within the geographical area known as eastern Europe. What is true of Kraków is not necessarily true of Warsaw or Kiev, and what is true of villages in western Galicia is not necessarily true of villages within the sphere of the Russian empire. As is well known, the inhabitants of Galicia lived under different historical and legal conditions from those of the Russian empire. Moreover, the ethnic minorities in whose midst Galician Jews lived possessed different national consciousnesses, different religions, and different cultures.

In order to answer these questions I will present, in the pages that follow, an extended description of the case of Deborah Lewkowicz, a young woman from a small village not far from Kraków. At the age of 18 Lewkowicz ran away from her home and spent several months in the Felician convent in Kraków before converting there in March 1901; in September of that year she returned to Judaism. The court file discussing her case, which is located in the State Archive in Kraków,[13] provides us with a rare glimpse into the life of someone who seems to have been an average Jewish girl of her time and place. Lewkowicz did not come from a particularly wealthy, learned, or well-connected family; under normal circumstances we would not possess written sources describing the actions, deliberations, and feelings of an 18-year old girl of similar circumstances. Yet because of the court case we have a substantial amount of documents, including testimonies from the young woman, her family, and her circle of acquaintances, that enable us to shed light on the questions raised above.

Deborah Lewkowicz's parents were tavern-keepers in the village of Rzeszotary, which had a tiny Jewish population at the time (twenty-one Jews and 1,207 Catholics).[14] The Catholics belonged to the parish of the neighbouring village of Podstolice, whereas the Jews belonged to the Jewish community of Wieliczka, a district town that was 14 kilometres from Kraków.[15] The village did not have ten adult Jewish males required for a prayer quorum; membership in the Wieliczka Jewish community enabled the Jews from the surrounding villages to participate in its synagogue on holidays and on special sabbaths (on regular sabbaths and during the week they would not attend synagogue), and to benefit from religious services such as ritual slaughter. Life in a village with a small number of Jews made contact with the Polish surrounding necessary and natural.

Deborah was born when her mother, Ciwie, was 27 and her father, Abraham, was 32. Three years later her sister Chaja was born, and two years after that her brother Mendele. At first Deborah attended the one-room schoolhouse in Rzeszotary; later she studied at the primary school for girls in Wieliczka.[16] At that time

[13] See APK, C. K. Sąd Krajowy Karny w Krakowie, 416—Vr 632/01 (hereafter referred to as the Lewkowicz file). [14] See *Słownik geograficzny Królestwa Polskiego*, x (Warsaw, 1889), 150–1.

[15] Surrounding the provincial town of Wieliczka were about a hundred small villages. The Jews of Wieliczka constituted about 15 per cent of the population and in 1900, 981 Jews lived there. See Shmuel Meiri (ed.), *Kehilat vilitchkah: sefer zikaron/The Jewish Community of Wieliczka: A Memorial Book* (Tel Aviv, 1980), 16. See also the remarks of Mosheh Yahrblum: 'On the surface, our community was no different from other communities in Galicia that shared the same way of life. Yet it seems that Jewish life in our town was more developed because of its proximity to Cracow, the metropolis of western Galicia . . . most townspeople often spent their time in Cracow either for pleasure or business. This was of significant influence upon our life. Unlike the other townlets that were resting on their oars, the people of Wieliczka brought home from the metropolis a gust of refreshing breeze that slowly changed their way of life' (ibid. 16–17).

[16] Lewkowicz file. Ciwie Lewkowicz, in her testimony of 18 Mar. 1901, relates that Deborah studied at first in the school in Rzeszotary; Deborah, in her testimony of 14 Mar. 1901, says that she attended the school in Wieliczka.

there were three primary schools in Wieliczka: two for boys, the one with five grades ('classes') and the other with three; and one for girls, with five grades.[17]

The number and variety of primary schools in Wieliczka doubtlessly reflected the relative prosperity of the city, famed for its salt mines, and the presence of a significant bourgeois element. But it was also an expression of the changes that had occurred in the second half of the nineteenth century with respect to the educational system in the Habsburg empire in general, and in Galicia in particular. To understand Deborah Lewkowicz's education in Wieliczka, and education for Jewish women of her social stratum in general, a few remarks about those changes are in order.

In the first half of the nineteenth century the typical school in the empire (*Normalschule*) had three grades, the third grade generally lasting two years. Following the 1848 revolution, and the founding of the Austrian Ministry of Education and Religion, a great effort was made to improve the educational system, and to add two more years to primary schools. In addition to the existing type of schools, a new model, with four grades, was developed; the first and fourth grades generally took two years to complete.

A major step forward in education reform came on 14 May 1869, when a law mandating education for all children between the ages of 6 and 14 in the Austrian empire was enacted. In effect, the law added two years to what had been up until then the maximum number of years of schooling. The law aroused opposition from a variety of groups: from traditionalists, who argued that education was the exclusive right and obligation of the family, and from Church circles, who were alarmed over the proposal to transfer control over the educational system from the religious to the state bodies, which they viewed as secular. These fears were not without foundation; the chief goal of the schools, as defined by the new law, was the ethical and religious education of the students, and the goal of that education was to raise citizens that respected God, the empire, and the state. The acquisition of knowledge was considered only a secondary aim.[18] The law was approved despite the conservative opposition, but since no system of enforcement of the law was put into place, its effect was limited,[19] and the debate over mandatory education continued.

Although the mandatory education law applied to boys and girls alike, there were large differences between the schooling of boys and girls in the second half of the nineteenth century. To be sure, the subject of girls' education was much discussed and numerous innovations were introduced.[20] Yet girls' school attendance was minimal until the first decades of the twentieth century[21] and the subjects studied by boys and girls differed considerably. For example, in the *lyzeum*, the

[17] *Słownik geograficzny Królestwa Polskiego*, xiii (Warsaw, 1893), 320.

[18] H. Engelbrecht, *Geschichte des österreichischen Bildungswesen. Erziehung und Unterricht auf dem Boden Österreichs*, iv (Krems, 1985), 114–19, 556–60.

[19] Ibid. 123.

[20] On women's education, see ibid. 278 ff.; on the opposition to women's education, see pp. 280–1.

[21] Ibid. 281.

first secondary school for girls, study of German and French constituted over 40 per cent of the curriculum. The other subjects, including religion, geography, history, arithmetic, nature, geometry, penmanship, and domestic crafts, were considered less important. The goal of the educational institutions for young women was to educate them to the ideal of 'true femininity', according to contemporary standards.[22]

In principle, the mandatory education law passed by the Austrian parliament was supposed to be binding on all the Crown lands of the Habsburg empire. But coalition considerations led to granting exemptions for several regions, and Galicia was one of these.[23] Moreover, beginning in 1879, when the Austrian government passed from the liberal coalition to the conservative and the clerical factions, repeated attempts were made to reduce the number of years of compulsory education from eight to six. Active in these attempts were Catholics and agriculturalists, among them Galician Poles. One of their arguments was that the children from the villages would have to make the long trek home at the end of the school day via forests and rivers, which could lead to immoral activity among 13- and 14-year-olds.[24]

A compromise formula was agreed upon in 1882 which kept the age of compulsory education as 6–14, but which also gave the parents living in villages and rural areas some flexibility with respect to fulfilling the law's obligations. Once again, Galician children were exempted from eight years of mandatory education. The aim of education was defined as guidance towards 'religious and ethical' conduct (instead of 'ethical and religious' in the 1869 formulation). It was expected of the students that they would finish their schooling with proficiency in the principles of religion and mastery of reading, writing, and arithmetic.

Educational institution for girls in Galicia developed slowly, with post-primary schools for women opening only in the 1870s. The typical school in the villages was a one-room schoolhouse for both boys and girls with one or two grades. In more developed rural areas there were co-educational schools for three, four, and even five grades. But separate schools for girls were only found in the provincial towns.[25] Deborah Lewkowicz attended a *szkoła wydziałowa* (multi-grade school) in Wieliczka, which was at a higher level than regular schools. Until 1898 twenty-six such schools for girls operated in Galicia: eighteen of them had three grades (generally four years of study), seven had five grades (seven years), and one had six grades (eight years).[26]

Galician schools, after the 1867 *Ausgleich*, became the principal vehicle of indoctrination of Polish patriotism for young people. The educational system was run by

[22] Ibid. 286.

[23] W. A. Jenks, *Austria Under the Iron Ring 1870–1893* (Charlottesville, Va., 1965), 125.

[24] Ibid. 125–6.

[25] Until the 1890s there were 3,726 public schools of all types in the seventy-eight school districts of Galicia, 127 of them for boys, 121 for girls, and the rest mixed. The division of village and city schools remained in effect until 12 Aug. 1895. See B. Czajecka, '*Z domu w szeroki świat . . .*': *Droga kobiet do niezależności w zaborze austriackim w latach 1890–1914* (Kraków, 1990), 53.

[26] Ibid. 55.

the newly formed Council of Education, all of whose members were Poles (only in 1906 was a Jew appointed to sit in the council), and Polish became the language of instruction in most educational institutions. Instruction in Polish literature, poetry, and history received special status and significance within the new educational framework. The educator Zevi Scharfstein, who was a teacher in western Galicia from 1900 to 1914, wrote in 1910 that Polish schools for girls were hotbeds of Polish nationalism, in which the teachers attempted to instil in their female students a 'fanatical devotion' to classical Polish literature and the Polish language.[27]

Thus, the primary school that Deborah Lewkowicz attended in Wieliczka would have been considered at the time to be one of the most progressive schools for girls in Galicia. The fact that her parents, traditional Jews from a small village, decided to send her to such a school testifies to their ambitions with respect to their daughter's education and their desire to give her the best schooling possible in their vicinity. And indeed, from the letters that Deborah wrote to her parents and to the convent, which are attached to the court file, we learn that she was fluent in Polish and German. She wrote in a beautiful and mature style, without any errors in spelling. Apparently she learned her lessons well.

Some of Deborah's correspondence to her parents appears at first glance to be in Yiddish, but in fact it is not Yiddish, certainly not Galician Yiddish, but a mixture of German and Yiddish, perhaps her attempt to adapt her German to the Yiddish of her parents. She writes the Hebrew characters in a beautiful hand, with the exception of the word 'Torah', which she mistakenly writes with a *tet* rather than with a *tav*. Her misspelling of such a basic word suggests that she was not familiar with the written term, or perhaps that she had not been exposed to it for some time. Jewish instruction for girls in Galicia during this period was generally limited to teaching the meaning of the prayers and blessings in Yiddish translation, and, in some cases, learning sufficient Hebrew to read from the prayer-book. That Deborah was able to write Hebrew characters clearly and beautifully is another testimony to her parents' efforts to give her what they considered to be the best possible Jewish education for a 'modern' Galician Jewish girl. It is likely that they hired a tutor to instruct her in the rudiments of the Hebrew language and especially penmanship.

Deborah belonged to the first generation of Jewish women in Galicia who attended primary schools for women. Her mother could not attend such a school because they did not then exist. Hence she could not have undergone the same process of Polonization and acculturation that was an essential part of her daughter's education. The openness of Deborah's parents to their daughter's education did not at all stand in opposition to their being traditional since there were no rabbinical rules or guidelines with respect to the education of daughters. In fact, the rabbis did not deal with the subject at all. It was simply the custom that western

[27] Z. Scharfstein, 'Meḥayei aḥeinu begalitsiyah: Ḥinukh habanot', *Ha'olam*, 26 Sept. 1910. See S. Stampfer, 'Gender Differentiation and the Education of the Jewish Woman in Nineteenth-Century Eastern Europe', *Polin*, 7 (1992), 53–85.

Galician girls from traditional Jewish homes attended the government schools, while their brothers attended *ḥeder*s and yeshivas.[28] The attitude of the traditional Jews to their daughters' education did not differ from that of non-Jews of the same economic class. In the absence of a specific Jewish practice or value with regard to female education, they behaved like their Polish neighbours.

The various testimonies in the legal file indicate that Deborah and her family led a peaceful life, in harmony with their surroundings, right up until the hour of her conversion. Their neighbours in the village were Andrzej Gadocha, a 33-year-old blacksmith, and his wife, Kunegunda, who was 23. Although both were illiterate and had resided in the village less time than the Lewkowiczes, the two families enjoyed good relations. Andrzej Gadocha testified that the Lewkowicz daughters visited him frequently at home and in his smithy, 'out of friendship as well as to request things, for example, to heat the clothes iron'.[29] Deborah also used to record his shop's bills for Andrzej.

The ties between Deborah and her Polish surroundings were not limited to her immediate neighbourhood. The school she attended in Wieliczka was a considerable distance from her home, and she made the journey either on foot or by wagon. On one occasion she encountered a young Pole named Stanisław Bakalarz, the son of a landowner from the neighbouring village of Podstolice, who worked as a supervisor of an agricultural co-operative. They would continue their conversations when Bakalarz waited at the blacksmith Gadocha's for his horses to be shod or his tools to be repaired; occasionally Bakalarz would visit Lewkowicz's tavern, where Deborah poured the beer and helped run the business.[30]

According to various testimonies, Bakalarz was a quiet and polite young man; Gadocha testified that Deborah's mother told him more than once that 'had they been gentiles, she would have willingly married off her daughter to Bakalarz, since she was fond of him, and he made a good impression on her'.[31] Deborah's younger

28 On the differences between the education of traditional boys and girls in western Galicia during the period, see the memoirs of a resident of Wieliczka: 'Though most orthodox sent their daughters to the governmental schools and their everyday language was Polish, the sons received their education solely in the Heder or Yeshivah' (Meiri (ed.), *The Jewish Community of Wieliczka*, 22). See also the memoirs of two sisters from Klasno, a small town next to Wieliczka: 'Our family, the Straussbergs, lived in a small and old Jewish settlement—Klasno. We were born to a very strict hassidic family. My grandfather, Sholem Straussberg, of blessed memory, was a ritual slaughterer . . . My father, Gershon Straussberg, of blessed memory, was a Belzer hassid. Many times he would leave his house and family and travel to his rebbe . . . we were five sisters, and all of us received public education in the primary schools. We were bilingual in the home. With our parents we spoke, of course, Yiddish, but between us we spoke Polish.' See Miriam and Sarah Gafni, 'Shetei aḥayot', ibid. 61.

It is interesting to note that among the list of Jewish female converts one finds an 'Etla Straussberg, age 15, daughter of the ritual slaughterer in Wieliczka Solomon Straussberg', who arrived at the Felician convent in January 1900. See APK, PMI 56.

29 Lewkowicz file, testimony of Andrzej Gadocha, 18 Mar. 1901.

30 Lewkowicz file, testimony of Abraham Lewkowicz, 6 Mar. 1901.

31 Lewkowicz file, testimony of Andrzej Gadocha, 18 Mar. 1901.

sister said in her testimony that Bakalarz was 'a respectable and bright young man, who behaved politely to all and to us'.[32]

In his own testimony Bakalarz confessed his love for Deborah and revealed that he had written her love letters. He added that he was unable to marry her since he was obliged to enlist in the military, but that he desired to marry her upon his release. Bakalarz was ambitious; although his present financial status was inconsiderable, he planned 'to live in a respectable manner in the future'. He claims that he was not the only Polish Catholic to receive letters from Deborah and denies that he tried to convince the young woman to convert, orally or in writing.[33] The denial came in response to Abraham Lewkowicz's complaint against Bakalarz and his friend Jan Śmieszkiewicz of enticing Deborah to convert.

This complaint was the legal basis for action against them. Because Austrian law allowed anybody of 14 years and older to choose his or her religious affiliation the Felician convent was perfectly free to convert whomever it wished.[34] But the convent had to verify that the potential convert was not enticed or threatened into leaving her home by a third party, but rather had arrived at the convent of her own free will. (The convent was also obliged to report to the Kraków police any new potential convert and her address at the convent for the purpose of civil registration.) The legal issue in the case of the conversion of young Jewish women was not one of involuntary conversion, but rather of inducing or aiding persons under the age of 24 (the Austrian age of majority) to leave their parents' homes. The law viewed such cases as tantamount to kidnapping, which is why the press used the terms 'abductions' and 'kidnappings' to describe cases in which young women left their homes. The state institutions, the police, and the courts were supposed to ensure that the minor be returned to his or her parents' home.[35]

The parents of the young women were often provided legal advice by the Österreichisch-Israelitische Union,[36] which employed the Kraków lawyer Dr Rafael

[32] Lewkowicz file, testimony of Chaja Lewkowicz, 18 Mar. 1901.

[33] Lewkowicz file, testimony of Stanisław Bakalarz, 18 Mar. 1901.

[34] See Gesetz vom 25. Mai 1868. Interconfessionelle Verhältnisse II, Art. 4: 'After the completion of his or her fourteenth year everyone without distinction of sex has the right to a free choice of religious confession according to his or her own conviction and shall in case of need be protected by the authorities in this free choice. He or she, however, must not at the time of choice be in a state of mind or spirit incompatible with his or her own free conviction' (cited in M. Burckhard, *Gesetze und Verordnungen in Cultussachen*, i (Vienna, 1895), 23).

[35] Para. 145 of the Civil Code gave parents the right to search after their missing children, to demand their return, and to have them brought home. The legal authorities were required to provide assistance to the parents. In certain cases a judge could intervene to prevent the minor's return, but this required an explicit judicial ruling. Para. 96 of the Criminal Code defined as a crime aiding a minor to flee home, either by threats or by promises. Para. 314 of the code stipulated imprisonment up to a month as punishment for this crime. See J. Ofner, 'Kinderraub in Galizien', Dr Bloch's *Österreichische Wochenschrift* (2 Nov. 1900), 780–5, esp. p. 783.

[36] Abraham Lewkowicz relates in his testimony of 10 Oct. 1901 that he appealed to the Union for assistance. On the Österreichisch–Israelitische Union, see J. Toury, 'Troubled Beginnings:

Landau especially for this purpose. The legal strategy of the Union was to treat each case as a problem of the non-enforcement of civil law, rather than as a religious struggle between Jews and the Church. But the inevitable conflict created between the interests of the convent and that of the parents ensured that the religious question would not be neglected. The minister of Galician affairs in the Austrian parliament went so far as to proclaim in reference to one of the cases: 'Secular authority stops at the convent's walls.'[37]

Deborah Lewkowicz's father, perhaps after receiving legal advice, also took pains to distinguish between his daughter's conversion and her leaving home. Blaming Bakalarz for the latter, he testifies: 'I, as her father, sense that an injustice has been done to me, regardless of whether my daughter Deborah converted or not. I request that my daughter be returned to me, for despite religious differences, I have paternal feelings for her.'[38]

To what extent did Bakalarz assist Deborah in leaving her parents' home, and did that assistance constitute being an accessory to 'abduction'? The various testimonies do not allow for a clear-cut answer. It was claimed in the police investigation that Deborah had initially hoped to be admitted to the Benedictine convent in Staniątki, near Bochnia, not far from her village,[39] and as a result, Bakalarz sent his friend Jan Śmieszkiewicz to find out whether this plan would work. But Bakalarz said that he could not remember whether Deborah has specifically requested him to find this out or not. Śmieszkiewicz testified that around a week before Deborah's flight he travelled to the Staniątki convent at Bakalarz's request. 'Of course I went there and explained [Deborah's] request to one of the nuns, mentioning that she wished to convert. But I received a negative response accompanied by explanation that Deborah should go to the Felician convent in Kraków. I reported this to Bakalarz.' Deborah's sister Chaja related in her testimony that Śmieszkiewicz afterwards travelled to the Felician convent in order to see whether they had a place for her sister. She added that on Saturday night, 29 December 1900, when he was at Gadocha's with Deborah, Śmieszkiewicz transmitted to her the affirmative response of the Felician convent.

Later on in the investigation Śmieszkiewicz changed his previous testimony to say that he went to the convent in Staniątki not merely because of Bakalarz's request but rather because of Deborah's, 'since she intended to convert, and she made that intention known to me when we met'. It is quite clear that both men

The Emergence of the Österreichisch–Israelitische Union', *Leo Baeck Institute Year Book*, 30 (1985), 457–75; R. S. Wistrich, *The Jews of Vienna in the Age of Franz Joseph* (Oxford, 1990), 309–43.

37 'An den Mauern des Klosters hat die weltliche Macht ein Ende' (Ofner, 'Kinderraub in Galizien', 781).

38 Lewkowicz file, testimony of Abraham Lewkowicz, 22 Apr. 1901.

39 The Benedictine convent in Staniątki was well known for its girls' school, considered to be one of the finest in Galicia. See I. H. Skąpska, 'Galicia: Initiatives for Emancipation of Polish Women', in R. Jaworski (ed.), *Women in Polish Society* (New York, 1992), 71–89, esp. p. 76.

feared that they would be accused of helping Deborah's flight, and hence they disavowed all connection with it.[40]

Deborah's mother testified that she had heard from the Bakalarzes' domestic servant that Bakalarz used to bring articles of clothing to Deborah when she was staying at the Felician convent. The servant herself said that Bakalarz's mother visited Deborah in the convent and even brought her a kerchief.[41] From all these testimonies it is clear that Bakalarz was very much aware of the plans for Deborah's flight and the flight itself. Even if he was not its initiator or the instigator, he offered her all the help she needed.

The first crack in Deborah Lewkowicz's conventional life resulted, then, from her love for Bakalarz, the young Pole whom everybody liked and respected. This youthful love lasted over three years, according to the various testimonies, and those immediately surrounding the couple knew of it. The love was expressed in letters that the couple exchanged clandestinely, often using Kunegunda Gadocha as an intermediary. Deborah testified that she would burn the letters she received so that they would not be discovered by her parents.[42] Chaja Lewkowicz, who knew about the romantic bond between the two, was privileged to read some of Bakalarz's letters, and in her court testimony was able to cite some of the affectionate terms he had employed. It appears also from the court testimony that Bakalarz and Deborah visited the market in Podstolice on one occasion, and there, while Bakalarz was intoxicated, they allowed themselves to utter terms of affection that others could also hear.[43]

There is no evidence during this early period that Deborah contemplated conversion or fleeing her parents' house. In a response to a query by the state's attorney-general, the local police chief described the chain of events leading up to the conversion. When Deborah's parents learned of the girl's romantic attachment to Bakalarz, they quickly sought a Jewish bridegroom for her, choosing a young man from Kraków, Mechel Hirschprung. A meeting was hastily arranged between the two and a date was then set for the wedding, against Deborah's will.[44]

Deborah related in her first testimony, which she gave while she was still in the

[40] Lewkowicz file, testimonies of Bakalarz, 18 Mar. and 24 Apr. 1901, and of Śmieszkiewicz, 18 Mar., 24 Apr., and 31 May 1901. The mother superior of the convent in Staniątki at first denied the entire story, then later admitted to its truth, although she claimed not to recall whether the young man had been referred to the Felician convent; see Lewkowicz file, testimonies of the Staniątki convent's mother superior, 24 Apr. and 11 June.

[41] Lewkowicz file, testimony of Anna Michalec, a 16-year-old servant in the Bakalarz household, 18 Mar. 1901.

[42] Lewkowicz file, testimony of Deborah Lewkowicz, 26 Apr. 1901. Bakalarz told investigators in his testimony of 18 Mar. 1901 that he also destroyed Deborah's letters so that his parents would not discover them.

[43] Lewkowicz file, testimony of Jan Jania, a friend of Śmieszkiewicz, 2 July 1901.

[44] Lewkowicz file, the police inspector's report to the attorney-general's office, 3 Mar. 1901, and the report of the investigating judge, 24 Oct. 1901.

Felician convent, that her parents forced the match and the marriage upon her, and that far from loving her intended bridegroom, 'he aroused within me antipathy'.[45] The night that Śmieszkiewicz informed her of the Felician convent's willingness to accept her, the night of 29 December, was three days before her wedding with Mechel. Her mind made up, she asked Śmieszkiewicz to meet her the very next day, Sunday, near the bridge from Podgórze to Kraków. She and her mother would be travelling to Kraków to pick up her bridal gown and to take care of some other business. According to her testimony, she did not inform Śmieszkiewicz of the purpose of the meeting.

Deborah was no stranger to Kraków nor the city to her. She and her mother would travel there frequently for shopping, and in her testimony the young girl spoke of her extensive knowledge of the city and its streets. Some time before her wedding she travelled to Kraków with her mother to be fitted for clothes. They left their village in a carriage in the morning and returned in the early evening; the distance was about 15 kilometres. According to the father's testimony, they rented a room in the Pod Czarnym Orłem (Under the Black Eagle) hotel in Podgórze,[46] where they changed out of their travelling clothes, and then crossed the bridge to Kraków to take care of their business.[47] One can assume that they had a special set of clothes for the city that differed from the clothes they wore in the village.

On Sunday 30 December Deborah and her mother travelled to Kraków for their final errands before the wedding. While still in the carriage, Deborah spotted Śmieszkiewicz waiting for her on the bridge and signalled him to follow them. After changing at their hotel in Podgórze, Deborah's mother left to see the notary. When she returned, she discovered that her daughter had disappeared. She then went looking for her in the places in Kraków where they were supposed to have visited. After several hours of fruitless attempts to find her, she returned to her home. In his testimony Abraham Lewkowicz related that after he had heard from his wife of the disappearance of their daughter, they suspected immediately that she had run away from home, and that she was hiding in one of Kraków's convents.[48]

These remarks of the father should not come as a surprise, for many young Galician Jewish women took refuge in the convent as a way to avoid their unhappy fate. The Jewish and non-Jewish papers were full of stories of girls who disappeared,

45 Lewkowicz file, testimony of Deborah Lewkowicz in the Felician convent, 14 Mar. 1901.

46 A town on the River Vistula facing Kraków. The inhabitants of the town in 1880 numbered 5,136 Catholics and 2,500 Jews. See *Słownik geograficzny Królestwa Polskiego*, viii (Warsaw, 1887), 380–1.

47 Lewkowicz file, testimony of Abraham Lewkowicz, 6 Mar. 1901.

48 Ibid. Deborah's flight two days before her wedding was reported in the Hebrew newspaper *Hamagid* (Kraków), 1 Jan. 1901, 5: 'A wedding between a Jewish youth from a very religious family and a young woman of his age from Wieliczka, the daughter of God-fearing Jews, was to have taken place here on Tuesday of this week. After the wedding had already been proclaimed in the synagogue on the sabbath, and the bridegroom had been called to the Torah, the news came by telegraph that the bride converted at the beginning of the week and that all the attempts of her parents and relatives to bring her back have so far been in vain!'

many of them on the eve of their wedding.[49] These stories were well known to other Jewish women, as Deborah Lewkowicz herself testified: 'I knew from various stories that the Felician convent in Kraków, in Smoleńsk, accepted catechumens. I knew where Smoleńsk was because I knew Kraków well, but I didn't know where exactly the convent was located.'[50] Nor was this knowledge something that only she, as a potential convert, sought. Her sister Chaja testified that she was present when Deborah read to her neighbour Kunegunda Gadocha a letter that she had received from Bakalarz. In that letter he explained that his friend had learned that the nuns at the convent at Staniątki were not interested in accepting new converts, 'because they had a problem in the past when people were searching for Araten'.[51]

Araten was Michalina Araten, a member of a well-to-do hasidic family in Kraków who had run away from her home, taken refuge in the Felician convent, and disappeared shortly thereafter.[52] Her father searched for her in various convents based on rumours that she was in them, including the convent in Staniątki. As extensively reported in the press, the father's demands to conduct searches in the convents aroused bitter opposition among the Catholic population, who viewed this as a Jewish affront to the Catholic religion. The convent in Staniątki was involved in one of the scandals, but what is important for us here is that the story of Michalina Araten was familiar to young Jewish women, even to a 15-year-old girl like Chaja Lewkowicz.

The Felician convent in Kraków indeed sheltered Jewish women who fled from their houses, offering them room and board and instruction in the Catholic religion as a preliminary to conversion.[53] The convent was even dubbed by the Jewish press a 'shmad fabrik [apostasy factory]'.[54] The Jewish girls lived in their own wing and

[49] Cf. Agnon, *The Bridal Canopy*, 71: 'It happened that a village girl, the daughter of a tax collector, had set her eyes on a gentile; so her father desired to marry her off before the whole country talked scandal about her.'

[50] Lewkowicz file, testimony of Deborah Lewkowicz in the Felician convent, 26 May 1901.

[51] Lewkowicz file, testimony of Chaja Lewkowicz, 27 Apr. 1901.

[52] R. Manekin, 'Tehilla's Daughter and Michalina Araten', *Ha'arets*, Literature and Culture suppl., 27 June 2003, 1.

[53] Rafael Landau, who provided legal representation for the family, wrote: 'Almost every Jewish girl in Galicia who in recent years has left her parents' home for any reason whatsoever has found shelter in the Felician Sisters' convent in Kraków; but the convent has never seen fit to notify the parents rendered disconsolate by the flight of their under-age daughter . . . The Felician Sisters' convent gives these girls shelter and essential instruction in the Christian religion' ('Interpellation des Abgeordneten Dr. Straucher und Genossen an Ihre Exzellenzen die Herren k. k. Minister des Inneren und der Justiz, betreffend geeignete Massnahmen zur Hintanhaltung von Kinderraub, beziehungsweise Mädchenentführung', in *Stenographische Protokolle über die Sitzungen des Hauses der Abgeordneten des Österreichischen Reichsrates*, xviii, Session am 29.1.1900, 14630).

[54] Cf. *Der Tog* (Kraków and Lemberg), 19 July 1911, where the paper claims that people initially made a big deal about the subject, but then got used to it, and that stories of the conversion of young women no longer caused a sensation. The newspaper added that at one time male or female apostasy was a stain that could not be cleansed. 'Now the matter has become quite simple', like transferring one's membership in a social club.

stayed mostly in the company of their co-religionists. The reputation of the convent as a place of conversions reached even Jewish women in the Polish part of the Russian empire, and 18 per cent of the Kraków converts arrived there from Russian Poland.[55]

Deborah planned her flight to the convent in complete secrecy from her family. Those who shared her secret denied completely that her boyfriend Bakalarz had a hand in it and insisted instead that Lewkowicz had thought of converting for a long time. Both Andrzej and Kunegunda Gadocha testified that Deborah had made up her mind to convert long before, and that she occasionally read from Catholic prayer-books. According to Kunegunda, Deborah 'said that she did not want to know about Jews, nor marry one, since she couldn't abide him'. She added that she had explained to Deborah that the best thing was 'to remain in her religion and in her situation, but she replied that she wished to be accepted into a convent'.[56]

Even if these testimonies are credible, and Deborah had decided to convert long before her marriage, there is no doubt that the impetus and timing of her flight was related to her impending marriage. For a young woman like Deborah it was virtually impossible to escape her parents. Where could she have gone? The flight to the convent may have been motivated by religious reasons, but the convent also provided a home far from her parents' house. The Felician convent was the only convent in the area in which was located a catechumenate, and girls who wished to be accepted were provided with room and board for several months.[57] At the turn of the century there were Jewish girls living there at almost any given time.[58]

For Deborah, who studied in school with Polish Catholics, made friends with her Polish neighbours, and entered into a romantic liaison with a Pole, the Polish Catholic environment was non-threatening, perhaps even friendly and understanding. Living in a Catholic area, she must have been familiar with Catholic processions, and attending a Polish primary school, where the Catholic religion was neither marginal or concealed,[59] she may have learned about other Catholic rituals.

[55] Thon, *Die Juden in Österreich*, 78.

[56] Lewkowicz file, testimonies of Andrzej and Kunegunda Gadocha, 18 Mar. and 24 Apr. 1901.

[57] Cf. the reply of the Austrian Staathalterei in Galicia of 29 Nov. 1910 to the Austrian minister of the interior, reacting to the 'Interpellation' of Benno Straucher: 'As regards the conduct of the Felician Sisters' convent in Kraków mentioned in the interpellation, the chief thing to note is that of the female monastic orders in Kraków only the said convent possesses a school for catechumens in which the persons who are to be received into the Christian Church are instructed in Christianity and prepared for baptism' (Tsentral'nyi derzhavnyi istorychnyi arkhiv Ukrayiny, L'viv, *fond* 146, *opys* 4, *sprava* 5067; microfilm copy in the Central Archives for the History of the Jewish People, Jerusalem, HM2/9440.7, p. 47).

[58] Some examples reported by the press: in February 1900 sixty Jewish young women were in the Felician convent (*Allgemeine Zeitung des Judentums*, 2 Mar. 1900, 163–4); thirty in May 1900 (ibid., 16 May 1900, 126); fifty in March 1910 (*Der Gemeindebote. Beilage zur Allgemeine Zeitung des Judentums*, 18 Mar. 1910, 4).

[59] See e.g. the description by Zevi Scharfstein: 'When the Catholic pupils rise at the beginning of the school day and sing the morning prayers, the tender Jewish pupils are also required to stand

In any event, there is no evidence that she had to overcome inhibitions or stigmas about Catholicism when she decided to convert.

The difficult part of the flight and subsequent conversion for Deborah appears not to have been the abandonment of her faith but rather the separation from her family, and the guilt she felt for causing them pain. Her sister and her parents testified that she was gloomy on the eve of her flight, and that she was easily brought to tears.[60] On the other hand, it appears that during a short period of time—five months—she made such strong ties with the people connected with the convent, chiefly priests, that she did not feel comfortable about returning to Judaism in Kraków. From complaints made against the Felician convent we learn that Polish noblewomen from Kraków visited the Jewish girls, bringing them flowers and candy, which instilled feelings of importance and belonging within the hearts of the young women.[61]

Because the convent not only prepared the young women for conversion but also tried to provide living situations for them afterwards, it was arranged for Deborah to be employed as a governess to the children of the local postmaster, Biliński. This ensured that she would continue to lead her life in a proper Polish Catholic atmosphere. The position also provided her with financial independence and the ability to survive in the big city.[62] A month after she began to work, the wife of her employer died, and propriety forced her to leave. According to the court records it appears that a similar position was found for her in the house of a local clerk in Krosno,[63] but

respectfully and in awe. As these ceremonies are repeated daily, they become more and more ingrained within the hearts of the Jewish maidens, who become fluent with the prayers from habit and repetition. The textbooks in Polish schools are replete with religious stories and with praises of the saints and of the wonders and miracles performed for the righteous of the Catholic faith. The Jewish girls are also required to learn these stories by heart and to stand and recite them before their teachers. At the times of the Catholic holidays, when the pupils present gifts to their teachers (and generally these gifts are of a religious character), the Jewish pupils are distinguished in such gift-giving. Jewish mothers, conscientiously assisting their daughters to receive high marks and report cards, provide their own money and urge the young girls to prepare worthy gifts for their teachers. If we add to this the scorn and ridicule that the Catholic teachers and students regularly heap upon the Jews and their customs, we will readily see how a love for the prevailing religion is ingrained within the hearts of the Jewish girls, as well as a contempt for the religion of their fathers' ('Meḥayei aḥeinu begalitsyah: Ḥinuch habanot', 11–12).

[60] Lewkowicz file, testimony of Abraham Lewkowicz, 6 Mar. 1901, and of Chaja Lewkowicz, 27 Apr. 1901.

[61] Ofner, 'Kinderraub in Galizien', 781. The newspaper *Der Tog*, 12 June 1912, 2, cites a report about the baptism of four Jewish girls that was accompanied by rejoicing and a procession. The enthusiastic baptism advisers were from the most important families of Kraków's nobility.

[62] The profession of governess was one of the few employment possibilities open to women during this period. According to Skąpska, 'They increased in number in the ranks of nursemaids and governesses, not only in the houses of gentry but also in those of well-to-do townsmen and higher orders of intelligentsia' (Skąpska, 'Galicia: Initiatives for Emancipation of Polish Women', 74–5).

[63] Lewkowicz file, request from the court in Kraków to the court in Krosno, 28 Sept. 1901, in an effort to locate Deborah's whereabouts.

for some reason Deborah declined the position. Perhaps she wished to stay in the familiar vicinity of Kraków. When she remained without work, her financial and emotional troubles increased, which finally led her to renew her contact with her family.

Deborah's first testimony to the police, within the context of its investigation into Abraham Lewkowicz's complaint against Bakalarz, was given on 4 March 1901 from inside the Felician convent. This was more than two months after she had entered the convent and a few days before her baptism. She testified that she had made up her mind to convert long before, but that she was waiting for the proper opportunity. That opportunity was her impending wedding, which had been thrust upon her. She emphasized that her flight and conversion were of her own free will and initiative, and that nobody had induced or enticed her in the matter. Displaying no hesitation or doubts, she was, at this point, utterly steadfast in her resolve to convert. And she took pains to sign her testimony 'Dorota Lewkowicz nie Deborah' ('Dorota Lewkowicz not Deborah'), a conscious act of estrangement from her Jewish past.

When she gave further testimony on 26 April, which she signed with her new Christian name, Anastasya Marya Lewkowicz, she denied the accusation that Bakalarz and Śmieszkiewicz were involved in finding a place for her in the convent at Staniątki, but she admitted that both of them visited her at the Felician convent, along with 'other people from Podstolice' whose names are not mentioned. On 26 May she gave further testimony, denying once again the involvement of the two men in her decision to convert. Apparently, Deborah did everything she could to protect them from a court case.

Marya Honorata Kummer, the mother superior of the Felician convent, also gave testimony to the police. According to her account, Deborah arrived at the convent out of breath, explaining that she had run away from her mother and had reached the convent of her own free will. The young woman then said that she had a Catholic fiancé, that she wanted to become a Catholic, and that she had wanted this for a long time. The fear of her parents' reaction had made this impossible. Deborah told her that had her parents known of her intention, 'they almost certainly would have sold her and would have not enabled her to convert'. It should be noted that in Deborah's own testimony there is no mention of her intention to marry Bakalarz.

According to the mother superior's testimony, a few days after Deborah's arrival her father came to the convent and met with her in the presence of a priest from the consistory of the bishop of Kraków, and Sister Rozalia Zagrabiska, who was in charge of the catechumenate.[64] The purpose of the father's visit was apparently to persuade Deborah to attend her wedding. This was the only visit of the father during the entire time that Deborah was at the convent. But after she left the convent and began to work, he renewed contact with her. This time he sent a young man named Józef Zoller, a commercial agent and business acquaintance, to speak to her. Zoller was a 32-year-old Jewish bachelor from Brody who lived near the centre of Kraków.

64 Lewkowicz file, testimony of Mother Superior Marya Honorata Kummer, 14 Mar. 1901.

Apparently Abraham Lewkowicz thought that a young urban Jew would find a better way to Deborah's heart. According to Deborah's testimony, Zoller pleaded with her to return to her father's home, and her father pleaded with her to return to Judaism. When she 'absolutely refused', her father asked her to return home, even as a Catholic.[65]

When Deborah was forced to leave her job as governess in the Biliński household, she found temporary quarters in the house of the midwife who had treated the postmaster's wife. There, in a suburb of Kraków, she began to look for new work. During this period she met with Zoller and members of her family often. Deborah emphasizes in her testimony that she did not initially intend to return to the Jewish religion, but her family kept pleading with her to do just that. 'I was confused,' she says, 'and I came to the conclusion that my situation was too much for me to bear.' She added that when she had entered the convent she did not consider the various implications, and so she decided to correct 'the step that had not been well-thought out' and to return to Judaism.[66] This decision clearly did not result from a new-found acknowledgement of the truth of the Jewish religion, or from any greater understanding or knowledge. Judaism never was an essential factor in Deborah's life; she never mentions it for good or for ill, at least not in her letters or testimonies that have been preserved.

Zoller relates that he did not visit Deborah in the suburb of Kraków where she was living, but rather that she would come to visit him in Kraków, where they would take long walks together. During this period Deborah frequently also took walks with her parents and her sister, 'And I discerned', the young businessman adds, 'the most harmonious relations among them.' During those conversations the issue of her return to Judaism came up, and finally 'she agreed to this of her own free will and without any coercion'.[67]

Zoller and Deborah's father both relate that after Deborah expressed her willingness to return to the Jewish religion she asked not to do so in Kraków, 'where she knows too many priests'. Deborah's father decided to take her to Vienna, and he asked Zoller, who knew the city well, to accompany them. The formalities of the young woman's return to Judaism were accomplished through the aid of the Österreichisch-Israelitische Union in Vienna, which was experienced in these matters. Both Zoller and Abraham Lewkowicz could only stay for a few days, so they left her in the care of a Mrs Menkes, who, if one can judge from the name, was originally from Galicia. With the Union's assistance, Deborah presented a declaration to the Viennese municipality in which she announced her intention to return to the Jewish religion, a formal step that was required of any act of conversion. Her declaration was accompanied by her baptismal certificate, which the Union had requested from Kraków.

Deborah's letters to her parents shed light on the process of her return to

65 Lewkowicz file, testimony of Deborah Lewkowicz, 12 Nov. 1901 (after her return to Judaism).

66 Ibid.

67 Lewkowicz file, testimony of Józef Zoller, 1 Oct. 1901.

Judaism. In a letter dated 5 August 1901 she writes to her father that 'Fleischer'[68] went with her to the Vienna Cultusgemeinde, where they were told that all she had to do was to go to city hall and afterwards to return to the Cultusgemeinde. She added that Fleischer told her that to spare her the unpleasantness he would do it for her in writing. When the process was completed, she went to the Cultusgemeinde, where she was congratulated by everybody in a friendly manner. She noted that Fleischer accompanied her everywhere and behaved towards her with great warmth. There is no mention in her letters of her performing any sort of Jewish ritual, such as immersion, as part of her return.

In that letter to her father Deborah thanks him for the money he had sent her, and asks her parents' forgiveness for all the trouble that she had caused them. 'I am your daughter once more,' she writes, 'who will try to bring sweetness and joy to your years.' She sends kisses to her younger brothers and regards to all her relatives, signing the letter 'Your daughter, Deborah'. As in the previous stages in her journey, the name under which she chooses to sign is revealing. At home she had been called not Deborah but Dorcia. But now apparently it was important for her to emphasize to her parents that she was once again a Jew.

Prominent in Deborah's letters to her family are her repeated requests for forgiveness for the pain and sorrow she caused them. She is especially moved by a letter from her father in which he reminisces about their past, prompting her to write that 'by these holy days [i.e. the high holidays] I declare that I will remain steadfast in my faith'. She adds that she committed one evil act—it is not clear whether she refers to her running away or to her conversion—but that she hopes that with God's help it will remain 'the first and last incident'.

The formal procedures for Deborah's return to Judaism continued for about four weeks, at the end of which her father returned to Vienna to bring her home. During her stay in the Austrian capital the family had commenced preparations for moving their residence to Podgórze, this time to a Jewish neighbourhood. Apparently many Jewish tavern-keepers in western Galicia at this time were forced to leave their villages and move to nearby towns. Changes in the tavern-leasing regulations led to a worsening of their financial situation. Perhaps this was why the Lewkowicz family moved to Podgórze.[69] Yet she was hesitant to live in Kraków or its vicinity

[68] The reference is to Siegfried Fleischer, the secretary of the Österreichisch–Israelitische Union. Fleischer apparently was an expert in matters pertaining to Galicia; cf. his remarks at the Union's general assembly in April 1905: 'Eine Spezialität Galiziens ist bekanntlich die Entführung minderjähriger jüdischer Mädchen in katholische Klöster.' See 'Protokoll', *Monatsschrift der Österreichisch–Israelitischen Union*, no. 5 (mid-May 1905), 8.

[69] See A. Sapir, 'Ha'antisemitizm bema'arav galitsyah', in M. A. Wiesen (ed.), *Luaḥ sha'ashuim shimushi vesifruti lishenat tarsa"g* (Kraków, 1902), 148–55, esp. 148–9. Interestingly, the author also writes: 'Throughout Galicia we have all heard of the bad consequences of the education of girls in taverns. Almost all the Jewish girls that are forcibly being held in the convents in recent times who had been swayed by their lovers and had converted of their own will—almost all are daughters of tavern-keepers in those villages' (ibid. 151).

as long as Bakalarz had not been called to military service. Zoller reported in his testimony that already on the trip to Vienna she had expressed reservations about meeting her former lover on her return, since Bakalarz often visited Kraków.[70] When that testimony was read to her, Deborah stated that she had not met Bakalarz since the time she had returned from Vienna, adding that although she did not fear him, nor had she feared him in the past, 'meeting him would cause me discomfort'.[71] Her aversion to encountering her former lover, and members of the Kraków clergy, after her return to Judaism and her reconciliation with her parents, suggests that she was still in a fragile and insecure emotional state. After she and her father spent three days in Kraków, they travelled together to Hungary, to the house of her maternal uncle Moses Schreiber, also a tavern-keeper. She wished thereby 'to breathe fresh air' and 'to rest from all the changes that she had undergone'. She stayed in Hungary until the end of October of that year.

From a letter Deborah wrote to her parents on 25 September we learn that they did indeed move to Podgórze, and that Deborah's uncle had arranged a match between her and a young Hungarian Jew named Blaufeder. The uncle attached a few lines to Deborah's letter in broken Hebrew announcing the match with the young man, whom he calls 'attractive'. Deborah herself writes in another letter:

> The wish that you, beloved Father, expressed, that I will be able to find a husband in Hungary, may in time be realized. The young man that Uncle has proposed for me, and about whom he has spoken to you, has been here already for the second time. We like each other, and, God willing, I will be a Hungarian citizen. *He is a young man, very capable, intelligent, and also can learn Torah.* He is a native Hungarian and also a citizen, which is considered very important in Hungary. The matter is not entirely settled yet, but I hope—if God wishes to bring it about—that I will be very happy.[72]

According to the uncle, Blaufeder was supposed to go to the army for six weeks. He expressed his hope that a wedding between the two would be forthcoming, because they liked each other.

We do not know whether in the end Deborah married Blaufeder (according to her 11 December testimony she returned to her parents' home in Podgórze at the end of October), but we can learn from her letter to her father that she wanted a husband compatible with her, a 'very capable, intelligent' young man. To please her father, presumably, she emphasizes that the young man knows how to learn Torah, but, as I mentioned above, the word 'Torah' is misspelled, and, indeed, it is the only misspelled word in the letter. Since she underscored the word it is unlikely that she made a careless error; she probably simply did not know (or did not know well) the proper spelling of this basic term.

Indeed, aside from knowledge of the Hebrew alphabet which she used to write her 'German Yiddish', her letters provide no evidence of any Jewish education or

70 Lewkowicz file, testimony of Józef Zoller, 1 Oct. 1901.

71 Lewkowicz file, testimony of Deborah Lewkowicz, 12 Nov. 1901 (after her return to Judaism).

72 Lewkowicz file, letter from Deborah Lewkowicz to her father, 20 Sept. 1901.

religious observance. Deborah does write that she fasted (on Yom Kippur), but not that she recited prayers or attended synagogue services, about which events, had they occurred, she would have certainly told her father. It should be noted that Galician Jewish girls and young women received, at best, a rudimentary Jewish education during this period that consisted of the ability to read basic prayers and the Hebrew alphabet. The Jewish communal leadership did not even consider the question of religious instruction for women.[73] It was left to publicists writing chiefly in newspapers to bring the subject to the public's attention, and to warn of the social and religious consequences of this neglect. There were indeed a few Jewish schools for women in Galicia during this period, but their curriculum had not changed since the 1840s.[74]

From what we have seen so far, Deborah's embrace of Christianity seems to have been a temporary affair, brought on by the hopelessness of her social situation, rather than by religious considerations. Yet the picture is more complex. While staying with her uncle in Hungary, she wrote a letter to Sister Rozalia, the nun in charge of the catechumenate at the Felician convent. Although the letter is undated and without a return address, we learn from the postmark that it was mailed on 5 September 1901. In the letter Deborah presents herself as a faithful Catholic and accuses 'the Jews' of holding her against her will and of not allowing her to fulfil the precepts and obligations of the Church. She relates that in Vienna the Jews compelled her to renounce her Catholicism and that she had pleaded to the court secretary for help. She adds that she was forcibly taken to Hungary as well, from where she is sending this letter; as just mentioned, she does not supply a return

[73] The question was discussed only once in a rabbinical forum, namely, in the rabbinical assembly that met in Kraków in the summer of 1903. At one session a rabbi from the Warsaw district brought up the subject of formal Jewish education for women, especially 'in light of the cases of young women leaving the Jewish religion that occur frequently in Galicia'. He proposed teaching the girls Torah and Jewish history in order to arouse their faith and to strengthen their bond with the Jewish people. Another rabbi attacked the proposal, citing the talmudic dictum 'Whoever teaches his daughter Torah is as if he taught her frivolity'. He added, 'God forbid that anything like this [i.e. formal religious education for women] be found in our midst!' The assembly approved a general proposal to educate the young women to faith and to modesty. One of the Galician rabbis proposed that the rabbis write, or ensure that others write, books in Polish to teach young women Jewish history and to emphasize the importance of the Torah and its commandments. He also proposed that parents who gave their daughters a general education should be required to provide them with the works of Rabbi Samson Raphael Hirsch and the stories of Markus Lehman, translated into Polish. These proposals were not approved. See J. Gutmann (ed.), *Mekits nirdamim* (Piotrków, 1904), 52–7.

[74] One of the oldest and most successful was the Jewish elementary school in Lviv, which was founded in the 1840s, and which had separate schools for boys and for girls. The school was recognized by the authorities as a public school with four grades, with the first grade lasting two years. The curriculum for the girls' school in 1881 included two hours a week for Jewish studies, which consisted mainly of translating the prayers. By contrast, religious studies for the boys included about seven to nine hours of instruction, mostly devoted to Bible and to Hebrew language. See Tsentral'nyi derzhavnyi istorychnyi arkhiv Ukrayiny, L'viv, *f.* 178, *op.* 2, *sp.* 228; microfilm copy in the Central Archives for the History of the Jewish People, Jerusalem, HM2/8672.4, p. 84.

address. 'For a month and a half I am without church, salvation, and confession,' adding,

> O, my Jesus, why have I been punished so harshly . . . would that I could participate just once in a mass, where Jesus sacrifices himself for me. O, God! Take mercy on me! The Jews are not harming me, but they are afflicting me in order that I become a Jew once more. I, however, show them nothing but contempt. I believe that soon somebody will come from Kraków and will release me from the Jews . . . I ask that the new catechumens should pray, and that Pepi should not go outside and meet the Jews, who will kidnap her, and that Ala—where is she?—should be on her guard.
>
> I conclude every prayer with 'Our Father who art in heaven' morning and evening, and I sing all the litanies and everything without a church. But I have hope that Jesus hears my prayer and will return me to the mother [i.e. the nun Rozalia], where I can tell everything personally.

Deborah signs the letter 'Anastasya Marya, who kisses the feet of the mother'.[75]

The first reaction of the convent upon receiving the letter was to complain to the police that Deborah's religious liberty had been infringed, a violation of a right guaranteed by the Austrian Constitution. The difficulty was that the police did not know Deborah's precise whereabouts. When she returned from Hungary, she was summoned to give testimony in court, where she claimed that the letter to the convent was not sincere, in contrast to her letters to her parents. She explained that she felt uncomfortable with the nuns since she had disappointed them, and that she didn't want them to know about her letters to her parents. She also added that she had regretted the trouble that she had caused, which is why she wrote to the convent.[76]

Deborah's explanation in this letter appears confused, vague, and unconvincing. The overall impression she leaves is one of a deeply conflicted young woman, torn between rival loyalties, who is anxious to please everybody. The letter may have been written out of fear that her friends would feel angry or betrayed by her return to Judaism. Her personal confusion was perhaps exacerbated by religious confusion and feelings of guilt: shortly after she wrote to the convent about her recitation of the daily prayers, she wrote to her father about her observance of the Yom Kippur fast.

In the clash of loyalties between Church and home, family ties prevailed. Still, after she returned to the family and to Judaism, Deborah took care not to offend the Felician convent or any of the Catholic Poles with whom she had been connected. She says nothing negative or derogatory about them in her letters and in her testimonies.[77] On the contrary, she feels guilty towards them, as if she had exploited

[75] Lewkowicz file. The letter to the mother superior is in Polish and translated into German.

[76] Lewkowicz file, testimony of Deborah, 12 Nov. 1901.

[77] A brother of one of the converts told a Viennese newspaper that the catechumens lived under difficult conditions in the Felician convent. According to him, the girls looked ill; they suffered from too much work and not enough food. They were allowed to go outside only once a day. After rising at six

their goodwill. She continues to insist that Bakalarz was not involved in her flight, even though she knows that her parents are pursuing a court case against him.

In a sense, Deborah lived on the boundary between the Polish Catholic and Jewish worlds. Her life in a small village, where there were very few Jews, contributed in no small measure to this reality. In the cities there were Jewish communities, Jewish neighbourhoods, Jewish stores, and a Jewish public space, of which one could feel a part. Moreover, in a city like Kraków many Jewish girls learned together in primary schools and thus could provide each other with a sense of social cohesiveness. By contrast, in a small village such as Rzeszotary the Jewish world was confined to family life. When Deborah walked out of her house she already was on the boundary between those worlds. This seems to be the principal reason why most of the converts came from villages.[78]

These young women were not provided with the means by which they could preserve their Jewish identity in their confrontation with Polish society. The dissonance between life at home and in the outside world became greater as they grew older, with the conflicts becoming deeper and more pronounced. The climax would come when the parents expected them to marry a young man from the 'old world', with whom they shared no language.[79] When such marriages were forced upon the young women, the equilibrium between parents and daughters was disturbed, and the latter felt free to run away and convert to Christianity.[80]

in the morning to say the morning prayers they were given only one cup of milk, and then they worked until twelve noon. For lunch they received only vegetables and bread. After praying for two hours they would do the laundry or some other difficult labour until the evening, when they would receive bread and milk. This would continue until they were pious enough to be married off to some dimwit, or to work as a maid in the household of a priest. The deliberate weakening of the body was intended to weaken their will. These remarks were quoted at one of the meetings of the Österreichisch–Israelitische Union. See Ofner, 'Kinderraub in Galizien', 782.

78 Some of the converts were city girls whose parents belonged to the Polonized intelligentsia, including members of the Jewish communal leadership. As a result, a writer in the *Togblat* demanded that the Jewish press publish a list of the converts' names, to ensure that their relatives would not be able to be elected to represent the Jewish community politically. See 'A rubrik far meshumadim', *Togblat*, 12 Aug. 1910, front page. The writer cited the example of the *Oesterreichische Wochenschrift*, edited by Bloch in Vienna, which published a regular column called 'Austritte aus dem Judentum' with the names of the converts. The notice influenced people not to vote for anybody connected to the converts for positions in politics. Cf. the condemnation of Adolph Lilien, a member of the Jewish communal council in Lviv, after he publicly led his niece to the church altar for the sake of her conversion and marriage to a Polish student, in *Ha'olam*, 21 July 1910, 12.

79 Cf. also Scharfstein's remark: 'The essential tragedy begins when the hour of the engagement arrives. The father wants to bequeath to his daughter a scholar with sidelocks, a bit learned, a hasid, in short, somebody like him. The daughter protests and fights—but in vain.'

80 Bertha Pappenheim, in her pamphlet *Zur Judenfrage in Galizien* (Frankfurt am Main, 1900), 5–6, complained about the fact that the Baron Hirsch Foundation established in Galicia only schools for boys. This was criticized by a Viennese Jewish newspaper, which wrote that there was no need to establish schools for women because most of them, including those from hasidic families, learned in schools: 'Imagine: a girl who has enjoyed a school education for many years has become acquainted

For young Jewish men, including those of the village, the Jewish world was fuller and more intensive. Men bore the external signs of Judaism such as the yarmulke and the *talit katan*, and their parents took care to send them to *ḥeder* rather than to primary schools. They went with their fathers to the synagogue in the neighbouring city, and a greater commitment to the observance of the daily religious obligations was demanded of them.

Regarding the geographical distribution of the converts, we find that a large majority came from western Galicia, i.e. from the villages and towns surrounding Kraków (the Wieliczka region, Nowy Sącz, Tarnów, etc.). Western Galicia was more homogeneous ethnically and religiously than eastern Galicia, where the majority of inhabitants were Ruthenians, a minority Armenians and Germans, and where several Churches were represented. Eastern Galicia was multicultural, with an emphasis on the German culture that had been the legacy of Austrian rule. Western Galicia was overwhelmingly Polish, and Polish Catholicism was the main religion. Kraków became the standard-bearer of Polish nationalism, from which Catholicism was inseparable. Hence, assimilation in western Galicia meant assimilation with the dominant Polish culture, of which the Catholic Church was a part.

At the turn of the century Kraków was the centre of the neo-Romantic movement Young Poland, which provided the younger generation with a refuge from the conservatism of their parents' generation.[81] The movement did not replace conservatism with liberalism, nor did it neglect Catholicism for secularism. Rather, emphasis was placed upon culture, especially literature and art. Perhaps the centrality of culture and literature during this period also played a part in making it easier for intelligent Jewish women to identify with Polish society, [82] and, on the other hand, made it easier for the Polish intelligentsia to accept these young Jewish women.

The attraction to Polish culture for educated Jewish women was not limited to progressive elements in Kraków. Jewish women from Orthodox and even hasidic

with a different life from that in the parental home, and through reading modern books has been made acquainted with modern ideas—and there are masses of such girls nowadays in Galicia—is tied to a young savage infinitely beneath her, of terrifying appearance, tongue-tied, with no manners and so on for her whole life! The consequences are not hard to gauge. From time to time a cry of distress reaches public attention, from time to time such an unfortunate creature escapes into the bosom of the Church, which willingly receives her . . .' (Dr Bloch's *Oesterreichische Wochenschrift*, 27 June 1900, 549–51, esp. p. 551).

[81] L. Wolff, 'Dynastic Conservatism and Poetic Violence in *Fin-de-Siècle* Cracow: The Habsburg Matrix of Polish Modernism', *American Historical Review*, 106 (June 2001), 735–64, esp. pp. 737–8.

[82] One of the institutions in Kraków where young Jewish women could acquire an advanced education in Polish literature was the Institute for Higher Education for Women, founded in 1868 by Adrian Baraniecki. The faculty of the institute included some of the poets and writers of the Young Poland movement, such as Lucjan Rydel, whose wedding served as the basis for Wyspiański's play *The Wedding* (see below). 691 Jewish women learned there between the years 1901 and 1924, as opposed to 3,023 Catholics. See J. Kras, *Wyższe Kursy dla Kobiet im. A. Baranieckiego w Krakowie 1868–1924* (Kraków, 1972), 79.

families, who were financially well off, though not necessarily wealthy, were drawn to the literary and cultural life of *fin-de-siècle* Kraków. With reference to this the Orthodox newspaper *Kol mahazikei hadat* wrote 'Ten measures of external education descended upon the daughters of Israel in our land; nine of them were taken by the city of Kraków.' Reporting on the wedding of the daughter of a wealthy hasid, the newspaper described the bride as 'a woman who in appearance, manner, and discourse was a Polish daughter in every sense of the term', and the groom as a 'small town idler behind the oven'.[83] The newspaper writes elsewhere:

> The rich, however, have committed a sin in educating their daughters that we cannot forgive. . . . All the daughters of rich Jews are educated and learned in every language and book, except for a Jewish one. In Kraków all[?] the daughters of the most scrupulously observant hasidim go to the university and hear exhortations and the pronouncements of Tarnowski . . . and when they are spoken of, they are given in marriage to faithful Jews whom they despise. Indeed, I have learned from honest men who speak the truth that some women who are graduates of schools such as these confessed to them that they are wives only in body, but not in soul and spirit.[84]

Polish education became the route taken by Jewish women to integrate into Kraków Polish society, but this route did not lead urban Jewish women, for the most part, to convert. They could continue to lead their lives, alienated from the lifestyle that their parents and husbands chose for them, since they had the support of similar women who shared a common fate. The situation of the educated women from the villages was completely different.

A writer who understood well the dissonance in the life of the Jewish educated village women was Poland's national playwright Stanisław Wyspiański (1869–1907). His play *Wesele* ('The Wedding'), first performed in 1901, describes the wedding of the Kraków poet Lucjan Rydel with a young Polish woman from the village of Bronowice, near Kraków. Marriage to village women became fashionable at the turn of the century among Kraków literati, who romanticized about a return to nature and authentic Polish roots. (Wyspiański himself married a village woman.) In the play the characters of the wedding guests are all based on real people from contemporary or historical Kraków, and the same is true of the play's Jews. The character of the tavern-keeper, 'the Jew', is based on Hirsch Singer, a bearded Orthodox Jewish tavern-keeper in Bronowice. The character of the Jew's daughter Rachel is based on Singer's own daughter Pepa (Józefa Perel) Singer.[85]

[83] See 'But We Are Guilty for the Sake of our Daughters', *Kol mahazikei hadat* (Lemberg), 14 Feb. 1902.

[84] See 'But We Are Guilty for the Sake of our Daughters', *Kol mahazikei hadat* (31 Jan. 1902), 4. Stanisław Tarnowski (1837–1917), the scion of Kraków nobility and an important literary critic, served as the rector of the Jagiellonian University in Kraków and as president of the Polish Academy of Sciences.

[85] On the characters in the play, including the Jews, see T. Żeleński [Boy], 'Plauderei über Wyspiańskis "Hochzeit" (Auszüge)', in S. Wyspiański, *Die Hochzeit. Drama in Drei Akten* (Frankfurt am Main, 1992). Cf. also Wolff, 'Dynastic Conservatism', 759–63.

Pepa Singer, who was born in 1881, lacked a formal secondary education. Like Deborah Lewkowicz she studied first in the school of the peasants' children in the village, and afterwards in primary school in Kraków.[86] We know that she loved modern Polish literature, and in the library of the Academy of Sciences in Kraków there is a copy of the Kraków literary annual *Życie* with the signature 'Józefa Singerówna 1898', i.e. a few years before *Wesele* was produced.[87] Pepa Singer also considered conversion to Christianity as a young woman, but her mother asked her not to do so as long as her father was alive. She converted in 1919.[88]

In *Wesele* the Jewish tavern-keeper boasts of his daughter Rachel to the poet bridegroom:

> As soon as books come, she reads them,
> But still she rolls out dough herself.
> At Vienna she's been to the Opera,
> But at home she still plucks chickens,
> She knows all of Przybyszewski
> And wears her hair in braided loops,
> Like angels in those Italian paintings . . .[89]

The father, aware of his daughter's attraction to the Polish literati, says to the poet:

> She will come here by herself;
> She told me that she couldn't sleep.
> She'd rather watch you gentlemen
> And your wedding—she's cultured.[90]

[86] See Helena z Rydlów Rydlowa, 'Ze wspomnień Heleny z Rydlów Rydlowej', in R. Brandstaetter (ed.), *Ja jestem Żyd z 'Wesela': Z wielogłosem i dokumentacją na temat 'Żyda' i 'Racheli'* (Kraków 1993), esp. p. 57. The daughter of the poet upon whom the play's hero is based writes that 'the Polish school and the Polish village transformed Józefa Singer into a Pole in heart and in spirit, if not in blood (ibid.).

[87] Ibid. 37. Żeleński notes that there were many girls in Kraków like Rachel. They could be found in the reading clubs, the libraries, the theatre, and the concert hall. See Żeleński, 'Plauderei über Wyspiańskis "Hochzeit"', 278.

[88] Brandstaetter, *Ja jestem Żyd z 'Wesela'*, 25.

[89] S. Wyspiański, *The Wedding*, trans. G. Kapolka (Ann Arbor, 1990), 50. Stanisław Przybyszewski was one of the central figures in the Young Poland movement, and his compositions were characterized by anarchism and Satanism. His books and personality contributed to the development of a cult of admirers around him, especially those who were attracted to Polish literature. Cf. Agnon's story 'With our Youth and our Aged', set in 1906: 'Just then Miss Ubershenkil walked in, her face lit up like a baker's oven in a year of plenty, and Przybyszewski's book *Snow* in her hand' (*Kol sipurav shel shemu'el yosef agnon: Al kapot hamanul* (Jerusalem, 1953), 323); cf. also Shmuel Werses, *Shay agnon kifshuto: Keriah bikhtavav* (Jerusalem 2000), 257). Agnon, who didn't read Polish, was apparently familiar with the book from its Yiddish translation. See also the statements of Y. L. Peretz: 'Hasidic girls, leave them alone! They comb their hair so nicely, use the best perfume, and look so pale . . . and they all read Przybyszewski . . .' (cited in C. Shmeruk, *Sifrut yidish bepolin: Meḥkarim ve'iyunim historiyim* (Jerusalem, 1981), 248). Shmeruk says that there were many literary compositions about young Jewish women leaving Judaism because the phenonemon was so widespread.

[90] Wyspiański, *The Wedding*, 50. Cf. also the following remark by Plach: 'Wyspiański's Rachel, for example, is so enveloped in Polish culture that one hardly notices that she is Jewish. Rachel becomes

He recognizes the consequences of this attraction but is powerless to stop his daughter:

> Let Rachel do as she pleases.
> You, sir, may loathe me as a Jew
> But her you must respect.
> She's not ashamed of her father.[91]

Later, when the poet tells Rachel,

> Your father has berated you
> For your literary tone,

she answers:

> He allows me everything
> And even boasts about me.
> It's interesting—isn't it?
> Exploitation, business, I and he?[92]

Wyspiański's Rachel knows that although her desires conflict with her father's faith and way of life, he appreciates her achievements and adopts an attitude of forgiveness towards her. She in turn appreciates his liberality and is not ashamed of him. Her father realizes the difficulty that such a woman will have in finding the proper husband, and he says to the poet:

> She says music carries her away.
> No husband has carried her off yet;
> Maybe she could work at the post office.
> My daughter, she's a woman,
> A thoroughly modern lady,
> Like a star.[93]

Rachel's problem does not lie in any discord or bad relations with her father, but rather in the conflict between the way of life she has chosen for herself and her father's traditional ways.

almost a parody of an assimilated Jew. Yet this is not to suggest that Jews like Rachel could not have existed; indeed, they did exist' (E. Plach, 'Botticelli Women: Rachel Singer and the Jewish Theme in Stanisław Wyspiański's *The Wedding*', *Polish Review*, 41 (1996), 309–27, esp. p. 320). Plach compares Rachel from the play to the literary critic Wilhelm Feldman.

[91] *The Wedding*, 52. See also Plach: 'With these words, however, the Jew reveals his own clear sense of the transitional nature of the turn-of-the-century period. The Jew is painfully aware of the distance that separates his traditional world from that of his daughter's modern one . . .' (Plach, 'Botticelli Women', 326).

[92] *The Wedding*, 77.

[93] Ibid. 50. Employment in a post office carried with it status, since postal workers formed part of the Austrian bureaucracy. Cf. e.g. the characterization of one of the newspapers of the period: 'Even the most hasidic father-in-law will rejoice if he is told that his daughter-in-law knows how to play the piano, knows French, bookkeeping . . .' (*Hamitspeh*, 2 Aug. 1901).

The father's inability to influence his daughter Rachel's way of life was typical of an entire generation of Jewish parents in the villages around Kraków whose daughters attended Polish primary schools. To a large extent, it was the problem of the Jewish community as a whole, which found expression in the confusion and ignorance over how to deal with 'the question of the daughters', or, more accurately, the question of the education of the daughters. Neither the classical rabbinical authorities nor the hasidic rabbis had anything to say about a situation in which daughters attended government schools by law, and comparatively little to say on the question of female education at all. Wyspiański portrays the father as proud of his daughter's accomplishments, yet at the same time apprehensive about her future in the traditional role of wife and mother.

In the play Rachel's mother never appears; the voice of the Jewish tradition is entirely that of the father. This also may be typical of the period; in many of the documented cases the mothers are conspicuously absent. Deborah Lewkowicz, for example, addresses all her letters to her father or to her parents, but never to her mother. In her letters she simply asks her father, the dominant figure in her life, to send her regards to her mother. It is her father who accompanies her to Vienna, and who brings her to Hungary, even though she is visiting her mother's brother. Of course, there may be many reasons for this. But one partial explanation is that Abraham Lewkowicz, a businessman who was in frequent contact with Poles, was better equipped to handle such matters, and to understand what was happening, than his wife. An examination of Ciwie Lewkowicz's signature on the protocol of her court testimony reveals that the letters were formed with great difficulty; in another place she signed with a circle rather than with her name.[94] It is almost certain that she did not master the skills of reading and writing Polish. Her daughter Deborah belonged to a different generation, the generation of girls who attended Polish schools; the cultural gap between mother and daughter was even wider than that between father and daughter.

POSTSCRIPT

In 1909 Benno Straucher presented before the Austrian parliament an interpellation that dealt with the question of the conversions of young Jewish women in the Kraków region. He related briefly the stories of close to thirty women who had arrived at the Felician convent, and accused the authorities of not discharging their legal obligation to help parents locate their daughters and return them home. Previously, other Jewish delegates had presented interpellations on specific cases. In a large number of cases the young women were romantically involved with Poles, and in some cases, they took money and valuables from their home. Following Straucher's interpellation, some of the young men were tried for aiding and abetting the girls'

[94] Lewkowicz file, protocols of Ciwie Lewkowicz's testimony from 18 Mar. and 22 Apr. 1901.

flight, usually for leading them to the Felician convent. Those convicted received prison sentences of up to a month.

In the parliamentary interpellations and in the Viennese Jewish press these conversions were called 'abductions'. But this was not the case in the Galician Jewish press, especially in the Yiddish and Hebrew newspapers. The Galician publicists made the connection between the phenomenon of young Jewish women converting and their education, and this led to some serious discussion in the Jewish community about how to combat the phenomenon. Involved in one of these discussions was Aaron Marcus (1843–1916), a scholar of kabbalah whose interest in hasidism had led him to move from Hamburg to Kraków. Marcus published in the Kraków Hebrew newspaper *Hamitspeh* two articles under the title 'Greetings to the People of Israel and Their Rabbis!' In them Marcus railed against the silence of the rabbinical leadership with regard to the conversion of the young women: 'Where there is desecration of God's name, respect shouldn't be paid to rabbis who turn a blind eye to the apostasy that has resulted from [young women attending] the schools of the Catholics, and which has steadily increased over the last thirty years. No one seeks a solution.' Marcus also criticized the parents' indifference to their girls' programme of studies, to the school's study trips (especially to churches), and to the content of the textbooks. He cited passages from a reading primer about the Trinity, as well as Catholic prayers, in an attempt to determine the factors that led girls to identify with Catholicism. In books used in the older grades he found selections of Jesus' assertions against the Jews.

Marcus writes that he decided to speak out on the subject because in 1874 he had advised the Jews of Kraków to cope with the compulsory education law by sending their daughters to school and thus 'to protect their brothers'. The idea was that since there were relatively few schools, and space was limited, the influx of girls would fill up the schools so that there would be no room for their brothers. This seemed all right to Marcus at the time because it was already the custom to send Jewish girls to school, even girls from hasidic families. But now he called upon the rabbis to alert the members of their communities to the dangers of such education, and to demand the removal of textbooks which included, illegally, religious matters and to oppose school trips to churches. As an alternative, he proposed that girls should no longer be sent to school but instead schooled at home, which was legal in Galicia.[95]

Marcus's proposals elicited a sceptical response in *Hamitspeh*, with at least one writer branding them impractical.[96] Parents would not substitute expensive private lessons for free education in the schools, he writes. And since rabbis were unable to reach a consensus on lesser problems, 'how will they render a decision on such a difficult question?' The solution, publicists suggested, was to combine Jewish

[95] *Hamitspeh*, 28 June and 5 July 1912, front page. Marcus was especially disturbed by the fact that even the daughters and granddaughters of rabbis were no longer faithful to Judaism.

[96] R. Pfeffer, 'The Education of the Daughters: A Reply to Aaron Marcus', *Hamitspeh*, 2 Aug. 1912.

religious education with general education, and even to establish religious schools for women.[97] *Hamitspeh* was a Zionist newspaper, and so it called for the provision of nationalist education through the study of Hebrew literature and Jewish history. None of these proposals received serious consideration at the time.[98]

It was not until after the First World War, when the women of Deborah Lewkowicz's generation—the first generation that had been educated almost entirely in Polish schools—became mothers of schoolchildren, that Jewish curricula for women began little by little to be developed.[99] In April 1925 one of the rabbis who had been involved in initiatives for change published the following:

The heart bleeds at the realization that a long list of accusations can be made against us, accusations of neglect of the lost Jewish generation that was torn from the body of the Jewish nation. It is true that from the standpoint of the Torah the question of the education of young women is sensitive and complex. It is true that for the upright, honest, and holy Jew of the previous generation, [the question of] entering the woman's gallery was difficult to resolve. But we should have taken our cue from the biblical verse 'Thus shall you say to the house of Jacob and tell the children of Israel' (Exod: 19: 3) . . . Hence, we cannot say that 'Our hands have not shed this blood' (Deut. ... 21: 8).

So if we now start to solve the problem of how to educate our daughters, we have to admit that we started too late, and that what we have lost we will never be able to regain . . . We are now speaking of a historic turning point. The great sages of our generation and the truly

97 See e.g. S. M. Lazar, '"The Precious from the Vile" (Concerning the Traitorous Girls)', *Hamagid*, 2 Aug. 1912. Even the Orthodox newspaper *Kol maḥazikei hadat* cited a proposal that called for teaching girls 'Scripture, Hebrew language, and Jewish history' in equal measure to the general studies and foreign languages that they learned. The writer saw his proposal as only a partial solution. See 'But We Are Guilty for the Sake of our Daughters', *Kol maḥazikei hadat*, 14 Feb. 1902.

98 See e.g. the remarks of Rabbi Moses Leiter, a Galician Jew who took refuge in Vienna during the First World War, after he was shocked to see young Galician women in the city working on the sabbath: 'This is the fruit of the strange and ruinous education that they received. Reading Polish novels, which are full of licentiousness and adulterous relations, is not enriched by any knowledge of the Hebrew religion. They do not know the nature of Judaism, and what it requires of them. Does the Russian government know the concept of justice, honesty, truth or mercy? So do our daughters understand the concept of Judaism, Torah and religion. What do you say, you rabbis of the Diaspora? "Let the wicked . . .". But do you know, you rabbis, upon whom you have pronounced this harsh sentence? On the majority of girls in Galicia, on the mothers and educators of the coming generation!' (M. Leiter, *Bein tikvah veye'iush (maḥshevot palit)* (Vienna, 1916), 9). Leiter does not blame the girls, but rather criticizes the indifference of the rabbis, who used the saying 'Let the wicked feed on it and die' (*Bava kama* 69*a*) as a halakhic ruling that exempted one from the need to be concerned with the Judaism of transgressors. With this approach, Leiter claims, the rabbis gave up on almost an entire generation of young women.

99 Cf. the proposal for the Beth Jacob schools for women, as presented in the Beth Jacob convention in Warsaw in 1925: *Beth Jacob* (Łódź) (Mar. 1925), 63–4. The curriculum alloted ten hours per week in each of the seven grades of the elementary school to Jewish subjects. Rabbi Dr Shmuel Deutschlander, who made the proposal, emphasized the importance of transmitting real knowledge of Judaism to the young women. He was opposed to education that appealed solely to their feelings.

pious must take care that this neglect not continue. Real practical steps must be taken for the organization of an educational system.[100]

Of course, not all the women of Deborah Lewkowicz's generation converted to Christianity. Of the different forms of alienation from Judaism that one finds among Jewish women at the turn of the century, conversion was the extreme. Different phenomena occurred in the cities and the villages, in the east and west of Galicia. In any event, the Jewish religious leadership's failure to meet head on the challenges posed by the changes in the educational system, and generally in Polish culture and society in Galicia, exacerbated the problem of conversions. Not surprisingly, perhaps, the first person to take concrete steps to solve the problem of religious education for women—the founder of the Beth Jacob movement, Sarah Shnirer—belonged herself to the 'lost generation' of Deborah Lewkowicz and Michalina Araten.

100 See Rabbi Tuvia Horowitz, 'What Is a Jewish Girl Lacking?', *Beth Jacob* (Apr. 1925), front page (free translation from Yiddish). Many writers treat the neglect of Jewish education for women as a problem specific to Polish Jews.

Feminism and Fiction: Khane Blankshteyn's Role in Inter-War Vilna

ELLEN KELLMAN

KHANE BLANKSHTEYN'S lifetime spanned an era during which east European Jews began to think in new ways about gender roles. Blankshteyn both modelled new female behaviours and agitated for change through her participation in the feminist, Folkist, and Labour Zionist movements and through her work as a fiction writer and publicist. During the final two decades of her life she fashioned a distinguished career as a Yiddish belletrist and journalist, a publisher and editor of her own feminist magazine, a political activist, and a leader in her community.

The available details of Blankshteyn's biography before the 1920s are sparse,[1] but her activities in inter-war Vilna were well documented in the Yiddish press.[2] Judging by accounts published at the time of her death, she was a figure of considerable renown there. She was at the centre of a feminist circle and in the leadership of various women's educational and political organizations.

Born in Vilna in the early 1860s to wealthy, assimilated parents, Blankshteyn led a privileged and, at the same time, adventurous life. Her father, Avrom Shorr, was a prominent merchant and property owner. She was educated privately in childhood and sent abroad to boarding school as an adolescent. A talented student, she later studied languages, literature, and philosophy at university level in France and Germany, mastering five languages and completing a course of piano study at the

1 The only known biographical essay about Blankshteyn was written by Hirsh Abramovitsh. It was, unfortunately, never published. All biographical information about Blankshteyn used in this chapter comes either from the entry about her in vol. i of *Leksikon fun der nayer yidisher literatur* (New York, 1956) or from obituaries and tributes published in the Polish Yiddish press at the time of her death. The entry on Blankshteyn in the *Leksikon* is based entirely on Abramovitsh's essay. When the entry was written, the essay was extant in the YIVO Archives in New York City, but it has since been lost. I have footnoted additional facts gleaned from newspaper articles, but not those taken from the *Leksikon* entry.

2 I mainly used two Vilna Yiddish dailies in my research on Blankshteyn's activities in Vilna: *Undzer tog* (also called *Vilner tog*) and *Tsayt*. Blankshteyn occasionally published her work in both papers, and both carried coverage of her death and funeral.

Dresden Conservatory.[3] Married and divorced twice, she raised a son and daughter as a single parent. After living for a time in Kiev with her second husband, she returned to Vilna with her children upon the dissolution of the marriage. During the First World War she served as a nurse with the Russian army. One biographical account mentions that she was active in an underground revolutionary movement.[4]

BLANKSHTEYN AND JEWISH AUTONOMISM

The Russian Revolution of 1917 found Blankshteyn again living in Kiev, where she joined the Folkspartey (People's Party), a Jewish nationalist group inspired by the autonomist ideology of Shimon Dubnov. The Folkspartey was active with other groups in endeavouring to establish autonomous Jewish institutions in Ukraine during the years of revolution and civil war.

When the Bolsheviks took control of Ukraine in 1920, the various Jewish parties and organizations that had sought to establish themselves during the period of civil war were forced to cease their operations. Blankshteyn, then already about 60 years old, returned to Vilna in 1922. Still committed to Jewish autonomism, she joined the Folkspartei in Poland, whose leader in Vilna was Dr Tsemakh Shabad. He encouraged her to write and speak on behalf of the Folkspartey.[5] During this period she learned Yiddish in order to use the language in her work as a publicist. She developed a fine command of the spoken language and was respected for her written style.[6]

Blankshteyn was also active in several feminist organizations and political campaigns in post-war Vilna. In time this involvement came to overshadow her work in the Folkspartey.

FEMINIST EDUCATIONAL WORK

Beginning in the mid-1920s, when the forces of economic depression and rising antisemitism severely curtailed employment options for Jewish youth in Poland,

[3] 'Intime noveles' ('Intimate Stories'), *Undzer tog*, 14 July 1939, 5. This unsigned review of Blankshteyn's short story collection *Noveles*, which appeared in July 1939, also contains biographical information.

[4] *Tsayt*, unsigned obituary, 30 July 1939, 3.

[5] 'Intime noveles'. The entry on Blankshteyn in *Leksikon fun der nayer yidisher literatur* states that she stood as a candidate for the Sejm within a few years of her return to Vilna. This seems unlikely. During the 1920s, elections to the Sejm were held in 1922 and 1928. It would have been too soon for Blankshteyn to become involved in the campaign of 1922, since she had barely returned to Vilna. By 1928 she had become deeply involved in feminist politics and had stood as a candidate for the Vilna City Council on a women's list in 1927.

[6] On Blankshteyn's command of spoken and written Yiddish, see the eulogy by Avrom Virshubski published in *Tsayt* on 30 July 1939, the eulogy by M. Volf published in *Folksvort* on 2 Aug. 1939, and 'Intime noveles'. Blankshteyn's rather sophisticated use of the Hebraic component in her Yiddish writing is evidence of her fluency in the language.

Blankshteyn became involved in the movement for Jewish productivization in Vilna. As it became evident that job opportunities in the professions and government service was shrinking, and that a large percentage of Jewish workers faced prolonged unemployment, several communal organizations initiated programmes to prepare Jewish youth to enter the skilled trades. In 1925 Blankshteyn was one of two women serving on the board of directors of the Vilna Tekhnikum, a technical high school for Jewish students.[7]

Blankshteyn was in the leadership of two important feminist organizations in Vilna, Yidisher Froyen-fareyn (Jewish Women's Union) and Froyen-shuts (Society for the Protection of Women), both of which sought to enable Jewish women to achieve personal autonomy by providing them with vocational training. Blankshteyn served on the board of directors of the Froyen-fareyn and was chairwoman of Froyen-shuts. Although they operated independently of one another, the membership of the boards of directors of the two groups overlapped somewhat and their members participated in several political campaigns together.[8]

The Froyen-fareyn was founded by a group of Vilna feminists in 1923 as an independent, *umparteyish* (non-partisan) organization. Its primary mission was to help impoverished Jewish girls and women from both working-class and middle-class backgrounds find productive employment.[9] It established training courses for young women who sought to enter the skilled trades, especially the needle trades. The organization also offered evening courses for adults in the needle trades, a diploma course in home economics for young people and evening courses in home economics for adults, a day care programme which served the children of the working poor, an array of cultural programmes and lectures, and a lending library of books in Yiddish and Polish. Blankshteyn served as a member of the board and worked with leading members of the organization on political campaigns and other projects.

Cognizant of the fact that the First World War had left a significant portion of the Jewish population of Vilna without the financial means to pursue their former business, vocational, or professional interests, the founders of the Vilna Froyen-fareyn held that 'it was not enough to give a hungry person a meal or a needy person an article of clothing . . . Help must now be tangible and constructive . . . It must

7 'Der vilner yidisher tekhnikum', in M. Grosman, *Yidishe vilne in vort un bild* (Vilna, 1925), 66–8.

8 On page 3 of the pamphlet entitled 'Froy, tsu di valn!' ('Woman, to the Polls!'), dated 18 June 1927, Blankshteyn's name appears with other candidates on the women's list. She is identified as a journalist and member of the board of directors of Froyen-fareyn. In a photograph accompanying her article entitled 'Di tsiln fun froyen-shuts in vilne' ('The Goals of Froyen-shuts in Vilna'), which appeared in A. I. Grodzenski (ed.), *Vilner almanakh* (Vilna, 1939), she is identified as chairwoman of the organization.

9 Information on the history of the Froyen-fareyn is taken from two articles by Fania Tsemel, a member of the board of directors. 'Di entshteyung fun vilner yidishn froyen-fareyn' appeared in E. H. Yeshurin, *Vilne—a zamlbukh gevidmet der shtot vilne* (New York, 1935). 'Der vilner yidisher froyen-fareyn' appeared in Grodzenski (ed.), *Vilner almanakh*.

fundamentally solve the problem of Jewish groundlessness, [by] making the Jew, and primarily the Jewish woman, productive.' Under the slogan 'Immediate constructive aid for the Jewish woman', the founders set to work with nothing except a desire to improve the material situation of Jewish women and their families.[10]

The ideology of productivization had been introduced in Vilna at the start of the twentieth century by the organization Hilf durkh Arbet (Help through Work). Its original purpose was to make it possible for impoverished Jews in Vilna, especially orphaned children, to enter the skilled trades by providing them with vocational training and employment. Hilf durkh Arbet established high-quality training courses in carpentry, furniture-making, shoemaking, and tailoring.[11] The organization was forced to suspend its educational activities during the First World War, but it re-established itself after the war and continued to operate throughout the inter-war period.

During the period of economic crisis that followed the establishment of the independent Polish state, many middle-class Jews were forced to abandon their aspirations towards higher education and the elite professions, as unemployment and antisemitism made job prospects more and more uncertain. Writing in the late 1930s about the accomplishments of the Froyen-fareyn, Fania Tsemel observed that massive economic and class restructuring had taken place in Jewish society since the war,[12] one result of which was that Jewish youth had come to understand that training for the professions was not likely to lead to secure employment, and that if anyone had a chance at making a living, it was the skilled tradesperson.[13]

> Fourteen or fifteen years ago . . . when the founders of the Froyen-fareyn spoke out [about this], it sounded like heresy. It was necessary to enter into a pioneering battle until [we] succeeded in breaking through the Chinese wall of prejudice that predominated in the mind of the Jewish woman with respect to work and the skilled trades.[14]

Although not officially aligned with any political party, the Vilna Froyen-fareyn was evidently modelled on the Warsaw-based feminist organization Farband fun Yidishe Froyen in Poyln (known as the Froyen-farband), which came into being immediately after women were granted voting rights under the Second Polish Commonwealth. The Labour Zionist feminist leader Puah Rakovsky and several of her associates from the Zionist women's organization Bnos Tsien led a campaign to transform the mainly middle-class-based Bnos Tsien into a new organization with the broad goal of persuading all classes of Jewish women 'to take advantage of our rights' under the newly established state.[15] According to Rakovsky, the newly formed Froyen-farband had no formal ties to the Zionist movement.

[10] Tsemel, 'Di entshteyung fun vilner yidishn froyen-fareyn', 332–3.

[11] H. Abramovitsh, 'Di vilner gezelshaft "hilf durkh arbet"', in his *Farshvundene geshtaltn* (Buenos Aires, 1958).

[12] Tsemel used the term *ibershikhtung*, transformation of one class into another, to describe this process.

[13] Tsemel, 'Der vilner yidisher froyen-fareyn', 281.

[14] Ibid. 282.

[15] P. Rakovsky, *My Life as a Radical Jewish Woman*, ed. P. Hyman (Bloomington, Ind., 2002), 133.

Its main task was to organize the masses of Jewish women, and it did not subscribe to any party so that its ranks could include women of all trends. As a Jewish national union with a positive position on the Land of Israel, the association had a special section for practical work in Palestine. But its main goal was to educate the lowest classes of Jewish women, to make young Jewish women productive, and to evoke in them an understanding of economic independence, a sense of society, and an interest in the collective.[16]

Early in 1924 the founding chairwoman of the Vilna Froyen-fareyn, Tatyana Epshteyn, requested help from the Froyen-farband in setting up the new organization. Rokhl Shteyn, the chair of the Froyen-farband, visited Vilna for that purpose.[17]

Writing ten years after its founding, Fania Tsemel described the accomplishments of the Froyen-fareyn in Vilna in broad terms:

During the ten years of its existence, the Froyen-fareyn has developed markedly, and has branched out in its activities so much that it is now one of the most respected of all the cultural and communal institutions in Vilna and the surrounding province. There is not one communal, political or cultural issue about which the Froyen-fareyn does not take an influential position.[18]

The central task of the Froyen-fareyn was, nevertheless, the vocational education of Jewish women. In 1935, 300 pupils from the ranks of the poorest strata of the Jewish population were receiving training in the needle trades through a variety of courses organized by the Froyen-fareyn. They included formerly middle-class women and other unemployed and déclassé individuals.[19]

The Froyen-fareyn conceived of its educational role more broadly, however. Supplementing its vocational courses with additional lectures in biology, literature, and Jewish history, and encouraging pupils to use its library of Yiddish and Polish books and to attend cultural events organized especially for them, the organization sought to raise the cultural level of the *masn-froy* ('woman of the masses').[20]

In addition to her ongoing involvement with the Froyen-fareyn proper, Blankshteyn chaired the board of the organization Froyen-shuts, which was closely allied with the Froyen-fareyn. Froyen-shuts conducted similar educational and social work, but its clients were women from the true underclass of Jewish Vilna—its prostitutes.

Froyen-shuts came into being in Vilna several years after the Froyen-fareyn.[21] It was founded as a branch of the Jewish Association for the Protection of Girls and

16 Ibid. 83.

17 Tsemel, 'Di entshteyung fun vilner yidishn froyen-fareyn', 333. Rokhl Shteyn was a Zionist leader and a member of the Warsaw City Council at the time. The Froyen-farband also called itself *umparteyish*, but many members were active in the Zionist movement. For more on the Froyen-farband, see Rakovsky, *My Life as a Radical Jewish Woman*, ch. 3.

18 Tsemel, 'Di entshteyung fun vilner yidishn froyen-fareyn', 334.

19 Ibid. 335.

20 Ibid. 336.

21 Information on the history of Froyen-shuts is taken from Blankshteyn, 'Di tsiln fun froyen-shuts in vilne'.

Women, an international organization based in London that had been in existence since 1885,[22] whose broad purpose was to combat prostitution in Jewish communities. Blankshteyn served as chairwoman of Froyen-shuts in Vilna. (Additional branches of the organization were established in Warsaw, Łódź, and Białystok at the same time.)

Jewish feminists had already been addressing the problem of Jewish involvement in prostitution and trafficking in women for several decades when Froyen-shuts came onto the scene. In Germany the Jüdischer Frauenbund (League of Jewish Women), whose charismatic leader was Bertha Pappenheim, had been founded in 1904. One of the original goals of Pappenheim's organization was to fight white slavery.[23]

A comparison of the activities of the two organizations suggests that Froyen-shuts may have modelled its programme for combating prostitution in Jewish Vilna partly on that of the Jüdischer Frauenbund, which founded girls' clubs, dormitories, and home economics schools especially to serve young, impoverished Jewish women from eastern Europe who came to German cities seeking employment and were felt to be at risk of becoming prostitutes.[24]

While both Froyen-shuts and Jüdischer Frauenbund were founded by middle-class feminists, there were some essential differences in their politics and attitudes towards their work in the area of prostitution. First, the membership of Jüdischer Frauenbund was made up of German Jewish women, while its clientele largely comprised Ostjuden. Secondly, Froyen-shuts emphasized the idea that, as a result of the massive economic and class restructuring that had taken place in Jewish society in Poland since the war, girls and women of middle-class origins were also at risk of falling into prostitution. As a result, Froyen-shuts did not present itself as an organization whose purpose was to serve a less educated, poorer, foreign-born class of women, but rather as a grass-roots organization that existed to serve its own kind.

The overall goal of Froyen-shuts was to prevent young unemployed Jewish women from turning to prostitution by offering them vocational training and a variety of services. Chief among these were a shelter for unemployed women, an employment bureau, a medical clinic, an office of legal aid which provided free legal representation in divorce cases, a bureau which aided deserted wives in tracing the whereabouts of their husbands and securing child support, and a training course for women aimed at enabling them to seek employment as domestic servants. The organization also sponsored cultural events for the women it served.

[22] M. A. Kaplan, *The Jewish Feminist Movement in Germany* (Westport, Conn., 1979), 108–9. The Jewish Association for the Protection of Girls and Women concentrated its efforts on exposing the activities of traffickers in women.

[23] Ibid. 86. Kaplan defines white slaves as 'women and girls who were lured, tricked, or forced to go abroad by traffickers who smuggled them across borders and sold them into prostitution' (p. 103). Pappenheim wrote extensively about Jewish involvement in prostitution in Galicia before and after the First World War.

[24] Ibid. 125–30.

Froyen-shuts was more than the sum of the services it provided to women at risk, however. Writing about the organization's goals in 1937, Blankshteyn emphasized its political role:

Froyen-shuts stands guard over women's rights and protects women in all areas of their professional and social activity. These are ominous, bitter times, especially for the Jewish woman, who always needs society's protection, but even more so in a time of anarchy and wildness, when we don't know what tomorrow will bring in the bleak struggle between fascism and democracy. At the present time it is more necessary than ever for Froyen-shuts to aid our helpless, unemployed female Jewish youth.[25]

SUPPORT FOR YIDDISH ELEMENTARY EDUCATION

Every aspect of Jewish cultural life in inter-war Poland was politicized, as parties and ideologies competed sharply for the allegiance of the Jewish masses. Privately run elementary schools offered a variety of curricula and languages of instruction. For the most part, schools where Yiddish was the primary language in the classroom served the children of working-class families.

In keeping with her Folkist and Yiddishist orientation, Blankshteyn became involved with the Vilna educational organization Shul un Kultur Farband (School and Culture Association, known as Shul-kult). Shul-kult was founded in 1928 as a result of a political conflict within the Tsentraler idisher shul-organizatsye (Central Yiddish School Organization, known as TsIShO) over instruction in Jewish history, Hebrew language, and Bible in the curriculum of the Vilna TsIShO schools.[26] The founder and subsequent leader of Shul-kult was Yisroel Gurevitsh. The organization's elementary school in Vilna prided itself on its up-to-date pedagogical methods and the fact that it served the children of the poorest Jewish families in the city, accepting pupils whether their parents could afford to pay school fees or not. Most subjects were taught in Yiddish, but the curriculum also emphasized instruction in Hebrew, Bible, and Jewish history. Blankshteyn served on the Shul-kult Committee in Vilna from at least 1934 until the end of her life.[27]

25 Blankshteyn, 'Di tsiln fun froyen-shuts in vilne', 281–2.

26 For more on the conflict that led to the founding of Shul-kult, see K. S. Kazdan, *Di geshikhte fun yidishn shulvezn in umophengikn poyln* (Mexico City, 1947), 536–46, the biography of Y. Gurevitsh in vol. ii of *Leksikon fun der nayer yidisher literatur* (New York, 1958), and 'Shul-kult in vilne', in *Vilner almanakh* (Vilna, 1939).

27 An invitation to the yearly general meeting of Shul-kult members that took place on 14 April 1934 lists Blankshteyn as one of three main speakers. Her topic was 'Thoughts and Reflections about Coeducation'. The invitation is found in the Vilna Collection in the Archives of the YIVO Institute, Record Group 29, folder 437. Blankshteyn appears in the group photograph of the Vilna Shul-kult Committee in the *Vilner almanakh* (1939). Another important indicator of the extent of her involvement in Shul-kult is the fact that Yisroel Gurevitsh delivered one of the eulogies at Blankshteyn's funeral.

BLANKSHTEYN'S ROLE IN ELECTORAL POLITICS

In addition to her work in feminist organizations, Blankshteyn was active in electoral politics in Vilna. In June 1927 her name appeared in the second position on list number 3, the Jewish Women's List (Froyen-liste) for election to the Vilna City Council.[28] The first position was filled by Tatyana Epshteyn, the chairwoman of Froyen-fareyn. Eight others, all members of Froyen-fareyn, appeared on the list.[29] The Women's List was an innovation in Vilna, apparently organized late in the campaign as a protest against the lack of female representation and the absence of advocacy for women's electoral interests in the Jewish National Bloc, the largest Jewish voting bloc in Vilna. The first three points in its programme were the following: (1) day care homes for children; (2) education in the skilled trades; and (3) protection of women (from prostitution).[30] The results of the election were disappointing; none of the candidates on the Women's List won a mandate.[31]

The next city council election took place in June 1934. There was no Women's List that year, and Blankshteyn did not stand as a candidate in the election. Two other representatives of the Froyen-fareyn appeared on the list of the Jewish National Bloc in the second municipal region. The Bloc won two seats on the city council in this region, but neither of the Froyen-fareyn candidates had a high enough position on the list to win a seat.[32]

The last election to the Vilna City Council before the outbreak of the Second World War took place on 21 May 1939. Blankshteyn ran on the list of a bloc called Poyle-Tsien, Hisakhdes un Tsienistishe Arbets-grupirungen (Labour Zionists, Confederation and Zionist Workers' Groups). This was, apparently, Blankshteyn's

[28] The Vilna Collection in the Archives of the YIVO Institute contains an assortment of election handbills for Vilna City Council elections and elections to the Sejm and Senate of Poland. Election handbills and leaflets issued by the Yidishe froyen-liste are found in the addendum to Record Group 29, box 1, folder 32.

[29] Position 3 was held by F. Komisarova; position 4 by N. Vaserman; position 5 by Dr Z. Levande; position 6 by M. Berger; position 7 by Sher-Antokolski; position 8 by S. Aronovski; position 9 by Khane Kats; position 10 by S. Broydo.

[30] The candidates also promised to fight for the following demands in the city council: full recognition of (and support for) Jewish schools; protection for widows and orphans; repeal of unfair taxes; immediate introduction of sewers and electricity in poor neighbourhoods; and inexpensive public transport between city and suburbs.

[31] In an article discussing the election results, *Vilner tog* (later known as *Undzer tog*) commented that the Froyen-fareyn had put out its own list because it was angry at the Jewish National Bloc, but that the inadvertent result was that the Jewish National Bloc got even more votes than it would otherwise have done. The article appeared on 21 June 1927, 1–2.

[32] In the second electoral region in Vilna, F. Komisarova held position 2 and Khane Kats held position 8. See *Tsayt*, 8 June 1934, 2. See also an editorial by Fania Tsemel that appeared in *Tsayt*, 6 June 1934, 2, in which Tsemel urged all Jewish women to vote for the list of the Jewish National Bloc, on the grounds that it alone represented women's interests and fought for children's education, equal rights for working women, and help for the most impoverished, unprotected women in the society.

first (and only) involvement in a Zionist electoral campaign.[33] She had the second position on the list in the region in which she ran, but only the candidate in the first position (Mark Dworzecki) won a mandate.

BLANKSHTEYN'S JOURNALISTIC WORK

In 1925 Blankshteyn founded a weekly magazine entitled *Di froy* ('The Woman') and served as its editor and publisher. Its subtitle, *Vokhnshrift gevidmet di interesn un shuts fun der yidisher froy* ('Weekly Devoted to the Interests and Protection of the Jewish Woman'), made its feminist orientation clear. Published in Vilna but intended to reach a national audience, *Di froy* was distributed in four urban centres in Poland: Vilna, Warsaw, Łódź, and Lemberg (Lviv).

A full assessment of the role that the magazine played in the feminist movement on the Jewish street in inter-war Poland will have to wait until more details about its history are recovered through research. It appears that only the first four numbers of *Di froy* are extant. Dated 8 April, 1 May, 8 May and 28 May 1925, they are found in the collection of the YIVO Institute in New York City. It is not presently known how many numbers were published in total.[34]

The four extant numbers are, however, very rich, and enable us to understand much about Blankshteyn's feminism and her Jewish nationalist political orientation.

A statement entitled 'Undzer ufgabe' ('Our Task') appeared on the front cover of the first number. In it the editor explained that the First World War and the economic crisis that followed it had forced working women in many countries to seek paid employment outside the domestic sphere. Working women were thus motivated to organize and voice demands arising from their new circumstances. As part of a repressed and persecuted people, Jewish working women were obliged to fight on two fronts, as feminists and as Jewish nationalists. They were becoming politi-

33 M. Volf, 'Khane Blankshteyn', *Folksvort*, 2 Aug. 1939. The author comments: 'Blankshteyn's death called forth especially profound sorrow in our movement, in which the deceased had recently become involved, even standing as a candidate in one of the first positions for the Bloc for workers of Erets Yisroel in the last city council elections in Vilna.'

34 Two bibliographies of Yiddish periodicals published in inter-war Poland provide information about *Di froy*. Yisroel Shayn's 'Materialn tsu a bibliografye fun yidisher periodike in Poyln, 1918–1939' appeared in J. A. Fishman (ed.), *Shtudyes vegn yidn in poyln* (New York, 1974). Shayn indicates that the magazine first appeared in 1925, but fails to note when it ceased publication or how many issues were published. In his *Preliminary Inventory of Yiddish Dailies and Periodicals Published in Poland Between the Two World Wars* (Jerusalem, 1986), the bibliographer Yechiel Szeintuch notes that the magazine was published from 1925 until 1933, but punctuates the latter date with two question marks. Other bibliographical sources, such as *Urzędowy wykaz druków* and *Urzędowy wykaz czasopism*, which were issued annually by the Polish Ministry of Education from 1929 until 1939, and supposedly include all the books and periodicals that appeared in Poland from 1928 onward, contain no mention of *Di froy*. Neither do the catalogues of the National and University Library in Jerusalem and the Biblioteka Narodowa in Warsaw.

cized, and had recently founded their own organization to represent their interests.[35] Now the time had come for Jewish women to have their own periodical as well.

Although attracted by the possibility of self-determination and opportunities to try their wings in a freer post-war society, Jewish women faced confusing, difficult dilemmas in the domestic sphere. How would their efforts to achieve economic and personal independence affect the lives of their husbands and children? Would their families not suffer as women took on more active roles in society? *Di froy* was intended to provide a forum where Jewish working women could take up these and other important questions.[36]

This statement of purpose positioned the magazine politically as much by what it neglected to mention as by what it actually discussed. No reference was made to either Zionism or socialism with regard to possible solutions to the problems Jewish women faced, although these were the leading political movements on the Jewish street in Poland at the time. Biographical sources suggest that when she founded *Di froy* in 1925, Blankshteyn was still active in the Folkspartei, whose political programme was based on the demand for cultural autonomy for Polish Jewry, with Yiddish as its official language, along with the right to full political participation in the democratic process of Polish society.[37] The Folkists advocated neither socialist revolution nor Zionism as solutions to the political dilemmas facing Polish Jews. Their programme, first issued in October 1917, called for the establishment of a fully democratic, secular state in Poland, where workers would have the right to unionize, women would have the right to vote, and the rights of all national minorities would be guaranteed. Within such a framework, they believed that 'a full and complete life' was attainable for Jews in the Diaspora.[38]

Emphasizing the demand for personal autonomy while affirming an individual's obligations to family and community, Blankshteyn's formulation of the aims of Jewish feminism was fully consonant with the programme of the Folkspartey. The Froyen-fareyn was scrupulously *umparteyish* in its self-presentation. In avoiding mention of party affiliations beyond Jewish feminist circles, Blankshteyn apparently sought to attract the most diverse possible readership for her magazine.

An article entitled 'Undzer lage' ('Our Situation'), whose purpose was to elucidate further the political stance of the magazine, also appeared in the first number. The author, Basye Lekerman, detailed the effects of the economic privations faced by both working-class and middle-class Jewish women as a result of the destruction and dislocations wrought by the First World War, pointing out the many recent suicides of impoverished women and the increasing numbers of Jewish prostitutes. She argued against the accusations, which she attributed to certain Jewish men, that

[35] Blankshteyn may have been referring to Vilna Froyen-fareyn, of which she was a member of the board of directors, or to the Froyen-farband, based in Warsaw.

[36] 'Undzer ufgabe' ('Our Task'), *Di froy*, no. 1 (8 Apr. 1925), 1–4.

[37] M. W. Kiel, 'The Ideology of the Folks-Partey', *Soviet Jewish Affairs*, 5/2 (1975), 75–89.

[38] Ibid. 81.

Jewish women, with their tendency towards extravagant spending and immodest sexual behaviour, their assimilationist attitudes and aversion to productive work, were to blame for many problems on the Jewish street. On the contrary, she contended:

Many Jewish women are active participants in the Jewish nationalist movement and in the creation of a modern Jewish culture, and in general, in the political, communal and social life of their people. It is also true that women are no longer afraid to work, and the desire to learn a trade and to be independent is very strong among Jewish women . . . If, however, it is hard for women of other ethnic groups, one can imagine how hard it is for the Jewish woman, as a daughter of a repressed and persecuted people . . . Therefore, the issue of the right to work is the most pressing for Jewish daughters now. In Poland there is no work: the Jewish working woman is pushed aside; the educated Jewish daughter can't get hired in government offices. The question of emigration is very timely for Jewish daughters. But where to? The little crack [in the wall] leading to the Land of Israel is also completely closed, as the number of certificates for Jewish girls is minuscule. All of this together leads to despair and the most terrible consequences.[39]

The article concluded with the author calling on women to take action:

One must not, however, sit with one's arms folded during such a period. Jewish women and girls must get organized and fight with united strength for their rights. The first item on the agenda is the right to work and to lead an independent life.[40]

FEMINIST FICTION IN *DI FROY*

Virtually all popular magazines and newspapers published in Yiddish during the twentieth century featured serialized novels. Very few of these were works of serious fiction. Most were formulaic romances that were primarily intended to entertain readers. *Di froy* followed this trend, but the subject matter of the novel it featured, entitled *Di fraye froy* ('The Free Woman'), turned the genre on its head. *Di fraye froy* is a novel about women's relationships with men, but its content is entirely different from that of other love stories, whose heroines may appear to be unconventional, but who wish, in their secret heart, to lead conventional lives. Most such novels conclude with the heroine's marriage to a partner of 'suitable' class and educational background. *Di fraye froy*, in contrast, is radically feminist in its outlook on women's choices.

Blankshteyn's decision to serialize this particular novel signified her intention to challenge the thinking of her east European Jewish readers about gender roles. Educated readers of the magazine would have realized this immediately, because the novel's author was notorious in post-war France as an iconoclast whose work advocated revolutionary ideas about women's roles in society.

[39] B. Lekerman, 'Undzer lage' ('Our Situation'), *Di froy*, no. 1 (8 Apr. 1925), 3–6.

[40] Ibid.

The author of *Di fraye froy* was the novelist Victor Margueritte (1867–1942).[41] Margueritte had made his reputation in the early twentieth century as a Naturalist author of social novels. His early works strongly criticized French attitudes towards marriage and the family. He was an active campaigner for a liberalized divorce law and for the rights of children born out of wedlock. Respected within the intellectual establishment, he was a prominent member of several prestigious French literary societies. During the course of the First World War he became an outspoken critic of the military and civilian leadership of France, coming to view the war as a symptom of a fundamentally flawed social structure.

In 1922 Margueritte's controversial novel *La Garçonne* became a runaway bestseller in France. The first of a trilogy entitled *La Femme en chemin*, the novel portrayed the revolt of its middle-class protagonist, Monique Lerbier, against the moral corruption of post-war society, and particularly against bourgeois gender relations. She rebels by imitating the dress and sexually promiscuous behaviour of middle-class men: she cuts her hair short, wears tailored clothing, uses drugs, and engages in a lesbian affair followed by a succession of liaisons with 'feminine' men whom she treats as sexual playthings. Even though Monique renounces her life as a gender outlaw to marry a war veteran at the end of the novel, *La Garçonne* scandalized French feminists and Catholic defenders of the traditional family alike. The archbishop of Paris denounced the novel as obscene and Margueritte was expelled from the Légion d'honneur. The notoriety of the book and its author sparked nationwide debates on gender roles in post-war society and on freedom of the press.[42]

The novel that Blankshteyn serialized in *Di froy* under the title *Di fraye froy* was the sequel to *La Garçonne*. It was first published in 1923 as *Le Compagnon*. It is not clear why the title was changed in the Yiddish translation. Perhaps Blankshteyn preferred a title that referred to the female protagonist and chose to adapt the French title of the trilogy for this purpose.[43]

Although lacking the sexual explicitness of its predecessor, *Di fraye froy* propounded corollary ideas about gender roles, but carried them further. While Monique Lerbier eventually retreats from her independent life as a *garçonne*, the protagonist of *Di fraye froy* puts her revolutionary ideas into lifelong practice.

[41] I am indebted to Nicholas Hewitt's article entitled 'Victor Margueritte and the Reception of *La Garçonne*: Naturalism, the Family and the *Ordre Moral*', *Nottingham French* Studies, 23/1 (May 1984), for biographical information on Victor Margueritte.

[42] The second chapter of Mary Louise Roberts's book *Civilization without Sexes: Reconstructing Gender in Postwar France, 1917–1927* (Chicago, 1994) contains an important analysis of the national debate sparked by *La Garçonne*.

[43] The instalments published in the four extant numbers of *Di froy* comprise a little more than half of the first chapter of the novel. A comparison with the original shows that Blankshteyn condensed the text slightly for publication in serial form. The entire trilogy was later translated into Yiddish by Puah Rakovsky. Rakovsky's translation of *Le Compagnon* appeared in 1927 under the Yiddish title *Der khaver*. *La Garçonne* appeared in 1928 under the title *Di bokherte*. The third novel in the trilogy, *Le Couple*, originally published in 1924, also appeared in 1928 as *Der nayer dor*. All three novels were published in Warsaw by Farlag Shloyme Goldfarb.

The novel opens as the 24-year-old heroine, Annik Raimbert, a lawyer by profession, described by the narrator as a *yunge kemferin* (young fighter), is having a bath in her tiny apartment in Paris, when her adoptive mother, Cécile Hardy, pays her a surprise visit. Cécile, a teacher in a provincial town, took the academically gifted Annik in when she was orphaned at the age of 13, and raised her to take pride in her physical being. Annik's elder sister Paule, who lived in a convent after their mother's death, lacks Annik's healthy attitudes:

> [Annik was] spiritually and physically healthy. Her body was lithe from the daily gymnastic exercises she did, and she was never embarrassed to be naked because she felt herself to be beautiful. When [Annik] was a girl in Yvelines, Miss Hardy got her used to cleanliness—the basis of self-worth—and raised her with full consciousness of all the natural functions of the human body. Her sister lived in the nearby convent during the same three-year period. There the boarders, who were forced into hypocrisy—the source of all sins—fantasized about 'forbidden things', while Annik developed in complete innocence, like an uninhibited flower.[44]

Annik has two suitors, Pierre Lebeau, the editor of an important Paris newspaper, a married man whom she distrusts but to whom she is strongly attracted, and Amédée Jacquemin, a socialist government deputy, whom she regards as a good friend but to whom she feels less physically drawn. She has grave doubts about the institution of marriage, having known many unhappy married couples:

> She had, in principle, decided that she would never give up the freedom and rights that an unmarried woman and mother had under the law. Except for political rights, which she hoped, sooner or later, to acquire, this freedom made her almost equal to men. By remaining single, she would have complete freedom to do as she wished, for herself and for her children.[45]

Paule, on the other hand, wants nothing more than to marry. Uneducated and underemployed, she works as a model in a clothing store and dreams of the 'golden chain that will assure her of a happy life'.[46]

Cécile Hardy is critical of Paule's attitudes and fiercely proud of Annik's. The fourth instalment of the novel concludes with her thoughts:

> In Annik, she recognized herself as she had been in her youth, when she first began to propagandize her belief that the world would remake itself with the emancipation of women. How much evil would be avoided when women stopped acquiescing to men's egoism and freed themselves from the disgraceful attitudes that they had been brought up to hold! If only everyone would want to unite, after the terrors they had experienced, in battle against the injustices and wrongs that bring unhappiness to humankind, against war more than anything—the source of all crimes![47]

[44] V. Margerit, 'Di fraye froy', *Di froy*, no. 1 (8 Apr. 1925), 10.

[45] 'Di fraye froy', *Di froy*, no. 2 (8 May 1925), 30.

[46] 'Di fraye froy', *Di froy*, no. 4 (28 May 1925), 62.

[47] Ibid.

Annik eventually enters into a long-term relationship with the socialist leader Amédée Jacquemin, and bears a child by him. Yet she refuses to marry her *compagnon*, and gives their child her own family name. In *Le Couple*, the third novel of the trilogy, which is set sixteen years in the future, Annik dies heroically in a pacifist–feminist-led effort to stop trains from carrying soldiers to fight a second world war.

With the serialization of a novel that preached women's economic, legal, and emotional independence from men as a means of correcting the ills of society, Blankshteyn further confirmed that the primary ideological position of her magazine was feminist.

FEATURE SECTIONS IN *DI FROY*

In addition to its articles with explicitly political content, *Di froy* offered a variety of feature sections, such as fashion, beauty, and hygiene, poetry by women, letters from readers, news about women's issues from around the world, and reviews of art exhibitions, concerts, and sporting events. Even the feature articles addressed their topics from a political perspective. For instance, Madame Li-Li, the pseudonymous author of the style section, reminded her audience that in addition to the influence of French designers on women's taste in clothing styles, commercial interests required that styles change every year, so that women would feel that the previous year's fashions were no longer becoming.[48] In a later article she reassured readers that even if they could not afford new dresses and suits every year, they could still give an impression of elegance, as long as their accessories were clean, neat, and matched their outfits.[49] In one article Madame Li-Li commented light-heartedly that the narrow-cut, knee-length, unbelted dress styles that continued to hold sway in Paris were highly becoming to slender women, but 'who gives a thought for the *shlimazlnitses* [unlucky women] who remain stout?'[50]

Articles on health and beauty addressed the most basic aspects of these topics, urging readers to bathe their faces and bodies frequently, to limit their use of cosmetics, to use massage to relieve stress and fatigue from physical labour, to rest their eyes frequently, and to expose their entire bodies to fresh air for at least five to ten minutes per day. The apparently pseudonymous authors of these articles, Dr B. and Dr Frume L.-G., emphasized that even working women who lacked bathtubs in their homes should take time daily to attend to their personal health and cleanliness.[51]

The first number of the magazine was twelve pages long, while each of the succeeding three was eight pages in length. The final page of each number was devoted

[48] 'Di mode', *Di froy*, no. 1 (8 Apr. 1925), 14–17.

[49] 'Di mode', *Di froy*, no. 2 (1 May 1925), 35–6.

[50] 'Di mode', *Di froy*, no. 1 (8 Apr. 1925), 14.

[51] 'Der sod fun sheynkeyt', *Di froy*, no. 1 (8 Apr. 1925), 11–13, and no. 2 (1 May 1925), 36–7; 'Higenye un sheynkeyt', *Di froy*, no. 3 (8 May 1925), 50, and no. 4 (28 May 1925), 66.

almost entirely to advertisements for goods and services. Most of these came from purveyors of dresses, corsets, hats, and cosmetics. Several private schools also placed advertisements, as did a number of magazines and newspapers.

BLANKSHTEYN'S FICTION

In addition to her work for *Di froy*, Blankshteyn worked as a freelance journalist, publishing pieces in several Yiddish and Polish periodicals, including the Vilna dailies *Tsayt* ('Time') and *Undzer tog* ('Our Day'), the Warsaw weekly *Velt-shpigl* ('World Mirror'), and the Polish Jewish feminist magazine *Ewa*. She also wrote short stories and sketches, some of which appeared in *Velt-shpigl* under the rubric 'Mir froyen' ('We Women').

A collection of Blankshteyn's short fiction was published several weeks before her death in July 1939. The volume, entitled *Noveles* ('Stories'), contains nine stories. All are set in the revolutionary period in Russia and in inter-war Europe; Jewish characters play leading roles in most of them. Although male protagonists are foregrounded in some of the stories, Blankshteyn was especially interested in portraying the experience of women who try to break free of traditional gender roles.

One of the most effective stories in the collection is entitled 'Shrek' ('Terror'), which depicts the anarchic, uncertain atmosphere of the revolutionary period through a narrative about an individual whose life is unexpectedly and arbitrarily endangered. A businessman travelling on an overnight train journey steps off the train to get a cup of tea at a brief station stop. To his dismay, the train begins to pull out of the station before he can reboard, and he is forced to run along the platform, jump onto the steps of a passing railway coach and grab the door handle. But the door is locked and the people inside refuse to open up for him. He soon grows weak from exertion and fright and is about to lose his grip on the handle when the door finally opens.

The unlucky passenger has inadvertently chosen a car full of political detainees who are being transported, under guard, to prison. Fearing that the shouting, desperate man was trying to initiate a prison break, the soldiers in charge had refused to open the door to him, until they finally realized that he was only a hapless passenger who had been left behind on the platform.

Blankshteyn's prose is spare and fast-paced. She succeeds here in evoking the terror of the nameless character, who represents the orderly, bourgeois society now profoundly threatened by revolutionary chaos.

While little is known about Blankshteyn's activities in Kiev from 1917 until her return to Vilna in 1922, several of the short stories in *Noveles* suggest that she was active in the revolution or was, at least, able to observe the newly developing revolutionary culture at close range. 'Der dekret' ('The Decree') is one of these. Set in a large city a year or two after the October Revolution, the story opens in a ruined villa that once belonged to a member of the nobility and is now used as a mess hall for members of the Communist Party. The young lawyer and party leader Shtoltsman, highly respected by his comrades for his 'sharply honed political line' has fallen in love with Leye, the granddaughter of a hasidic *rebbe* from a provincial shtetl, who came to work in the big city to escape the dangerous situation in her region, where counter-revolutionary bands were roaming the countryside. While Shtoltsman believes that the institution of marriage will soon be abolished, he proposes to Leye in order to lay claim to her as a life partner. The situation grows ideologically complicated for Shtoltsman when Leye insists that she will only agree to marry him on the condition that they have a Jewish wedding, as she has promised her grandfather. He tries to persuade her to make do with civil registration of the marriage, but she holds firm to her demand.

'You're silent, Leye? Don't you know that I can't do differently?' he said, making an impatient gesture. 'Don't be a child, Leye. Don't you understand that my convictions won't allow me to go to the rabbi with you? You know this very well. You're playing with me. You're an empty-headed girl. You don't love me.'

'If I didn't love you, I wouldn't kiss you.' She straightened up. The languid yearning had disappeared from her eyes.[52]

Leye proceeds to ignore Shtoltsman for the next few days. He suffers from sleeplessness and headaches until he realizes that the only way to win her is by compromising his revolutionary principles and marrying her under a *khupe* ('bridal canopy').

The concluding section of the story is observed from the point of view of the rabbi in a provincial town not far from Leye's shtetl. The couple have arrived there by sleigh in the middle of a wintry night, whereupon Shtoltsman demands that the rabbi perform an impromptu marriage ceremony for them. Recognizing Shtoltsman from a newspaper photo as the party leader who has recently announced the abolition of religious marriage ceremonies, the rabbi savours the irony of such a man marrying into the family of a hasidic *rebbe*. He understands Shtoltsman's capitulation to Leye as a triumph of love over ideology, and takes pleasure in that understanding.

The story is not only interesting in terms of its content, but also successful as a literary work. Blankshteyn writes convincingly of the fears, suspicions, and pretences of the various characters, who are called upon to assume unfamiliar roles and modes of behaviour during the early stages of revolution. Everyone seems to take false steps except for Leye, who knows exactly what she wants and goes after it with quiet resolve and inner fortitude. When, for instance, the terrified rabbi seems about to refuse to perform the marriage ceremony in the middle of the night at bayonet point, Leye speaks up to reassure him of the unspoken purpose of the impromptu wedding: 'A melodious girlish voice interrupted [the tension]: "Comrade Rabbi, we're going to see my grandfather in Gostinyets." The elderly doctor of philosophy

[52] K. Blankshteyn, 'Der dekret', in her *Noveles* (Vilna, 1939), 125.

straightened his stooped shoulders, smiled to himself and thought: "This is some *shidekh* [marriage arrangement] for the hasidic court of Gostinyets!" '[53]

Though perhaps less impressive as a work of literature than the two stories described above, 'Di ershte hant: Geshikhte fun a por yidishe farvoglte neshomes' ('The Head Artisan: The Story of a Pair of Homeless Jewish Souls') cogently expresses Blankshteyn's feminist cultural politics. First published in *Velt-shpigl* in 1928,[54] it chronicles the development of a young working-class Parisienne, Andrée, in 1920s Paris. Its theme is similar to that of 'Di fraye froy', published in 1925 in Blankshteyn's magazine: given the opportunity to work and develop her unique talents and her sense of personal autonomy, a young woman will figure out how to chart her own course professionally and eventually make a satisfying, companionate marriage. Blankshteyn adds a Jewish twist to this story, though. Andrée is the illegitimate daughter of a French Catholic mother and a Jewish artist from eastern Europe whom she never knew, but whose painting of a group of men at prayer in a shtetl study house intrigued Andrée as a small child. Orphaned, she grows up in a children's home and dreams of visiting her father's birthplace one day. In her mid-teens she gets a job with a clothing design firm and works her way up to the position of head artisan, thereby becoming economically self-sufficient, self-confident, and emotionally self-reliant. Powerfully drawn to the fine arts, she spends her free time studying and copying paintings in the Louvre. There she eventually meets Miguelo, a Spaniard employed as an engineer in the developing automobile industry. They fall in love and conduct a chaste courtship, maintaining separate apartments. When Miguelo returns to Spain to visit his parents, Andrée fears that they will pressure him to abandon his relationship with her. He surprises her by returning with a marriage proposal and a confession that his parents are descendants of the Marranos and have raised him as a Jew. In spite of their objections, he had insisted on marrying Andrée, and they reluctantly gave their consent. During the marriage ceremony Andrée reveals that her father was Jewish, which pleases her new parents-in-law, who welcome her into their family. Andrée and Miguelo are each delighted to have found, through a chance encounter, 'a second homeless soul'.

Its happy ending notwithstanding, 'Di ershte hant' is more than a piece of lightweight entertainment fiction culminating in a mutual recognition scene with *basherte* ('preordained') lovers. It also has ideological content, namely that Andrée's love for Miguelo is made possible because she leads a self-sufficient life. She understands this very well, and is committed to continuing along the same path. This is seen clearly at the end of the story, which concludes on the morning after the wedding, as Andrée prepares to go off to work.

The first delicate rays of the sun were barely visible through the window when Andrée quietly rose, dressed and began to clean the apartment. After she had finished and put away

[53] Ibid. 133.

[54] K. Blankshteyn, 'Di ershte hant', *Velt-shpigl*, no. 40 (4 Oct. 1928), no. 41 (11 Oct. 1928).

the cleaning implements, she watered the flowers in the vase that stood on the table. Then she had something to eat, prepared breakfast for Miguelo and got ready to leave the house. Miguelo woke up and caught up with her at the door.

'You're leaving so early today?'

'I have to fit a couple of dresses for a loyal customer. She's leaving town tomorrow.'

He embraced her and didn't want to let her go. Laughing, she freed herself from his arms. Her peals of laughter sounded like silver bells as she said to him: 'Be well, my husband, be well!' and quickly ran down the stairs.

In 'Di ershte hant' Blankshteyn attempted to enact an ideological principle in prose form; namely, that when a young woman finds meaningful work that affords her the opportunity to develop her talents and to become financially self-reliant, she will eventually be capable of both becoming professionally productive and creating a healthy relationship with a marital partner. As she had done in publishing Victor Margueritte's *Di fraye froy* three years earlier, Blankshteyn made use of that familiar entertainment medium, the magazine serial, to introduce a critique of gender roles to female readers of the popular weekly *Velt-shpigl*.

Because of the close proximity between the publication of *Noveles*, Blankshteyn's death, and the Nazi invasion of Poland, there was little opportunity for critical response to the collection. In his rather meagre introduction to the volume Maks Vaynraykh remarked that Blankshteyn published her work irregularly and was not a professional writer, allowing that 'the understanding of life that reveals itself in writing [such as this] can sometimes be greater and more multifaceted than that of people who observe life for the express purpose of writing about it [professionally]'.[55]

An unsigned review of the book appeared in *Undzer tog* on 14 July 1939. Calling it a modest collection of interesting, easy-to-read stories, the reviewer observed that there was 'an intimate tone' in the stories, 'as though you were sitting around with friends of a quiet evening and, while the samovar seethes, listening to stories that have taken place in real life'.[56] Further damning the collection with faint praise, the reviewer continued: 'Khane Blankshteyn has stories to tell and knows how to make them exciting. And even if many of her artistic methods and her way of structuring her stories are not new, the stories possess an intimate charm and an individuality which merits recognition.'[57]

Although it appeared in *Undzer tog*, a paper that had published Blankshteyn's journalism over the years, and where she probably had good friends on the editorial board, the review patronizes Blankshteyn by insinuating that her stories are valuable more as mementoes of the author's life than as works of literature. Apparently, it did not occur to the reviewer that Blankshteyn had written several of the stories as entertainment fiction in order to reach readers of women's magazines with her feminist message, while other pieces were more ambitious as literary works.

[55] M. Vaynraykh, 'Araynfir', in Blankshteyn, *Noveles*.

[56] 'Intime noveles', *Undzer tog*, 14 July 1939, 5.

[57] Ibid.

The contemporary reader can find much of interest in Blankshteyn's stories. Some, such as 'Di ershte hant', were apparently written with propagandistic aims in mind, while others, such as 'Shrek' and 'Der dekret', are keenly observed portraits of individuals as they experience cataclysmic changes in the social order of Jewish eastern Europe in the inter-war period.

CONCLUSION

Blankshteyn died of cancer on 30 July 1939. In spite of the fact that the city of Vilna was at that moment braced for an attack by Germany, the Vilna *kehile* organized an elaborate funeral and provided a burial plot in a section reserved for highly respected members of the community in the Vilna Jewish cemetery.[58] The funeral began at the office of Froyen-shuts at Strashun 6, where a *hazkore* ('memorial service for the dead') was sung and eulogies were given. The funeral procession traversed several streets in the Jewish quarter and stopped in front of the premises of the Froyen-fareyn in Breyter gas.[59] According to the account in *Tsayt*, 'masses' of people attended.[60] Distinguished community figures gave eulogies at the graveside and delegations from all of the organizations in which Blankshteyn had been active participated.

Blankshteyn's role in inter-war Jewish Vilna was an unusual one, in that she sought to integrate feminism and Jewish nationalism in her social activism and belletristic work. In a eulogy published in the newspaper *Tsayt* on the day of her death, Blankshteyn's friend and colleague from the Froyen-fareyn and Froyen-shuts, Sore Zaydshnur, wrote that

> in the final years of her life, [the highly educated, formerly assimilated] Blankshteyn grew close to the Jewish masses in general and to the masses of Jewish women in particular . . . She developed a deep understanding of their psychology, which had previously been entirely alien to her . . . and with sadness united her easygoing nature with Yiddish culture and language.[61]

In another eulogy published in the same issue of the paper, the Vilna communal leader Dr Avrom Virshubski wrote that Blankshteyn's intellectual gifts and dedication to social activism combined to make her a 'yekhide bedoyre' ('a unique figure in her generation').[62]

58 *Tsayt*, 31 July 1939, 4, and *Undzer tog*, 31 July 1939, 4. Blankshteyn was buried in the first section of the Zaretshe Cemetery near the grave of A. Vayter, a beloved Bundist leader who was murdered in Vilna in 1919 by Polish legionnaires.

59 Details of the funeral are found in the following newspaper accounts: 'Di levaye fun khane blankshteyn', *Undzer tog*, 31 July 1939, 4, and 'Levaye fun khane blankshteyn', *Tsayt*, 31 July 1939, 4.

60 *Tsayt*, 31 July 1939, 4.

61 'Geshtorbn khane blankshteyn', *Tsayt*, 30 July 1939, 3.

62 Ibid.

Feminism and Nationalism on the Pages of *Ewa: Tygodnik*, 1928–1933

EVA PLACH

In an article written in January 1932 Paulina Appenszlakowa (d. 1976), the editor of the Warsaw-based Polish-language Jewish women's weekly newspaper *Ewa: Tygodnik* ('Eva: A Weekly') (1928–33), described the budget discussions that had taken place earlier in the month in the Warsaw *kehilah*, the self-governing organization of the local Jewish community. The *kehilah* had just passed a motion to build a 'new, luxuriously appointed *mikveh*', the ritual bathhouse for women. 'One among this crowd of reactionaries', as Appenszlakowa referred to the motion's supporters in the *kehilah*, 'declared publicly that a *mikveh* would contribute to higher fertility.'[1] Appenszlakowa was stunned by this apparent misdirection of funds as well as by the absurdity of trying to increase the birth rate during a period of widespread depression and pauperization. The problem was both the persistence in the *kehilah* of what Appenszlakowa described as backward-looking Orthodox views on society, as well as the fact that there were no progressive, modern women—or any women—present in the *kehilah* to speak on behalf of women's concerns; women did not have suffrage rights in the *kehilot* of Poland's Second Republic (1918–39).[2]

In the column next to Paulina's, Jakub Appenszlak (1894–1950), Paulina's husband, expressed similar indignation at the situation in the *kehilah*, and wondered, as Appenszlakowa had in her piece, why the budget had elicited so little reaction from Jewish women. From Appenszlak's point of view, the explanation ironically lay in the fact that Jewish women of the bourgeoisie and the intelligentsia—who formed the milieu from which *Ewa*'s readership was drawn—were 'unusually progressive'.

Support for this research was generously provided by the Social Sciences and Humanities Research Council of Canada, the Jewish Community Foundation of Montreal (Frances and Isaac Zlotowski and Krisha Zlotowska Starker Award), and the Hadassah–Brandeis Institute. The phrase 'Boy in a dress' comes from F. Stendigowa, 'Zadania i cele prasy kobiecej', *Ewa*, 4 (24 Jan. 1932), 2.

[1] Editor, 'Wymowne milczenie', *Ewa*, 5 (31 Jan. 1932), 1. Articles signed by the editor and unsigned articles are assumed to have been written by Paulina Appenszlakowa, *Ewa*'s editor from 1928 to 1933.

[2] Ibid. On the *kehilah* institution, see J. Tomaszewski, *Zarys dziejów Żydów w Polsce w latach 1918–1939* (Warsaw, 1990), 37–41.

Many had read the works of the most fashionable social–sexual reformers of the day—such as Magnus Hirschfeld (a 'sexologist' who ran the Institute for Sexual Science in Germany), Ben Lindsey (a proponent of 'companionate marriage'), and Tadeusz (Boy) Żeleński (Poland's leading advocate of birth control and abortion rights)—and were ready to fight for the causes these men advocated. The trouble was, according to Appenszlak, that Jewish women were *au courant* with what was going on in European capitals, but they had little idea about their own local Jewish communities.

Appenszlak suggested that perhaps the time had come for Jewish women to become better informed about local politics and to stop devoting a disproportionate amount of attention to those 'marginally radical' topics that, in his opinion, they evidently favoured.[3] Appenszlak acknowledged that his views might earn him the titles of 'boor, idiot, reactionary, hooligan' from *Ewa*'s readers. He nevertheless stayed his course and concluded his article with a characteristically witty summary emphasizing the distance that separated the modern progressive feminist politics of *Ewa*, on the one hand, and, on the other, the unfortunate reality of 'our Jewish medieval times' in which women were denied even the right to participate fully in the Jewish communal government. *Ewa* was rather ahead of its time: 'Yes, Mesdames. You still live in the year 1332! How long you have to go before you reach Lindsey! Birth control—that is an illusion—the naked truth is in the *mikveh*!'[4]

With these two lead articles appearing in 1932, *Ewa* reminded readers—as it had been doing since its inception four years earlier—that the *kehilah* would function as a real representative of the Jewish nation only when women achieved suffrage rights in the *kehilah* elections.[5] In the February 1928 founding statement of *Ewa*, the battle for women's suffrage in Poland's *kehilot* appeared as a key objective of the emerging modern Jewish feminist movement, at the forefront of which, the statement proclaimed, *Ewa* would stand.[6] But these two articles reveal a great deal more about the newspaper's goals, profile, and reputation. As Appenszlak had suggested, *Ewa*'s editorial position was indeed 'unusually progressive'. Appearing on the pages of *Ewa* from 1928 to 1933 were amazingly frank articles about birth control and abortion, marriage, divorce, adultery, the keys to a happy marriage, prostitution, and the sexual double standard, in addition to pieces about Jewish women's philanthropic activity, women's legal rights, women and work, and fashion. *Ewa*'s willingness 'to bring out into the light of day those topics which in the past were only whispered about', as Appenszlakowa described it, reflected the specific elite milieu out of which

[3] Pierrot, 'Czy panie wiedzą?', *Ewa*, 5 (31 Jan. 1932), 1. 'Pierrot' was Jakub Appenszlak's pseudonym. See M. Fuks, *Prasa żydowska w Warszawie, 1823–1939* (Warsaw, 1979), 269.

[4] Pierrot, 'Czy panie wiedzą?', 1.

[5] On women's suffrage in the *kehilah*, see P. Appenszlakowa, 'Gmina bez kobiet', *Ewa*, 2 (26 Feb. 1928), 1; R. Klingberg, 'Księgi święte po naszej stronie', *Ewa*, 22 (15 July 1928), 2; and I. Krantz, 'Przed wyborami do gminy', *Ewa*, 15 (19 Apr. 1931), 1.

[6] 'Ogól inteligentnych kobiet żydowskich zdobył własną trybunę prasową', *Nasz Przegląd*, 9 Feb. 1928, 3.

the publication emerged.[7] *Ewa* was a newspaper directed at the secular, acculturated, and cosmopolitan Polish-speaking Jewish woman, and its goal was to serve as the conduit through which women of the bourgeoisie and the intelligentsia would develop a decidedly modern and progressive feminist consciousness. As Appenszlakowa proclaimed, *Ewa* existed to 'awaken' Poland's Jewish women from their lethargy and to propel them into informed activism on behalf of their national community: 'We have set swinging in Poland the bell of the Jewish women's movement.'[8]

Inseparable from *Ewa*'s feminism was its Zionism. Zionism was but one of many nationalist identities that Jews embraced during the Second Republic, and even within Zionism there existed numerous competing perspectives and parties. *Ewa* was not associated with any specific Zionist party. Its publishers were, however, committed to carving out a meaningful place for women in the Zionist fold and to creating a new nationally committed Jewish woman citizen: she would be politically and socially equal to the new Jewish man, and together they would work to subvert what they regarded as the traditional and backward aspects of Jewish culture in favour of the dynamic Zionist future.[9] What *Ewa* showed was that Zionist ideology in inter-war Poland was sophisticated enough to accommodate debates about the status of women and, in turn, that a progressive and modern Jewish feminism was nationally committed enough to support a grand-scale national rebirth that harnessed women's full potential to work for the collectively imagined ideal. The publishers of *Ewa* understood themselves as forming an integral part of a developing Jewish nationalism as well as of a progressive Jewish feminism; from *Ewa*'s perspective, nationalism and feminism were each absolutely necessary to effect a wholesale 'rebirth of the Jews'.[10] By stimulating the foundations of good citizenship, good nationalism, and good feminism, and by creating a forum in which Polish-speaking Jewish women from across the country could make connections with one another, *Ewa* hoped that it would also inspire a Jewish nationalist revival. *Ewa: Tygodnik* offered a promising start. As Appenszlakowa announced in the first issue, the historical Eve, after all, was the 'mother of life'.[11]

This chapter will begin with an analysis of *Ewa*'s attempt to fashion itself as a feminist and secular Zionist paper during a period marked both by great socio-economic challenges and by exciting cultural and nationalist growth. As the first extended discussion of the publication *Ewa*, this chapter introduces an effort that was bold and expectant, however short-lived it ultimately proved to be.[12] Though in the

[7] P. Appenszlakowa, '10 lat kobiety', *Nasz Przegląd*, 18 June 1933, 19. *Ewa* was no longer publishing in June 1933.

[8] 'Refleksje noworoczne', *Ewa*, 52/1 (1 Jan. 1930), 1.

[9] These general ideas about Zionism are influenced by D. Biale, *Eros and the Jews: From Biblical Israel to Contemporary America* (New York, 1982), ch. 8.

[10] The term appears in S. Lewite, 'Bez ideału', *Ewa*, 5 (18 Mar. 1928), 1.

[11] P. Appenszlakowa, 'Kwestja zjednoczenia kobiet żydowskich', *Ewa*, 1 (19 Feb. 1928), 1.

[12] On *Ewa*, see Fuks, *Prasa żydowska w Warszawie*, 282–5; M. Fuks, '*Ewa*', in Z. Borzymińska and R. Żebrowski (eds.), *Polski słownik judaistyczny: Dzieje, kultura, religia, ludzie*, i (Warsaw, 2003), 407; and M. C. Steinlauf, 'The Polish-Jewish Daily Press', *Polin*, 2 (1987), 232.

last decade Polish historiography has started to develop women's history topics, these have remained almost exclusively concerned with the ethnic Polish community. Within Jewish historiography, attention has been paid primarily to Yiddish-speaking and to socialist–feminist nationalism. Little has been said about feminist–nationalist politicization within a Polish-speaking middle- and upper-class milieu.[13]

The second part of the chapter focuses on the ways in which *Ewa*'s publishers approached one of the 'marginally radical' subjects which, as Appenszlak had observed, were often found on its pages: reproductive politics. From *Ewa*'s perspective, birth control and abortion were anything but marginal. Indeed, the discussions that formed around these issues constituted one of the most compelling public debates of the entire inter-war period. The timing of the debates was no coincidence: in the late 1920s and into the early 1930s the Polish Codification Commission, established right after independence to write co-ordinated laws for the new state, began submitting proposals on a number of delicate questions, including whether to keep abortion in the Criminal Code. *Ewa*, as the self-proclaimed voice of modern Jewish feminism, would not be left out of these discussions. *Ewa*'s associates believed that, by providing the impetus for a debate within Jewish circles about abortion, family planning, and modern sexual morality more generally, it was helping to create the engaged Jewish woman citizen who was vital to the flourishing of the Zionist conception of the future. The reproductive issue fitted perfectly into the newspaper's general aim of fashioning a new Zionist woman, of subverting what it regarded as outmoded foundations of social, sexual, and moral organization, and of articulating bold links between so-called private affairs and public needs.

UNDER THE BANNER OF NATIONAL JEWISH FEMINISM

On 19 February 1928 *Ewa* appeared as the first and only Polish-language Jewish women's weekly in the Second Republic. From then until 1932 it was published each Thursday in a format that ranged from six to ten pages. In June 1932 the paper became a bi-weekly, and so it remained until its 242nd and final issue—which came with no warning or explanation—on 12 March 1933.[14] Throughout its existence

[13] For an overview of the latest work in Polish women's history during this period, see A. Żarnowska and A. Szwarc (eds.), *Równe prawa i nierówne szanse: Kobiety w Polsce mi ędzywojennej* (Warsaw, 2000). On Jewish women in inter-war Poland, see A. Cała, 'Kobiety wobec tradycyjnych norm życia rodzinnego w społecznościach żydowskich w Polsce międzywojennej', in A. Żarnowska and A. Szwarc (eds.), *Kobieta i kultura życia codziennego* (Warsaw, 1997); P. Rakovsky, *My Life as a Radical Jewish Woman: Memoirs of a Zionist Feminist in Poland*, ed. P. E. Hyman, trans. B. Harshav with P. E. Hyman (Bloomington, Ind., 2002); and D. Blatman, 'National-Minority Policy, Bundist Social Organizations, and Jewish Women in Inter-War Poland', in Z. Gitelman (ed.), *The Emergence of Modern Jewish Politics: Bundism and Zionism in Eastern Europe* (Pittsburgh, 2003).

[14] A note pinned to p. 242 of the 12 Mar. 1933 (no. 6) issue of *Ewa* found in Poland's National Library confirms this. The date is further confirmed in K. Zawadzki, *Bibliografia czasopism warszawskich 1579–1981*, ii (Warsaw, 1996), 27.

Ewa was edited exclusively by Paulina Appenszlakowa, who, along with Iza Wagmanowa, published the paper.[15] Women predominated as contributors to *Ewa*, though articles written by men also appeared regularly.[16] Contributors were professional journalists and authors for the most part, but given its commitment to stimulating Jewish women's participation in the debates that shaped their lives, the paper often published readers' submissions, too. *Ewa* was rhetorically directed at 'all' Polish-speaking Jewish women and claimed a readership that came from across Poland, as well as from other parts of Europe and even from America and Palestine.[17] Despite this claim, however, the paper likely only reached a narrow elite of women who formed part of Poland's numerically small Jewish middle and upper class and intelligentsia.[18]

Regularly throughout *Ewa*'s five-year existence, Poland's largest and most important Polish-language Jewish daily, *Nasz Przegląd* (1923–39) ran advertisements that enticed readers to pick up an issue of *Ewa*, which, the daily said, 'contains interesting topical reading for every intelligent woman'.[19] The two papers shared a general Zionist orientation and had readers and associates in common. Most notably, Jakub Appenszlak was one of the principal editors of *Nasz Przegląd*, and while writing regularly for that premier Warsaw daily, he also occasionally contributed articles to *Ewa*.[20] The journalist and historian Samuel Hirszhorn also wrote for both papers, while the likes of Majer Bałaban and Bernard Singer, along with Appenszlakowa's second husband, Zygmunt Fogiel,[21] were listed as associates

[15] *Ewa*'s publishing offices were located first on Rymarska Street and, by 1930, at 13 Nowolipki, in the midst of Warsaw's Yiddish-speaking Jewish district. (*Nasz Przegląd* was published at 7 Nowolipki.) See Fuks, *Prasa żydowska w Warszawie*, 263.

[16] Among the most frequent female contributors to *Ewa* were Dr Julia Blay, Róża Gryncendlerowa, Dr Marta Hoffman, Judyta Horn, Mira Jakubowiczowa, Rachela Klingberg, Celina Meersohn-Beckerowa, Róża Melcerowa, and Thea Weinberg.

[17] 'Po roku', *Ewa*, 46 (30 Dec. 1928), 1.

[18] A 21 Sept. 1930 issue of *Ewa* located in Poland's National Library bears the number 2,000 on the cover; this likely referred to the number of copies printed. Determining circulation figures for the inter-war Jewish press is generally difficult and is all the more so for a seldom mentioned women's newspaper. On circulation statistics generally, see Steinlauf, 'The Polish-Jewish Daily Press', 224–7. Andrzej Paczkowski estimates that Jewish intellectuals and large entrepreneurs, together with their families, numbered around 400,000 to 500,000 people during the inter-war period. See A. Paczkowski, 'The Jewish Press in the Political Life of the Second Republic', *Polin*, 8 (1994), 178.

[19] The quotation comes from an advertisement in the 26 Aug. 1932 issue of *Nasz Przegląd*. Other such advertisements are found, for example, in the following issues: 16 May 1929, 8 Aug. 1930, 22 Oct. 1931, and 10 Mar. 1933. For *Nasz Przegląd*, see [M.LAN.], '*Nasz Przegląd*', in *Encyclopedia Judaica* (Jerusalem, 1971), xii. 843; Steinlauf, 'The Polish-Jewish Daily Press', *passim*; and Fuks, *Prasa żydowska w Warszawie*, 259–82.

[20] On Appenszlak, see A. Hertz, *Żydzi w kulturza polskiej* (1961), trans. R. Lourie as *The Jews in Polish Culture* (Evanston, Ill., 1988), 125, 154, and R. Żebrowski, 'Jakub Appenszlak', in Borzymińska and Żebrowski (eds.), *Polski słownik judaistyczny*, i. 96–7.

[21] Appenszlakowa married Zygmunt Fogiel in Israel. Both Jakub and Paulina had left for New York before the outbreak of war in 1939, but Paulina returned to Poland shortly thereafter and then, during the war, escaped to Palestine, where she remained. See J. Solarz, 'Paulina Appenszlakowa', in Borzymińska and Żebrowski (eds.), *Polski słownik judaistyczny*, 97.

of each paper.[22] Appenszlakowa herself occasionally contributed to *Nasz Przegląd* (on whose editorial board she sat), even while she edited *Ewa*.[23] *Ewa* is best understood as having been a 'sister publication' of *Nasz Przegląd* (to use the daily's own description of the relationship),[24] rather than as a formal supplement to it in the way that, for example, Janusz Korczak's *Mały Przegląd* was. For their part, *Ewa*'s publishers were proud of the fact that their newspaper had been founded without party affiliations and without private capital, and of the fact that it was maintained by subscriptions, advertising, and readers' 'moral support' alone.[25]

Perhaps the clearest indication of *Ewa*'s general identity and target audience is that this self-styled nationalist paper published not in Yiddish or Hebrew, but in Polish. Though many Zionists promoted the use of Hebrew as the Jewish national language, only a small percentage of the 3 million Jews in the Second Republic actually knew Hebrew, and as a result it was not uncommon for the inter-war Zionist press to publish in both Yiddish and Polish. Linguistic Polonization among Jews in the Second Republic was widespread, even for the vast majority who used Yiddish as an everyday language, and so it happened that Polish proved to be one of the more effective means of delivering a 'Jewish paper'.[26] The popularity of Polish-language Jewish dailies (*Nasz Przegląd*'s print run was about 40,000 copies) attests to this.[27] In general, Polish-language papers, including *Nasz Przegląd* and *Ewa*, were directed at a readership that was part of the acculturated middle and professional classes, but that, in an era of growing nationalism, looked increasingly for some acknowledgement of and engagement with their national identity in their daily and weekly newspapers.[28]

As a Zionist women's paper, one of *Ewa*'s goals was to prepare women for a future in the Jewish homeland.[29] The second page of many issues of *Ewa* was devoted to Palestine, and *Ewa*'s publishers regularly included articles on the work of the

[22] A full list of associates is found in 'Ogół inteligentnych kobiet żydowskich', 3. Not all of the listed associates actually contributed articles to *Ewa*.

[23] Fuks, *Prasa żydowska w Warszawie*, 270. *Nasz Przegląd* fashion articles were written by 'Paulinette'. One can speculate that this was Paulina's pseudonym.

[24] See Lektor, 'Jak skończyć z piekłem kobiet', *Nasz Przegląd*, 20 Dec. 1931, 11.

[25] 'Po roku', 1.

[26] In the 1931 census 80 per cent of Jews claimed Yiddish as their mother tongue, 12 per cent claimed Polish, and 8 per cent claimed Hebrew. On the meaning and reliability of this census, see C. Shmeruk, 'Hebrew–Yiddish–Polish: A Trilingual Jewish Culture', in Y. Gutman, E. Mendelsohn, J. Reinharz, and C. Shmeruk (eds.), *The Jews of Poland Between Two World Wars* (Hanover, NH, 1989), 28–9, 300–5. The Yiddish press in the Second Republic reached 1,715 titles. The number of Polish-language titles ranged from 271 to 415, depending on the types of publications included in the count. See J. Tomaszewski, 'Niepodległa Rzeczpospolita', in Tomaszewski (ed.), *Najnowsze dzieje Żydów w Polsce* (Warsaw, 1993), 261.

[27] [M.LAN.], '*Nasz Przegląd*', 843.

[28] On readers of the Polish-language Jewish press, see Steinlauf, 'The Polish-Jewish Daily Press', 222.

[29] A., 'Czynnik fanatyzmu a nasza sprawa', *Ewa*, 42 (2 Dec. 1928), 1. On women in Zionism, see E. Mendelsohn, *Zionism in Poland: The Formative Years, 1915–1926* (New York, 1981), 339–41, and P. E. Hyman, *Gender and Assimilation in Modern Jewish History: The Roles and Representation of Women* (Seattle, 1995), 79–85.

Women's International Zionist Organization (WIZO). Established in London in 1920 and working in Poland since 1925, WIZO existed to promote the Zionist cause, especially among middle- and upper-class women, and it also engaged in philanthropic work with women and children in Palestine.[30] Appenszlakowa, a member of the group's central committee who herself had visited Palestine, described the kind of woman that WIZO wished to create in the countries of the Diaspora: 'A culturally and nationally conscious Jewish woman, an idealist participating in the work of the Jewish national renaissance. Using various methods, the Organization attempts to combat assimilation and the indifference of the Jewish woman to social issues.'[31] *Ewa* assumed this responsibility of spreading the Zionist message and harnessing Jewish women's potential to become committed nationalists working for the good of the whole community.

The enemies of this effort, according to *Ewa*'s editorial position, were 'neither those who hate us, nor those who do not know us. We have an enemy more dangerous because it is internal, an enemy from whom we expect help and friendship: "Indifferent Women". How dangerous these words sound to us.'[32] *Ewa* began from the assumption that Jewish women in the Diaspora were becoming assimilated and were increasingly showing indifference to the Jewish aspects of their identity. The problem, according to Dr Salomea Lewite, president of the Federation of Jewish Women and an *Ewa* contributor, was not the 'outward' assimilation that Jews adopted to live and succeed in Poland, but it was, rather, an 'internal assimilation' that saw many Jews, especially from the intelligentsia and upper classes, moving away from Jewish national affiliation entirely.[33] Appenszlakowa herself had come from an assimilated Jewish family (as did her first husband, Jakub, for that matter), but as an adult found her way to Zionism and, as such, was living proof of the possibility of overcoming assimilation and of submitting to the power of the Zionist draw.[34] From *Ewa*'s editorial perspective, it was especially important in this process to target women, who, as wives and mothers, wielded great influence in the lives of their husbands and children and who were the guardians of tradition, culture, and national identity. *Ewa* hoped to overturn Jewish women's indifference and to stimulate in them a sense of collective responsibility and active citizenship. It would only be through a collective effort, beginning in the Diaspora, that Zionist

30 WIZO represented Zionist women in over forty countries. On WIZO, see S. Lewite, 'Żądamy szacunku', *Ewa*, 12 (23 Mar. 1930), 2; id. , 'Perspektywy rozwoju wszechświatowego WIZO', *Ewa*, 34 (20 Nov. 1932), 2; and J. Bełcikowski, *Warszawa kobieca* (Warsaw, 1930), 77–8.

31 'Ogólny krajowy zjazd Zrzeszenia Kobiet Żydowskich WIZO', *Ewa*, 10 (22 Apr. 1928), 10.

32 'Po roku', 1.

33 S. Lewite, 'Problemy wychowania', *Ewa*, 9 (15 Apr. 1928), 1. On women and assimilation, see also C. Prylucki, 'Rola kobiety w żydostwie nowoczesnem', *Ewa*, 15 (27 May 1928), 5. An analysis of assimilation as both a 'sociological process' and 'project' is provided in Hyman, *Gender and Assimilation*, ch. 1.

34 For a brief reference to Appenszlakowa's assimilated background, see Steinlauf, 'The Polish-Jewish Daily Press', 231. For a reference to Appenszlakowa's childhood milieu, see M. Ciesielska, *Jerzy Abramów: Redaktor, Małego Przeglądu* (Warsaw, 2003), 4.

women could hope 'to build Jewish national life' and to prepare themselves and the Jewish people generally for life in a future Jewish state.[35]

In promoting a model of nationally engaged Zionist femininity, *Ewa* offered an alternative to what it regarded as the existing outdated expressions of Jewish women's identity. Appenszlakowa drew a contrast between the progressive-modern and secular women who formed the newspaper's readership and the Orthodox women. She suggested that these two groups inhabited nothing less than 'two separate worlds'.[36] In the aftermath of a large meeting of Orthodox women held in Warsaw in 1931, for example, *Ewa*'s editorial position was to lament the fact that there existed 'so much darkness among Jewish women' and that, in general, 'the forces of reaction are so powerful'.[37] *Ewa* existed, in part, to show that Orthodox women, and Orthodoxy generally, did not have a monopoly on an authentic Jewish identity, and loyalty to the Jewish people did not need to come from within traditional circles, but could instead emerge from modern and secular ones. *Ewa* defined respectability in terms of this radical break with the Jewish past.[38]

But the associates of *Ewa* also differentiated themselves from women's groups on the left. Political ideology, class, language, and approaches to Jewish nationalism separated *Ewa* from the Jewish Labour Bund and its women's group, the Jewish Working Women's Organization (Yidishe Arbeter-froyen Organizatsye), for example.[39] And though *Ewa*'s associates found some common cause with the feminist Zionist activist Puah Rakovsky,[40] especially around support for women's suffrage in the *kehilah*, WIZO, and women's education rights, what ultimately divided socialist Zionists from the *Ewa* milieu was political ideology and class. 'We have to admit', Appenszlakowa sated, 'that we are far removed from the Jewish working woman. We know so little about her, we have so little contact with her.'[41] *Ewa* did not wield Marxist frameworks for its analyses of social problems and did not see itself as speaking primarily for, or to, the Jewish lower middle class and proletariat, which constituted the majority of Poland's Jewish population (though in their

[35] Editor, *Ewa*, 1 (19 Feb. 1928), 1; and see also Appenszlakowa, 'Kwestja zjednoczenia kobiet żydowskich', 1.

[36] 'Wywiad *Kurjera Warszawskiego* z redaktorką *Ewy*', *Ewa*, 26 (30 June 1929), 2. On the Orthodox party Agudat Yisrael, see G. C. Bacon, 'Agudat Israel in Inter-War Poland', in Gutman *et al.* (eds.), *The Jews of Poland Between Two World Wars* , 20–35.

[37] Editor, 'Wielki Zjazd Kobiet Ortodoksyjnych w Warszawie', *Ewa*, 17 (3 May 1931), 1.

[38] 'Wywiad *Kurjera Warszawskiego* z redaktorką *Ewy*', 2. On Zionism and the break with the past, see Biale, *Eros and the Jews*, 177.

[39] On the Bund, see Blatman, 'National-Minority Policy, Bundist Social Organizations, and Jewish Women in Inter-War Poland', 54–70.

[40] On Puah Rakovksy (1865–1955), see Rakovsky, *My Life as a Radical Jewish Woman*, 14–15, 64, and 82–4. Rakovsky, as ' Rakowska', is listed as an associate of *Ewa* in 'Ogól inteligentnych kobiet żydowskich zdobył własnątrybunę prasową', 3.

[41] 'Robotnica żydowska (*Ewa* w Zrzeszeniu Kobiet Pracujących)', *Ewa*, 5 (3 Feb. 1929), 2. On the servants that *Ewa* assumed its readers kept, see R.Gr. [Róża Grycendlerowa], 'Dziecko i służąca', *Ewa*, 7 (16 Feb. 1930), 5.

social reform work *Ewa*'s many collaborators did target these constituencies, especially in their approaches to family planning, as discussed below).[42]

By virtue of its location within the Second Republic, *Ewa* was naturally linked with Polish expressions of feminism. *Ewa*'s editorial position had the most in common with the Polish feminist and middle- and upper-class milieu that comprised the readership of *Kobieta Współczesna*, which was, just as Appenszlakowa described *Ewa*, a 'representative of progress and enlightenment'.[43] *Ewa*'s editorial goals were typically feminist ones aimed at improving the contemporary reality in which 'all' women—Polish and Jewish—functioned, as women. Reflecting on what divided the Polish and the Jewish 'feminist camps' in Poland, Appenszlakowa stated, 'Not much!' She added that what linked the two movements was 'Almost everything. The economic, legal, social and political situation [of women].'[44] As such, Appenszlakowa believed that Catholic and Jewish women in the Second Republic needed to co-operate in order to realize changes that would serve the cause of 'women in Poland' generally.[45]

At the same time, the publishers of *Ewa* realized that Jewish women's concerns could not be included easily in 'general' women's issues and that Polish women did not have a good track record of promoting Jewish women's interests in their feminist campaigns.[46] At any rate, even if such Polish–Jewish feminist co-operation could exist, it would only satisfy *Ewa*'s feminist identity at the expense of its nationalist identity. As it stood, Jewish women were handicapped as a result of what Appenszlakowa described as the 'tragic situation' of Jews generally and, in her opinion, this fact needed to be incorporated into Jewish feminism. In the 1928 founding issue of *Ewa*, Appenszlakowa outlined the view that Jewish women suffered a 'double oppression' as Jews, widely discriminated against in society, and as women. She argued that as a result of this double oppression, Jewish women in Poland found themselves behind other women in the struggle to gain rights and equality.[47] Jewish women's exclusion from the *kehilah* provided the clearest evidence of this and it meant, as Jakub Appenszlak once remarked, that Jewish feminism in the Second Republic remained, at least in part, in a 'suffrage stage'.[48] Though Jewish women had achieved the national suffrage in 1918, they had shown exceptionally weak participation in the political life of the new state.[49] In 1928 not a single Jewish

[42] On Jewish social structure in inter-war Poland, see E. Mendelsohn, *The Jews of East Central Europe Between the World Wars* (Bloomington, Ind., 1983), 23–32.

[43] Editor, 'Wielki Zjazd Kobiet Ortodoksyjnych w Warszawie', *Ewa*, 17 (3 May 1931), 1. On *Kobieta Współczesna*, see M. Dołęgowska-Wysocka, 'Tygodnik *Kobieta Współczesna*', in *Kwartalnik Historii Prasy Polskiej*, 21/3–4 (1982), 56–72.

[44] P. Appenszlakowa, 'Polski i żydówski', *Ewa*, 6 (25 Mar. 1928), 1.

[45] Ibid.

[46] Ibid. and I. Krantz, 'List do Redakcji', *Ewa*, 31 (16 Sept. 1928), 6.

[47] Appenszlakowa, 'Kwestja zjednoczenia kobiet żydowskich', 1. On the 'double oppression' of Jewish women, see also R. Lemkin, 'Kobieta żydowska a feminizm', *Ewa*, 3 (4 Mar. 1928), 2.

[48] Pierrot, 'Między wierszami, *Ewa*', *Nasz Przegląd*, 19 Feb. 1928, 11.

[49] Editor, 'Tym razem nie ustąpimy', *Ewa*, 35 (7 Sept. 1930), 1.

woman was in the Polish parliament, the Sejm, and the national Jewish political parties did not make putting women on their electoral lists a priority, much to *Ewa*'s great disappointment: 'The lack of women should bring shame on us,' declared an *Ewa* editorial.[50] Changing these facts was a matter of both feminist and Jewish pride.[51] *Ewa* existed to help Jewish women 'catch up' with Polish feminism as well as to assist them in realizing their rights and responsibilities as citizens of the Second Republic and of a future Jewish state.

Though this process of catching up and of stimulating engaged feminist activism among Jewish women occurred on many fronts, the remainder of this chapter will focus on just one general area to which *Ewa* devoted sustained attention throughout its existence: reproductive politics. *Ewa*'s editorial position was to support 'voluntary motherhood' (*Świadome macierzyństwo*). Its associates advocated the use of birth control to limit fertility, supported the decriminalization of abortion, and argued that 'rational family planning', especially during economically challenging times, would lead to a better Poland for women generally and for Jews specifically. *Ewa*'s associates further believed that the very act of discussing reproductive politics would stimulate precisely the kind of collective-minded social activism that was vital to realizing the Zionist vision. The attention to the controversial subject of reproductive politics in *Ewa* reflects its dual identity as a progressive feminist paper, conversant with Europe-wide trends surrounding population politics and social-scientific management, and a Jewish nationalist paper eager to reform and improve the local community.

EWA ON 'VOLUNTARY MOTHERHOOD'

The concept of voluntary motherhood was introduced into the lexicon of the Second Republic by Tadeusz Żeleński (1874–1941), commonly referred to by his pen-name, Boy. Though he was also a medical doctor, cabaret writer, and prolific translator, Boy is perhaps best remembered as a controversial feuilletonist who opposed clericalism, mocked what he regarded as a pervasive Polish provincialism, and broadcast, as one critic stated, the 'immorality in morality'.[52] From the late 1920s to the early to mid-1930s, Boy led what many called a 'sexual revolution' in the Second Republic through his public advocacy of voluntary motherhood. Specifically, Boy hoped that he would be able to influence Poland's Codification Commission to remove from the Criminal Code those paragraphs which punished

[50] 'Rozmyślania przedwyborcze', *Ewa*, 36 (14 Sept. 1930), 1. See also R. Melcerowa, 'Echa naszej akcji w sprawie wyborów do przyszłych ciał parlamentarnych', *Ewa*, 37 (21 Sept. 1930), 1. During the Second Republic women held 1.9 per cent of all Sejm seats and 3.8 per cent of all Senate seats. See M. Śliwa, 'Udział kobiet w wyborach i ich działalność parlamentarna', in Żarnowska and Szwarc (eds.), *Równe prawa i nierówne szanse*, 53. For a criticism of (Polish) female Sejm members' efforts on behalf of general women's causes, see J. Horn, 'Niepokojące milczenie na szachownicy wyborczej', *Ewa*, 39 (5 Oct. 1930), 1.

[51] 'Refleksje noworoczne', 1.

[52] M. Piszczkowski, 'O trzech Boy'ach i jednym Żeleńskim', *Myśl Narodowa* (3 Jan. 1932), 6.

both the woman who underwent an abortion and the abortion provider. Few other writers and activists, male or female, and few women's groups and papers did as much to spark public debate about reproductive questions and about various aspects of modern sexual morality.[53]

There were, of course, important exceptions. The women's newspaper of the Polish Socialist Party, *Głos Kobiet*, took a strong stand in favour of decriminalization and improved birth control access. The middle-class Polish women's newspapers *Kobieta Współczesna* and *Bluszcz* also devoted a great deal of attention to these topics.[54] *Ewa*, over its five-year existence, published over forty articles that dealt with different aspects of voluntary motherhood. The amount of attention that *Ewa*'s publishers gave to these questions was not lost on anyone who was paying attention. Certainly Jakub Appenszlak had noticed it.[55] For its part, *Nasz Przegląd* had expressed 'great satisfaction' with *Ewa*'s willingness to stimulate debate on such fundamental issues.[56] Boy himself recognized *Ewa* as a major voice of the progressive camp and, in *Jak skończyć z piektem kobiet?* ('How to End Women's Hell'), a collection of his previously published feuilletons on reproductive topics, Boy thanked the women of *Ewa* for doing that which other Polish Catholic 'ladies', he said, were apparently too afraid to do.[57] *Ewa* took great pride in being associated with what it regarded as a 'progressive' stand on voluntary motherhood. One contributor stated that the very name Ewa in fact obliged the paper to take up these 'most vital postulates'.[58] Another contributor, Felicja Stendigowa, called *Ewa* 'a chief advocate of progress', one that 'boldly appeared in defence of the newest social reforms'. As Stendigowa suggested, *Ewa* fulfilled the role of 'Boy in a dress' by fearlessly inciting debate on socially and morally controversial subjects.[59] *Ewa* actively encouraged 'all women' to read Boy's works.[60]

Ewa's editorial support for voluntary motherhood satisfied its purpose as a feminist paper: encouraging women to work collectively on improving women's socio-economic and legal standing. Further, in linking its identity to what were considered some of the era's most advanced ideas about rational family planning

[53] Boy's feuilletons on these topics were published in *Kurier Poranny* and in *Wiadomości Literackie*. They were later published in book form as *Piekło Kobie* ('Women's Hell') and *Jak skończyć z piekłem kobiet* ('How to End Women's Hell') (each of which is reprinted in T. Żeleński [Boy], *Pisma*, xv (Warsaw, 1958). See also M. Gawin, 'Planowanie rodziny—hasła i rzeczywistość', in Żarnowska and Szwarc (eds.), *Równe prawa i nierówne szanse*.

[54] On the other participants in the debates, see Gawin, 'Planowanie rodziny', 221–42.

[55] Pierrot, 'Czy panie wiedzą?', 1.

[56] Lektor, 'Jak skończyć z piekłem kobiet', 11.

[57] Żeleński, *Pisma*, xv: *Dziewice konsystorskie, Piekło kobiet, Jak skończyć z piektem kobiet?, Nasi okupanci*, ed. Henryk Markiewicz (Warsaw, 1958), 247. See also 'W obronie wolności kobiecej: Dlaczego kobiety milczą?', *Ewa*, 51 (22 Dec. 1929), 1. This reference contains a list of the major articles published in *Ewa* that deal with voluntary motherhood. See also 'Co pisze Boy o *Ewie*', *Ewa*, 49 (13 Dec. 1931), 2.

[58] R. Melcerowa, 'Dlaczego milczą kobiety?', *Ewa*, 52/1 (1 Jan. 1930), 2.

[59] Stendigowa, 'Zadania i cele prasy kobiecej', 2.

[60] N. Bender, 'Krzyk życia', *Ewa*, 14 (6 Apr. 1930), 2.

and social-scientific thinking on population management, *Ewa* was able to present itself as part of a decidedly modern and liberal–progressive movement that contained no traces of religious traditionalism, provincialism, or false modesty; it was able to show that Zionist feminism had arrived to take its place among the secular and modern movements of the day. As one contributor suggested, *Ewa*'s stand on voluntary motherhood allowed the paper to cement an identity for Jewish women as 'leaders of all progress', distinct both from traditional Orthodox Jewish women and from traditional Catholic women.[61]

In the voluntary motherhood debates, *Ewa* espoused typical neo-Malthusian views, which in turn had much in common with eugenic approaches to defining and solving social problems.[62] The term 'neo-Malthusian' was used from the nineteenth century and appeared frequently in inter-war Poland, as it did in Europe generally, to describe supporters of the idea that birth rates should suit the socio-economic profile of a given period.[63] As one *Ewa* contributor summarized, neo-Malthusians argued that one should have as many children 'as the socio-economic circumstances of a given epoch could support'.[64] Neo-Malthusians maintained that in an economic depression, as the Second Republic was experiencing in the late 1920s and into the 1930s, fewer children meant healthier and stronger children, happier families, and therefore more productive members of society, which would in turn guarantee a better foundation for the nation as a whole. Neo-Malthusians in Poland advocated the use of artificial means of birth control as a way of managing population growth and supported the right of a woman to terminate a pregnancy.

The earliest article in *Ewa* on the topic of birth control appeared in the spring of 1928, less than two months after *Ewa* started publishing. This piece was written by Samuel Hirszhorn, a frequent contributor to *Nasz Przegląd* and that paper's author of its series on birth control. Hirszhorn's introductory article, entitled simply 'Birth Control', defined neo-Malthusianism and made the case for rational family planning as a constituent component of sound social policy.[65] In the months following this introductory piece, *Ewa*'s publishers continued to develop the standard neo-Malthusian view that reproductive issues were inseparable from wider social questions. They did so by printing articles and interviews with major activists, as well as by presenting the views of their own associates and readers. A regular *Ewa* contributor and former parliamentarian, Róża Melcer-Pomeranc, for example, was a devoted exponent of neo-Malthusian arguments for controlling the number of

[61] R. Melcer, 'Jak to zrobić?', *Ewa*, 49 (13 Dec. 1931), 2.

[62] See J. Horn, 'Regulacja urodzeń pod względem społecznym', *Ewa*, 32 (16 Aug. 1931), 1. On eugenics, which *Ewa* discussed directly from time to time, see 'Zapobieganie ciąży: Odczyt Dr. Babeckiego w Tow. Eugenicznem', *Ewa*, 52/1 (1 Jan. 1930), 6.

[63] For an introduction to the history of neo-Malthusian and eugenic thought, see W. H. Schneider, *Quality and Quantity: The Quest for Biological Regeneration in Twentieth-Century France* (New York, 1990), ch. 1.

[64] Horn, 'Regulacja urodzeń pod względem społecznym', 1.

[65] S. Hirszhorn, 'Kontrol urodzeń', *Ewa*, 7 (1 Apr. 1928), 6. A study could profitably be done of *Nasz Przegląd*'s position on birth control and abortion.

births in society as a means of raising healthier children and building stronger communities.[66] Melcer argued that the widespread adoption of birth control would guarantee the well-being of mothers, and even of fathers, who would be spared the burden of having to provide for too many children. The end result would be the higher general achievement of the community as a whole, owing to 'the longer and more productive life of parents and children'.[67] Judyta Horn, another regular *Ewa* contributor on reproductive questions, argued forcefully that abortion rights, together with the wide availability of contraception, were especially pressing issues for the working poor, who were often unable to provide adequately for the children that they already had.[68] The newspaper's general approach to reproductive questions was marked by this emphasis on economics, class, and the greater social good. The specific appeal of neo-Malthusianism to feminist Zionists lay in the solutions it offered to the socio-economic problems of the present and, by implication, in the possibility it provided for the long-term biological, social, and national regeneration of the Jewish people.

Neo-Malthusians, like those associated with *Ewa*, understood that they were part of an educated and prosperous segment of the population for whom acquiring birth control posed relatively few problems, financial or other. Low birth rates in the Polish and Jewish intelligentsia and upper classes supported this view.[69] Moreover, women from these social strata could always find a doctor willing to provide a 'pressing medical reason' for the termination of a pregnancy and could afford to pay a doctor the high fee that was demanded for having performed an illegal service.[70] But the situation for women of modest means was different. They often did not have access to reliable contraceptives and, once pregnant, they had few options but to give birth to a child they did not want. An unwanted child would further strain the already limited resources of the family and would diminish the standard of living for each of the family members. Alternatively, pregnant women who were determined not to bring another child into the family could pursue unsafe back-room abortions performed by the local *babka* (old woman); in doing so, they risked death or serious injury, both of which would also compromise the lives of the remaining family members.[71] What was at stake, therefore, as Boy himself argued, was the democratization of the latest advances in social and scientific approaches to

[66] Melcer won a seat as a Zionist in the 1922 elections. See C.B., 'Róża Melcer-Pomeranc', in J. Majchrowski (ed.), *Kto był kim w Drugiej Rzeczypospolitej* (Warsaw, 1994), 399.

[67] R. Melcerowa, 'Jeszcze o kontroli urodzeń', *Ewa*, 10 (22 Apr. 1928), 2. See also W.H.v.C., 'Regulacja urodzeń', *Ewa*, 18 (17 June 1928), 5.

[68] J. Horn, 'Barbarzyństwo śród cywilizacji', *Ewa*, 20 (1 July 1928), 3.

[69] Horn, 'Regulacja urodzeń pod względem społecznym', 1. On the Polish intelligentsia's attitudes towards family planning, see K. Sierakowska, 'Macierzyństwo—wizje a rzeczywistość', in Żarnowska and Szwarc (eds.), *Równe prawa i nierówne szanse*, 212; and Żeleński, *Pisma*, xv. 207.

[70] Bender, 'Krzyk życia', 2.

[71] According to one estimate, 100,000 abortions were performed in Poland every year. See 'W obronie wolności kobiecej (II)', *Ewa*, 52/1 (1 Jan. 1930), 6.

family planning and giving the poor the same privileges that the rich had.[72] According to Judyta Horn, the real challenge was to reach the working classes with the latest information and resources.[73]

Part of the general neo-Malthusian strategy was to support the opening of birth control clinics that would teach people how to prevent conception in the first place. Poland's first family planning clinic was opened in Warsaw in 1931 under the auspices of the Workers' Society for Social Service (Robotnicze Towarzystwo Służby Społecznej) and under the direction of the socialists Dr Justyna Budzińska-Tylicka and Dr Henryk Kłuszyński, though it was popularly referred to as 'Boy's clinic'.[74] The main clients of the clinic were working-class women, precisely those who, according to the neo-Malthusians, could least afford to raise a large number of children. The clinic served an educational function, teaching women about family planning, and made birth control available either at a small cost or for free. It did not offer abortions—and neo-Malthusians were always clear that abortion should not be used as a form of birth control[75]—though critics fanned controversy by suggesting that the clinic really existed only to provide abortions.[76] Dr Rubinraut, a leading doctor at the clinic and a recurrent reference for discussions of birth control in *Ewa*, outlined his hope that the clinic would become 'a small consulate for the citizen of the New, Better Epoch'.[77] Rubinraut defined the purpose of the clinic as educating people about the benefits of birth control and attacking the 'backwardness' that caused many to shun and to fear rational family planning.[78] For their part, *Ewa*'s editor and contributors were great supporters of an effort that, as Appenszlakowa stated, popularized the use of 'reason and will' in conception.[79] An emphasis on the emancipatory potential inherent in education, science, and reason suited *Ewa*'s secular nationalist vision for a modern society that had overcome 'Jewish backwardness' and had replaced it with 'enlightened' approaches to the Jewish future.

Moreover, this whole discussion about limiting fertility, especially among the

[72] 'W obronie wolności kobiecej', 1. See also H. Rubinraut, 'Wycinki', *Ewa*, 21 (29 May 1932), 2.

[73] Horn, 'Regulacja urodzeń pod względem społecznym', 1.

[74] M. Gawin, 'Boyownicy i boyowniczki: Środowisko *Wiadomości Literackich* wobec problemu regulacji urodzeń', in Żarnowska and Szwarc (eds.), *Kobieta i kultura życia codziennego*, 141. The first English birth control clinic was established by Marie Stopes in 1921. See R. A. Soloway, 'The "Perfect Contraceptive": Eugenics and Birth Control in Britain and America in the Inter-War Years', *Journal of Contemporary History*, 30/4 (Oct. 1995), 639.

[75] See T. Weinberg, 'Dwa głosy wciąż o par. 218', *Ewa*, 2 (12 Jan. 1930), 1.

[76] On the clinic, see J. Budzińska-Tylicka, 'Poradnia świadomego macierzyństwa dobrze prosperuje', *Ewa*, 19 (15 May 1932), 2. In 1932 the Warsaw clinic served about 4,000 women. See also M. Gawin, 'Liberalizm społeczno-obyczajowy: Czyli rzecz o Boyownikach', *Społeczeństwo Otwarte*, 6 (1997), 26–7; and M. Dołęgowska-Wysocka, *Poboyowisko* (Warsaw, 1992), 48.

[77] H. Rubinraut, 'O prawo do szczęścia', *Ewa*, 48 (6 Dec. 1931), 1.

[78] H. Rubinraut, 'Macierzyństwo w niewoli', *Ewa*, 41 (18 Oct. 1931), 1.

[79] 'Przychodnia świadomego macierzyństwa', *Ewa*, 40 (11 Oct. 1931), 1. See also Z. Gottliebowa, 'Zarzut niesłuszny', *Ewa*, 47 (29 Nov. 1931), 2.

lower classes, opened up debates about 'national degeneration' in the post-First World War era. Anxiety about national degeneration was pervasive in the post-war period, but in much of Europe this anxiety was fuelled by declining birth rates and by fears that a small population would have an adverse impact on a given state's military and political potential. Unlike France or England, for example, Poland's aggregate birth rates were comparatively high in the post-war era.[80] In view of this, neo-Malthusians in Poland argued that national degeneration would emerge not because of a declining birth rate, but as a result of maintaining a high birth rate during a period of severe economic depression.[81] A high birth rate, especially among the rural and ethnically Polish population, led to high infant mortality and high unemployment, which in turn only exacerbated economic and social problems for everyone, and thereby provided the fertile ground in which fears of national degeneration could grow.[82]

From the perspective of *Ewa*'s associates, limiting family size in Poland suited the overall needs of a state unable to provide adequately even for the existing population, Polish or Jewish. *Ewa*'s advocacy of rational family planning as part of a general solution to economic and social circumstances reflected its status as a participant in what was a national debate. But as a Jewish newspaper, *Ewa* was especially interested in applying neo-Malthusian perspectives to the situation in the Jewish community specifically.

Jews in the Second Republic had a birth rate that was lower than that of the general population, owing in part to the overwhelmingly urban character of the Jews and to their concentration not in agriculture, but in commerce and the professions.[83] But according to the neo-Malthusian viewpoint, birth rates in the large Jewish urban lower middle class and proletariat were still too high for the socio-economic conditions of the day. In an article entitled 'Neomaltuzjanizm a żydzi' ('Neo-Malthusianism and the Jews'), one contributor, Dr Gliksman, outlined this argument for *Ewa*'s readers. Gliksman reasoned that as the economic situation in Poland deteriorated and the competition for jobs grew ever greater, antisemitism also increased. As a result of antisemitism, Jews had a harder time landing decent

[80] Between 1926 and 1930 the birth rate in Poland was 15.5 per 1,000 inhabitants. By contrast, it was 4.4 in Britain. See Gawin, 'Planowanie rodziny', 223; and Budzińska-Tylicka, 'Poradnia świadomego macierzyństwa dobrze prosperuje', 2. On French anxiety about a low birth rate, see M. L. Roberts, *Civilization Without Sexes: Reconstructing Gender in Postwar France, 1917–1927* (Chicago, 1994).

[81] On the economic situation in Poland, see Z. Landau and J. Tomaszewski, *The Polish Economy in the Twentieth Century* (London, 1985).

[82] Dr Kłuszyński calculated the infant mortality rate for the late 1920s and early 1930s as 20.3 children for every 100 born. The rate in France for 1928 was 9.4 and in the United States 7.2. See H. Kłuszyński, *Regulacja urodzeń: Rzecz o świadomem macierzyństwie* (Warsaw, 1932), 36–7.

[83] Statistics on Jewish birth rates in this period are hard to provide. See L. Dobroszycki, 'The Fertility of Modern Polish Jewry', in P. Ritterband (ed.), *Modern Jewish Fertility* (Leiden, 1981), 66–71. On fertility among Jews in Imperial Russia, see C. Y. Freeze, *Jewish Marriage and Divorce in Imperial Russia* (Hanover, NH, 2002), 58–62.

employment and found themselves in economic and social conditions that were far worse than those which the Polish working classes faced. Jews were therefore the least able to support large families.[84]

The *Ewa* contributor Róża Grycendlerowa added a related perspective to this discussion by focusing on women's experiences of economic depression and antisemitism. She stated that, while so-called protective legislation in Poland restricted where and when a female person of any ethnicity or religion could work, antisemitism introduced yet another layer of restrictions against Jewish women; Jewish women again suffered a 'double oppression'.[85] Yet the deteriorating economic conditions in the late 1920s and into the 1930s had made women's paid contributions to the family economy absolutely vital. For a Jewish woman who had to work to help support her family, but who, owing to antisemitism, could not find adequate employment, children became 'only a responsibility and a burden'.[86] Access to birth control and to safe, legal, and affordable abortions was thus especially important to the Jewish working poor. The Warsaw clinic recognized the importance of attracting Jewish clients and accordingly one of the brochures that it put out was published in Yiddish.[87]

The fact that the neo-Malthusian position found support in parts of the Jewish community was exploited by Catholic nationalist antisemites. Some of these argued that it was Jews who were in fact spearheading the neo-Malthusian campaign for voluntary motherhood as part of a sinister plot perpetrated against the Polish Catholic nation. Samuel Hirszhorn explained this antisemitic argument in a speech he gave to WIZO, which was later printed in *Ewa*. Neo-Malthusianism, the antisemites said, was one big 'Jewish swindle' in which Jews actively promoted birth control and abortion as a way of effecting a reduction in the birth rate of *goyim* (non-Jews). At the same time, as Hirszhorn described the argument, Jews were said to be promoting a high birth rate for themselves in an effort to increase their presence, first in Poland and then in the world.[88] Elsewhere, even Boy himself was implicated in these plots and swindles. As the symbolic leader of the voluntary motherhood campaigns, Boy was often caricatured by his critics as an 'artificial Jew': a Jew in spirit and intellect, if not actually by blood (though even this was disputed).[89] This

[84] A. Gliksman, 'Neomaltuzjanizm a żydzi', *Ewa*, 33 (23 Aug. 1931), 2. See also 'O prawo do pracy', *Ewa*, 26 (12 Aug. 1928), 1.

[85] R. Grycendlerowa, 'Kobieta w domu', *Ewa*, 20 (25 May 1930), 5; and 'O prawo do pracy', *Ewa*, 26 (12 Aug. 1928), 1. On women and work in the Second Republic, see the various articles in A. Żarnowska and A. Szwarc (eds.), *Kobieta i praca: Wiek XIX i XX* (Warsaw, 2000).

[86] A. Trusiewiczowa, 'Macierzyństwo nie zawsze jest radosne', *Ewa*, 1 (1 Jan. 1933), 2.

[87] 'Co czynią kobiety przeciwko "piekłu kobiet"?', *Ewa*, 50 (20 Dec. 1931), 1.

[88] S. Hirszhorn, 'Neomalthuzjanism a kwestja żydowska', *Ewa*, 12 (22 Mar. 1931), 2.

[89] The stereotype of Boy as a Jew is taken up in S.H. [S. Hirszhorn], 'Żydzi wobec reform seksualnych', *Nasz Przegląd*, 28 Dec. 1931, 3. The distinction between a real and artificial Jews is made in K. M. Morawski, 'Na marginesie polemiki z Boyem', in C. Lechicki (ed.), *Prawda o Boyu-Żeleńskim: Głosy krytyczne* (Warsaw, 1933), 29, repr. from *Przegląd Katolicki* (1929).

strategy of blaming Jews for anything that was perceived as dangerous to the collective possessed a long and ignoble history, not only in Poland, but throughout Europe, where Jews formed the classic 'Other'. In the Second Republic, Jews were categorized as morally perverted elements in the pure Polish Catholic body; Jews would undermine the Polish nation with their pernicious liberalism, modernity, and secularism.

Cultural and moral liberalism and an embrace of secular-modern and scientific approaches to social problems were precisely the qualities that *Ewa* in fact hoped to promote by its activism. It used these qualities to separate itself from what it regarded as religious conservatism, anti-modernism, and cultural backwardness of the kind represented by the Catholic nationalist right—and by Jewish traditionalists. Hirszhorn outlined for *Ewa*'s readers the criticism of the voluntary motherhood campaigns, emanating this time from Jewish quarters. Some argued that Jewish unhappiness was linked directly to the fact that Jews were a minority. If the Jewish population were greater, this position held, then Jews would constitute a stronger political force and would therefore be in a position to wield real power and to make a positive impact on Jews' daily lives in Poland.[90] Perhaps a *mikveh* to increase the birth rate? Other than this reference, *Ewa*'s contributors did not engage directly or specifically with Jewish opponents of neo-Malthusianism and preferred instead to address only general criticism of the overall neo-Malthusian position. The standard neo-Melthusian response to an argument like the one that Hirszhorn repeated for *Ewa*'s readers emphasized that numbers were not what mattered, but that overall strength and health was—and that this was all the more important to understand during the contemporary period of economic depression. Hirszhorn summarized his own position with the often repeated neo-Malthusian phrase 'The quality of people is more important than the quantity'.[91] Neo-Malthusians generally argued that addressing fears about national prestige and potential by simply advocating an increase in the birth rate was entirely irresponsible and short-sighted and would not produce the desired end result of a vital and productive population. Instead, only rational family planning, which would teach people how to match births 'to political-economic potential', offered the hope of producing this 'quality' population which could serve as the foundation for a national rejuvenation of any kind.[92]

The publishers of *Ewa* were also well aware that opponents derided neo-Malthusians as advocates of an immoral and hedonistic lifestyle (as sex for purposes other than procreation apparently implied) that threatened the most basic principles of family life. As such, the paper went to some lengths to argue that, as supporters of neo-Malthusianism and as self-described feminist women, they could simultaneously fulfil the roles of moral and responsible wives and mothers.[93] Responding to critics' charges that neo-Malthusians were feminists gone wild who

[90] Hirszhorn, 'Neomalthuzjanism', 2. [91] Ibid. [92] Ibid.

[93] See e.g. R. Melcerowa, 'Ankieta *Ewy* na temat: Winna czy niewinna?', *Ewa*, 34 (25 Aug. 1929), 1.

aimed to destroy the family, Judyta Horn, for instance, stated that a 'real and true feminist' aimed not to destroy the family, but rather to 'strengthen it': 'She does not deny either motherhood or love. Just the opposite: through the limiting of *surplus* offspring, she improves immeasurably how she can feed and raise her children.'[94] Throughout the discussions in *Ewa* about voluntary motherhood, Horn developed the position that the advocacy of birth control and of legal abortion constituted not a wholesale denial of women's traditional roles, but rather 'a variation of the protection of motherhood'.[95]

Ewa also had little patience with those who argued that aborting the development of a foetus was morally suspect. In one editorial entitled 'W obronie wolności kobiecej' ('In Defence of Women's Freedom'), Appenszlakowa simply stated the view that a foetus could not exist apart from the mother, especially in the early stages, and so terminating a pregnancy was in no way a morally ambiguous act. The editorial posed a rhetorical question directed at 'the moralists' who advocated a strict prohibition on abortion rights: Would they prefer that a child be born to poverty and with little hope for a decent life? This kind of child would be neither a good person nor a good citizen, and so the real immorality was located in the fact that society allowed children to be born into unacceptable circumstances.[96]

Similarly, in an interview with a regular *Ewa* contributor, Thea Weinberg, Dr Kłuszyński of Warsaw's birth control clinic shared his view that discussing abstract notions of morality in relation to family planning, while ignoring real socio-economic concerns, was entirely wrong. Kłuszyński posed what were also rhetorical questions: 'Is the senseless and unlimited birth of children, who later die of hunger, cold, bad hygienic conditions, moral? . . . Is it really moral to force a woman to give birth to a foetus that she doesn't even want to carry when there are no [social] provisions for children or for mother . . . ? This is exactly what immorality is.'[97]

Ewa further presented the argument that what was in fact immoral was a prevailing contemporary 'double morality' that held women to standards that men did not have to meet. *Ewa* suggested that society needed to question the archaic moral codes that determined what was appropriate and inappropriate behaviour for women and to recognize that sometimes the sexual double standard actually created the problems that neo-Malthusianism aimed to solve. One reader of *Ewa*, writing under the apparent pseudonym of Tea Hajot, contributed an extraordinary article that summarized the attitudes which reappeared in successive *Ewa* issues. Hajot asked what was worse: a 15-year-old boy with a venereal disease or a 15-year-old pregnant girl? Hajot guessed that a boy in such a situation would succeed in getting medical attention and would have the chance to grow into a 'decent citizen'. 'But the girl? Her life is forever ruined', Hajot declared, if she were to unable to arrange secretly

[94] J. Horn, 'Czy wolno burzyć rodzinę?', *Ewa*, 10 (8 Mar. 1931), 1. This article also contains a singularly unique and brief criticism of Boy's popularization of a radical, sensational feminism.

[95] J. Horn, 'Na straży własnych interesów', *Ewa*, 11 (15 Mar. 1931), 1.

[96] 'W obronie wolności kobiecej (II)', 6.

[97] Weinberg, 'Dwa głosy wciąż o par. 218', 1.

and successfully for an abortion. 'We embrace the legality of abortion as a sign of the greatest kindness,' she stated categorically. Hajot presented an impassioned set of demands that contemporary women should make:

> We demand that . . . those of us who have 'fallen' continue to have the same right to live life as those who wear a wedding band or those who were able to avoid getting pregnant. We demand social welfare and rights for ourselves as well as for our children. . . . We demand that . . . the child who carries the name of its mother is received by the world in the same way as the child who carries the name of a father. That which is natural [sex] cannot be and is not immoral, and so neither the sex drive nor the satisfaction of that drive can be considered immoral, just as motherhood, even without marriage, cannot be immoral.[98]

Hajot called for a wholesale change to the way in which society held women to unfair standards and argued that, until society implemented these changes, it was positively ludicrous, and indeed immoral, to think about criminalizing abortion.

Similarly, another contributor used the example of a young unmarried woman's pregnancy and suicide to argue for the need 'to change outdated views' about marriage and motherhood. Society categorically condemned out-of-wedlock pregnancy but, at the same time, it put incredible pressure on young women to find a marriage partner and, from an early age, taught members of the female gender that they would find meaning and value only in being wives and mothers.[99] Women needed to be taught instead that they had options and that they were living in a modern age, one in which they were free to choose the specific paths that their lives would take. While in no way denying the centrality of women's roles as wives and mothers, *Ewa*'s editorial position was not to reach for marriage and motherhood as the crowning achievement of every women's identity. Rather, *Ewa* encouraged women to blend the identities of wife and mother with a commitment to social reform work and to feminist and nationalist causes; women would gain confidence and respect through their activism and would make better choices in all areas of their lives.[100] From *Ewa*'s perceptive, the voluntary motherhood campaigns were so important not only because they aimed to create tangible changes in behaviour and legislation, but also because they helped popularize the view that a narrow understanding of 'proper femininity' was stifling and ultimately destructive to individuals, families, and the larger national community.

The approach to voluntary motherhood that we read about in *Ewa* was multipronged: it outlined the socio-economic benefits of rational family planning to society at large and, to Jews specifically, it opposed the criminalization of abortion and stimulated discussions about the deleterious effects on women of the moral double standard. Like neo-Malthusians generally, *Ewa*'s contributors on the subject further argued that it was absurd to think about criminalizing abortion when the state made

[98] T. Hajot, 'Dyskusja czytelniczek *Ewy*: O podwójnej moralności', *Ewa*, 15 (13 Apr. 1930), 4. 'Hajot' stands for 'H.J.'.

[99] A. Rappel, 'Już czas', *Ewa*, 4 (26 Jan. 1930), 5.

[100] On social activism, see R. Grycendlerowa, 'Zacznijmy od małego', *Ewa*, 17 (4 May 1930), 2.

no adequate provision to care for mothers and children in need. *Ewa* was therefore a great advocate of strengthening social aid to women and their children.[101] The women who read *Ewa* understood, however, that in mixed Polish–Jewish organizations, Jews confronted resentment from antisemitic Poles who argued that, in funding Jewish relief efforts, the Polish state government essentially 'stole bread' from the mouth of a Polish child.[102] Consequently, *Ewa*'s associates supported the concept of Jewish-run social welfare organizations that would focus exclusively on Jewish women and children, and it reported regularly on the work of, for example, the Society for the Protection of the Jewish People (Towarzystwo Ochrony Ludności Żydowskiej) and the Jewish Society for the Protection of Women (Żydowskie Towarzystwo Ochrony Kobiet). Both of these groups, which maintained branch organizations across Poland, provided the kinds of services which *Ewa* believed might alleviate the burdens and temptations that women, especially young and vulnerable women, faced in contemporary society.[103]

This again brings the issue of Jewish women's exclusion from the *kehilot* to the forefront. Though women were often the ones who staffed and ran charitable organizations that dealt with women's welfare generally, their exclusion from community councils prevented them from having full input into the priorities established by those groups.[104] The fact that Jewish women were not represented in the Polish national parliament further limited what they could do for their communities, whether with respect to the abortion issue or any number of other causes. Given Jewish women's absence from state-national and local governmental bodies alike, *Ewa*'s publishers saw the newspaper as providing an especially important forum in which Jewish women could agitate for specific policy changes.

Ewa's involvement in the voluntary motherhood question ended when the Poland-wide debates generally subsided. This occurred in 1932, when the Polish Codification Commission delivered its final draft of what would become Poland's new abortion legislation. *Ewa*'s front-page verdict on the Commission's draft called it a setback in the fight for women's rights, one that 'should serve as a cautionary warning . . . especially given that the enemies of women's emancipation are not asleep'.[105] This apparent defeat was not, at any rate, so surprising, according to the article's author, Judyta Horn. This was the case, Horn argued, because women's journals generally—with the exception of *Ewa*—were 'indifferent' to the issue, while Christian and Jewish 'reactionary-clerical' forces were especially active for this cause.[106]

[101] Z.Kł., 'Dzieciobójstwo i spędzenie płodu', *Ewa*, 33 (18 Aug. 1929), 8; and see P.A., 'Macierzyństwo, a prawo spędzania płodu', *Ewa*, 28 (26 Aug. 1928), 5.

[102] R. Rakowska, 'Praca społeczna czy filantropja?', *Ewa*, 11 (17 Mar. 1929), 1.

[103] See 'Co "TOŻ" uczynił dla kobiet i dzieci?', *Ewa*, 20 (1 July 1928), 1. The Jewish Society for the Protection of Women worked with the Polish Society for the Protection of Women and Children to fight the so-called 'white slave trade'. See J. Zylbermincowa, 'Handel żywym towarem', *Ewa*, 8 (8 Apr. 1928), 2.

[104] Klingberg, 'Księgi święte po naszej stronie', 2.

[105] J. Horn, 'Lekcja ostrzegawcza', *Ewa*, 27 (14 Aug. 1932), 1.

[106] Ibid.

From Horn's perspective, the final proposal was, at best, a middle-of-the-road position. The new legislation would read that Articles 231 and 232 of the Criminal Code were not contravened, if the abortion was performed by a doctor and was necessary for the health of the mother, or if the pregnancy was the result of certain conditions, such as rape. Socio-economic reasons for wanting to terminate a pregnancy—which neo-Malthusians strongly advocated—were insufficient. The punishment for breaking the law was up to three years' imprisonment for the woman and up to five for the abortion provider. What would happen under this system was clear to Horn: Rich women would pay a doctor, as they always had, to swear to the 'medical need' for an abortion, and cultural and class norms would ensure discretion from all parties involved. Poor women would be unable to afford this and thus they would remain trapped by precisely the same unfortunate circumstances that they had always known.[107]

CONCLUSION

One of the important causes that had occupied *Ewa* from its inception in 1928 had ended, if not in a wholesale defeat, then in a disappointing compromise. The women of *Ewa* did not really 'win' any major feminist or nationalist battles from 1928 to 1933. By 1933 women still did not sit in Poland's *kehilot* and Jewish women remained absent from the Polish parliament. Antisemitism continued to limit women's (and indeed men's) choices in economically challenging times—and the situation was only getting worse. How, then, do we judge *Ewa*? What do we make of a newspaper that reached only small numbers of women and that stopped publishing just five years after its inception, in March 1933?[108]

We need to evaluate *Ewa* not in terms of the longevity of its publication or by counting its concrete victories on specific issues; we need, rather, to evaluate its symbolism, context, and aspirations. Ultimately, what the paper represents is a bold attempt at a great transformation: transforming indifference into feminist and nationalist consciousness on the part of the modern Jewish woman. *Ewa* also stands as an eloquent example of the Zionist attempt to 'normalize' the Jewish experience and, in this case, to normalize a Jewish middle- and upper-class feminism.[109]

Ewa's sustained focus on voluntary motherhood constitutes but one example of how the paper approached the goal of normalization. *Ewa* had absorbed a

[107] Ibid.

[108] Economic problems, in part, may explain *Ewa*'s fate. In 1931 *Ewa* had reduced the price per issue from 60 to 30 groszy, making it the least expensive weekly in all of Poland. See '*Ewa* dla wszystkich!', *Ewa*, 36 (13 Sept. 1931), 1. Note that in January 1934 Appenszlakowa started a new journal directed at the Polish Jewish and the Polish intelligentsia, entitled *Reading: A Literary–Social Weekly* (*Lektura: Tygodnik Literacko-Społeczny*). It lasted only until May 1934.

[109] On the 'ideology of normalization', see D. Biale, *Power and Powerlessness in Jewish History* (New York, 1986), 130–6, and A. Shapira, introduction to J. Reinharz and A. Shapira (eds.), *Essential Papers on Zionism* (New York, 1996), 11–13.

Europe-wide language of and anxiety about degeneration. It had embraced neo-Malthusianism's promise of the possibility for national regeneration and had applied these preoccupations to the nationalist cause. As the self-defined representative of progressive Jewish feminist Zionists, *Ewa* would not be left out of debates in which the progressive, Western-oriented, and liberal intelligentsia across Europe took part. This very public placement of its identity alongside these Europe-wide trends formed at least some part of *Ewa*'s aim. The specific content of its publishers' stand—support for voluntary motherhood, through improved access both to contraception and to legal and safe abortions—did more than any other issue might have to announce the arrival of a progressive feminism within Zionist nationalism. By articulating bold support for neo-Malthusian approaches to social management, *Ewa* cemented for itself a secular modern identity that carried within it a rejection of traditional, conservative Judaism, a definitive break with the past, and an embrace of the Zionist future. It announced to Europe, Poland, and to Jews themselves, the arrival of the socially active and politically engaged Jewish woman; it announced the potential for co-operation between a modern Jewish feminism and a secular nationalism.

Interview with Professor Jadwiga Maurer

KATARZYNA ZECHENTER

JADWIGA MAURER'S writing is exceptional. She began to write late in life and published three volumes of short stories: *Liga ocalałych* ('The League of the Saved', 1970), *Podróż na wybrzeże Dalmacji* ('A Voyage to the Coast of Dalmatia', 1982), and *Sobowtóry* ('The Doubles', 2002). These short stories, written in the first person, appear autobiographical; yet they are works of fiction centred on post-Holocaust life. The main character, a girl whom the reader might view as Maurer's alter ego, survives the war and moves with her mother to Munich, always remaining an outsider. She never truly participates in life; instead she observes it and ponders the absurdity of life in general. Yet she is unable to free herself from the fascination aroused by others' hunger for life, their desire for success, and most of all their need to find some purpose in the world after the Holocaust.

Maurer was born in Kielce, Poland, in 1932, into an educated, Polonized, non-religious Jewish family. Her mother studied at the Jagiellonian University in Kraków and later taught Polish literature; her father taught Polish, Hebrew, and geography as principal of a high school in Kielce. The whole family survived the war mainly in Kazimierz, the Jewish part of Kraków, under 'Aryan papers' (false papers declaring the person to be Christian) with help from Żegota (the Council for Aid to Jews in Occupied Poland), an agency run by the Polish Home Army. Maurer devotes a few short stories to the years in Kazimierz, years that she calls 'somewhat happy'. In 1944 Żegota tried to evacuate her family from Poland to Hungary, but they never reached their destination because of further German occupation. Instead, they stayed in Prešov, a small town in Slovakia, where Jadwiga was hidden by nuns in a Franciscan school. Her knowledge of and interest in Catholicism date from that time. After the war her family briefly returned to Poland but, fearing the spread of communism, decided to leave for Munich, as many other Polish Jews did at that time. Maurer studied Polish literature and received her doctorate in Slavonic studies. She eventually went to America, where she taught Polish literature at Berkeley, Indiana, and eventually at the University of Kansas.

Maurer does not write about the Holocaust per se, though the majority of her short stories are set in wartime Kraków and in post-war Munich. In her work, the

Holocaust is always present as an event that marked all Jews as the eternal 'Others'—and the surviving Jews as the most lonely of Others because they did not share the fate of the dead. Maurer's protagonist is alive, but her life is punctuated by constant questions about post-war existence and existence in general. Surprisingly she never asks 'why', as if this question and its answer(s) never make any sense. Such an existence on the fringes of reality, devoid of ambition, passion, or even humble desire, marks the protagonist as an unusual witness to the heritage of survival. Maurer's protagonist does not see an overriding purpose in life, yet the writer is determined to chronicle the remnants of Polish Jews who lived in Munich after the war. Maurer has no desire to discuss the Jewish fate in general, but only to depict the people she saw, knew, befriended, and later immortalized in her prose, because they have no other chroniclers.

The following interview with Jadwiga Maurer took place on 26 May 1999 at the University of Kansas. At the time I was an assistant professor of Polish literature and Jadwiga Maurer was about to retire. My goal was to commemorate the sixtieth anniversary of the beginning of the Second World War on 1 September 1939 by interviewing nine Poles who survived the war and eventually moved to Lawrence, Kansas. Each story I recorded was remarkable. Among others, I interviewed a hero of the 1944 Warsaw uprising, a survivor of the Warsaw ghetto uprising in 1943, a survivor of Soviet occupation, and the daughter of the Polish ambassador to Estonia in 1939. Jadwiga Maurer was one of those people who survived thanks to their intelligence, wit, bravery and, most importantly, a miracle—as she says in her short story 'There Was an Old Man and a Woman'.

The interview was conducted in Polish and later translated into English.

KATARZYNA ZECHENTER. *In your short stories, the narrator is a girl or a young woman who survived the Second World War and whom the reader almost automatically identifies with the author, that is with you. Your stories, however, do not form an autobiography. Although they do contain many autobiographical elements, they are a unique transformation of autobiographical material. How do you conduct this transformation?*

JADWIGA MAURER. What I write is not autobiography and I am glad that you understand this. Many of my readers do not and therefore ask me for further details. In my short stories, I place some characters, who are fictitious, in 'real' and 'true' situations, that is in situations that appear real to me. Sometimes the exact opposite is true. Some unreal situations happen to people who in my understanding are 'real', as I remember them. I believe that 'true' autobiography does not exist, because everything we remember is filtered through our own minds, through our unique feelings and memory. And it often happens that two or three people will remember things differently. I want my readers to understand that I don't write autobiography. Sometimes, I am confounded when someone asks whether something 'really' happened; it did and it did not. It is a literary truth, not the 'true' truth.

K.Z. *Your stories tell about the end of the world of Polish Jews, about their lives after the war. The narrator pretends that one can live normally after the war, which of course is not really possible. To her identity as a Jew—born in pre-war Poland, raised on Polish literature, having survived the war on Aryan papers, and having spent time in a convent school in Slovakia—she adds other identities. For instance, she adds a Catholic identity and even a German one as a literature student in Munich after the war. Finally, she adds an American identity. How do you unite these sometimes even contradictory identities?*

J.M. First of all, I would like to go back to the word 'pretend'. I do not believe that my narrator 'pretends' in the way we commonly understand this word. She is who she is; she tries to live the way she believes she ought to live. Her identity does change a little, but identity changes in everyone. Our identity when we are young is different from our identity in middle age. A child identifies herself differently than she does as an adult. It is easy to explain the Catholic identity of my narrator. Catholicism was the first religion for both the narrator and the author, because she came from a family which did not practise any religion—as was the case for the vast majority of children who survived under Aryan papers. The Catholic religion is very attractive. The narrator talks for instance about month of May evening devotions to the Blessed Virgin and about the liturgy, which is very attractive, especially to a child. Later, she resides in the very heart of the Church: a Catholic school. Despite the fact that she is still a child, she begins to orient herself pretty well in various dogmas and even in the history of the Church. This is not a difficult identification for someone who had not known any other religion.

People often used the term 'to pretend on Aryan papers'. I have the impression—here I need to add that the author agrees with the narrator—that the word 'pretend' can only be used in the context of an adult. But, for a child, even for a young adult, such identification resulted from the fact that these young Jewish people wanted to be Poles, the same as other Poles. Yet they knew early in pre-war Poland that they were not completely Polish.

Here I would like to add something about the experiences of the author herself. My mother told me that she remembered a warm May afternoon day when she was sitting on the stairs of the house where she lived and was born. People were going to a Blessed Virgin evening devotion. She longed to go, too, because everybody else was going. This was impossible, since she came from a strictly hasidic home. This rush to identification with Poles was common, not only among assimilated Jews or Jewish intelligentsia. Besides, pre-war Poland was antisemitic. Even the children knew that there were borders that could not be crossed. For example, Jewish children were not allowed to join Scout groups. Thus their longing for identification with Catholicism is not difficult to understand.

K.Z. *What about later identifications? Your narrator has girlfriends who are German. Is there a real friendship between them?*

J.M. On some level, this is a true friendship. The narrator always remembers the past, because it is impossible completely to erase it from her memory. If she had stayed in Germany, she would have had problems marrying a German, for example. Starting a family in Germany would have created an even greater problem. However, identification with German culture, literature, or with the new state was not difficult for her. Her friends from the Jewish Student Organization simply waited for emigration. They were mostly orphans and experienced everything differently. As refugees, they neither needed support from the German culture, nor were they looking for it. They wanted to finish their studies and leave as soon as possible; this is why they chose such practical professions. My narrator, on the other hand, searches for German support.

K.Z. *Did leaving Germany mean forgetting the past?*

J.M. I don't know. It seems to me that they wanted to begin a new life in a naive and idealistic manner. They thought that once they left Germany and began to work and make money, a completely new life would begin. As I write in *Liga ocalałych*, they did not think that they needed a new language, a new start, new people. For them, the world ended and began with leaving Germany.

K.Z. *In your short story 'A Place that did not Exist on a Map', the narrator says that she would like to be a 'chronicler of places that did not exist on a map and events that history did not note'. What did you mean in writing these words?*

J.M. Actually, this is a concrete question and the answer is concrete as well. Namely, not only Jews, but also Ukrainians or Poles lived in post-war countries, especially in Germany in the DP [displaced persons] camps and in small towns where they received meagre stipends. German authorities—also American authorities and most probably British and French as well, although I am not sure—wanted to get rid of these thousands of people who terrified them simply by their presence. It was as if these camps were extraterritorial. They were places that were not noted anywhere. Today, when I mention 'DP', everybody asks, what is that? Nobody remembers any more; there is a gap in people's memory. Yes, these people and their fate in post-war Germany are not remembered. These places literally did not exist on maps, but some literature does exist about them. The writer Tadeusz Nowakowski, a friend of my parents, wrote a novel called *The Camp of All Saints* about the DP camps, in which he presented this hopeless world. These places were not prisons, but a world 'outside'. Though people later somehow managed, they existed outside almost everything.

K.Z. *Would you agree that you write to 'rescue from forgetting' or rather that your writings create another reality?*

J.M. Yes, you could say that. People are often surprised that I wrote about the post-war world, about the Holocaust, about German occupation—that these are my subjects. They know that in so-called 'real life' they talk to me about fashion or which hairdresser is the best in town. I do think that all writers, if their work has artistic merit, return to the central episodes in their lives. The war, the Holocaust, and the German occupation are the central episodes not only in my life, but also in the life of our century. Writers always come back to pivotal events, like Hemingway, who kept returning to the war in Spain until his death, or like Faulkner, who kept going back to his South even though his South did not really exist at the end of his life. I find this perfectly normal. 'Not normal', if I can put it this way, is the amazing interest in the Holocaust in the past ten years.

K.Z. *Why do you consider this interest 'not normal'?*

J.M. Because I thought that before the fall of communism, the Holocaust was almost forgotten, swept under the carpet. Suddenly, it turned out that many people born after the war, who could not have remembered, have a great—and I might add private—consciousness and awareness of what happened. I do not mean 'not normal' as craziness, but rather 'not normal' because, generally, first we remember and then we forget. And here is a total reversal. I also believe that it has something to do with the fall of communism, because under communism it was impossible to talk about it. Today people remember and want to talk about it.

K.Z. *You write mostly about the war. Over sixty years have passed since September 1939. How have these years influenced your understanding of what happened and consequently your writing?*

J.M. This is a difficult question because my belief is probably similar to yours: we will never fully understand what happened. And when we attempt to analyse it, even such events as Hitler's accession to power remain a mystery. Our understanding of what happened is similar to that right after the war: it remains a shock, a tragedy. One can, of course, use the clichés, but we will never understand exactly what happened. It seems to me that those who survived and those who read about what happened react in a somewhat similar manner: shock. The concept of Holocaust is outside our knowledge of Holocaust. Museums that are now beginning to display Holocaust writings, Holocaust memoirs, somehow exist outside the Holocaust itself. This is an incredibly difficult concept that cannot be understood.

K.Z. *Do you think that current interest in Holocaust might be somewhat influenced by globalization—by the shrinking of the world which causes people to become interested in what is local? Could the interest in the Holocaust be such a phenomenon?*

J.M. Perhaps. Globalization exists and surely helps in dissemination of our knowledge of the Holocaust. On the other hand, it is very misleading when people assume that life is similar everywhere in the world—which of course is not correct. What we know about the Holocaust and about the German occupation belongs to ethnic studies. The writer Hanna Krall wrote that the fact that a story is improbable does not mean that the story is not true. Her statement absolutely reflects the human fate, in particular, because we can talk about survival only in the context of a miracle. And, if someone is trying to search for the 'true' truth that contains logic, then such a search cannot be successful. What if we realize that all Jews who survived the Holocaust and all Poles who survived the German occupation or German camps survived only by a miracle, not by any logic? Then maybe we are beginning to understand a little of what happened.

K.Z. *We were talking about the war that robbed you of your first home, which for every child is the 'the home'. What does the word 'home' mean to you?*

J.M. For me and also my narrator, this first home, although very happy, was not ideal because of antisemitism in pre-war Poland. Home means family. Home as a place to live should be rather secondary. However, many people are strongly attached to the landscape of their childhood. I have to admit that, although it might sound offensive to Holocaust specialists, I am attached to Kraków's Kazimierz section where I lived under Aryan papers during the war. It would seem that it should not have been a happy childhood. But I do have many fond memories, despite the constant threat at the time. I have many memories of running through Wolnica Square, playing with children. The human mind and the human memory are such that we can simultaneously exist on various levels.

K.Z. *So, you do not have a place, an apartment, a home that you miss?*

J.M. No, I don't, because I moved so many times and I don't have the kind of place that my parents did. I never stayed in any place long enough to be attached to the landscape. I was most attached to Berkeley, California, where I lived for seven years and where my daughter was born.

K.Z. *Do you feel homeless?*

J.M. I felt most homeless in Munich after the war. If something can be deduced from my stories in *Liga ocalałych*, it is that life is so temporary, so provisional—not because life had to be this way, but because people wanted to leave as soon as possible. Some were even doing very well—they had friends—and yet they thought only of leaving.

K.Z. *How were you able to live among Germans after the war? You were surrounded by them; you had to speak German.*

J.M. My parents knew German very well, because they came from Galicia and they went to Polish schools where German was taught. Yet I had not heard even one German word before coming to Munich at the age of 14. Life in Munich existed on various levels. I always had a subconscious feeling that life there was not normal, that it was not for me. On the other hand, life in a DP camp, in itself, was not normal, because it was temporary and all acquaintances were circumstantial.

K.Z. *Home means identity. Who are you? You went through hell, survived, left the country. Now you have a family, you live in the United States.*

J.M. There is not one definition that would describe me, because we are also defined by others. I consider myself Polish. With Jews, I have a common past and consciousness of the history of Polish Jews. Because I am not religious and I do not practise Judaism, I don't really have the common religious bond with other Jews. Despite everything we say about secular Jews, still, it is the religion which is bonding. I live in the United States, I work here, my husband is an American. My children were born here, though they probably have a consciousness of their European descent.

K.Z. *You said that you feel Polish.*

J.M. Yes, I consider myself Polish.

K.Z. *Are you a Polish Jew?*

J.M. That depends on who calls me that. If some Pole were to say that you are Polish and I am a Polish Jew, I would disagree. If, however, someone would say that you are a *krakowianka* (a native of Kraków) and I am a Polish Jew, then maybe I would agree. This would depend on my interlocutor and on what such description is supposed to serve.

K.Z. *How do you understand the expression 'Jewishness'?*

J.M. Around ten years ago in Jerusalem, I attended a conference about the culture of Polish Jews. They adopted a terminology that I really liked. They talked about Jews and Poles. They did not use euphemisms such as 'of Jewish extraction'. For me, the Jewishness of Polish Jews (that is, Jews who have origins similar to mine) means the consciousness of a common fate, a common past; a realization that Polish Jews no longer exist, that we are the last Polish Jews; and the consciousness of common history in Poland. I suspect that in other countries such identification is connected with religion. There exists some community among Jews but, like all communities, it is difficult to describe, since it is somewhat mythical.

K.Z. *There are initiatives in Poland to revive a Polish Jewish community. In Warsaw, for example, there is a Jewish primary school, a Jewish kindergarten, and a synagogue. Similar attempts are taking place in Kraków. Do you think that these initiatives can succeed?*

J.M. Perhaps, but this will not be the Polish Jews who were there earlier. Some time ago Jews constituted some sort of community, but I don't believe that this is possible now. Jewish towns do not exist; Jewish communities do not exist; Jewish intellectual currents do not exist. In pre-war Poland, in the generation of my parents, many Jews were completely assimilated and some took the final step of becoming Christians. This group must have been large. Many Jews who were scholars and professors, for whom scholarly careers were difficult in pre-war Poland, were baptized along with their families. These groups of people embraced total assimilation. Today, everything is different. I read in *Midrasz* [a Polish Jewish journal] that anyone who does not believe in any other religion and who is of Jewish origin can belong to the Jewish community, forgoing the rule that a Jew is someone whose mother is Jewish. These requirements are very liberal and perhaps will attract some people of Jewish origin. In Poland there are many people of Jewish extraction who do not admit to it or are even unaware of it.

K.Z. *The next question cannot be overlooked in the context of Polish–Jewish relationships. Are Poles antisemitic or are some Poles antisemitic?*

J.M. It is a mystery for me and for many people of my generation how antisemitism can still exist in Poland, though Polish Jews no longer exist. This is a strange form of antisemitism—almost traditional—that is passed from generation to generation. I read in *Kultura* [a Paris journal] that in some high schools a new word has appeared: *żydzić* or 'to Jew', the same way as *cyganić* or 'to lie' comes from the word Cygan, Gypsy. For a majority of Jews, it is not possible to understand this. In Polish society there still exists a huge gap between the intelligentsia and the rest of the society. The writer Boy-Żeleński said that noble status was replaced by a high school diploma. [In pre-war Poland a high school diploma suggested an educated person.] I agree with this. The Polish intelligentsia was not and is not antisemitic, even those on the political right. Those coming from the countryside, the peasants, the so-called masses including the lower ranks of clergy, were antisemitic, though I don't know why. Perhaps some ideals or concepts simply did not reach them. Perhaps this is connected with the fact that the Polish intelligentsia, even the intelligentsia of People's Poland, is still to some degree of post-gentry origin. But the culture of Polish gentry was not and is not antisemitic. Sometimes I believe that these are two nations. In other countries, in America, in Germany, or in France, the difference between the intelligentsia and the rest of society is not so tremendous; there is no such division. In Poland, however, this division still exists.

K.Z. *I have an impression that anti-Polish tendencies in the Jewish communities in the United States are growing stronger. These abated for a short time during the era of Solidarity when the press was presenting Poland's struggle for freedom. Now these tendencies seem to have grown stronger.*

J.M. I do not have an established opinion on this topic, although American culture interests me a lot. I do not understand it. I know that American Jews are anti-Polish and, when you ask them about it, you cannot get a sensible answer. They absorbed anti-Polonism—when, how, and in what way I do not know. I have heard different opinions on that subject. One opinion is that the first Jews who strongly influenced American culture came from Germany and that these German Jews did not have a positive attitude towards Poles. Later came Jews from Russia. Both groups were anti-Polish and somehow they influenced the general opinion. This is still a mystery for me, but it is a fact that American Jews are anti-Polish. Perhaps, to some degree, they feel guilty about the past because they did not help.

Bibliography: Jewish Women in Eastern Europe

KAREN AUERBACH

THIS bibliography includes historical sources, as well as literary, sociological, religious, and linguistic studies of a historical nature, related to the lives of Jewish women in eastern Europe. It is limited geographically to the area of present-day Poland, Russia, Ukraine, Belarus, Lithuania, Latvia, and other countries traditionally considered part of eastern Europe. However, several sources related to countries in central Europe, such as the former Czechoslovakia, are included for the period after the Second World War, when these countries were politically aligned with eastern Europe. The bibliography excludes sources about women during the Holocaust, because this important topic comprises a separate category. In the memoirs section, only those sources that deal significantly with life in eastern Europe are included; memoirs that describe only experiences after emigration from eastern Europe or during the Second World War are not listed.

For a comprehensive bibliography of sources on Jewish women, generally, see Emily Taitz, Sondra Henry, and Cheryl Tallan, *The JPS Guide to Jewish Women: 600 BCE to 1900 CE* (Philadelphia: Jewish Publication Society, 2003), 325–46.

Memoirs

ALPERIN, MENUCHE, *Unter fremde un eygene himlen* ('Under Foreign and Familiar Skies'), 2 vols. (Tel Aviv: Nay Lebn, 1972).

Memoirs of childhood in the small town of Pohost, near Pinsk, Belarus. The author describes relations between Jews and Christians, Jewish occupations, family life, holiday rituals, the influence of Zionism on young people, generational conflicts, and other topics. The first half of the first volume recounts experiences before the Second World War. The remainder relates the author's wartime experiences and the post-war years.

I am grateful to ChaeRan Freeze, Ellie Kellman, Gennady Kulikov, Joanna Nalewajko-Kulikov, Simon Rabinovitch, Jim Rosenbloom, and Sarah Silberstein Swartz for their help in compiling this bibliography.

ANTIN, MARY, *The Promised Land* (Boston: Houghton Mifflin, 1912; repr. 1969).

About one-half of this memoir recounts experiences in Plotsk (Płock), Poland, and elsewhere in eastern Europe in the last decades of the nineteenth century before emigration to the United States. Antin describes Jewish–Christian relations, holiday rituals, a cholera epidemic, restrictions on education for girls, the education of other female family members, marriage and wedding customs, *mikveh* customs, and other issues. The chapter 'The Tree of Knowledge' describes her and her sister's religious and secular education and Antin's intellectual development. Other writings by Antin include *From Plotzk to Boston* (Boston: W. B. Clarke, 1899; repr. New York: M. Wiener, 1986), and *Selected Letters of Mary Antin*, ed. Evelyn Salz (Syracuse, NY: Syracuse University Press, 2000). However, only *The Promised Land* deals extensively with Antin's life in eastern Europe.

AZARYAHU, SARAH, *Pirkei ḥayim* ('Chapters of a Life') (Tel Aviv: M. Nyuman, 1957).

Memoir of childhood in Dinaburg (Dvinsk, Daugavpils), Latvia, and Pinsk in the last quarter of the nineteenth century, including her education and involvement in early Zionist circles in Białystok and elsewhere.

BALABANOFF, ANGELICA, *Erinnerungen und Erlebnisse* ('Memories and Experiences') (Berlin: E. Laubsche Verlagsbuchhandlung, 1927); trans. into Yiddish as *Zikhroynes un iberlebenishn* by I. Rapaport (Warsaw: Ch. Brzoza, 1929), with introd. by Balabanoff: 'Vi azoy fun a rusish-yidishn privilegirtn meydl iz oysgevaksn an italyenisher sotsialist' ('How a Russian Jewish Privileged Girl Became an Italian Socialist').

The introduction to the Yiddish translation describes the author's childhood in the Kiev region in a wealthy Jewish family. The author recounts restrictions on her education, attitudes towards Russian and Yiddish, her efforts to acquire an education, and rebellion against her wealthy upbringing. The remainder focuses on socialist thought and her leadership in socialist politics and the Communist Party.

BALABANOFF, ANGELICA, *My Life as a Rebel* (New York: Harper, 1938).

Recounts the author's political activities, describing in the first chapter her privileged childhood and rebellion against her family with no reference to her Jewish background. She writes about her early education, language studies, university studies, and intellectual development before focusing on her leadership in revolutionary politics.

BAS YONAH [Sheyndl Dvorin], *Em labanim* ('A Mother of Children') (Pinsk: Dolinko, 1935).

BERG, REBECCA HIMBER, 'Childhood in Lithuania', in Leo W. Schwarz (ed.), *Memoirs of My People: Jewish Self-Portraits from the 11th to the 20th Centuries* (New York: Schocken Books, 1963), 269–80.

The author recounts her childhood in Yaneshok (Joniškis), Lithuania, in the last quarter of the nineteenth century, with descriptions of family and religious life, marriage customs, living quarters, her father's business as a petty merchant, and other topics.

BERGNER, HINDA ROSENBLATT, *In di lange vinternekht: Mishpokhe-zikhroynes fun a shtetl in galitsie, 1870–1900* ('In the Long Winter Nights: Family Memories from a Shtetl in Galicia') (Montreal: privately published, 1946); trans. into Hebrew as *Beleilot haḥoref ha'arukim* by Aryeh Aharoni (Tel Aviv: Am Oved, 1982).

The author recounts her childhood and the early years of her marriage in the small Galician town of Redim (Radymno), Poland. She describes her religious home, efforts to acquire an education and to avoid marriage proposals, scenes from family life, living quarters, helping her father in his grain business, marriage and childbirth, the influence of modernity on dress, and other matters. Bergner is the mother of the Yiddish writers Melech Ravitch and Herz Bergner.

BERLIN-PAPISH, TOVA, *Tselilim shelo nishkeḥu: Mimohilev ad yerushalayim* ('Sounds that Were Not Forgotten: From Mogilev to Jerusalem') (Tel Aviv: Reshafim, 1988).

The author recounts her experiences in Mogilev (Belarus), Leningrad, and Berlin, as well as her emigration to Palestine in 1924. Includes journal entries.

BERMAN, ZEHAVAH, *Bedarki sheli* ('My Ways') (Jerusalem: Elyashar, 1982).

Memoirs of a woman from Białystok, describing her education, study of Hebrew, involvement in Zionist circles, and emigration to Palestine.

BOBROVSKAYA, CECILIA, *Twenty Years in Underground Russia: Memoirs of a Rank-and-File Bolshevik* (New York: International, 1934).

The author describes her Jewish childhood in Velizh, near Vitebsk, Belarus, including access to books and reading, education and work in Warsaw in the 1890s, underground reading circles, and involvement in revolutionary politics throughout the Russian empire.

BROIDO, EVA LVOVNA, *Wetterleuchten der Revolution* (Berlin: Bücherkreis, 1929); trans. into English as *Memoirs of a Revolutionary* by Vera Broido (London: Oxford University Press, 1967).

The author recounts her childhood as the daughter of a talmudic scholar in Sventsyany (Švenčionys), Lithuania, and her leadership in the Russian revolutionary movement. She describes family life, her education in a boys' *ḥeder*, private tutoring, reading habits, university studies, work in a chemist's shop, marriage, her political awakening to socialism, and other topics. The author focuses on her involvement in revolutionary politics, later as a Menshevik. She ends her memoir in 1917.

CHAGALL, BELLA, *Brenendike likht* (New York: Book League of the Jewish People's Fraternal Order, IWO, 1945); trans. into English as *Burning Lights* by Norbert Guterman (New York: Schocken Books, 1962).

The author, the wife of Marc Chagall, describes in short sketches her childhood in a hasidic home in Vitebsk in the context of the cycle of the Jewish week and year, including sabbath, meals, Jewish holidays, rituals, and family life.

CHAGALL, BELLA, *Di ershte bagegenish* ('The First Encounter') (New York: Book League of the Jewish People's Fraternal Order, IWO, 1947).

CHAGALL, BELLA, *First Encounter*, English trans. of *Brenendike likht* and *Di ershte bagegenish* by Barbara Bray, 1 vol., with some changes in chapter sequence (New York: Schocken Books, 1983).

Recollections of the author's first meetings with Marc Chagall and her childhood in Vitebsk, including descriptions of her father's watchmaking shop, wedding rituals, and other sketches of family life.

COHEN, ROSE, *Out of the Shadow* (New York: George H. Doran, 1918); repr. as *Out of the Shadow: A Russian-Jewish Girlhood on the Lower East Side* (Ithaca, NY: Cornell University Press, 1995).

The first section recounts the author's childhood in the 1880s in a 'small Russian village' before her emigration to New York at the age of 12. Included are descriptions of family life and religious beliefs. The sections on life in eastern Europe are dominated by preparations for emigration.

COSOW, PAULINE [Pesil] L. SHER, *A lebn farn folk* ('A Lifetime for My People') (New York: Shulsinger, 1971).

Early sections describe the author's family and childhood in Vilna in the late nineteenth and early twentieth centuries, before her emigration to the United States in 1905. She describes her own and her sisters' limited education, her work learning a trade, attendance at a night school for women workers, and her encounter with Theodor Herzl. Includes journal entries, poems, and letters.

DAYAN [Daian], DEBORAH, *Be'osher uveyagon* ('In Happiness and in Sorrow') (Ramat Gan: Massada, 1956–7); trans., abridged, into Yiddish as *In glik un in troyer* (Tel Aviv: Farlag Y. L. Peretz, 1960); trans., abridged, into English as *Pioneer* by Michael Plashkes (Ramat Gan: Massada, 1968).

In the first chapter the mother of Moshe Dayan relates her experiences in Ukraine, including her education in a Russian gymnasium, her work in local government, and her awakening to Zionism. The remainder of the book recounts her experiences in Palestine and Israel.

DINUR, BILHA, *Lenekhdotai: Zikhronot mishpaḥah vesipurei ḥavayot* ('For My Granddaughters: Family Memories and Stories of Experiences'), ed. Ben Zion Dinur (Jerusalem: privately printed, 1972).

DRACH, LISA, *Les Fantômes de Lisa, juive polonaise émigrée* (Paris: L'Harmattan, 1996).

The first chapter relates experiences of family life in Mińsk Mazowiecki, Poland, before the First World War until the author's emigration to France before the Second World War.

DUBNOVA-ERLIKH, SOFIYA, *Khleb i matsa: Vospominaniya, stikhi raznykh let* ('Bread and Matzah: Recollections, Poems of Various Years') (St Petersburg: Maksima, 1994).

The author is the daughter of the historian Simon Dubnow.

EDELMAN, FENI [Fannie], *Der shpigl fun lebn* (New York: Shulsinger, 1948); trans. into English as *The Mirror of My Life* by Samuel Pasner (New York: Exposition Press, 1961).

The author recounts in the first three chapters her early years in a poor family in a small Galician town near the Russian border, describing the life of the town, relations between Jews and Christians, childhood sickness and medical care, the economic roles of her parents, marriage customs, and other issues. The remainder of the memoir describes life in the United States.

EDELSTEIN [Adelshtein], ZELDA, *Bedarkhei avot* ('The Ways of the Fathers') (Jerusalem: privately published, 1970).

Memoirs of pre-Second World War life in Stavisk (Stawiski), in the Łomża region, Poland, including family, local personalities, religious life, communal life, disease, education, and marriage.

FEIGENBERG [Feygenberg], ROKHEL, *Di kinder-yorn* ('The Childhood Years') (Warsaw: Hatsefirah, 1909–10).

This novel, which bears strong similarities to the author's early life, describes a girl's childhood, education, and family history in a small town in Lithuania, from education in Torah, secular studies, and love of books to the premature death of the narrator's father and her taking charge of the family's store during her mother's illness. The narrator describes her grandmother's education, reading habits, and attitudes towards her daughters' education; customs of arranged marriage; her mother's store and bakery, which she opened after her husband's death; education at her mother's behest in Hebrew, Russian, and Yiddish; sabbath rituals; her own reading habits and obstacles to obtaining new books; and her mother's long illness and death.

FISZMAN-SZNAJDMAN, RÓŻA, *Mayn lublin: Bilder funem lebns-shtayger fun yidn in farmilkhomadikn poyln* ('My Lublin: Pictures of the Way of Life of Jews in Pre-War Poland') (Tel Aviv: Farlag Y. L. Peretz, 1982).

Memoir of childhood on Lubartowska Street in Lublin before the Second World War. The writer describes the everyday lives of working-class families in a courtyard of apartment buildings, including occupations, family life, experiences during the First World War, education and teachers, medical care, colonies of Jewish summer vacationers, and political movements of Jewish youth.

FOGELMAN, BELLA, *Mibeit aba ad halom* ('From My Father's House to Here') (Kiryat Motzkin: privately published, 1974).

GORSHMAN, SHIRE, *Ikh hob lib arumforn* ('I Love to Travel') (Moscow: Sovetsky Pisatel, 1981).

Short essays by the Yiddish writer about life in the Soviet Union.

GORSHMAN, SHIRE, *Lebn un licht: Dertseylungen un noveln* ('Love and Light: Stories and Novels') (Moscow: Sovetsky Pisatel, 1974).

Autobiographical stories describing childhood in the small town of Krok (Krakės), Lithuania, and beyond.

GRADE, CHAIM, *My Mother's Sabbath Days: A Memoir*, trans. Channa Kleinerman Goldstein and Inna Hecker Grade (New York: Knopf, 1986; repr. Northvale: Jason Aronson, 1997).

The writer's memoir of life in Vilna before the Second World War. The first half centres on Grade's mother, including her prayers and religious observance, holiday rituals, family life, and Jewish women in economic life.

GREENBLATT, ALIZA [Eliza], *Baym fenster fun a lebn* ('By the Window of a Life') (New York: Farlag Aliza, 1966).

Early sections recount the Yiddish poet's childhood in Mogilev-Podolsky and the nearby small town of Azarenits (Ozarintsy) in the 1890s, before her emigration to

Philadelphia with her family in the early twentieth century. She describes daily life in Azarenits, occupations, the market fair, dress, sabbath preparations and rituals, charity customs, attitudes towards orphans, marriage customs, her father's early death, her mother's remarriage, and her early poetry. She mentions briefly her and her sisters' education and their recital of kaddish for their father.

GROBER, CHAYELE, *Tsu der groyser velt* ('To the Greater World') (Buenos Aires: Bialystoker Farband, 1952).

An actress in the Yiddish theatre in Montreal recounts her childhood, family life, and education in Białystok and the surrounding region at the beginning of the twentieth century, and her work in the Hebrew and Yiddish theatre in eastern Europe. Included are descriptions of childhood friends, a pogrom in Białystok, experiences as a refugee in Kharkov during the First World War, her start as an actress, and sketches of personalities in the Jewish theatre in eastern Europe.

GROBER, CHAYELE, *Mishnei tsidei hamasakh* ('On Both Sides of the Curtain') (Haifa: Pinat Hasefer, 1973); Hebrew trans. of *Tsu der groyser velt* and *Mayn veg alein* ('My Way Alone') (Tel Aviv: Farlag Y. L. Peretz, 1968).

Grober's account of her life in the Yiddish theatre after emigrating from eastern Europe.

GUBER, RIVKA, *Morashah lehanḥil* ('A Legacy to Pass On') (Jerusalem: Kiryat Sefer, 1979).

Memoir describing her childhood in a family of farmers in Ukraine, her education and university studies, experiences during the First World War and the Russian Revolution, and her activities in Zionist circles before her emigration to Palestine.

GURVITS, FRUMAH, *Zikhronoteiha shel rofah: Im yehudei lita biyemei hasho'ah* ('Memoirs of a Doctor: With the Jews of Lithuania in the Days of the Holocaust') (Tel Aviv: Beit Loḥamei Hagetaot, Hakibuts Hame'uhad, 1981).

Recollections of a woman doctor from Kovno (Kaunas). About one-third of the memoir recounts experiences before the Second World War.

HAUTZIG, ESTHER [Rudomin], *The Endless Steppe: Growing up in Siberia* (New York: Thomas Y. Crowell, 1968).

Memoir of her childhood in Vilna and her Second World War experiences in Rubtsovsk, Russia. Brief recollections of pre-war childhood, including education.

HERSCH, ITA, The Writings of Ita Hersch (Melamed) in Hebrew, Yiddish, and English (Johannesburg: Ammatt, 2000).

Hersch's memoir recounts her childhood in Trishik (Tryškiai), Lithuania, including her education in Hebrew and Torah in the late nineteenth century, and her involvement in Zionist and literary circles in Warsaw after her marriage. She emigrated to South Africa in 1904, where she became a Hebrew teacher. The book also includes an essay by her on the *Tsenerene* and essays about her life. The memoir was initially published from 1956 to 1958 in a Hebrew journal.

HILF, MARY ASIA, *No Time for Tears*, as told to Barbara Bourns (New York: Thomas Yoseloff, 1964).

The first third of the memoir recounts the author's childhood in Teofipol, near Kremenets, Ukraine, in the last quarter of the nineteenth century. The author describes her struggles to gain an education, her reading habits, work, family life, the childhood deaths of siblings, marriage customs, and other issues. The rest of the memoir recounts experiences after emigration to the United States.

HOLTMAN, ROKHL KIRSH, *Mayn lebns-veg* ('My Life's Path') (New York: Rokhl Holtman Book Committee, 1948).

The writer recounts her childhood in the small town of Plungyan (Plungė), Lithuania, in the Memel region in the 1880s and 1890s, and her education in her home town. The chapter 'Mayn gezelshaftlekhe arbet' ('My Communal Work') describes the establishment of a night school and an illegal library by the author and other young women in Plungyan as well as her own reading habits and desire for learning. In later chapters she describes travelling to Vilna, Warsaw, and Berlin to study. About one-third of the memoir describes life before emigration.

HUBERMAN, HAYAH, *Tsurikgemishte bletlekh: Zikhroynes* ('Recalled Pages: Memoirs') (Paris: Schipper, 1966).

Memoir of the author's childhood in a small town near Warsaw and her work as a union organizer in the Warsaw and Łódź regions from the late nineteenth century, including the First World War, the Polish–Soviet War, and the inter-war period.

KAHAN, ANNE, 'The Diary of Anne Kahan, Siedlce, Poland, 1914–1916', trans. from Yiddish by A. Kahan, *YIVO Annual Jewish Social Science*, 18 (1983), 141–371.

Diary entries from 31 Dec. 1914 to 26 Sept. 1916. The author, who was 14 years old in May 1915, writes about her life in Siedlce during the First World War, with descriptions of her work as a seamstress in a hat shop, reading habits, education, religion and family life, popular culture, politics, antisemitism, Zionism, wartime refugees, and other topics.

KALISH, ITA, *A rebishe heim in amolikn poyln* ('A Rabbinic Home in Poland of the Past') (Tel Aviv: I. L. Peretz, 1963); pub. in Hebrew, with some revisions, as *Etmoli* ('My Yesterday') (Tel Aviv: Kibuts Hame'uhad, 1970).

The author, a daughter of the Vorker (Warka) hasidic *rebbe*, describes her childhood in a hasidic court and the history of her family through the First World War and the inter-war period. The memoir takes place in Matshayevits (Maciejewice), Otwock, and Wyszków, Poland.

KAMIŃSKA [Kamiński], ESTHER RACHEL, *Briv fun ester rokhl kaminski* ('Letters of Esther Rachel Kamiński') (Vilna: B. Kletskin, 1927).

Letters from the Polish Jewish actress to her family and friends, written from 1908 to 1925, the year of her death.

KAMIŃSKA, IDA, *My Life, My Theater*, ed. and trans. Curt Leviant (New York: Macmillan, 1973).

Memoirs of the Polish Jewish actress in the Yiddish theatre, a daughter of Esther Rachel Kamińska, from childhood to her emigration from Poland during the 'anti-Zionist' campaign in 1967–8.

KAMIŃSKA, RUTH TURKOW, *I Don't Want to Be Brave Anymore*, introd. Harrison E. Salisbury (Washington: New Republic, 1978).

Memoirs of the actress Ida Kamińska's daughter, who recounts experiences in eastern Poland and the Soviet Union during the Second World War, until her repatriation to Poland from the Soviet Union in 1955 or 1956.

KIRSHENBAUM, HAYA, *Me'ir huladeti, melits* ('From the City of My Birth, Melitz [Mielec]') (Ramat Gan: privately published, 1976).

KORNGOLD, SHEYNE, *Zikhroynes* ('Memoirs') (Tel Aviv: Idepress, 1968).

The author, the elder sister of Golda Meir, describes her childhood and youth in Pinsk and Kiev at the start of the twentieth century. She writes about family life and awakening to Jewish political movements by her and her siblings. The first half of the memoir recounts life before emigration from eastern Europe.

KOSITZA [Kositsa], ROKHL [Rachel Anna], *Zikhroynes fun a bialystoker froy* ('Memoirs of a Woman from Białystok') (Los Angeles: Schwartz Printing, 1964).

The author recounts the story of her family, childhood, and adulthood in Białystok in the last three decades of the nineteenth century and early years of the twentieth century before her emigration to the United States in 1906.

KOVÁLY, HEDA MARGOLIUS, *Under a Cruel Star: A Life in Prague, 1941–1968*, trans. Franci Epstein, Helen Epstein, and Heda Margolius Kovály (Cambridge, Mass.: Plunkett Lake Press, 1986; repr. New York: Penguin Books, 1989; New York: Holmes & Meier, 1997).

The author's account of childhood survival during the Second World War and subsequent experiences in Czechoslovakia, including her husband's conviction and death sentence in the 1952 show trials of the Communist Party general secretary Rudolf Slánský and thirteen co-defendants.

LANG, LUCY ROBINS, *Tomorrow Is Beautiful* (New York: Macmillan, 1948).

The first chapter, 'Matriarch Versus Patriarch', recounts the author's childhood in Kiev and nearby small towns. She describes marriage customs, attendance at a boys' *ḥeder*, her mother's refusal to shave her head, men's and women's dress, her father's emigration to avoid being drafted, and issues of family life and observance. Most of the remaining book recounts life after emigration to the United States.

LAZEBNIK, EDITH, *Such a Life* (New York: William Morrow, 1978).

The author focuses on the Minsk region, describing the complicated family life of her father, his move away from tradition, business activities, women's employment in factories and shops, the impact of early marriage, education, divorce, and other family issues.

LEDER, MARY M., *My Life in Stalinist Russia: An American Woman Looks Back*, ed. Laurie Bernstein, introd. Laurie Bernstein and Robert Weinberg (Bloomington: Indiana University Press, 2001).

Memoirs of an American Jewish girl from California, the daughter of Jewish immigrants from Ukraine, who as a teenager moved with her family to Birobidzhan. The memoir describes her experiences in Birobidzhan, Moscow, and elsewhere in the Soviet Union from 1931 primarily until 1953, including university studies, work in publishing, and employment in the Soviet news agency.

LEE, MALKA, *Durkh kindershe oygn* ('Through Child's Eyes') (Buenos Aires: Farlag 'Yidbukh', 1955).

The poet describes her childhood in a small town in Galicia in a hasidic family, including education in a Polish school, a cholera epidemic, and experiences during the First World War.

LIPSHITZ, SHIFRA, *Khaloymes un virklekhkeit: Birobidzhan un arbetslagern* ('Dreams and Reality: Birobidzhan and Labour Camps') (Tel Aviv: Eygens, 1979).

The author recounts her childhood in the Łomża region in the early twentieth century, her work in Warsaw and the Soviet Union, her experiences in Birobidzhan in the 1930s, and life in Soviet labour camps.

LISHANSKY, SHOSHONA, *Mitseror zikhronotai* ('From the Bouquet of My Memories') (Jerusalem, 1942).

LONDYN[SKI], HELEN, *In shpigl fun nekhtn: Zikhroynes* ('In the Mirror of Yesterday: Memoirs') (New York: Helen Londynski Book Committee, 1972).

The author recounts her rebellion against her wealthy hasidic family in Warsaw and her involvement in Warsaw Yiddish literary circles. She describes her efforts to obtain an education despite her father's protests; attitudes towards the Yiddish, Polish, and Russian languages; founding a kitchen for refugee children during the First World War and her help in establishing a Yiddish nursery school for the refugees; marriage to the Yiddish writer and poet Shmuel Londynski; the establishment of the Yiddish publishing house Di Tsayt in Warsaw; the Londynskis' involvement in Polish and Yiddish intellectual circles in Paris in the 1920s and 1930s; and their lives as wartime refugees before reaching the United States in 1942.

LOWN, BELLA, *Memories of My Life: A Personal History of a Lithuanian Shtetl* (Malibu, Calif.: Joseph Simon/Pangloss, 1991).

The author recounts her childhood as the daughter and granddaughter of rabbis in Filipoveh (Filipów, Poland) and Shirvint (Širvintos, Lithuania), and her married life in Utyan (Utena), Lithuania, until her departure from Lithuania in 1936. She describes holiday rituals, her father's visit to Palestine, typhus epidemics, medical care, wedding customs, a female relative's suicide, secular and religious education, reading habits, the First World War and experiences as refugees, work as a teacher and translator, the Russian Revolution, her marriage and childbirth, Jewish communal life, Zionist youth groups, and other topics. The last third of the memoir describes life in the United States.

MARGOLINA, RAKHEL PAVLOVNA, *Rakhel Pavlovna Margolina i ee perepiska s Korneem Ivanovichem Chukovskim* ('Rakhel Pavlovna Margolina and her Correspondence with Korney Ivanovich Chukovsky') (Jerusalem: Stav, 1978).

MARKISH, ESTHER, *The Long Return*, trans. D. J. Goldstein, foreword David Roskies (New York: Ballantine, 1978); first pub. as *Le Long Retour*, trans. from the original Russian by Léon Kroug, preface Georges Bortoli (Paris: Laffont, 1974); trans. Imanuel Bikhovski as *Laḥzor miderekh arukah* (Tel Aviv: Kibuts Hame'uhad, 1977).

The author was the wife of the Soviet Yiddish poet and writer Peretz Markish. Her memoir recounts her early years in Ekaterinoslav (Dnipropetrovsk), Ukraine, and Baku in an assimilated, wealthy Jewish family, describing her father's activities in the oil business, attitudes towards religion, the Russian Revolution, pogroms, education, antisemitism, the impact of Soviet politics on her family, and marriage. The bulk of the memoir describes life with Markish, including Soviet Jewish literary circles, the Second World War, her husband's arrest, and her efforts to emigrate to Israel after her husband's death.

MEDEM, GINA, *A lebensveg* ('A Way of Life') (New York: Gina Medem Book Committee, 1950).

The author, who was married to the writer and Bund activist Vladimir Medem, recounts her childhood near Piotrków and in Łódź as the daughter of an assimilated father and a mother from a rabbinic home in Memel. She describes family life, her education and intellectual development, revolutionary politics in Łódź, her studies abroad in Estonia and elsewhere, her involvement in the Bund in Poland, and her life with Medem.

NUDEL, IDA, *A Hand in the Darkness: The Autobiography of a Refusenik*, trans. Stefani Hoffman (New York: Warner, 1990).

Autobiography of a Soviet Jewish dissident, including her exile to Siberia and her emigration to Israel in 1987. The memoir briefly describes her childhood in Moscow and the Crimea, and adulthood as an economist, before focusing on her efforts on emigrating to Israel and her experiences of antisemitism. The autobiography also includes letters written to and from Nudel from 1972 to 1986.

PESOTTA, ROSE, *Days of our Lives* (Boston: Excelsior, 1958).

The author recounts her Jewish youth in Derazhnya, Ukraine, focusing on aspects of economic and religious life, life-cycle events, and political awakening. She describes holiday preparations and rituals, wedding customs, childbirth and funeral rituals, reactions to political events, food rituals, attendance at an elementary school for girls, study of Hebrew and Russian, reading habits, involvement in a reading circle, and underground political activities. The last three chapters describe her journey to the United States and life as an immigrant.

PROZANSKAYA LACKOW, MANYA, 'In the Russian Gymnasia', *Lilith*, 15/1 (Winter 1990/5750), 15–20.

Excerpt from a memoir in which the author describes her education at a Hebrew school and a Russian government primary school in the small town of Lyubeshov and at a Russian gymnasium in Pinsk beginning in 1912.

RAKOVSKY, PUAH, *My Life as a Radical Jewish Woman: Memoirs of a Zionist Feminist in Poland*, ed. Paula E. Hyman, trans. Barbara Harshav with Paula E. Hyman, introd. Paula E. Hyman (Bloomington: Indiana University, 2002); pub. in Yiddish as *Zikhroynes fun a yidisher revolutsionerin* (Buenos Aires: Tsentral-Farband fun Poylisher Yidn in Argentine, 1954); trans., abridged, as *Lo nikhnati* ('I Did Not Yield') (Tel Aviv: N. Tversky, 1951); also excerpted as 'A Mind of My Own', in Lucy S. Dawidowicz (ed.), *The Golden Tradition: Jewish Life and Thought in Eastern Europe* (Syracuse, NY: Syracuse University Press, 1996).

The author recounts her childhood and education in a religious family in Białystok, her career as an educator in private schools for Jewish girls, her work as a Zionist and feminist activist in Poland, primarily in Warsaw, and her private life, including her arranged first marriage and divorce. The memoir, which was written in 1940–2, begins in the 1860s and ends with her emigration to Palestine in 1935.

ROSENTHAL-SHNAIDERMAN, ESTHER, *Birobidzhan fun der noent: Zikhroynes, gesheenishn, perzenlikhkaitn* ('Birobidzhan from Up Close: Memories, Experiences, Personalities') (Tel Aviv: H. Leyvik-Farlag, 1983); trans. into Hebrew as *Birobizan mekarov: Zikhronot, me'oraot, ishim* by Shelomoh Even-Shoshan (Tel Aviv: Kibuts Hame'uhad, 1990).

ROSENTHAL-SHNAIDERMAN, ESTHER, *Oyf vegn un umvegn: Zikhroynes, gesheenishn, perzenlikhkaitn* ('Of Roads and Detours: Memories, Experiences, Personalities'), 3 vols. (Tel Aviv: Hamenora, 1974, 1982); trans. into Hebrew as *Naftulei derakhim: Zikhronot, me'oraot, ishim*, 3 vols. (Tel Aviv: Kibuts Hame'uhad, 1970–89).

The first volume recounts the author's childhood and youth in Częstochowa, Poland, in the early twentieth century; the second follows her life and political work among Jews in the Soviet Union; the third describes personalities and events in Soviet Jewish life. The author was repatriated to Poland in 1958 and settled in Jerusalem in 1962.

ROZENTHAL, ANNA HELLER, 'Bletlekh fun a lebns-geshikhte' ('Pages from a Life Story'), in A. Tsherikover (Elias (Eliahu) Tcherikower) (ed.), *Di yidishe sotsialistishe bavegung biz der grindung fun 'Bund'* ('The Jewish Socialist Movement Until the Establishment of the Bund'), *Historishe shriftn*, 3 (Vilna: YIVO, 1939).

Memoirs of a Bund activist, a dentist by profession, from the Grodno region who lived in Vilna. The author died in the 1940s in a Soviet prison, according to the *Leksikon fun der nayer yidisher literatur* ('Biographical Dictionary of Modern Yiddish Literature').

RUBIN, RIVKE, *Yidishe froyen: Fartseykhenungen* ('Jewish Women: Jottings') (Moscow: Der Emes, 1943).

Sketches of Jewish women's lives in the Soviet Union by the Yiddish writer and literary critic.

RUSINEK, ALLA, *Like a Song, Like a Dream: A Soviet Girl's Quest for Freedom* (New York: Scribner, 1973).

Memoir of a Soviet Jewish activist. The author describes her childhood with little attention to Jewish matters, then focuses on her awakening to Zionism as a young woman and her increasing involvement in Zionist circles in Moscow, including her requests to emigrate and her eventual emigration to Israel.

SCHENIRER [Shnirer], SARAH, *Gezamlte shriftn* ('Collected Writings') (Łódź: Beys Yakov, 1932–3); pub. in Hebrew as *Em beyisra'el: Kol kitvei sarah shenirer* ('Mother in Israel: Collected Writings of Sarah Schenirer'), 3 vols. (Tel Aviv: Netsah, 1955–60); excerpt, with biographical information, pub. as 'Mother of the Beth Jacob Schools', in Lucy S. Dawidowicz (ed.), *The Golden Tradition: Jewish Life and Thought in Eastern Europe* (Syracuse, NY: Syracuse University Press, 1996).

Autobiographical essays by Schenirer, founder of the Beth Jacob religious schools for girls in Poland.

SCHULMAN, FAYE, with the assistance of Sarah Silberstein Swartz, *A Partisan's Memoir: Woman of the Holocaust* (Toronto: Second Story Press, 1995).

The first two chapters recount the author's childhood in Lenin, Belarus, including descriptions of economic life, religious observance, political activities of youth, a Jewish women's volunteer organization, her sister's working life and marriage, her family's business activities, antisemitism, and education.

SHECHTER, ESTHER, *Di geshikhte fun mayn lebn* ('The Story of My Life') (Winnipeg: Dos Yidishe Vort, 1951).

The author, the daughter of a maskil, describes in the first sections her childhood in a well-to-do family in Medzhybizh (Medzhibozh), Ukraine, in the last quarter of the nineteenth century. She recounts her education in a *ḥeder* and a Russian gymnasium, reading books and newspapers, the town's library, studies in Odessa, marriage and divorce, her printing shop in Odessa, political involvement, and remarriage. The remainder of the memoir describes her life in Canada beginning in 1905 and includes correspondence and essays written after emigration.

SHOHAT, MANYA, 'The Woman in the Bund and in Poalei Zion (1937)', in Paul Mendes-Flohr and Jehuda Reinharz (eds.), *The Jew in the Modern World: A Documentary History*, 2nd edn. (New York: Oxford University Press, 1995).

In this excerpt from a speech in Tel Aviv, Shohat, a leader of Labour Zionism, describes the role of women in socialist parties in eastern Europe and the status of Jewish women.

SHULNER, DORA, *Azoy hot es pasirt, 1905–1922* ('This Is How It Happened') (Chicago: Radomishler Ladies' Auxiliary, 1942).

The author describes life in Ukraine, including education, work experiences, and political involvement.

SHULNER, DORA, *Miltshin un andere dertseylungen* ('Miltshin and Other Stories') (Chicago: 'A Group of Friends', 1946).

Autobiographical short stories.

SIVAK-KIRSH, CHAIKA, *Fun mayn nekhtn: Zikhroynes* ('From My Yesterdays: Memoirs') (Tel Aviv: Farlag Problemen, 1981).

The first two sections recount the author's childhood near Kiev, until her emigration to Montreal in 1923.

SPERBER [Shperber], MIRIAM, *Miberditsev ad yerushalayim: Zikhronot leveit ruzin* ('From Berdichev to Jerusalem: Recollections of the House of Ruzin') (Jerusalem: M. Shperber, 1980).

Memoir of childhood and family history beginning in the 1870s in Berdichev, Ukraine, and her travels to Odessa, Romania, and London before emigration to Palestine after the Second World War.

STONE, GOLDIE, *My Caravan of Years: An Autobiography* (New York: Bloch Publishing, 1945).

The first quarter of the memoir recounts the author's childhood and young adulthood in a small town in the Suwałki region of Poland. She describes her education in Hebrew, attitudes towards marriage and divorce, friendship with Christian children and Jewish–Christian relations, women's participation in the synagogue, fear of a pogrom, knowledge of languages, a neighbour's suicide, medical care, her father's death, her brother's efforts to gain a university education, and her emigration to the United States.

WEIZMANN-LICHTENSTEIN, HAYA, *Betsel koratenu: Pirkei zikhronot mibeit aba* ('In our House: Chapters of Memories from My Father's House') (Tel Aviv: Am Oved, 1947–8).

The author, a sister of Chaim Weizmann, describes childhood in Motele (Motol), Belarus, including family life, religious observance, and the beginnings of her Zionist involvement, as well as her experiences in Warsaw, Vilna, and elsewhere in eastern Europe.

WEIZMANN-LICHTENSTEIN, HAYA, *El hagevul hanikhsaf* ('To the Long-Awaited End') (Tel Aviv: Am Oved, 1952–3).

Continuation of *Betsel koratenu*. The first quarter of this volume continues to recount the author's life in eastern Europe before emigration to Palestine in the 1920s.

WENGEROFF, PAULINE, *Rememberings: The World of a Russian-Jewish Woman in the Nineteenth Century*, ed. Bernard D. Cooperman, trans. Henny Wenkart (Potomac: University Press of Maryland, 2000); first pub. as *Memoiren einer Grossmutter* (Berlin, 1908, 1910); also excerpted as 'Memoirs of a Grandmother', in Lucy S. Dawidowicz (ed.), *The Golden Tradition: Jewish Life and Thought in Eastern Europe* (Syracuse, NY: Syracuse University Press, 1996).

Memoir of childhood in a religious, well-to-do, mitnagdic family in Bobruisk and Brest, Belarus, and the impact of the Haskalah on education, youth, and Jewish observance. The memoir covers the period from about 1840 to her husband's death in 1892. Wengeroff intersperses her personal experiences with analysis of the impact of modernity and general societal changes on Jewish life. Included are descriptions of her education, Jewish holidays and rituals, wedding customs, reading habits, her arranged marriage, married life in various cities of the Russian empire, childbirth, Jewish dress, her children's baptism, and other topics.

YELLIN, ITA [Etta], *Letse'etsa'ai* ('For My Descendants') (Jerusalem: Hama'arav, 1937–41).The author describes childhood in a small town near Grodno and in Mogilev before emigration to Palestine.

ZUNSER, MIRIAM SHOMER, *Yesterday: A Memoir of a Russian Jewish Family*, ed. Emily Wortis Leider (first pub. 1939; New York: Harper & Row, 1978).

Story of the author's family beginning with her maternal grandparents and their children in the first half of the nineteenth century. The author, a daughter of the Yiddish writer whose pen-name was Shomer, recounts her parents' involvement in the Yiddish theatre in Odessa and the family's lives in Odessa and Pinsk. Most of the memoir recounts the family's history before their emigration to the United States in 1889 and 1890. With a postscript by Leider, the author's granddaughter, recounting Zunser's life in the United States.

Secondary Sources

ADLER, ELIYANA R., 'Educational Options for Jewish Girls in Nineteenth-Century Europe', *Polin*, 15 (2002), 301–10.

ADLER, RUTH P., 'Devorah Baron: Chronicler of Women in the Shtetl', *Midstream*, 34/6 (Aug.–Sept. 1988), 40–2.

—— 'Dvora Baron: Daughter of the Shtetl', in Judith R. Baskin (ed.), *Women of the Word: Jewish Women and Jewish Writing* (Detroit: Wayne State University Press, 1994).

—— 'The Rabbi's Daughter as Author: Dvora Baron Views the Rituals and Customs of a Lithuanian Shtetl', *Proceedings of the Eleventh World Congress of Jewish Studies*, 3/3 (1994), 53–60.

—— *Women of the Shtetl: Through the Eyes of Y. L. Peretz* (Rutherford, NJ: Fairleigh Dickinson University; London: Associated University Presses, 1980).

AGUDAT ISRAEL, *Programm und Leistung. Keren Hathora und Beth Jakob, 1929–1937* ('Programming and Achievements of Keren Hatorah and Beth Jacob, 1929–1937') (London: Verlag der Keren Hatora-Zentrale, 1937).

ALEKSIUN, NATALIA, 'Gender and Nostalgia: Images of Women in Early "Yizker Bikher"', *Jewish Culture and History*, 5/1 (2002), 69–90.

ARASZKIEWICZ, AGATA, *Wypowiadam wam moje życie: Melancholia Zuzanny Ginczanki* ('I Express to You My Life: The Melancholy of Zuzanna Ginczanka') (Warsaw: Fundacja OŚKa, 2001). About the life and literature of Zuzanna Ginczanka, an inter-war Polish poet of Jewish background involved in Polish literary circles in Warsaw.

ARATEN, RACHEL SARNA, *Michalina: Daughter of Israel* (Jerusalem: Am Yisra'el Hai, 1986). Story of a Polish Jewish girl who was kidnapped in 1899 and raised as a Catholic.

ASHKENAZI, SHLOMO, *Ha'ishah be'aspaklarit hayahadut* ('The Woman in the Mirror of Judaism'), 2 vols. (Tel Aviv: Hotsa'at Tsiyon, 1979).

—— 'Meḥaberot piyutim, teḥinot utefilot' ('Women Authors of *Piyutim* [Liturgical Poems], *Teḥinot* [Supplicatory Prayers], and Prayers'), *Maḥanayim*, 109 (1967), 75–82.

BACON, GERSHON C., 'The Missing 52 Percent: Research on Jewish Women in Inter-War Poland and its Implications for Holocaust Studies', in Dalia Ofer and Lenore J. Weitzman (eds.), *Women in the Holocaust* (New Haven: Yale University Press, 1998).

—— 'Woman? Youth? Jew? The Search for Identity of Jewish Young Women in Interwar Poland', in Judith Tydor Baumel and Tova Cohen (eds.), *Gender, Place and Memory in the Modern Jewish Experience: Re-placing Ourselves* (London: Vallentine Mitchell, 2003).

BAKER, MARK, 'The Voice of the Deserted Jewish Woman, 1867–1870', *Jewish Social Studies*, 2/1 (1995), 98–123. About deserted women in eastern Prussia, Russia, and Poland, based largely on information in *Hamagid*, a newspaper in eastern Prussia.

BALIN, CAROLE B., *To Reveal our Hearts: Jewish Women Writers in Tsarist Russia* (Cincinnati: Hebrew Union College, 2000).

BASKIN, JUDITH R. (ed.), *Women of the Word: Jewish Women and Jewish Writing* (Detroit: Wayne State University Press, 1994). Individual articles are listed by author.

BAUM, CHARLOTTE, 'What Made Yetta Work? The Economic Role of Eastern European Jewish Women in the Family', *Response, A Contemporary Jewish Review*, 18: *The Jewish Woman: An Anthology* (1973), 32–45.

BENISCH, PEARL, *Carry Me in Your Heart: The Life and Legacy of Sarah Schenirer, Founder and Visionary of the Bais Yaakov Movement* (Jerusalem: Feldheim, 2003).

BEN-ZVI, RACHEL YANAIT, *Manyah shoḥat* (Jerusalem: Yad Yitshak Ben-Tsevi, 1976); trans. into English as *Before Golda: Manya Shochat. A Biography* by Sandra Shurin, introd. Marie Syrkin (New York: Biblio Press, 1989).

BERGER, RUTH, 'Frauen in der ostjüdischen Volkserzählung' ('Women in East European Jewish Folk Stories'), *Aschkenas*, 8/2 (1998), 381–423.

BERGER, SHULAMITH Z., '*Tehines*: A Brief Survey of Women's Prayers', in Susan Grossman and Rivka Haut (eds.), *Daughters of the King: Women and the Synagogue: A Survey of History, Halakhah and Contemporary Realities* (Philadelphia: Jewish Publication Society, 1992).

BIALE, DAVID, 'Childhood, Marriage and the Family in the Eastern European Jewish Enlightenment', in Steven M. Cohen and Paula E. Hyman (eds.), *The Jewish Family: Myths and Reality* (New York: Holmes & Meier, 1986).

—— 'Eros and Enlightenment: Love Against Marriage in the East European Jewish Enlightenment', *Polin*, 1 (1986), 49–67.

—— *Eros and the Jews: From Biblical Israel to Contemporary America* (New York: Basic Books, 1992).

BILIK, DOROTHY SEIDMAN, 'Jewish Women and Yiddish Literature', *Transactions of the Seventh International Congress on the Enlightenment*, iii (Oxford: Voltaire Foundation, 1989).

—— '*Tsene-rene*: A Yiddish Literary Success', *Jewish Book Annual*, 51 (1993), 96–111.

BLATMAN, DANIEL, 'National Minority Policy, Bundist Social Organizations, and Jewish Women in Interwar Poland', in Zvi Gitelman (ed.), *The Emergence of Modern Jewish Politics: Bundism and Zionism in Eastern Europe* (Pittsburgh: University of Pittsburgh Press, 2003).

—— 'Women in the Jewish Labor Bund in Inter-War Poland', in Dalia Ofer and Lenore J. Weitzman (eds.), *Women in the Holocaust* (New Haven: Yale University Press, 1998).

BRISTOW, EDWARD J., *Prostitution and Prejudice: The Jewish Fight Against White Slavery 1870–1939* (New York: Schocken Books, 1983).

BRUMLIK, MICHA, 'Jüdischer Alltag in Polen' ('Jewish Everyday Life in Poland'), in Kristine von Soden (ed.), *Rosa Luxemburg* (Berlin: Elefanten Press, 1995).

COHEN, STEVEN M., and PAULA E. HYMAN (eds.), *The Jewish Family: Myths and Reality* (New York: Holmes & Meier, 1986). Individual articles are listed by author.

COHEN, TOVA, *Ha'aḥat ahuvah veha'aḥat senuah: Bein metsiut ledimyon bete'urei ha'ishah besifrut hahaskalah* ('One Beloved and the Other Hated: Between Reality and Fiction in Haskalah Depictions of Women') (Jerusalem: Magnes Press, 2002).

—— '"Information About Women Is Necessarily Information About Men": On Iris Parush's "Reading Women"', *Journal of Israeli History*, 21/1–2 (2002), 169–91.

——*Min hateḥum haprati el hateḥum hatsiburi: Kitvei maskilot ivriyot* ('From Private Sphere to Public Sphere: The Writings of Nineteenth-Century Enlightened Jewish Women'), in David Assaf *et al.* (eds.), *Mivilna li-yerushalayim: Meḥkarim betoledoteihem uvetarbutam shel yehudei mizraḥ eiropah mugashim leprofesor shmuel verses* ('From Vilna to Jerusalem: Studies in East European Jewish History and Culture in Honour of Professor Shmuel Werses') (Jerusalem: Magnes Press, 2002).

——'Reality and its Refraction in Descriptions of Women in Hebrew Haskalah Literature', in David Sorkin and Shmuel Feiner (eds.), *New Perspectives on the Haskalah* (London: Littman Library, 2001).

CZAJECKA, BOGUSŁAWA, 'Działalność żydowskich stowarzyszeń kobiecych (zawodowych, oświatowych i charytatywnych) w Krakowie w latach 1869–1939' ('The Activities of Jewish Women's Associations [Professional, Educational, and Charitable] in Kraków, 1869–1939'), in Krzysztof Pilarczyk (ed.), *Żydzi i judaizm we współczesnych badaniach polskich: Materiały z konferencji, Kraków 21–23 XI 1995* ('Jews and Judaism in Contemporary Polish Research: Materials from the Conference in Kraków, 21–3 November 1995') (Kraków: Księgarnia Akademicka, 1997).

DAVIS-KRAM, HARRIET, 'The Story of the Sisters of the Bund', *Contemporary Jewry*, 5/2 (1980), 27–43.

DEUTSCH, NATHANIEL, *The Maiden of Ludmir: A Jewish Holy Woman and her World* (Berkeley: University of California Press, 2003).

——'New Archival Sources on the Maiden of Ludmir', *Jewish Social Studies*, 9/1 (2002), 164–72.

DEUTSCHLANDER, LEO, *Bajs Jakob. Sein Wesen und Werden* ('Bais Jacob: Its Character and Development') (Vienna: Verlag der Keren Hatora-Zentrale, 1928).

DOBROSZYCKI, LUCJAN, 'The Fertility of Modern Polish Jewry', in Paul Ritterband (ed.), *Modern Jewish Fertility* (Leiden: E. J. Brill, 1981).

ELAZAR, DAHLIA S., '"Engines of Acculturation": The Last Political Generation of Jewish Women in Interwar East Europe', *Journal of Historical Sociology*, 15/3 (2002), 366–94.

ENDELMAN, TODD M., 'Gender and Radical Assimilation in Modern Jewish History', in Marc Lee Raphael (ed.), *Gendering the Jewish Past* (Williamsburg, Va.: College of William and Mary, 2002).

ENGELSTEIN, LAURA, 'Die Auslöschung der jüdischen Frau. Antisemitische Klischees von Mädchenhandel und Ritualmord im Russland der Jahrhundertwende' ('The Erasing of the Jewish Woman: Antisemitic Stereotypes of Traffic in Young Women and Ritual Murder in Russia at the Turn of the Century'), in

Jutta Dick and Barbara Hahn (eds.), *Von einer Welt in die andere. Jüdinnen im 19. und 20. Jahrhundert* ('From One World to the Other: Jewish Women in the Nineteenth and Twentieth Centuries') (Vienna: Verlag Christian Brandstätter, 1993).

ETKES, IMMANUEL, 'Marriage and Torah Study Among the *Lomdim* in Lithuania in the Nineteenth Century', in David Kraemer (ed.), *The Jewish Family: Metaphor and Memory* (New York: Oxford University Press, 1989). Discusses the economic role of Jewish women in the family and the portrayal of women in east European Enlightenment literature.

ETTINGER, ELŻBIETA, *Rosa Luxemburg: A Life* (Boston: Beacon Press, 1986). Includes aspects of Luxemburg's Jewish background as a child and young woman in Zamość and Warsaw.

FEINER, SHMUEL, 'Ha'ishah hayehudiyah hamodernit: Mikreh-mivḥan beyaḥasei hahaskalah vehamodernah' ('The Modern Jewish Woman: A Test-Case in the Relations of the Haskalah and Modernity'), *Zion*, 58 (1993), 453–99.

FEINGOLD, BEN AMI, 'Feminism in Hebrew Nineteenth Century Fiction', *Jewish Social Studies*, 49/3–4 (1987), 235–50.

FIESELER, BEATE, 'Dziedzictwo żydowskie i socjaldemokracja: Kobiety w Bundzie i SDPRR na przełomie XIX I XX wieku' ('The Jewish Legacy and Social Democracy: Women in the Bund and the Russian Social Democratic Workers' Party at the Turn of the Nineteenth and Twentieth Centuries'), in Feliks Tych and Jürgen Hensel (eds.), *Bund: 100 lat historii, 1897–1997* ('The Bund: 100 Years of History, 1897–1997') (Warsaw: Jewish Historical Institute, 2000).

FORMAN, FRIEDA, ETHEL RAICUS, SARAH SILBERSTEIN SWARTZ, and MARGIE WOLFE (eds.), *Found Treasures: Stories by Yiddish Women Writers*, introd. Irena Klepfisz (Toronto: Second Story Press, 1994).

FRANKEL, GIZA, 'Notes on the Costume of the Jewish Woman in Eastern Europe', *Journal of Jewish Art*, 7 (1980), 50–7.

FREEZE, CHAERAN Y., 'Gendering Marital Conflict and Divorce Among Jews in Tsarist Russia', in Marc Lee Raphael (ed.), *Gendering the Jewish Past* (Williamsburg, Va.: College of William and Mary, 2002).

——*Jewish Marriage and Divorce in Imperial Russia* (Hanover: University Press of New England, 2002).

——'The Litigious "Gerusha": Jewish Women and Divorce in Imperial Russia', *Nationalities Papers*, 25/1 (1997), 89–101.

FRIEDLANDER, JUDITH, 'The Jewish Feminist Question', *Dialectical Anthropology*, 8 (1983), 113–20.

GITELMAN, ZVI, 'Correlates, Causes and Consequences of Jewish Fertility in the USSR', in Paul Ritterband (ed.), *Modern Jewish Fertility* (Leiden: E. J. Brill, 1981).

GLENN, SUSAN, *Daughters of the Shtetl: Life and Labor in the Immigrant Generation* (Ithaca, NY: Cornell University Press, 1990).

GOLDBERG, JACOB, 'Jewish Marriage in Eighteenth-Century Poland', *Polin*, 10 (1997), 3–39.

GOLDSTEIN, YA'AKOV, *Manyah vilbushevits shoḥat: Perek hamanhigut mahpekhanit* ('Manya Vilbushevitz-Shochat: Her Revolutionary Leadership in Russia') (Haifa: Haifa University Press, 1991).

GOVRIN, NURIT, *Hamaḥatsit harishonah: Devorah baron, ḥayeiha vitsiratah, 1887–1923* ('The First Half: Dvora Baron, Her Life and Work, 1887–1923') (Jerusalem: Mosad Bialik, 1988).

GREENBAUM, ALFRED ABRAHAM, 'The Girls' "Heder" and Girls in the Boys' "Heder" in Eastern Europe Before World War I', *East/West Education*, 18/1 (1997), 55–62.

HAVER, CHARLOTTE E., 'Vom Schtetl in die Stadt. Zu einigen Aspekten der Migration ostjüdischer Frauen um die Jahrhundertwende' ('From the Shtetl to the City: On Some Aspects of the Migration of Eastern European Jewish Women at the Turn of the Century'), *Aschkenas*, 5/2 (1995), 331–58.

HELLERSTEIN, KATHRYN, 'Gender Studies and Yiddish Literature', in Naomi B. Sokoloff, Ann Lapidus Lerner, and Anita Norich (eds.), *Gender and Text in Modern Hebrew and Yiddish Literature* (New York: Jewish Theological Seminary of America; Cambridge, Mass.: Harvard University Press, 1992). Annotated bibliography.

—— 'The Name in the Poem: Women Yiddish Poets', *Shofar*, 20/3 (2002), 32–52.

—— *Paper Bridges: Selected Poems of Kadya Molodowsky*, introd. Hellerstein (Detroit: Wayne State University Press, 1999).

—— 'A Question of Tradition: Women Poets in Yiddish', in Lewis Fried (ed.), *Handbook of American Jewish Literature: An Analytical Guide to Topics, Themes and Sources* (New York: Greenwood Press, 1988).

—— 'Songs of Herself: A Lineage of Women Yiddish Poets', *Studies in American Jewish Literature*, 9/2 (1990), 138–50.

—— (ed. and trans.), 'Canon and Gender: Women Poets in Two Modern Yiddish Anthologies', in Judith R. Baskin (ed.), *Women of the Word: Jewish Women and Jewish Writing* (Detroit: Wayne State University Press, 1994).

HENRY, SONDRA, and EMILY TAITZ, *Written Out of History: A Hidden Legacy of Jewish Women Revealed Through their Writings and Letters* (New York: Bloch, 1978). Reprinted as *Written Out of History: Our Jewish Foremothers* (Fresh Meadows: Biblio Press, 1983).

HUNDERT, GERSHON DAVID, 'Approaches to the History of the Jewish Family in Early Modern Poland–Lithuania', in Steven M. Cohen and Paula E. Hyman (eds.), *The Jewish Family: Myths and Reality* (New York: Holmes & Meier, 1986).

HUNDERT, GERSHON DAVID, 'Jewish Children and Childhood in Early Modern East Central Europe', in David Kraemer (ed.), *Jewish Family: Metaphor and Memory* (New York: Oxford University Press, 1989).

HYMAN, PAULA E., 'East European Jewish Women in an Age of Transition, 1880–1930', in Judith R. Baskin (ed.), *Jewish Women in Historical Perspective* (Detroit: Wayne State University Press, 1998).

—— *Gender and Assimilation in Modern Jewish History: The Roles and Representation of Women* (Seattle: University of Washington Press, 1995).

—— 'Gender and the Jewish Family in Modern Europe', in Dalia Ofer and Lenore J. Weitzman (eds.), *Women in the Holocaust* (New Haven: Yale University Press, 1998).

—— 'The Jewish Body Politic: Gendered Politics in the Early Twentieth Century', *Nashim: A Journal of Jewish Women's Studies and Gender Issues*, 2 (1999), 37–51.

—— 'Memory, Gender and Identity in Modern Jewish History', in Michael A. Signer (ed.), *Memory and History in Christianity and Judaism* (Notre Dame, Ind.: University of Notre Dame Press, 2001).

—— 'Puah Rakovsky; ou, Le Défi des conventions', *Cahiers du Judaïsme*, 12 (2002), 25–33.

—— 'Two Models of Modernization: Jewish Women in the German and the Russian Empires', *Studies in Contemporary Jewry*, 16 (2000), 39–53.

KAPLAN-MERMINSKI, ROKHL, *Froyen-problem* ('Women's Problem') (Warsaw, 1927).

KÄSTNER, INGRID, 'Aufstieg durch Bildung? Das Schicksal der Jüdinnen unter den ersten russischen Ärztinnen' ('Advancement Through Education? The Destiny of Jewish Women under the First Russian Female Doctors'), in Albrecht Scholz and Caris-Petra Heidel (eds.), *Medizinische Bildung und Judentum* (Dresden: Goldenbogen, 1998).

KATZ, JACOB, 'Family, Kinship and Marriage Among Ashkenazim in the Sixteenth to Eighteenth Centuries', *Jewish Journal of Sociology*, 1/1 (1959), 4–22.

KAUFMAN, SHIRLEY, GALIL HASAN-ROKEM, and TAMAR S. HESS, *The Defiant Muse: Hebrew Feminist Poems from Antiquity to the Present: A Bilingual Anthology* (New York: Feminist Press at the City University of New York, 1999). With introductory overview of the history of Hebrew poetry by women.

KAY, DEVRA, 'An Alternative Prayer Canon for Women: The Yiddish *Seyder Tkhines*', in Julius Carlebach (ed.), *Zur Geschichte der jüdischen Frau in Deutschland* (Berlin: Metropol Verlag, 1993).

——'Words for God in Seventeenth Century Women's Poetry in Yiddish', in Dovid Katz (ed.), *Dialects of the Yiddish Language: Papers from the Second Annual Oxford Winter Symposium in Yiddish Language and Literature, December 1986* (Oxford: Pergamon Press, 1988).

KAYE (Kantrowitz), MELANIE, and IRENA KLEPFISZ (eds.), *The Tribe of Dina: A Jewish Women's Anthology* (Boston: Beacon Press, 1989).

KAYSERLING, M., *Die jüdischen Frauen in der Geschichte, Literatur, und Kunst* ('Jewish Women in History, Literature, and Art') (Leipzig: F. A. Brockhaus, 1879).

KLIRS, TRACY GUREN, *The Merit of our Mothers: A Bilingual Anthology of Jewish Women's Prayers*, trans. Tracy Guren Klirs, Ida Cohen Selavan, and Gella Schweid Fishman, annot. Faedra Lazar Weiss and Barbara Selya (Cincinnati: Hebrew Union College Press, 1992). Compilation of *tkhines* in Yiddish and English.

KOESTLER, NORA, 'Jüdinnen in der Habsburger Monarchie und Emanzipation' ('Jewish Women in the Habsburg Monarchy and Emancipation'), *Acta Poloniae Historica*, 86 (2002), 57–72.

——'Kobieta w społecznościach żydowskich w monarchii habsburskiej: Etapy emancypacji' ('The Woman in Jewish Communities in the Habsburg Monarchy: Stages of Emancipation'), in Anna Żarnowska and Andrzej Szwarc (eds.), *Kobieta i świat polityki: Polska na tle porównawczym w XIX i w początkach XX wieku* ('Woman and the World of Politics: Poland Against a Comparative Background in the Nineteenth and the Beginning of the Twentieth Centuries') (Warsaw: Instytut Historyczny Uniwersytetu Warszawskiego, 1994).

KORMAN, E. (ed.), *Yidishe dikhterins: Antologye* ('Yiddish Women Poets: Anthology') (Chicago: Farlag L. M. Shtayn, 1928).

KOZLOWSKA, TERESA, 'Rodzina żydowska w swietle akt notarialnych powiatu skalbmierskiego z lat 1817–1835' ('The Jewish Family in Light of Notarial Records of Skalbmierz District, 1817–1835), *Kwartalnik Historii Żydów* (formerly *Biuletyn Żydowskiego Instytutu Historycznego*), 202 (2002), 227–32.

KRAEMER, DAVID (ed.), *The Jewish Family: Metaphor and Memory* (New York: Oxford University Press, 1989). Individual articles are listed by author.

KRAMER, SYDELLE, and JENNY MASUR (eds.), *Jewish Grandmothers* (Boston: Beacon Press, 1976). Three interviews in the first section portray the lives of three Jewish women in eastern Europe in the early twentieth century.

KUGELMASS, JACK, and JONATHAN BOYARIN (eds.), *From a Ruined Garden: The Memorial Books of Polish Jewry*, 2nd expanded edn. (Bloomington: Indiana University Press, 1998). See 'Girls' *Kheyders*', 'Esther-Khaye the Zogerin ("Sayer")', 'Reb Dvoyre Mash', and 'My Grandmother Sews her Own Burial Shroud'.

KUMOVE, SHIRLEY, 'Drunk from the Bitter Truth: The Life, Times and Poetry of Anna Margolin', in Sarah Silberstein Swartz and Margie Wolfe (eds.), *From Memory to Transformation: Jewish Women's Voices* (Toronto: Second Story Press, 1998).

LERNER, ANNE LAPIDUS, 'Lost Childhood in East European Hebrew Literature', in David Kraemer (ed.), *The Jewish Family: Metaphor and Memory* (New York: Oxford University Press, 1989).

LEVY, ROBERT, *Ana Pauker: The Rise and Fall of a Jewish Communist* (Berkeley: University of California Press, 2001). Biography of a post-Second World War leader of Romania's Communist Party.

LIEBLICH, AMIA, *Conversations with Dvora: An Experimental Biography of the First Modern Hebrew Woman Writer*, ed. Chana Kronfeld and Naomi Seidman, trans. Naomi Seidman (Berkeley: University of California Press, 1991).

LOWENSTEIN, STEVEN M., 'Ashkenazic Jewry and the European Marriage Pattern: A Preliminary Survey of Jewish Marriage Age', *Jewish History*, 8 (1994), 155–75.

MAGNUS, SHULAMIT S., 'Pauline Wengeroff and the Voice of Jewish Modernity', in T. M. Rudavsky (ed.), *Gender and Judaism: The Transformation of Tradition* (New York: New York University Press, 1995).

MIRON, DAN, *Imahot meyasedot, aḥayot ḥoregot* ('Founding Mothers, Stepsisters') (Tel Aviv: Kibuts Hame'uhad, 1991). Examines the emergence of women's poetry in Hebrew.

—— 'Why Was There No Women's Poetry in Hebrew Before 1920?', in Naomi B. Sokoloff, Anne Lapidus Lerner, and Anita Norich (eds.), *Gender and Text in Modern Hebrew and Yiddish Literature* (New York: Jewish Theological Seminary of America; Cambridge, Mass.: Harvard University Press, 1992).

NATIONAL COUNCIL OF JEWISH WOMEN, NEW YORK SECTION, *Di froyen: Women and Yiddish. Tribute to the Past, Directions for the Future*, Conference Proceedings (New York: Jewish Women's Resource Center, 1997). See esp. Chava Weissler, 'Contrasting Views of Women as Religious Subjects in the *Tkhines* of Leah Horowitz and Sarah bas Toyvim'; Ellie Kellman, 'Women as Readers of Sacred and Secular [Yiddish] Literature: An Historical Overview'; Sheva Zucker, 'The Fathers on the Mothers and the Daughters: Women in the Works of the *Klasikers*/Classical Writers'; Paula E. Hyman, 'Memoirs and Memories: East European Jewish Women Recount their Lives'; Rochelle Goldberg Ruthchild, 'Esther Frumkin: Jewish Women Radical in Early Soviet Russia'; Rozka Luksamberg Aleksandrowicz, 'YAF and Women in the Bund'; Dina Abramowicz, 'Forsherin: Women Scholars at YIVO'; Ethel Raicus, 'Rokhl Brokhes'.

NIGER, SHMUEL, 'Di yidishe literatur un di lezerin', *Der pinkes* (Vilna, 1913); repr. in Shmuel Niger, *Bleter geshikhte fun der yidisher literatur* ('Studies in the History of Yiddish Literature') (New York: Sh. Niger Book Committee of the World Jewish Cultural Congress, 1959); trans. into English as 'Yiddish Literature and the Female Reader' by Sheva Zucker, in Judith R. Baskin (ed.), *Women of the Word: Jewish Women and Jewish Writing* (Detroit: Wayne State University Press, 1994).

NORICH, ANITA, 'The Family Singer and the Autobiographical Imagination', *Prooftexts*, 10 (Jan. 1990), 91–107.

PARUSH, IRIS, *Nashim korot: Yitronah shel shuliyut baḥevrah hayehudit bemizraḥ eiropah beme'ah hatesha-esreh* (Tel Aviv: Am Oved, 2001); trans. as *Reading Women: Marginality and Modernization in Nineteenth Century Eastern European Jewish Society* (Hanover: University Press of New England for Brandeis University Press, 2004).

—— 'The Politics of Literacy: Women and Foreign Languages in Jewish Society of 19th-Century Eastern Europe', *Modern Judaism*, 15/2 (1995), 183–206.

—— 'Readers in Cameo: Women Readers in Jewish Society of Nineteenth-Century Eastern Europe', *Prooftexts*, 14/1 (1994), 1–23.

—— 'Women Readers as Agents of Social Change Among Eastern European Jews in the Late Nineteenth Century', *Gender and History*, 9/1 (1997), 60–82.

PLAKANS, ANDREJS, and JOEL M. HALPERN, 'An Historical Perspective on Eighteenth Century Jewish Family Households in Eastern Europe', in Paul Ritterband (ed.), *Modern Jewish Fertility* (Leiden: E. J. Brill, 1981).

PRATT, NORMA FAIN, 'Anna Margolin's *Lider*: A Study in Women's History, Autobiography, and Poetry', *Studies in American Jewish Literature*, 3 (1983), 11–25.

—— 'Culture and Radical Politics: Yiddish Women Writers, 1890–1940', *American Jewish History*, 70/1 (1980), 68–91.

RABINOWICZ, HARRY M., 'Lady Rabbis and Rabbinic Daughters', in Rabinowicz (ed.), *The World of Hasidism* (Hartford, Conn.: Hartmore House, 1970).

RAICUS, ETHEL, 'Women's Voices in the Stories of Yiddish Writer Rokhl Brokhes', in Sarah Silberstein Swartz and Margie Wolfe (eds.), *From Memory to Transformation: Jewish Women's Voices* (Toronto: Second Story Press, 1998).

RAKOVSKY (Rakowska), PUAH, *Di moderne froyen-bavegung* ('The Modern Women's Movement') (Warsaw: Yidisher Froyen-Farband in Poyln, 1928).

—— *Di yidishe froy*, 1: *Di yidishe froy un di tsyonistishe bavegung*; 2: *Far vos darfn mir a spetsiele froyen-organizatsye* ('The Jewish Woman', 1: 'The Jewish Woman and the Zionist Movement'; 2: 'Why We Need a Special Women's Organization') (Warsaw: Bnos Tsiyon, 1918).

RANSEL, DAVID L., 'The Ethno-Cultural Impact on Childbirth and Disease Among Women in Western Russia', *Jews in Eastern Europe*, 2/45 (2001), 27–47.

RAPOPORT-ALBERT, ADA, 'On Women in Hasidism: S. A. Horodecky and the Maid of Ludmir Tradition', in Ada Rapoport-Albert and Steven J. Zipperstein (eds.), *Jewish History: Essays in Honor of Chimen Abramsky* (London: Peter Halban, 1988).

REINHARZ, SHULAMIT, 'Manya Wilbushewitz-Shohat and the Winding Road to Sejera', in Deborah S. Bernstein (ed.), *Pioneers and Homemakers: Jewish Women in Pre-State Israel* (Albany: State University of New York, 1992).

—— 'Toward a Model of Female Political Action: The Case of Manya Shohat, Founder of the First Kibbutz', *Women's Studies International Forum*, 7/4 (1984), 275–87.

ROSKIES, DAVID, 'Yiddish Popular Literature and the Female Reader', *Journal of Popular Culture*, 10/4 (1977), 852–8.

RUBINRAUT, H., *Yidishe froy, dervakh! Vi azoy zikh tsu farhitn fun umgevunshener shvangershaft* ('Jewish Woman, Awake! How to Avoid Unwanted Pregnancy') (Warsaw: Towarzystwo Ochrony Zdrowia, 1934). Not seen. Located at the Jewish National and University Library, Hebrew University, Jerusalem.

RUTHERS, MONICA, *Tewjes Töchter. Lebensentwürfe ostjüdischer Frauen im 19. Jahrhundert* ('Tevye's Daughters: Sketches of the Lives of East European Jewish Women in the Nineteenth Century') (Cologne: Böhlau, 1996).

SALKIND, S., 'The Jewish Women of Latvia: Their Progress in Social Work', *Jewish Woman*, 3/1 (1923), 2–3. Periodical published until 1931 in New York.

SALMON, TAMAR, *Gerushei nashim lo shaoyot bepolin bemayot ha-17 veha-18* ('Mad Women and Divorce Among Polish Jews in the Seventeenth and Eighteenth Centuries'), *Gal-Ed*, 7 (2000), 37–61. Summary in English.

SALZMAN [Zalcman], MOJSHE, *Bela Shapiro: Di populere froyen-geshtalt* ('Bela Shapiro: The Popular Women's Figure') (Paris: no publisher listed, 1983); trans. into French as *Bela Szpiro: Militante socialiste du Bund à Lublin (1890–1944)* by Irene Kanfer, preface by Marc Hillel (Quimperlé: La Digitale, 1988).

SEEMAN, DON, and REBECCA KOBRIN, '"Like One of the Whole Men": Learning, Gender and Autobiography in R. Barukh Epstein's *Mekor barukh*', *Nashim: A Journal of Jewish Women's Studies and Gender Issues*, 2 (1999), 52–94.

SEIDMAN, NAOMI, 'Gender Criticism and Hebrew–Yiddish Literature: A Report from the Field', *Prooftexts*, 14/3 (1994), 298–310.

—— 'Lawless Attachments, One-Night Stands: The Sexual Politics of the Hebrew–Yiddish Language War', in Jonathan Boyarin and Daniel Boyarin (eds.), *Jews and Other Differences: The New Jewish Cultural Studies* (Minneapolis: University of Minnesota Press, 1997).

—— *A Marriage Made in Heaven: The Sexual Politics of Hebrew and Yiddish* (Berkeley: University of California Press, 1997).

SHEPHERD, NAOMI, *A Price Below Rubies: Jewish Women as Rebels and Radicals* (Cambridge, Mass.: Harvard University Press, 1993).

SHERMAN, JOSEPH, 'Money, Revolution and Women in Russia and America in Pre-World War I Yiddish Prose Fiction', *Jews in Eastern Europe*, 1–2/47–8 (2002), 125–33.

SHMERUK, CHONE, 'Di mizrekh-eyropeishe nuskhoes fun der Tsenerene (1786–1850)' ('The East European Versions of the *Tsenerene*'), in *For Max Weinreich on his Seventieth Birthday: Studies in Jewish Languages, Literature and Society* (The Hague: Mouton, 1964); trans. into Hebrew as 'Hanusaḥot hamizraḥ-eiropeyot shel hatsenah ure'enah', in C. Shmeruk (ed.), *Sifrut yidish bepolin* (Jerusalem: Magnes Press, 1981).

—— *The Esterke Story in Yiddish and Polish Literature: A Case Study in the Mutual Relations of Two Cultural Traditions* (Jerusalem: Zalman Shazar Center for the Furtherance of the Study of Jewish History, 1985).

—— 'Hasoferet hayehudit harishonah bepolin: Rivkah bat me'ir tiktiner veḥibureiha' ('The First Jewish Woman Author in Poland: Rivkah bat Meir Tiktiner and her Work'), in Me'ir Vunder (ed.), *Ateret rivkah: Arba'ah sifrei teḥinot nashim. Im targum lileshon hakodesh; meneket rivkah* ('Rivkah's Crown: Four Books of Women's *Teḥinot*. With translation into the Holy Tongue [from Yiddish]; Rivkah's Nurse') (Jerusalem: Hamakhon Lehantsaḥat Yahadut Galitsiyah, 1991–2).

SINCLAIR, CLIVE, *The Brothers Singer* (London: Allison & Busby, 1983). Includes information on Esther Kreitman Singer.

SION, ARIEL, 'L'Éducation des jeunes filles à Lodz (Pologne) entre 1919 et 1939' ('The Education of Young Girls in Łódź (Poland) Between 1919 and 1939'), *Cahiers d'Études Juives*, 2 (1991), 75–107.

SOKOLOFF, NAOMI B., 'Gender Studies and Modern Hebrew Literature' (annotated bibliography), in Naomi B. Sokoloff, Anne Lapidus Lerner, and Anita Norich (eds.), *Gender and Text in Modern Hebrew and Yiddish Literature* (New York: Jewish Theological Seminary of America; Cambridge, Mass.: Harvard University Press, 1992).

—— ANNE LAPIDUS LERNER, and ANITA NORICH (eds.), *Gender and Text in Modern Hebrew and Yiddish Literature* (New York: Jewish Theological Seminary of America; Cambridge, Mass.: Harvard University Press, 1992). Individual articles are listed by author.

SOMOGYI, TAMAR, 'Jüdische Hochzeitsbrauche in Osteuropa im 18. und 19. Jahrhundert' ('Jewish Marriage Customs in Eastern Europe in the Eighteenth and Nineteenth Centuries'), in Gisela Völger and Karin von Welck (eds.), *Die Braut, geliebt, verkauft, getäuscht. Zur Rolle der Frau im Kulturvergleich* ('The

Bride, Loved, Sold, Deceived: On the Role of the Woman in Cultural Comparison') (Cologne: Rautenstrauch-Joest-Museum, Museum für Völkerkunde, 1985).

STAMPFER, SHAUL, 'Gender Differentiation and Education of the Jewish Woman in Nineteenth-Century Eastern Europe', *Polin*, 7 (1992), 63–87.

—— 'Marital Patterns in Interwar Poland', in Yisrael Gutman, Ezra Mendelsohn, Jehuda Reinharz, and Chone Shmeruk (eds.), *Jews of Poland Between Two World Wars* (Hanover: University Press of New England, 1989).

—— 'Remarriage Among Jews and Christians in Nineteenth-Century Eastern Europe', *Jewish History*, 3/2 (Fall 1988), 85–114.

STROBL, INGRID, 'Family Origins and Political Motivations of Jewish Resistance Fighters in German-Occupied Europe', in Judith Tydor Baumel and Tova Cohen (eds.), *Gender, Place and Memory in the Modern Jewish Experience: Replacing Ourselves* (London: Vallentine Mitchell, 2003).

SUCHMIEL, JADWIGA, 'Kariery naukowe Żydówek na Uniwersytecie Jagiellońskim do czasów Drugiej Rzeczypospolitej' ('The Academic Careers of Jewish Women at the Jagiellonian University [Kraków] Until the Time of the Second Republic'), with summary in German, in Aleksandra Bilewicz and Stefania Walasek (eds.), *Rola mniejszości narodowych w kulturze i oświacie polskiej w latach 1700–1939* ('The Role of National Minorities in Polish Culture and Education, 1700–1939') (Wrocław: Wydawnictwo Uniwersytetu Wrocławskiego, 1998).

—— *Żydówki ze stopniem doktora wszech nauk lekarskich oraz doktora filozofii w Uniwersytecie Jagiellońskim do czasów Drugiej Rzeczypospolitej* ('Jewish Women with the Degree of Doctor of Medicine as well as Doctor of Philosophy at the Jagiellonian University Until the Time of the Second Republic') (Częstochowa: Wydawnictwo WSP, 1997).

SULITEANU, GISELA, 'The Traditional System of Melopeic Prose of the Funeral Songs Recited by the Jewish Women of the Socialist Republic of Rumania', *Folklore Research Center Studies*, 3 (1972), 291–349.

TAITZ, EMILY, 'Kol Ishah, the Voice of Women: Where Was It Heard in Medieval Europe?', *Conservative Judaism*, 38/3 (1986), 46–61.

—— 'Women's Voices, Women's Prayers: Women in the European Synagogues of the Middle Ages', in Susan Grossman and Rivka Haut (eds.), *Daughters of the King: Women and the Synagogue. A Survey of History, Halakhah and Contemporary Realities* (Philadelphia: Jewish Publication Society, 1992).

TIKTINER, RIVKAH BAT ME'IR, *Ateret rivkah: Arba'ah sifre teḥinot nashim. Im targum lileshon hakodesh; meneket rivkah* ('Crown of Rivkah: Four Books of *Tkhines* of Women. With translation into Hebrew [from Yiddish];

Rivkah's Nurse'), ed. Me'ir Vunder (Jerusalem: Hamakhon Lehantsahat Yahadut Galitsiyah, 1991–2). Includes reprint of Rivkah bat Me'ir Tiktiner, *Meneket rivkah* (Prague, 1609).

TZUR, ELI, 'The Forgotten Leadership: Women Leaders of the Hashomer Hatzair Youth Movement at Times of Crisis', in Judith Tydor Baumel and Tova Cohen (eds.), *Gender, Place and Memory in the Modern Jewish Experience: Re-placing Ourselves* (London: Vallentine Mitchell, 2003).

UMIŃSKA, BOŻENA, *Postać z cieniem: Portrety Żydówek w polskiej literaturze od końca XIX wieku do 1939 roku* ('A Figure with a Shadow: Portraits of Jewish Women in Polish Literature from the End of the Nineteenth Century to 1939') (Warsaw: Wydawnictwo, 2001).

WEINBERG, SYDNEY STAHL, *World of our Mothers: The Lives of Jewish Immigrant Women* (Chapel Hill: University of North Carolina Press, 1988).

WEISSLER, CHAVA, '"For the Human Soul Is the Lamp of the Lord": The *Tkhine* for "Laying Wicks" by Sarah bas Tovim', *Polin*, 10 (1997), 40–65.

—— '"For Women and for Men Who Are Like Women": The Construction of Gender in Yiddish Devotional Literature', *Journal of Feminist Studies in Religion*, 5/2 (1989), 7–24.

—— '"Mitzvot" Built into the Body: *Tkhines* for Niddah, Pregnancy and Childbirth', in Howard Eilberg-Schwartz (ed.), *People of the Body: Jews and Judaism from an Embodied Perspective* (Albany: State University of New York Press, 1992).

—— 'Prayers in Yiddish and the Religious World of Ashkenazic Women', in Judith R. Baskin (ed.), *Jewish Women in Historical Perspective* (Detroit: Wayne State University Press, 1998).

—— 'The Religion of Traditional Ashkenazic Women: Some Methodological Issues', *Association for Jewish Studies Review*, 12/1 (1987), 73–94.

—— '*Tkhines* for the Sabbath Before the New Moon', in Judit Targarona Borrás and Angel Sáenz-Badillos (eds.), *Jewish Studies at the Turn of the Twentieth Century: Proceedings of the 6th EAJS Congress*, ii (Leiden: Brill, 1999).

—— 'The *Tkhines* and Women's Prayer', *CCAR Journal* [Central Conference of American Rabbis journal of Reform Judaism], 40/4 (1993), 75–88.

—— 'The Traditional Piety of Ashkenazic Women', in Arthur Green (ed.), *Jewish Spirituality*, ii (New York: Crossroad, 1987).

—— *Voices of the Matriarchs: Listening to the Prayers of Early Modern Jewish Women* (Boston: Beacon Press, 1998).

—— 'Woman as High Priest: A Kabbalistic Prayer in Yiddish for Lighting Sabbath Candles', *Jewish History*, 5/1 (1991), 9–26.

WEISSLER, CHAVA, 'Women in Paradise', *Tikkun*, 2/2 (1987), 43–6.

——'Women's Studies and Women's Prayers: Reconstructing the Religious History of Ashkenazic Women', *Jewish Social Studies*, 1/2 (1995), 28–47.

WEISSMAN, DEBORAH, 'Bais Yaakov: A Historical Model for Jewish Feminists', in Elizabeth Koltun (ed.), *The Jewish Woman: New Perspectives* (New York: Schocken Books, 1976).

——'Bais Ya'akov as an Innovation in Jewish Women's Education: A Contribution to the Study of Education and Social Change', *Studies in Jewish Education*, 7 (1995), 278–99.

——'Education of Jewish Women', *Encyclopedia Judaica Year Book, 1986–1987*, 29–36.

WISTRICH, ROBERT (ed.), *Revolutionary Jews from Marx to Trotsky* (London: Harrap, 1976). See the chapter 'Rosa Luxemburg the Internationalist'.

YIVO INSTITUTE FOR JEWISH RESEARCH, *Ida Kaminska (1899–1980): Grande Dame of the Yiddish Theater* (New York: YIVO, 2001).

ZAREMSKA, HANNA, 'Rachela Fiszel: Żydowska wdowa w średniowiecznym Krakowie' ('Rachela Fiszel: A Jewish Widow in Kraków in the Middle Ages'), *Kwartalnik Historii Żydów* (formerly *Biuletyn Żydowskiego Instytutu Historycznego*), 207 (2003), 381–90.

ZITRON, SAMUEL LEIB, *Barimte yidishe froyen: Zeyer lebn un virkn* ('Notable Jewish Women: Their Life and Works') (Warsaw: Ahisefer, 1928). Includes brief biographies of several women from eastern Europe: Chava Frank, Chaya Voloski, Dinah Val, and Chana-Rachel Werbermacher, the Maid of Ludmir.

Theses

ADLER, ELIYANA R., 'Private Schools for Jewish Girls in Tsarist Russia', Ph.D. thesis (Brandeis University, 2003).

ATKIN, ABRAHAM, 'The Beth Jacob Movement in Poland (1917–1939)', Ph.D. thesis (Yeshiva University, 1959).

BALIN, CAROLE B., 'Jewish Women Writers in Tsarist Russia, 1869–1917' [Miriam Markel-Mosessohn, Chava Shapiro, Rashel Khin, Feiga Kogan, Sofiya Dubnowa-Erlikh], Ph.D. thesis (Columbia University, 1998).

CARUSO, NAOMI, 'Chava Shapiro: A Woman Before her Time', MA thesis (McGill University, 1991).

FREEZE, CHAERAN Y., 'Making and Unmaking the Jewish Family: Marriage and Divorce in Imperial Russia, 1850–1914', Ph.D. thesis (Brandeis University, 1997).

GLASER, KAREN MELISSA, 'Female Émigrées from the "Shtetl" and their Interpretations of the Past: An Oral History', MA thesis (University of Windsor, 1990).

GONSHOR (Fishman), ANNA, 'Kadye Molodowsky in *Literarishe bleter*, 1925–1935: Annotated Bibliography', MA thesis (McGill University, 1997).

KAUFMAN, MARIANNA B., 'Two Women of the Zionist Socialist Youth Organizations: Warsaw, 1939–1943' [Frumka Plotnitzka, Lonka Kozibrodska], MA thesis (Emory University, 2000).

KLIRS, TRACY GUREN, 'Bizkhus fun sore, rivke, rokhl un leye: Through the Merit of Sarah, Rebekah, Rachel, and Leah: The *Tkhine* as the Jewish Woman's Self-Expression', Ph.D. thesis (Hebrew Union College, Jewish Institute of Religion in Cincinnati, 1984).

KOLODZIEJ, JOYCE STORY, 'Eliza Orzeszkowa's Feminist and Jewish Works in Polish and Russian Criticism', Ph.D. thesis (Indiana University, 1975).

LEVY, ROBERT, 'Ana Pauker: A Case Study of Jewish Communists in East-Central Europe', Ph.D. thesis (University of California, Los Angeles, 1998).

LITWIN-GRINBERG, RUTH R., 'Lives in Retrospect: A Qualitative Analysis of Oral Reminiscence as Applied to Elderly Jewish Women', DSW thesis (University of California, Berkeley, 1982).

RICAR, SONDRA LEE, 'A Portrait of Russian Revolutionary Women', Ph.D. thesis (University of California, Santa Cruz, 1995).

SCOTT, MARK CHAPIN, 'Her Brother's Keeper: The Evolution of Women Bolsheviks', Ph.D. thesis (University of Kansas, 1980).

SEIDMAN, NAOMI SHEINDEL, '"A Marriage Made in Heaven?" The Sexual Politics of Hebrew–Yiddish Diglossia' [Mendele Abramovitsh, Sholem Yankev, Dvora Baron], Ph.D. thesis (University of California, Berkeley, 1993).

WEISSMAN, DEBORAH, 'Bais Ya'akov, A Women's Educational Movement in the Polish Jewish Community: A Case Study in Tradition and Modernity', MA thesis (New York University, 1984).

ZAIDIN, NURIT, 'Haḥaverah batenuot hano'ar hatsiyoniyot bepolin bein shetei milḥamot olam' ('The Female Member in Zionist Youth Movements in Poland Between Two World Wars'), Ph.D. thesis (Ben-Gurion University of the Negev, 2000). With abstract in English.

ZUCKER, CHARLOTTE SHEVA, 'The Emergence of the Modern Woman in Yiddish and Western Literature', Ph.D. thesis (City University of New York, 1987).

PART II

New Views

Jewish Settlement in the Polish Commonwealth in the Second Half of the Eighteenth Century

ZENON GULDON and WALDEMAR KOWALSKI

POPULATION and settlement statistics are undoubtedly key factors in the analysis of the history of Polish Jewry. Previous attempts at the generalization of demographic processes have been based on fragmentary observations and/or methods that do not correspond to the needs of contemporary historiography. In this chapter we would like to present data on Jewish settlement in the lands of the Polish Commonwealth, including both the Kingdom of Poland (the Crown) and the Grand Duchy of Lithuania between 1764 and 1795. This period was one of decline for the Republic of Nobles and was formative in the modernization of east European Jewish communities; thus it is important in the history of both peoples. Its importance arises also from the fact that it was precisely in this era of reform that fiscal registers began to be recorded on a scale unparalleled in Polish history. Of course, there are limitations one must be aware of in using these sources or works based upon them. Nevertheless, some findings seem undisputed as well as methodologically instructive. Last but not least, we hope that the bibliographical references presented here will be useful to the vast number of professional and amateur historians engaged in genealogical studies.[1]

The Jewish population of Europe around 1490 is estimated at 600,000, including 250,000 in Spain, 120,000 in Italy, 80,000 in the Holy Roman Empire, 80,000 in Portugal, and 30,000 (or 5 per cent) in Poland–Lithuania. The Jewish population of Poland–Lithuania is supposed to have grown to 23 per cent of world Jewry by the mid-seventeenth century, to 33 per cent by about 1772, and to 42–6 per cent in the period 1800–1900. In 1764 Jews supposedly constituted approximately 7 per cent of the Commonwealth's population.[2] Thus the data fully justify the long-lasting

This chapter is an expanded and updated version of a paper presented at the conference 'Erfahrungen jüdischer Existenz im Zeitalter der Aufklärung. Mittel- und Osteuropa im Vergleich', which was organized by the Simon-Dubnow-Institut für jüdische Geschichte und Kultur e.V. and held at Leipzig University, 27–9 Aug. 1996.

[1] See e.g. *Avotaynu*, a leading periodical in this field; <http://www.avotaynu.com>.

[2] S. W. Baron, *A Social and Religious History of the Jews*, xvi: *Poland–Lithuania 1500–1650* (New

and commonly repeated opinion that Poland–Lithuania was 'the demographic power-house of modern European Jewry'.[3]

Until recently, the works of Ignacy Schiper published in 1914 and 1932 were the only global presentations of Jewish settlement in the Commonwealth in the sixteenth to eighteenth centuries.[4] Now, the studies of Salo Wittmayer Baron for the years 1500–1650 and those by Raphael Mahler for the mid-eighteenth century are regarded as the broadest and most accurate analyses of the demographic history of Polish Jewry.[5] The sources and methods of the population estimates have been thoroughly discussed by Zenon Guldon,[6] who is also the author (with Jacek Wijaczka) of an overview describing the results of investigations conducted in this field.[7]

Investigations into Jewish settlement in the different territories of the Commonwealth have not advanced to the same level thus far. The process of the Jewish settlement in Małopolska by the end of the sixteenth century has been described recently by Feliks Kiryk and Franciszek Leśniak, and that in the second half of the seventeenth century by Guldon.[8] Jewish settlement in Lublin province (*województwo*) in 1764–5 has been described by Mahler, and the works of Władysław Ćwik and Tomasz Opas concern the following decades of that century.[9] Furthermore,

York, 1976), 207; id., 'Population', in *Encyclopedia Judaica*, xiii (Jerusalem, 1972), 878; Z. Sułowski, 'Jewish Population Figures for the Polish Territories During the Last Millennium', in *International Conference on the History and Culture of Polish Jews: Abstracts* (Jerusalem, 1989), 110.

[3] J. I. Israel, *European Jewry in the Age of Mercantilism, 1550–1750* (London, 1998), 198; cf. esp. J. Czyński, 'La Question juive en Pologne', *Archives Israélites* (1864), 452.

[4] I. Schiper, 'Rasselenie evreev v Pol'she i Litve ot drevneishikh vremen do kontsa XVIII v.', in J. Hessen, S. M. Ginzburg, and M. Wischnitzer (eds.), *Istoriya evreiskogo naroda*, xi: *Istoriya evreev v Rossii*, pt. i (Moscow, 1914); id., 'Rozwój ludności żydowskiej na ziemiach dawnej Rzeczypospolitej', in I. Schiper, A. Tartakower, and A. Hafftka (eds.), *Żydzi w Polsce odrodzonej*, i (Warsaw, 1932). See also E. Feldman, 'The Earliest References to Jews in Polish Towns in the Fourteenth to Sixteenth Centuries', *Bleter far geshikhte*, 1 (1934), 59–73.

[5] Baron, *A Social and Religious History of the Jews*, *passim*; R. Mahler, *Yidn in amolikn poyln in likht fun tsifrn* (Warsaw, 1958).

[6] Z. Guldon, 'Źródła i metody szacunków liczebności ludności żydowskiej w Polsce w XVI–XVIII wieku', *Kwartalnik Historii Kultury Materialnej*, 34/2 (1986), 249–63; id., 'Osadnictwo żydowskie i liczebność ludności żydowskiej na ziemiach Rzeczypospolitej w okresie przedrozbiorowym: Stan i program badań', in K. Pilarczyk (ed.), *Żydzi i judaizm we współczesnych badaniach polskich* (Kraków, 1997); id., 'Skupiska żydowskie w miastach polskich XV–XVI wieku', in K. Pilarczyk and S. Gąsiorowski (eds.), *Żydzi i judaizm we współczesnych badaniach polskich* (Kraków, 2000).

[7] Z. Guldon and J. Wijaczka, 'Die zahlenmässige Stärke der Juden in Polen-Litauen im 16.–18. Jahrhundert', *Trumah*, 4 (1994), 91–101.

[8] F. Kiryk and F. Leśniak, 'Skupiska żydowskie w miastach małopolskich do końca XVI wieku', in F. Kiryk (ed.), *Żydzi w Małopolsce* (Przemyśl, 1991); Z. Guldon, 'Ludność żydowska w miastach małopolskich w drugiej połowie XVII wieku', in Kiryk (ed.), *Żydzi w Małopolsce*; id., 'Żydzi wśród chrześcijan w miastach małopolskich w XVI–XVIII wieku', *Nasza Przeszłość* (*NP*), 78 (1992), 187–222.

[9] R. Mahler, 'Statystyka Żydów województwa lubelskiego na przełomie 1764–1765 roku', *Młody Historyk*, 2 (1929), 67–108; W. Ćwik, 'Ludność żydowska w miastach królewskich Lubelszczyzny w II

Zenon Guldon and Karol Krzystanek have estimated the Jewish population on the left-bank territories of Sandomierz province in the sixteenth to eighteenth centuries.[10] In addition, Jadwiga Muszyńska has recently published a detailed study of the demographic aspects of Jewish history in the provinces of Lublin and Sandomierz in the second half of the eighteenth century.[11] Jakub Goldberg has commented on demographic features of the Jewish family in this period on the basis of censuses preserved from Małopolska.[12]

In his widely respected volume Maurycy Horn sets the population changes within the context of the whole of Jewish life in Red Ruthenia up to 1648.[13] Zdzisław Budzyński, Zenon Guldon, and Jerzy Motylewicz have taken up the question of the same region in the decades that followed.[14]

The Jewish population in Volhynia and Podolia in the second half of the seventeenth century has been presented by Zenon Guldon.[15] Ivan M. Kamanin has provided a detailed picture of Jewish settlement in the part of the Ukraine that belonged to the Commonwealth (on the right bank of the Dnieper) in the second half of the eighteenth century.[16]

We are still comparatively less knowledgeable about Jewish settlement in Wielkopolska. Thus, for the western part of the region, the work of Aaron Heppner and Isaak Herzberg is still the landmark.[17] Jewish settlement in the provinces of Poznań

połowie XVIII wieku', *Biuletyn Żydowskiego Instytutu Historycznego w Polsce* (*BŻIH*), (1966), 59: 29–62; T. Opas, 'Sytuacja ludności żydowskiej w miastach szlacheckich województwa lubelskiego w XVIII wieku', *BŻIH* (1968), 67: 3–37.

10 Z. Guldon and K. Krzystanek, *Ludność żydowska w miastach lewobrzeżnej części województwa sandomierskiego w XVI–XVIII wieku: Studium osadniczo-demograficzne* (Kielce, 1990).

11 J. Muszyńska, *Żydzi w miastach województwa sandomierskiego i lubelskiego w XVIII wieku* (Kielce, 1998); ead., 'The Urbanised Jewry of the Sandomierz and Lublin Provinces in the 18th Century: A Study in the Settlement of Population', *Studia Judaica*, 2/2 (1999), 223–39.

12 J. Goldberg, 'Jewish Marriage in Eighteenth-Century Poland', *Polin*, 10 (1997), 3–39; Z. Guldon and W. Kowalski, 'The Jewish Population and Family in the Polish–Lithuanian Commonwealth in the Second Half of the Eighteenth Century', *The History of the Family*, 8 (2003), 517–30.

13 M. Horn, *Żydzi na Rusi Czerwonej w XVI i pierwszej połowie XVII wieku* (Warsaw, 1975), 9–82.

14 Z. Budzyński, *Ludność pogranicza polsko-ruskiego w drugiej połowie XVIII wieku: Stan, rozmieszczenie, struktura wyznaniowa i etniczna* (Przemyśl, 1995), i. 241–58; Z. Guldon, 'Ludność żydowska w miastach małopolskich i czerwonoruskich w drugiej połowie XVII wieku', in his *Żydzi i Szkoci w Polsce w XVI–XVIII wieku* (Kielce, 1990); J. Motylewicz, *Miasta ziemi przemyskiej i sanockiej w drugiej połowie XVII i w XVIII wieku* (Przemyśl, 1993), 101–9 and table 18.

15 Z. Guldon, 'Żydzi na Podolu i Wołyniu po zniszczeniach z połowy XVII wieku', in his *Żydzi i Szkoci*.

16 I. Kamanin, 'Statisticheskie dannye o evreyakh v Yugo-Zapadnom krae vo vtoroi polovine proshlogo veka (1765–1791)', in *Arkhiv Yugo-Zapadnoi Rossii*, v/2 (Kiev, 1890), 1–239; see also M. Kędelski, 'Zaludnienie prawobrzeżnej Ukrainy w drugiej połowie XVIII wieku', *Przeszłość Demograficzna Polski* (*PDP*), 18 (1990), 53–90.

17 A. Heppner and J. Herzberg, *Aus Vergangenheit und Gegenwart der jüdischen Gemeinden in Posener Landen* (Koschmin, 1909). Kędelski's output is based mainly upon the Prussian censuses from the

and Kalisz has been traced by Guldon and Wijaczka.[18] Paweł Fijałkowski has provided an overview of these problems in the provinces of Łęczyca (that is, the eastern part of Wielkopolska) and Rawa (in Mazovia).[19] Research on the region has been enlarged upon recently by Guldon in a work on Kujawy and in another study of his (with Wijaczka) on Wielkopolska as a whole.[20]

Jewish settlement in Royal Prussia (Westpreussen) has been described by Max Aschkewitz, Samuel Echt, and Zenon Hubert Nowak.[21]

Late medieval Jewish settlement in Mazovia was examined by Emanuel Ringelblum.[22] This research has been continued for the early modern epoch by Marek J. Wieczerski and Paweł Fijałkowski, and the Jewish communities in Podlasie drew the attention of Anatol Leszczyński.[23]

Scholarly output on the Grand Duchy of Lithuania is far less developed. The monograph by Sergey A. Bershadsky published at the end of the nineteenth century is still instructive.[24] However, noticeable progress in research has been made recently thanks to Shaul Stampfer.[25] In his unpublished thesis Leib Flaks tackled the status of the Jewish population in the Grand Duchy in the second half of the

period after the second partition; see his works: 'Ludność ziemi wschowskiej w drugiej połowie XVIII wieku', *Rocznik Leszczyński* (*RL*), 8 (1987), 57–76; 'Stan i struktura wyznaniowa ludności powiatu kościańskiego w drugiej połowie XVIII wieku', *RL* 9 (1989), 43–61; 'Ludność północno-zachodniej Wielkopolski w XVIII wieku', *Studia i Materiały do Dziejów Wielkopolski*, 18/2 (1991), 27–56 (Wałca district); *Rozwój demograficzny Poznania w XVIII i na początku XIX wieku* (Poznań, 1992).

18 Z. Guldon and J. Wijaczka, 'Osadnictwo żydowskie w województwie poznańskim i kaliskim w XVI–XVII wieku', *BŻIH* (1992), 2/3: 63–77.

19 P. Fijałkowski, 'Początki i rozwój osadnictwa żydowskiego w województwach rawskim i łęczyckim', *BŻIH* (1989), 4: 3–15; id., *Żydzi w województwach łęczyckim i rawskim w XV–XVIII w.* (Warsaw, 1999).

20 Z. Guldon, 'Żydzi w miastach kujawskich w XVI–XVIII wieku', *Ziemia Kujawska*, 9 (1993), 99–108; Z. Guldon and J. Wijaczka, 'Ludność żydowska w Wielkopolsce w drugiej połowie XVII wieku', in J. Topolski and K. Modelski (eds.), *Żydzi w Wielkopolsce na przestrzeni dziejów* (Poznań, 1995); Guldon and Wijaczka, 'Żydzi wśród chrześcijan w miastach wielkopolskich w okresie przedrozbiorowym', *NP* 79 (1993), 149–96.

21 M. Aschkewitz, 'Die Juden in Westpreussen am Ende der polnischen Herrschaft (1772)', *Zeitschrift für Ostforschung*, 6/4 (1957), 557–72; see also S. Cackowski, 'Wiejscy Żydzi w województwie chełmińskim w 1772 r.', *Acta Universitatis Nicolai Copernici: Historia*, 28 (1993), 61–72; S. Echt, *Die Geschichte der Juden in Danzig* (Leer, 1972); Z. H. Nowak, 'Dzieje Żydów w Prusach Królewskich do roku 1772', in J. Basista, A. Link-Lenczowski, and A. Polonsky (eds.), *Żydzi w dawnej Rzeczypospolitej* (Wrocław, 1991).

22 E. Ringelblum, *Żydzi w Warszawie*, i (Warsaw, 1932).

23 M. J. Wieczerski, 'Żydzi w województwach środkowego dorzecza Wisły w XVI i pierwszej połowie XVII w.', *BŻIH* (1998), 3: 63–76 (eastern Wielkopolska and part of Mazovia); P. Fijałkowski, 'Żydzi na ziemi zawkrzeńskiej do 1795 roku', *BŻIH* (1995–6), 3/2: 27–35; A. Leszczyński, *Żydzi ziemi bielskiej od połowy XVII w. do 1795 r.* (Wrocław, 1980), 14–47; id., 'Z dziejów Żydów Podlasia (1487–1795)', *Studia Podlaskie*, 2 (1989), 7–24.

24 S. A. Bershadsky, *Litovskie evrei* (St Petersburg, 1883).

25 S. Stampfer, 'Some Implications of Jewish Population Patterns in Pre-Partition Lithuania', in A. Teller (ed.), *Studies in the History of the Jews in Old Poland in Honor of Jacob Goldberg*, Scripta Hierosolymitana: Publications of the Hebrew University of Jerusalem, 38 (Jerusalem, 1998).

eighteenth century.[26] Leonid Żytkowicz used the Russian census for 1795 for similar research.[27] Other works that must be consulted regarding the Jewish population in the part of Lithuania called Samogitia (Żmudź) are those by Grzegorz Błaszczyk.[28]

Both the sources and the literature provide data that were collected within different administrative units of Poland, Austria, Prussia, and the Russian empire, and for this reason they cannot be conflated. Thus, an encyclopaedia of all Jewish settlements and colonies up to the turn of the eighteenth century should be prepared as a starting point for an overview of this sub-field of historical geography and demography.

The basis for estimation of the numbers of Jews in the second half of the sixteenth century is the amount of Jewish capitation (which was imposed by the Diet for the first time in 1563). The tax proclamations required a payment of 1 zloty per head, irrespective of sex and age, and only the poor were to be released. In the years 1569 and 1578 the Jewish capitation brought in, respectively, just over 6,000 and 10,000 Polish zlotys. Thus, based upon the same sources, the Jewish population in the Polish Commonwealth in that period has been calculated between 30,000 to 300,000. Numerous estimates ranging between these extremes are based on the supposition that an unknown part of the Jews avoided taxation. However, there is no consensus on the number of those who did so. Some historians who interpret the tax proclamation almost literally maintain that the capitation must have been paid by individuals and because of this the number of Jews who evaded taxation was minimal. Others assume that the capitation was actually paid by families, or even households, and multiply the sums collected.[29]

The Jews suffered heavy losses during the Cossack rebellions, and also during the wars that Muscovy and Sweden waged on Poland in the mid-seventeenth century.[30] In the second half of this period the Commonwealth is said to have been inhabited by 180,000 to 350,000 Jews.[31] It seems that these estimates are significantly exaggerated.[32] Unfortunately, there are no grounds for calculating the

26 L. Flaks, 'Regulacja spraw żydowskich przez Komisję Skarbową Litewską: Studium z dziejów gospodarczych Żydów na Litwie za Stanisława Augusta' (University of Vilna, 1931) (Biblioteka Narodowa, Warsaw, MS IV. 7666).

27 L. Żytkowicz, *Rządy Repnina na Litwie w latach 1794–1797* (Vilna, 1938).

28 G. Błaszczyk, 'Liczebność Żydów na Żmudzi w XVI–XVIII wieku', pts. 1–3, *BŻIH* (1987), 1: 21–38; (1988), 1/2: 23–31; 3/4: 29–55.

29 Z. Guldon and W. Kowalski, 'Between Tolerance and Abomination: Jews in Sixteenth-Century Poland', in R. B. Waddington and A. H. Williamson (eds.), *The Expulsion of the Jews: 1492 and After* (New York, 1994).

30 L. Lewin, *Die Judenverfolgungen im zweiten schwedisch-polnischen Kriege 1655–1659* (Posen, 1901); J. Schamschon, *Beiträge zur Geschichte der Judenverfolgungen in Polen während der Jahre 1648–1658* (Bern, 1912); Z. Guldon, 'Straty ludności żydowskiej w Koronie w latach potopu', in J. Muszyńska and J. Wijaczka (eds.), *Rzeczpospolita w latach potopu* (Kielce, 1996).

31 Schiper, 'Rozwój ludności żydowskiej na ziemiach dawnej Rzeczypospolitej', 32; Baron, *A Social and Religious History of the Jews*, 207.

32 Z. Guldon and W. Kowalski, 'The Jewish Population of Polish Towns in the Second Half of the 17th Century', in Teller (ed.), *Studies in the History of the Jews in Old Poland.*

number of Jews in the Commonwealth at the end of the seventeenth and in the first half of the eighteenth centuries. However, a 1717 poll tax tariff sheds some light on Jewish settlement around that year.[33]

In 1764 the Diet voted for new capitation, and this time only children not older than 1 year were to be excluded. Registrations were carried out in 1764–6, 1775, 1778, 1781–4, 1787, and 1790–1. Shaul Stampfer has recently reprinted the Crown census for 1765, and he has also published a 1765 Lithuanian census.[34] Similar sources for the following decades are regarded as far less credible and are therefore rarely employed in research. All the censuses in Ukraine for the years 1765–91,[35] as well as the censuses for Lithuania[36] and some Crown provinces for 1790,[37] have been published. Many such registers are preserved in archives and have been exploited only to a very small extent.

The validity of the Jewish censuses of the second half of the eighteenth century has already been thoroughly discussed. Considerable omissions in the registration were pointed out by Tadeusz Czacki as early as 1788,[38] and also, among others, by an enumerator for the district of Kremenets (in Volhynia) in 1790.[39] The very low rate of people per homestead, which supposedly results from the inconsistent inclusion of children, also attests to the inaccuracy of the counts.[40] Registration of the poor was also far from complete.[41] The census for 1765 is well known for its credibility, which is proven by a 15 per cent decrease in the number of Jews who lived in the territories under the Crown in the years 1765–87 (Table 1). These territories were curtailed after the 1772 partition. The number of Jews living in the *kahal* centres of Sandomierz district (*powiat*) dwindled from 6,055 in 1765 to 2,874 in 1787 (47.5 per cent of the 1765 total), and 3,383 Jews (55.9 per cent of the 1765

[33] J. Muszyńska (ed.), 'Dyspartyment pogłównego żydowskiego w Koronie w 1717 roku', *Czasy Nowożytne*, 5 (1998), 119–31.

[34] S. Stampfer, 'The 1765 Census of Polish Jewry', *Bar-Ilan: Annual of Bar-Ilan University*, 24–5 (1989), 60–147; S. Stampfer, 'The 1765 Census of Lithuanian Jewry and What It Can Teach Us', in S. Della Pergola and J. Even (eds.), *Papers in Jewish Demography 1993 in Memory of U. O. Schmelz* (Jerusalem, 1997).

[35] I. Kamanin (ed.), 'Perepisi evreiskogo naseleniya v Yugo-Zapadnom krae v 1765–1791 gg.', in *Arkhiv Yugo-Zapadnoi Rossii*, v/2.

[36] R. Jasas and L. Truska, *Lietuvos Didžiosios Kunigaikštystės gyventojų surašymas 1790 m.* (Vilnius, 1972), 31–73.

[37] Z. Guldon and L. Stępkowski, 'Spis ludności żydowskiej z 1790 roku', *BŻIH* (1986), 3/4: 126–30.

[38] Archiwum Główne Akt Dawnych w Warszawie, Zbiór Popielów, MS 131, fos. 506^{v}–515.

[39] Z. Guldon and N. Krikun, 'Przyczynek do krytyki spisów ludności żydowskiej z końca XVIII wieku', *Studia Źródłoznawcze*, 23 (1978), 156–7.

[40] Mahler, 'Statystyka Żydów województwa lubelskiego na przełomie 1764–1765 roku', 15.

[41] Z. Guldon, 'Uwagi o spisach ludności żydowskiej w drugiej połowie XVIII wieku', in his *Żydzi i Szkoci*, 132–3.

Table 1. Number of Jews in the Kingdom of Poland (Korona), 1765 and 1787

Province	**Population in the territories (1765)**		**1787**
	Before first partition[a]	**After first partition**[b]	
Wielkopolska			
Brześć Kujawski, Inowrocław, and the Land of Dobrzyń	3,771	2,184	1,507
Kalisz	12,995	7,130	5,901[c]
Łęczyca	2,903	2,749	2,167
Poznań	19,913	16,021	10,267
Sieradz	7,990	7,930	6,977
Total	47,572	36,014	26,819
Małopolska			
Kraków	18,677	7,392	6,323
Lublin	20,191	17,685	15,912
Sandomierz	42,972	29,875	16,936
Total	81,840	54,952	39,171
Mazovia and Podlasie			
Mazovia	10,662	10,407	10,362
Płock	3,960	3,960	4,939
Podlasie	19,043	19,033	13,426
Rawa	5,332	5,340	4,543
Total	38,997	38,740	33,270
Red Ruthenia and Ukraine			
Bełz	16,442	—	—
Bratslav	20,337	20,327	27,562
Chełm	9,787	5,329	—
Kiev	22,352	22,409	27,194
Podolia	38,384	20,327	27,562
Ruthenia	100,111	—	—
Volhynia	50,792	48,744	39,363[d]
Total	258,205	127,944	119,702
Royal Prussia			
Culme	577	—	—
Marienburg	87	—	—
Pomerania	2,731	—	—
Total	3,395	—	—
TOTAL	430,009	257,650	218,962

[a] Comprising data collected in 1765 for the whole province.
[b] Comprising the same census figures but only for those lands that were part of the Polish Crown after 1772.
[c] Incl. the province of Gniezno, founded in 1768.
[d] Incl. the Land of Chełm.

Source: Z. Guldon, *Żydzi i Szkoci w Polsce w XVI–XVIII wieku* (Kielce, 1990), 130.

Table 2. Number and percentage of urbanized Jews in selected provinces of the Kingdom of Poland, 1765

Province	Total no.	No. in towns	% in towns
Bratslav	20,271	14,018	69.2
Inowrocław	1,422	1,290	90.7
Kalisz	12,995	12,814	98.6
Kiev	21,600	13,520	62.6
Kraków	18,677	12,911	69.1
Land of Wieluń	2,988	2,161	72.3
Łęczyca	2,903	1,926	66.3
Lublin	20,191	14,105	69.9
Mazovia	10,379	4,092	39.4
Podolia[a]	20,334	15,606	76.7
Sandomierz[b]	29,749	20,280	68.2
Sieradz	5,022	3,878	77.2
Volhynia	51,736	37,301	72.1

[a] District of Kamieniec.
[b] Districts of Pilzno, Sandomierz, and Wiślica.

Sources: R. Mahler, *Yidn in amolikn Poyln in likht fun tsifern* (Warsaw, 1958), tables; I. Kamanin, 'Statisticheskie dannye o evreyakh v Yugo-Zapadnom krae vo vtoroi polovine proshlogo veka (1765–1791)', in *Arkhiv Yugo-Zapadnoy Rossii*, v/2 (Kiev, 1890), 236–9 (his data for Ukraine are different from Mahler's).

total) were listed in 1790.[42] The Jewish population in Samogitia decreased from 15,591 in 1765 to 12,105 in 1784; that is, by just over 20 per cent.[43]

According to Mahler, poll tax was paid by 587,658 Jews in 1765, of whom 450,009 lived in the Crown territories. In an attempt to estimate the total numbers of Jews, the author estimated the number of those who had been excluded from the levy and added it to the census data. Thus, with infants (6.35 per cent of the total population) and the 20 per cent of the population that avoided payment, he arrived at a figure of 750,000 Jews in the Commonwealth.[44]

It is possible to trace changes in the Jewish population. In the second half of the sixteenth century, Jews living in Wielkopolska constituted as much as 28.6 per cent of all Polish Jewry, but in 1765 their proportion was no more than 11.7 per cent. More and more Jews settled in the south-eastern regions of the Commonwealth. Further, the data show that the percentage of Jews living in the Crown's urban centres was lowest in Mazovian towns (only some 40 per cent of all the Jews in that province lived in urban centres) (see Table 2). Possible explanations for this must

[42] Z. Guldon and K. Krzystanek, 'The Jewish Population in the Towns on the West Bank of the Vistula in Sandomierz Province from the Sixteenth to the Eighteenth Centuries', in A. Polonsky, J. Basista, and A. Link-Lenczowski (eds.), *The Jews in Old Poland, 1000–1795* (London, 1993), table 4.
[43] G. Błaszczyk, 'Liczebność', *BŻIH* (1988), 5/4, tables 1–2.
[44] R. Mahler, 'Żydzi w dawnej Polsce w świetle liczb', *PDP* 1 (1967), 154.

include the ban on Jewish dwelling in the region from the beginning of the sixteenth century to 1768. Restrictions on living in the towns led the Jews to set up *kehilot* in the countryside with the *kahal* located in a principal village. This unique arrangement was possible thanks to the protection of noble landlords. In other territories of central and south-eastern Poland, between 62.6 and 77.5 per cent of the Jewish population was urbanized. In western Kujawy urban dwellers constituted more than 90 per cent of the total Jewish population. Furthermore, in the province of Kujawy itself as many as 98.6 Jews lived in towns. The size of the Jewish population and its economic role were inversely proportional to the development of a regional market. Thus, Jewish innkeepers were rarely seen in the western part of Wielkopolska, while in the eastern lands of Poland–Lithuania 'there was Jewish activity vital to the latifundium economy, which otherwise would have been as a living organism without blood'.[45]

According to the census for 1787, there were 218,962 Jews in Crown Poland at that time (Table 1). In 1790, 75,177 Jewish people were counted in eleven districts of Lithuania. During that year 3,936 Jews were born and 3,445 died. The demographic ratios were high: a birth rate of 25.8 to 130.5 per 1,000 (52.4 on average) in the various territories and a death rate of 29.4 to 108.4 (45.8 per 1,000 on average). Such figures have led the editors of the census to speculate that the actual number of Jews was twice as large as stated in the register.[46] In any case, there can be no doubt that more than 300,000 Jews of both sexes were counted in the Commonwealth in 1787–90. On the other hand, according to Czacki, the last census lists 308,516 men in the state. He remarks: 'More than a dozen reports have convinced me that the number of men can be estimated at 450,000 at least.' Adding the same number of women, the above assumption allowed him to estimate the total number of Jewish inhabitants at the end of the eighteenth century at 900,000.[47] This assessment was accepted by Tadeusz Korzon and Zygmunt Sułowski.[48] In this way the territory of the Commonwealth, which was 211,000 km^2 smaller than it was before the first partition, was said to have been inhabited by a greater number of Jewish people than in 1765. This supposed increase in the number of Jews in the years 1765–90 seems extremely doubtful. However, this conclusion does not prevent further speculations about the real numerical force of Polish Jewry in that period.

Once again ecclesiastical censuses and parish records have proven their usefulness as demographic sources. According to the 1777–87 Poznań diocese visitation

45 J. Topolski, 'Uwagi o strukturze gospodarczo-społecznej Wielkopolski w XVIII wieku, czyli dlaczego na jej terenie nie było żydowskich karczmarzy', in Topolski and Modelski (eds.), *Żydzi w Wielkopolsce na przestrzeni dziejów*, 81.

46 Jasas and Truska, *Lietuvos Didžiosios Kunigaikštystės gyventojų surašymas 1790 m.*, 31–73, 89.

47 T. Czacki, *Dzieła* (Poznań, 1845), iii. 254.

48 T. Korzon, *Wewnętrzne dzieje Polski za Stanisława Augusta* (Kraków, 1897), i. 218; Z. Sułowski, 'Mechanizmy ekspansji demograficznej Żydów w miastach polskich XVI–XIX wieku', *Zeszyty Naukowe KUL*, 1 (1974), table 1.

Table 3. Population of the Kujawy region of the diocese of Włocławek, 1779–1781

Deanery	Catholics	Protestants	Jews	Total
Bobrowniki	4,735	398	89	5,222
Brześć Kujawski	9,603	74	879	10,556
Fordon	3,507	950	505	4,962
Gniewkowo	4,781	1,240	59	6,080
Inowrocław	4,111	1,085	890	6,086
Izbica Kujawska	5,009	470	161	5,640
Kowal	10,041	35	312	10,388
Kruszwica	6,889	133	47	7,069
Nieszawa	3,859	379	14	4,252
Radziejów	6,716	48	485	7,249
Służewo	6,074	977	275	7,326
TOTAL	65,325	5,789	3,716	74,830
% of total	87.3	7.7	5.0	100.0

Sources: Archiwum Diecezjalne we Włocławku, MSS 88–90; Archiwum Archidiecezjalne w Gnieźnie, MS E. 19.

protocols, there were 363,246 people in Poznań province, including 21,010 Jews (5.8 per cent of the total).[49] The number of Jews is slightly higher than that of the 1765 census (19,913). A report on the population of the diocese of Włocławek, whose territory comprised East Pomerania (with Danzig), most of Kujawy, and part of the Land of Dobrzyń, found 288,678 people in 1768, including just 1,535 Jews (0.5 per cent of the total).[50] As Emil Waschinski's research has shown, in 1766 the ten Pomeranian deaneries were inhabited by 101,830 Catholics, 39,399 Protestants (mainly Lutherans), and approximately 2,500 Jews (constituting just 1.7 per cent of the total).[51] These data may be supplemented with information collected during an inspection of the Kujawy region of that diocese in 1779–81. These records list only 3,716 Jews, who constituted approximately 5 per cent of the total population (Table 3). However, the bishop's inspector did not visit every parish in those years. Similar records have been also preserved for the Pomeranian part of that diocese for the years 1779–82.[52]

According to the Church census for 1787, Jews constituted 7.2 per cent of the total population of Kraków diocese, but made up 23 per cent of all the urban inhabitants (Table 4). This census lists 4,527 Jewish townsfolk in the Sandomierz district,

[49] J. A. Lewicki, 'Stosunki wyznaniowe w wielkopolskiej części diecezji poznańskiej w II połowie XVIII wieku', in E. Wiśniewski (ed.), *Z badań nad dziejami zakonów i stosunków wyznaniowych na ziemiach polskich* (Lublin, 1984), 110–11.

[50] Z. Chodyński (ed.), *Statuta synodalia diocesis Wladislaviensis et Pomeraniae* (Warsaw, 1890), p. ix.

[51] E. Waschinski, *Wie gross war die Bevölkerung Pommerellens, ehe Friedrich der Grosse das Land übernahm?* (Danzig, 1907), 47–8.

[52] Archiwum Diecezjalne w Pelplinie, MSS G. 69–72.

Table 4. Population of the diocese of Kraków, 1787

Province	Total	Jews		Urban population		
		No.	%	Total	Jews	
					No.	%
Duchy of Siewierz	18,564	10	0.05	33,204	—	0.0
Kraków	279,944	12,172	4.3	50,986	7,617	14.9
Lublin	223,315	24,220	10.8	47,791	15,602	32.6
Sandomierz	341,317	25,758	7.5	63,988	14,937	23.3
TOTAL	863,140	62,160	7.2	166,099	38,156	23.0

Source: J. Kleczyński (ed.), 'Spis ludności diecezji krakowskiej z r. 1787', *Archiwum Komisji Historycznej*, 7 (1894), 320, 326.

whereas the state registration that took place in the same year counts only 2,874—that is, 36.5 per cent fewer.[53] This does not mean that the Church enumeration is complete. The Revd Krokowski, the rector at Skotniki, commented on the Jewish counts in 1787 as follows: 'Not more than half of them go to the registration, and where there are ten, only five of them are listed.' The same relates to the Catholics, who fled their houses and even parishes to avoid being counted.[54] Similar problems occurred during the enumeration of Jews in the Uniate eparchy of Przemyśl in 1767. One of the priests explained that 'counting infidel Israelites is a difficult task as they hide themselves'.[55] Taking into consideration the ecclesiastical census for 1787 and the hearth tax in 1790, Stanisław Jop arrived at a total population of 263,568 for Lublin province, including 30,945 Jews (11.7 per cent of the total). Jews made up 4.5 per cent of the rural population and 32.5 per cent of the townsfolk. In all, 71.8 per cent of the Jews in the province lived in towns.[56]

The census for the diocese of Płock, which comprised part of Mazovia and the Dobrzyń region, lists 331,448 people in 1773, including 18,103 Jews (5.5 per cent of the total).[57] Three years later a total of 333,357 was reported, with 18,919 Jews (5.7 per cent of the total) (Table 5).

Finally, we must stress the importance of censuses carried out by the states which partitioned Poland. Approximately 225,000 Jews were counted on the territories that had been subjected to the Austrian administration with the first partition

[53] Guldon and Krzystanek, 'The Jewish Population', in Polonsky *et al.* (eds.), *The Jews in Old Poland*, table 4.

[54] J. Kracik, 'Wokół spisu ludności diecezji krakowskiej z roku 1787', *Studia Historyczne*, 28/1 (1985), 35–6.

[55] Budzyński, *Ludność pogranicza polsko-ruskiego w drugiej połowie XVIII wieku*, 249.

[56] S. Jop, 'Rozmiary jednostek administracji państwowej oraz gmin wyznaniowych (parafie rzymskokatolickie i greckokatolickie, kahały) na terenie woj. lubelskiego w ostatniej ćwierci XVIII w.', *Rocznik Lubelski*, 16 (1973), 117, 121, 125, 135.

[57] After the 1765 data in Table 2; cf. Mahler, 'Żydzi w dawnej Polsce', 155–6.

Table 5. Population of the diocese of Płock, 1776

Province	Catholics		Protestants	Jews	Total
	Aged ≥	Aged <7			
Land of Dobrzyń	24,137	6,420	3,392	1,235	35,184
Mazovia	169,189	41,941	1,135	13,558	225,823
Płock	52,197	11,605	586	4,012	68,400
Rawa	3,103	664	69	114	3,950
TOTAL	248,626	60,630	5,182	18,919	333,357

Source: B. Kumor (ed.), 'Spis ludności diecezji płockiej biskupa Michała Jerzego Poniatowskiego z 1776 r.', *Przeszłość Demograficzna Polski*, 9 (1976), 94.

Table 6. Population of Galicia, 1773

Province	Settlements			Population		
	Towns	Villages	Total	Total	Jews	
					No.	%
Bełz	22	353	375	149,567	21,413	14.3
Kraków	40	1,437	1,477	480,029	11,833	2.5
Lublin	6	81	87	22,480	2,763	12.3
Podolia	19	157	176	71,725	3,202	4.5
Ruthenia	165	2,704	2,869	1,318,070	174,148	13.2
Sandomierz	28	735	763	266,106	11,622	4.4
TOTAL	280	5,467	5,747	2,307,977	224,981	9.7

Source: A. Brawer, *Galizien, wie es an Österreich kam* (Leipzig, 1910), 25.

(Table 6). Only 155,000 Jews had been counted there in 1765.[58] Another Austrian registration from 1774 counts only some 172,000 Jews, while the census for 1786 counts 215,000. The Austrian authorities compelled poor Jews to leave Galicia; between September 1781 and the end of 1782, 1,192 paupers were expelled.[59] According to a description of similar events in 1783, 'a group of Galician Jews was driven to the customs house and forced to cross the border to the Polish side. Our sentry who was keeping guard there tried his best to prevent them from crossing, but, having been driven off the toll-gate, he gave way to the armed [Austrian] ruffians.'[60] This policy of the Habsburgs was continued until 1789, when the Edict of Toleration was proclaimed.[61] In the lands occupied by Austria after the third

[58] J. Korytkowski, *Arcybiskupi gnieźnieńscy, prymasowie i metropolici polscy od roku 1000 aż do roku 1821* (Poznań, 1892), v. 156.

[59] M. Bałaban, *Dzieje Żydów w Galicji i w Rzeczypospolitej Krakowskiej 1782–1868* (Lwów, 1918), 21, 27–8.

[60] Guldon and Krzystanek, 'The Jewish Population', in Polonsky *et al.* (eds.), *The Jews in Old Poland*, 325.

[61] J. Karniel, 'Das Toleranzpatent Kaiser Joseph II für die Juden Galiziens und Lodomeriens', *Jahrbuch des Institut für Deutsche Geschichte*, 11 (1982), 55–89.

Table 7. Jewish population in Lithuania, 1765

Province	District	No. of Jews
Vilna	Vilna	5,560
	Oshmyana	7,124
	Lida	5,291
	Vilkomir	6,976
	Bratslav	2,476
Troki	Troki	5,905
	Grodno	13,815
	Kovno	6,148
	Upita	6,335
Duchy of Samogitia	Samogitia (Żmudź)	15,996
Polotsk	Polotsk	3,060
Novogrudok	Novogrudok	12,024
	Slonim	4,289
Vitebsk	Orsha	4,753
Pinsk	Brest	14,979
	Pinsk	7,000
Minsk	Minsk	7,191
	Mozyr	2,251
	Rechitsa	4,729
TOTAL		135,902[a]

Note: The data have been taken from the 1775 tariff, which repeats the totals in the 1765 Jewish census.

[a] The census excludes the provinces of Mstislav and Vitebsk as well as Livonia, which were inhabited by 7,979 Jews; K. Korobkov, 'Statistika evreiskogo naseleniya Pol'shi i Litvy vo vtoroi polovine XVIII veka', *Evreiskaya starina*, 4 (1911), 541–62.

Sources: L. Flaks, 'Regulacja spraw żydowskich przez Komisję Skarbową Litewską: Studium z dziejów gospodarczych Żydów na Litwie za Stanisława Augusta' (University of Vilna, 1931), 62–8 (census dated 1775); S. Stampfer, 'The 1764 Census of Lithuania Jewry', *Bar-Ilan: Annual of Bar-Ilan University*, 24–5 (1989), 120–1.

partition (western Galicia), there were some 118,000 Jewish inhabitants constituting 9.4 per cent of the total population.[62]

For the lands of the first Prussian partition, the *Contributionis catastrum*, or tax cadastre, is of vital importance. It was conducted in 1772–3, and the originals are preserved in archives in Bydgoszcz and Marburg.[63] In those years 3,062 Jews were registered in Royal Prussia (Westpreussen)[64] and 9,432 were counted in towns of northern Wielkopolska and part of Kujawy (Netzedistrikt). On the strength of the instruction of 1 March 1773, all Jews whose property was valued at less than 1,000

[62] J. Buzek, 'Wpływ polityki żydowskiej rządu austriackiego w latach 1772 do 1788 na wzrost zaludnienia żydowskiego w Galicji', *Czasopismo Prawnicze i Ekonomiczne*, 4 (1903), 102, 129.

[63] S. Cackowski, 'Z dziejów polityki ekonomicznej pruskiego absolutyzmu: Kataster podatkowy z r. 1772/73 dla ziem pierwszego zaboru pruskiego', *Zeszyty Naukowe Uniwersytetu M. Kopernika w Toruniu: Historia*, 3 (1967), 41–76.

[64] Aschkewitz, *Die Juden*, 568.

Table 8. Population of the Lithuanian gubernatorial territory, 1795

District	Jews and Karaites	Total
Braslav	1,091	42,775
Brest	4,600	81,680
Grodno	4,968	71,048
Kovno	2,984	39,142
Kobrin	3,225	84,866
Lida	4,361	82,128
Novogrudok	2,917	93,899
Oshmyana	2,212	92,725
Pruzhana	2,732	54,776
Roshenie	8,590	126,074
Shavle	5,545	100,627
Slonim	3,236	76,982
Telshe	3,499	82,858
Troki	2,679	51,774
Upita	5,856	94,665
Vilkomir	6,088	150,648
Vilna	6,721	107,914
Volkovysk	3,185	62,540
Zavileisky	1,173	71,200
TOTAL	75,662	1,568,321
%	4.8	100.0

Source: L. Żytkowicz, *Rządy Repnina na Litwie w latach 1794–1797* (Vilna, 1938), table A.

thaler were to have left the state by 1 May 1773. This order caused apprehension among the nobility, who were concerned about a possible desertion of the towns.[65] In fact the number of Jews increased from 6,936 in 1783 to 13,297 in 1799 in the urban centres of Netzedistrikt.[66]

Descriptions from the years 1793–4 of the towns in the lands under Prussia after the second partition (Südpreussen) have been published as well.[67] At that time 31,640 Jews lived in the towns of western Wielkopolska, and they constituted 21.6 per cent of the urban population.[68] Prussian descriptions of towns in 1799 are also available in print.[69] For the towns of Podlasie, the Polish census for 1790 counts

[65] M. Bär, *Westpreussen unter Friedrich dem Grossen* (Leipzig, 1909), i. 425–6; ii. 711–12.

[66] O. Kossman, *Die Deutschen in Polen seit der Reformation. Historisch-geographische Skizzen. Siedlung—Sozialstruktur—Wirtschaft* (Marburg, 1978), table 2.

[67] J. Wąsicki (ed.), *Opisy miast polskich z lat 1793–1794*, pts. 1–2 (Poznań, 1962). On the 1793–5 Prussian censuses, see D. Łukasiewicz, 'Nowe źródła do dziejów Wielkopolski na przełomie epok (1793–1806)', *Acta Universitatis Nicolai Copernici: Historia*, 30 (1997), 117–24, and S. Cackowski, *Miasta dobrzyńskie i kujawskie w końcu XVIII i na początku XIX wieku (1793–1807)* (Włocławek, 1995).

[68] Kossman, *Die Deutschen in Polen seit der Reformation*, table 1.

[69] J. Wąsicki (ed.), *Pruskie opisy miast polskich z końca XVIII wieku: Departament białostocki* (Poznań, 1964).

3,944 Jews; but the Prussian census carried out nine years later counts 9,324 Jews—an increase of 136 per cent.[70]

Approximately 136,000 Jews were counted during a registration in Lithuania in 1765 (Table 7). A contemporary witness to that process remarked that 'the knavish Jewish tribe concealed their number by a half, at least'.[71] According to the Russian census for 1795, there were over 75,000 Jews and Karaites there, who made up just under 5 per cent of the total population (Table 8). However, this is also considered a low estimate.[72]

On the basis of the material discussed here, we are able to draw the following conclusions. There are absolutely no grounds for the belief that between 1765 and 1790 the Jewish population in the territories that remained after the first partition of Poland increased from 750,000 to 1 million. Moreover, there can be no doubt that it is futile to compare sets of statistical data that have been collected according to different procedures. Thus, only an encyclopaedia of settlements, written on the basis of all available sources, would make it possible for us to approach critically the subjects of Jewish settlement and Jewish demography in Poland–Lithuania in the early modern epoch.

[70] Z. Guldon, 'Ludność żydowska w miastach województwa podlaskiego w końcu XVIII wieku', *Studia Podlaskie*, 2 (1989), 53.

[71] Flaks, *Regulacja spraw żydowskich przez Komisję Skarbową Litewską*, 61.

[72] Żytkowicz, *Rządy Repnina na Litwie w latach 1794–1797*, 170–1.

Julian Ursyn Niemcewicz on Polish Jewry

JAKUB GOLDBERG

AT the beginning of the nineteenth century Tadeusz Czacki became the first author in Polish literature to write about the customs, laws, and history of the Jews in a complex and synthetic manner.[1] Following his example, Julian Ursyn Niemcewicz began to take a passionate interest in this field of study. Although he enjoyed a reputation as a scholar, he did not write scholarly works in the area of Jewish history, culture, and social life, but rather wrote from the point of view of a writer, journalist, and diarist who saw the subject differently and more broadly than did Czacki. His opinions on the national character of the Jews of Poland were emotional and contradictory, but none of his predecessors was interested to the same degree in their culture and fate, or was sensitive to all of the issues connected with the subject. His three novels *Lejbe i Siora: Romans żydowski* ('Lejbe and Siora: A Jewish Romance'), *Moszkopolis: Rok 3333 czyli sen niesłychany* ('Moszkopolis: The Year 3333, or The Incredible Dream'), and the as yet unpublished 'Powóz złamany' ('The Broken-Down Carriage')—are all dedicated to Polish Jewish matters.[2] In *Rok 3333*, which provoked a sharp reaction, he stated simply: 'my excitable imagination produced nothing other than Jewish characters'. He expressed himself on this subject on many occasions, highlighting the significance of issues concerning the Jewish community in Poland.

Niemcewicz's memoirs also testify to his attitude towards Jews. Written when he was already advanced in years, they reveal that, even as a boy, he interacted with Jews on his parents' estate. He tells how a Jewish innkeeper warned members of the Bar Confederation, organized to oppose the submissiveness of King Stanisław August to the Russians, that the Muscovite forces were approaching. These notes are a perfect complement to the report found in Władysław Konopczyński's work on the Bar Confederation concerning a group of Jews who were sent to Siberia for

[1] T. Czacki, *Rozprawa o Żydach* (Vilna, 1807).

[2] See Z. Libera, 'Żydzi w polskiej literaturze pięknej w okresie późnego Oświecenia', in J. Michalski (ed.), *Lud żydowski w narodzie polskim* (Warsaw, 1994), 107–15; R. Brandstaetter, 'Moszkopolis', *Miesięcznik Żydowski*, 2 (1932), 20–41.

similar actions together with ultra-Catholic residents of Bar.[3] However, Niemcewicz passes over in silence the open acts of repression that were taking place at the time, including the hanging of Jews suspected of co-operating with the Russians by Bar confederates.[4] Surely, with his deep interest in matters concerning the Jewish community he had heard news of these executions. But in his *Listy litewskie* ('Lithuanian Letters') of 1812, he sharply criticizes the Jews of Brest for welcoming the entering Muscovite divisions and trying to gain the soldiers' goodwill.[5] As a Polish patriot he could not forgive them this, nor could he understand that these actions were provoked by the fear that there would be a repetition of the excesses and the accompanying looting of Jewish property that had taken place in similar circumstances.

As a boy, Niemcewicz became acquainted with the Jewish innkeeper who leased the inn on his parents' property. He writes: 'My father often ordered me to go to the inn to perfect my German.'[6] But the innkeeper knew German words in the forms in which they had been absorbed into the Yiddish language; Niemcewicz thus lamented that 'the German exam did not go well. When the aforementioned innkeeper, Chaim, mumbled to me in guttural Hebrew German, I could understand barely one-tenth and didn't answer, except falteringly.'[7] Although he believed that the Jews should completely abandon Yiddish, Niemcewicz nevertheless uses a few words that he happened to pick up in this language reproduced in a Polonized form in *Lejbe i Siora*; for example, 'mother went to skim the *łokszyn*'; 'kugiel'; 'bachury, bachurzęta'; 'siksele', 'bajgełe', 'kaczkes'; the garbled 'boruchy' (Hebrew: *berachot*, 'blessings'); and 'tatełe' and 'mamełe'.[8] In addition he recalls the Jewish doctors who treated a pair of lovers who were infected with 'the courtly disease'.[9]

However, Niemcewicz was not able to overcome the widespread perception of acts of oppression and humiliation against Jews as pleasurable and fun; nor was he able to eliminate the resentment that this caused. This can be seen from an incident described in his memoirs, in which the psychopath Mikołaj Bazyli Potocki, the *starosta* of Kaniów, killed a Jew from a village on his neighbour's estate. After the neighbour lodged a formal complaint, Potocki ordered that a cart be filled with randomly seized Jews and rolled into the neighbour's courtyard. Niemcewicz saw only the humour in this, acknowledging the incident in one laconic and unequivocal sentence: 'People laughed about this witty joke for a long time.'[10] However, in the same memoir he recalls with approval his father's forbearing attitude towards the

[3] J. U. Niemcewicz, *Pamiętnikiczasów moich* (Warsaw, 1957), i. 47; W. Konopczyński, *Konfederacja barska* (Warsaw, 1938), ii. 407–10. Cf. J. Goldberg, 'Żydzi wobec wrogów Rzeczypospolitej', in J. Tomaszewski (ed.), *Żydzi w obronie Rzeczypospolitej* (Warsaw, 1997), 14.

[4] See *Pamiętnik księdza Pstrokońskiego kanonika katedralnego gnieźnieńskiego* (Wrocław, 1844), 147.

[5] J. U. Niemcewicz, *Listy litewskie* (Warsaw, 1812), 160–6.

[6] Niemcewicz, *Pamiętniki czasów moich*, i. 86.

[7] Ibid.

[8] J. U. Niemcewicz, *Lejbe i Siora, czyli listy dwóch kochanków* (Kraków, 1931), 2, 3, 54, 62, 63, 66, 175.

[9] Niemcewicz, *Pamiętniki czasów moich*, i. 43.

[10] Ibid. 147.

Jewish tailors employed on his estate, and with a sense of humour he describes his father's fruitless efforts to persuade them to accept the Catholic religion.[11] Niemcewicz was, after all, attracted to satire, as we can see in the controversial *Rok 3333*, a satirical picture of a Poland ruled by Jews.

Of all of Niemcewicz's works dedicated to Jewish themes, the novel *Lejbe i Siora* has enjoyed the greatest fame. Niemcewicz admitted that he had written this epistolary romance in order to 'return the Jews to the true light, to cure them of their superstitions, show them that in clinging to the inhuman superiority of their rules, they are plunging themselves into degradation and poverty, blocking their own way to all advantages in human society; this is the only object of this work. I will be happy if I even partially fulfil my design.' Thus it was not just literary inspiration, but above all a desire to introduce sweeping social and cultural reforms into the Jewish community of Poland, that led Niemcewicz to write this work. This type of literary inspiration was not exceptional in his work; his conception of the history of Poland, as well as *Śpiewy historyczne* ('Historical Songs'), which was based on it, were intended to support the slogans of Polish national liberation that he propagated.[12] Just as Niemcewicz's history of Poland 'like a lever of national consciousness was to be a prerequisite to the success of Poles' future efforts to win independence',[13] his postulates concerning the social and cultural reform of Jewish society were based on a 'specifically conceived history of the Jews'. [14]

In 1825, four years after the publication of the original version of *Lejbe i Siora*, the work appeared in German translation.[15] At the time Niemcewicz was president of Warsaw's Warszawskie Towarzystwo Przyjaciół Nauk (Association of the Friends of the Arts and Sciences), and the publisher in Berlin therefore remarked in the prologue that the author was 'one of the most distinguished living Polish scholars'.[16] This opinion held in the following years and led to the announcement in 1850 of the first historical writing competition in Niemcewicz's honour.[17] In 1828 a Dutch edition of the novel was published, followed by an English translation in 1830. These three translations served to inform Europeans about the largest concentration of Jews in the world at that time, which was located in territories that had until recently belonged to the republic. Likewise, the Polish readers of *Lejbe i Siora* learned about the culture, religion, and customs of the Jews with whom they lived side by side, but who were isolated to a certain degree and about whom they knew little. The author himself was no exception to this, although he realized that, as a proponent

[11] Ibid. 86–7. See also J. Goldberg, 'Żydowscy konwertyci w społeczeństwie staropolskim', in A. Izydorczyk and A. Wyczański (eds.), *Społeczeństwo staropolskie* (Warsaw, 1986), 203.

[12] A. F. Grabski, 'Koncepcja dziejów Polski Juliana Ursyna Niemcewicza', *Przegląd Humanistyczny*, 1 (1979), 66–7.

[13] Ibid. 67.

[14] See M. Janion, *Do Europy tak, ale razem z naszymi umarłymi* (Warsaw, 2000), 116.

[15] J. Niemcewicz, *Levi und Sara. Briefe polnischer Juden. Ein Sittengemälde* (Berlin, 1825).

[16] Ibid., p. v.

[17] A. F. Grabski, *Historiografia i polityka: Dzieje konkursu historycznego im. Juliana Ursyna Niemcewicza* (Warsaw, 1994).

of the social and cultural reform of Polish Jewry, he should acquire a certain store of Judaic knowledge.

In *Rok 3333*, Niemcewicz remarks that 'in recent times, often in fact, I have been so bold as to express myself' on the matter of the reform of the Polish Jewry. In doing so he drew on his experiences from the time of the Four Year Sejm and the Grand Duchy of Warsaw, particularly since at the time of the Great Sejm he moved in the circles of Hugo Kołłątaj and Józef Pawlikowski, each of whom had a different opinion on the Jewish question. He also used the term 'organization of the Jews', a reference to the proposal on 'the Organization of the Jewish People in the Entire Polish Nation'. This proposal had arisen in the Deputacja do Spraw Żydowskich (Committee on the Reform of the Jews), which in the final phase of the Sejm was headed by Hugo Kołłątaj.[18] In *Listy litewskie*, Niemcewicz includes his own proposal for such reform, which he then summarizes in *Przestroga dla współziomków na rok 1809* ('A Warning for My Compatriots for the Year 1809')[19] and in *Lejbe i Siora*. Niemcewicz's proposals, like others made at the time, assumed that assimilation was a panacea for all the ills of the Polish Jews and was the only road to the resolution of all misunderstandings and conflicts between the Jews and their Christian neighbours.

In Niemcewicz's attitude towards the Jews there appeared a lack of tolerance for other cultures that was characteristic of proponents of the ideas of the Enlightenment. He stressed that the culture of the Jewish community made its modernization impossible, and in *Przestroga dla współziomków na rok 1809* he stated bluntly that it would not be possible to recognize Jews as citizens unless they completely abandoned this culture.[20] This opinion is put forward by one of the characters in *Lejbe i Siora* as he attempts to persuade the Jews to change: 'First prove yourselves by speech, dress, education, customs, adherence to the laws, and love similar to the Poles, and then we Poles will gladly accept you as compatriots.'[21] However, in *Śpiewy historyczne*, Niemcewicz suggests that, if Poles want to win independence, they should follow the example of the Jews of remotest antiquity: 'Displaced from the Holy Land, the people of Israel on the banks of the waters of Babylon recalled the Jordan. In their melancholy songs they crooned about their homeland, about the deeds of their ancestors; in the end they recovered that land because they thought of it, never stopped sighing for it.'[22] And in *Lejbe i Siora*, through the mouth of the old man Abraham, Niemcewicz expresses the hope that the Jews will likewise recover the country of their ancestors, but he cautions that 'if we return to

[18] On this proposal, see J. Michalski, 'Sejmowe projekty reformy położenia ludności żydowskiej w Polsce w latach 1789–1792', in Michalski (ed.), *Lud żydowski w narodzie polskim*, 27–42.

[19] J. U. Niemcewicz, *Przestroga dla współziomków na rok 1809* (Breslau, 1809), 12; cf. A. Eisenbach, *Emancypacja Żydów na ziemiach polskich na tle europejskim* (Warsaw, 1988), 162, 583.

[20] Niemcewicz, *Przestroga dla współziomków na rok 1809*, 12.

[21] Artur Eisenbach deals with this issue in his 'Prawa obywatelskie i honorowe Żydów (1790–1861)', in W. Kula (ed.), *Społeczeństwo Królestwa Polskiego* (Warsaw, 1965), i.

[22] J. U. Niemcewicz, *Śpiewy historyczne*, 4th edn. (Kraków, 1835), ii–iii.

the land of Canaan in the darkness and superstition in which the talmudists are keeping us today, then Abraham, Isaac, and Jacob would shudder at the sight of us, and David and Solomon would never accept us as their people'. Niemcewicz's proposal for assimilation, so unrealistic at the time, was to modernize the Jewish community and lead it to union with the Polish community. He draws attention to the biblical genealogy of the Jews living in the countries of Europe at a time when this was mentioned most often for the purpose of recalling their guilt for the crucifixion of Jesus. In keeping with his formula, assimilation and modernization were to cleanse Jewish culture and tradition of deviations and accretions acquired in the Diaspora and were necessary conditions for the eventual rebirth of the Jewish nation in its primeval homeland.

Niemcewicz realized that a nation that had suffered so much in the course of its long history might be suspicious of any attempt to intervene in its internal affairs, saying: 'Far be it from me to condemn this unhappy nation to extermination or exile; correct it, lead it to commemoration, to recognition of its own good: that is what Christian teachings recommend.' He asserted that the Jews could be made equal to Christians if they would renounce their customs and their obedience to the elders of the *kahal*. This attitude was widespread at the time, and at the beginning of the nineteenth century the economist Wawrzyniec Surowiecki, though presenting himself as a defender of the Jews, used even harsher arguments, asserting that 'the Jewish nation, with its immoral character in commerce and crafts, has many talents for harming the country: superstitious, clever, dishonest, criminal'.[23] Niemcewicz's views were closer to Jan Alojzy Radomiński's than to Surowiecki's; in a treatise published almost simultaneously with *Lejbe i Siora*, entitled *Co wstrzymuje reformę Żydów w kraju naszym*, Radomiński asserted that the supposedly negative characteristics of the Jews did not result from adherence to Jewish tradition, but arose in circumstances created by the Christian nations.[24] Among proponents of the Enlightenment in Poland, only Jacobin Józef Pawlikowski was opposed to efforts to assimilate the Jews. In *Myśli polityczne dla Polski*, published anonymously in 1789, he came out against Kołłątaj, who thought Jews should be encouraged to forsake their distinctive dress and declared: 'We will not be to them like the ancient Spaniards, we will not force them to change their attire; let us behave towards them so that they will see it not as a disadvantage, but as good fortune to be Poles.'[25]

To justify his arguments, Niemcewicz presents one group of Jewish characters positively, and contrasts them with negative characters from the opposite camp. So, on the one hand, we have Lejbe and Siora, and Siora's friend Rachela; the aforementioned Abraham, a maskil who is 'wise, handsome, noble, and venerable, more than 80 years old . . . wealthy from constant labour, beloved of the people close to him'; and Chaim, a simple, positive character, a carter (a common profession among

[23] W. Surowiecki, *Wybór pism*, ed. J. Grzywicka and A. Łukaszewicz (Warsaw, 1957), 213.

[24] J. A. Radomiński, *Co wstrzymuje reformę Żydów w kraju naszym* (Warsaw, 1824).

[25] [J. Pawlikowski], *Myśli polityczne dla Polski* (Warsaw, 1789), 244.

Jews at the time). On the other side are the negatively depicted figures of the hasidim and their leader Jankiel, as well as his father, Herszko, and Sara's father, Moszko.

The hasidim, who were enjoying ever greater approval among the Polish Jews at the time, are presented extremely negatively in *Lejbe i Siora*. Before Niemcewicz, the only mention of hasidim in Polish literature came from Stanisław Wodzicki, the future president of the senate of the republic of Kraków, whose attitude towards Jews was negative. In 1787, as the leaseholder of Olkusz, he accused local Jews of murdering a Christian girl,[26] and he remarked in his diary that, 'although the blood of animals is prohibited to Jews, as evidenced by the de-veining of kosher meat, there exists the sect of the *chassydym* [hasidim], who despite that law hunger for the blood of Christian children for their rituals', and that, 'although not all Jews use Christian blood for Passover, the hasidim certainly and indisputably do'.[27] In response to this, representatives of the Kraków *kahal* successfully appealed to Stanisław Augustus, who ordered Wodzicki to withdraw his accusation of murder from the court.[28] None of the many researchers on hasidism has drawn attention to the fact that the repeated assertion that hasidim needed Christian blood for their rituals derives from the rumour that the rabbis had excommunicated them for using a new kind of knife in the ritual slaughter of cattle and poultry.[29] According to the hasidim, knives used for this purpose should be sharper, better polished, and of harder steel than those that the ritual slaughterers had been using up to that point. Wodzicki and his ilk used this requirement as a basis for spreading the rumour that such knives were used for ritual murder.[30] But neither Niemcewicz nor Jan Alojzy Radomiński accuse the hasidim of this type of crime. Niemcewicz in particular, as a proponent of Enlightenment ideas, fought against backwardness as a matter of policy, and asserted that 'of all the illnesses of the human mind, prejudice and superstition are the most dangerous'.

Niemcewicz's criticism of Polish Jews in *Lejbe i Siora* concentrates on the hasidim as an extremist group within the Jewish community. It is possible that his negative attitude towards hasidim arose as a result of his contacts with the maskilim who were hostile to them. In order to demonstrate the need for the reform of Jewish society, he presented a supposedly authentic but in fact skewed picture of the lifestyle and customs of the Jews (mainly hasidim and *kahal* elders). He acquired his knowledge

[26] See M. Bałaban, *Historja Żydów w Krakowie i na Kazimierzu 1304–1868* (Kraków, 1936), ii. 500, 526–9; Z. Guldon and J. Wijaczka, *Procesy o mordy rytualne w Polsce w XVI–XVIII wieku* (Kielce, 1995), 41.

[27] S. Wodzicki, *Wspomnienia z przeszłości od roku 1768 do roku 1840* (Kraków, 1840), 204; cf. Bałaban, *Historja Żydów w Krakowie i na Kazimierzu 1304–1868*, ii. 500, 529.

[28] Wodzicki, *Wspomnienia z przeszłości od roku 1768 do roku 1840*, 204. See also I. Schiper, *Przyczynki do dziejów chasydyzmu w Polsce* (Warsaw, 1992).

[29] See C. Shmeruk, 'Chasydyzm i kahał', in K. Link-Lenczowski (ed.), *Żydzi w dawnej Rzeczypospolitej* (Wrocław, 1991), 62; cf. Schiper, *Przyczynki do dziejów chasydyzmu w Polsce*.

[30] Shmeruk, 'Chasydyzm i kahał', 62. In writing about the question of knives used for slaughter, the author does not discuss the reaction to the issue in Polish society.

of Jewish society and its religion and culture primarily through personal observation as well as from foreign literature that was misleading and hostile to Jews; it is possible that he supplemented this knowledge with information he received from the maskilim. Earlier anti-Jewish Polish literature was of little use for his purpose because it was dominated by authors of a middle-class urban background, whose motives for attacking the Jews were primarily economic.[31] Nor did he use pamphlets presenting the Jews as murderers of Jesus who desecrated the host and performed ritual murders.[32] His choice of arguments indicates that he made use of known anti-Jewish works in German from the sixteenth and seventeenth centuries by Pfeferkorn and Eisenmenger and their imitators. Earlier authors, as well as contemporaries of Niemcewicz in other countries, also drew on this literature. Niemcewicz repeated their views uncritically. To be sure, the text of *Lejbe i Siora* reveals that he was aware of the kind of laws that were contained in the *Shulḥan arukh* (the Hebrew compendium of Jewish religious practices); however, the language barrier prevented him from becoming more closely acquainted with them.

The Jewish way of life and the enmity of the hasidim towards Christians that Niemcewicz presented constituted his proof of the need for far-reaching and comprehensive changes within the Jewish community. The hasidic characters in *Lejbe i Siora* assert that the Talmud calls for Jews to cheat 'goys', and Moszko, Siora's father, even says that cheating them brings him joy. This hatred is shown as being so great that Siora is forbidden to drink from a cup after a Christian has drunk from it. In *Rok 3333* Niemcewicz wrote satirically about the supposed Jewish belief that the Jews should rule over other nations; in *Lejbe i Siora* this idea is repeated with almost every instance of anti-Jewish propaganda, and Jankiel, the leader of the hasidim, states that 'the entire hope for the greatness and rulership of our people on earth lies in the complete eradication of the "goyim" and our increase'. These are the rare instances in which Niemcewicz uses arguments taken from anti-Jewish pamphlets to win support for the idea of the social and cultural reform of the Jews.

In the novel Niemcewicz draws attention to the difficult circumstances of the Jews and to the poverty spreading throughout Jewish society, providing little-known details of Jews' daily and holiday fare. In one of her letters Siora writes: 'My father, though rich, is abstemious and thrifty. A pickle or a clove of garlic and a piece of bread are his lunch; for supper a cup of goat's milk sated me, my mother, and the boys.' Elsewhere, Niemcewicz presents the preparation of the sabbath meal

[31] See K. Bartoszewicz, *Antysemityzm w literaturze polskiej XV–XVII w.* (Warsaw, 1914).

[32] See H. Olszewski, *Doktryny prawno-ustrojowe czasów saskich* (Warsaw, 1961); W. Kowalski, 'W obronie wiary: Ks. Stefan Żuchowski między wzniosłością a okrucieństwem', in W. Kowalski and J. Muszyńska (eds.), *Żydzi wśród chrześcijan w dobie szlacheckiej Rzeczypospolitej* (Kielce, 1996); J. Goldberg, 'Die sächsisch-polnische Verbindung und die polnische Juden', in *Schriftenreihe des Vereins für Geschichte Sachsens*; J. Goldberg, 'August II wobec polskich Żydów', in K. Link-Lenczowski and M. Markiewicz (eds.), *Rzeczpospolita wielu narodów i jej tradycje* (Kraków, 1999).

in this way: 'I prepare *lokshn* [noodles], spice the pike with pepper and onion, and assemble a delicate kugel and place it in the oven.' These descriptions of material culture, though not free from errors and misunderstandings (for they were not just based on personal observation but were also spun out of conjecture), are nevertheless more realistic than the information Niemcewicz provides on Jewish laws, customs and religious life.

Let us, for example, turn our attention to the figure of the praying Jew described in *Lejbe i Siora* and undoubtedly familiar to Niemcewicz from personal observation. As was the accepted custom for married men, this character wraps himself in a *talit* (which Niemcewicz refers to as a 'tsitsele', a corrupt version of 'tsitsis', a garment worn at all times by adult Jewish men). On his brow and arm the praying Jew wears phylacteries (*tefilin*). Niemcewicz calls Jewish prayers 'boruchs', which means actually 'blessings' (*berachot*, or *bruches* in the Ashkenazi dialect). Moreover, he did not know what to call the phylacteries and simply called them 'armbands'. Nor did he understand that, while phylacteries are worn only at morning services on weekdays, the prayer shawls (*talitot*) are worn at morning services and on the sabbath and other holidays. It becomes clear from the text that the author observed Jews at their daily afternoon and evening prayers, when in accordance with the laws they wore neither striped shawls nor phylacteries, and he misinterprets this in concluding that it is a sin, even suggesting, in the novel, that this is one of the reasons why Lejbe is excommunicated by the rabbis.

Niemcewicz was interested in the question of excommunication among Jews, and he created fruitful ground for the negative presentation of the Jewish customs of which he was critical. Excommunication was after all an uncompromising means of punishing a serious departure from the norms of behaviour and the religious obligations prescribed in the Talmud. This is particularly so since, in contrast to Catholic excommunication, Jewish excommunication is not a corrective punishment but a retaliatory one; the excommunicated person is placed beyond the bounds of society and deprived of the means of material existence.[33] Thus, after Lejbe is excommunicated, even the ever-faithful carter Chaim, who is ready to serve anyone, begins to avoid him. Such matters were widely discussed in the literature that was known to Niemcewicz, and he was able to give the actual Hebrew term (*ḥerem*) and even to distinguish certain of its forms (*nidui* and *shamta*) However, he gives an incorrect example when he shows his hero Lejbe being placed under *ḥerem* for failure to observe laws concerning food, and above all because, 'during the Feast of Tabernacles, inside his hut he ate salad with vinegar': the assertion that Jews may not use vinegar and that violation of this law supposedly resulted in excommunication is also mistaken. Niemcewicz likewise exaggerates when he writes that refusing to wear the distinctive Jewish attire carried the same punishment. He exaggerates the methods of censure applied in Jewish society, asserting that the hasidim—

[33] I. Lewin, *Klątwa żydowska na Litwie w XVII i XVIII wieku* (Lviv, 1932), 18.

Jankiel's followers—demanded the stoning of Siora. But no Jew, even in a state of fervour, would demand the stoning of his opponent.

Niemcewicz fails to understand the custom, widespread among Jews, of leaving small rocks on gravestones. In one of Lejbe's letters to Siora we read that if an excommunicated person 'should die . . . during the period of excommunication, then a stone should be placed on his gravestone as a sign that he deserved to be stoned'. This indicates among other things that Niemcewicz visited Jewish cemeteries and observed the stones left on gravestones there. But this custom, which is practised even today, has nothing to do with attitudes towards excommunicates. As is well known, Jews place stones on gravestones as a sign that they have visited the resting place of members of their family or of their friends. But Niemcewicz was aware of the role that respect for the dead played in Jewish culture and that Jews visit cemeteries often. In this connection he describes the meeting in the cemetery between Rachela and Siora, who writes to Lejbe that they both 'sat on gravestones . . . among the dwelling places of death . . . and we spoke of those alone for whom our hearts beat'.

In *Lejbe i Siora*, Niemcewicz raises the question of the burial societies, usually called holy brotherhoods (*ḥevrah kadisha*), which were the most troubling of institutions for Jews. Not only did they run the cemeteries, but they also conducted charitable activities and were famous for collecting excessive fees for burials. They were not above blackmail and by delaying burials they cheated Jewish families in mourning of contributions.[34] In his novel Niemcewicz describes the case of Efraim, Lejbe's deceased uncle: the burial brotherhood refuses to bury his remains, although Jewish custom requires that this should be done as soon as possible after death; Lejbe writes to Siora that, 'despite my requests and interventions, Efraim's remains lay unburied for four days'. In his presentation of this incident, Niemcewicz gets to the heart of the matter of burial societies, but he is wrong to say that the requirement to proceed quickly with burials was introduced by the burial societies; in fact it is an ancient Jewish custom.

Niemcewicz's satirical presentation of the Jewish custom of marrying at an early age and without the previous consent of the partners touched on a crucial aspect of the proposals for the social and cultural reform of Polish Jewry put forward from the mid-eighteenth century onwards. Traditional Jewish marriage is based on the realistic principle—which is in contrast to Catholic optimism—that in general people are not able to restrain their sexual urges. The custom of forming matrimonial unions at an early age was intended to create the conditions that would eliminate extramarital sexual relations. The ideal was for girls to marry before the age of 16 and boys to marry before they turned 18. In this way young people at the beginning of sexual maturity could begin their adult lives in the framework of marriage. At the same time, this created the possibility for young people to marry

[34] See J. Goldberg, 'Bieda i dobroczynność Żydów polskich w dawnej Rzeczypospolitej', *Kultura i Społeczeństwo*, 1 (1997), 7.

while their parents were still living. In the context of average lifespans much shorter than today's, parents had little chance of surviving until the marriage of fully grown children or of providing a means of existence for the young couple.[35] In past centuries, even representatives of the Polish middle classes, who were not favourably inclined towards the Jews, as well as other enemies of that nation, and even Catholic priests, praised the Jewish model of marriage.[36] But Niemcewicz's criticism of the institution of Jewish marriage is entirely in keeping with the views expressed by the maskil Jakub Kalmanson at the end of the eighteenth century. At this time, the growing poverty of the Jewish community had led to a drop in the proportion of early marriages among Jews: only about 42 per cent of girls and just over 19 per cent of boys entered into marriage between the ages of 15 and 19.[37] In the letters of Lejbe and Siora, Niemcewicz presents this type of marriage in a clear though somewhat exaggerated manner. But he gets right to the heart of the matter when Herszko writes to Moszko: 'Your son Dawidek is eleven, my daughter Lyje is nine. Let's marry them: I'll give two thousand roubles in dowry with my daughter, and after the wedding I will take my daughter home.' He refers here to yet another Jewish custom, according to which the parents provide for the young couple, who are not yet able to provide for themselves, and give them a roof over their heads for several years. This custom, referred to in Yiddish as *kest*, was known in the first half of the eighteenth century by the Polish term *ojcowski stół* ('father's table').[38] This 'table' turned out to be indispensable, and Niemcewicz illustrates this in a letter from Moszko to Herszko: 'My Dawidek is very happy to be married; although married, he still runs after sparrows with a bow and arrows', so it was necessary to educate and nourish him together with his bride. For her part, in a letter to Lejbe, Siora draws attention to another negative characteristic of Jewish marriage, namely the lack of feeling between the two who are bound as partners in this way. She remarks that 'neither love, nor mutual recognition, nor inclination, nor respect unites our couples. Two fathers reach an agreement on price, that is on dowry; one gives over his son, who has never seen his betrothed, the other gives over his daughter, who has never heard of her fiancé.'

Likewise, the problem of the hasidim is presented in *Lejbe i Siora* in connection with the two fathers' plan to marry Siora to the *tsadik* Jankiel. Niemcewicz briefly describes the genesis of this movement as well as the customs and ceremonies of the hasidim, but he mistakenly calls the founder of the movement, the Ba'al Shem Tov, by the name Ba'al Achen. As noted above, Jan Alojzy Radomiński, who also wrote about the spread of hasidism, published a book just as the first edition of *Lejbe i Siora* was published. But Radomiński was interested above all in comparing the situation of the Jews in Poland with that of Jews in other countries, and not in the essence and customs of hasidism. However, Niemcewicz writes that hasidim

35 See J. Katz, *Masoret umashber* (Jerusalem, 1962), 172.

36 J. Goldberg, 'Jewish Marriage in Eighteenth-Century Poland', *Polin*, 10 (1997), 3–18.

37 Ibid. 18–26, 32–9.

38 Ibid. 27–31.

'believe . . . that because the rabbi is a kabbalist, he becomes therefore a heavenly being; he understands the language of the beasts, trees, and flowers; through secret arts he can avert evil'. He was aware that this movement constituted a link in the socio-religious messianic ferment that was taking place among Jews in the Diaspora. He points to the similarity between hasidism and the sect of Shabbetai Tsevi, which arose in the second half of the seventeenth century. He was familiar with the general structure of the hasidic movement and was aware that it was divided into several branches under different leaders, but he did not understand the function of the hasidic courts. To be sure, he mentions that 'some thirty or forty Jews and Jewesses at a time go on pilgrimages' to particular hasidic courts, but in fact the numbers were much higher. He describes the character of Jankiel as the head of the hasidic movement in Poland, but by that time the movement no longer had a single leader. He provides colourful descriptions of hasidic practices and the cult of the *tsadik*, who is personified by the aforementioned Jankiel. He notes the increasing influence of the hasidim in Jewish society in a letter from Herszko to Moszko, in which we read that 'the entire body of our elders—the *kahal* elders and the rabbi—take off not only their hats but also their yarmulkes before [the *tsadik*]'. In a letter from Siora to Lejbe we find the following very typical description of the manifestations of the cult of the *tsadik*: 'Suddenly I see Jews flying along the street with a terrible cry, and with them a slowly moving carriage drawn by two horses. . . . All of Jewry began to crowd around the carriage. Finally, with cries of joy they brought out a large black shape. . . . They kissed his hands and feet.' In Polish literature after Niemcewicz no one would paint such a suggestive picture of hasidic customs until Julian Stryjkowski did so in his *Austeria*.

We turn now to the question of the model Niemcewicz used for the portrayal of Jankiel, the leader of the hasidim in the novel. It is worth noting Jankiel's physical similarity to the figure of Mendel Lefin of Satanów, the leading representative of the first generation of supporters of the Haskalah in Poland. Lefin came from the Podolian village of Satanów (hence the name Satanover), on the property of Prince Adam Czartoryski, Lefin's patron.[39] Niemcewicz moved in Czartoryski's circles and could have met Mendel Lefin on his estate. According to the account of his contemporary, the Hebrew author Abraham Ber Gottlober, Lefin suffered from a disease of the eyes brought about by his incessant poring over books; he was ugly and his face was pock-marked.[40] In *Lejbe i Siora*, Niemcewicz ascribes similar features to Jankiel, '[he is] hump-backed and his eyes drip with pus', 'ugly, hump-backed', 'imagine a figure of barely four feet in height with . . . long thin little legs . . . a pale face, with eyes set in eyelids bloody from constantly sitting over the Talmud, tossed in the gloomy flame of funerary candles'. This was perhaps paradoxical, but Niemcewicz presented representatives of opposing positions as ugly people, and

[39] See M. N. Gelber, 'Mendel Satanower, der Verbreiter der Haskalah in Polen und Galizien. Ein Kulturbild aus dem jüdischen Polen an der Wende des XVIII. Jahrhunderts', *Mitteilungen zur jüdischen Volkskunde*, 43 (1914).

[40] A. B. Gottlober, *Zichronot umasaot* (Jerusalem, 1976), 198–9.

the stunted and deformed figure of Mendel Lefin, one of the leading opponents of hasidism, was a likely model.

Niemcewicz is the first author in Polish literature to criticize equally both Jewish and Polish societies, tracing the failings and deformities of both. In Rachela's letter to Siora he includes an entire paragraph setting down the characteristics of Jews and Poles, beginning with the words: 'They accuse us [Jews] of laziness, of wanting to earn easy money, but let's consider—is it possible to call Poles lovers of work? The rich man and the poor man alike hate it, and they think only of how to avoid labours and live as freely and luxuriously as possible.' Niemcewicz believed that the transformation of the Jews is possible, so in *Lejbe i Siora*, as well as in his unpublished novel 'Powóz złamany', he includes examples that are meant to demonstrate that his postulates are entirely realistic. In the range of Jewish national and cultural values that he recognizes, he placed the question of language at the forefront.[41] He demanded that the Jews should stop speaking Yiddish: since 'the Jews have forgotten Hebrew . . . the most natural thing is for them to use the language of the people among whom they were born'. At the same time he requires that the Poles abandon the fashion of speaking French. He points to the equality of rights of assimilated Jews, and in creating the character of the Jewish governess and Polish teacher for the countess, he opens a new chapter in Polish literature on Polish–Jewish relations.

Niemcewicz's attitude towards Polish Jews must be examined in the context of his engagement in the cause of improving the fate of downtrodden ethnic and social groups, which found expression in his addresses to the Sejm in defence of townspeople and peasants, and his condemnation of the enslavement of blacks in North America that he had observed first-hand. His attitude towards the Jews was the same, and he strove for the improvement of their situation through programmes of reform that aimed to deprive them of their traditional Jewish culture and to end the dominance of the *kahal* elders. In this regard, Maria Janion has recently stressed that *Lejbe i Siora*, as a sentimental '"Jewish romance", is . . . at the same time—in keeping with the spirit of the Enlightenment—a tendentious novel on "the Jewish question"'.[42] Niemcewicz combined his utopian, pre-Zionist prophecies with sharp criticism of the customs and relationships reigning in old Jewish society—a society in which, he felt, the worst evil was the ever-increasing influence of hasidism. In order to develop a proposal for reform and condemn traditional Jewish culture, he had to acquire some knowledge in this field. Although he was not able to familiarize himself properly with all aspects of Polish Jewish culture, and made many serious errors in presenting it, he nevertheless tried to bring the Polish and Jewish communities closer to each other. Niemcewicz's attitude towards the Jews, like that of other Poles before him and among his contemporaries, was not always coherent; at times he would speak of them positively; at others he would

[41] See Grabski, 'Koncepcja dziejów Polski Juliana Ursyna Niemcewicza', 65.

[42] Janion, *Do Europy tak . . .*, 102.

condemn or criticize their behaviour.[43] It sometimes happened, even during his lifetime, that, on the basis of individual facts rather than his general stance, it was asserted that he hated Jews.[44] But Niemcewicz used comical or unfavourable terms for Jews in order to convey meanings that he believed would help to introduce positive changes into bosom of the Jewish community. This is particularly so as he also declared his positive attitude towards the Polish Jews and stressed that he was striving for their integration into the Polish nation.

Translated from Polish by Claire Rosenson

[43] On this question, see J. Goldberg, 'Wystąpienie na uroczystości nadania tytułu doktor *honoris causa* Uniwersytetu Warszawskiego', *Biuletyn Żydowskiego Instytutu Historycznego*, 1/2 (1993), 127–30.

[44] Jan Nepomucen Janowski, who circulated in the Polish émigré circles in Paris, described Niemcewicz's attitude towards the Jews with these words: 'The author of *Lejbe i Siora*, though not a very zealous Catholic himself, but I hear a very legitimate one, hated the Jews and disliked converts' (N. Janowski, *Notatki autobiograficzne 1803–1853* (Kraków, 1960), 189). Janowski even asserted that Niemcewicz disliked the Frankist Krysiński because of his origins. Ryszard Löw, a researcher on Polish–Jewish literary contacts, drew my attention to these remarks.

Translation as a Weapon for the Truth: The Bund's Policy of Multilingualism, 1902–1906

SUSANNE MARTEN-FINNIS

PROLOGUE

TRANSLATION can be a weapon: a cutting tool or a hatchet. This characterization may seem surprising, for we are told too often that translations should be smooth, natural, and elegant; that translation distorts and betrays, and is in more than one sense a false friend; that it is like glass—impersonal, anonymous, transparent gauze. And that is so, sometimes.[1]

But translation fulfils various functions. In the eyes of translators of religious works, from Luther to the martyr Dolet to the modern translators of the Koran and the Bible, translation is a weapon for truth. In the eyes of political thinkers like Engels, who supervised many translations of his own and Marx's works, it was a weapon for communism. Similarly, the United Nations Charter and the Universal Declaration of Human Rights, which is translated into many languages and to which translators subscribe, is a weapon for morality. And, of course, translation is used as an instrument for disseminating general and technological knowledge.[2]

In the present essay I wish to discuss translation as an implicit, indirect critical tool that is used on the source-language text. The original language is stripped of much of its own culture and exposed to the harsh light of a different culture and language, as well as perhaps to some universal truths of morality and common sense.

THE BUND'S MULTILINGUAL ACTIVITIES: A SURVEY

Bundist journalism functioned in a social environment that included more than one speech community. It used Yiddish to address its primary audience, the Jewish workers.[3] A second target group consisted of potential confederates of other nation-

[1] P. Newmark, *About Translation*, Multilingual Matters 74, ed. D. Sharp (Clevedon, 1991), 162.

[2] Ibid.

[3] Since the decision had been made to leave the narrow circles of Russian propaganda and to start mass agitation in Yiddish, literary output had been published mainly in Yiddish. Among such publica-

alities living in Russia at the time; as the Bund's first May Day proclamation in April 1898 expressed it, 'in its struggle the Jewish proletariat had to go hand in hand with its Russian, Polish, Lithuanian, and other comrades, who live in Russia, and with the development of our workers' movement national hostility will become weaker and weaker'.[4]

This proclamation was, at the time, translated into Russian.[5] However, it was not until May 1901, at its Fourth Convention, that the Bund decided to address Polish- and Russian-speaking target groups more systematically. This decision was preceded by a period of reappraisal, as a result of which the Fourth Convention emphasized the importance of co-operating with the Christian movements and recommended that material be issued in Polish and Russian. This was necessary, the delegates believed, in order for the movement to 'fight the terrible antisemitism that had been spread among Christian society and the less conscious masses by the government and the reactionary press, and to inform our Christian comrades about the Jewish workers' struggle for liberation'.[6] In the following year the question of whether it was necessary 'to spread literary activities into those areas where no other revolutionary organizations existed, and to revolutionize the Polish, Russian, and German population there' was repeatedly debated among members of the Bund Central Committee and the Bund Committee Abroad.[7]

In addition to informational material in Polish and Russian, the Bund published another category of its journalism in translation: literature representing the Bund to the international socialist movement. Among these documents, which were sent out to socialist movements and newspapers worldwide, were progress reports presented at the international congresses of social democracy, press releases, and appeals for donations. The documents were issued mainly in German, but some press releases and appeals for donations were also issued in English and French. This type of publishing activity began with the International Weavers' Congress,

tions were the early brochures printed in London beginning in 1895, the central organ *Di arbeter shtime* issued by the Vilna-based Bund Central Committee for the Jewish masses beginning in September 1897, and from December 1896 the Yiddish journal *Der yidisher arbayter*. The latter was a so-called '*visnshaftlekher organ*', a journal in which political and economic topics were discussed and made digestible for a more educated readership. After March 1899 responsibility for the content of the journal was shifted to the Geneva-based Bund Committee Abroad. The chronicles of various local committees in Bund centres such as Minsk, Vilna, Warsaw, and Białystok were also published in Yiddish.

[4] Tsentraler sotsyal-demokratisher komitet, *Oyfruf tsum ershter May*, pamphlet (Vilna, Apr. 1898).

[5] 'Russkii perevod proklamatsii Ts.K. Bunda k 1-omu maya 1898-ogo goda', Rossiiskii gosudarstvennyi arkhiv sotsial'no-politicheskoi istorii (RGASPI), *fond* 271, *opis'* 1, *delo* 41, fo. 2.

[6] Ruslander sotsyaldemokratishe arbayter-partay (Russian Social Democratic Workers' Party), Fun tsentraln komitet fun algemeynem yidishn arbayter bund in lite, poyln un rusland, *Oyfruf tsu ale arbayter un mitfilnde fun der gezelshaft* (Vilna, Nov. 1901).

[7] 'Pis'mo Noikha Dzhonu o vysylke russkoi i pol'skoi literatury' (Warsaw, Oct. 1902), RGASPI, *f.* 271, *op.* 1, *d.* 138, fo. 4.

which took place in Berlin in April 1900,[8] and received a significant boost after the Bund's divorce from the Rossiiskaya sotsial-demokraticheskaya rabochaya partiya (Russian Social Democratic Workers' Party, RSDRP). After this parting of ways the Bund's need to distinguish itself became all the greater.

It is important to differentiate here between two groups of texts: those produced by the Bund Central Committee or the local committees inside tsarist Russian (i.e. under clandestine conditions), and those produced outside Russia by the Geneva-based Bund Committee Abroad. It is largely the latter group of publications to which Weinreich refers when he states in his *History of the Yiddish Language* that 'the Bund Committee Abroad proved to have a marked influence on the fashioning of a Yiddish style in journalism and in the social sciences'.[9]

The focus of this chapter is on the former group; namely, on the Bundist journalism produced inside Russia by the Vilna-based Central Committee, and in particular on press releases and appeals that were originally produced in Yiddish and then *re*-produced in Russian, Polish, or German. The reason why I have chosen press releases and appeals rather than newspaper or journal articles is that the former were usually stimulated by special occasions, and therefore most strongly reflect in their language the Bund's attitude and policy at a particular point in time. This makes them an especially valuable source for monitoring and tracking the changes in the Bund's use of language. My thesis is that the authenticity of the voice of the Bund was not only maintained in the Yiddish original of a press release or appeal, but to a certain extent also reproduced in its Russian, Polish, or German versions.

It is with some reservation that I call these versions 'translations', as they were not translations in the sense that they were aiming at the greatest possible correspondence between source text and target text.[10] They were rather intended to reach as wide as possible an audience of both addressees and chance recipients. The easiest way to accomplish this under the prevailing conditions was to translate an existing Yiddish appeal or press release into Russian, Polish, or German, omitting or replacing certain paragraphs depending on the respective audience at which they were directed, while at the same time preserving the main body of the text and translating it word for word into the other language.

In this essay I will examine the omissions and replacements—which usually revealed the strategy of how a certain target group was approached—as well as the main body of the texts that were translated from the Yiddish original into another language. As for the latter, I will apply a form of translation criticism that is based on comparative analysis of source and target texts. In this analysis I will proceed,

8 'Spravka ob otchetakh Bunda k internatsional'nym sots. Kongressam', RGASPI, *f.* 271, *op.* 1, *d.* 25, fos. 1–2.

9 M. Weinreich, *History of the Yiddish Language*, trans. S. Noble with the assistance of J. A. Fishman (Chicago, 1973), 289.

10 C. Nord, *Text Analysis in Translation: Theory, Methodology, and Didactic Application of a Model for Translation-Oriented Text Analysis* (Amsterdam, 1991), 22–3.

as it were, in reverse, working backward from the result—i.e. from the Russian, Polish, or German version—to the Yiddish original.[11]

PERIODIZATION AS A METHODOLOGICAL TOOL: DIMENSIONS OF TIME AND SPACE

Before I proceed, I will establish a frame of reference and specify dimensions of time and space (that is, the cultural and political conditions of the production, distribution, and consumption of texts). A text published in a country where literature is censored must be read in a different light from a text whose author has not been subject to any restrictions; authors under censorship often wrote 'between the lines'. As a result of the fact that the Jewish press in eastern Europe emerged in the first half of the nineteenth century in imperial Russia, censorable writing,[12] in which symbolism and deliberate ambiguities were used in order to get the text past the censor, was always a characteristic feature of Jewish publications. The development of an independent journalism was hampered by strict regulations and censorship; as a consequence, writers developed a phraseology that formed a kind of secret language designed to slip past the censors and to be recognized and understood only by a specific readership.[13]

This phenomenon was further cultivated after the emergence of radical Haskalah journalism in the 1870s—for example, in Michel Levi Rodkinson's Hebrew-language journal *Hakol* ('The Voice'),[14] with its Yiddish supplement *Kol la'am* ('Voice of the People'),[15] or in *Asefat ḥakhamim* ('The Gathering of Scholars'),[16] which Rodkinson launched in 1877 as a substitute for Aaron Liberman's banned Vienna journal *Ha'emet* ('The Truth').[17] *Ha'emet* advocated socialist ideas but mostly concentrated on articles on science and cultural history. Only three editions appeared.[18] According to Morris Vinchevsky, the striking literary–philosophical title *Asefat ḥakhamim* was intended to lead the Russian censors away from the journal's political agenda and to 'araynganvenen undzere ideyen in Rusland—durkh a hinter-tir' ('smuggle our ideas into Russia through the back door').[19]

[11] W. Wilss, *The Science of Translation: Problems and Methods* (Tübingen, 1982), 220.

[12] I. P. Foote, 'In the Belly of the Whale: Russian Authors and Censorship in the Nineteenth Century', *Slavonic and East European Review*, 68/2 (Apr. 1990), 295–8.

[13] J. Lin, *Die hebräische Presse. Werdegang und Entwicklungstendenzen*, Schriften der jüdischen Sonderschau, Bibliothekar der jüdischen Gemeinde zu Berlin (Berlin, 1928), 17–18.

[14] M. Vinchevsky, *Gezamlte shriftn*, ix (New York, 1927), 161–7.

[15] Ibid.

[16] Vinchevsky's best-known contribution to the journal is probably his series of socio-critical articles written by a *meshugenem filosof* (crazy philosopher).

[17] Liberman was a former graduate of the Vilna Rabbinical School, and the first to try to create a socialist movement among Russian Jews in the 1870s. In the history of the social movements he is considered 'the father of Jewish socialism'.

[18] 'Materialy ob Arone Libermane i ego kruzhke. Protsess Libermana v Vene 13 noyabrya 1878 g. i v Berline 26 aprelya 1879', RGASPI, *f.* 271, *op.* 1, *d.* 3, fos. 85–6.

[19] Vinchevsky, *Gezamlte shriftn*, ix. 193.

However, whether the readership was always able to decode the messages conveyed by the authors remains questionable. From a letter found in Liberman's possession at his arrest in Vienna we learn about the '3rd, 4th and 5th Books of Moses. . . . The content is meaningless to the uninitiated. Another letter, postmarked 16 April 1877, says: What use is the Hebrew language? You can fool the censor once or twice, but not a third time. But if you write in such a coded fashion that the readers don't understand you either, what use is that?'[20]

In his time Liberman wrote for an audience that could understand Hebrew.[21] He insisted on Hebrew as the language of socialist propaganda for practical rather than nationalistic reasons: Hebrew, he thought, was the best literary vehicle for training revolutionaries among yeshiva students.[22]

Yeshiva students eventually did play a constitutive role in shaping Bundist journalism, in a rather different way, however, than Liberman had anticipated: in the mid-1890s, when Yiddish became the language of the revolution, former yeshiva students (*polintelligenty*, or semi-intellectuals, as they were called) were recruited to assist the intellectual leaders. More often than not the Bund leaders were acculturated to the Russian language. The semi-intellectuals formed an intermediate group of authors between the Jewish masses and the intellectual leadership. They were young men who had been brought up within the Jewish tradition, and were usually former yeshiva students who knew Yiddish and Russian well enough to convey their Russian-speaking mentors' ideas to the masses in Yiddish.[23]

Thus, it is important to bear in mind that Bundist journalism in its original (Yiddish) form did not simply differentiate between editorship and readership, or text producers and text consumers; one has to deconstruct the text producers into animators (the intellectual leadership) and authors (semi-intellectuals),[24] and note their different cultural backgrounds.

It is through the authors that Jewish oral and written traditions—for example, the use of symbolism or deliberate ambiguities derived from Jewish religious or folkloric sources as didactic constructs—became a constitutive feature of Bundist revolutionary discourse. Such journalistic practice was dictated by the Bund's policy

[20] The original is as follows: 'Der Inhalt ist dem Nichteingeweihten unverständlich. Ein anderer Brief mit dem Poststempel vom 16. April 1877 sagt: Was nützt die hebräische Sprache? Du kannst den Zensor einmal oder zweimal täuschen, das dritte Mal nicht. Schreibst du aber so dunkel, dass dich auch die Leser nicht verstehen, wo bleibt der Nutzen?' ('Materialy ob Arone Libermane i ego kruzhke. Protsess Libermana v Vene 13 noyabrya 1878 g. i v Berline 26 aprelya 1879', RGASPI, *f.* 271, *op.* 1, *d.* 3, fos. 86–7).

[21] Ibid. 87.

[22] B. Sapir, 'Liberman et le socialisme russe', *International Review for Social History*, 3 (1938), 25–87.

[23] T. M. Kopelson, 'Evreiskoe rabochee dvizhenie kontsa 80-kh i nachala 90-kh godov (Stenogramma vospominanii, zachitannykh na zasedaniyakh sektsii 16 fevralya i 9 marta 1928 g.)', in S. Dimanshtein (ed.), *Revolyutsionnoe dvizhenie sredi evreev* (Moscow, 1930); S. Gozhansky, 'Evreiskoe rabochee dvizhenie nachala 90-kh godov (Stenogramma vospominanii, zachitannykh na zasedaniyakh sektsii 5 i 20 yanvarya 1928 g.)', in Dimanshtein (ed.), *Revoliutsionnoe dvizhenie sredi evreev*; A. Litvak, *Geklibene shriftn* (New York, 1945), 16.

[24] E. Goffman, *Forms of Talk* (Oxford, 1981), 144.

of propaganda and education during its formative period and the subsequent years until 1902.

It is also important to bear in mind that texts are consumed differently in different social contexts; this is partly a matter of the sort of interpretative work that is applied to them, and partly a matter of the modes of interpretation that are available. To a large extent, the mode of interpretation depends on whether consumption of a text was individual or collective.[25] The latter was the case for the texts analysed here.

As for the dimension of time, the appeals on which I have based my analysis originate from the years 1902 to 1906, which is to say, the years immediately before and after the revolution of 1905. The period begins in 1902, following the Bund's 1901 decision to approach target groups within speech communities other than Yiddish more systematically. It is important to note two aspects of this period that influenced contemporary Bundist journalism: first, this period coincided with the period of the Bund's transition from its previous tactics of propaganda and education to the use of violence as a tactical means of (joint) political struggle. Secondly, this was a period of severe political stress for the Bund because of growing competition from the Zionists and the divorce from the RSDRP.

During the period under discussion, appeals were issued on special occasions rather than on a regular basis, usually in the aftermath of events that had a deep emotional impact and marked the beginning of severe political or emotional stress. The three occasions I refer to and on which I have based this essay were the May Day events in Vilna[26] in 1902,[27] the Bund's withdrawal from the RSDRP in 1903,[28] and the events of October 1905.[29] Three texts (two appeals and a press release) corresponding to these three events are the subject of the analysis that follows. The 1902 and 1903 appeals were reproduced in Polish and Russian. The third text is a press release that was sent to socialist newspapers abroad and was reproduced in Polish and Russian.[30]

[25] N. Fairclough, *Discourse and Social Change* (Cambridge, 1992), 79.

[26] The new governor, von Wahl, called in troops to break up the May Day celebrations in Vilna. A number of workers were arrested. The next day twenty Jewish prisoners and six Polish prisoners were whipped while the other prisoners were forced to look on. This was a blow to the pride that the Bund had fostered among the Jewish workers—to that sense of dignity that had led them to fight together. See H. J. Tobias, *The Jewish Bund in Russia: From Its Origins to 1905* (Stanford, Calif., 1972), 150.

[27] Tsentraler komitet fun bund, *Tsu ale yidishe arbayter un arbayterinen* (Vilna, May 1902); Od Centralnego Komitetu Ogólnożydowskiego Związku Robotniczego na Litwie, w Polsce i Rosji, *Odezwa do polskich towarzyszy-robotników* (Vilna, May 1902); Rossiiskaya sotsial-demokraticheskaya rabochaya partiya: Ot tsentralnogo komiteta Vseobshchego evreiskogo Rabochego Soyuza v Litve, Pol'she i Rossii, *Vozzvanie k russkim tovarishcham-rabochim* (Vilna, May 1902).

[28] Tsentraler komitet fun bund, *Vegn der aroystretung funem bund fun der rusisher sotsyaldemokratisher arbayter-partay* (Vilna, Dec. 1903); Centralny Komitet Bundu, *Z powodu wystąpienia Bundu z Soc.-Dem. Partji Robotn. Rosji* (Vilna, Dec. 1903); Tsentral'nyi komitet Bunda, *Po povodu vystupleniya Bunda iz Rossiiskoi sotsial-demokraticheskoi rabochei partii* (Vilna, Dec. 1903).

[29] During the Bund's first decade, there was only one other event that had such a deep emotional impact, namely the Kishinev pogrom in 1903.

[30] Bund Central Committee, *Kontr-revoliutsiya idet*, press release (Vilna, Nov. 1905), 1; German version: *Der Vormarsch der Kontrerevolution* [*sic*] (Vilna, Nov. 1905).

BUNDIST JOURNALISM IN TRANSLATION

In this section I will discuss two issues, namely the different approaches and strategies that the Bund chose for approaching a particular audience, and secondly, the language used in a translation from the Yiddish into Russian, Polish, or German.

As noted above, a more serious attempt to address the Polish and Russian comrades was made in the spring of 1902. This effort followed the Russian government's implementation of its new rigid policy of applying the strictest possible interpretation of the law.

A document referring to the May Day beatings in Vilna, and directed to the Polish and Russian workers, stated: 'For the first time we, organized Jewish workers and social democrats, are turning to you with an appeal on behalf of our league. It is a unique event for us! But what drives us is also unique.'[31]

Only one earlier appeal had been translated for these two target groups, in September and November 1901, following the Russian government's introduction of the new restrictions on Jews' right to education;[32] in addition, the twenty-fifth anniversary edition of the Bund central organ *Di arbayter shtime* was issued in December 1901 in Yiddish, Russian, and Polish.[33]

Appeals directed to the Polish workers generally built on shared experience—Jews and Poles lived in a region that was mainly 'inhabited by those despised by the Russian government: Poles, Lithuanians, and Jews'[34]—and on shared suffering: 'Prison, exile, batons, bullets, total destruction—this is the response to us from the tsar's government! You know it all very well, as you too are exposed to it as badly as we are.'[35] This may have been an attempt to resume the Polish–Jewish cooperation (the concept of 'brothers-in-deed'[36]) of an earlier struggle 'for our freedom and yours!', and thus to provide a basis and perhaps an additional motivation for further collaboration in the present revolutionary struggle: 'While we Jews and Poles are exposed to such persecution, our Russian comrades have absolutely no idea about it. We, like you, belong to a nation that is particularly hated by the Russian

[31] Polish version: *Odezwa do polskich towarzyszy-robotników*; Russian version: *Vozzvanie k russkim tovarishcham-rabochim*. The quotation is translated from the Polish edition.

[32] Rossiiskaya sotsial-demokraticheskaya rabochaya partiya: Ot tsentral'nogo komiteta Vseobshchego evreiskogo Rabochego Soyuza v Litve, Pol'she i Rossii, *Vozzvanie k evreiskomy obshchestvu [popovodu poslednikh ogranichenii prava obrazovaniia evreev]* (Vilna, Sept. 1901). *Odezwa Centralnego Komitetu Ogólno-Żydowskiego Związku Robotniczego na Litwie, w Polsce i Rosyi do żydowskiego społeczeństwa z powodu ostatnich ograniczeń prawa kształcenia się Żydów* (Vilna, Nov. 1901).

[33] *Di arbayter shtime*, 25 (Dec. 1901).

[34] *Odezwa do polskich towarzyszy-robotników*.

[35] Ibid.

[36] As a character in Józef Ignacy Kraszewski's novel *Żyd* put it, 'be our brothers in spirit rather than in words; brothers in deed rather than in appearance' (cited in B. Porter, *When Nationalism Began to Hate: Imagining Modern Politics in Nineteenth-Century Poland* (New York, 2000), 40).

government, and this government exploits, persecutes, humiliates, and embarrasses us twice as much.'[37]

The list of four successive verbs as well as the five successive nouns in the previous quotation ('prison', 'exile', 'batons', 'bullets', 'total destruction'), all of them indicating various degrees of suffering, is rather unusual in both Polish and Russian and indicates the Yiddish origin of the text. In Yiddish sources, lists of similar epithets or qualities of comparable importance are used often. Such reinforcement is meant to catch the ears of the listeners, and through their ears to reach their hearts. It was a proven device for reaching as many people as possible when the idea was to establish a mass audience for solidarity and protest. However, even taking into account the fact that the text is an appeal, both listings sound somewhat awkward in their translated form; the translators here have not taken into account the different cultural background of the readers. The style of their translation, close as it is to the original, would not have been appreciated by the readers for whom it was intended. It might even have irritated some readers as it may have jarred against their concepts of natural usage of social language, or made them laugh or feel embarrassed when this wasn't the author's intention, which is a common first reaction to close translation. We see here that the atmosphere of suffering and misery—or of merriment and joy—characteristic of many Yiddish source texts does not always lend itself to translation.

The strategy of emphasizing the shared suffering and shared past seems to have been applied above all to the Polish workers living nearby; however, the Russian comrades, located mainly in the southern provinces, such as Ekaterinoslav, Kiev, Kharkov, Nikolaev, Odessa, and Kremenchug,[38] far away from the Bund's original bases in Poland, Lithuania, and Belarus, needed first of all to be *reached*. This becomes clear from both the Russian and the Polish versions of the appeal, which include the remark: 'but we Jewish workers are exposed to yet more persecution, which you cannot imagine'.[39] The Russian version, however, lacks the paragraphs referring to a shared past and the suffering of 'us Jews and Poles';[40] instead, towards its end it contains an additional paragraph referring to the common search for dignity, which leads the workers to stand together to fight tsarism:

> Comrades, we revolutionaries can endure a lot, but we cannot and must not allow our personality to be mocked. The insult against our Vilna comrades is at the same time a deep insult against every worker combating Russian tsarism; we are sure that you personally feel the humiliation to which we have been subjected in public, and we have no doubt that curses will fly from your lips as soon as the news reaches you of the Tatar violence that has been inflicted upon us.[41]

37 *Odezwa do polskich towarzyszy-robotników.*
38 Tobias, *The Jewish Bund in Russia*, 117.
39 *Vozzvanie k russkim tovarishcham-rabochim.*
40 *Odezwa do polskich towarzyszy-robotników.*
41 *Vozzvanie k russkim tovarishcham-rabochim.*

Both the Polish and the Russian versions of this appeal are somewhat shorter than the Yiddish original. While they provide information about the Vilna May Day events, they lack the extended and lamenting prologue of the Yiddish original.[42] Similar lamentations can also be found as introductions to other appeals directed to the Jewish workers after February 1902. Such appeals usually called for organized revenge;[43] their aim was to stir up among Bund members and their supporters 'hatred and scorn towards the Russian government', as well as to 'awaken the thirst for holy revenge. . . . So far our struggle has confined itself to peaceful means, and it is not our aim to shed human blood. However, there is a limit to all patience. It is no fault of ours if people's revenge, hatred, and excitement turn into violence.'[44] In other words, these appeals contained a strong element of justification in order to prepare the ground for a certain degree of violence, which was deemed necessary for the destruction of the existing regime.

[42] 'Comrades! Never before has the Russian government displayed its whole insolence, madness, and cruelty as openly as on 1 May this year. Never before has the mad arbitrariness of the despotic band of robbers governing our unfortunate country achieved such a high level of impertinence. More than once, we Jewish workers happened to endure the most cruel, violent deeds of the mad tsarist servants; more than once we have felt on our backs the gashes of the Cossacks' sling whips; more than once we have been thrown en masse into gaols, when we have attempted to improve our situation just a little; more than once they have banned the best of our comrades to cold Siberia, without trial and without any evidence of guilt. However, what occurred this year on 1 May in Vilna is worse than everything that we have had to endure so far. Comrades! Before 1 May in Vilna, when the rumour was spread that for the demonstrations they would apply physical punishment, not one person believed it. Everyone thought that this would be impossible, that the Russian government will not allow itself to do so. This opinion was, however, a mistake. When our Vilna comrades went out on 1 May to demonstrate, Cossacks and policemen threw themselves upon them. They encircled some of the demonstrators and beat them ruthlessly with sling whips and truncheons; the standard-bearer was beaten even as he lay unconscious on the ground. Bloodied and destroyed, the demonstrators were incarcerated in the police station. On the next day, the terrible, cruel execution took place. On the next morning our comrades were badly tortured in the presence of Governor von Wahl, Chief of Police Nazimov, Dr Mikhailov, policemen, Cossacks, and guards. Comrades! The blood freezes in our veins when we visualize this cruel Asiatic image. When we were stepping out to combat tsarist rule, we knew what to expect. We knew that our path would be strewn with piercing thorns, that long years of prison, Siberia, hunger, and cold awaited us along this way. And we have already proved that all of this cannot frighten us, that we are able to endure all this. Always and everywhere in the most difficult moments of our lives, we revolutionaries have guarded and defended our human person and our human dignity. To insults we have responded with insults, to violence we have responded with violence. We cannot keep quiet about what has happened in Vilna. From thousands of honest hearts is torn a general cry for revenge: *Nekome! Rakhe!*' (italic is shown as bold in the original).

[43] Algemeyner yidisher arbayterbund in lite, poyln un rusland: Tsentraler komitet fun bund, *Tsu ale yidishe arbayter un arbayterinen* (Vilna, Feb. 1902); Der algemeyner yidisher arbayterbund in lite, poyln un rusland: Vilner sotsyal-demokratisher komitet, *1-ter mart* (Vilna, Feb. 1902).

[44] Tsuzamengekumene komitetn fun di ortige organizatsyonen; Vilner sotsyal-demokratisher komitet fun bund; Vilner sotsyal-demokratisher komitet fun sotsyal-demokratisher partay in poyln un lite; Vilner arbayter komitet fun litvishe sotsyal partay un a vilner grupe fun ruslander sotsyal-demokratisher arbayter partay, *Khoverim arbayter!* (Vilna, May 1902).

While the justification of the party line was the theme in the Yiddish original, the versions directed to the Polish and Russian fellow-workers and international social democracy focused on the call for solidarity and on protest against the suffering of the 'pariah among the proletarians'[45] rather than on encouraging destructive actions. Thus, the Polish and Russian versions of this appeal constitute adjustments or adaptations of the source text to the party line propagated at the time by the Bund, rather than translations strictly speaking.

The function of the next appeal was to inform the Jewish masses and their Polish and Russian fellow workers about the Bund's decision to leave the ranks of the RSDRP. It attempted to justify what was clearly an about-face: in spite of having advocated to that point the speedy unification of all revolutionary forces, the Bund was now going to pursue its own course. No paragraphs were omitted and no changes were made for the respective target groups; both the strategy of justification and the rhetoric of lamentation thus entered the Polish and Russian versions.

In the appeal on the Vilna beatings, the strategy of justification was confined to the Yiddish original and was aimed at sweeping aside the addressees' moral scruples. In the text on the decision to separate from the RSDRP, the strategy involved labelling the Russian social democrats renegades and declaring them to be politically immature, while presenting the Bund as continuing along the right path. The idea of *going off course* as opposed to remaining *true* advocates of the socialist ideal is presented with the help of positive and negative phrases as italicized in the following quotation:

> The representatives of the Russian social democrats who were present at the Congress do not have even the faintest idea either about the nature and direction of the activism of the Bund, or about the role history has forced on the Bund because of the specific social and political conditions and the psychological conditions that prevail, created by twenty centuries of persecution of the Jews. . . . The requests that . . . were formulated by the Bund at the second Party Congress were met by the majority of delegates with such *utter ignorance* and *irresponsibility* (which could be described in stronger language). . . . It is *absolutely true* that only an organization that grew up within this community and lives the same life as the community, whose blood pulses to the same historic beat, can be *successful* in propagating in this society the idea of class struggle and socialism. Only such an organization can carry out our *fruitful* work in order to unite the Jewish proletariat with the international family of the proletariat. . . . The *blinkered uncompromising* centralization *blindly* mangles everything that crosses its path. Such a centralization would be suitable for a group of conspirators but does not correspond to the requirements of a party—and this is what most of the Russian delegates wanted. However, behind this *utopian* ideal of centralization in reality there hides the

[45] This refers to the status of being a proletarian, a Russian, and a Jew. See Karl Kautsky's letter of 20 May 1899 to the Bund: 'Pis'ma Bebelya i Kautskogo k Bundu o rabote evreiskikh organizatsii v Rossii', RGASPI, *f.* 271, *op.* 1, *d.* 67, fos. 19–22. See also Tsentraler komitet fun algemeynem yidishn arbayter bund in lite, poyln un rusland: Vilner sotsayl-demokratisher komitet, *Vegn der aroystretung fun bund fun der ruslender sotsyaldemokratisher arbayter-partay* (Vilna, Dec. 1903).

desire to settle the interests of those closest to them, interests which they *do not fully understand*—and to remove them from the basic principles of the *true* revolutionary socialist movement. They show organizational *immaturity*, stemming in large measure from a *false* understanding of the international socialist ideal. . . . We will not cease in our struggle to ensure that there will be a *real* unification of all the revolutionary and socialist forces of the Russian state.

The irony, as well as the highly emotional declamatory and sometimes pathetic style that dominated the Yiddish original (and was often expressed with the help of tautological pairings of listings, as well as with anaphoric or metaphorical use of language, as in the following three sections), now enters the translations.

Tautological pairing:

The suicide of the Bund would have meant the suicide of the movement within the Jewish proletariat. Had this happened the international family of the proletariat would have lost one of its *energetic and resolute* members. Nonetheless, the *saddest and most frightful* fact arising from that historic moment is the fratricidal struggle that will doubtless now break out.

Anaphorism:

The organization that in the course of the last five years has been generally considered to be one of the most energetic revolutionary forces in the Russian Party; the organization that in its activism among the Jewish proletariat has achieved such splendid results; the organization that strove so hard to achieve the speediest unification of all the revolutionary strengths of Russia—this organization has suddenly left the ranks of the party.[46]

Many metaphorical fields, in which one image gives rise to the next one or is closely related to it, are included. The following is but one example:

The Bund was a social anomaly. The Bund only harmed the development of the revolution. The Bund was a nationalistic and bourgeois movement and it ought to disappear from the surface of the earth! . . . In response to our request the second Party Congress contemplated offering the Bund a silk garrotte with which it could strangle its own lifeline. The Congress was considerate enough to offer the Bund conditions in which its death would not be instantaneous but would take place by degrees.

Metaphors are to be understood as the transfer of words from their expected and familiar use into a context in which they are not normally used.[47] For readers to

[46] Tsentraler komitet fun bund, *Vegn der aroystretung funem bund fun der rusisher sotsyaldemokratisher arbayter-partay*; Centralny Komitet Bundu, *Z powodu wystąpienia Bundu z Soc.-Dem. Partji Robotn. Rosji*; Tsentral'nyi komitet Bunda, *Po povodu vystupleniya Bunda iz Rossiiskoi sotsial-demokraticheskoi rabochei partii*.

[47] M. Pöttner, 'Metaphors of Universal Love', in R. Bishops and J. Francis (eds.), *Metaphor, Canon and Community: Jewish, Christian and Islamic Approaches*, Religions and Discourse (Bern, 1999), i. See also E. A. Hermanson, 'Recognizing Hebrew Metaphors: Conceptual Metaphor Theory and Bible Translation', *Journal of Northwest Semitic Languages*, 22/2 (1996), 67–78. As for the cognitive conceptual metaphor theory, see G. Lakoff and M. Johnson, *Metaphors We Live By* (Chicago, 1980).

understand metaphors, they need to be aware of their original settings; the author thus has to presume a certain level of familiarity with a particular metaphor and its meaning on the part of his addressees. In Yiddish texts produced during the Bund's early years (1897–1902), metaphors served mainly as didactic constructs for explaining to the Jewish masses the Marxist teaching of class struggle. After 1902 a more complex use of metaphors can be observed, and this indicates the beginning of a more strategic use of language.

Whether the irony and metaphors in the sections quoted were recognized and interpreted in the desired way by the new (Polish- and Russian-speaking) audience remains, however, doubtful. In any case, no attempt has been made by the translators to clarify the irony or to compensate the Polish and Russian readers for the semantic loss that occurs in the translation of metaphors.

In comparing the appeal on the Vilna beatings and the appeal on the Bund's withdrawal from the Russian Party, several points can be made. First, both appeals are significant for their period; the former is typical for the beginning of a period of severe political stress that results in a greater effort to establish new partnerships, while the latter marks the (preliminary) end of such a partnership. Secondly, both Yiddish originals are characterized by a passionate discourse of justification. While in the first appeal this justification confines itself to the Yiddish original, as the relevant passages remain untranslated, in the latter it dominates both the Yiddish original and the translated Russian and Polish versions (no passages were omitted). Thirdly, appeals issued in the aftermath of events marking the beginning of stressful periods, rather than as part of a regular series of statements, share a common characteristic: their language is much stronger than that used in Yiddish appeals that were directed to the Jewish workers exclusively and therefore remained untranslated.

With its divorce from the Russian Social Democrats, the image of the Bund as an international force was damaged, and on its home front in the Pale of Settlement it faced ever increasing competition from the Zionists.[48] In the following years the Bund increased its efforts to influence the international political scene by issuing information in English and German.[49] Some of their press releases called for workers to show their solidarity, more often than not by sending monetary contributions for the purchase of weapons.[50] The aim of others was self-presentation or differen-

[48] In 1903–4 more than half a dozen publications authored by various Zionist groups made their appearance. Though the Bund still heavily dominated the political literary scene, its near monopoly in the Pale was broken. Tobias, *The Jewish Bund in Russia*, 252.

[49] European Committee of the Bund, *The Bund and Self-Defence*, appeal (Geneva, July 1905); Bund Committee Abroad, *The Military Massacres in Gomel*, press release (Geneva, Feb. 1906); Bund Central Committee, *An alle Rekruten!*, appeal (Vilna, Nov. 1905); id., *Der Vormarsch der Kontrerevolution*; id., *Der schachernde Liberalismus und das kämpfende Proletariat*, appeal (Vilna, Jan. 1906); Bund Committee Abroad, *Die Wahrheit über Homel*, press release (Geneva, Feb. 1906).

[50] '. . . but the principal difficulty lies in the fact that notwithstanding all our efforts, we lack financial means and are therefore short of arms. All of this demands large sums of money, which we cannot

tiation.[51] The latter appears to have become increasingly important to the Bund after it broke ranks with the Russian Social Democrats, and particularly when it argued that it should be allocated one of the Russian delegation's two votes (or even a third vote). The Bund's motion was denied, however; the International Bureau in Amsterdam expressed the view that the Bund differed from the Russian Party only in organizational matters and not in matters of principle, and consequently allocated the second vote to the Social Revolutionaries.[52]

The last text I have chosen for analysis—a press release issued following the events in the autumn of 1905—belongs to the former group, however. Some 120,000 Yiddish copies were distributed, as were 40,000 Russian copies and 20,000 Polish copies.[53] The full German version appeared two months later in an American German-language newspaper under the headline 'Aus der russischen Revolution. Aufrufe und Schriftstücke erlassen von dem "Bund", der jüdischen revolutionären Kampforganization' ('From Revolutionary Russia: Appeals and Pamphlets Released by the Bund, the Jewish Revolutionary Organization').[54] Such press releases presented the Bund's revolutionary struggle in Russia to an international audience. They were sent out to socialist movements and newspapers worldwide through the Bund Committee Abroad.

For this analysis I have examined the German and Russian versions of this revolutionary appeal. While the former is a verbatim translation from the Yiddish original into German (I suspect it was written with translation in mind), the Russian version is again what I would call an adaptation, designed to make the text palatable to the Russian audience.

Both texts begin with lengthy descriptions of the 'bloody doings of the counter-revolution' but, as it turns out, they pursue rather different aims. The German version focuses mainly on explaining the concept of counter-revolution to the readers, who are assumed to be far away from Russia. It leans heavily on the Yiddish original, with its typical didactic constructs, such as similes ('Bloodthirsty as a wolf and cunning as a fox is the counter-revolution'), metaphors ('The young blossoms of freedom should be drowned in blood and buried under a mound of corpses'), and

raise in Russia. We consider it the moral duty of all men who sympathize with the heroic struggle of the organized Jewish defenders . . . to assist the Bund financially in organizing self-defence work' (European Committee of the Bund, *The Bund and Self-Defence*, 4).

[51] Bund-Auslandskomitee, *Bericht über die Tätigkeit des Allgemeinen Jüdischen Arbeiterbundes in Litauen, Polen und Russland ('Bund') nach seinem V. Parteitag*, Bericht für den Internationalen Sozialistischen Kongress in Amsterdam 1904 (Geneva, 1904). Staatsbibliothek zu Berlin, Preussischer Kulturbesitz, Abteilung Historische Drucke, Haus 1, Unter den Linden 8, *Sammelband zur Russischen Revolution*, 10 Schriften: Jüdischer Arbeiterbund. Zeitschriften und Flugschriften im Jargon, Sign.: gr20 Fc 7595/45-3RAR.

[52] 'Pis'ma Bebelya i Kautskogo k Bundu o rabote evreiskikh organizatsii v Rossii', letter from Karl Kautsky, 1 Nov. 1904, RGASPI, *f.* 271, *op.* 1, *d.* 67, fos. 8–10.

[53] *Kontr-revolyutsiya idet*, 1.

[54] 'Revolutionsaufruf des Central Comites des Bundes: Der Vormarsch der Kontrerevolution (übersetzt aus dem jüdischen Jargon)', *Arbeiterzeitung* (St Louis), 3 Feb. 1906, 1.

personifications ('Up to her neck in blood the counter-revolution goes on, sowing strife and hatred on her way and encouraging the animal instincts of humanity. . . . With its bloody hands, it throws Russia back into the old kingdom of darkness and slavery'). The aim, as is revealed towards the end, is to prepare the ground for making an appeal for a speedy donation:

All the quicker and more powerful must be the onward march of the revolution. All the quicker and more powerfully must the revolution regain the country's freedom. The counter-revolution is armed. Machine guns and cannons are at its disposal. The revolution must have weapons, too. Its heroic army must be as well armed as possible. . . . To the concerted attack of the counter-revolution the revolution must respond with a general armed popular revolt.

The Russian version, too, begins with an extensive description of the counter-revolution, and uses similar Jewish didactic constructs, such as metaphors ('Tsarism in presentiment of its death agony wants to pour blood over the dawn of freedom, torrents of blood, and to bury the revolution under the dead bodies of the fighters'), similes ('jackals'), and personification ('The counter-revolution, up to its knees in blood, stepping through mountains of dead bodies, sowing on its way death and atrocity . . .'). Unlike the German version, in which this language prepares the ground for pleas for donations, the Russian version is much more focused on accelerating activities leading to a quick final battle in order to complete the project, while at the same time communicating to its audience that this battle will be cruel and bloody: 'The final battle is already near! . . . The dark army of the counter-revolution stands face to face with the righteous army of freedom. . . . There will be a battle, a cruel and painful battle, but its outcome has already been settled! The victory belongs to us! Freedom will triumph!'

Some of the language of appeal used in the Yiddish text may have been lost in translation. Effects such as phonetically supported messages, for example in rhymes and rhythms or alliterations, were particularly difficult to preserve. Only rarely can alliteration survive in a translation—as in the case of the phrase *fintster un faykht*, meaning 'dark and dank'. Usually the alliterations get lost, as in the case of *hader un has*,[55] the English translation of which is 'strife and hatred'. However, in the Russian version of this pamphlet, *hader un has* is not literally translated into 'strife and hatred' but becomes *smert' i uzhas* ('death and atrocity').[56]

What happened in this case? Presumably, it was more important to the translator to maintain the special effect in the translation, rather than the meaning of the idiom. Consequently, he replaced the special effect conveyed in the Yiddish original through sound with another special effect in the Russian version: namely, epithets or the hyperbolic use of language. This translation strategy appears to be aimed at *moving* people rather than instructing them or making them understand something.

55 'Revolutionsaufruf des Central Comites des Bundes', 1.

56 *Kontr-revolyutsiya idet*, 1.

CONCLUSION

During the period 1902–6 both the composition and 'translation' of Bundist texts were clearly subordinated to the proclamation and justification of the Bund's party line, rather than to the aim of making the readers understand something. Promoting loyalty to the party line was not only the reason for composing a text, but also a principal factor in the nature of its 'translation'. It determined the translators' strategy when they were transferring a written message from Yiddish into another language. This feature of Bundist revolutionary discourse spread into Polish, Russian, and German socialist, and later on communist, language, where its style penetrated and remained evident in public discourse throughout the twentieth century.

The 'translators' of the Bund's messages, although for most purposes having a satisfactory command of both source and target language, often failed to overcome the cultural difficulties presented by the task of translation, because they were not always able to compensate their Polish, Russian, or German readers for the semantic loss of the connotations inherent in devices such as metaphors or irony in the Yiddish source text. In this sense the inadequacies of the Polish, German, or Russian 'translations' tended not to be due to a lack of linguistic competence on the part of the 'translators', but to the fact that they were unable to anticipate the possible reactions of a reader and thereby to judge the adequacy of their own translations. Recipient orientation as a fundamental factor for translation played no part in the Russian, Polish, or German reproductions of Yiddish source texts. In other words, those press releases and appeals were sender-oriented rather than recipient-oriented and could therefore be fully understood only by a narrow target group. The authors and translators appear to have been unaware of the obvious conflict with their aim of reaching as wide an audience as possible in order to establish a basis for solidarity and protest. This intention sits uneasily with the conventional pattern of Jewish discourse, which concentrates on 'putting the message across', no matter to how few people. Perhaps the gap is widened here by a Jewish tradition of providing tailored translations to defined target groups, with little ambition, however, to provide translations to a naïve audience, especially when compared with the typically Christian translation models that are ambitious enough to target a more general audience.

Poles in the German Local Police in Eastern Poland and their Role in the Holocaust

MARTIN DEAN

THE recent publication of *Neighbors* by Jan Gross has unleashed an intense debate in Poland about the active participation of Poles in the Holocaust.[1] A careful re-examination of the available evidence supports the thesis that a unit of the Sicherheitspolizei and the Sicherheitsdienst (German security police (Sipo) and SD) probably initiated the pogrom in Jedwabne, although, as eyewitness reports confirm, the murders were actually carried out almost exclusively by the Polish inhabitants of the town.[2] In the broader context of German occupation policy in eastern Poland, Jedwabne is an extreme case, but it was by no means an isolated incident.

Although Jan Gross's short book has been much criticized in Poland, his previous works on the Soviet occupation of eastern Poland and the German occupation of the country demonstrate that he is well acquainted with the suffering of the Polish people during the Second World War.[3] Both the weakness and the strength of the work lie rather in its limitation to the study of a single event; the book ultimately raises more questions than it answers. Recent research on the participation of Ukrainians and Belarusians in the Holocaust as policemen has also shown that hundreds of local Poles participated alongside these groups in the anti-Jewish massacres orchestrated by the Germans in the eastern districts of Poland.[4]

This chapter was previously published as 'Polen in der einheimischen Hilfspolizei. Ein Aspekt der Besatzungsrealität in den deutsch besetzten ostpolnischen Gebieten', in B. Chiari (ed.), *Die polnische Heimatarmee. Geschichte und Mythos der Armia Krajowa seit dem Zweiten Weltkrieg* (Munich, 2003). The opinions stated in this chapter are those of the author alone and do not necessarily reflect those of the United States Holocaust Memorial Museum or the United States Holocaust Memorial Council.

[1] J. T. Gross, *Neighbors: The Destruction of the Jewish Community in Jedwabne, Poland* (Princeton, 2001); on this debate, see e.g. J. Borkowicz *et al.*, *Thou Shalt Not Kill: Poles on Jedwabne* (Warsaw, 2001).

[2] A. B. Rossino, 'Polish "Neighbours" and German Invaders: Anti-Jewish Violence in the Białystok District During the Opening Weeks of Operation Barbarossa', *Polin*, 16 (2003), 431–52.

[3] See J. T. Gross, *Revolution from Abroad: The Soviet Conquest of Poland's Western Ukraine and Western Belorussia* (Princeton, 1988); id., *Polish Society Under German Occupation* (Princeton, 1979).

[4] M. Dean, *Collaboration in the Holocaust: Crimes of the Local Police in Belorussia and Ukraine, 1941–44* (London, 2000), 85, 96.

Gross uses documents from the post-war investigations of the Main Commission for the Investigation of Crimes Against the Polish Nation (now renamed the Instytut Pamięci Narodowej, Institute for National Remembrance) as the primary source material in his reconstruction of the events of Jedwabne.[5] The Main Commission has conducted hundreds of other war crimes investigations into occurrences in the former eastern districts of Poland (Kresy wschodnie) under German occupation.[6] Many of those who were accused in the Polish trials—especially in cases related to the territory of present-day Belarus—can be identified as ethnic Poles in the files of the Main Commission. Dozens of these Poles were indicted for the murder or betrayal of Jews and convicted by Polish courts. This research is based primarily on investigative files preserved at the Main Commission.[7] Criminal investigations conducted by the Soviet, German, and British authorities provide strong independent corroboration of the findings from the Polish cases. The main focus here is on the activity of individual Poles who served within the German local police.

Before entering into this highly sensitive subject, it is important to clarify certain key points about German policy towards the Poles in the occupied eastern territories. In those former Polish territories that now form part of present-day western Belarus and western Ukraine, the German occupation forces were highly suspicious of the Polish ethnic minority. They were acutely aware that most Poles were committed to the restoration of their national independence in the form of a Polish state.[8] Accordingly, the German occupying force directed severe repressive measures against what they perceived to be the Polish intelligentsia. The Nazis murdered or imprisoned many Polish priests, officials, lawyers, doctors, and teachers.[9] Nevertheless, because of the shortage of experienced administrators, particularly at the beginning of the occupation, the Germans were compelled to employ many Poles in the police and local administration. In certain districts, such as the area around Lida, Poles had not yet been replaced with Belarusians by the autumn of 1943, so that much of the region remained under the control of police posts run by Poles.[10] Moreover, in the Polish eastern territories the attitude of the Poles themselves was ambivalent: Soviet mass deportations, arrests, and confiscations between 1939 and 1941 had led many Poles to view the Germans as the lesser of the two evil occupying powers.

[5] Gross, *Neighbors*, 26–32.

[6] I would like to thank Elżbieta Kobierska-Motas of the former Polish Main Commission for the Investigation of Crimes Against the Polish Nation, who made available to me an extensive annotated list of these trials.

[7] I should like to thank the historians Jolanta Choińska-Mika, Rita Röhr, and Richard Butterwick for assisting me with this work.

[8] See e.g. P. Klein (ed.), *Die Einsatzgruppen in der besetzten Sowjetunion 1941/42. Die Tätigkeits- und Lageberichte des Chefs der Sicherheitspolizei und des SD* (Berlin, 1997), 126, 207.

[9] A. Galiński, 'Eksterminacja inteligencji polskiej latem 1942 r. w. nowogródzkiem', *Biuletyn Głównej Komisji*, 23 (1972); Dean, *Collaboration in the Holocaust*, 100.

[10] B. Chiari, *Alltag hinter der Front. Besatzung, Kollaboration und Widerstand in Weissrussland 1941–1944* (Düsseldorf, 1998), 275.

It would be impossible to conduct a detailed analysis here of the strength and significance of indigenous Polish antisemitism; however, a few key points must be clarified. Both German and native antisemitic propaganda sought to link the Jewish population with a supposed 'Jewish–Bolshevik' conspiracy. Those who had suffered personally under Soviet repressive measures were particularly inclined to support this line of argument. In the eastern districts of Poland the radical political and economic changes that took place during the brief period of Soviet occupation served to intensify social and ethnic tensions within the population. Many Poles were galled by their perception that Jews were now taking their places within the local administration and even the police force. At the same time, they overlooked the practical reality that Soviet repressive measures affected Jewish communal organizations, businesses, and refugees just as severely as they did the Poles.

The role of the Polish underground must also be taken into account, as there is some evidence of a systematic attempt by the Polish underground to infiltrate the local police.[11] In this context it should be stressed that throughout the occupation the Polish underground army, the Armia Krajowa, remained a rallying point for Poles from across the political spectrum.

The goal of this research is to assess the extent of Polish participation in the anti-Jewish actions on the basis of an extensive investigation of the personnel and activities of the local police units in various regions. The direct participation of individual Poles in the crimes of the local police is of course only one aspect of a highly complex situation; there were also many Poles who saved Jews or bravely resisted the German occupation.[12]

On 25 July 1941 Himmler issued an order to the senior SS and police leaders that 'additional protection forces were to be raised from Ukrainians, the inhabitants of the Baltic States, and Belarusians' in the territories formerly occupied by the Soviets.[13] Reference to participation of Poles was intentionally omitted. Nevertheless, some Poles did join the local police, as there were often too few qualified Belarusians or Ukrainians available; the same held true for the selection of local mayors and other administrative posts.

In the Mir *raion* (district), close to Baranowicze on the territory of contemporary Belarus, a local auxiliary police force was established within a few days of the arrival of the German troops. The police force consisted mainly of Belarusians, although some Poles and Tatars were also members. The men were between the ages of 18 and 35 and reported for police service voluntarily.[14] In a retrospective report

11 This important aspect requires detailed analysis on the basis of the available Polish sources.

12 See e.g. S. Spector, *The Holocaust of Volhynian Jews, 1941–1944* (Jerusalem, 1990), 248–51.

13 Bundesarchiv-Militärarchiv, Freiburg (BA-MA), RW 41/4 RFSS, to the Higher SS and Police Leaders, Berlin, 25 July 1941.

14 Magistrates' Court, Dorking, Surrey, committal proceedings against Semion Serafinowicz (hereafter Dorking), statement of Ivan Yatsevich on 21 Mar. 1996; see also Gosudarstvennyi arkhiv Rossiiskoi Federatsii, Moscow, *fond* 7021, *opis'* 148, *delo* 364. (Hereafter the standard Russian archival notation will be used: *f.* (*fond*), *op.* (*opis'*), *d.* (*delo*).)

Commander Klepsch of the Ordnungspolizei (Order Police) in Minsk noted that the Ordnungsdienst (Order Service), as it was called, was recruited on a voluntary basis and that prior military training was not a necessary requirement for acceptance.[15] Among the main motivations for joining the Ordnungsdienst was the regular pay and food provided by the Germans, as well as other material benefits. As one Belarusian put it: 'At the beginning nobody was forced to join the police. . . . Those people joined who were hungry for power or had an eye for easy pickings.'[16] For some, motives of personal revenge also played a role. For example, some recruits had been arrested by the Soviets just before the German attack, or members of their families had been deported to Siberia. According to some local witnesses, there were also a few notorious antisemites among the initial voluntary recruits to the Ordnungsdienst in the Mir *raion*.

There are a number of documented cases of local policemen actively supporting the mass shooting of Jews in Belarus and Ukraine in the autumn of 1941. On 9 November 1941 there was a veritable hunt for Jews on the streets of the small town of Mir. Several eyewitnesses describe the active participation of the Ordnungsdienst, which, together with the 8th Company of German Infantry Regiment 727, shot about 1,500 Jews on that day. The Belarusian witness Boris Grushevsky described the scene at the grave site:

> The policemen were sitting on the top of this pit. They had sub-machine guns. There were also several Germans. It was the policemen who shot. The Jews were standing in columns in front of the pit. The police were guarding at the sides of the pit. The Jews were made to take off their clothes a few at a time and approach the pit and enter it. They lay down and were shot.

The local policemen came from Mir and the surrounding villages. Grushevsky noted that it appeared to him as if the policemen were enjoying their murderous work. They were drunk and 'behaved themselves as if they were celebrating a wedding'. In fact, one local policeman did get married on that terrible day in Mir.[17]

The non-Jewish local inhabitants of Jody, in the Glubokoe district in Belarus, recounted a similar 'celebratory' mood during the massacre of the Jews of the town. The local police, mostly Belarusians, Russians, and a few Poles, who were also mostly drunk, carried out the murder in December 1941. Some local inhabitants, especially the policemen, enriched themselves from the property left behind by the Jews.[18]

In the summer and autumn of 1941 a German civil administration replaced the

[15] Natsional'niy arkhiv Respubliki Belarus', Minsk (NARB), *f.* 370, *o.* 1, *d.* 1263, Klepsch Report, Apr. 1943; see also US National Archives, RG-242 (captured German records), T-580, roll 96, Vortrag über den Kräfte- und Kriegseinsatz der Ordnungspolizei im Jahre 1941.

[16] War Crimes Unit, Scotland Yard (WCU), D7341.

[17] Dorking, statement of Boris Grushevsky, 18 Mar. 1996.

[18] P. Silverman, D. Smuschkowitz, and P. Smuszkowicz, *From Victims to Victors* (Concord, Ont., 1992), 82–3.

military administration in the western districts of Belarus and Ukraine. Shortly thereafter, small units of the Ordnungspolizei (the gendarmerie in the countryside and the Schutzpolizei in the larger towns) took over police authority. These units of the Ordnungspolizei consisted mostly of older police reservists from the 1890 to 1910 cohort, although a core of career policemen provided the leadership. The gendarmerie posts in the countryside took over the local militia units (known as the Miliz, Ordnungsdienst, or Hilfspolizei) that had been set up in the villages. Thereafter these units became known as the Schutzmannschaft-Einzeldienst. A gendarmerie order issued in the Zhitomir general district instructed that

> The existing militia units in the districts are to be dissolved in so far as they are difficult to control and unreliable. . . . The creation of a new Schutzmannschaft force, corresponding to our needs, is to commence right away. The Schutzmannschaft should assist the police and gendarmerie by carrying out the dirty work (*Schmutzarbeit*). Its strength will vary according to the tasks; generally some 20 or 30 men for each *raion* town will be sufficient.[19]

The Germans used this reorganization at the end of 1941 and beginning of 1942 as an opportunity to reduce the influence of the Poles within the local police.[20] In Nieśwież, for example, the Germans questioned the local policemen about their nationality in December 1941; one man recalled: 'I replied that I was Polish and could not lie about my nationality. After the questioning a list was drawn up of all those who said that they were Belarusians. . . . Then I was dismissed from the police service.'[21] A Polish policeman from the nearby town of Nowa Mysz said that he was advised by his colleagues to reply that he was Belarusian because the Germans were firing the Polish policemen.[22]

In the Nowa Mysz *raion* members of a Polish underground organization (which apparently was affiliated with the Armia Krajowa) infiltrated the Schutzmannschaft. Several former policemen from Nowa Mysz stated in post-war interrogations that they had joined the Belarusian police on instructions from the Polish underground. Before signing up, they had sworn oaths of loyalty to General Sikorski and adopted pseudonyms. From early 1942 the Polish underground appears to have intentionally infiltrated the Schutzmannschaft for the purpose of obtaining military training for its members. The chief of police in Nowa Mysz, Henryk Zaprucki, was at the same time a commander in the Polish underground. While serving in the Schutzmannschaft, Polish policemen smuggled weapons, munitions, and food to Polish partisans. During the German retreat from Belarus, the Polish policemen from the Nowa Mysz police post were split up and assigned to different

[19] Derzhavnyi arkhiv Zhitomirs'koyi oblasti, *fond* 1182, *opys* 1, *sprava* 17, fo. 132, extracts from the Gendarmerie Captaincy Orders concerning the establishment of the Ukrainian Schutzmannschaften, n.d.

[20] NARB, *f* 370, *o.* 1, *d.* 1262, fos. 147–58, Klepsch speech at the meeting of the district commissars, 10 Apr. 1943.

[21] WCU, D9084; see also D8661 and S135B, which indicate that some Polish policemen remained in the police service at this time.

[22] WCU, D6104.

German police units; some deserted and died in a battle against the Germans near Słonim.[23]

This example from Nowa Mysz cannot be seen as typical of the whole of eastern Poland. However, it is probable that the Polish underground also attempted to infiltrate the police in other areas, just as the Ukrainian nationalists did on a large scale. A thorough examination of the files of the Polish underground would reveal the extent to which Poles temporarily 'collaborated' with the Germans by serving in the police forces in order to combat their enemies in the Soviet or Ukrainian partisan forces.

Despite their membership in the Polish underground movement, some Polish policemen actively participated in German atrocities against the local Jewish population. For example, the following incident, which took place in late 1943, was reported in the post-war testimony of a former Polish policeman in the Nowa Mysz *raion*:

> While we were eating breakfast and drinking vodka, the policeman P. entered the house and reported to Zaprucki that the policemen had arrested a Jew and a Jewess. Then Zaprucki said to the policeman L., 'Go and deal with them.' L. and P. left the house and we remained as before. After a while when we were inside the house I heard some individual shots, but I didn't see who was shooting at whom. Subsequently P. told me and the other policemen that he and . . . W. had shot the Jews who had been arrested. After the shots, L. returned to the house on his own and reported to Zaprucki that the Jews had been dealt with.[24]

The signature of the same Zaprucki can be found in the Brest regional archive on a captured German document concerning the shooting of four Jews by the local police in December 1942.[25]

The ghetto in Nowa Mysz was liquidated in the summer of 1942. A former policeman described the murders as follows in an interview after the war:

> Germans came from Baranowicze and they brought a Lithuanian murder squad with them. The local police escorted the Jews to the collecting point. The local police chief [Zaprucki] was in charge during the action. He had said that he was a Belarusian (to avoid dismissal). The SD officer was Lieutenant Amelung. A cordon was set up around Nowa Mysz so that the Jews could not escape. In the town there was a marketplace with a fire station that served as the collecting point. The local police from the surrounding outposts had been called in. . . . The Jews were taken from the fire station and shot behind a stand of trees. Several hundred people, perhaps 600 altogether, were shot.[26]

According to eyewitnesses, local policemen shot a number of Jews during this

[23] Instytut Pamięci Narodowej, Warsaw (IPN), SWSz 77, fos. 1697–1713, statement by W.W., Jan. 1971; fos. 1736–71, statement by J.R. before the court, Jan. 1971; and fos. 1840–4, statement by B.L., 24 Mar. 1971; IPN, I ZH KPP 50/93, statement by B.B., 10 Aug. 1994.

[24] IPN, SWSz 69, fos. 96–7, statement by B.B., 24 Nov. 1962.

[25] Gosudarstvennyi arkhiv Brestskoi oblasti (GABO), *f.* 995, *o.* 1, *d.* 4, fo. 456, gendarmerie report, 5 Dec. 1942.

[26] WCU, D6104.

action and in the course of the next few days.[27] The Germans established a reinforced cordon around the execution site to protect it and set up machine gun posts pointing away from the graves to guard against possible partisan attack during the shootings.[28] After the action at least one Polish member of the Schutzmannschaft took up residence in a formerly Jewish-owned home.[29]

Members of the Polish resistance movement within the Schutzmannschaft in Nowa Mysz also participated in reprisals against Soviet partisans. These included shooting the parents of known partisans. Non-commissioned officers in the local police in Nowa Mysz, including a few Poles, were particularly implicated in such actions.[30] After the war several former policemen from Nowa Mysz were tried and convicted by Polish courts. A cautious evaluation of these sources, together with captured German documentation, confirm the active participation of Polish local policemen in the various punitive and murderous actions carried out by the Schutzmannschaft against the local population.

Another stronghold of the Poles was the Schutzmannschaft in the town of Iwieniec in the Naliboki forest. Here the force consisted almost exclusively of Poles, and many members subsequently defected to the so-called Polish Legion under the command of Zdzisław Nurkiewicz. Of fifty-four members of the Legion, it is known that twenty-eight had already joined the police or the local self-defence force by 1941.[31] Some members of the Legion were tried in Poland after the war. One was indicted for the murder of Jews in Iwieniec in his police capacity, as well as for the murder of Soviet partisans and their families as a member of the Legion.[32] Some former members of the Legion denied any direct participation in the shooting of Jews despite the fact that at least one witness reported that Polish policemen in Iwieniec had served as perimeter guards during the action in the summer of 1942. The same witness also maintained that Polish policemen were active participants in the shooting of Soviet partisans.[33] Another witness, who apparently worked for the Armia Krajowa in the Vilna district, testified that Nurkiewicz failed to carry out all of the orders that he received from central command and had to be punished for this reason.[34] Although they have to be treated with considerable caution and must be compared with other relevant sources where possible,[35] the extensive investiga-

27 IPN, SWB 221, fo. 115, statement by M.P., 23 Jan. 1964; fo. 41, statement by E.L., 20 June 1963.

28 IPN, SWSz 69–78.

29 IPN, SWO 12, statement by A.W.

30 Arkhiv Komiteta gosudarstvennoi bezopasnosti, Belarus, file 25547, archive 16890, statement by the accused, F.A.M., Aug. 1957.

31 Chiari, *Alltag hinter der Front*, 292–3.

32 IPN, SSWr 79, trial of P.K., 1961, act of indictment.

33 Ibid., fo. 105, statement by the accused, P.K., 21 Nov. 1961; fo. 120, statement by the witness Z.B.

34 Ibid., fo. 117.

35 For example, a German Security Police report from July 1943 referred to the events in Iwieniec as a justification for investigating whether Polish corporals in the Schutzmannschaft were already secretly organizing the Polish resistance movement, as was widely suspected in Nowogródek; report from Baranowicze, 11 July 1943, on the 9 July operation in Nowogródek, in H. Friedlander and S. Milton (eds.), *Archives of the Holocaust: An International Collection of Selected Documents*, xx: *Zentrale Stelle der Landesjustizverwaltungen, Ludwigsburg* (New York, 1993), doc. 76, pp. 165–7.

tive files on the Polish Legion in the archives of the Main Commission shed light on the complicated local conditions in the Iwieniec area during the war.[36]

A considerable number of Poles lived in the Słonim area, and some served in the police force there. As one Jewish survivor recalled, after the arrival of the Germans 'the Belarusian police was formed from young men from Słonim and the surrounding villages, including some Poles'.[37] One former partisan gave a detailed description of the activities of the local police:

> The Belarusian police worked closely together with the Germans and carried out the German orders. Their uniforms were black, they wore a white armband with the word 'Schutzmannschaft' written on it. I think they had round black caps. The collars and cuffs I believe were brown. Most of those who joined the police were local people—Poles and Belarusians, no Jews. Among those who joined were a wide variety of types. Some were just hanging around and had no jobs. They joined the police in order to earn some money. In total there were some 200 or 300 men in the Belarusian police in Slonim and the surrounding villages. They worked like other policemen, but only for the Germans. I assume that they had to carry out their orders.[38]

In one of the Polish trials from the 1960s—which were generally more thorough than the trials that took place shortly after the war—the witness J.R. provided detailed information about the local police personnel in Słonim. He claimed that he himself worked mainly as a tailor while serving in the Schutzmannschaft. He named more than ten Poles, including several non-commissioned officers, who had served with him. According to his recollection the local police were used mainly as guards during the anti-Jewish actions in Słonim and the surrounding areas. However, he explicitly named two Polish local policemen who murdered Jews. Since there was no active investigation against either of the two men at that time, it is unlikely that these allegations were intended to deflect guilt from the witness.[39] Moreover, a second witness, who was not a policeman, reported that one of the Polish policemen named had participated in escorting Jews to the execution site.[40]

At the end of 1943 a Polish police commander from Słonim by the name of Chmielewski, who had disguised himself as a Polish resistance fighter, was apparently killed during an attempt to desert to the partisans. It is likely therefore that the Polish underground had infiltrated the Schutzmannschaft in Słonim just as they had in Nowa Mysz.[41]

[36] See also IPN, SWZG 20–6, investigation of Zdzisław Nurkiewicz (more than 1,000 pages in total); other possible sources include, for example, the Polish Underground Study Trust Archive in London, memoirs of Stanisław Gąsiewski and others; J. Trznadel, 'Drobiazg', *Arka*, 49/1 (1994), 159–66; as well as reports by the Soviet Partisan units (NARB, *f.* 3500, *o.* 2, *d.* 32) and the Polish underground (Archiwum Akt Nowych, Warsaw (AAN)).

[37] WCU, D7852, statement by L.I.A., 25 Sept. 1995.

[38] WCU, statement by V.A.F., 28 Sept. 1995.

[39] IPN, SWZG 29, statement by J.R., 6 Oct. 1962.

[40] Ibid., statement by M.B., 16 Nov. 1962.

[41] Ibid., statement by J.R., 6 Oct. 1962; A. Nachum, *The Destruction of Slonim Jewry* (New York, 1989), 35–7.

The Schutzmannschaft-Einzeldienst in the German-occupied eastern territories numbered more than 100,000 members by December 1942 and continued to expand thereafter.[42] In the eastern Polish regions of what is now Belarus there were some 10,000 members in service, of whom probably some 15 per cent were Poles. An analysis of the membership of various police units and the Belarusian Selbstschutz (Self-Defence Force) in the Słonim district reveals that of more than 300 named individuals, just under 10 per cent appeared to be of Polish nationality. The members of the Schutzmannschaft in the Baranowicze district, which in June 1944 had a total strength of 2,263,[43] were primarily Belarusian (approximately 75 per cent) and of the Greek Orthodox religion. About 20 per cent were Polish Catholics who had survived the anti-Polish purges of 1941 and 1942, and the rest were mainly Russians and Tatars.[44]

In the Brest-Litovsk district, which today is part of Belarus, Ukrainians made up some 70 per cent of the Schutzmannschaft; Poles made up about 20 per cent, and the rest were Russians and Belarusians. The gendarmerie district leader in Brest-Litovsk reported on 5 December 1942 that the SD had shot two Polish local policemen in Domaczewo because it had come to light that they were members of the Polish underground resistance movement.[45] This report, which is corroborated by local witnesses, demonstrates that the Polish underground was active within the Schutzmannschaft and also that German punishment of underground members who were discovered was harsh.

However, a Polish underground report from the same period (the end of December 1942) confirms that the Schutzmannschaft, which had many Polish members, was active in the liquidation of the Brest ghetto:

> Brest. The liquidation of the Jews has been continuing since 15 October. During the first three days about 12,000 people were shot. The place of execution is Bronna Góra. At present the rest of those in hiding are being liquidated. The liquidation was being organized by a mobile squad of SD and local police. At present the 'finishing off' is being done by the local police, in which Poles represent a large percentage. They are often more zealous than the Germans. Some Jewish possessions go to furnish German homes and offices, some are sold at auction.[46]

Not all of the Polish members of the Schutzmannschaften joined during the initial months of the occupation. Many were recruited more or less by force from the

[42] US Holocaust Memorial Museum Archive, RG-11.001M.15 Tsentr khraneniya istoriko-dokumental'nykh kollektsii (formerly Osobyi arkhiv), Moscow, reel 81, *f.* 1323, *o.* 2, *d.* 267, Bericht über den Kräfte- und Kriegseinsatz der Ordnungspolizei im Jahre 1942 abgegeben am 1. Februar 1943.

[43] Chiari, *Alltag hinter der Front*, 164.

[44] Dean, *Collaboration in the Holocaust*, 74.

[45] Bundesarchiv Lichterfelde, R 94/7, Gendarmerie-Gebietsführer Brest-Litowsk, report, 5 Dec. 1942.

[46] AAN, 202/III/7, vol. 1, p. 187, report of the Polish underground, 252/A-1, 17 Dec. 1942. On the active participation of the local police in the hunt for Jews after the ghetto liquidations in Volhynia, see Spector, *The Holocaust of Volhynian Jews*, 176.

summer of 1942 for the purpose of reinforcing the police in their struggle against the partisans. Most of those who were recruited after the liquidation of the ghettos were not directly involved in the persecution of Jews.

An analysis of post-war trials in Poland has made it possible to assess more effectively the extent of Polish collaboration with the Germans in the eastern territories as well as Polish participation in crimes against the Jewish population. In 1993 almost 500 files relating to the trials of individuals from the territories of present-day Belarus and Ukraine were located in the archives of the former Main Commission in Warsaw. The nationality and the wartime activities of the accused are summarized in Table 1. The number of people who could be identified on the basis of the available summaries as having been tried explicitly for crimes against Jews is listed separately. A closer examination of some of the trial files clearly confirms that this number is an underestimate, as there are many cases in which the brief summary gives no specific information about the victims, but in fact crimes against Jews are mentioned in the documents.

As the table shows, more than half of all the accused in the cases from present-day Belarus were Poles who had served in the Schutzmannschaft. Of these, at least 25 per cent were accused of participating in crimes against Jews. The actual number of convicted collaborators is relatively small—a few hundred. However, doubtless many other Poles were active in the Schutzmannschaft and later fled to the West, were tried in the Soviet Union, or were killed in the war (and therefore not tried in Poland).[47] Of particular significance is the large number of Poles who were accused of working for the Schutzmannschaft as compared to the local administration, or the SD or Kripo (Criminal Police), and also as compared to the number of Poles who were accused of denouncing others. With regard to the issue of Polish col-

Table 1. Analysis of Polish trials in the former eastern districts

	Belarus	**Ukraine**
Total accused	273	222
Of which, no. of Poles	181–200	51
Poles in the Schutzmannschaft	160	17
Crimes against Jews	41	5

Source: Summaries prepared by the Main Commission (Elżbieta Kobierska-Motas) of trials in Poland after 1945 for war crimes in the former Polish eastern territories (Belarus and Ukraine), 1993 (unpublished list provided by the Instytut Pamięci Narodowej, Warsaw). The list is not complete as a few trial files at this time were stored regionally outside Warsaw. Trials of people from the territory of present-day Lithuania (about 30 cases) have not been included as the proportion of Poles in the local police in these areas was very low.

[47] Cf. the post-war fates of local policemen from the Mir *raion* (mostly Belarusians) in Dean, *Collaboration in the Holocaust*, table 8.1, p. 155.

laboration with the Germans in the former Polish eastern territories, the Schutzmannschaft was by far the most important institution, in terms of both the number of Polish members and the direct participation of Poles in the Holocaust. Of the fifty or so convicted Polish war criminals who did not serve in the Schutzmannschaft, only about ten (according to the summaries) were tried primarily for crimes against Jews. Of this group, those who served in the civil administration or worked for the SD were most likely to have participated actively in the persecution of the Jews.

The considerable discrepancy between the figures for Belarus and those for the Ukraine requires some explanation. As mentioned above, the German occupation authorities in Belarus were heavily dependent on Poles to fill leadership positions within the local administration and the police, as there were too few qualified Belarusians for these posts.[48] In Ukraine it was easier to find local Ukrainians for the equivalent jobs. In addition, a number of Ukrainian nationalist leaders from western Ukraine accompanied the advancing German troops and helped to set up the local administration. By comparison, only a small number of Belarusian exiles were available to the Germans. It is also important to take into account the tensions that existed between Poles and Ukrainians in Volhynia and Galicia. In 1943 widespread armed clashes broke out as Ukrainian bands attempted to wipe out small Polish settlements in these areas. A further explanation for the smaller number of investigations against Poles from Ukraine can perhaps be found in the much poorer post-war co-operation between the Ukrainian KGB and its Polish counterpart than between the Polish and Belarusian security administrations.[49]

As Jan Gross argues with regard to the criminal investigations into the events in Jedwabne in 1941 (supported independently by research conducted by the Instytut Pamięci Narodowej), such investigations were primarily of a criminal nature and without strong political undertones. In fact, the post-war Polish authorities displayed a relative lack of interest in them.[50] As a consequence, the results of these trials concerning the participation of Poles and people of other nationalities in German war crimes can be viewed in many cases as reliable.[51] Somewhat more care is required in cases in which Polish partisans were accused of killing Soviet partisans, as there may have been some political pressure here to influence the outcome.

48 See e.g. BA-MA, RH 26-707/15, Kommandantur des Sicherungs-Gebietes Weissruthenien (707. Inf. Div.), Abt. Ic, report of 8 Jan. 1942.

49 I would like to thank Ray Brandon, who assisted me by examining a number of IPN files with respect to this issue.

50 Gross, *Neighbors*, 26–32; P. Machcewicz and K. Persak (eds.), *Wokół Jedwabnego*, 2 vols. (Warsaw, 2002); see esp. the contributions by Andrzej Żbikowski and Andrzej Rzepliński (short abstracts in English were available on the Internet at <http://www.ipn.gov.pl/summary_1.pdf> on 25 Mar. 2004).

51 See esp. B. Musiał, 'NS-Kriegsverbrecher vor polnischen Gerichten', *Vierteljahreshefte für Zeitgeschichte*, 47/1 (1999), 25–56. Musiał compares the trials against Nazi war criminals directly with other 'political' trials conducted against opponents of the communist government.

However, in terms of the circumstances that initially led to the indictment and the amount of evidence gathered, most of the Polish cases were broadly comparable to the war crimes investigations conducted by the Allies in Germany and other countries at this time.[52] Though the witness evidence taken in the Polish trials did not always rise to the prevailing standards of criminal trials conducted by civilian courts in the West, the Polish war crimes proceedings nevertheless bore some resemblance to those of the American and British post-war military tribunals in that they could achieve little more than summary justice in the face of an overwhelming and difficult task. The following brief examples give an indication of the nature of these Polish trials.

Significantly, in virtually all cases in which the defendants were alleged to have served in the Schutzmannschaft, there was no doubt about the basic facts of the case. In many cases the names of the defendants were listed in captured German documents found in the archives. In addition, there were witness statements from other policemen or town residents who attested to the defendant's service in the police, so that the question of actual collaboration was rarely in doubt. More important for the assessment of the activities of a defendant, however, was the date on which he entered into police service and whether he entered voluntarily.

Eyewitness testimony describing the direct participation of the accused in war crimes was rare in these trials. Only 'excessive perpetrators' were occasionally convicted on the basis of the testimony of several reliable eyewitnesses. In most cases against former policemen there was only general information about the accused's participation in specific anti-partisan actions or in escorting members of particular victim groups (sometimes Jews) to execution sites. Many witnesses were themselves compromised by their own police service and had been tried (and convicted) previously. Usually the question was not whether a defendant had collaborated with the Germans, but whether he had played an active role in the German repressive measures, or, as defendants often claimed, had only gone along with the Germans passively out of fear for himself and his family. The Polish authorities were able to carry out investigations at crime scenes in what was now the Soviet Union only in a few cases. Instead, they had to rely on the co-operation of their Belarusian colleagues, and it was only in the later trials that they were able to bring Belarusian witnesses to Poland to testify before the court. In a number of cases, the Belarusian authorities made available extracts from investigations that had been concluded earlier.

Sentencing varied considerably in the Polish courts. Many of those convicted received sentences of between five and fifteen years in prison for their collaboration, which usually consisted of participation as police officers in anti-partisan actions and in escorting Jews and other prisoners to their deaths. Amnesties and parole

[52] See also D. Pohl, *Nationalsozialistische Judenverfolgung in Ostgalizien 1941–1944. Organisation und Durchführung eines staatlichen Massenverbrechens* (Munich, 1996), 392.

policies meant that many prisoners actually served only about half of their sentences, and sometimes less. Severer punishment was meted out primarily to those who had held leadership positions or who could be proven to have participated in brutal atrocities and were therefore classified as 'excessive perpetrators'.

In a case in the town of Sielec, near Pružana in Belarus, three Polish local policemen were sentenced in the 1960s to between five and seven years for their participation in killings and reprisals, although no eyewitness testimony demonstrating their personal responsibility in these acts was presented. Members of the Schutzmannschaft in Sielec, however, were also engaged in escorting Jews during the liquidation of the ghetto there. During the course of the investigation the Polish authorities uncovered a great deal of incriminating evidence against a fourth member of the Schutzmannschaft, identified as S.B., who was apparently also of Polish nationality. Two eyewitnesses reported having seen S.B. shooting Jews. In one case he was alleged to have personally shot seven Jews in a ditch behind the town's school. Apparently on this occasion he remarked that there was no point in escorting the Jews to Bereza Kartuzka as the Germans there would shoot them in any case. Unfortunately this criminal could not be located in Poland.[53]

Many of the punishments were surprisingly mild, however.[54] For example, in 1954 a local policeman from Stołpce in Belarus was sentenced to only two years' imprisonment, although he had apparently taken part in the liquidation of the ghetto there. He was released after only one year of detention.[55] In another case, though, a Polish policeman in the town of Dzisna was sentenced to death in 1965 for his participation in the liquidation of the ghetto and in other killing actions against partisans and civilians. Shortly afterwards his punishment was commuted to a sentence of twenty-five years, sixteen of which he actually served.[56] A Polish policeman from the town of Mizocz, in Zdołbunów (Zdovbuniv) district in Ukraine, who was also accused of killing Jews, was sentenced to death in Poland in 1963. He died in 1971 while still in gaol.[57]

The statements of the accused and of the witnesses in the Polish trials provide few insights into the motives of Polish perpetrators and have to be treated with considerable caution. Experience gained from more recent British investigations can help to put this evidence into context. For example, the questioning of a Polish former member of the Schutzmannschaft in Baranowicze by the British police in England in 1994 reveals certain key aspects of the mentality of Polish collaborators. The defendant's father was working in the town administration in Wołkowysk, but after being tipped off, the family fled to Baranowicze in 1939 to avoid arrest and deportation to Siberia. The defendant stated that the Russians and the Germans were both the enemies of Poland, but that the Germans had been 'better' than the Russians. He served in the mobile anti-partisan squad, or Jagdzug, of the Schutz-

[53] See IPN, SwSz 68.

[54] On this point, see Musiał, 'NS-Kriegsverbrecher vor polnischen Gerichten', 47–8.

[55] IPN, SWGd 27.

[56] IPN, SWGd 53–4.

[57] IPN, SWOl 36–7.

mannschaft and participated in some actions against Soviet partisans. During his questioning he was able to recall the names of only a few of his Polish colleagues from his police service, and none of the names of his Belarusian comrades in arms.[58] A file from the Brest regional archives indicates that he was probably already a member of the Baranowicze town police by January 1942, which means that he must have volunteered for police service with the Germans.[59] Additional witnesses describe the active participation of the Baranowicze Jagdzug in reprisals against partisan families, including the burning of civilians in a barn towards the end of the occupation at Nowe Sioło, near Turzec in the Mir *raion*.[60]

These comments on the complex issue of Polish collaboration with the Germans in what had been the eastern territories of Poland and on the direct participation of Poles in the murder of the Jews are intended only as an introduction to the extensive records held in the archives of the former Main Commission. A comprehensive analysis of these important sources remains to be carried out. The ongoing debate about the events in Jedwabne has already been extended to cover similar pogrom-like events in the Białystok region and other parts of eastern Poland. However, my aim here is to draw attention to the widespread service of Poles within the Schutzmannschaft in the former eastern territories. The majority of convicted Polish war criminals from these areas served in the Schutzmannschaft; many others escaped justice by emigrating, or died before they could be brought to trial.

Although the use of these difficult sources entails certain methodological problems, in almost all cases there is little doubt that the defendants in the Polish trials had actually collaborated with the Germans. As mentioned above, despite the instinctive German distrust of Poles, at least 10 per cent of the local police in Belarus were of Polish nationality. The active participation of the Schutzmannschaft in the liquidation of the ghettos in much of the former Polish territories in 1942 and 1943 has already been demonstrated.[61] However, further research remains to be done, especially on the role of the Polish underground in the penetration of the Schutzmannschaft. This research will help us to assess the scale and nature of Polish collaboration, as well as the responsibility of organizations and individuals.

[58] WCU, interrogation conducted on 18 Jan. 1994.

[59] GABO, *f.* 995, *o.* 1, *d.* 5, fos. 21–2, list of the police in Baranowicze, Jan. 1942.

[60] See esp. the record of the trial of Stanisław Boguszewicz before the court in Zielona Góra completed in 1974, fos. 27–37, statement of P.K., 7 Aug. 1967.

[61] See Dean, *Collaboration in the Holocaust*, 78–104.

PART III

Reviews

Communist Questions, Jewish Answers: Polish Jewish Dissident Communists of the Inter-War Era

JACK JACOBS

In a perceptive essay that is certainly well known to the readers of *Polin*, Isaac Deutscher once described a particular set of brilliant revolutionaries, including Marx, Luxemburg, and Trotsky, as 'non-Jewish Jews'. These figures, Deutscher pointed out, were all of Jewish origin, all lived on the margins of their societies, and all found Jewry narrow, archaic, and constricting. It is important to recognize, Deutscher added, that 'the Jewish heretic who transcends Jewry belongs to a Jewish tradition' and thus that in one significant sense, Marx, Luxemburg, and Trotsky were 'very Jewish indeed'.[1] These were, however, Jews who moved, so to speak, beyond Jewishness.

Tamara Deutscher has suggested that her husband, Isaac, thought of himself as fitting into this category.[2] But it strikes me as worth noting that Deutscher's great insight into the most prominent Jews ever to have been affiliated with the communist movement simply does not apply to many Polish Jewish communists, including, notably, a large proportion of those with whom Deutscher himself worked most closely during much of the 1930s, that is, the leaders of the KPP Opozycja (KPP Opposition), which first crystallized in 1932.

A number of Jews adhered to the Komunistyczna Partia Robotnicza Polski (Communist Workers' Party of Poland, which later became the Komunistyczna Partia Polski, Communist Party of Poland, KPP) following the creation of the party in 1918. It has been conservatively estimated that Jews made up approximately 20 per cent of the total membership by the end of 1923.[3]

[1] Deutscher, 'The Non-Jewish Jew', in T. Deutscher (ed.), *The Non-Jewish Jew and Other Essays* (New York, 1968), 26–7.

[2] T. Deutscher, 'Introduction: The Education of a Jewish Child', in Deutscher (ed.), *The Non-Jewish Jew and Other Essays*, 22.

[3] M. Mishkinsky, 'The Communist Party of Poland and the Jews', in Y. Gutman, E. Mendelsohn, J. Reinharz, and C. Shmeruk (eds.), *The Jews of Poland Between Two World Wars* (Hanover, NH, 1989), 62. A second source suggests that Jews may have constituted 22–26 per cent of the party's membership at varying points (J. Brun-Zejmis, 'The Origin of the Communist Movement in Poland

However large the proportion of individuals of Jewish ancestry active in the KPP may have been, it was apparently still higher in the KPP Opposition. Indeed, it seems that all of the founders of the Opposition were Jewish—though their reasons for establishing a new political tendency most assuredly were not. Communist questions, not Jewish questions, led them away from the party.

And yet in the latter half of the 1930s a majority of the Opposition's leaders—including Hersz Mendel Sztokfisz, Pinkus Minc, Issakhar Eichenbaum, Szlama (Shloyme) Erlich, and Leon Erlich—joined the Jewish Workers' Bund. Sztokfisz, Minc, and Eichenbaum, moreover, survived the Second World War and lived out the rest of their lives within specifically Jewish movements.

In order to make some sense of this tale, and of its significance, it is necessary to reconstruct the backgrounds and life paths of these leading members of the KPP Opposition. And it is precisely because of its critical importance in this process that I applaud the appearance of *The History of a False Illusion*, an English translation of the memoirs of Pinkus Minc (first published in Yiddish in 1954).[4]

Though neither the brief introduction by Bryan Palmer nor Robert Michaels's tendentious preface to the English-language edition will be of great use to the scholarly world, Michaels's translation is accurate, and so are the editorial footnotes sprinkled through the text.

If, however, the introductory apparatus is not very instructive, the same cannot be said of the text itself. Minc's story is of considerable significance.

Born in 1895 and raised in Łódź in a middle-class hasidic family, Minc became a member of the Bund before the First World War.[5] He was deeply stirred by the success of the Bolsheviks, and helped to stimulate the creation of the Polish Kombund. When, in September 1922, the Kombund was absorbed into the KPP, Minc—known to his comrades as Aleksander—was co-opted onto its Central Committee. *The History of a False Illusion* is largely concerned with the policies of the KPP and with Minc's activities in the party. His reports on the Bolshevization of the party, on Soviet espionage, and on prison life, though not shocking today, are likely to be of interest to historians of inter-war Poland.

Minc's depiction of the emergence of the KPP Opposition in the 1930s is rare and thus of greater importance. Indeed, there is only one other book-length memoir describing the crystallization of the KPP Opposition—Sztokfisz's *Memoirs of a Jewish Revolutionary*, which have also been translated into English by Michaels.[6]

and the Jewish Question, 1918–1923', *Nationalities Papers*, 22, suppl. 1 (Summer 1994), 29). The proportion of Jews in the party may well have risen in later years. Official Communist sources have estimated that 35 per cent of the party's membership was Jewish in 1930 (C. S. Heller, *On the Edge of Destruction: Jews of Poland Between the Two World Wars* (New York, 1977), 254).

[4] P. Minc, *The History of a False Illusion: Memoirs on the Communist Movements in Poland (1918–1938)*, trans. R. Michaels (Lewiston, NY, 2002); 1st pub. as *Di geshikhte fun a falsher iluzie* (Buenos Aires, 1954).

[5] Minc, *Lodzh in mayn zikhorn* (Buenos Aires, 1958).

[6] H. Mendel, *Memoirs of a Jewish Revolutionary*, preface by I. Deutscher (London, 1989).

Hersz Mendel Sztokfisz, born in the early 1890s, was raised in Warsaw by observant parents. He became a Bundist in 1911, was attracted to anarchism during the course of the First World War, and, deeply impressed by Lenin's work *State and Revolution*, entered the Communist movement in 1919. In the early and mid-1920s Sztokfisz, best known under his party name, Hersz Mendel, was active in the Jewish Central Bureau of the KPP, and in 1928 began what was supposed to have been a three-year course of study at the Lenin School in Moscow intended for individuals who would become functionaries of the Comintern.[7] Sztokfisz's experiences in Moscow, however, during which he became aware of toadying and widespread fear even among prominent Communists, led him to question key portions of Stalinist orthodoxy. He resolved to return to Poland, where, he hoped, the Communist Party had, in his words, 'not yet lost its untarnished idealism'.[8] Sztokfisz succeeded in leaving the USSR at the very end of 1930, was appointed secretary of the KPP's Jewish Central Bureau, and was entrusted with a sensitive position with *Literarishe tribune*, a Yiddish-language organ of the Left Writers' Group. According to Dovid Sfard, a Yiddish writer who was affiliated with the Group, Sztokfisz and one Yoshke Rabinovitsh acted as KPP 'mashgikhim' (supervisors who ensure that food is prepared in a kosher manner) for *Literarishe tribune*, and were responsible for ensuring that the paper's content was 'kosher'.[9]

It was apparently while he was working with *Literarishe tribune* that Sztokfisz began to discuss his political doubts with Minc. Minc ran into him in Warsaw, and complained to Sztokfisz that the theory of social fascism 'was having a devastating effect on the workers' movement'.[10] Sztokfisz and Minc proceeded to develop a three-point programme underscoring their differences with the KPP. The first point endorsed the notion of a united front with social democrats in the struggle against fascism. The second endorsed unity in the trade union movement (rather than the fostering of a separatist union movement dominated by Communists). The final point of this initial programme advocated democracy within the

[7] As Daniel Singer has pointed out, 'for a communist, fighting underground for a problematical future victory, a journey to the birthplace of revolution was like a trip to the promised land for a zionist' ('Armed with a Pen: Notes for a Political Portrait of Isaac Deutscher', in D. Horowitz, *Isaac Deutscher: The Man and his Work* (London, 1971), 27).

[8] Mendel, *Memoirs of a Jewish Revolutionary*, 265.

[9] *Literarishe tribune* allegedly attracted a great deal of attention. Sfard indicates that the organ was read not only by leftist Jewish youth but also by members of the intelligentsia and of literary circles with non-leftist orientations. These broader circles were apparently attracted to *Literarishe tribune* because of the cutting-edge writers it published, i.e. Binem Heller, Moyshe Shulshtayn, Kalmen Lis, and Moyshe Knaphays, among others. From Sfard's perspective, the relative success of *Literarishe tribune* was also due to the fact that it presented a new perspective on the nature of proletarian literature, of socialist realism, and of aesthetics (D. Sfard, *Mit zikh un mit andere: Oytobiografie un literarishe eseyen* (Jerusalem, 1984), 52–3). My thanks to Samuel Kassow for suggesting that I examine Sfard's work. Sztokfisz reports, with reference to *Literarishe tribune*, that 'in my capacity as secretary of the Central Bureau I was responsible for its political line' (Mendel, *Memoirs of a Jewish Revolutionary*, 283).

[10] Mendel, *Memoirs of a Jewish Revolutionary*, 281.

Communist Party, and criticized 'bureaucratic wrongdoing'. Thus, it must be underscored that it was not explicitly Jewish concerns of any kind that motivated these members of the KPP to criticize Communist orthodoxy.

In the wake of their initial meetings, Sztokfisz and Minc began to approach others likely to be sympathetic to their views. The third known adherent of what eventually became the KPP Opposition was Abraham ('Black Abe') Pflug. Pflug, born in 1896, was a prominent member of the Bund from 1915 until 1921. Like Minc, he had played an active role in the Polish Kombund. He had entered the KPP in 1922, served as Secretary of its Jewish Central Bureau from 1927 to 1929, and, like Sztokfisz, had been a student at the Lenin School in Moscow.[11]

Sztokfisz also solicited the support of Isaac Deutscher—whose career is too well known to warrant retelling here.[12] Deutscher had been appointed editor of *Literarishe tribune* in 1930,[13] and in 1931 was sent by the KPP to the USSR. However, as with Sztokfisz, Deutscher's direct exposure to the situation in Russia led him away from Communist orthodoxy rather than reinforcing his allegiance to it.[14]

Matters came to a head when, in July 1932, Deutscher, in a piece which appeared in *Literarishe tribune*, suggested that the Communist Party of Germany and the Social Democratic Party of Germany should work together against the Nazi threat.[15] It was to be his last issue as editor. The KPP—stunned by Deutscher's apostasy—removed him from his position, and had a strongly worded rebuttal published in the subsequent issue.[16] When a group of members of the KPP—now formally referring to themselves as the KPP Opposition—declared themselves to be in solidarity with Deutscher, not only Deutscher but also his supporters were expelled from the party, on the grounds that they were agents of 'social fascism'.[17]

[11] H. Goldfinger, M. Mirski, and S. Zachariasz (eds.), *Unter der fon fun k.p.p. zamlbukh* (Warsaw, 1959), 363–4; Minc, *The History of a False Illusion*, 247–8.

[12] For additional information on Deutscher's life, see L. Syré, *Isaac Deutscher: Marxist, Publizist, Historiker* (Hamburg, 1984).

[13] Deutscher did not make a good impression on Sfard, who found his 'self-confident tone, badly masked stuck-up-ishness', and habit of speaking as if he were the final arbiter on matters under discussion very off-putting (Sfard, *Mit zikh un mit andere*, 52).

[14] 'The misgivings [Deutscher] was beginning to have about some of the trends and practices within his own party were rather strengthened by his visit to the international headquarters of the movement' (Singer, 'Armed with a Pen', 27–8). When Deutscher returned to Poland, Sztokfisz has noted, he and Deutscher 'often used to speak to one another about the sad state of the party' (Mendel, *Memoirs of a Jewish Revolutionary*, 283).

[15] A. Krakovski [I. Deutscher], 'Di gefar fun kultur-barbarizm in daytshland', *Literarishe tribune*, 7/30 (July 1932), 1–4.

[16] M. Levi, 'Tsu der frage fun "kultur-barbarizm" in daytshland (oyfn rand fun kh'krakovskis artikl in forikn num. "lit. tribune")', *Literarishe tribune*, 8/31 (Aug. 1932), 3–8.

[17] M. K. Dziewanowski, *The Communist Party of Poland: An Outline of History* (Cambridge, Mass., 1959), 137. Cf. I. Deutscher to M. K. Dziewanowski, 21 June 1952, International Institute of Social History, Amsterdam, Isaac Deutscher Papers, file 5. The expulsions apparently took place at the Sixth Party Congress of the KPP, which was held in the USSR in October 1932. Neither Deutscher nor any of those sympathetic to him attended this Congress (Minc, *The History of a False Illusion*, 272).

In 1933 these one-time members of the KPP—led by Deutscher, Minc, Sztokfisz, Pflug, and several other Communists of Jewish origin, namely Szlama Erlich,[18] Leon Erlich,[19] and Arthur Redler—attempted to conduct political work as an independent tendency. The Opposition attracted a modest number of supporters, including a small number of non-Jewish Poles.[20] At one point some 300 people in Warsaw were members.[21]

The Opposition, however, initially included Communist dissidents from a variety of perspectives and was plagued by internal disagreements. Pflug attempted to lead a small group back into the KPP during the course of 1933, only to find that he and his followers were no longer welcome.[22] But with Pflug's departure from the

18 Szlama (Shloyme) Erlich, born in 1907, was also known as Stein (Ludwik Hass, 'The Bolshevik Leninist (Fourth International) Movement in Poland up to 1945', *Revolutionary History*, 3/1 (Summer 1990), 17). His parents were well-off (Minc, *The History of a False Illusion*, 268). He was apparently raised in Będzin, and moved to Palestine (possibly with his parents) and, somewhat later, to Switzerland. He returned to Poland in the 1930s at the request of the international Trotskyist movement (Ludwik Hass, 'Trotskyism in Poland up to 1945', *Revolutionary History*, 6/1 (Winter 1995–6), 18). Minc reports that Erlich agitated on behalf of Trotskyist ideas in the Communist Party of Palestine (Minc, *The History of a False Illusion*, 268).

19 According to Minc, 'Little Leon' Erlich, who was from Warsaw, was responsible for the Opposition's publications in Yiddish and Polish (Minc, *The History of a False Illusion*, 268).

20 Two attempts were made by individuals sympathetic to the Opposition to create a Yiddish-language periodical that would present their perspective: *Unzer gedank* and *Shtern*, each of which appeared briefly in Warsaw (I. Szajn [Y. Shayn], *Bibliografie fun oysgabes aroysgegebn durkh di arbeter-parteyen in poyln in di yorn 1918–1939* (Warsaw, 1963), 163). Trotsky may have had direct contact with one or both of these periodicals, as evidenced by his essay entitled 'Evreiskii organ oppozitsii v Pol'she', cited by Dziewanowski, *The Communist Party of Poland*, 335 n. 51. Sztokfisz reports that 'the' Yiddish-language newspaper of the Opposition had a higher circulation in Warsaw than the Yiddish-language periodical of the KPP. 'I cannot', he adds, 'say the same for our Polish edition' (Mendel, *Memoirs of a Jewish Revolutionary*, 289). Deutscher wrote for *Unzer gedank* (under the pseudonym A. Kra-ski), and also wrote a response to the Bundist left under this name (*Aktuele problemen fun der arbeter-bavegung (an entfer khmurnern)* (Warsaw, 1933)). My thanks to Dr Hans-Juergen Boemelburg for his help in obtaining copies of this and other relevant sources.

21 The KPP itself had no more than 1,000 members in the Polish capital during the period in question—and maybe as few as 800 (I. Deutscher, 'The Tragedy of the Polish Communist Party', in T. Deutscher (ed.), *Marxism in our Time* (Berkeley, 1971), 153). It is impossible to identify more than a tiny handful of those who were members of the Opposition.

Julek Kanfer (a son of the editor of the Zionist-oriented *Nowy Dziennik*, which was issued in Kraków), Aron Szpicberg, and Palia Meisner (a one-time member of the Bundist Tsukunft who had later joined the KPP) are explicitly named by Minc as fellow Oppositionists (*The History of a False Illusion*, 277, 290, 294). Noyakh Zshelazo, who was raised in the same shtetl as Sztokfisz's wife, Miriam Shumik, seems to have been one of those who was involved first in the KPP and then in the Opposition (N. Zshelazo, 'Hersh-Mendl—der yidisher revolutsioner', *Yisroel-shtime*, 8 Mar. 1988, 7).

22 Pflug was imprisoned (Minc, *The History of a False Illusion*, 248), and died in 1938. When the KPP declined to arrange a funeral for him, his family turned to the Bund, which apparently covered the costs of the funeral of its one-time member (J. S. Hertz [I. S. Herts], 'Der bund in umophengikn poyln, 1918–1925', in S. Dubnow-Erlich [Dubnov-erlikh] (ed.), *Di geshikhte fun bund*, iv, ed. J. S. Hertz [I. S. Herts], K. S. Kazdan, and E. Scherer [Sherer] (New York, 1972), 172).

Opposition, the rump group found itself to be more united than had earlier been the case, and to have a decidedly Trotskyist orientation. It renamed itself the Związek Komunistów-Internacjonalistów Polski (Union of Communist Internationalists of Poland),[23] and established formal ties to the International Secretariat of the Left Opposition.[24]

It soon became apparent to Leon Trotsky, however, that his supporters not only in Poland but also in other countries would be unable to make much of an impact unless they affiliated with far larger, broader, movements. He therefore advised his followers to join the social democratic parties of the countries in which they lived. His followers in France, Italy, and Belgium did in fact do so; those in Poland, on the other hand, initially hesitated.

Significantly, however, the Bund actively encouraged Polish Trotskyists to enter its ranks. An internal document written by the Bund's Central Committee at the end of May 1935, and distributed to the local organizations of the Bund, explicitly declared that bringing Trotskyists into the Bund was one of the Bund's primary political tasks.[25]

While the Bund welcomed Trotskyists with open arms, Poalei Zion Left did not. A number of one-time members of Poalei Zion had entered the KPP in the early 1920s (as had a number of members of the Bund), including Saul (Shaul) Amsterdam, Gerszon Dua-Bogen, Alfred Lampe, and Józef Lewartowski. But, though there are cases one could point to in other countries, no prominent one-time Labour Zionists became Trotskyists in Poland, nor did any prominent Polish Trotskyists join Poalei Zion Left in Poland before the beginning of the Second World War. Unlike the Bund, which was critical of Stalinism in the mid-1930s, Poalei Zion Left proclaimed in 1935 that Stalin was right and Trotsky was wrong on two basic issues: the feasibility of creating socialism in one country and relations to the peasantry. *Arbeter-tsaytung*, an organ of Poalei Zion Left published in Warsaw, insisted that Soviet reality demonstrated that Trotsky's theory was completely bankrupt.[26] Thus, it is hard to imagine that a Polish Trotskyist seeking a broader context within which to work would have considered Poalei Zion Left as a viable alternative to the Bund in 1935.[27]

[23] Hass, 'Trotskyism in Poland up to 1945', 27.

[24] Ibid. 20. Certain key figures, including Deutscher, continued to carve out positions differing from those of Leon Trotsky on specific questions.

[25] Central Committee of the Bund in Poland, Circular 11, end of May 1935, YIVO Institute for Jewish Research, New York, Bund Archives of the Jewish Labor Movement (henceforth Bund Archives), MG 2 (470).

[26] Y. Vronski, 'Di likvidatsie fun trotskizm', *Arbeter-tsaytung*, 10/23 (7 June 1935), 4.

[27] In the period following its founding, the Communist movement attracted not only Bundists and Labour Zionists, but also members of the Fareynigte (the United Jewish Socialist Workers' Party), e.g. Izaak (Yitskhok) Gordin, Pinkus Bukshorn (Julian), and Izrael (Yisroel) Gajst (Goldfinger *et al.* (eds.), *Unter der fon fun k.p.p. zamlbukh*, 346, 349–50; Mendel, *Memoirs of a Jewish Revolutionary*, 196, 218–19; Minc, *The History of a False Illusion*, 259–60). Gutman-Zelikowicz, another former member

But the Bundists took a dramatically different stance from Poalei Zion Left on this, as on many other issues. In an editorial published in the Bundist *Naye folkstsaytung* in May 1935 Henryk Erlich, one of the Bund's most eminent leaders, proclaimed that it was high time that the Trotskyists of Poland acted like the major Trotskyist organizations elsewhere and joined the socialist movements of Poland.[28] Erlich did not sketch out why the Bund wanted to attract the Trotskyists, but it would have been clear to him that the Bund and the Polish Trotskyists had much in common. The Bund, after all, considered itself to be a revolutionary party, was committed in principle to socialist unity, and condemned both the policies of the Polish regime and those of Stalin. It was, moreover, certainly known to the leading Bundists that Minc and Sztokfisz had Bundist roots.

The first sign that Erlich's hopes would be realized manifested itself in August 1935, when Issakhar Eichenbaum (who used the party name Oskar) indicated that he, for one, was eager to become a member of the Bund. Eichenbaum, born in 1903 into a petit-bourgeois family, was briefly a member of the Bundist youth organization Tsukunft, and at various later points became a member of the Central Committee of the Communist Youth Association, and a member of the Warsaw Party Committee.[29] Eichenbaum came to share the misgivings that those in the Opposition had concerning the practices of the KPP, left that party at the end of 1933, and joined the Trotskyist group.[30]

It is of considerable importance that the statement by Eichenbaum in which he declares his desire to enter the ranks of the Bund does not mention the Bund's positions on Zionism, antisemitism, or Yiddish. Eichenbaum indicates that he had reached the conclusion that there was no room on the Polish political map for small, independent leftist groups, that the Bund was the socialist party in Poland closest to revolutionary Marxism, and that, therefore, he had decided that his place was in the Bund.

Several months after Eichenbaum took this step, the second conference of the

of the Fareynigte, joined the KPP somewhat later. Unlike the one-time Bundists Sztokfisz, Eichenbaum, and Minc, Gordin, Bukshorn, and Gajst never broke from the KPP.

28 H.E. [H. Erlich], 'Oyf vos vartn zey?', *Naye folkstsaytung*, 26 May 1935, 3.

29 Y. Ludin, 'I. artuski—der simbol', in *Yid, mentsh, sotsialist: I. artuski ondenk-bukh* (Tel Aviv, 1976), 27; J. S. Hertz [I. S. Herts], 'Ideyishe erlikhkayt', in *Yid, mentsh, sotsialist*, 44–6. Though Sztokfisz, Minc, Pflug, and Eichenbaum are all examples of Jews who were affiliated with the Bund, joined the Communist Party, and broke from that party, there were former Bundists in the KPP who remained Communists throughout the history of the KPP, e.g. Samuel (Shmuel) Bursztyn and Benyomin Racianowicz (Ratsianovitsh) (Goldfinger *et al.* (eds.), *Unter der fon fun k.p.p. zamlbukh*, 346, 367).

30 Oskar [Issakhar Eichenbaum], 'A por verter ofyklerung vegn mayn arayntrit in "bund"', in *Yid, mentsh, sotsialist*, 135. Ludwik Hass has indicated that Eichenbaum was one of those who was 'especially active' in the work of the Opposition (Hass, 'Trotskyism in Poland up to 1945', 20). Minc, on the other hand, has noted that Eichenbaum was ideologically close to the Opposition but did not formally belong to it (Minc, *The History of a False Illusion*, 289). However, since Eichenbaum himself explicitly asserts that he was a member of the Trotskyist group, it appears that Minc is mistaken.

Trotskyists of Poland followed his lead. Those attending the conference formally declared that while the Trotskyist organization did not resign its principles, it was prepared to resign its organizational independence, and to have its members enter the Bund or the Polska Partia Socjalistyczna (Polish Socialist Party, PPS). The conference declaration also stated that the Trotskyists were prepared to accept party discipline if admitted into these parties, and asked only for the right to agitate on behalf of their ideas.[31] Both the Bund and the PPS agreed, and the Trotskyists followed through. According to *Naye folkstsaytung*, 'the great majority' of the Trotskyists entered the Jewish socialist movement rather than the Polish one.[32] Deutscher and Redler, to be sure, opted for the PPS.[33] But Sztokfisz, Szlama Erlich, Leon Erlich, and an unknown number of Trotskyist rank and file became card-carrying Bundists. Minc was initially sceptical about the advisability of this step, decided to leave Poland, and worked with Trotskyists in Prague, Danzig, and Copenhagen. In 1938, however, while living in France, he too joined the Bund.

The movement of these Trotskyists into the ranks of the Bund, I hasten to add, was a tactical decision, and should by no means be taken to suggest that these one-time members of the KPP had come to accept the Bund's position on Jewish affairs. Indeed, an article by Eichenbaum published in *Naye folkstsaytung* in December 1935 suggests that many Polish Communists and ex-Communists who were eager to find a new organizational home had deep misgivings about entering an exclusively and explicitly Jewish party. 'It is difficult', Eichenbaum writes, 'for Communists who have been used to being in a party with the proletariat of other nations to join a party made up only of Jewish workers.'[34]

Moreover, as the tactics of the worldwide Trotskyist movement shifted once again, many of the Polish Trotskyists resolved to make another stab at organizing an independent political organization, and left the Bund.[35] But Sztokfisz, Minc, and Eichenbaum did not go with them.

[31] 'Trotskistn arayngetrotn in "bund" un p.p.s.', *Naye folkstsaytung*, 10/347 (23 Nov. 1935), 5. Dziewanowski suggests that the 'Trotskyist faction began to disintegrate' because it was 'riddled with internal tensions and lack of central leadership'.

[32] Ibid. In an internal document meant for its own members, the Central Committee of the Bund provided additional details, i.e. that the Trotskyist organizations of Warsaw, Kraków, and Zagłębie had dissolved and that 'the former Trotskyists have entered in the Bund' (Central Committee of the Bund in Poland, Circular 25, 20 Nov. 1935, Bund Archives, MG 2 (470)).

[33] Stefan Purman was also among the Trotskyists who joined the PPS (Hass, 'Trotskyism in Poland up to 1945', 34).

[34] *Yid, mentsh, sotsialist*, 143.

[35] Sztokfisz suggests that the decision on the part of some of the Trotskyists to leave the Bund in 1937 may have been motivated (in part) by 'their hopes that better conditions had been created for winning over the Communist masses in the wake of the dissolution of the Communist Party' (Mendel, *Memoirs of a Jewish Revolutionary*, 317). The KPP was not formally dissolved until 1938, but it is plausible that the Polish Trotskyists believed that the Great Purge (which began in 1937) provided them with opportunities that had not previously existed. In any event, the movement of Trotskyists out of the Bund was sparked primarily not, as Sztokfisz's account might lead one to believe, by local factors, but rather by a shift in Trotsky's thinking. 'Trotsky now felt that, as the German debacle had dis-

The History of a False Illusion ends with the beginning of the Second World War. It ought to be noted, however, that Minc survived the war in France, and emigrated to Argentina in the early 1950s. During his years in Argentina he was a member of the Coordinating Committee of the Bund, was active in the Society for Yiddish Secular Schools, and eventually became editor-in-chief of the Bund's Argentine periodical *Undzer gedank*. He died in Buenos Aires in 1962.[36]

There is precious little biographical information on other one-time members of the KPP Opposition. Certain of them disappear altogether from the historical record once the Second World War begins. However, four other men known to have been sympathetic to the Opposition—Eichenbaum, Sztokfisz, Redler, and Deutscher—also survived the war.[37]

Though Deutscher may well have thought of himself as a non-Jewish Jew in the post-war era, the same cannot be said about all Polish Jewish one-time leaders of the KPP Opposition. Eichenbaum, who, like Minc, remained a Bundist during the war, became editor of the Bund's Parisian newspaper, *Unzer shtime*, in the late 1940s. He moved to Tel Aviv at the behest of the Bund's Coordinating Committee in the 1950s, became General Secretary of the Bund's group in Israel, and edited the Bund's Israeli organ, *Lebns-fragn*. He died in Israel in 1971.[38]

Sztokfisz too remained in the Bund during the first years of the war. However, he later worked with Poalei Zion Left in France, made *aliyah*, joined Mapam, and still later became a member of Aḥdut Ha'avodah.[39] At the time of his death in Israel in 1968 Sztokfisz was no longer party-affiliated, but he remained a (critical) Zionist.[40]

credited the Second and Third Internationals, the defeat of the [Spanish] Loyalists would show the need for a Fourth International . . . the new line was to break loose from embarrassing "centrist" entanglements' (D. Bell, *Marxian Socialism in the United States* (Princeton, 1967), 176). Thus, those Trotskyists in the United States who had entered the Socialist Party also left that party in 1937 (by engaging in actions which led to their being expelled).

36 'Geshtorbn kh'aleksander mints', *Undzer gedank*, 17/153 (Mar. 1962).

37 In 1940 Szlama Erlich began to edit a Trotskyist periodical, *Czerwony Sztandar*. He died in the Warsaw ghetto in 1943 (Hass, 'Trotskyism in Poland up to 1945', 41–2, 46; Hass, 'The Bolshevik Leninist (Fourth International) Movement in Poland up to 1945', 17). Leon Ehrlich apparently died in the USSR (conversation with Solomon Krystal (who knew Leon Erlich in the period before the Second World War), New York, 27 Jan. 2003). Redler lived in New York in the decades following the Second World War. He died there in 1984 (my thanks to Itzhak Epstein for obtaining this information for me from the Surrogate's Court).

38 *Yid, mentsh, sotsialist*, 48–9.

39 I.A. [Eichenbaum], 'Hersh mendl', *Lebns-fragn* (July–Aug. 1968), 24.

40 K. Shimon, 'Hersh m[e]ndls "zikhroynes fun a yidishn revolutsioner"—in daytsh', *Letste nayes*, 15 Feb. 1980, 8: 'Biz zayn letste otem hot er nisht oyfgehert tsu gloybn in ideal fun yoysher un felker-farbriderung, ober di eyntsike hofnung fun yidishn folk hot er gezen nor in eygenem land.' At the time of Sztokfisz's death Eichenbaum indicated that Sztokfisz had frequently visited the office of the Bund in Tel Aviv, and that they had chatted regularly. 'He used to attempt to unite Trotskyism with Zionism and at the same time spoke with great sentiment about the Bund. As if he wanted to find a synthesis among all of these ideological tendencies, which he went through over the years of his life' (I.A. [Eichenbaum], 'Hersh mendl'). Tamara Deutscher describes Sztokfisz in 1968 as 'an embittered and tired man, half-reconciled to Zionism' (Deutscher (ed.), *Marxism in our Time*, 9).

In an afterword to his autobiography, first published in Yiddish in 1959, Sztokfisz explained a portion of his political evolution:

I experienced the deepest moral crisis when Hitler's armies invaded France. . . . I asked myself, as a Jewish worker what must I do? . . . It was soon clear to me that Hitler's victory meant the destruction of Jewry in every country in Europe. . . . After wrestling with this question for a long period of time . . . I became convinced that only the Jewish workers in Israel were now capable of struggling for socialism, for it was only in Israel that the Jewish people would gather once again and begin to create a new and free life under the rule of the workers.[41]

Minc and Eichenbaum would not have agreed. Yet for them as well as for Sztokfisz there simply was no question, as the Holocaust gathered force, that they belonged in the Jewish socialist world. Even Redler, who had opted for the PPS in the 1930s rather than enter an explicitly Jewish political movement, ultimately had a change of heart. In the mid-1970s he was an active member of the Jewish Socialist Community (a small, short-lived, New York-based group).[42] The Opposition began with 'Communist questions'—but Minc, Eichenbaum, Sztokfisz, and Redler were ultimately led to (somewhat different) Jewish answers.

Deutscher was, so far as can be ascertained, the only one of the leading pre-war Polish Trotskyists who survived the war and who did not establish a primary affiliation with an explicitly Jewish political movement in the last decades of his life.[43] Indeed Minc may well be more representative of the circle of which Deutscher was a part than was Deutscher himself.

Two interrelated facts—revolving around age and prior affiliation—may help to explain the differences between Deutscher's life path and those of Sztokfisz, Minc, and Eichenbaum. Deutscher was several years younger than these other Oppositionists, and thus did not enter the political arena until after the founding of the KPP. Whereas Sztokfisz, Minc, and Eichenbaum had cut their political teeth in Jewish socialist movements before entering the Communist Party, and apparently found it relatively easy to return to such movements when they became disillusioned with the KPP, Deutscher had had no such prior experience.[44]

Minc, Sztokfisz, and Eichenbaum, on the other hand (and an unknown number of other former leaders and members of the KPP Opposition), began their political lives in the Jewish socialist world and ended it there as well. The pre-war experiences of Minc and of certain other of his communist-affiliated comrades may best

[41] Mendel, *Memoirs of a Jewish Revolutionary*, 327.

[42] 'Jewish Socialist Community Active List as of May 1974', unpub. document in my possession.

[43] Deutscher allowed his work to be published in certain Jewish periodicals in the post-war decades, and accepted some invitations to speak under the auspices of Jewish groups. He maintained regular friendly relations with Sztokfisz and Redler, and also corresponded briefly with Minc (International Institute of Social History, Amsterdam, Isaac Deutscher Papers).

[44] There is not enough biographical information available on Redler to ascertain whether or not his decision to become a member of the Jewish socialist community can also be explained in this manner.

be seen as 'internationalist' chapters in their lives, bracketed by direct, active involvement in explicitly Jewish movements. *The History of a False Illusion* helps to document this under-studied phenomenon. I therefore welcome the publication of this English translation.

On Solzhenitsyn's 'Middle Path'

YOHANAN PETROVSKY-SHTERN

CONTROVERSIES over Aleksandr Solzhenitsyn's attitude towards the Jews and his alleged antisemitism date back at least to his cycle of novels entitled *The Red Wheel*, in which the Jewish role in Bolshevism was emphasized. These arguments have resurfaced with the publication in Russian of his history of Russian–Jewish relations. *Dvesti let vmeste* ('Two Hundred Years Together')[1] has sparked such intense controversy that, in August 2002, the *New Yorker*'s editor-in-chief, David Remnick, felt it necessary to assert that 'Solzhenitsyn, in fact, is not antisemitic; his books are not antisemitic, and he is not, in his personal relations, anti-Jewish.' However, a close examination of the first volume of this book makes it doubtful whether such a categorical statement can withstand scrutiny.

For Solzhenitsyn, now in his mid-eighties, the choice of subject for his new book might seem surprising. When he re-emerged in 1956 after years of imprisonment in Stalin's camps, Solzhenitsyn became the spokesman for ordinary people who had been thrown into the fearsome pit of the Soviet penitentiary system. Quite unexpectedly for many, and for Solzhenitsyn himself as well, the fusion of his personal experiences as a former *zek* (inmate), his astonishing creative will, and his intent to perpetuate the memory of millions of other *zek*s produced the ground-breaking masterpieces *One Day in the Life of Ivan Denisovich* and *The Gulag Archipelago*. Naturally, the Soviets could not tolerate a champion of undesirable truths in their midst, and in 1974 they expelled him from the USSR.

During his twenty years of exile, Solzhenitsyn wrote his multi-volume literary version of the Russian Revolution in *The Red Wheel*; he also alienated a good many admirers by publicly vilifying the West and praising the Russian monarchy, thereby becoming an object of sharp criticism, if not derision, among liberal-minded Russian intellectuals. After returning to Russia in 1994, the former prophet, who was as instrumental as any other person in bringing down Russian communism, was slowly but steadily transformed into a living icon whose desire to see the revival of patriarchal Russia was out of step with the vibrant neo-capitalism that the country had chosen in 1991.

If Solzhenitsyn planned to recapture the public imagination by publishing a book on relations between Russians and Jews in the last 200 years, he seems to have

[1] *Dvesti let vmeste (1795–1995)* (Moscow: Russkii put', 2001).

succeeded. In Russia the book sold out immediately. It has also enjoyed impressive commercial success among Russian Jews in Israel and the United States. Russian literary critics and scholars have rushed to publicize their opinions, many of which are half-baked. Some journalists have praised the book, saying that it fulfils a long-standing need for the 'unravelling of the Russian–Jewish knot'. Others have praised the author's courage in examining such a pivotal cultural and political issue. Outside Russia, Mikhail Heifets, a renowned Israeli journalist, Natalia Gorbanevskaya, a poet from Paris, and Mikhail Krutikov of the US-based *Forward*, have all assessed Solzhenitsyn's undertaking positively. So, too, did the eminent historian of Russia, Richard Pipes. A few reviewers were more moderate in their assessments, and some were even sharply critical.

Until recently, because of his praise of the Russian empire and his calls for the restoration of a 'good old' tsarist regime, Solzhenitsyn seemed to have become an unpopular figure among Russian intellectuals. However, his unexpected and remarkable return to the centre of public debate demonstrates that it is too early to dismiss him as outdated. Solzhenitsyn observes correctly in his newly published book that two opposing concepts have shaped the image of Russian Jewry in the Russian public imagination. One is that Russia is inherently antisemitic and that Jews are hostages to its policies, and the other is that Jews developed Bolshevism to destroy Russia. Solzhenitsyn, claiming to adopt a fresh approach, sets out to illuminate 'objectively' the 'red-hot issue' of Russian–Jewish relations. He asserts that his goal is to revisit the history of those relations from a new vantage point, purporting to distance himself from those who accuse Jews of Russophobia and those who accuse Russia of antisemitism.[2] On another occasion, he dubs his stance 'the middle path'.[3] No wonder that the book has become a major topic in contemporary Russian–Jewish discourse. My goal here is to determine whether it does indeed follow Solzhenitsyn's middle path between the Russophobia and the antisemitism laid out on its first page.

ETHICS AND HISTORY

The English-speaking reader will miss what the Russian reader will understand immediately: the Russian title *Dvesti let vmeste*, 'Two Hundred Years *Together*',

[2] To translate Solzhenitsyn's highly charged literary metaphors into rational scholarly statements is difficult, if not impossible. My aim is accurately to convey his basic message as set out in his two brief introductions to the book (Solzhenitsyn, *Dvesti let vmeste*, 5–7, 8–9). Without resorting to such notions as Russophobia or antisemitism, Solzhenitsyn, however, describes two approaches that coincide with these notions: 'But more often we find unilateral reproaches: either that the Russians are guilty in relation to the Jews, or even that the Russians are inherently corrupt—such reproaches abound. Or, from the opposite side, those Russians who have written about this mutual issue have done so in anger, exaggerating (*pereklonno*), and refusing to find in their opponents any virtues worth mentioning' (ibid. 5).

[3] Ibid. 440. Solzhenitsyn uses the metaphor 'the middle path' to depict the activities of Petr Stolypin, the Russian prime minister whom Solzhenitsyn admired, who sought, as it were, a middle path between the right-wing Russian government and a society increasingly under the influence of revolutionaries.

contains a pun, since the similar-sounding phrase *dvesti let v mesti* means 'two hundred years *in revenge*'. This double meaning is echoed in the theme of the book. According to Solzhenitsyn, Russia has always wanted to adopt a friendly and sympathetic attitude towards her Jews, while the Jews themselves did not share this goodwill, and paid Russia back in the currency of violence and revolution.

The pun embedded in the title is part of a carefully designed plan. Solzhenitsyn eloquently describes how the rulers of Russia showered privileges upon the Jews. Russia, he claims, treated her Jews with empathy and appreciation, wholeheartedly embracing them. From the time of Catherine II (1762–96), Russia granted Jews rights equal to those of Christians. Alexander I (1801–25) postponed and later cancelled the expulsion of Jews from rural areas. Nicholas I (1825–55) went so far as to give Jews the right to own land, and Alexander II (1855–81) considerably amplified their civil liberties.

But, Solzhenitsyn continues, Jews never reciprocated. Rather, they responded with pure ingratitude. They reacted inappropriately—indeed offensively. They responded to Catherine II's benevolence with attempts to transform Russian peasants into drunkards, to undermine the Russian economy by smuggling, and to strangle Russian trade in Moscow. Later, they contemptuously rejected Alexander I's generous offer of the right to an education. Under Nicholas I, who allowed Jews to have Christian servants, Jews seduced into Judaism thousands of followers of Russian Orthodoxy.[4] Finally, when the Russian state allowed Jews to own arable land, Jewish colonists who were totally unsuited to agricultural labour ruined the colonies and squandered the money allotted by the state for this purpose.[5]

The situation deteriorated further in the late nineteenth and early twentieth centuries. The more Russia strove to win over her Jews, the more she was repaid in Jewish hatred. For example, Solzhenitsyn argues, Russian reformers such as Alexander II and Prime Minister Stolypin endowed the Jews with a genuine sense of belonging to the Russian fatherland, triggered the rise of the Russian Jewish intelligentsia, legalized Jewish emigration, defended the Jews during pogroms, and eased certain Jewish civil disabilities. Yet what was the response of the ungrateful Jews? They plotted the assassination of Alexander II on 1 March 1881; they emigrated to avoid army service; they blemished the international reputation of Russia by spreading calumnies about the Kishinev pogrom; and they murdered Stolypin.[6]

Russia's benevolent attitude towards the Jews deteriorated under the influence of foreigners and people of alien (not Russian Orthodox) beliefs. Those who were to blame for the anti-Jewish riots of the 1900s were aliens: politicians and journalists of Ukrainian, Moldavian, or German origin. Liberals and revolutionaries were also to blame: according to Solzhenitsyn, it was the populists (*narodniki*) who instigated the pogroms in Odessa and Ekaterinoslav. Besides, it was not only Ukrainians, Poles, and Germans who were at fault, but the Jews themselves were guilty of

[4] Ibid. 39–41, 47, 87–8, 98.
[5] Ibid. 106–13.
[6] Ibid. 174–5, 309, 329–32, 425.

causing their own misfortunes.[7] Solzhenitsyn goes so far as to make Dmitry Bogrov's assassination of Stolypin in 1911 into an indirect cause of the 1941 Babi Yar massacre, in which some 100,000 Jews were shot:

I personally feel here the gigantic paths of History, its amazingly unexpected results. Bogrov killed Stolypin, defending the Jews of Kiev from oppression. The tsar would have dismissed Stolypin in any case, and would have called him up again in the periodic absence of efficient staff in 1914–16, and with Stolypin we would not have ended up so terribly either in the war or in the revolution.

The first step: Stolypin is dead—nerves are lost in the war, and Russia lays herself down under the boots of the Bolsheviks.

The second step: the Bolsheviks, with all their rage, turned out to be even more inept than the tsarist government, and in a quarter of a century they expediently ceded half of Russia to the Germans—Kiev included.

The third step: Nazis swiftly passed through Kiev and—destroyed Kievan Jewry. The same Kiev, the same September, but 30 years after Bogrov's shot.[8]

Solzhenitsyn is so deeply convinced of the correctness of his argument that he calls his logic 'the compass of God's morality'.[9] Indeed, Solzhenitsyn's understanding of how the wheel of history turned and punished the Jews vividly illustrates his philosophy of history.

SOLZHENITSYN'S IMAGE OF RUSSIAN JEWS

The image of the Jews in *Dvesti let vmeste* is entirely negative. Like the blatantly anti-Jewish polemicists of the nineteenth century, Solzhenitsyn depicts Jews as unproductive people who never work in the field or in factories.[10] Wherever they went—to Russia, Argentina, or Palestine—Jews possessed an innate revulsion against the land and an intrinsic hatred of agricultural labour.[11] Incapable of productive labour, Jews always and everywhere exploited others. Throughout their interaction with Russians, from the times of Kievan Rus to the end of the nine-

[7] *Dvesti let vmeste*, 195, 207, 377, 449, 480. Solzhenitsyn argues, for instance, that the Pale of Jewish Settlement in Russia was too narrow because Jews as a group were almost exclusively traders and not because the government imposed restrictions (p. 120). Likewise, restrictive measures had to be adopted for the Jews because they proved to be bad patriots who did their best to avoid military service (p. 210). In 1914–15 Jewish purveyors gained control of the stock of bread and horses; this unscrupulous economic activity caused state prices for victuals to soar and triggered the rise of state antisemitism (p. 483).

[8] Ibid. 444.

[9] 'I edinstvennoe spasenie ot takikh promakhov—vsegda rukovodstvovat'sia tol'ko *kompasom Bozh'ei nravstvennosti*' (ibid. 444; my emphasis).

[10] The metaphors that emphasize the unproductive nature of the Jewish people appear on pp. 52 and 59 and those of Jewish aversion to productive labour on pp. 244–5 and 308.

[11] Solzhenitsyn, who perceives the peasantry as the embodiment of Russia's virtues, spends much time proving the incompatibility of Russian Jews and agricultural labour; ibid. 73, 76, 256, 257, 258, 267, 268.

teenth century, Jews were tax-collectors, well-to-do contractors, distillery owners, vodka purveyors, smugglers, and bankers. They were constantly conspiring with the enemies of Russia: the belligerent nomadic Khazars 1,200 years ago, the rebellious Poles in the late eighteenth and early nineteenth centuries, and the hostile Germans at the end of the nineteenth century (one might easily have predicted their post-Second World War pro-American sympathies); in a word, they associated themselves with any potential internal or external enemy of Russia.[12]

Solzhenitsyn implies that the main characteristic of Russian Jewry was its propensity not only for exploitation but for *destruction*. Early in the Russian–Jewish encounter Jews manifested their destructiveness through their control of liquor production, which enabled them to exploit the Russian people. However, once the state introduced its own liquor monopoly, Jews were unable to continue their concealed destruction of Russia at the same pace. Hence, they chose an open form of destruction: revolution. 'Rabbi-talmudists' blessed their revolutionary children, encouraging them to eradicate Russian statehood. Earlier, Jews had made Russian peasants drunk, but now they fomented revolution in the village. And whatever the role of Jews, Solzhenitsyn characterizes them as a people of 'ardent groundlessness'[13]—a charge that is reminiscent of Stalin's 1948 assessment of Jews as 'rootless cosmopolitans'.

Wherever possible, Solzhenitsyn hints, Jews conspired against Mother Russia. Although he rejects *The Protocols of the Elders of Zion* as absolutely untrustworthy and a police forgery, the imagery of the *Protocols* is clearly present in the book. Jews in *Dvesti let vmeste* enticed naïve Russians with kabbalah, tempted the Russian Orthodox with rationalism, fostered the rise of Russian sectarianism, instilled fear and spiritual slavery in their own people, and undermined the work of the Russian State Committee and the State Treasury.[14] The next step for Solzhenitsyn should have been to call a spade a spade and openly discuss the notorious anti-Russian Judaeo-Masonic plot, yet he does not care to go that far. It does not seem to be necessary. There are enough metaphors in the book and an attentive reader will at once connect all the hints.[15]

In place of the old-fashioned explanation of the Jewish Diaspora based on the image of the 'wandering Jew' doomed to eternal exile, Solzhenitsyn creates a new historical image of the Diaspora. This image involves the continuous expansion of Jewry in the warmth of the Russian environment. Solzhenitsyn has argued elsewhere that no country on earth welcomed Jews with such spiritual and physical

12 See pp. 16–17 (Khazarian Jews and their negative impact on Kievan Rus); pp. 32–3, 45–8 (Polish Jews together with the Polish *szlachta* oppress the local rural population); p. 241 (on Jews transplanting anti-Russian German Marxism onto Russian soil); p. 477 (Jews during the First World War overwhelmingly sympathized with the Germans); pp. 498–9 (Rasputin's court Jews were German spies).

13 'plamennaya bespochvennost'' (p. 238).

14 Ibid. 20, 21, 35, 50, 70, 87.

15 Solzhenitsyn's use of the imagery of the *Protocols of the Elders of Zion* in his book on Russian Jewry has become the focus of analysis in a sharp article entitled 'Protokoly siamskikh bliznetsov' by Sergey Ivanov, the leading Russian scholar of Byzantium (*Neprikosnovennyi zapas*, 4 (2001), 62–9).

warmth as did Russia.[16] And it is a well-known fact, especially to Solzhenitsyn, a former physics teacher, that matter expands when exposed to heat. That is why, he argues, a continuous expansion of Jews across the world started only after they found themselves in Russia's warm, human, and natural environment. But, he argues, the Jews realized that Russia's embrace was too hot for them, and the empire too narrow. They were no longer satisfied with being, in his words, 'the most important influence on Russia'.[17] Russia's warmth, so to speak, bolstered the Jews' expansion and their desire to conquer the world. Hence, Jews appear in the book as a mysterious and 'rapidly growing self-persistent species'.[18] Having begun in Russia, the triumphant Jewish expansion swiftly achieved the stage at which 'the restless dynamics of Jewish commerce' mobilized 'entire states',[19] and the Jews finally started to 'define the destinies of all the earth in the twentieth century'.[20] In light of these remarks, this work could easily be seen as a sequel to the *Protocols of the Elders of Zion*.

SOURCES CONVENIENT AND INCONVENIENT

Solzhenitsyn seems unaware of recent publications, both in Russian and in English, that have established a picture of Jewish life in Russia very different from his own. One looks in vain for references to the work of such scholars as John Klier on nineteenth-century Russian–Jewish relations, on the rise of Russian Jewry, on the Jewish theme in the Russian press, and on the complex picture of the pogrom; Michael Stanislawski on Nicholas I's Jewish policies and on the Enlightenment movement in Russia; or Ezra Mendelsohn on the Jewish workers' movement. Nor is there any reference to books by Oleg Budnitsky on Jews in the Russian Revolution, or to those by Simon Markish on Russian Jewish literature—not to mention such classic sources as the monographs by Salo Baron, Isaac Levitats, and Louis Greenberg, or the plethora of Moscow and St Petersburg periodical publications on nineteenth-century Russian Jews that have appeared in the last fifteen years. These scholars, who have made a major contribution to research on pre-1917 Russian Jewry and who have provided, to use Solzhenitsyn's own phraseology, 'a multi-faced and balanced elucidation of this issue', are clearly not on the list of voices approved by Solzhenitsyn's personal censorship.

The author claims that he is an impartial observer because he also ignores any nineteenth- or twentieth-century source that is either blatantly antisemitic or profoundly philosemitic. Yet this leads him to neglect important sources and legal compilations. In this context, his treatment of the Pale of Jewish Settlement in

[16] On Russia welcoming the Jews and embracing them with love, see *Dveste let vmeste*, 31, 32, 43, 107, 108, 110, 120, 309, 329, 345, 460, 468.

[17] Ibid. 121.

[18] 'stremitel'no rastushchii samoupornyi organizm v rossiiskom gosudarstvennom tele' (ibid. 127).

[19] 'neutomimaya dinamika evreiskoi kommertsii, dvizhushchaya tselymi gosudarstvami' (ibid. 300).

[20] Ibid. 307.

Russia is revealing. According to Solzhenitsyn, this was nothing else but 'a considerably expanded region of Jewish residence'.[21] Solzhenitsyn remarks repeatedly that the Pale was a legal fiction and that Jews could freely move and settle throughout the Russian empire. Solzhenitsyn's repetitions could hardly sweeten the bitter pill of the Pale of Settlement. And although the issue of the Pale in a variety of epochs and for a variety of Jewish social strata was far from simple, Solzhenitsyn treats its complexity as irrelevant. His vantage point becomes particularly unambiguous if one takes into consideration the availability and accessibility of some of the basic Russian sources that he neglects. Before the First World War there appeared about ten systematic reviews of Russian legislation on Jews. These were huge volumes of up to a thousand pages containing senate explanations, corrections, and amendments of legislation, as well as complaints, pleas, and petitions from ordinary Jews.

A brief glance at these sources would suffice to make it clear that the Pale of Settlement represented one of the most important forms of social disability and inequality imposed on Russian Jews. Contrary to Solzhenitsyn's opinion, the Pale operated effectively, and became all the more effective as time passed. The complaints to the senate corroborate that, at the end of the nineteenth century, the Pale was steadily *contracting*, not expanding. In the first years of Alexander III's reign (1881–94) the right to settle outside the Pale that had been granted to Jewish artisans in the mid-1860s was cancelled. In 1891 the right to live in Moscow, which had been granted to Jewish Nicholaevan soldiers who had served the full twenty-five years in the pre-reformed army, was rescinded; during the week of Passover elderly retired soldiers, together with their families, were banished from the city. The 'benevolent gesture' of Nicholas II allowing the Jewish soldiers who participated in the Russo-Japanese War to settle outside the Pale never came into effect. It is unclear why Solzhenitsyn overlooks the senate documents that explain the curtailment of the civil rights of the Jews of the Pale of Settlement. Yet in his book he quotes extensively from the memoirs of those high-ranking Jewish lawyers and doctors who lived in Moscow or in St Petersburg and for whom the Pale was porous indeed. Solzhenitsyn allows those Jews who lived in the capitals, and who represented less than 3 per cent of Russia's Jewish population, to speak out. Yet the voices of the 6 million Jews living in the Pale are absent from the book.

As a result, Solzhenitsyn bypasses some key developments in Russian–Jewish history and highlights others that are by and large secondary and of dubious significance. He passes over the pauperization of the shtetl and the proletarianization of Russian Jews, the primary characteristics in the life of late nineteenth-century Russian Jewry. Solzhenitsyn discusses the Bund (the Jewish socialist workers' party) and its role in twentieth-century Russian politics at considerable length; yet the emergence of the Bund in Solzhenitsyn's story is almost inexplicable because in

21 Ibid. 43, 118, 119. (Elsewhere in the book Solzhenitsyn offers the whole gamut of versions of the word combination 'rasshirennyi krai evreiskogo prozhivaniya'.)

his view the Jewish working class does not exist. Solzhenitsyn's Jew always exploits others, and is therefore inconceivable as a proletarian. Likewise, Solzhenitsyn describes the Jewish revolutionary movement as a senseless and destructive imitation of the Russian Revolution. Jewish revolutionary activities, claims Solzhenitsyn, had no social, economic, or cultural bases. They represented yet another slap in the face to the Russian state, yet another ungrateful Jewish response to the generous state decision not to implement the barbaric 1882 May laws.[22] And thus Solzhenitsyn sketches a picture of Jews as the people who never work but become revolutionaries en masse.

One might argue that it is quite normal to omit sources that undermine one's theory. However, one must bear in mind that there are fields in the humanities—and especially in the humanities—where this selective approach to the sources makes one's point of view unscholarly, if not unethical. This is exactly what happens when Solzhenitsyn analyses the Jewish pogroms.[23] To strengthen his claim that Jews themselves were to blame for the pogroms, he omits from his narrative any reference to the increasing penetration of the state administration by the ideology of the Russian far right after 1900. He dismisses the proto-fascist Union of the Russian People, of which Nicholas II himself may have been a member, as a 'pitiful, inept, and under-funded party' hardly capable of accomplishing anything. He then eloquently recounts how well-organized and effective revolutionaries of Jewish origin killed state officials, threw bombs, and attempted to seize power. It comes as no surprise that against Solzhenitsyn's backdrop of the inept Black Hundreds and the lazy and incompetent police, the 1905 Jewish self-defence organizations are depicted as groups of insolent, over-armed young Jews. It is also no surprise that, having sketched this picture, Solzhenitsyn defines the anti-Jewish violence of this period as the only form of self-defence available to a beleaguered Russian government beset by revolutionary, armed Jewish youths.

Solzhenitsyn provides only one type of source material relating to the pogroms: documents that originated in the offices of the police and state administration. He dubs this type of evidence 'the highest level of trustworthy investigation'.[24] He draws extensively from these police reports, which are self-serving and were intended to justify police actions. Moreover, Solzhenitsyn deploys his sources

[22] According to Solzhenistyn's extensive analysis, the goal of Ignatev's May laws was to stop Jewish exploitation of Russia's weak peasantry, and not to expel the Jews from the townlets or limit their economic activities. See *Dvesti let vmeste*, 201–5.

[23] Solzhenitsyn analyses the pogroms in Gomel (pp. 321–9), Kishinev (pp. 333–43), Kiev (pp. 371–84), Odessa (pp. 384–400), and Białystok (pp. 408–12). Whatever the historical circumstances, he claims that in most cases either unnecessary and premature Jewish self-defence or Jewish involvement with the revolutionary terrorists groups triggered the pogroms (pp. 323, 343, 373–4). Moreover, he does not hesitate to resort to the most staunchly antisemitic accusations of the Union of the Russian People and its like, arguing, for example, that the pogrom in Gomel was 'anti-Russian', not 'anti-Jewish' (p. 343), and even that there were never any anti-Jewish pogroms in Russia before 1917 (p. 321).

[24] 'vysshyi klass dostovernogo rassledovaniya' (ibid. 371).

carefully here as well. Sources that are inconvenient for him, such as reports by government clerks detailing atrocities committed by the authorities, are simply ignored. For example, the minutes of the Duma for 1906 contain a detailed account of the Białystok pogrom extending over several hundred pages; Solzhenitsyn often cites such minutes, but not in this particular case. He relies only on police reports and right-wing denunciations, and as a result, judges the victims rather than the perpetrators.

If Solzhenitsyn rules out most of the crucial sources, then what *does* he cite? He seems to welcome the testimony of state bureaucrats who reproach Jews for the exploitation of peasants; of assimilationists and converts who reject the Jewish tradition; of Zionists who mock the Jews' struggle for social and cultural equality in Russia; of traditionalists who condemn Jewish participation in the Russian Revolution; of revolutionary Bolsheviks who criticize the nationalism of the Bundists; and of Russian officials angered by the 'over-representation' of Jews in universities. In a word, he relies on all those whose words can be employed to show that it is the Jews who are at fault in their relations with the Russian government and Russian society.

Solzhenitsyn's use of many different points of view, which is praised by his critics, is deceptive. In fact, his book is not polyphonic but monophonic. In his narrative the right to discuss Russian Jewry is restricted to critical and hostile voices. Quotation marks become almost unnecessary as the author's voice fuses stylistically with those of his sources. The harsher and more subjective the criticism articulated in the sources, the better it is for Solzhenitsyn. He claims revealingly at the beginning of the book that his intention is to dissipate 'false accusations' against Jews and resurrect 'justified accusations'.[25] But he operates as a prosecutor who does not allow the defendant to defend himself. Both the unfounded and the well-grounded accusations cited in the book thus become denunciations. The defendant, Russian Jewry, does not have and *must not* have the last word. Imagine the history of the 'gulag archipelago' written not on the basis of *zek*s' memoirs, but rather on the basis of KGB denunciations and testimonies signed by victims under torture. This is the type of narrative Solzhenitsyn has written. It is the obverse of the historical methodology he employed in his earlier non-fiction and it is the product of the double standard he now uses.

IN THE MARGINS

Solzhenitsyn's book is also rich in errors and misunderstandings. For example, Egor Perets, the Secretary of State in the 1880s, was a second-generation Christian. Solzhenitsyn describes him as a Jew in order to demonstrate that tolerant tsarist Russia allowed Jews to become high-ranking officials. Similarly, he introduces

[25] 'rasseyat′ neponimanie oshibochnoe i obvineniya lozhnye, a napomnit′ i ob obvineniyakh spravedlivykh' (ibid. 8–9).

von Kankrin (Fedor Frantsevich Kankrin), a Russified German and a hereditary nobleman with absolutely no Jewish connections, who was Nicholas I's minister of finance, as 'the Rabbi's son'. Sometimes he fails to distinguish between converts and Jews, claiming—contrary to common knowledge—that under Peter the Great, Jews were allowed into Russia. For instance, the eighteenth-century Saxon merchant Grunshtein was a Lutheran who converted to Russian Orthodoxy; no previous scholar has detected in him even feelings of sympathy towards Judaism, yet in Solzhenitsyn's narrative he figures as a Jew who occupied a high position at the Russian queen Elizabeth's court.

Solzhenitsyn's distortions and errors echo the underlying thesis of the book and even seem to be shaped by it. Thus, Solzhenitsyn justifies Russian governmental policies towards Jews by arguing that 'if a considerable number of Jews had not moved from constricted Poland into extensive Russia, the notion of the "Pale of Settlement" would not have emerged at all'. That is to say, it was not the case that Russia acquired its Jewish population with the newly annexed territories of partitioned Poland; rather, the Jews moved to Russia of their own free will. Consequently, the Jews themselves are to blame for the establishment of the Pale of Settlement.

THE CONTEXT

Solzhenitsyn's narrative consistently ignores any historical context, which makes it even more problematic from a scholarly point of view, if not from an ethical one, and reveals his basic intention. Territorially, Ukraine west of the Dnieper was part of the Polish–Lithuanian Commonwealth. Only at the end of the eighteenth century, after the partitions of Poland, did this area become part of the Russian empire. Together with this territory, Russia acquired between 800,000 and 1,200,000 Jews who had long enjoyed the privileges of residence and trade granted to them by the Polish Crown and the Polish nobility.

Rather than attempting to unravel the complex Russian–Jewish–Ukrainian–Polish 'knot' (to use Solzhenitsyn's favourite metaphor), the author cuts through it with a single stroke, taking Poland (and sometimes Ukraine) out of the picture. He presents Ukraine ('Malorossiya') as native Russian territory and describes the presence of Jews in Ukraine between the thirteenth and eighteenth centuries not as a legal arrangement between the rulers and nobility first of the Grand Duchy of Lithuania and then of the Polish–Lithuanian Commonwealth and the Jews, but as the result of the political benevolence of Russian tsars. Right-bank Ukraine, with its highly Polonized towns, never existed for Solzhenitsyn. Consequently, Solzhenitsyn makes another 'discovery' (repeating Russian classic antisemitic sources): the Ukrainian towns declined economically because Jews transformed independent Russian urban-dwellers into serfs. Solzhenitsyn ignores the political context as well, and especially the policies of Alexander III, which were intended to reverse the policies aimed at Jewish acculturation. He presents the *numerus clausus* that radically reduced higher education opportunities for the Jews as merely another measure of self-defence by the state, rather than as a severe limitation of the reforms initiated by Alexander II.[26]

Solzhenitsyn depicts the Russian state as one that granted the Jews everything: 'every bit of education and every bit of wealth', and even 'the Yiddish-language press, which never existed before'. One might ask at this point whether the author is unaware that Yiddish (or at least Judaeo-German) existed in print from as early as the sixteenth century, beginning with the publication of the *Tsenerene*, a paraphrase of the Pentateuch that enjoyed a vast readership among Jewish women. Does he not know that in the last quarter of the nineteenth century, Russia banned the Yiddish theatre for some twenty years, or that Russian bureaucrats outlawed the Jewish press because they believed Yiddish to be a worthless and dangerous language—the 'jargon' of Moscow swindlers? Is he unaware of the fact that during the First World War the Russian authorities shut down all Yiddish publications on the charge of anti-Russian espionage and that rank-and-file soldiers were forbidden to write letters home in Yiddish, the only written language they knew? One assumes that he is aware of these facts. Yet, he eliminates the cultural context in which they are embedded from his narrative.

THE READER AND THE BOOK

Despite his clear ideological bias, Solzhenitsyn does not neglect his readership, which is largely Jewish, liberal, and critical. For those who read his book with a secret hope of finding at least some truth and some reason for optimism about future Russian–Jewish dialogue, Solzhenitsyn has provided a whole set of attention-grabbing and eloquent aphorisms. Criticizing the revolutionary zeal that was rampant at the beginning of the century, he identifies 'a spiritual helplessness of both our peoples'. Underscoring mutual—Jewish and Russian—responsibility for the fate of the Russian state, Solzhenitsyn argues that 'we dug the precipice from both sides'. He does not hesitate to flatter the Jewish reader with such claims as: 'the Jews are the closest to us, most tightly linked with us' (in the cultural and historical sense).[27] Many readers have seized on such observations and praised their wisdom, straightforwardness, and sincerity. Even Geoffrey Hosking, the eminent English historian of Russia, who reviewed the book for the *Times Literary Supplement*, appeared to accept its analysis without reservation.

Alas, contrary to his promise, Solzhenitsyn's book does not provide a 'middle path' in the Russian–Jewish dialogue. Rather, it is vociferously anti-Jewish, of pseudo-scholarly substance, wrapped in pseudo-ethical claims, and presented for mass—mostly Jewish—consumption. Notwithstanding his liberal use of quota-

[26] *Dvesti let vmeste*, 181. [27] Ibid. 468.

tions, sources, and authoritative names, Solzhenitsyn is unable to conceal the one-sidedness of the picture of Russian–Jewish relations set out in his book. Whether he is aware of it or not, his book repeats all the mendacious, hostile, and biased perceptions of Jews elaborated by the likes of Yakov Brafman, the author of the notorious *The Book of Kahal* (1869), Georgy Butmi, the author of *The Enemies of the Human Race* (1906), or Vasily Shulgin, the author of *What We Do Not Like About Them* (1929).

This allegedly neutral book is merely one more in a long series of denunciations of the Jews and their conspiracies against Russia. It is a fitting sequel to *The Red Wheel* series of novels, which relates how Russian anti-heroes together with the Russian left, with its large Jewish component, destroyed Russia. Perhaps, therefore, the book should not be seen merely as a straightforward attack on the Jews. To use Solzhenitsyn's own metaphor, his book on Russian Jews belongs only in the moderate 'first circle' of antisemitism. Yet the slopes are slippery and the pit is deep. In light of this, how should Russian Jews read *Dvesti let vmeste*? What does it signify for them—as well as for all those readers of Solzhenitsyn for whom, as the author of *Matryona's Place* and *The First Circle*, he remains the unsurpassed champion of truth? How can these readers continue to read and love Solzhenitsyn? What should they say, all those who in the 1970s and 1980s risked their careers, their freedom, and even their lives to circulate samizdat copies of *One Day in the Life of Ivan Denisovich* and who experienced the great joy of participating in a common act of civil courage and intellectual resistance? How can they now square that joy with the confusion and embarrassment triggered by Solzhenitsyn's new book?

Three Books on the Łódź Ghetto

HELENE J. SINNREICH

THE destruction of documents produced during the war has made the writing of Holocaust history, and particularly the history of its victims, a difficult challenge. Łódź, the second largest city in Poland and the site of the second largest ghetto in Nazi-occupied Europe, sustained far less damage than Warsaw. As a result, there is more surviving documentation from the Łódź ghetto than from any other. Of particular importance was the survival of the *Chronicle of the Łódź Ghetto*, written under the direction of the Jewish ghetto administration, which recorded the daily events and statistics of the ghetto.

The *Chronicle*, originally written half in Polish and half in German, has appeared as a whole or in part in three languages. The late Lucjan Dobroszycki, an eminent scholar and survivor of the Łódź ghetto, served as an editor of each of these editions. The first half of the *Chronicle of the Łódź Ghetto*, which was written in Polish, was edited by Dobroszycki and Danuta Dąbrowska and published in the original language in the mid-1960s. In 1987 Dobroszycki published an English version of the *Chronicle*, but this abridged version contains only one quarter of the original document. The unabridged *Chronicle* was not published until Yad Vashem released a Hebrew translation in four volumes between 1986 and 1989. Scholars wishing to examine the complete *Chronicle* are currently limited unless they are fluent in both Polish and German or in Hebrew. Soon, however, a German edition and a Polish edition of all four volumes will be published as part of a joint project between the universities of Giessen and Łódź.

The *Chronicle* was written with the knowledge of the Nazi authorities and with an awareness that the Germans were able to read the material; it was therefore heavily self-censored. Its authors, however, had access to a vast number of documents produced inside and even outside the ghetto, and had the opportunity to conduct interviews with individuals from all parts of the ghetto administration and society; thus, they were privy to information not necessarily available to the average ghetto dweller. They used this information to create documents that did not appear in the *Chronicle*, and some of the chroniclers also kept private journals. These secondary works are of extraordinary historical value. It is therefore quite fortunate that in recent years a number of these works have been published: the writings of

Oskar Singer, the former head of the ghetto archives, Oskar Rosenfeld, and Józef Zelkowicz have all appeared as monographs.

Oskar Singer's writings, edited by Sascha Feuchert, Erwin Leibfried, and Jörg Rieke, appeared in 2002 as *'Im Eilschritt durch den Gettotag . . .': Reportagen und Essays aus dem Getto Lodz.*[1] This publication is particularly important as some of the papers included in it were unknown before their recent discovery by the editors. Feuchert, a scholar of Holocaust literature at the University of Giessen, contextualizes the writings in his introductory essay. For this essay Feuchert was able to interview Lucielle Eichengreen, a survivor who has published two sets of memoirs; more significantly, she was Oskar Singer's secretary.

Singer's own writings are, of course, the most noteworthy of the documents. The essays presented, drawn from various archives, cover a vast range of topics. Coming from Vienna, Singer considered himself a 'Western Jew'. As such, he writes with great sympathy about the deportation of the 'Western Jews' from the ghetto (the destination, unbeknownst to the deportees, was the Chełmno death camp). He also writes on relations between Jews from the East and Jews from the West in the ghetto, a topic explored by Abraham Barkai in his article 'Between East and West: Jews from Germany in the Lodz Ghetto', published in *Yad Vashem Studies*.[2] Though he only had partial access to Singer's writings, Barkai was able to use certain fragments. Singer also wrote essays in which he illustrated the difficulties of ghetto conditions through his sympathetic portraits of the plight of individuals. These accounts speak to the scholar and the human soul alike. Lastly, the collection includes Singer's texts for an album on ghetto workshops. Numerous albums were prepared in the ghetto. The official ones, including the one for which Singer wrote the text, extolled the virtues of the ghetto leadership and ghetto production. The history of these albums were recently discussed by Irene Kohn at the United States Holocaust Memorial Museum in Washington.

Several essays follow Singer's text. The first, by Jörg Rieke, analyses the language used in the *Chronicle* and in Singer's writing. The second, written by the archivist Julian Baranowski, is a short history of pre-war Łódź and the Łódź ghetto. While Baranowski's history provides a background on the ghetto for the layman, it could have provided more background on the specific issues that Singer raises in his essays.

Throughout Singer's essays, there are copious footnotes dealing not only with the history but with the language used. There is also information in the footnotes about the dates of each handwritten original document, the document's reference number, and whether it came from YIVO archives. A Polish translation of this work entitled *Przemierzając szybkim krokiem getto: Reportaże i eseje z getta łodzkiego* appeared in 2002.

[1] O. Singer, *'Im Eilschritt durch den Gettotag . . .'. Reportagen und Essays aus dem Getto Lodz*, ed. S. Feuchert, E. Leibfried, and J. Rieke (Berlin: Philo Verlagsgesellschaft mbH, 2002).

[2] A. Barkai, 'Between East and West: Jews from Germany in the Lodz Ghetto', in A. Weiss (ed.), *Yad Vashem Studies*, 16 (Jerusalem, 1984).

Oskar Rosenfeld, another 'Western' Jew from Vienna, was an important contributor to the *Chronicle*. In addition to writing essays and entries for the *Chronicle*, he kept a private diary, which appeared in print as *Wozu noch Welt. Aufzeichnungen aus dem Getto Lodz*. This volume, edited by Hanno Loewy and published in Frankfurt am Main in 1994, has recently appeared in English translation as *In the Beginning Was the Ghetto: Notebooks from Lodz*.[3] Just as Sascha Feuchert does in his introductory text on Oskar Singer, Loewy provides a detailed biography of Oskar Rosenfeld in his introduction. Additionally, he provides a brief history of the ghetto, and, in the English edition, a history of the diaries themselves as well. The translation, which attempts to leave the original multilingual character of the diaries intact, is an appealing element of this work. Another positive feature is the footnotes; in addition to providing commentary on the text, they include references to other works.

It is unfortunate that Rosenfeld's drawings were not reproduced in the published work. Also, the published text is not the entirety of Rosenfeld's diary and unfortunately the structure of the diaries was not maintained but rather edited for the sake of readability. Loewy comments on this, and also on the fact that the editing will no doubt be controversial. Scholars wishing to utilize this work should thus pay careful attention to the Editorial Notes.

Rosenfeld's text is invaluable as historical material. He was an extraordinarily talented writer who wrote with incredible insight and sensitivity. His notebooks were written in a fragmentary style, as notes to himself, but this stark writing is particularly moving. Minor details tell of the brutality of ghetto life. The notebooks begin with the arrival of the 'Western Jews' in the ghetto. Rosenfeld describes the new ghetto inhabitants' physical and mental breakdown as they encounter hunger and other difficulties inherent in ghetto life. The diary contains fragmentary images of daily life in the ghetto, with descriptions of the rising food prices, the unbearable idleness of talented people without work, and the arrival and departure of more Jews; it includes impressions of the Germans, short sketches, and personal notes such as memories of the pre-war period and of loved ones. This emotionally difficult text is a portrait both of the community in the ghetto and of an intelligent man in tragic circumstances.

Józef Zelkowicz was the only Polish Jew among the *Chronicle* writers to appear in print. His writings, which were originally composed in Yiddish, were edited by Michal Unger and published in Hebrew in 1994 as *Bayamim hanora'im hahem*; they were recently translated and published in English as *In Those Terrible Days: Writings from the Lodz Ghetto*.[4] Michal Unger provides two introductory chapters to the work, including a piece on Zelkowicz and a brief history of the Łódź ghetto.

[3] O. Rosenfeld, *In the Beginning was the Ghetto: Notebooks from Lodz*, ed. H. Loewy, trans. B. M. Goldstein (Evanston, Ill.: Northwestern University Press, 2002).

[4] Y. Zelkovitsch, *In Those Terrible Days: Writings from the Lodz Ghetto*, ed. M. Unger, trans. N. Greenwood (Jerusalem: Yad Vashem, 2002).

Given Unger's depth of knowledge on the history of the ghetto (her doctoral thesis at the Hebrew University was entitled 'Internal Life in the Łódź Ghetto 1940–1944'), one would have wished for more introductory material. However, except for a few pictures, she reserves space for Zelkowicz's words, which cover nearly 350 pages. She leaves it to this articulate writer to tell the sad history of the ghetto.

The monograph begins with Zelkowicz's collection of essays entitled 'A Bruise and a Welt in Every Dwelling', in which he chronicles his journey with a welfare case worker to the homes of the poverty-stricken of the ghetto. Through these essays, the stories of the most destitute of the ghetto are preserved. His anger against the injustices barely contained, Zelkowicz relates the tragic stories of the starving. In the second section, 'Hold a Pot for Me . . .', he sketches ghetto scenes. In 'The Carpenters' Strike', he gives a report of the little-known rebellion against Rumkowski in the ghetto, interviewing various witnesses and gathering documents to provide a description of the strike and the reasons for it. He follows the strike from the time it starts until it is broken by the hunger of the striking workers. He reports on the difficulties of finding employment in the ghetto and on the resourcefulness of workers who create useful items from garbage and scraps in 'At the Paper Resort'. The most tragic portion of the work is the last section, 'In Those Terrible Days', which relates the story of the deportation of the children and elderly people of the ghetto to the Chełmno death camp in September 1942. The section begins with a description of the removal of the sick from the hospitals and continues with the reactions of the ghetto dwellers upon learning that the children and the elderly are to be deported. Zelkowicz relates scenes between parents and children, complete with dialogue. The tragedy of the events is brought to life through stories of individuals and how they faced this painful moment.

The availability of these materials is useful to scholars, but their translation into English makes them particularly welcome to educators, who will find in them sensitive writings by Holocaust victims. Until now, the most substantial collection of Łódź ghetto documents in English was Alan Adelson's *Lodz Ghetto: Inside a Community Under Siege*, which was created for his documentary film.[5] Because of deficiencies in translation, editing, and citation, this work has been regarded by scholars as problematic. These new volumes present an alternative for classroom use. An additional work, Isaiah Trunk's *Lodzher geto: A historische un sotsyologishe shtudye* ('The Łódź Ghetto: A Historical and Sociological Study') originally published in New York in 1962, will soon be available in English. Trunk's former student Robert Moses Shapiro is translating the work from Yiddish.

[5] A. Adelson and R. Lapides (eds.), *Lodz Ghetto: Inside a Community Under Siege* (New York, 1989); A. Adelson (producer), *Lodz Ghetto* (Alexandria, Va.: PBS Home Video, 1992).

REVIEWS

IRIS PARUSH

Nashim korot: Yitronah shel shuliyut baḥevrah hayehudit bemizraḥ eiropah bame'ah hatesha-esreh

(Tel Aviv: Am Oved, 2001); pp. 345

The field of Jewish women's studies has reached a level of maturity in the past decade, particularly in the United States. Books that address gender and its role in classical Jewish texts and in the narratives of the Jewish past have proliferated. It is rare indeed to find a new book dealing with Jewish history or culture that does not at least raise the questions of gender and women even if the author has no intention of addressing them in a sustained way. But there are few books that provide such a combination of research and interpretation that they can lay claim to being a milestone in the development of a field. Iris Parush's *Reading Jewish Women: Marginality and Modernization in Nineteenth-Century Eastern European Jewish Society*[1] is one.

Parush's thesis is a simple one: that the 'benign neglect' of women's education in the traditional communities of eastern Europe allowed women to be taught foreign languages and have access to secular learning that would have been anathema if boys had been the students. Because traditional Jewish society was highly gendered, with the highest status learning—that is, the study of rabbinic texts—reserved for males, as secular learning was increasingly promoted both by maskilim and by the Russian government in the course of the nineteenth century, girls were available to be taught the new subjects. In prosperous families in particular, girls were often privately tutored as a mark of the family's economic status. As they acquired foreign languages, they had access to foreign literature as well, and adopted values that were foreign to traditional Judaism.

Parush's interdisciplinary book goes far beyond this grossly simplified summation of her thesis. She has mined the Russian Jewish press, Haskalah literature in both Yiddish and Hebrew including the writing of women, memoirs, and the available secondary sources to explore the issues of how women were educated in traditional Jewish society, how they modernized, and how they influenced the larger Jewish society. She has paid close attention to the gendered forms of learning available in traditional Jewish society and to the possibilities made available to women

[1] The book has been translated under this title by Saadya Sternberg (Waltham, Mass., 2004).

through modernizing leaders. In other words, her interest in literature and literacy leads her to pose questions that are more commonly raised by social historians. In doing so, she moves the story of educated females from the margins to a position closer to the centre of the narrative of the secularization of Jews in eastern Europe. In addition to looking at representations of women and attitudes towards their education, she posits a plausible account of the ways in which reading women brought new ideas into their families and the circles of their friends.

By focusing on the ways in which students acquire knowledge of languages and the meanings that they attach to their language learning, Parush deepens our understanding of the gender divide in east European Jewish society. She suggests great differences between men and women even when they both acquired secular knowledge. Boys were forced to study maskilic Hebrew literature in secret, and novels remained disparaged in their circles. Maskilim learned foreign languages like Russian and German late, and many never achieved fluency. Girls, on the other hand, read a variety of languages and literature, in public, without a sense of entering forbidden territory. They learned languages in a systematic way. Women's widespread reading of popular Yiddish literature, however simplistic and sentimental, both eased women with secular education to a reading of Russian literature and introduced modern ideas even to those women who never moved beyond Yiddish.

PAULA HYMAN
Yale University

CAROLE B. BALIN

To Reveal Our Hearts: Jewish Women Writers in Tsarist Russia

(Cincinnati: Hebrew Union College Press, 2000); pp. x + 270

Historians of east European Jewry have contributed generously to the biographical genre, but until recently few works have been devoted to Jewish women's lives. With the publication of *To Reveal Our Hearts*, Carole Balin offers an immensely readable and impressively researched study of five Russian Jewish women writers: Miriam Markel-Mosessohn (1839–1920), Chava Shapiro (1879–1943), Rashel Mironovna Khin (1861–1928), Feiga Israilevna Kogan (1891–1974), and Sofiya Dubnowa-Erlikh (1885–1986). The result is a monograph that will prove useful in the classroom and is of interest to specialists and general readers alike.

Balin's research identified sixty-seven Jewish women who, from 1869, either contributed to the Russian Jewish press or published volumes of literature, poetry, history, or biography. The five writers she focuses on in *To Reveal Our Hearts* were the most prolific of this group, producing works in these genres as well as memoirs, correspondence, autobiographies, and diaries.

All five of Balin's subjects were secularly educated urban women and members of the middle class, and all struggled to enter what Balin calls 'the interior of Russia's cultural landscape' (p. 202). Markel-Mosessohn translated German works into Hebrew and worked as a foreign correspondent for the Hebrew newspaper *Hamelits*; Shapiro penned short stories and journalistic works in Hebrew; Khin wrote short stories and plays in Russian; Kogan was a poet in the Symbolist style, writing first in Russian and later in Hebrew. Dubnowa-Erlikh, too, wrote poetry, as well as essays and a biography of her father, the historian and cultural theorist Simon Dubnow. Balin concludes: 'These Jewish women writers do not conform to the accepted stereotypes of Jewish women in Tsarist Russia. Neither *balebustes* nor revolutionaries, they resemble their Western European sisters far more than their cousins in the romanticized Pale' (p. 7).

The five subjects of *To Reveal Our Hearts* were also complex women, and in every case (except, perhaps, that of Dubnowa-Erlikh), they lived the turbulent lives one associates with turn-of-the-century Russian intellectuals. Balin tells of great bursts of creative and romantic passions for literature, for the Russian and Hebrew languages, and for men, as well as of children nurtured and abandoned. She tells of acceptance and at times unwitting condescension on the part of male luminaries such as Yehuda Leib Gordon, Moshe Leib Lilienblum, Abraham Mapu, Reuven Brainin, Y. L. Peretz, and Menahem Gnessin, and of the challenge of determining what, exactly, it meant to live and work as a Russian Jewish woman writer in that period.

Balin's study devotes a chapter to each of her five subjects in turn. This format allows the reader to become absorbed in the personal history of each individual *maskelet* (enlightened woman), but it also raises the question—as Balin herself does—of whether a more organic history (what the author calls a 'composite biography') of female Russian Jewish writers could be written. Perhaps the result would be condescending, perhaps complimentary; in any case, Balin does not set out to take on this challenge. As she points out in her conclusion, personal histories tie her subjects together far more closely than does the nature of their prose. This might explain Balin's tendency to view her subjects' prose as an illustration of their private lives (or, as the book's title suggests, their hearts) rather than as something larger. And yet one cannot help but feel that such fascinating and unusual private lives have the potential to alter the way we understand the Haskalah, Russian Jewish culture, and modern Russian society as a whole.

In any case, the act of being representative may be too awesome a responsibility to assign to any historical figure; certainly, as others have argued, it is a standard with which scholars of women's history are unfairly saddled. Balin's study provides the reader with a rare glimpse into the lives of five extraordinary Russian Jewish women. Precisely because of the unusual texture of their lives, *To Reveal Our Hearts* makes fascinating reading.

SARAH ABREVAYA STEIN
Department of History,
Henry M. Jackson School of International Studies,
University of Washington

DOV LEVIN

The Litvaks: A Short History of the Jews in Lithuania

(Jerusalem: Yad Vashem, 2000); pp. 282

The history of the Jews in Lithuania has been the subject of an increasing number of publications in recent years. In most cases, the authors do not deal with the subject directly but approach it rather through one or another topic in the fields of politics, social life, and so on. However, 'Jewish' history is still discussed separately from the general history and historiography of Lithuania. The 'cold war' in scholarship continues, and as a result the research developed through several decades in different countries remains to be integrated.

Dov Levin's extensive bibliography in the field qualifies him as an expert in the area of Lithuanian Jewry and Lithuanian history. His latest work, *The Litvaks: A Short History of the Jews in Lithuania*, is divided into four chapters. The first provides an overview of Lithuanian history. The second is devoted to Jewish history in Lithuania, with special focus on the period 1569–1918. The author covers the topics raised most frequently by students of Lithuanian Jewish history, including among many others Jewish economic and social status, Jewish self-government, and demographic change. He stresses autonomous Jewish life, the striving for Palestine, and 'the concern that Lithuanian Jewry experienced for Eretz Israel' (p. 101). The third chapter presents an overview of Jewish life in independent Lithuania during the inter-war years. Among other things, in this chapter the author describes Jewish politics in the newly born Lithuanian state and provides statistics on demographics, education, and culture. However, most of the chapter is devoted to a description of the Jewish parties of the times: the Zionists, the ultra-Orthodox, and the Folkist-Communist Camps. The events of the Soviet occupation and World War Two are covered in Chapter 4. Additionally, several pages are devoted to sketches and insights on post-war Lithuania.

In this short history, Levin attempts to provide the reader with a concise version of Jewish history in Lithuania. Unfortunately, the work is an example of the pitfalls of attempts to produce 'short' and hermetic versions of history. The book has little resemblance to modern scholarship, which would have integrated different visions and narratives of the Jewish ideologies popular at the time, and would have discussed the Lithuanian part of the story (or at least would have attempted to do so in presenting the history of a country that has had so much influence on the contemporary and past life of the Jews).

The narrative presents a one-sided version of the history: Lithuanian Jews are viewed ahistorically as having been, through the ages, nationalist, patriotic, and dedicated to contemporary ideologies. Thus Lithuanian Jewry, a minority people, becomes retrospectively a kind of Israel in Diaspora, a micro-cosmos of contemporary Israel. Levin claims, for example, that in the nineteenth century Lithuanian Jews used Hebrew *even for day-to-day communication* (p. 96). In the same way, he argues, the Jewish educational system was dominated by Hebrew-language education.

In the first volume of *Polin*, Jerzy Tomaszewski observed that a tradition had developed 'of treating the Jews as a kind of alien body within Polish society' ('Some Methodological Problems in the Study of Jewish History in Poland between the Two World Wars' (1986), 162). The article was critical primarily of scholarship produced in Poland. Levin's narrative shares the defects described by Tomaszewski. The Jews are shown in isolation from the surrounding society and as possessing a modern national consciousness. Such an approach ignores much recent research on the political and social history of Lithuanian Jewry. It ignores the political visions and cultural and social achievements of the Yiddish-speaking religious or leftist Jews of Lithuania, who constituted the majority in the pre-war years. It was their vision and culture that dominated the Jewish street in the inter-war period alongside the growing strength the Zionist camp. In addition, Levin bases his conclusions largely on the Israeli and Lithuanian secondary sources of the 1960s and 1970s. He ignores newer, more multi-faceted research based on primary sources by respected scholars in Lithuania, Poland, and the United States.

No wonder, then, that even Joshua Trigubov, the primary sponsor of this publication, notes modestly that: 'As to the Jewish situation between 1918 and 1939, my personal recollections differ somehow from those of Professor Dov Levin' (p. 250). Because of its ideological bias and subjectivity, Levin's work is not so much a scholarly monograph as an extended essay. He is above all interested in advancing a thesis and the factual material he adduces is employed for illustration rather than analysis and is often inaccurate. This seriously diminishes the value of the work as a short reference book on Lithuanian Jewry.

For example, Levin states that the Magdeburg Law for the inhabitants of the Karaite Trakai Quarter was promulgated in 1441 (p. 44), while the actual date is 1444 and the law was applied to Trakai, not only the Quarter. Vilna was not re-annexed on 30 October 1939 (p. 12) but on 10 October 1939. The Great Northern War did not take place between 1700 and 1715 (p. 26), but between 1700 and 1721. The ban on the Lithuanian press was lifted not in 1905 but on 7 May 1904 (p. 75). The Šiauliai organization was founded not in 1920 (p. 117), but in 1919. Lithuania declared its independence on 11 March 1990 and not in 1991 (p. 38). These are only a few of the many errors to be found in the book. The figures cited are also frequently inaccurate. Levin claims that 25,000 refugees (Polish and Jewish) fled to the Vilna region from Poland after the Polish defeat in 1939 (p. 35). However, the Red Cross registered only 12,000 Poles and 'assumed' that at most 7,000 Jews arrived in the Vilna region from Poland (the actual registration lists contained only 2,379 people). He claims that the Lithuanian army numbered about 50,000 men in the inter-war period (p. 34), but the actual size of the military barely exceeded 28,000 in 1935 and was at the same level in 1940. The Lithuanian army was at its largest in December 1920, with a total of 45,314 persons (including civilian employees).

Likewise, the description of events often includes incorrect information. Thus on page 76 Levin claims that Hirsh Lekert *assassinated* the provincial governor because he had ordered the beating of all Jewish participants in the 1 May demonstrations in 1902, while in fact the Russian governor got away slightly wounded. Further, the book contains stereotypical views that can no longer be sustained. For example, it states that the pogrom that broke out in Vilna on 29 October 1939 was incited by the Lithuanian police (p. 191). In fact, the event occurred despite the efforts of the police, as is accepted even by right-wing Polish historians. Similar in nature is the claim that, with the outbreak of war between the Nazis and the Soviets, 'the Lithuanian population in at least forty different towns and settlements brutally attacked and murdered their Jewish neighbours even before the German army reached them'. Such claims must be based on research and not on opinion. The history of such localities at the outbreak of war has been well researched by many academic institutions, including the Lithuanian State Jewish Museum. The facts and sequence of the events are well established and are bad enough without the need for exaggeration.

These errors have been chosen randomly as illustrations; similar statements, misinterpretations, and confusions in the sequence of events abound in the book. There are some evident *lapsus linguae*, such as the claim on page 48 that Vilijampolė is in Grodno province, while it is actually part of Kovno. Similarly, the Jews fleeing from Tsar Alexey are described as have taken a 'north-eastward' direction (p. 51), when in fact they fled northwest. In an equally careless fashion, Levin writes that 'the outbreak of war and the conquest of Lithuania by the German army left some 220,000 Lithuanian Jews under Soviet [*sic*] control' (p. 200).

There are some orthographic issues as well. For instance, what purpose does it serve to provide the Lithuanian-language equivalents of the Polish administrative terms originally used in the Polish–Lithuanian Commonwealth, such as *województwo* or *powiat* (*pviat* in the book), when Lithuanian translations of the terms emerged only at the end of the nineteenth and beginning of the twentieth centuries? Further, there is a great deal of inconsistency in the use of place names. Sometimes Vilnius is Vilna, Samogitia is Zamut, Kovno is Kaunas, and so forth.

Lastly, the pictures in the book have no relevance to the text, especially when the author discusses pre-modern times. The visual materials are predominantly from the inter-war period, and this greatly diminishes the book's emotional and visual appeal.

Ultimately, there are positive aspects to the publication of a book with so many inaccuracies and mistakes. It teaches us the lesson that scholarship does not stand still and that past discoveries very quickly become the mistakes of today.

SARUNAS LIEKIS
University of Vilnius

BENJAMIN NATHANS

Beyond the Pale: The Jewish Encounter with Late Imperial Russia

(Berkeley: University of California Press, 2002); pp. xviii + 424

Students of the modernization of nineteenth-century Russian Jewry have generally concentrated on the Jews of the Pale of Settlement and the Congress Kingdom of Poland, an area that was home to 4.9 million Jews in 1897, 94 per cent of the empire's Jewish population. In structuring their work, some have identified the Russian government as the engine of change that drove the community to modernity, while others have looked to those emerging intellectual currents and non-traditional perspectives within the community that challenged authority and welcomed modernity. Another group of scholars have focused on the radical political ideologies that emerged within the community as a way of documenting a modern political consciousness that strove for emancipation and civic equality for all. Finally, some writers have drawn our attention to Jewish experiences in the rapidly developing urban settings, the location they identify as the laboratory where modernity should be studied.

In this book Benjamin Nathans treats the experiences of those Jews permitted to settle in the historic heartland of Russia in the second half of the nineteenth century. Since the Reform Era policies of Alexander II brought with them a new approach to the Jews of the empire, Nathans directs our attention to the impact of these changes on Jewish life after 1856. He is quick to note that since Alexander II did not change any of the social or political structures of Russia, the transformations studied here fell far short of the emancipation experienced by Jews in western and central Europe. In Russia these ameliorations touched the lives of relatively few, only those able to take advantage of the new approach identified by Nathans as selective integration. Methodologically, then, this work falls into that category of scholarship that views official policy as driving Jewish change. However, unlike earlier studies using this approach, Nathans directs his attention to a community of Jews already prepared for change and especially eager to move out of an exclusively Jewish orbit and to participate in the new Russia being created in the post-Crimean era. While the author's insights and conclusions are extended broadly to Jewish life in those areas of residence opened to Jews since 1859, the principal target of his observations is the new and growing Jewish community of St Petersburg.

This study is systematic and thorough. Nathans offers readers both a demographic and a cultural survey of St Petersburg Jewry. He describes a community that, while Russifying linguistically, was not necessarily integrating physically and culturally. In fact, Nathans discerns the emergence of a distinctive Russian Jewish subculture in the capital city, thereby challenging the expectations of those policymakers who anticipated full and complete Jewish assimilation into Russian life as a by-product of selective integration. The chapters on education, especially at university level, and the legal profession are particularly rich and illuminate patterns of Jewish integration and self-definition.

Since a university degree offered professional and residential opportunities, it became the object of Jewish efforts in the early 1860s, testifying to the Jewish acceptance of the quid pro quo being offered by the tsarist government. Nathans documents this magnetic pull of the university on both Jewish men and women, noting that nearly 15 per cent of students in the heartland in the mid-1880s were of Jewish origin. (The percentage in universities situated within the Pale was even higher.) The fact that the Russian *studenchestvo* was, unlike the case in contemporary Germany and Austria, free of explicit anti-Jewish expressions, made the university, generally, a comfortable environment for Jewish youth in the age of Alexander II. The depiction here of that university experience reminds us of Jacob Katz's introduction of the concept of the neutral or semi-neutral society in his own presentations of German Jewish life at the close of the eighteenth century. However, the imposition of a quota system on Jewish enrolments in 1887, both within and outside of the Pale, served notice that after thirty years the government was abandoning the path of selective integration.

The creation of an autonomous judiciary in 1864 proved to be extremely attractive to many contemporary Jewish young people, too. Nathans finds that, by the mid-1880s, 13 per cent of the empire's lawyers were Jewish, and in St Petersburg 21 per cent of the city's lawyers were of Jewish origin. This new reality and the growing number of Jewish students preparing for careers in law created a backlash within the profession that led to later self-regulatory practices meant to identify and restrict non-Christian attorneys. Here, too, we are offered evidence of a broader retreat from selective integration not just within governmental circles but within that segment of civil society that should have been committed to the ideals of equal opportunity and individual mobility. However, since these reversals came after more than a quarter of a century of Jewish acceptance of a new relationship with the larger society, they hit a Jewish community that had been unalterably transformed in the interim.

The discussion of the law in this analysis goes beyond the number of Jews in the legal profession. Nathans also explores the importance of the law as a tool used by a new cadre of Jewish leaders in order to combat discrimination, to seek redress for victims of assault, and to delineate a conception of citizenship and identity that fused Russianness with Jewishness. Nathans introduces readers to the career of Genrykh Sliozberg, the exemplar of the Jewish advocate articulating a vision of a harmonious Russian–Jewish coexistence. In Sliozberg, Nathans has found the individual who brings together all of the threads of this story: here is a modern, educated St Petersburg Jewish lawyer denied the right to practise and thus forced to turn to Jewish defence, and thereby moved to construct a future reality in which individuals such as himself could find self-realization and fulfilment in Russia.

Benjamin Nathans has written an important and creative book. It is methodologically sophisticated and based on archival research buttressed by a commanding control of a wide-ranging set of secondary and published sources. He has addressed and grappled with large and important questions that explore the experiences of Russian Jewry, and he relates that story to key issues of modern Jewish life and the nature of its evolution. We are indebted to him for his effort.

ALEXANDER ORBACH
University of Pittsburgh

YEKHEZKEL KOTIK

Journey to a Nineteenth-Century Shtetl: The Memoirs of Yekhezkel Kotik

EDITED BY
DAVID ASSAF

TRANSLATED BY
MARGARET BIRSTEIN

(Detroit: Wayne State University Press, 2002); pp. 540

This first volume of Yekhezkel Kotik's memoirs presents a fascinating and informative picture of shtetl life in the period around 1860. Kotik (1847–1941) is an excellent storyteller who graphically describes his family, his town of Kamenets, and life in the province of Grodno. First published in Yiddish in 1913 as *Mayne zikhroynes* ('My Memoirs'), this English translation by Margaret Birstein has been supplemented by David Assaf's masterful notes.

Kotik depicts many facets of everyday life in the nineteenth-century shtetl such as business, Jewish education, religious life, home life, dealings with the Polish nobles, and secular leanings. The inner conflicts between the hasidim and the mitnagedim take on special significance for Kotik, because his father joined the small circle of hasidim in Kamenets. He also gives accounts of broader historical events such as the liberation of the serfs and the Polish revolt of 1863.

A reader who has only vague notions of how Jews worked for Polish nobles has much to gain from this book. Kotik's grandfather was a powerful community leader who worked with the local estate owners, held leases on their properties and on vodka sales, and sometimes became involved in their personal affairs. According to Kotik, Lord Sihowski attended a family wedding and 'went into raptures over Shepsl's [klezmer] music, maintaining that he'd never heard the likes of it during his entire life' (p. 276); after that occasion, 'Shepsl and two other players would perform four times a year at the balls given by the Sihowskis for the surrounding gentry' (p. 276).

Kotik is highly critical of the traditional Jewish education he received. The *ḥeder* education seems to have been dominated by rote learning, legends, and whippings. His father—more concerned that he become a God-fearing hasid than that he receive a rigorous training—opposed his wish to study at the famous yeshiva in Volozhin.

Among the many customs Kotik describes are the exorcism of a dybbuk (p. 231) and cholera weddings[1] at the cemetery (p. 383).

Perhaps the most horrific chapter describes the press-gangs (*khapers*; lit. 'kidnappers') who were sent to capture young boys for military service. Yiddish readers may be familiar with a comic portrayal of this phenomenon in S. Y. Abramovitsh's *The Brief Travels of Benjamin the Third* (1878). During the Crimean War (1853–6) 8-year-old boys were conscripted, and the sordid reality of this practice is the subject of chapter 9, which tells how Kotik's friend Yosele was kidnapped by a press-gang. When the townspeople caught sight of him again, 'his face was swollen and pale, like that of a corpse. . . . He had become like a log' (p. 236).

Yet David Assaf points out that Kotik's memoirs focus more on the consequences of modernization than on catastrophic events. Unlike post-Holocaust memoirists, Kotik 'did not view his past through the threatening storm of physical destruction' (p. 70).

Kotik tells anecdotes that make it easier to visualize well-known historical events. For example, he describes how the liberation of the serfs was announced in 1861:

On Sunday at twelve noon, when the market was teeming with peasants, the *ispravnik* [district chief of police] . . . read the proclamation out to them.

[1] It was believed that a wedding of young people in a cemetery could halt the progress of a cholera epidemic.

After hearing the proclamation, the peasants went home and refused to work, although, according to the proclamation, they were supposed to do so until the end of the summer. They didn't want to wait until then, and, since the lord was forbidden to flog them, they instigated a revolt. (p. 340)

Kotik then explains how this development impoverished both the estate owners and the Jews. Next he turns to the Polish rebellion of 1863, which made matters even more difficult for the Jewish inhabitants of Kamenets. Although he is not entirely reliable with regard to historical details, Kotik makes up for this in vivid portrayals of the conflict.

Kotik writes at length about the internal Jewish conflict between the dominant mitnagedim and the emerging hasidim of Kamenets. He points out that, in traditional rabbinic Judaism, prestige was measured by 'lineage of wealth and lineage of learning' (p. 400). Hence 'the penniless and the illiterate felt degraded and humiliated by their treatment in the synagogues and study houses', whereas 'to the simple Jew Hasidism brought genuine happiness. He became worthy' (pp. 400, 406). Yet Kotik himself was put off by the hasidic adulation of the *rebbe*; moreover, he was shocked by the poverty and hunger among hasidic families, in which the men seemed unconcerned about the fate of their wives and children (p. 409). The conflict touches close to home when Kotik recalls how his father fought his decision to leave hasidism.

This English translation by Margaret Birstein (edited by Sharon Makover-Assaf) reads well. The notes and bibliography by David Assaf greatly enrich the text by providing explanatory materials and some critical commentary. Assaf does not blindly accept Kotik's assertions, which sometimes seem hyperbolic. For example, he provides historical data indicating that Kotik's statements suggesting that there was a sharp rise in the divorce rate between the 1860s and the 1890s are inaccurate (p. 475 n. 14).

David Frishman once wrote that, if 'some flood came over the world and effaced from the earth the entire universe of Jewish street life', S. Y. Abramovitsh's fictional works could help a researcher reconstruct that world. It would seem, however, that Kotik's memoirs could serve an equally important role in such a reconstruction.

Kotik's memoirs should contribute to a more thorough understanding of shtetl life in the second half of the nineteenth century. In doing so, this book provides a welcome antidote to shtetl nostalgia and kitsch.

KEN FRIEDEN
Syracuse University

PUAH RAKOVSKY

My Life as a Radical Jewish Woman: Memoirs of a Zionist Feminist in Poland

EDITED BY

PAULA E. HYMAN

TRANSLATED BY

BARBARA HARSHAV

(Bloomington: Indiana University Press, 2002); pp. xii + 204

My Life as a Radical Jewish Woman is a fascinating account of the life of Puah Rakovsky (1865–1955), pioneering educator of Jewish girls, ardent feminist, Zionist activist, and role model for the 'New Jewish Woman' of the late nineteenth and early twentieth centuries. An excellent introduction and the editorial notes throughout the text place the personal life and political activities of this revolutionary Jewish woman in historical context and supply the reader with insights that help to illuminate the traditional world of east European Jewry, the impact of the Haskalah on women, and the development of the Zionist movement. By making this work available to a broad audience, Paula Hyman has made a very important contribution to the scholarship on east European Jewish women.

Previously available to English readers only as excerpts entitled 'A Mind of My Own' in Lucy Dawidowicz's anthology *The Golden Tradition: Jewish Life and Thought in Eastern Europe* (Boston, 1967), this rich memoir, originally written in Yiddish in Palestine in 1942, is a welcome addition to the growing collection of European Jewish women's memoirs. Organized both chronologically and topically and ably translated by Barbara Harshav, *My Life as a Radical Jewish Woman* reads very well and serves as a valuable introduction to the life and times of a remarkable Jewish woman. It deserves to become a staple of all courses dealing with Jewish women's history and should find its rightful place in personal as well as institutional libraries.

In both her private and her public life Puah Rakovsky protested against the social and cultural conventions of her day to become an independent and self-supporting woman with a strong secular Jewish identity. Born in Białystok in 1865, she was the eldest daughter in a large traditional family but received an unusually good Jewish as well as secular education. Although her parents would not allow her to attend gymnasium, she continued her studies privately, learning Hebrew, French, and German, as well as Russian. She criticized rabbis for not allowing girls to study Torah, and was very aware of explicit gender roles within the Jewish community. After entering into an arranged marriage against her will and bearing a son at the age of 17 and a daughter at 20, Rakovsky rebelled and decided to become a teacher so that she could support herself and her children. Threatening to convert to Christianity, she finally managed to get a divorce and find a job teaching Hebrew in Warsaw. She would later experience a brief companionate marriage, widowhood, and a long-time partnership with a younger man, with whom she bore another daughter. In her description of her early years in Russian Poland, Rakovsky explores many crucial issues relating to Jewish family life, marital relations, and gender roles, as well as the problems inherent in arranged marriages, divorce, motherhood, and relationships between men and women.

Much of the memoir deals with Puah Rakovsky's struggles to become and remain financially independent and to support her children and later her grandchildren. She always stressed the vital importance of educating girls and teaching them a trade in order to liberate them. For many years before the First World War, she ran her own school for girls, with Russian as the language of instruction but teaching subjects in Hebrew as well; she also organized and directed summer boarding schools for Jewish children in the countryside. Her elder children and her partner, whom she refers to as Comrade Birnbaum, often taught in her schools and camps. Her home in Warsaw was a haven for her extended family and friends, many of whom were involved in illegal socialist activities.

During the inter-war years Rakovsky earned her livelihood largely by working for Jewish women's and Zionist organizations, including ORT, the Jewish Women's Association (YFA), and the Palestine Office in Poland, as well as by doing translations into Yiddish. It is both sad and ironic that a woman who began her career as a successful Hebrew educator in Poland ended her days barely eking out a living as a Yiddish translator for the Jewish Agency in Palestine after making *aliyah* in 1935, at the age of 70.

Very much aware of the marginalization of women within the Jewish community and its organizations, Puah Rakovsky worked hard on behalf of women's rights in Russia, Poland, and Palestine and was actively involved in both the World Zionist Organization (WZO) and the Women's International Zionist Organization (WIZO), attending several Zionist Congresses. Although a socialist Zionist, affiliated with the left-of-centre Tse'irei Zion (Youth of Zion), and often sympathetic to the Soviet Union, she was a bourgeois feminist who strongly believed in the need for separate women's organizations to fight for women's education, women's suffrage, and equality for women. This memoir describes in considerable depth the activities of various Jewish women's and Zionist organizations in Poland with which Rakovsky was involved. It also sheds light on the ideological differences and personal relationships among Zionists, Bundists, and communists in the early twentieth century.

During her long life Puah Rakovsky experienced many personal losses and hardships; she lived through pogroms not only in Russia and Poland, but also in Palestine in 1921, but she had the courage of her convictions and fought for what she believed was right. As a lifelong Zionist, she opted to make *aliyah* twice, settling permanently in Palestine in 1935, even though she often despaired of the future of the Jewish homeland. *My Life as a Radical Jewish Woman* is an inspiring memoir chronicling the trials and tribulations of a remarkable individual and helping us understand east European Jewish history from a Zionist feminist perspective. It is a wonderful resource for both the general reader and the specialist, and should become essential reading on the syllabus of all courses in modern Jewish history.

HARRIET FREIDENREICH
Temple University

MARC B. SHAPIRO

Between the Yeshiva World and Modern Orthodoxy: The Life and Works of Rabbi Jehiel Jacob Weinberg, 1884–1966

(London: Littman Library of Jewish Civilization, 1999); pp. viii + 284

Jehiel Jacob Weinberg is not exactly a household name in most Jewish circles. His halakhic writings have had some impact, and some of his writings about the Musar movement have attracted attention. However, his influence on halakhah or *musar* is limited. During the pre-Holocaust years Rabbi Weinberg was an important figure in German Orthodoxy. However, he spent much of his lifetime successfully avoiding the limelight. After the war he lived in relative obscurity in Switzerland, even though he was held in high regard in rabbinical circles in Israel and elsewhere.

However, with this brilliant biography by Marc Shapiro, the life of Rabbi Weinberg has become a key to understanding some of the more complex and misunderstood issues of modern Jewish history, including the process of modernization in eastern Europe and the appearance of modern Orthodoxy. This book is required reading for anyone who deals with these topics and should make the complicated and tragic story of Rabbi Weinberg's life known to a wide audience who otherwise would never have come across his Hebrew writings. Luckily for the students who will be assigned the book, it is wonderfully written, with a sense of both drama and human sensitivity. It will be hard to put down even if it is required reading.

Rabbi Weinberg was born in 1884 and studied in the famous *musar* yeshiva of Slobodka. While studying in the yeshiva he developed an interest in general studies. This was quite typical of young men of his generation. Somewhat less typical was the attachment of the head of the yeshiva to Rabbi Weinberg. As a student and later as a young rabbi, Weinberg was constantly examining developments both in the traditionalist camp and among the modernists. At this stage he was already attracted to the model of German Orthodoxy. Here Shapiro's analysis of Weinberg's changing views on secular knowledge is sensitive and enlightening. This is one of the few analyses I know of that detail how a young, committed traditionalist in eastern Europe dealt with the challenges of modern thought.

It is not just Rabbi Weinberg's treatment of intellectual issues that attracts attention. Shapiro's account of Weinberg's unhappy marriage is also very significant. Weinberg was pressured into entering into a very incompatible marriage as a condition of a rabbinical appointment; after much foot-dragging, the marriage ended in divorce. At this point Shapiro makes one of the few points on which I disagree with him. He shares the widely held view that 'divorce was very uncommon in traditional Lithuanian Jewish society, and among members of the rabbinate it was unheard of'. This may have been the case at the beginning of the twentieth century, but half a century earlier divorce was very common in almost every circle and certainly among rabbis. For example, Rabbi Joseph Soloveitchik of Volozhin was divorced as a youth, while Rabbi Berlin of the same yeshiva married a divorcee in his second marriage.

The outbreak of the First World War found Rabbi Weinberg in Berlin, where he had been seeking medical treatment. He remained there for the duration of the war and, after its end, began to study at the University of Giessen. Many former students of the Slobodka yeshiva had gone on to academic study, though almost none did so while maintaining standing in Orthodox society. Rabbi Weinberg took a position as a lecturer in Jewish studies in Giessen, teaching both Jews and non-Jews. This appeared to violate a rabbinic prohibition against the teaching of Torah to non-Jews even though there were many precedents for it. However, Weinberg issued one of the responsa that made him a well-known figure in modern Orthodox circles and an anomaly in rabbinic circles. In it he claimed that the rabbinic prohibition against the teaching of Torah to non-Jews did not apply when this teaching was academic in nature. From Giessen, Weinberg went on to teach at the Rabbiner Seminar zu Berlin, the Orthodox rabbinical seminary that had been founded by Rabbi Hildesheimer.

Rabbi Weinberg remained in Berlin almost until the outbreak of the Second World War. He was at first optimistic that the Nazi regime would not harm the Jews, and later became deeply involved in the efforts to preserve *sheḥitah* (the kosher slaughtering of animals for meat) and the rabbinical seminary itself. He took an active role in the Jewish intellectual revival that took place in the last years before the Holocaust. His Lithuanian citizenship saved his life: classified as a Soviet citizen, he survived the war in a special German camp for Soviet prisoners.

After the war Rabbi Weinberg settled in Switzerland and taught at the small yeshiva in Montreux. He carried on a prolific correspondence with other scholars and carefully followed developments in the Jewish world. However, he did not take upon himself a leadership role.

Rabbi Weinberg was a man of great potential, but of limited achievement—in part due to the course of events and in part due to his personality. What, then, makes this such an important and valuable study? In writing this biography and assessment of the works of Rabbi Weinberg, Shapiro has undertaken to provide a deep analysis of the nature of east European Orthodoxy and its counterpart, Western neo-Orthodoxy, as well as the complex attitudes of Orthodox circles and individuals towards modern methods of study. These are exceptionally complicated issues and Shapiro deals with them with remarkable clarity, precision, and comprehensiveness. The result is a book that is far more than the biography of a tragic individual. It delivers what it promises: a profound analysis of the world of the east European yeshiva and the varieties of modern Orthodoxy. That he manages to accomplish this in a very readable fashion is an achievement that the casual reader will appreciate without ever realizing how different it could have been. The book contains lucid analyses of Rabbi Weinberg's views on a number of significant halakhic issues. Here, as well, Shapiro takes very complex topics, provides the necessary context for assessing Weinberg's responsa, and enables a reader with a limited halakhic background to appreciate both the halakhic problematic and the novelty (or lack of novelty) in Weinberg's response.

One additional point that deserves comment has to do with Shapiro's moral approach to historical writing. The fact that this topic is often overlooked does not mean that it is unimportant. In preparing this study, Shapiro had access to many personal papers that Rabbi Weinberg never intended to publish. In the hands of a less sensitive writer they could easily have been used—or, to be more precise, abused—as material for scandalmongering or sensationalism. Shapiro uses these sources and develops the potential in them without cheapening either Rabbi Weinberg or the individuals referred to in the sources. This book could easily be used as a model in a course on the ethics of historical writing—just as the works of some critics of historical studies can be taken as models of scurrilous and unethical writing.

Between the Yeshiva World and Modern Orthodoxy is a book that is a pleasure to read and that deserves to be read. It is serious without being heavy, and enlightening without being preachy. It is a crucial introduction to the inter-war religious life both of east European Jewry and of German Jewry, and provides unique insights into religious thought in Palestine–Israel. It deals with history and halakhic thought in a thoroughly integrated fashion, and has much to offer both to the reader who was previously familiar with Weinberg's works and to the reader with no background in Jewish studies. It is an admirable book.

SHAUL STAMPFER
Hebrew University of Jerusalem

SHIMON FROST

Schooling as a Socio-Political Expression: Jewish Education in Interwar Poland

(Jerusalem: Magnes Press, 1998); pp. 176

According to informal data, approximately half a million Jewish children of school age lived in Poland during the 1930s. One-third of these children attended private Jewish schools. At first glance 180,000 seems like a small number. This group of Jewish pupils becomes more significant, however, when we consider, on the one hand, that the Polish government did almost nothing to fulfil its obligation to support Jewish (and other minority) education and schools, and, on the other hand, the existence of a whole network of public schools for sabbath observers (*szabasówki*). While the authorities fully subsidized the public schools for Jews, private Jewish schools were provided with only a 'one-time allocation in the [symbolic] sum of 45,000 zloty granted in 1927' (p. 25). Jewish private schools thus had to depend on local Jewish communities, donations from abroad, and tuition fees. Bearing in mind the rapid impoverishment that Polish Jews experienced during this time, the existence of a network of private Jewish schools becomes even more remarkable. Knowing that upon graduation their children would have to pass the state's matriculation exams in order to continue their studies, these parents chose to demonstrate their commitment to the Jewish community. Even the arbitrary closing of Jewish schools by the authorities under all kinds of pretexts did not stop them (the most common pretexts were that the teachers were communists, the curriculum was subversive, or the physical conditions of the school were substandard).

Approximately 55 per cent of the children attending Jewish schools received a traditional education. These schools operated, for the most part, under the auspices of the Agudat Yisrael party, which also did pioneering work in formal education for girls in the form of the Beit Yaakov schools. About one-quarter of all Jewish pupils attended the Zionist-oriented Hebrew Tarbut schools, making it the largest Jewish secular education network. The largest secular Yiddish (i.e. socialist) educational network was Tsisho, identified with the Bund and the left Poalei Zion parties, which attracted 9.5 per cent of the children attending Jewish schools. Other children attended the Zionist Orthodox Yavneh network (8.5 per cent) and the bilingual ('bourgeois') network, Shul-kult (less than 0.5 per cent). For gymnasiums and high schools, the proportions were completely different: only some 6–6.7 per cent of the students attended the small number of high schools in which the language of instruction was either Hebrew or Yiddish. Others attended private schools that declared themselves to be Jewish but used Polish as the language of instruction and offered very little, if anything, that was Jewish in their curriculum.

All of this well-known information is put into a new perspective in the late

Shimon Frost's book. Dr Frost, an educator in his own right, sheds new light on the impressive Jewish school network in the Second Polish Republic. Frost preferred to divide the types of schools by language, rather than by political inclination, into the following categories: schools with Hebrew or Yiddish as the language of instruction; bilingual schools (Polish–Hebrew or Polish–Yiddish), in which all subjects were taught in Polish with the exception of Jewish topics; and private Jewish schools offering the full Polish state curriculum including a course in Jewish religion, as required by Polish law, with an occasional smattering of instruction in prayer-book Hebrew (p. 34). Frost did not view the last type as Jewish in any sense, but as an agent for encouraging acculturation and assimilation.

Frost's book is divided into eight chapters. The first focuses on the fruitless struggle of Polish Jews for recognition as a national minority under the Minority Rights Treaty, which Poland had been forced to sign in 1919. The second chapter, based on sources, some better known than others, including some general and particular statistics, draws a vivid picture of the different school networks. Since both Jewish education and Jewish cultural activities were strongly bound to politics and politicians, Frost devotes the third chapter to a concise review of the various ideological concepts upon which each of the educational systems was founded.

In the fourth chapter Frost describes the state school system (both general and Jewish) on the basis of the Revised National Education Act of March 1932, beginning with pre-school levels, various types of elementary school (grades 1–6), the gymnasium (grades 7–10), and the lyceum (grades 11–12). Polish law required that each school include a certain number of hours of instruction in various subjects, and each Jewish school network integrated Polish state requirements into its own curriculum. To illustrate how these schools coped with the situation, Frost provides detailed information on the curricula of different school systems. He includes the Jewish gymnasiums, for which the information in previous publications was quite limited, and emphasizes the significance of the Beit Yaakov network. Setting up the curriculum was not an easy task: because the curriculum had to reflect the school's exclusivity, the issue received much attention and was the subject of many debates that are discussed in the fifth chapter. In the Tsisho network, among the questions raised were the meaning of 'nationalism' and the importance of teaching Hebrew and the Bible; significant differences in approach appeared between the central Poland and the Vilna branches of the network. Similar differences of opinion occurred within the Tarbut network regarding the use of Yiddish and the meaning of prayer in a secular school. On the other hand, Agudat Yisrael thinkers and politicians had to clarify for themselves their attitude towards general studies.

The sixth and seventh chapters are devoted to a subject that has been relatively neglected until now. In them Frost examines educational theory and values education by analysing a variety of statements, evaluations, and deeds in the field of Jewish education. He shows that Jewish educational theory reflected a broad interest in Polish pedagogy and was strongly influenced by contemporary Western educational and psychological methods. Because 'the typical Jewish school in inter-war Poland, irrespective of ideological orientation, was not a knowledge-dispensing agency but sought to educate the total child' (p. 147), each school system aimed to impart its own Jewish (religious, national, and/or cultural) and general human values to the young generation—the leaders of the future. Ideologists and educators were constantly seeking the proper pedagogic and didactic methods for achieving such a goal. Frost writes, 'It was a total commitment and an active/direct involvement in the pursuit of a particular ideological/educational goal. As these leaders of all nuances on the ideological spectrum state repeatedly, an education worthy of its name cannot be neutral' (p. 132).

The last chapter reviews some of the achievements of the young and vibrant Jewish schools and tries to find links between them and post-Second World War Western Jewish school systems. Although there was some influence, one must not ignore the uniqueness of the Polish context, in which the Jewish educational system was not just a tool for 'socializing' children into ideological and cultural norms but a manifestation of autonomous Jewish cultural life in a place where Jews' civil rights were constantly violated.

Despite the lack of any discussion of the role of youth movements in the Jewish educational system, as well as the absence of reference to the evening school networks that operated throughout the country, Shimon Frost's book reveals important aspects of the Jewish educational system in Poland and is a most important contribution to research on Jewish cultural life in inter-war Poland. One hopes that this new study will encourage more research on the topic and lead to a comprehensive work on this key issue in our understanding of the history of Polish Jewry in the inter-war period.

NATHAN COHEN
Bar-Ilan University

JEFFREY SHANDLER (ED.)

Awakening Lives: Autobiographies of Jewish Youth in Poland Before the Holocaust

INTRODUCED BY
BARBARA KIRSHENBLATT-GIMBLETT, MARCUS MOSELEY, AND MICHAEL STANISLAWSKI

(New Haven: Yale University Press in co-operation with the YIVO Institute for Jewish Research, 2002); pp. lii + 438

In 1932, 1934, and 1939 the Yidisher Visntshaftlekher Institut (YIVO) in Vilna organized three contests inviting young people to submit their autobiographies.

The organizers' aim was to document the lives of Polish Jewish youth and to gather sources for the planned sociological studies called *Yugnt forshung*, with a selection of sources to be published.

The project, an independent initiative of YIVO, was similar to projects being undertaken at that time by the Instytut Gospodarstwa Społecznego (Institute for Social Economy) in Warsaw, as well as other institutions that held autobiography contests for various social groups (the unemployed, emigrants, peasants, etc.), and published their works before 1939. (Three further volumes of emigrants' memoirs were published much later, in 1971 and 1977.) I do not agree, therefore, with the authors of the introduction that the YIVO autobiographies 'were gathered in the most unusual manner' (p. xi). At that time the YIVO autobiography contest was one of several such projects in Poland.

However, there was one unusual aspect to the YIVO contests: no such projects were carried out by other national minorities in Poland. Historians therefore have a unique opportunity not only to acquaint themselves with the fates, feelings, and views of young Jews living in Poland before 1939, but also to gain insight into the life of an important section of inter-war Poland's national minorities. A significant feature of these autobiographies was that the majority of authors described their families, often giving basic facts concerning the lives of their parents, and I am deeply convinced that they are of the utmost importance not only to Jewish historians but to Polish scholars as well.

In the three contests, YIVO received a total of 627 autobiographies. The institute specified a minimum length of twenty-five pages, but there was no maximum, and the longest manuscript was some 800 pages long. Unfortunately, it was impossible to publish the autobiographies before 1939 and a significant portion of them was lost during the war, but 350 manuscripts were reclaimed after 1945 by YIVO's New York branch. Thirty-nine more were received in the 1990s, together with other archival collections, after Lithuania regained independence. A committee chaired by Marcus Moseley reviewed the documents, and a small selection of them, consisting of fifteen autobiographies by girls and boys between 17 and 23 years of age, was prepared for printing. The originals, written in Polish, Yiddish, or Hebrew, were carefully translated into English.

Awakening Lives contains only a small portion of the real treasures preserved in YIVO and it would be risky to draw any general conclusions about Jewish youth in inter-war Poland from the fifteen autobiographies that appear in the book. Furthermore, a reader who has no opportunity to become acquainted with the whole collection cannot appreciate the principles of the selection. However, regardless of any possible criticism, *Awakening Lives* is a valuable collection that can be a useful aid to understanding Jewish life in Poland.

The introduction stresses that these documents of individual lives call into question the idealized picture that includes the traditional Jewish family living in harmony in an atmosphere of mutual help in a shtetl. One significant value of the collection is that its authors came from families of various religious and political views and expressed a range of attitudes towards these issues. Most often, however, they were critical of existing social relations. A striking feature of *Awakening Lives* is that all but one of the autobiographies were written by poor or very poor people, some of whom survived difficult times as beggars. It would be useful to know whether this proportion corresponds to that of the entire group of contestants. In any case it would be unsafe to conclude that the socio-economic structure of the group of respondents more or less accurately represented the structure of Jewish youth in Poland. A more probable explanation is that those whose living conditions were very harsh were most likely to write autobiographies: they may have hoped to receive some money (YIVO promised small prizes for the best autobiographies), or perhaps they simply felt the need to take advantage of the anonymity of the contest to vent their sorrows, even on questions that were strictly personal. Those who were in a relatively good situation and were employed may have been less inclined to sacrifice their free time in such a way. Even so, this collection is important for historians who are able to understand properly its flaws and advantages and to use it critically as a historical source. This is the case particularly where it would be difficult to find equally reliable archival sources; for example, in research on the attitude of the police towards Jews, especially relating to the question of bribes.

The autobiographies are preceded by an introduction that will serve as an excellent aid to scholars and laymen who are interested in the everyday lives of young Polish Jews. It includes basic information on YIVO and explains the history of the contests and the *Yugnt forshung* project led by Max Weinreich. In addition, it describes the social, political, and intellectual atmosphere that influenced scholars and society at large in Poland before 1939. The comments of those who are familiar with both the published and the unpublished autobiographies are integral. The autobiographies are supplemented by notes that include, where possible, basic data on towns mentioned in the text, although the names of the towns in which the authors lived remained secret. They also contain explanations of words, places, and events, and quotations from the Bible and other sources alluded to in the text. Several researchers mentioned in the book helped to compile this supplementary information. There are also separate lists of persons and organizations, together with a glossary of foreign words and terms.

I have found only two errors. A *feldsher* was not a 'traditional healer, who use[d] folk remedies instead of modern medical treatment' (p. 434), but a kind of medical assistant with secondary vocational education. Older *feldsher*s often had vast medical experience that they had gained in practice. In addition, the Jewish use of the word 'Greens' (Polish: Zieloni) to refer to the National Democrats did not derive from the Polish slang for 'ignoramus' (p. 413): there existed in Poland the so-called Liga Zielonej Wstążki, the League of the Green Ribbon, an association inspired by radical nationalists who organized boycotts of Jewish shops. The word *zieloni* has a second meaning closer to the American word 'greenhorns'. These two errors are nonetheless minor compared to the important contribution that *Awakening Lives* makes to the literature on Polish Jewry between the two world wars.

Another collection of autobiographies has also been published in Poland: *Ostatnie pokolenie: Autobiografie polskiej młodzieży żydowskiej okresu międzywojennego ze zbiorów YIVO Institute for Jewish Research w Nowym Jorku. Opracowała i wstępem opatrzyła A. Cała* (Warsaw, 2003). The book comprises twenty texts, of which sixteen were written in Polish and four in Yiddish (translated into Polish by Michał Friedman). Fourteen were not included in the American edition.

JERZY TOMASZEWSKI
Warsaw University

JANUSZ BARDACH AND KATHLEEN GLEESON

Surviving Freedom: After the Gulag

(Berkeley and Los Angeles: University of California Press, 2003); pp. xiii + 252

In recent years the number of memoirs devoted to surviving the Gulag has soared. However, the vast majority of memoirists devote only a few pages to their experiences after the Gulag. It was enormously difficult to adjust to a relatively free life outside Soviet prisons and camps: not only were former prisoners made to sign a document stating that they would never 'disclose any information about places of confinement', but they had to fit into the very system that had put them into a prison or camp. In his memoirs *Surviving Freedom: After the Gulag*, Janusz Bardach focuses on the years immediately following his release from the Gulag in August 1945.

He did not arrive in Moscow until March 1946 since it was almost impossible, even for a free man, to leave Kolyma—the ship from Vladivostok was booked a year in advance and Bardach had to bribe the pilot of a commercial plane to fly to Khabarovsk, where he bought an onward ticket to Moscow. Bardach's elder brother Julek, a high-ranking diplomat in the Polish embassy, who had been instrumental in his release from the Gulag, helped Bardach to settle in the city. One of the first things Julek did was to have Bardach's Polish citizenship reinstated: no longer a Soviet citizen and an ex-convict, he was now a 'respectable foreigner'. Although Polish citizenship did not give Bardach any immunity against the Soviet authorities, he gained some privileges that put him above the daily lot of an ordinary Soviet citizen. In his own words, 'Being a Polish citizen I felt safe, but not safe enough to quell my fear of being rearrested again and sent back to Kolyma' (p. 210).

Bardach had to conceal his past imprisonments from both Polish embassy staff and Soviet acquaintances. He also had to learn to live with his newly invented life story. If the transition from the barracks of the Gulag to the life in the Polish embassy, with its receptions, official dinners, and social events, wasn't hard enough, the news that his family, including his wife, had perished in the Holocaust shattered the foundations of his self-identity. So hard was the truth that he had to go back to his native town of Vladimir in Volhynia to convince himself that indeed nobody had survived and there was no return to his pre-war life.

Bardach describes his bitter loneliness among free people. In the camps, life had been unbearably hard, but his friendships there 'were the strongest [he] had ever known' (p. 173). In Moscow he was alone among strangers: he had never been close to his brother and he did not have any close friends. He entered the Moskovsky Institut Stomatologii (Medical Stomatological Institute) in Moscow without any serious intention of graduating, but a year later he realized that medicine was his vocation and that he should follow what had been his father's profession. He retained his connections with Poland and re-established his connections with the Jewish community there, and in the summer of 1947 he travelled to Łódź, where he traced some of his pre-war friends. He gives a vivid account of heated political discussions in the Jewish community in the town, the main issues being Zionism and emigration, the legacy of the Holocaust in Poland, and tense relations with the Polish people who had resisted the Soviet occupation. Bardach became a keen observer of the emerging Polish pro-Soviet administrative elite. As one of the first Polish students to study in Moscow, he was invited to the houses of the new bureaucrats to talk about Moscow, Stalin, and the Soviet lifestyle.

In Poland, Bardach had witnessed the sweeping political changes when the Communists banned all other political parties. Julek, a member of the Polska Partia Socjalistyczna (Polish Socialist Party), had to resign from the embassy in Moscow and move back to Poland, but in spite of the new wave of terror and raging antisemitism, Bardach stayed in the city to graduate from medical school. Realizing that the rules of survival in the Gulag were quite applicable to the 'free' world outside Soviet forced labour camps, he learned to live a quiet life, focusing on his studies: 'one has to be lower than grass, quieter than still water' (p. 219). And yet, life in the Soviet Union drew him to the brink of breaking one of Stalin's new laws: Soviet citizens were prohibited from marrying foreigners and Bardach was in love with Lena, his classmate at the medical institute. Only Stalin's death and the subsequent liberalization of some Soviet policies prevented another tragedy in his life.

Janusz Bardach's *Surviving Freedom: After the Gulag* is the sequel to his camp memoir *Man is Wolf to Man*: *Surviving the Gulag* (Berkeley and Los Angeles: University of California Press, 1998). *Surviving Freedom* fills a gap in the memoirs of former prisoners of Soviet forced labour camps—that of adjustment and survival after the Gulag. Moreover, the book perfectly describes life in the 'big zone' outside the Gulag and juxtaposes it with life in the 'small zone' inside it. The memoir is an unusually balanced account of a Polish Jew who made a decision to stay and study in the Soviet Union and return to Poland as a specialist who could make 'a strong physical and psychological impact on patients' lives' (p. 205). It is well written and the authors include concise summaries of the most significant historical events and characters. It is a welcome addition to the fields of Jewish and Slavonic studies.

VERONICA SHAPOVALOV
San Diego State University

JOSHUA D. ZIMMERMAN (ED.)

Contested Memories: Poles and Jews During the Holocaust and its Aftermath

(New Brunswick, NJ: Rutgers University Press, 2003); pp. xx + 324

Polish ice, Jewish fire: such were, as readers of *Polin* well know, the incompatible properties that long made joint habitation of the intellectual field of modern Polish–Jewish relations almost impossible. Since the time of the Solidarity movement, the flames of self-discovery have risen among the Poles, while on the Jewish side the rage and grief that Polish antisemitism inspired coexist in the post-Holocaust generations with a cooler acceptance of the need for deeper historical understanding. This valuable book, dedicated to the memory of the Polish underground courier Jan Karski—who risked his life to learn at first hand of the Polish Jews' martyrdom and to communicate it, among other things, to the West—bears witness to these changes in its twenty-two well-documented and conciliatory essays. Though they focus mainly on the years of the German occupation and the Holocaust, they also open new windows on the post-war and contemporary eras. The book will be indispensable both for its empirical and interpretative findings and for its excellent bibliographies.

Taken together, these studies do not construct any new master narrative. Yet one finishes the book impressed by the degree to which its individual chapters combine to underscore, through documentation rather than reproachful assertion, the exceptional gravity of the problem of antisemitism in modern Polish history. This problem was made much worse by failure on the part of both the post-war state and society to respond to the central challenge described with perfect clarity in 1944 by Władysław Sikorski's Democratic Party's underground publication *Nowe Drogi*: '*We must come around to an honest attitude to the dying*. The Germans will someday answer before a tribunal of free nations for what they have done to the Jews. Let us not suppose, however, that our turn will not also come to give an accounting for our attitude to what happened before our eyes. . . . The Jewish question lives, as a question of the nation's moral health' (p. 185).

Yet, as recent surveys have shown, it is precisely those generations of Poles who witnessed the Holocaust, as adults or children, who still harbour today the strongest antisemitic hostilities and delusions (p. 264). The reason why this should be the case is not addressed at any length in these pages, which offer instead various psychological hypotheses. But long before Jan Gross's book sparked the Jedwabne controversy, the fact that in 1945–6 Polish mobs staged pogroms, at Kielce and elsewhere, in the shadow of the departing Nazis, and that in the same post-war years Poles murdered some 1,000 or more Jewish Holocaust survivors, often merely to prevent them from reclaiming their homes and businesses, raised chilling questions about Polish antisemitism. In her well-documented account of the Kraków pogrom of August 1945, Anna Cichopek cites testimony given under interrogation of a soldier involved in the pogrom who said, 'the old hatred of Jews started boiling in me so I simply let it out', while a militiaman declared that he 'acted out of personal motives, namely the hatred towards Jews' (pp. 227, 230). Even today, as the Warsaw University philosophy professor and Polish Jewish activist Stanisław Krajewski writes, 'the most obvious' impediment to the recovery of Jewish identity among Poles of Jewish parentage 'is fear of antisemitism. Virtually all Polish Jews feel that antisemitism is widespread and that sensitivity of Poles to Jewish concerns is low' (p. 301).

Though they do not express it, these essays support the vital distinction that must be made between antisemitism as, anthropologically speaking, a cultural structure—that is, a significant mentality embedded and institutionalized in social life—and antisemitism as an attribute which individuals may or may not possess. One must be intellectually and emotionally prepared to accept such statements as that of the Holocaust survivor Eva Safszycka, whose words Nechama Tec quotes in her eloquent essay 'Hiding and Passing on the Aryan Side'. Safszycka, the daughter of once prosperous parents who spent the war years in the household of a landed estate belonging to a Polish businessman, recalled that 'I met with so much kindness from the Poles, so many were decent and helpful that it is unbelievable.' Tec cites too the recollection of Chava Grinberg-Brown, the daughter of impoverished Jews, who survived the war as a defenceless girl desperately working in villages. Peasants once saved her from an informer by threatening to beat him. 'I have no bad feelings towards the Christians. I survived the war thanks to them. They helped me'; but she adds that 'no one did me any favors'. Rina Eitani, who lived by smuggling, recalled that 'the peasants were nice to us. They would feed us and sometimes, in exchange, we worked for them' (pp. 201–3). Nechama Tec, though a sociologist, offers no sociology of humaneness. Individual qualities are unpredictable and irreducible to broad categories such as religion or class.

Yet, if there is some truth in Shoshana Felman's ironic remark that the Holocaust remains 'an event without a witness', it is because the public sphere in post-war Poland displayed no free and broad discussion of Polish–Jewish relations during the Holocaust (p. 263). Whether the Jedwabne debate is now repairing that deficit or simply releasing a parade of denials, self-exculpations, and self-righteousness is perhaps still an open question. Certainly, though, this book helps considerably to summon evidence, not from tortured personal memory, valuable though that is, but soberly from the documentary record.

The editor, Joshua Zimmerman, offers an expert review of the relevant historiography, emphasizing the greater refinement of judgement and goodwill on both sides. Emanuel Melzer's study of Polish Zionist involvement in the pre-war government's territorial projects for Jewish emigration argues that it weakened Zionism in Jewish opinion, while official propaganda accustomed the Polish public to the idea of Jewish superfluity, probably contributing to Polish indifference towards the Holocaust. David Engel shows how, even as the mass murders were occurring, Polish government-in-exile officials self-deludingly berated Polish Zionists for Jewish 'betrayal' of Polish interests by remaining neutral in the fighting over Lwów in November 1918.

The Polish sociologist Barbara Engelking-Boni measures the 'psychological distance' between Poles and Jews under Nazi occupation, emphasizing Polish fear of the doomed Jews, both then and subsequently. 'There was no social approval for hiding Jews' (p. 52). Addressing Jewish survival strategies under Soviet rule in 1939–41, Andrzej Żbikowski documents the widespread welcome Jews gave the Soviets in 1939 and their partly willing, partly forced 'collaboration' over the following years. He endorses Karski's wartime view, which was meant without animosity, that 'the Jews created the situation in which the Poles regard them as devoted to the Bolsheviks'. Ben Cion Pinchuk, treating the same theme, acknowledges the Jews' understandable search for security under Soviet rule, illusory though it may have been. He rejects Polish rhetoric of collaborationism as unwarrantedly self-referential.

Jan Gross contributes a descriptive section from his Jedwabne book, but his co-authors do not comment at length on the bloody massacre. Looking at the Polish government-in-exile in London, Dariusz Stola emphasizes its deference to the more or less anti-Jewish warnings of the Armia Krajowa (Home Army) against provoking Polish opinion by advocating Jewish interests. It took the Warsaw ghetto rising to elicit Sikorski's (largely fruitless) public call for support of the Jews. Israel Gutman's essay emphasizes other failings of the Armia Krajowa. Shmuel Krakowski analyses the Polish underground press's views, finding more encouragement for aid to the Jews than has hitherto been thought. Yet the underground's hostile responses to Jewish escapees from the ghettos, whose numbers may have reached 300,000, doomed most of them, though a few survived in communist-protected forest camps in the east. On Polish Catholics' wartime relations with the Jews, John Pawlikowski rejects the equation of religious anti-Judaism with antisemitism, the more so as some anti-Judaists risked their lives to save Jews through the underground Żegota organization. It was Catholic anti-liberalism, Pawlikowski holds, that underlay its animosity towards the Jews.

Daniel Blatman's illuminating essay on the (mainly secular, leftist) Jewish underground press's view of the Poles describes one of his main findings as 'nostalgia for the future' (p. 129), which desperately imagined at the war's end a purge of antisemitism from a democratized and pacified Poland. Feliks Tych's survey of the Holocaust as it figures in some 450 published and unpublished memoirs reports sombrely that most Polish authors maintained a 'complete or near-complete silence about the Holocaust', while Jewish memoirs mostly report a 'resoundingly negative attitude on the part of most Poles' during and after the war (pp. 137, 140). Contemplating the evolution of Emanuel Ringelblum's views on Polish–Jewish relations, Samuel Kassow finds them skewed by Ringelblum's optimistic leftism but ultimately unsparing towards (in Ringelblum's words) 'Polish fascism and its ally, anti-Semitism' (p. 154).

Henry Abramson pursues the empirically difficult question of Orthodox Jewish reactions among the Holocaust's victims. Rabbi Kalonimus Kalman Shapiro's wartime writings show how he interpreted the Nazis as embodiments of the 'intensely evil' Amalek, while, seemingly, his discussion of 'Egyptians', indifferent or passively hostile to Jewish fate, referred to the Poles. But the enigmatic problem derived from the all-controlling divine will, which made of the Jews' murderers mere 'instruments by which the cosmic drama unfolds'. Rabbi Shapiro condemned the Jewish embrace of secular (Amalek's) knowledge, writing that 'now you see and feel with intensity just how attractive his wisdom is' (pp. 163, 165).

Gunnar S. Paulsson's innovative comparison of the survival of Jews in Poland and the Netherlands through Christian assistance concludes, contrary to Ringelblum's expectations and much contemporary opinion, that 'once the ghetto had time to respond to the [first, unexpected, and devastating Nazi] deportations, the proportion of Jews who escaped to the Aryan side was . . . slightly higher than it was in the Netherlands'. He reckons that, in Warsaw, out of a population of a million, 1,000–2,000 Poles worked against the Jews as blackmailers, while 50,000–60,000 aided them significantly. 'The remaining 94–95 per cent, whatever their thoughts or feelings about Jews, remained passive' (pp. 189–90). Nechama Tec's essay, mentioned above, found that women survived better on the 'Aryan side' than men, partly because they tended to speak better Polish and partly because they were psychologically more adaptable. Both sexes tried to avoid discovery by hiding 'the sadness of Jewish eyes' (p. 199).

On the post-war years, Anna Cichopek's study of the 1945 Kraków pogrom emphasizes the centrality of the belief in ritual murder in an ill-educated and impoverished urban proletarian setting not unlike that of Kielce and numerous other Polish towns where pogroms also occurred or threatened. Bożena Szaynok underscores the anti-Jewish hostility of post-war Polish society both in spurring mass Jewish emigration and in engendering the abandonment of Jewish identity and embrace of Polish communism among those who stayed. Natalia Aleksiun's newly researched study of the Zionist-dominated post-war Centralny Komitet Żydów w Polsce (Central Committee of Jews in Poland, CKŻP) shows how the provision of an armed defence against Polish antisemitism came unexpectedly to dominate the agenda. While the Polish communists aimed to protect the surviving Jews, they were too weak to do so effectively, as was the CKŻP. After the 1946 Kielce pogrom, they both, against their earlier support for maintaining the Jewish population in Poland, acceded to fear-stricken Jewish pressure for permission to emigrate.

Michael Steinlauf's well-researched essay on the treatment of the Holocaust in post-war Polish school textbooks and other semi-official publications reveals crude propagandizing of anti-Jewish positions, actively supported by the state in the Communist years and passively tolerated since then. Zvi Gitelman marshals substantial survey data showing, in comparison with other central and east European countries, the relatively high (though recently declining) degree of antisemitic attitudes in Poland, though these are expressed by minorities of 15 to 30 per cent, depending on the question asked. As a guide working with Jewish tours of Poland, including the March of the Living, Gitelman is struck by American Jewish indifference to the Polishness of the Jews of Poland, and their ambivalence towards the survival and growth of a Jewish community there, 'perhaps because the only Polish Jews are supposed to be dead Jews' (p. 285). Finally, Stanisław Krajewski's 'personal account' of post-war attitudes among the progeny of Holocaust survivors, many raised without knowledge or acknowledgement of their Jewish origins, is a riveting document. Among the dilemmas that 'marginal Jews' face in contemplating whether to embrace a Jewish identity is that of confronting the central role Poles of Jewish heritage played in the Communist Party: 'the numerous Jews in the power elite'. Krajewski adds that 'Jews were not only victims but victimizers', though 'it was not Judaism or Jewish traditions but the social situation that led Jews to Communist involvement' (p. 300).

These short characterizations can only hint at the freshness and interpretative vigour of the essays assembled in this collection. They are professional but also humane. They honour the memory of both Jan Karski and the Polish Jews he sought to save.

WILLIAM W. HAGEN
University of California, Davis

MAREK JAN CHODAKIEWICZ

After the Holocaust: Polish–Jewish Conflict in the Wake of World War II

(Boulder, Colo.: East European Monographs, 2003); pp. viii + 266

In 1998 I published a study of anti-Jewish violence in post-war Poland, based primarily upon case records compiled by the Polish Ministerstwo Administracji

Publicznej (Ministry of Public Administration) in Warsaw between September 1944 and September 1946 and supplemented by contemporary intelligence and press reports. I noted the incompleteness of the available data and the highly tentative nature of any conclusions that might be drawn from them. In particular, I insisted that 'it does not seem possible to determine with any reasonable degree of certainty the total number of Jews killed by Poles in the years following the liberation' ('Patterns of Anti-Jewish Violence in Poland, 1944–1946', *Yad Vashem Studies*, 26 (1998), 60). I stated that the most commonly quoted estimates, which placed the number of Jewish victims at 1,000–1,500, seemed to me too high. In a sentence that was excised by the editors and did not appear in the article I speculated that, 'if complete data could be assembled, chances are that the total number of casualties would fall in the range of 500–600, with the probability of a greater or lesser figure declining fairly sharply with distance from that range'. This is the approximation I have used in subsequent discussions of the matter, even though it remains only a best guess. As far as I know, no new evidence has surfaced to date that would suggest a substantially higher or lower figure.

Indeed, in a new study of the same subject, based largely upon exploration of records in provincial archives that I was not able to consult, Marek Jan Chodakiewicz has concluded that 'probably a minimum of 400 and a maximum of 700 Jews and persons of Jewish origin perished in Poland from July 1944 to January 1947' (p. 213). Chodakiewicz, too, recognizes the problematic nature of the sources and stresses that he can make only rough estimates. Still, the fact that two scholars working independently from different source bases and from different historiographical perspectives (of which more later) should make similar extrapolations ought to provide ground for a broad scholarly consensus.

Chodakiewicz has also explicitly endorsed my finding that the violence in question should not be understood 'simply as a continuation of ancient hatreds that the Nazi Holocaust either intensified or, at the very least, failed to uproot' ('Patterns of Anti-Jewish Violence', 85; cf. Chodakiewicz, *After the Holocaust*, 7), noting that I 'most plausibly postulated a multitude of factors' behind the killing of Jews (p. 7). At this point, however, the similarity between us ends. In particular, where I have sought to depict the intricate interplay of conceptual and contextual motives, of long-standing animosities and contemporary political concerns among those who attacked the small communities of Holocaust survivors returning to their pre-war homes, and to elucidate the difficulty in separating the two analytically, Chodakiewicz locates the origins of the violence in the contemporary context only. Moreover, he represents the violence as almost entirely a rejoinder to provocative behaviour by the Jews as a group. 'In reality,' he writes, 'violence against Jews stemmed from a variety of Polish responses to at least three distinct phenomena: the actions of Jewish Communists, who fought to establish a revolutionary Marxist–Leninist regime in Poland; the deeds of Jewish avengers, who endeavoured to exact extrajudicial justice on Poles who allegedly harmed Jews during the Nazi occupation; and the efforts of the bulk of the members of the Jewish community, who attempted to reclaim their property confiscated by the Nazis and subsequently taken over by the Poles' (p. 1). In other words, the large majority of the Jews who died brought their deaths upon themselves through their own actions; had they only thrown in their lot with the right-wing nationalist insurgents who took military action against the de facto governmental authority in liberated Poland, not availed themselves of the legal mechanisms established by that authority for pursuing grievances against Polish citizens who allegedly co-operated with the Nazis in their murder campaign, and avoided seeking legal restitution of possessions taken from them during the German occupation, the insurgents would have protected them instead of targeting them for execution. Indeed, it is difficult not to hear the refrain of the murderesses' tango from the musical *Chicago*—'They had it coming!'—echoing throughout the volume.

Perhaps this echo would not sound quite so pathetic had the situation in post-war Poland been in fact as Chodakiewicz represents it. To his mind, Poland and the Polish nation were victimized from the end of the Nazi occupation by a small but ruthless band of Stalinist subjugators, who 'established a puppet Communist state in central Poland' in July 1944 (p. 16). This state, he maintains, had virtually no support among the non-communist majority of the Polish population, except for a few 'renegade leaders of radical leftist splinter groups' who appropriated the names of 'respectable pre-war organizations' like the Polskie Stronnictwo Ludowe and the Polska Partia Socjalistyszna (the Polish Peasant Party and Polish Socialist Party) (pp. 16–17). Instead, according to his account, the Poles as a whole rallied behind 'hundreds of . . . secret [armed] organizations' for whom 'anti-Communism and anti-Sovietism were synonymous with freedom and independence' (p. 24). The dogged resistance of these 'independentists' is said to have inspired 'a spontaneous insurrection . . . against the Soviets' in the spring of 1945, which succeeded in confining 'Communist power . . . to the large cities only' until it was brutally suppressed by 'Soviet reinforcements' (p. 25). To be sure, Chodakiewicz claims, the 'independentist' leadership 'wanted to limit the armed struggle to necessary self-defense' in order 'to prevent further bloodshed', but 'secret police terror caused the insurgents to step up their operations' during 1946 (p. 25). Chodakiewicz is convinced that it was the terror that eventually allowed a veritable handful of communist criminals to withstand and repel this intensified insurrectionist drive. Yet for him the most significant detail about the terror, one that he claims other scholars have failed to note, is that Jews were largely responsible for its success: 'Jewish participation in the institutions of the Communist regime, especially the secret police, as manifested in concrete anti-insurgent deeds', together with 'free-lance informing, which often took the form of squaring accounts with anti-Semitic perpetrators, real or alleged, with the assistance of the NKVD [the Soviet secret police] and the UB [Urząd Bezpieczeństwa (Security Office)]', brought about the 'den[unciation], abuse, and despoil[ment of] at least 7,000 Poles', and perhaps, according to another estimate, over 13,000 (131,213).[1] Attacks on Jews, he thus suggests, were part of the 'necessary self-defense' to which the 'independentist' leadership 'wanted to limit the armed struggle'; breaking the Jewish–communist axis of collaboration was vital to the cause of free Poland.

Such a portrayal of the state of affairs in Poland between 1944 and 1947 may bring some comfort to zealous guardians of the Poles' long-standing representation of themselves as history's most valiant martyrs for the cause of human freedom, but in the event it is more the product of an active imagination informed largely by hindsight (and perhaps by politics) than of any real understanding of the situation on the ground at the time in question. For much of this interval the de facto authorities in Poland, who enjoyed Soviet backing—first the Polski Komitet Wyzwolenia Narodowego (Polish Committee of National Liberation), then the Rząd Tymczasowy Rzeczypospolitej Polskiej (Provisional Government of the Polish Republic), and finally (after June 1945) the Tymczasowy Rząd Jedności Narodowej (Provisional Government of National Unity, TRJN)—pursued a policy of obtaining the assent of non-communist Polish political groups to their rule. On the whole the policy was successful; as early as 29 August 1944 the London-based anti-communist Polish government-in-exile publicly declared its willingness to share power with the Communists in the future Poland, and following the Yalta Conference in February 1945 most Polish political circles acknowledged that the Communists would have to be accorded a position of primacy in governing the liberated homeland. Even before the Yalta agreements had been announced, on 8 February 1945, the government-in-exile ordered all armed resistance to Soviet and Soviet-backed forces on its behalf to cease. The TRJN was formed following negotiations in Moscow in which representatives of all but the most extreme positions on the Polish political spectrum participated, including the legendary peasant leader Wincenty Witos and the eminent historian Stanisław Kutrzeba, long associated with the Polish National Democratic movement. On 28 June 1945 the former prime minister of the government-in-exile, Stanisław Mikołajczyk, chairman of the Polskie Stronnictwo Ludowe, joined TRJN as deputy premier and minister of agriculture; he was joined by Jan Stańczyk, former minister of labour and social welfare in the exile regime, who assumed the same portfolio in the new national unity government. On 5 July 1945 TRJN was recognized by Great Britain, the United States, and virtually every other state as the legitimate government of Poland. To be sure, the Polish

[1] Chodakiewicz's presentation of statistics contains several confusing inconsistencies. In a table on page 213, for example, he lists a minimum of 3,128 Poles denounced by Jews, 2,408 arrested (by 'direct and indirect actions of Jewish security men in the Communist employ'; p. 125), 63 'killed directly', and 195 'caused to be killed'. Maximum figures in these categories were 6,238, 6,625, 125, and 455, respectively. How these numbers tally with the statement on the same page that 'persons of Jewish origin . . . denounced, abused, and despoiled at least 7,000 Poles' is not clear. Nor is it clear how they chime with the assertion on page 223 that 'perhaps between 3,128 and 6,625 Poles were victimized by Jewish perpetrators', or with the table on page 113 that gives considerably lower minimum and maximum figures for the four categories.

communists and their Soviet backers eventually scuttled the promise that the provisional unity government would transform itself into a true coalition supported by a free popular vote, but they began to signal their intentions publicly only from late February 1946, and the process of communization did not begin in earnest until the following July, after the peak of anti-Jewish violence had passed. Until that time relatively few Poles anticipated the Stalinist dictatorship that was to take power with the deposition of Władysław Gomułka and the creation of the Polska Zjednoczona Partia Robotnicza (Polish United Workers' Party) in late 1948, and fewer still, Jews and non-Jews alike, regarded the government of post-war Poland as so lacking in legitimacy as to make any accommodation with it a crime.

In other words, during the months between August 1944 and September 1946, when some 500–600 Jews (or 400–700 in Chodakiewicz's estimate) lost their lives as a result of violent actions by Poles, the 'puppet Communist state in central Poland' against which Chodakiewicz claims the 'independentists' fought did not yet exist. In the event, the struggle of the relatively small number of insurrectionists (who were in active rebellion against a government whose legitimacy was not widely questioned) was directed not only against the spectre of a communist government but against the possibility that Poland would be governed by *any* party or combination of parties that did not share their vision of what a Polish state should be. That vision had been formed long before any serious threat of a communist takeover in liberated Poland had materialized, and it hardly left room for Jews as equal claimants upon the resources of a Polish state. Indeed, as the emissary Jan Karski (hardly a communist or a communist sympathizer) explained as early as 1942, the parties of the nationalist and extreme nationalist right envisioned 'a ruthless struggle against Jewry' (*bezwzględna walka z żydostwem*) following liberation and even went so far as to excoriate the *exile* government (not a future communist one) for 'depending upon the Jews for support'.[2] The association of Jews with communism by the 'independentists' was thus at no time anything more than a cruel diversionary tactic, designed to obscure the actual aims of their struggle and to win sympathy by playing upon a long-standing stereotype; the 'independentists' would have dangled it before the Polish public with the same degree of ferocity and indignation no matter how many or how few Jews or non-Jews resisted their efforts to upset public order and to derail a political agreement that until mid-1946 was generally believed to be consistent with multi-party democracy. That Chodakiewicz could give it credence indicates at the very least his failure as a historian to distinguish between 1945 and 1948.

Actually, it may indicate more. Chodakiewicz claims that one of his primary purposes in writing his book was to dispel a common stereotype about the per-

[2] Karski to Sikorski, 'Prasa tajna', n.d. (*c.*15 December 1942), Hoover Institution Archives, Stanford, Calif., Jan Karski, box 1, file 6. Karski noted further that 'with regard to the Jews [the extreme nationalist underground press] assumes a stance that is completely hostile, not even expressing the slightest sympathy in the face of the German terror against the Jewish population'.

vasiveness and strength of 'Polish antisemitism'. In this connection he might well have pointed with pride to the fact that the large majority of the Polish population rejected the 'independentist' red herring and that the extent of deadly violence against Jews, while sufficient to reinforce deep feelings of insecurity among them and to colour their experience after the Holocaust in unexpectedly dark tones, ultimately claimed the lives of less than 0.2 per cent of the total number of Jews who set foot on Polish soil during the two years following liberation. Instead, however, he chose not to follow the majority example but to rehabilitate the 'good name' of a small, extreme political minority by endowing its propaganda with the imprimatur of historical research. In the event his book seems less an act aimed at promoting inter-group understanding than one of advocacy for certain exponents of a radical politics not easily harmonizable with the commonly accepted canons of Western morality. If so, then it is not only a poor piece of craftsmanship (its exposure of newly discovered archival documents notwithstanding); it is a misguided and regrettable effort.

DAVID ENGEL
New York University

ANTONY POLONSKY AND MONIKA ADAMCZYK-GARBOWSKA (EDS.)

Contemporary Jewish Writing in Poland: An Anthology

(Lincoln: University of Nebraska Press, 2001); pp. 1 + 350

When I was a young reader in Poland in the 1950s, I believed Adolf Rudnicki, the author of *Żywe i martwe morze* ('The Live and the Dead Sea'), to be the world's best living writer. The tragic stories and their protagonists—members of the Polish intelligentsia, who because of their Jewishness were marked for annihilation—were not unfamiliar to me, but Rudnicki's voice, at once intensely emotional and ironic, seemed capable of revealing the exact and always particular nature of the horrendous transition from the mundane to the catastrophic. Every character in those tales from the recent years of mayhem—a worldly, assimilated pre-war writer, who in the course of persecutions transforms himself into an Orthodox Jew; a woman who tries to protect her schizophrenic husband; a young artist whose determination to prove his innocence against an accusation of treason is stronger than his fear of death—had a luminous individuality that defied the statistics of mass murder and collective grief.

After Rudnicki's work, next on my list of the best books was Kazimierz Brandys's *Samson*. The scene in which its young hero, Jakub Gold, emerges from yet another exposed hideout into the daylight of Warsaw in August 1943 and is met by the shocked glances of the passers-by still stands out in my mind as one of the most unforgettable I have ever read. Then came Julian Stryjkowski's novels of Jewish communities before the destruction, and his confessional *Sen Azrila* ('Azril's Dream'), the lament of an old Jew who is tormented by his betrayal of his God and his people. Then another Rudnicki: *Kupiec łódzki* ('The Merchant of Łódź'), a literary biography of Chaim Rumkowski, the grotesquely tragic 'king of the Łódź ghetto'. There was no end to that descent into a man-made hell. Then Bogdan Wojdowski's *Chleb rzucony umarłym* ('Bread for the Departed') came out, followed by Henryk Grynberg's 'non-artistically true' (in his phrase) short novels about his family's experience of the Holocaust. By that time, the great modern masterpieces of Western literature, which were then available in Poland, seemed to me irrelevant and obsolete. I was not alone in thinking that soon the world would take what we had to offer: our literature of testimony and our reflections from the epicentre of the century's most horrible human catastrophe.

But this did not happen. It could not happen, not only because the West did not trust Jewish writers who chose to stay in the communist cum antisemitic Poland, as the editors of *Contemporary Jewish Writing in Poland* rightly note in their introduction, but also because works of art from peripheral cultures do not easily travel to the centre, regardless of their universal significance and superior quality. And, let's be candid about yet another reason: few books about the Holocaust sold well. If there were some limitations to what the writers in the post-war communist bloc could write about their recent history, publishers in the West, particularly in the United States, also favoured books and films that adhered to certain political and commercial formulas. No matter how earnestly we say that we must not forget, the market for complex, 'non-artistic truth' about the Holocaust is still rather small; it is as if the story were too painful for the Jewish reader, and too uncomfortable for non-Jews.

Of course Professor Antony Polonsky, a true bookman and keeper of history's flame, has never been particularly concerned about the marketing of the books he brings out, although he does perform miracles in finding financial support for his rescue operations. We owe to him, in addition to *Polin* and many other publications, the appearance in English of Abraham Lewin's diary from the Warsaw ghetto, *A Cup of Tears* (Oxford, 1988), and of *The Jews in Poland* (Oxford, 1986). And now, together with Monika Adamczyk-Garbowska, the head of the Centre for Jewish Studies at Maria Curie-Skłodowska University in Lublin, he has produced the first English-language anthology of works by Jewish writers who were born in the past century in Poland and wrote in Polish. The editors made a wise decision to dedicate their anthology to the writers, few of whom are known here, rather than to the one subject—the Holocaust—that all of them were compelled to address. Artists ought not to be herded into thematic categories, no matter how noble a criterion; the Jewish artists in Poland deserve recognition based on the merit of their art, and all the more so because of their distinct tribulations.

The editors had to resolve several difficulties in selecting the authors and the texts. The first was how to establish which of the writers qualified as Jewish. This used to be a sensitive issue in Poland, in part as a result of the Nazi racist theories and practice, and later because of communist antisemitic manoeuvres. The editors decided to include those writers who were assertive about their Jewishness and who devoted most of their work to Jewish topics. Hence, to my regret, the absence here of Kazimierz Brandys, his *Samson*, and his fictionalized memoir of growing up in Łódź. The next difficulty, which is not fully acknowledged in the introduction, concerns the definition of a writer. By choosing only those who wrote fiction or poetry, the editors excluded authors of diaries and memoirs. Was Anne Frank a writer? I think so, and so was Dawid Sierakowiak, a multilingual teenage genius who kept his diary from 1939 until he died in 1943 in the Łódź ghetto. The publication of the five recovered notebooks of his diary in the United States in 1998 should have been a major event, but instead the book was met with scant notice; the subject was still too disturbing. If I were to include one memoir in the anthology, or to recommend one book containing all there is to know about the Holocaust, it would be Arnold Mostowicz's *Żółta gwiazda i czerwony krzyż* ('The Yellow Star and the Red Cross', London, forthcoming). Mostowicz was a young doctor in the Łódź ghetto and then a prisoner in Auschwitz and several German transitional camps. After the war he became a man of letters, the editor-in-chief of a satirical magazine, *Szpilki*, and the editor of several anthologies of, yes, humour. His memoir is that of an old man in full control of his recollections from the lowest rungs of hell. One of only a handful of survivors from the Łódź ghetto and a doctor who received his medical degree from a French university, Mostowicz notes that he was never called 'to a witness stand in any court of justice'.

This anthology, however, is intended not for those who know the literature it presents, but for those who do not. Its purpose is to offer a sample from a rich and diverse complex of works that in their entirety could fill a library. Both the richness and the diversity are splendidly reflected in one ground-breaking volume. Four of the book's twelve authors, Julian Stryjkowski (1905–96), Adolf Rudnicki (1912–90), Bogdan Wojdowski (1930–94), and Henryk Grynberg (b. 1936), are among the most prominent writers in Poland's post-war literature. They have little in common besides their desire to commemorate the life and death of the Polish Jews. Another, Antoni Słonimski (1896–1976), achieved his high artistic and intellectual status in the period between the two world wars. They came from different geographic and cultural backgrounds and experienced the Holocaust as adults or children, inside or outside the ghetto walls or, in the case of Stryjkowski and another of the writers, Leo Lipski (1917–97), in the Soviet Union. More importantly, their creative personalities are as distant from each other as, for example, those of Cynthia Ozick and Philip Roth.

Julian Stryjkowski is a magical realist in his evocation of what he called in his afterword to *Judas Maccabeus* 'the Atlantis that seemed to be lost and drowned forever'. In this he is not unlike Isaac Bashevis Singer; but unlike Singer—a faithful Yiddishist—Stryjkowski is profoundly concerned with the complicated issues of identity, loyalty, and betrayal. The main characters in all his novels are torn between their attachment to their Jewish roots and their striving to escape the tight grip of that bond. Can one be a Polish writer, a communist, a Marrano, and remain a good Jew? Stryjkowski's pained and passionate probing into such questions elevates his work above the boundaries of region and history. The fragment from his *Voices in the Darkness* that is included in the anthology illustrates well the power of his voice.

Rudnicki's novella *Ascension* was a perfect choice for the anthology. It presents Rudnicki at his best, as a Conradian neo-Romantic and a brilliant explorer of the human condition in utterly inhuman conditions. The scene in which Raisa gets ready to poison her insane husband in order to save him from a likely death in the gas chamber, and then realizes that she cannot do it, is as revealing of the enormity of the horror of the Holocaust as it is of Rudnicki's talent for exemplifying it in terms of intimate personal tragedy. I disagree with the authors of the introduction (I detect here the hand of Professor Adamczyk-Garbowska) that Rudnicki's realism 'was tempered by his attempts at complex psychological analysis' (p. xxiii). The evil was simplistic, but its victims were complicated people, and so are Rudnicki's characters, whose shattered, or strengthened, inner lives he documents in a darkly ironic style. A different kind of realism, that of lucid remembrance of a childhood lost in the Warsaw ghetto, triumphs in Bogdan Wojdowski's *Chleb rzucony umarłym*. The choice of an excerpt in which the boy's deeply religious grandfather urges him to run away from the ghetto, and from his Jewishness, is again excellent. Some critics lauded Wojdowski's novel as a Proustian masterpiece. Needless to say, here it is a chunk of stale bread, not a madeleine, that unlocks the flow of memory.

Henryk Grynberg is perhaps the last great Jewish writer from Poland with childhood memories of the Holocaust, although the less prolific but equally astounding Jadwiga Maurer (alas, not included in the anthology) is equally deserving of this title. In *Fatherland*, printed in full in the anthology, Grynberg investigates the murder of his father by, as he will find out, a couple of Polish neighbours from their native village. What he does here, as in all of his compact books, is relentlessly assemble evidence of what exactly had happened: to his father, to other members of his family, to the Jews they or he had known, and, as the circle expands, to Jews from anywhere in the Holocaust's range. Like his predecessor in such unsparing documentarism, Tadeusz Borowski, Grynberg does not varnish the represented reality of the victims' suffering, and their sometimes unheroic struggle for survival, with even the slightest touch of romantic rhetoric. He does, however, draw a clear line between the victim and the murderer. He is also the most convincing explorer of the relations between Jews and Poles during and after the war, as he is uninterested in pleasing either of the sides. In his *Memorbuch* (2000), he tells several life stories of the Jews who remained in Poland after the war, and who were nearly or actually destroyed by the outburst of antisemitism in 1968. (His previous book, *Drohobycz, Drohobycz*, was nominated for the highest literary prize in Poland.) Grynberg is also a gifted poet, and fifteen of his poems appear in the anthology. The only other poet represented here is Stanisław Wygodzki (1907–91), a survivor of Auschwitz, where he witnessed the death of his wife and small daughter, and where he mourned the murder of his mother. A talented writer and a superb poet, he was too burdened by grief to make full use of his artistic potential. He died in Israel, alone and depressed.

A writer who did find a home in Israel is Ida Fink (b. 1921), the author of several collections of stories that were published in English and brought her deserved recognition. Here we have four true pearls born of Fink's pain (beautifully translated by the invaluable Madeline G. Levine and Francine Prose). Quietly, these brief tales of barely visible wounds that cannot heal take us into the heart of darkness. In comparison, the two short stories by Stanisław Benski (1922–88) seem strained in the effort to find an original voice. There are stories that talk and stories that listen; in this volume they are Wojdowski's and Grynberg's, Fink's and Zofia Grzesiak's (b. 1914). Grzesiak, born Nachume Szwarcblat, was a poorly educated, unassimilated country girl, and as she was rescued from the Holocaust by her Polish future husband, she rewarded him with her marvellous gift of storytelling. He encouraged her to write, and even a small sample of her extensive work, the story titled 'Marriage', proves that he rescued a true talent.

In Poland there is a generation of Jews who, like Moses, were foundlings—perhaps a couple of thousand saved from the millions who perished. Some of them were reclaimed by Jewish relatives, but some might never have learned about who they were; most stayed with their adoptive Polish parents who, at some point, revealed to them their identity. Such is the case of Hanna Krall (b. 1937), a distinguished journalist and later a writer of fiction based loosely on interviews and her own experience. The three short stories included in the anthology are characteristic of her great care in accurately representing the always unique circumstances of the protagonists' survival, and her resistance to attempts to bundle them together or to turn them into spokespersons for this or that side in disputes about Poles and Jews (either in Poland or in the United States, where her objectivity has met with disapproval). In all her writing she echoes the line in a poem by her contemporary, now a Polish Jewish American, Anna Frajlich: 'I am distinct'.

No one on Poland's post-war literary scene was more distinctive than Artur Sandauer (1913–89). Though he was best known for his fiercely independent literary criticism and for his major contribution to the revival of interest in Bruno Schulz, he also wrote fiction. Most of this work was autobiographical and focused on his experience of the Holocaust. A secular Jew from an assimilated background, he chronicled the particular tragedy of the liberal members of the Polish Jewish intelligentsia. These Jews either chose or were forced to share the fate of the Jewish masses. The protagonist of his 'Death of a Liberal' takes upon himself the role of an accommodating intermediary between the Jews in a small ghetto and the German overseers of its gradual destruction. (Such a role was played by *Judenräte* as well.) He uses old illusions about 'civilized Germans' to justify his position, and as the atrocities progress, he resorts to a desperate notion of lesser evil. In the end he, too, perishes—'the last one from the town' (p. 142).

The authors of the introduction are somewhat harsh on Sandauer. Perhaps confusing him with the characters in his stories, they write that his character was much less attractive than Wygodzki's. They describe one of his characters as 'a nihilist' who believed in nothing, and conclude that therefore, 'not entirely surprisingly, he takes his own life' (p. xxxviii). Yet those old liberals and young 'nihilists' who were legion in eastern Europe deserve no less sympathy than the idealistic true believers. Sandauer himself never lacked courage.

With regret, I admit that I have not read any of Leo Lipski's works. The two fragments included here attest to the originality of his voice, which is described by the editors as 'a combination of Tadeusz Borowski's brutal behavioural presentation with Bruno Schulz's sensitivity to images'. He stands apart from other contributors to this volume as a former prisoner of the Soviet camps. His internment destroyed his health. He left the Soviet Union with General Anders's Polish Army and settled in Israel, where, paralysed and isolated by the otherness of his experience, he struggled to write and to publish. Faced with a similar fate—isolation from his native land and readers—Antoni Słonimski, a beacon of Poland's progressive liberalism, decided to return to Poland from his exile in London. Until the end of his life he played a leading role in the dissident community in his beloved Warsaw. His bitter-sweet piece about the second coming of Jesus, who arrives to comfort a dying Jewish tailor in post-war Warsaw, closes the book. An apt choice for the last page of the book would have been Słonimski's best-known poem, 'Elegy for Small Jewish Towns', paired, perhaps, with Anna Frajlich's powerful 'Wciąż przechodzę nad Mostem Gdańskim' ('I keep crossing the Gdańsk Bridge').

But all good anthologies carry within them a counter-anthology; the editors apologize for the omissions of, among others, Jadwiga Maurer and Anna Frajlich. Their extensive introduction is addressed to the reader unfamiliar with most of the many authors included and, in all likelihood, those distant crosswinds of history from whose devastating force they escaped. The result is a thorough presentation of writers from a complex background, with thoughtful analysis of such problems as identity, moral choices in extreme situations, and, above all, finding one's own best way to give voice to the world of the silenced. More impatient readers will be satisfied with the informative biographical notes. The translations are clearly labours of love and deserve applause, if not in equal measure. Beyond its value as a reference, this is the book that will help the Future in its search for its most crucial Past.

JOANNA ROSTROPOWICZ CLARK
Princeton Research Forum

ANDRZEJ KRAKOWSKI (DIR.)

Farewell To My Country

(Pine Hill Productions, 2002)

The children born to Holocaust survivors who remained in Poland after the Second World War shared common threads of experience that shaped their generation. The post-war waves of emigration in the 1940s and 1950s resulted in a largely assimilated Jewish population in Poland, and the families that remained by the 1960s, the children of the survivors, often had only a limited understanding of their Jewish roots. Many of their parents were communists and, as atheists, believed communism would solve the problem of antisemitism. Their parents, who had survived the war as refugees in the Soviet Union or, less frequently, in hiding or in camps in Poland, had few or no other relatives, so their children's extended families often consisted of family friends with similar backgrounds.

In 1968 these children of survivors in Poland were students and young adults during the defining experience of their generation. In March of that year the communist government used the student demonstrations against censorship to further the 'anti-Zionist' campaign that had begun to simmer the previous year, following the Six-Day War in Israel. Jewish students were singled out as leaders of the demonstrations and arrested; others were harassed or expelled from university, while their parents were dismissed from their jobs. These events resulted in the emigration from Poland of at least 12,000 Jews, including those who had had no involvement in Jewish life. For the assimilated Polish Jews of this generation of survivors' children in Poland, the 1968 campaign challenged their identity as Poles and, in many cases, prompted them to re-evaluate their attitude towards their Jewish roots.

Andrzej Krakowski's documentary *Farewell To My Country* sketches the experiences of this generation. Its historical narrative asserts a continuity between the antisemitism of Poland before the Second World War, during the Holocaust, and after the war, leading up to 1968. Furthermore, the documentary argues that the events of 1968 were rooted not only in internal Communist Party politics, which historians of the period cite as the main impetus behind the campaign, but also in antisemitism within Polish society. The richness of the documentary lies in its portrayal of individual stories: in the break-up of families, struggles with identity, and the rootlessness of the experience of emigration. Yet *Farewell To My Country* is hampered by a lack of historical context, making it difficult for anyone unfamiliar with the history to place the individual stories within a meaningful narrative or to gain a deeper understanding of the underlying issues.

The documentary is more effective on the level of personal history. Krakowski himself left Poland for the United States in 1968 with his sister, while their father,

Józef, was initially unable to obtain permission to emigrate. The experiences of the Krakowski family, told through letters from Krakowski's father to his children in the United States, and through voice-overs and interviews with the director himself, form the thread of the narrative, along with interviews with a dozen or so other members of Krakowski's generation (though the interviewees are played by actors, a fact that the audience does not learn until the closing credits). Their recollections, interspersed with news footage from the period, convey the traumatic disruption that the 1968 events created in the lives of individuals and their families.

Framing post-war Jewish history in Poland as generational history highlights the common historical factors that shaped individual identities, and brings out the dynamics that made the experiences of post-war Polish Jews distinct from those of non-Jews despite assimilation. Jaff Schatz, in his sociological sketch of the generation of pre-war Jewish communists in Poland—the parents of Andrzej Krakowski's generation—wrote:

> Sociological generations—communities shaped by the trinity of demography, identity, and action—do not jump forth out of nothing. Whether sudden and traumatic or accumulated and prolonged, the sequences of significant experience under whose impact generations are created operate on the deeper layer of background factors that are similar or common for all those who will form the new generation. (*The Generation: The Rise and Fall of the Jewish Communists of Poland* (Berkeley, 1991), 20)

The experiences and identities of the generation of the children of survivors were shaped by background factors that were different from those of their parents, for whom the 1968 events resulted in their 'existential defeat', in Schatz's phrase (p. 11). Yet the events, and the light they shed on the identities of these young assimilated Polish Jews, were essential in forging the common experiences of this generation.

Although the generational approach shapes the stories conveyed in *Farewell To My Country*, Krakowski views the narrative almost entirely through the lens of antisemitism. This angle obscures other experiences common to the individual stories, which echo themes that both Henryk Grynberg and Hanna Krall convey in their literary portrayals of the 1968 events (Grynberg's *Memorbuch* is based on the life of Adam Bromberg, a top official in the state publishing bureaucracy in post-war Poland who was targeted in the 'anti-Zionist' campaign; parts of Krall's *Sublokatorka* ('The Subtenant') also deal with the 1968 events). These themes are: the ways in which assimilated Polish Jews had either suppressed their Jewishness or sought to synthesize it with their Polish identity, and the subsequent shock to this identity when they were targeted as Jews in 1968; the search for historical truth; and the physical and spiritual rootlessness of the experience of emigration, heightened by the loss of family and community during the war.

For Krakowski, the Jewish identity of these second-generation post-war Polish Jews is rooted almost entirely in the experience of antisemitism, which the narrative suggests was pervasive and overt even before the events of 1968. The first two sections, about identity and childhood, and much of the third section, on adolescence, focus on playground taunts and other stories of harassment through which some of the interviewees learned about or came to understand their Jewish identity. One interviewee quotes from Jean-Paul Sartre's *Anti-Semite and Jew*: 'That little word Jew appeared in his life one day and he has not been able to get rid of it ever since.' Antisemitism, Krakowski's narrative suggests, preserved Jewish identity as an unwanted label among the children of assimilated Jews.

Other interviews convey the ways in which post-war Polish Jews retained affirmative elements of Jewishness even when religious observance and conscious cultural identity were entirely absent. Michał K., for example, who emigrated to Israel in 1968, remembers, 'As far back as I can remember, I knew I was a Jew, even though at home we didn't have any Jewish culture. Except one thing—in April Mum brought home a box of matzah, but I really didn't know what it was and what it was for.' Another interviewee describes her participation in Jewish youth groups and summer camps during adolescence.

The core of *Farewell To My Country*—through sections on adulthood, the bureaucratic process of obtaining emigration documents, and departure—describes the individual experiences of the 1968 events: the student demonstrations, disillusionment and fear as the government and state-controlled press singled out Jewish students, conscription into military service, difficulties finding a job. The documentary is strongest in its portrayal of how individual decisions and experiences converged in a wave of emigration, particularly the trauma of family separation and the bureaucratic obstacles that blocked departure even as the government left these people with no other choice. (Perhaps it is only coincidence that the documentary refers to Krakowski's father as Józef K., recalling Kafka's *The Trial*, since all of the characters are cited by first name and last initial.)

Farewell To My Country does not address extensively the political involvement and ideology of the older generation of Polish Jews in post-war Poland, or the ways in which Krakowski's generation, both during the 1968 events and as a result of them, challenged the system that represented their parents' world-view. Through the letters from Krakowski's father and from a young woman named Zosia R. who left Poland for Paris in 1968, the documentary conveys the feeling of betrayal experienced by the older generation, as well as the anger of Krakowski's generation, but the political context—the closing of the play *Dziady* ('Forefathers'), which created the spark for the student demonstrations; the literary protests against censorship and cultural policy; and the internal politics of the communist government—is absent. The documentary's focus is less on the 1968 events than on the experiences of those who were forced to emigrate. As a result, it does not address the repercussions of 1968 on the remaining Jewish population, or the significance of the events for post-war politics. Nevertheless, an important theme is the gap between political rhetoric and reality during the 1968 events, a dissonance that brought to the surface what Schatz called the 'political bankruptcy of the Communist system' (p. 11). As footage shows Gomułka proclaiming that 'the only way to judge a citizen is by his attitude towards socialism and the vital interests of our fatherland', and that 'every citizen defines his own nationality with his own conscience', young Polish Jews describe harassment and discrimination at work and at school because of the anti-Jewish campaign. Just before snippets of Gomułka's speech, the documentary quotes from a letter written by Zosia R. in September 1968 in which she says: 'I'm trying at any cost not to hate Poland, but sometimes it's not that easy. I can forgive them a lot, but I can't forgive them for lying to us all this time and for treating us with such contempt.'

In seeking to understand the background to his own story, Krakowski gives voice to his anger at having been uprooted from his country, separated from his family, and treated as disloyal to Poland because of an identity about which his generation had only limited knowledge. However, in trying to understand the historical factors that affected his own life, he paints a picture of Polish Jewish history that does not acknowledge its complications; for example, his sweeping assertion that 'for every Pole who helped the Jews under German occupation, there were dozens who denounced them' expresses his own anger more than it addresses the difficult issue of Polish–Jewish relations during the Second World War and its significance for post-war Poland. However, although his view from inside the events proves an obstacle to a distanced and contextualized approach, the individual stories contribute to our understanding of the events of 1968 and the role of Krakowski's generation in recent Polish Jewish, and Polish, history. One individual interviewed in *Farewell To My Country* describes the importance of the stories in this way:

> All the colours, the full rainbow of it, those who were okay and those who suffered, those who had deep personal reasons or those who wanted to leave because their pride was hurt, or out of fear; all the nuances of individual life—illness, pregnancy, love, death, immediately, let's wait a little bit, later, all together, alone, with the children, without the children, only the children, to Denmark, to Chicago . . . to Israel, no, not to Israel, never to Israel—all difficult, individual, gut-wrenching decisions under every Jewish roof in Poland. And because those were our lives, and because those were our feelings, we have to respect them all.

KAREN AUERBACH
Brandeis University

LARRY N. MAYER

Who Will Say Kaddish? A Search for Jewish Identity in Contemporary Poland

PHOTOGRAPHS BY
GARY GELB

FOREWORDS BY
THANE ROSENBAUM and MARC RIBOUD

(Syracuse: Syracuse University Press, 2002); pp. xii + 194

The title of this book could just as well have been a somewhat bitter joke circulating in Poland in the years 1968 to 1971, when Jews were yet again forced to leave their homeland. At that time, people were saying that when the last Jew left Poland, fifty other Jews would see him off at the station. In this saying, which undoubtedly arose in Jewish circles, there is both sorrow and hope.

The world has accepted as axiomatic that there are no more Jews in Poland, and that if there are some, then they themselves are somehow guilty. From time to time Jewish tourists who have come wandering to Poland have noted with amazement that those 'guilty ones' continue to exist. This astonishment has sometimes resulted in a publication, for example, Earl Vinecour's interesting album (with photographs by Chuck Fishman) *Polish Jews: The Final Chapter* (New York, 1977), whose title betrays the authors' feelings. They photographed the last guardians of the graves and ruins; after the departure of these elderly Jews, they suggest, the only remaining trace of their presence, culture, and history will be Auschwitz.

The title of this latest publication seems to display a similar emotional attitude. The tone is the same in its two forewords. Thane Rosenbaum, the author of the first foreword, writes about the book in a rather maudlin style: 'It was grounded in the haunted soil of contemporary Poland. Without ever having met before, we had . . . observed the same continuing tragedy, searched for the same touchstones, and wept at the vastness of vanished Jewish life.' Rosenbaum goes on to place the book in 'the Holocaust canon'. Marc Riboud, the author of the second foreword, put it more succinctly and in a significantly better style: 'When I was there [in Poland] in 1980 I felt an absence, an emptiness as an immense and poignant hollow.'

If this book was to be, as Rosenbaum in particular suggests, a therapeutic 'internal journey' for himself and for Larry Mayer, who both suffer from 'second-generation syndrome' (which I believe was invented by American psychotherapists who wanted to make a profit, and who forgot that they could broaden their pool of clients to include Poles, Russians, Ukrainians, Belarusians, Lithuanians, Hungarians, Serbs, Bosnians, Frenchmen, and even Germans born after the war), then why did they bother all the people they spoke with and photographed in Poland? Would it not have made more sense to describe their own feelings and internal problems without taking on the inconvenience of a trip? Why should Poland be 'haunted soil' for those—both Jewish and Polish—living here in modern Poland? And do the authors not feel it is less than tactful to reproach Polish Jews for living on 'haunted soil'?

The rather pompous title and the pretentious statements in the two forewords are mistaken, however. Perhaps in spite of their own intentions, in their 'travel journal' the authors have accurately captured the phenomenon of the Jewish life that exploded in Poland after 1989 and which, though limited to a small group of people, is very rich. Their discovery that 'there are Jews here' determined their point of departure, which was a very personal one, but at the same time one that reveals their distance from what they wanted to see. They made their way to Poland with the same attitude that nineteenth-century Jewish travellers probably had when they discovered members of the Jewish faith in China or the interior of India. Thus their book is also a record of their attempt to overcome this distance and to establish contact with and try to understand these exotic Jews who insist on living in Poland.

They focus on the middle and younger generations of Polish Jews, describing their lives and exploring their attitudes towards Jewishness, Israel and Poland, the cultural heritage, and Jewish nationality. The book is divided into five chapters, entitled respectively: 'Amnesia', 'A Time to Gather Stones', 'From Generation to Generation', 'A New Testament', and 'Bearing Witness'. The authors do not maintain a rigid thematic order, but the contents are loosely connected to the section titles. In the first section they describe their first meetings with Jews who are active in the various Jewish institutions, such as the *gmina* (the administration of the Jewish community), the synagogue, and the Children of the Holocaust organization. They write about the complexity of these Jews' attitudes towards Jewishness and their complicated double or triple identifications. Mayer continually relates these to his memories of his own parents, who came from Poland and knew Polish. He writes of the conflict between information about the post-war history of Poland that is new to him and the painful memories of his parents. At times his formulations arouse objections, for example, in the statement: 'The first generation of this new "race" of Jews was more biologically Jewish than anything else.' He had in mind here the Jewish communists, who did not speculate on the subject of their origin, or their national belonging, convinced as they were that in the new order these concepts would lose their meaning. To call this type of consciousness 'biologically Jewish' is not accurate, however—not to mention that the formulation has an unfortunate similarity to the assertions of racist antisemitism, whose propagators believed in the biological conditioning of the Jewish 'character' or 'psyche'.

There is also discussion here of the assistance of American Jews in the search for national and religious roots, and particularly of the Ronald S. Lauder Foundation, whose financial and organizational contribution has determined that a large proportion of the younger generation of Polish Jews identifies more with Judaism than with Jewish nationality. It is thanks to the Lauder Foundation that summer camps have been organized at which several hasidic rabbis have taught the Orthodox tradition of Judaism. This undertaking demands of them great tolerance towards their 'disconnected' brothers and sisters, who stubbornly mix dairy and meat dishes, are accustomed to frying their eggs in pork fat, or, through a lapse of memory, flip light switches on the sabbath. At the same time they sing Hebrew songs with great enthusiasm at the sabbath table. This observation escaped the authors' notice.

The second section is a sentimental and very painful journey through ruins and recollections of the past. Its point of departure is the Holocaust and the exceedingly accurately observed and startling fact of the lack of care for Jewish relics—evidence of the degree to which the memory of the Jews has been expunged from Polish consciousness. Although they do not dwell on this subject, they note the evidence of antisemitism in Poland; for example, they include a photograph of anti-Jewish graffiti on a wall. This is embarrassing for my country, the more so as manifestations of antisemitism are not limited to graffiti, but include the propaganda of hate in several legally published journals and in the broadcasts of a Catholic radio station and the verbal aggression of certain public figures. Despite the fact that such actions violate existing laws, the Polish justice system is afraid to react, or else calls them acts of 'negligible social harm'.

I could point out here the lack of any mention of the Poles who are making efforts to change this state of affairs, and whose numbers are increasing. Particularly striking is the omission of any reference to the Żydowski Instytut Historyczny (Jewish Historical Institute), which has been in operation uninterruptedly since 1947, and in which Poles and Jews jointly research the history of the Jews. The authors visited it, if I remember correctly. But I won't carp, because the authors' intention in this book is 'Judaeocentric', if not egocentric. Poles are not necessary to the inner journey of the authors, and if they exist, it is in the distant background. As a rule they are suspected of holding a hostile attitude towards Jews (for example, on page 178: 'There is something menacing about being in a post-Communist Eastern European city in the late evening, under a drizzling sky in 1991, near the Ukrainian border, in a place where everyone supposedly hates Jews'); or they are seen as accidental and unimportant guides to forgotten and abandoned Jewish places, whose good intentions are ignored so as not to destroy assumptions constructed a priori.

In the third chapter the authors visit the centres of the religious and social lives of Polish Jews. They observe services and meals in kosher cafeterias. They talk with people who are active in the community and with a young couple who were married beneath a *ḥupah* (wedding canopy), the parents of a newly circumcised son. They meet the old and the young, including the founders of the Polska Unia Studentów Żydowskich (Polish Union of Jewish Students). They visit a Jewish school. They reflect on the gulf dividing the oldest from the youngest generation, as a result of which the younger ones are learning about their Jewish heritage from community workers who come from the United States and Israel rather than from their parents or grandparents. I am tempted to point out here the authors' lack of knowledge of the phenomenon and ideology of assimilation and of the post-war process of secularization. But I will resist, with difficulty, because after all this is not a scholarly treatise.

In chapter 4 the authors present even more complicated examples of Jewish identity. They talk with a priest who learned from his dying mother that he was the son of her Jewish friend. He then established contact with his hasidic family in Israel and, after many difficulties, persuaded them to accept that they had a priest for a relative. The authors also attend a meeting at which the participants speak in turn about how they came to their Jewish consciousness and about 'what it means to be a Jew here'. This question has become the favourite subject of discussion among the majority of young Jews in the Diaspora (not excluding the authors), but is barely comprehensible to the majority of Israelis; it infuriates some, and in others provokes a rather paternalistic attitude towards their co-religionists' 'suffering in the *galut*'. Next the authors discover 'Polish Jewish craziness' as exemplified by the devout Catholic parents who have joyfully accepted the fact that their son has become a believing Jew, or by the Jewish parents, one of whose two children has chosen Judaism and the other Catholicism. They speak with the young editors of the Polish-language journal *Jidełe* about the intricacies of consciousness and of intergenerational relations.

The role of the fifth and final chapter is to complete and summarize the journey. It is impressionistic, mixing several seemingly unrelated images. It records a conversation with a drunken organist, whom the authors assume to be antisemitic although they do not know Polish, in the town on the Ukrainian border mentioned above. Then there are the meetings between the author and his relatives, one of whom does not know that there is a synagogue in Warsaw, and another of whom, a devout Catholic, follows the Pope to every city he visits on his pilgrimages to Poland. These two scenes are presented along with a history of Mayer's parents, as well as some reflections by the author on the subject of his own complexities, as evidenced by his marriage to a Catholic, and on the difficulty of transmitting the experience of the Holocaust.

In the end, my obligation as a reviewer is to give my verdict. In this case, however, I refuse to come down on one side. This is a strange book, and one that provokes various reactions—from sympathy to irritation. Its writing style is equally strange. It is difficult to say whether this is belletristic writing, or the description of a journey, or an analysis of the authors' psyches. This stylistic indecision is truly exasperating. As a belletristic work it seems to me far from perfect—though at the same time intriguing. In assessing the educational value of the work, it is difficult not to note that the authors could have benefited from reading the most ordinary introductory textbook on the history of modern Poland and of Polish Jews. Perhaps this would have delivered them of their false conviction that they knew everything they needed to know about this country, and would have led them to visit it with eyes wide open. This would have prevented them from making exasperatingly stereotyped evaluations, and would have given the book some originality. Perhaps they would have perceived more than that which arose from their conversations with more or less Jewish Jews. Or perhaps their statements could have been interpreted in more than one way, and not only in regard to themselves. This would have done the book no harm either. I felt worst in the role of witness to the authors' journey into their inner selves. These inner selves were presented without enough complexity; one could not identify with these people, become interested in their personalities, or grow to like them. Nevertheless, the book is absorbing. I read it almost in one breath, although it delivered a large dose of adrenaline. And so I am making my way to the pool to work it off, and what I wish for the authors is that on their next visit they may take note of some more sympathetic Poles.

ALINA CAŁA
Jewish Historical Institute, Warsaw
Translated from Polish by Claire Rosenson

Dora Kacnelson

1921–2003

In his introduction to Dora Kacnelson's last major publication, *Skazani za lekturę Mickiewicza* ('Condemned for Reading Mickiewicz'), Dr Andrzej Paluchowski of the Catholic University of Lublin writes:

> in scholarly matters she appears to be the leading expert on historical and literary Polish documents and manuscripts in the archives and libraries of Russia (especially eastern Siberia), Ukraine, Lithuania, and Belarus. . . . Among her works, the studies of the reception and suppression of Mickiewicz's works in the Russian empire and under the Habsburg monarchy are of particular significance.

Dora Kacnelson's biography is a canvas for the fascinating story of a Polish Jewish woman raised in the language and culture of Yiddish—the language spoken in her childhood home. Her parents, especially her mother, developed a love of Russian literature, while young Dora fell in love with the Polish language and literature. This duality—her Polishness and her Jewishness—was for Kacnelson a source of vexation and even persecution over the course of many decades.

Dora Kacnelson was born in Białystok on 19 April 1921. Her parents, Berl Kacnelson and Batsheva Dejno Kacnelson, came from the town of Bobruisk. Her mother was an elementary school teacher and her father, a would-be rabbi, was an activist in the Bund. In 1920 they fled the Bolshevik terror and settled in Białystok. It was here that Dora attended Polish schools and where she fell wholeheartedly in love with Polish history and Polish poetry. In various autobiographical texts she mentions her early teachers, both Polish and Jewish: it was they who decisively influenced the sensibility and spiritual life of the future scholar.

After the outbreak of the Second World War the family took refuge with relatives in Leningrad. There, on the banks of the Neva, Kacnelson began her studies in the field of Russian philology and Slavonic studies with an emphasis on Polish studies. Her teachers were the leading scholars Paweł Berkov, Jarek Azadovsky, and Grigory Tsukowsky. They all travelled a road of suffering because of their independent research and their Jewishness.

Kacnelson's parents died in 1942 during the German blockade of the city of Peter the Great. After the war the young researcher's life within the Soviet system was not easy, as she writes in a couple of her autobiographical works. She obtained permission to begin her doctoral studies only with difficulty. In 1953 she defended her thesis, which was written in Russian and entitled 'Adam Mickiewicz and Popular Literature'. She planned to take a position at the University of Minsk, but this turned out to be impossible. With difficulty, she found work at the Higher Pedagogical School in Polotsk, from where she often travelled to nearby Vilna, where she conducted research in the archives.

From 1961 to 1966 Kacnelson lived in eastern Siberia, first in Ulan-Ude, and then in Chita. Here she conducted intensive research on the history of Polish exiles and labour camp inmates in Siberia. In 1966 she took a position as Assistant Professor at the Ivan Franko Pedagogical Institute in Drohobycz, Bruno Schulz's home town, where she researched Polish folklore and its ties to 'high' Polish literature, songs of nineteenth-century uprisings, links between Polish, Russian, and Ukrainian folklore, and the role and reception of Polish literature, especially poetry, in the life of Polish exiles in Siberia. She almost always published her works in professional journals, and always with great difficulty, for publication required the approval of the authorities and the party committees. Her articles were scrupulously researched, and it is impossible to say how many hours she spent over the course of her lifetime in the archives of St Petersburg, Vilna, Lviv, and Chita. Among other topics she wrote and published, in Polish, Russian, and Ukrainian, about the rich Ukrainian threads in the poetry and dramas of Juliusz Słowacki, about Aleksander Herzen, about the Hungarian national poet Sandor Petőfi, and about Józef Bem, the Polish general active during the Springtime of Nations.

In an article published in the journal *Arcana*, Kacnelson wrote:

> Using directives from the police and the Galician regional administration, I wrote the biographies of Polish participants of the Hungarian Revolution of 1848–9. I dream of publishing a biographical dictionary of these heroes of the period of the Springtime of Nations. The co-author is the Hungarian professor István Kovacs, but it is difficult to find a publisher.

István Kovacs, a poet, essayist, and translator of Polish poets as well as a historian, is now the Hungarian consul in Kraków. Publication of this biographical dictionary would honour the memory of the deceased.

Kacnelson published many of her studies and essays in Poland, in journals, collections, and monographs. For example, the Wrocław publishing house Ossolineum (formerly in Lviv) published her work *Z dziejów pieśni powstańczej XIX wieku* ('History of Insurgent Songs of the Nineteenth Century'), and the Kraków publishing house Universitas published her equally broad and insightful study entitled *Poezja Mickiewicza wśród powstańców: Wiek XIX* ('Mickiewicz's Poetry Among the Insurgents: The Nineteenth Century'). For many years Kacnelson worked with the editorial board of the *Polish Biographical Dictionary*, writing the biographies of prominent Poles who died or disappeared in Siberia in the nineteenth century.

When, after many years, the *gmina*, or Jewish communal administration, was reconstituted in Drohobycz, Professor Kacnelson began to work for the city's decimated Jewish community. (Despite her accomplishments, Kacnelson did not officially achieve the title of professor; however, everyone knew that she was a true scholar.)

Throughout her modest, quiet life Kacnelson served several nations and several cultures: Polish, Jewish, Ukrainian, and Russian. She was a demon for archival research, and the deeper she delved into the archives, the more boundless her area of research became. In the introduction to her book *Poezja Mickiewicza wśród powstańców*, she wrote: 'As I have uncovered new archival sources on the history of the cult of the bard among the insurgents, I have become ever more convinced that these sources are so numerous and abundant that one lifetime is not enough to gather and systematize them.'

Kacnelson's works also appeared in the pages of the Paris publications *Kultura* and *Zeszyty Historyczne*. For example, in 1992 she published there her valuable text entitled 'Losy Ossolineum we Lwowie w latach 1961–1991' ('The Fate of the Ossolineum in Lviv 1961–1991') and in 1993 her profile 'Kustosz Władysław Abramowicz' ('Curator Władysław Abramowicz').

On the two-hundredth anniversary of Mickiewicz's birth Kacnelson edited a collection of studies entitled *Skazani za lekturę Mickiewicza: Z archiwów Lwowa i Wilna* ('Condemned for Reading Mickiewicz: From the Archives of Lviv and Vilna'); the volume was published by the Lublin publishing house Norbertinum. The poet was banned not only during the Russian partition, but also during the 'liberal' Austrian partition—particularly such works as *Konrad Wallenrod*, *Dziady*, *Księgi Narodu i Pielgrzymstwa Polskiego*, and *Pan Tadeusz*. Among those condemned for reading and distributing Mickiewicz's works were graduates of the Roman Catholic seminary in Lviv, including the historian and writer Karol Szajnocha, who later became much respected. In the last book she published, Kacnelson confides, 'I intend to keep publishing the materials I have collected.' Sadly, her death put an end to these plans.

Towards the end of 2002, during a stay in Kraków and at the urging of many people, Kacnelson was working on a draft of her autobiography entitled 'Ukochałam obydwa narody: Pamiętnik polskiej Żydówki' ('Attached to Both Nations: Memoirs of a Polish Jew'). The book was to have five chronological chapters as well as a prologue and an epilogue. An epigraph was also chosen—a couplet from Artur Oppman's 'Or-Ot': 'Tylko mi ciebie Mamo | Tylko mi Polski żal' ('Only you Mama | I pity only Poland'). Did she write the book, or even fragments of it? We will only know after an examination of her enormous archive.

On 29 December 2003 the newspaper *Rzeczypospolita* reported:

> In the more than one hundred cardboard boxes in the apartment of Ewa Mackiewicz, the executor of Dora Kacnelson's will, there are manuscripts, old prints, an archive on Polish exiles to Siberia, and many valuable documents. . . . Her extensive archive collected in Drohobycz also awaits return to Poland. . . . In keeping with Dora Kacnelson's will, the Siberian archives will be transferred to the University of Wrocław and the Lviv and Vilna archives will be transferred to Warsaw University.

Defiant and independent, Kacnelson brought down the wrath of the administrative and political bosses upon herself, committing such 'crimes' as publishing books in Poland without the approval of the party authorities of her college in Drohobycz and participating—also without permission—in the World Congress of Slavists in Kiev. In far-off Chita, in a little one-room apartment with a shared kitchen, she organized an informal seminar for students of history, Russian studies, and Slavonic studies. But unconventionality was a sin. For many years Kacnelson experienced great difficulty in her travels not only to the West, but also to the countries of the so-called Eastern Bloc, and particularly Poland. Whenever possible, she eagerly attended scholarly conferences and symposia in Poland. She wanted to settle in Poland at the end of her life, but it was not to be. She died in Berlin on 1 July 2003, 'leaving no family'. Her friends published a touching obituary for her (*Gazeta Wyborcza*, 11 July 2003): 'Knight of the order Polonia Mater Nostra Est, righteous person, distinguished Mickiewicz scholar, great advocate for Polish–Ukrainian–Jewish rapprochement, researcher of the fate of Polish exiles. . . . For thirty-five years she lived in Drohobycz, where she preserved the memory of Bruno Schulz. Say Kaddish for her, if you can.'

Many scholars and humanists have spoken about the life and achievements in research and writing of Pani Dora. Let Professor Maria Janion of the Polish Academy of Sciences speak for them all:

> For many years Dora Kacnelson's publications and data have served as an aid to historians of Romantic and late Romantic literature. The author undertook the exceptionally great labour of searching the archives of Lviv, Vilna, and eastern Siberia to find materials which more often than not had been confiscated in the course of police investigations, and which testified to the widespread and lively reception of Mickiewicz among nineteenth-century conspirators and insurgents in the Russian and Austrian partitions. The wealth of the evidence presented is impressive.

We may hope that from these exceedingly rich and already partially edited materials, through the efforts of the next generation of scholars, Dora Kacnelson's next—posthumous—books will be published.

RYSZARD WASITA

Translated from Polish by Claire Rosenson

Adam Penkalla

1944–2003

ADAM ROMAN PENKALLA was born on 17 November 1944 in Ostrowiec Świętokrzyski. His parents, Ludwik and Maria (neé Lipa), were members of the intelligentsia. Penkalla went to school in his home town, and in 1963 left to study history in the Humanities Department of the Catholic University of Lublin (KUL). His master's thesis, completed in 1968, was entitled 'The Reform of the Lay Clergy According to the Reports of Apostolic Nuncio Jan Andrzej Caligari (1578–1581)'; it was supervised by the distinguished historian Professor Jerzy Kłoczowski.

In recognition of his talent and industriousness, Penkalla was offered an assistant professorship at the university, and he held this position until 1972. In 1969 he spent a year studying in Groningen and Louvain on a KUL scholarship.

In 1972 Penkalla became editor of the Catholic periodical *Słowo Powszechne*, while at the same time engaging in postgraduate studies in journalism at the Jagiellonian University in Kraków; these he completed in 1974. In 1975–6 he returned to scholarly research, working in the National Archives in Kielce. In 1976 he joined the Kielce Workshop for the Conservation of Monuments, where he worked primarily on the documentation of Jewish synagogue architecture and sepulchral art. From 1991 he was also employed in the Radom section of the National Service for the Preservation of Monuments, overseeing the documentation of monuments and the preservation of the tombstones in these cemeteries. In 1981 he received an award from the Conservator-General of Monuments for his work in documenting the Jewish cemetery in Przytyk, and in 1983 a scholarship to conduct research on methods of documenting monuments of Jewish material culture in Czechoslovakia, particularly Prague.

At the same time Penkalla was preparing his doctoral thesis on the Jewish population of the Kielce region in the mid-nineteenth century to 1862 at the Institute of History at the Polish Academy of Arts and Sciences, under the supervision of Professor Artur Eisenbach; he received his doctorate in 1984. Shortly afterwards he started research on changes in the structure of the Jewish population of the province of Kielce in the nineteenth century. As part of this research he took a course at the École des hautes études en sciences sociales in Paris, and in 1997 he studied at the International Center for Holocaust Studies in Jerusalem.

In 1991, while continuing his work on the documentation of Jewish material culture in the province of Kielce, Penkalla became a lecturer at the Pedagogical

College in Kielce. Meanwhile, he was preparing a treatise (in co-operation with the Mordechaj Anielewicz Centre for the Study of the History and Culture of the Jews in Poland) on the process of assimilation and acculturation among the Jewish population of the province of Radom in 1867–1914; this work remains unfinished.

Penkalla began to publish the results of his research in the early 1970s. His areas of interest reflected the successive stages of his professional life, which was constantly enriched by exploration in new directions. His lengthy co-operation, between 1973 and 2002, with the *Catholic Encyclopaedia* in Lublin attests to his interest in the history of Christian thought. His mastery of the archivist's craft gave him the ability to read and interpret sources, particularly those related to the history of the Jewish population of the province of Radom, to which he devoted his later years, researching the lives of rabbis in the Kingdom of Poland.

Penkalla's work as a conservator of monuments allowed him to become an unquestioned expert on the synagogue architecture and cemeteries of the Jews of the province of Kielce, but he was also interested in Protestant and Russian Orthodox cemeteries, as well as First World War military cemeteries. The academic community of Kielce, which had researched the economic, social, political, and cultural life of the Jews, inspired him to reflect on the Jewish communities of the small towns of the province of Kielce in the nineteenth and twentieth centuries. Although the nineteenth century was the period dearest to his heart, during the 1990s Penkalla also focused on the history of the Jews of the province of Kielce in the twentieth century. His enthusiasm infected his students, and several dozen theses devoted to the problems of the ethnic minorities in the province of Kielce in the nineteenth and twentieth centuries were completed under his supervision.

As a professional journalist Penkalla was keen to work with journals such as *Folks-sztyme* and popular periodicals such as *Spotkania z Zabytkami*. However, he published primarily in national and regional professional journals such as *Kwartalnik Historii Kultury Materialnej*, *Rocznik Pracowni Konserwacji Zabytków*, *Biuletyn Żydowskiego Instytutu Historycznego*, and *Acta Polonia Historica*. His works also appeared in Israeli and French publications. He began his co-operation with *Polin* in 1988.

Penkalla's work was valued and acknowledged, as his numerous honours and diplomas testify. Among other awards he received a Certificate of Recognition for Services to the Cause of Preserving Jewish Cultural Monuments in Poland from the Israeli Embassy in Warsaw in 1998, and in the same year he was awarded Poland's Gold Medal for the Preservation of Monuments by the Minister of Culture and Art.

He left a rich legacy: nearly one hundred articles, collections of studies and conference materials, entries in dictionaries, encyclopedias, and lexicons, and numerous book reviews. He died prematurely on 25 July 2003.

MARTA MEDUCKA
Higher Pedagogical School, Kielce

Translated from Polish by Claire Rosenson

Notes on the Contributors

ELIYANA R. ADLER is currently a postdoctoral Fellow at the Joseph and Rebecca Meyerhoff Center for Jewish Studies at the University of Maryland. She completed her dissertation, on private schools for Jewish girls in tsarist Russia, at Brandeis University in 2003.

KAREN AUERBACH is a doctoral candidate in modern Jewish history at Brandeis University. Her main areas of interest are Polish Jewish history, assimilation and Jewish identity, and Jewish history during the Communist period in eastern Europe. Her dissertation research focuses on the social history and assimilation of Jewish families in Poland after the Second World War.

CAROLE B. BALIN received her Ph.D. at Columbia University and is an Associate Professor of History at the Hebrew Union College–Jewish Institute of Religion in New York. Her book *To Reveal Our Hearts: Jewish Women Writers in Tsarist Russia* (Cincinnati, 2000) won a Koret Foundation Publication Prize.

TOVA COHEN teaches in the Department of Hebrew Literature at Bar-Ilan University, where she also chairs the Interdisciplinary Program in Gender Studies. Her latest book is *One Beloved, the Other Hated: Between Fiction and Reality in Haskalah Depictions of Women* (Jerusalem, 2002). She is currently compiling, with Shmuel Feiner, an anthology of Hebrew writings by women writers of the Haskalah.

MARTIN DEAN is a Research Scholar at the Center for Advanced Holocaust Studies, United States Holocaust Memorial Museum (USHMM). He is the author of *Collaboration in the Holocaust*, published in association with the Museum in 2000, and of several other articles on different aspects of the Holocaust. He worked from 1992 to 1997 as Senior Historian for the Metropolitan Police War Crimes Unit.

CHAERAN FREEZE is Associate Professor of East European Jewish History at Brandeis University. Her book *Jewish Marriage and Divorce in Imperial Russia* (Hanover, NH, 2002) won the Salo W. Baron Award of the American Academy of Jewish Research for the best first book in Jewish studies and the Koret Foundation Publication Prize.

JAKUB GOLDBERG is Professor Emeritus of the Hebrew University in Jerusalem and doctor *honoris causa* (1993) of the University of Warsaw. He taught previously at the University of Łódź and has been Visiting Professor at a number of European universities. He has published over forty books and articles on the social and economic history of the Jews in the Polish–Lithuanian Commonwealth. Among his books are *Stosunki agrarne w miastach ziemi wieluńskiej w drugiej połowie XVIII wieku* ('Agrarian Relationships in the Towns of the Wieluń District in the Second Half of the Seventeenth and Eighteenth Centuries') (Łódź, 1960) and *Jewish Privileges in the Polish Commonwealth: Charters of Rights Granted to Jewish Communities in Poland–Lithuania in the Sixteenth to Eighteenth Centuries: Critical Edition of Original Latin and Polish Documents with English Introduction and Notes* (Jerusalem, 1985 (vol. i) and 2001 (vols. ii and iii)).

ZENON GULDON is Professor Emeritus at the Akademia Świętokrzyska in Kielce. Early modern economic history, especially Jewish demography and settlement in Poland–Lithuania, is his main research field. He has published numerous works on Polish Jewry, including *Ludność żydowska w miastach lewobrzeżnej części województwa sandomierskiego w XVI–XVIII wieku* ('The Jewish Population of the Towns of the Eastern Part of Sandomierz Province in the Sixteenth to the Eighteenth Centuries', Kielce, 1990) and *Żydzi i Szkoci w Polsce w XVI–XVIII wieku* ('Jews and Scots in Poland in the Sixteenth to the Eighteenth Centuries', Kielce, 1990).

PAULA HYMAN is the Lucy Moses Professor of Modern Jewish History at Yale University. Among her books are *Gender and Assimilation in Modern Jewish History* (Seattle, 1995) and *The Jews of Modern France* (Berkeley, 1998). She is co-editor of the prizewinning encyclopedia *Jewish Women in America* (New York, 1997) and of the forthcoming *Jewish Women: A Comprehensive Encyclopedia*.

JACK JACOBS is Professor of Political Science and Deputy Executive Officer of the Ph.D./MA Program in Political Science at the Graduate Center, The City University of New York (CUNY), and is also a Professor of Government at John Jay College, CUNY. He is the author of *On Socialists and 'The Jewish Question' After Marx* (New York, 1992), which has also appeared in German and is scheduled to be published in Hebrew; he is the editor of *Jewish Politics in Eastern Europe: The Bund at 100* (New York, 2001).

ELLEN KELLMAN is Lecturer in Yiddish with the rank of Assistant Professor at Brandeis University. She also teaches at the Uriel Weinreich Yiddish Program at Columbia University and in Warsaw at the Jewish Historical Institute's Summer Yiddish course, which she founded in 1999. She has published several articles on Jewish women and on Yiddish culture.

WALDEMAR KOWALSKI is Professor at the Akademia Świętokrzyska in Kielce. His studies concern various aspects of ethnic and religious relations in late medieval and early modern Poland. He has published several books and co-edited various volumes including *Żydzi wśród chrześcijan w dobie szlacheckiej Rzeczypospolitej* ('Jews Among Christians in the Period of the Republic of Nobles', Kielce, 1996); he has also contributed to a variety of journals including *Studia Judaica*, *Church History*, and *The Sixteenth Century Journal*.

SHULAMIT MAGNUS is an Associate Professor in the History Department of Oberlin College, where she is Chair and Director of the Program in Jewish Studies. She is completing an annotated translation of, critical commentary on, and introduction to the memoirs of Pauline Wengeroff (1833–1916), *Memoiren einer Grossmutter*, a major piece of writing by a Jewish woman about the emergence of Jewish modernity and its cultural and familial travails in tsarist Russia. Magnus is the author of *Jewish Emancipation in a German City: Cologne 1798–1871* (Stanford, Calif., 1997), and articles about Jewish social and women's history and feminist Jewish ritual.

RACHEL MANEKIN teaches at the Hebrew University and works at the Central Archives for the History of the Jewish People in Jerusalem. Her main interest is the social and political history of the Jews of Galicia. She received her Ph.D. in Jewish history from the Hebrew University and an MA in history from the University of Maryland.

SUSANNE MARTEN-FINNIS studied general linguistics, translation and interpreting, Russian language and literature, and English language and American literature at Leipzig University. She completed a postgraduate degree in media studies at Tübingen University and went on to take a Ph.D. in applied linguistics. She followed courses in Yiddish and the history of the Jews in Poland, Lithuania, and Russia. In 1995 she joined the Queen's University of Belfast, where she is now a Reader in German Studies. Her main area of research is the Jewish press in central and eastern Europe before the Second World War.

YOHANAN PETROVSKY-SHTERN is an Assistant Professor in the History Department and the Crown Center for Jewish Studies at Northwestern University and a Fellow at the Davis Center for Russian Studies at Harvard University. He received his Ph.D. in modern Jewish history at Brandeis University (2001) and a Ph.D. in comparative literature at Moscow University (1988). His articles have appeared in the *Association of Jewish Studies Review*, *Jewish Social Studies*, *Jewish Quarterly Review*, *East European Jewish Affairs*, *Ab Imperio*, *KRITIKA: Explorations in Russian and East European History*, and *Polin*. His book *Evrei v russkoi armii* ('Jews in the Russian Army') appeared in Moscow in 2003. At present he is working on a monograph, *Drafted into Modernity: Jews in the Russian Army*.

EVA PLACH is Assistant Professor of History at Wilfrid Laurier University, Waterloo, Ontario. She specializes in modern Polish history and is currently working on a book entitled 'The "Clash of Moral Nations": Imponderabilia in the Second Polish Republic, 1926 to 1935'.

MOSHE ROSMAN teaches Jewish history at Bar-Ilan University in Israel. He is the author of *The Lords' Jews: Magnates and Jews in the Eighteenth Century Polish–Lithuanian Commonwealth* (Cambridge, Mass., 1990) and *Founder of Hasidism* (Berkeley and Los Angeles, 1996). Currently he is researching the subject of Jewish women in the Polish–Lithuanian Commonwealth.

HELENE J. SINNREICH has taught in the History Department at Brooklyn College and is at present Assistant Lecturer and Director of the Jewish Studies Program at Youngstown State University, Ohio. She recently completed her doctoral thesis, 'The Supply and Distribution of Food to the Lodz Ghetto: A Case Study in Nazi Jewish Policy 1939–1945', at Brandeis University.

KATARZYNA ZECHENTER teaches Polish literature and culture at the School of Slavonic and East European Studies, University College London. She has written on contemporary Polish literature, Polish Jewish writers, and the concept of displacement and loss. Her book *Curse or Glory: Polish History and Politics in Tadeusz Konwicki's Fiction* is forthcoming. Currently she is working on the concept of the sacralization of space in Polish national culture, focusing on Kraków.

Glossary

aggadah (Hebrew; lit. 'narrative') That portion of rabbinic teaching that is not concerned with religious laws and regulations (halakhah). For the most part it consists of an amplification of those portions of the Hebrew Bible that include narrative, history, ethical maxims, and the reproofs and consolations of the prophets.

agunah (pl. *agunot*; Hebrew) An 'anchored woman'—one who cannot remarry because her first marriage was not terminated through either divorce or the death of her husband.

aliyah (Hebrew; lit. 'ascent') Emigration to the land of Israel. It is used in two senses: first, to describe the coming of Jews to the land of Israel as immigrants (*olim*); secondly, to describe the Jews who came from a particular region or during a particular period (as in 'second *aliyah*', e.g. the emigration from Russia in the first decades of the twentieth century).

arenda A lease of monopoly rights, usually of an estate.

arendar, arrendator The holder of an arenda.

ba'alei batim (Hebrew; lit. 'householders') The wealthier section of traditional Jewish society.

ba'al shem (pl. *ba'alei shem*; Hebrew; lit. 'Master of the Divine Name') The title given in popular usage and in Jewish literature, especially kabbalistic and hasidic works from the Middle Ages on, to one who possessed secret knowledge of the Tetragrammaton and other 'Holy Names' and who knew how to work miracles by the power of these names.

ban (Hebrew: *ḥerem*) Denotes the various degrees of religious and social ostracism imposed by rabbinical courts. Frequently used as a deterrent: transgressors would be threatened with the ban when an edict was promulgated.

beit midrash (Hebrew) Study house.

Bund The General Jewish Workers' Alliance; a Jewish socialist party founded in 1897. It joined the Russian Social Democratic Labour Party, but seceded from it when its programme of national autonomy was not accepted. In independent Poland it adopted a leftist, anti-communist posture, and from the 1930s co-operated increasingly closely with the Polish Socialist Party.

commonwealth (Polish: *rzeczpospolita*) The term *rzeczpospolita* is derived from Latin *res publica*. It is sometimes translated as 'commonwealth' and sometimes as 'republic', often in the form 'Noblemen's republic' (Rzeczpospolita szlachecka). After the union of Lublin in 1569 it was used officially in the form Rzeczpospolita Obojga Narodów (Commonwealth of Two Nations) to designate the new form of state that had arisen. In historical literature this term is often rendered as the Polish–Lithuanian Commonwealth.

eshet ḥayil (Hebrew; lit. 'a woman of valour') The opening words of the praise of the virtuous woman contained in Proverbs (31: 10–31). In many families this passage is recited by the husband, alone or together with the children on Friday evenings before the Kiddush. This practice originated in kabbalistic circles and initially referred to the *shekhinah* (divine presence) as the mystical mother and wife. Later this became a domestic ceremony in which the family pays homage to the housewife and mother. It may also have legitimized situations in which the wife was the breadwinner.

ezrat nashim (Hebrew) Women's sections in the synagogue.

halakhah (Hebrew; lit. 'the way') A word used to describe the entire prescriptive part of Jewish tradition. It defines the norms of behaviour and religious observance. (*Halakhot*: individual rulings.)

ḥalitsah (Hebrew) Levirate divorce. According to Jewish law, a widow whose husband died without issue is obliged to marry his brother (Deuteronomy 25: 5–6). The brother is known as a 'levir'. When the levir does not wish to marry such a widow, the ceremony of *ḥalitsah* takes place and the woman is released from the levirate tie and free to marry someone else.

hasidism A mystically inclined movement of religious revival consisting of distinct groups with charismatic leadership. It arose in the borderlands of the Polish–Lithuanian Commonwealth in the second half of the eighteenth century and quickly spread through eastern Europe. The hasidim emphasized joy in the service of God, whose presence they sought everywhere. Though their opponents the mitnagedim pronounced a series of bans against them beginning in 1772, the movement soon became identified with religious orthodoxy.

Haskalah (Hebrew; lit. 'learning' or 'wisdom', but used in the sense of Enlightenment) A movement that arose in the wake of the general European Enlightenment in the second half of the eighteenth century and continued into the second half of the nineteenth century. Its adherents were known as maskilim. Its most prominent representative was Moses Mendelssohn (1729–86). The Haskalah was particularly important and influential in German and Slav lands. It advocated secular education, the acquisition of European languages, the adoption of productive occupations, and loyalty to the state. In eastern Europe there was considerable emphasis on Hebrew as opposed to Yiddish, which was rejected by most maskilim.

ḥeder (Hebrew; lit. 'room') Colloquial name for a traditional Jewish elementary school in which teaching was carried out by a *melamed*.

kahal (pl. *kehalim*), *kehilah* (pl. *kehilot*) (Hebrew) Although both terms mean 'community', *kahal* is used to denote the institution of Jewish autonomy in a particular locality, while *kehilah* denotes the community of Jews who live in the town. The *kahal* was the lowest level of the Jewish autonomous institutions in the Polish–Lithuanian Commonwealth. Above the local *kehilot* were regional bodies, and above these a central body, the Va'ad Arba Aratsot (Council of Four Lands) for the Kingdom of Poland and the Va'ad Medinat Lita (Council of Lithuania). The Va'ad Arba Aratsot was abolished by the Polish authorities in 1764, but autonomous institutions continued to operate legally until 1844 and in practice for many years after this date in those parts of the Polish–Lithuanian Commonwealth directly annexed by the tsarist empire and until the emergence of the Polish state in the Kingdom of Poland and Galicia. Here the reorganized communal body, which no longer had the power to punish religious heterodoxy, but administered synagogues, schools, cemeteries, and *mikvaot*, was often called the *gmina* (commune). In inter-war Poland the legal status of the *kehilot* was regulated by statute in October 1927 and March 1930. The legislation gave them control over many aspects of Jewish communal life with both religious and social functions. All adherents of the 'Mosaic faith' were required to belong to a *kehilah*, and one could not withdraw except through baptism or by declaring oneself an atheist.

kasher (Hebrew; Ashkenazi pronunciation: 'kosher') A term originally used in the Bible in the sense of 'fit' or 'proper' and later used in the sense of ritually correct or faultless. Usually used to denote food that is permitted in contrast to that which is non-*kasher* (*tref*).

kashrut (Hebrew) The quality of being *kasher*.

kest (Yiddish) An arrangement by which men supported their Torah scholar sons-in-law for a number of years after marriage.

maskil (pl. maskilim) See Haskalah.

maskilah (pl. maskilot; Hebrew) A woman supporter of the Haskalah.

melamed (pl. *melamedim*; Hebrew; lit. 'teacher') A teacher in a *ḥeder*. A distinction is made between a *melamed dardeki*, who taught children of both sexes to read and write Hebrew and also a chapter or two of the weekly lessons from the Pentateuch, and a *melamed gemara*, who taught Bible and Talmud to boys and also, when they were older, *Shulḥan arukh*.

mikveh (pl. *mikvaot*; Hebrew) A pool or bath of clear water, immersion in which renders ritually clean a person who has become ritually unclean through contact with the dead or any other defiling object or through an unclean flux from the body, especially menstruation.

mitnaged (pl. mitnagedim; Hebrew; lit. 'opposer') The rabbinic opponents of hasidism.

mitsvah (pl. *mitsvot*; Hebrew) A commandment, precept, or religious duty derived from the Hebrew *tsavah* 'to command'.

Musar movement A movement for the establishment of strict ethical behaviour in the spirit of halakhah which arose in the nineteenth century among the mitnagedim of historical Lithuania. Its influence remained strong in the area until the Second World War, and it was particularly influential in the yeshivas there.

pilpul (Hebrew) A collective term describing a method of talmudic study and exposition making use of subtle legal, conceptual, and casuistic differentiations. The term is derived from *pilpel* (pepper) to indicate metaphorically the sharp type of argumentation employed.

pinkasim (Hebrew) Minute-books.

raion (Russian) District.

seder (Hebrew) Passover eve ritual meal.

Sejm The central parliamentary institution of the Polish–Lithuanian Commonwealth, composed of a senate and a chamber of deputies; after 1501 both of these had a voice in the introduction of new legislation. It met regularly for six weeks every two years, but could be called for sessions of two weeks in an emergency. When it was not in session, an appointed commission of sixteen senators, in rotation four at a time, resided with the king both to advise and to keep watch over his activities. Until the middle of the seventeenth century the Sejm functioned reasonably well; after that the use of the *liberum veto* began to paralyse its effectiveness. Also used for the local parliament in Galicia as in 'Sejm Galicyjski'.

starosta (Polish) A royal administrator, holder of the office of *starostwo*. From the fourteenth century three distinct offices were covered by this term: the *starosta generalny* (general *starosta*) in Wielkopolska, Rus′, and Podolia represented the Crown in a particular region; the *starosta grodowy* (castle *starosta*) had administrative and judicial authority over a castle or fortified settlement and its surrounding region; and the *starosta niegrodowy* (non-castle *starosta*), or *tenutariusz* (leaseholder), administered royal lands leased to him.

szlachta The Polish nobility. A very broad social stratum making up nearly 8 per cent of the population in the eighteenth century. Its members ranged from the great magnates, such as the Czartoryskis, Potockis, and Radziwiłłs, who dominated political and social life in the last century of the Polish–Lithuanian Commonwealth, to small landowners (the *szlachta zagrodowa*) and even to landless retainers of a great house. What distinguished members of this group from the remainder of the population was their noble status and their right to participate in political life in the dietines, the Sejm, and the election of the king.

tkhines (Yiddish) Topical supplicatory prayers that women said at home, or in the synagogue, *mikveh*, or cemetery.

tsadik (pl. *tsadikim*; Hebrew; lit. 'the Righteous One') The leader of a hasidic group was called a *tsadik* or *rebbe*. Often his hasidim credited him with miraculous powers, seeing him as mediator between God and man.

vajbershul (Yiddish) Women's annexes in the synagogue.

Wielkopolska (Polish; lit. 'Great Poland' or 'Greater Poland') Western Poland, the area around Poznań.

yeshiva A rabbinical college, the highest institution in the traditional Jewish system of education.

Index